T0339574

Routledge Handbook of Environmental Displacement and Migration

The last twenty years have seen a rapid increase in scholarly activity and publications dedicated to environmental migration and displacement, and the field has now reached a point in terms of profile, complexity, and sheer volume of reporting that a general review and assessment of existing knowledge and future research priorities is warranted. So far, such a product does not exist.

The *Routledge Handbook of Environmental Displacement and Migration* provides a state-of-the-science review of research on how environmental variability and change influence current and future global migration patterns and, in some instances, trigger large-scale population displacements. Drawing together contributions from leading researchers in the field, this compendium will become a go-to guide for established and newly interested scholars, for government and policymaking entities, and for students and their instructors. It explains theoretical, conceptual, and empirical developments that have been made in recent years; describes their origins and connections to broader topics including migration research, development studies, and international public policy and law; and highlights emerging areas where new and/or additional research and reflection are warranted.

The structure and the nature of the book allow the reader to quickly find a concise review relevant to conducting research or developing policy on particular topics, and to obtain a broad, reliable survey of what is presently known about the subject.

Robert McLeman is a former foreign service officer specializing in migration management and is presently Associate Professor of Geography and Environmental Studies at Wilfrid Laurier University in Waterloo, Canada.

François Gemenne is Director of the Hugo Observatory at the University of Liège, Belgium, the first research centre dedicated to the interactions between environmental change and human migration. A political scientist by training, he is also the executive director of the research programme Politics of the Earth at Sciences Po in Paris, where he is a lecturer in environmental politics.

"Environmental migration and displacement is a massive phenomenon, a new wicked universality whose political influence is felt everywhere. This book is important not only for those who document the pace and size of the phenomenon, but also for those in receiving countries who must learn how to cope with it."

Bruno Latour, sociologist and philosopher, France

"This handbook allows us to anticipate impending disasters, such as the 2004 Indian Ocean tsunami which was one of the first topics of discussion for my government, and the volume calls for rapid solutions. I am optimistic and I believe that we can save the planet, because the world has equipped itself with the knowledge and technology to do so. This is a most helpful guide for political parties who want to formulate responsible and vote winning polices. It's a blueprint for NGOs interested in doing good. It's the definitive guide on the subject and a good read."

Mohamed Nasheed, former President of the Maldives

"This handbook is essential reading and a key teaching resource for everyone interested in an interdisciplinary approach to climate change and migration. McLeman and Gemenne succeed in bringing together a state of the art collection of articles that provide a comprehensive survey of current thinking, not only on the theoretical and methodological underpinnings of a quickly expanding field of research, but also on the available empirical evidence as well as current developments in the areas of law and policy."

Walter Kälin, Special Envoy of the Chairmanship of the
Platform on Disaster Displacement

"This handbook will be a resource for policy makers to identify the current state of the science on the impacts, responses and best practices relating to environmental migration and displacement."

Mary Robinson, President, Mary Robinson
Foundation – Climate Justice, Ireland

Routledge Handbook of Environmental Displacement and Migration

Edited by Robert McLeman and François Gemenne

Routledge
Taylor & Francis Group
LONDON AND NEW YORK

First published 2018 by Routledge

2 Park Square, Milton Park, Abingdon, Oxfordshire OX14 4RN

52 Vanderbilt Avenue, New York, NY 10017

Routledge is an imprint of the Taylor & Francis Group, an informa business

First issued in paperback 2020

British Library Cataloguing-in-Publication Data
A catalogue record for this book is available from the British Library

Library of Congress Cataloging-in-Publication Data
A catalog record for this book has been requested

ISBN: 978-1-138-19446-5 (hbk)
ISBN: 978-0-367-52150-9 (pbk)

Typeset in Bembo
by Apex CoVantage, LLC

Contents

Contents

Contents

Foreword

If you have picked up this book (or accessed it online), you are probably already aware that people in many parts of the world are, at this very moment, on the move for reasons linked to changes and variations in the natural environment. You probably also did not need to be persuaded that this is a serious challenge for policymakers, for institutions, for communities, and for households and individuals, one that becomes increasingly serious the longer we put off taking meaningful action at global, regional, and local scales to tackle the root causes of land degradation, deforestation, biodiversity loss, climate change, and pollution on water and on land. And (hopefully) you may also be ready and willing to contribute in a meaningful way to creating responses, innovations, and actions to help people who are vulnerable to the impacts of environmental change, who may be at risk of displacement, who migrate reluctantly, who must make the best of a bad situation, or who find themselves trapped in worsening circumstances with no apparent way out. You may be a student thinking about doing research in this field, or are already doing it. You may be an established researcher who has already worked in this area, or are approaching it as a new initiative. You may work in a government agency, a multilateral organization, a development NGO or other organization that has some responsibility for policy or programming, and you want or need to learn more about the 'who, what, where, when, how and why' of environmental migration and displacement. Maybe you read something in a newspaper or in social media about climate refugees or environmental migrants, and simply out of curiosity want to know more about what's going on, from a reliable source. This Handbook has been prepared for you – all of you.

This Handbook is intended to be a handy desk reference, a starting place for newcomers to the field and a resource people already working in the field can refer back to when needed. It is not an encyclopedia (though for those holding a physical copy, it may feel like one), and does not pretend to be an exhaustive collection that defines and describes every term and concept used in discussions of environmental migration and displacement. Neither is it a thematic, edited collection of academic research intended to be representative of the broad field of environmental migration and displacement, for the extent of knowledge in the field today is so wide and so deep that any such collection that is not focussed on a specific subset of the field would be little more than a miscellany. Consider that the University of Neuchâtel maintains a database of research and policy publications about environmental migration; at time of writing in the summer of 2017, the database contained more than 1,700 documents, most of which were published in the last fifteen years. Any book that pretended to provide an encyclopedic or comprehensive overview of this rapidly expanding and diversifying field would be too big to carry, and outdated on the day of publication.

As with any rapidly expanding field of research, a handbook is, well, handy. In assembling this Handbook, we have done two things. First, we asked a variety of established and emerging researchers from around the world to submit chapters that describe – in concise, accessible terms – overviews of the past and present state of research in their respective areas of expertise. Some have written about theoretical or methodological considerations, others about particular regions where they work and the key issues they face, and still others about the legal and policymaking challenges. Each of these chapters has been peer-reviewed, and contains a useful list of references to guide the reader to additional readings. Second, we asked representatives of the leading global multilateral organizations that engage on a daily basis with environmental migration and displacement to provide a concise overview of their experience, interests, and challenges they face. In addition to all this, we were also able to persuade Professor Lori M. Hunter – who was until recently the long-time editor of *Population and Environment*, the leading scholarly journal in the field – to contribute a concluding summary of the key unanswered questions and future challenges for researchers and policymakers. And, as you will also see, none other than Mary Robinson – former President of Ireland, United Nations High Commissioner for Human Rights, and activist for climate justice – has provided a formal introduction to this volume. If there is any truth to the old saying that, 'you are judged by the company you keep', we are fortunate and honoured to be in her company.

As editors, we have strived to ensure that the sum of these contributions captures, as best as we can muster, the important topics and conversations that engage established experts in the field, and with which newcomers to the field will want to become familiar. Despite containing thirty-six chapters, there will inevitably be gaps in the coverage of topics in this Handbook; that is our fault as editors, though not for lack of effort. Our concluding hope is that you, the reader, will find this volume to be a useful resource for inquiry into this subject of critical importance to achieving a sustainable future.

Robert McLeman and François Gemenne

Foreword

It is with pleasure that I write a foreword to this important *Routledge Handbook of Environmental Displacement and Migration*, coming as it does during a period of international cooperation and interest in this field. We have seen migration and human mobility on an unprecedented scale in recent years, and a corresponding deepening of understanding within the international community of drivers and root causes of mobility, including as a result of climate change and environmental impacts.

My Foundation, the Mary Robinson Foundation – Climate Justice, has been an advocate for action on climate displacement for some time, across international processes. A stark reality of this work has been the recognition that lack of a deeper understanding based on research and data in the international conversations is holding back effective solutions. I hope that this book will go some way to addressing that gap. This Handbook will be a resource to policy makers to identify the current state of the science on the impacts, responses and best practices relating to environmental migration and displacement.

Communities at risk of displacement as a result of environmental degradation, often exacerbated by climate change, have a lot to lose. And losses for these communities are not limited to material and economic impacts; they are also deeply personal. This is something I want to underline. The land one comes from is often deeply embedded within an understanding of self. It can act as the social fabric that binds communities together and from it stems culture and identity. This was something I learned from my friend Ursula Rakova, who is currently undertaking a move with her community from their ancestral lands in the Carteret Islands to Bougainville Island due to sea level rise. She explained that her communities' move was not just difficult because of the problems of management and guaranteeing livelihoods, but also included a significant trauma from leaving behind the 'bones of their ancestors'. This is a hugely valued asset these communities cannot get back, and it is a moral imperative for action. Sadly, a recognition of the loss of cultural identity has been largely missing from international conversations on environmental displacement.

It is this deeply personal aspect of displacement and migration that I hope readers of this Handbook will engage with and utilise to inform future policy work. Climate change is happening, we are seeing its impacts, including displacement, right now. Even in a best case scenario, in which we limit warming to the 1.5°C goal of the Paris Agreement, we are likely to see more people on the move. In Agenda 2030, countries agreed to take steps on migration, climate change, and development, and more importantly to 'leave no one behind' and 'reach the furthest behind first'. A person who loses their home and livelihood due to environmental impacts must be included within that category. The international community needs to come together to recognise these realities and to acknowledge that the people first to move are often those who did least to contribute to the problem. This is the injustice of climate change. Responses must acknowledge these people as representing a critically vulnerable group and protect their human rights in a spirit of equality and burden sharing.

Environmental displacement is happening right now yet it is often unrecognised by governments. However, there is hope; the New York Declaration of September 2016, and the commitment to a Global Pact on Migration by 2018, demonstrate the renewed vigour with which the world is facing the challenges of displacement and migration. As people increasingly lose their homes, livelihoods, and culture to climatic and environmental impacts, we need to develop people-centred, rights-based policy responses. Climate change and environmental degradation are matters of grave urgency, and the impacts on the most vulnerable are persistent and unconscionable. This cannot be seen as a problem that is considered too complex for the global community to solve. As Nicolas Hulot stated, in his introduction to the *Atlas of Environmental Migration*: 'The challenge lying ahead is to allow a population that has never been so large to attain a quality of life without precedent' (Ionesco et al. 2017, p. vii).

Mary Robinson

About the Mary Robinson Foundation – Climate Justice

The Mary Robinson Foundation – Climate Justice is a centre for thought leadership, education, and advocacy on the struggle to secure global justice for those people vulnerable to the impacts of climate change who are usually forgotten – the poor, the disempowered and the marginalised across the world. It is a platform for solidarity, partnership, and shared engagement for all who care about global justice, whether as individuals and communities suffering injustice or as advocates for fairness in resource-rich societies. The Foundation provides a space for facilitating action on climate justice to empower the poorest people and countries in their efforts to achieve sustainable and people-centred development.

Mary Robinson is President of the Foundation. She served as President of Ireland from 1990–1997 and UN High Commissioner for Human Rights from 1997–2002.

Acknowledgements

The editors wish to thank Margaret Farrelly, Annabelle Harris, and Matt Shobbrook of Routledge for their guidance and support in assembling this Handbook. Rashari Henry provided excellent editorial assistance in preparing the final manuscript. The following individuals were instrumental in helping us ensure the quality of this volume (listed alphabetically by surname): Simon Batterbury, Ingrid Boas, Clark Gray, Colin Harvey, Matt Hauer, Shirley Laska, Simon Léger, Phil McMichael, Mohammad Moniruzzaman, Meena Poudel, Mariana Rufino, Johanna Wandel, Elissa Kate Waters, and Brooke Wilmsen. Dr. McLeman would like to thank the Department of Geography at Trinity College Dublin for allowing him to use their facilities during the preparation of this book.

Figures

Tables

Boxes

Contributors

Dr. W. Neil Adger is Professor of Human Geography at the University of Exeter (UK). His research includes contributions on social dynamics of global change, ecosystem services, wellbeing, demography, and migration.

Sonja Ayeb-Karlsson researches mobility and immobility decisions in Bangladesh in the context of environmental stress and livelihood sustainability at University of Sussex (UK) and United Nations University Institute for Environment and Human Security (UNU-EHS). Her research emphasises storytelling methodology and the development of anthropological approaches to interact with people facing environmental stress.

Ling Bai is a PhD student in the Department of Sociology at University of Southern California. Her research focuses on how demographic factors shape social inequality and mobility, and it fits broadly in the areas of stratification and inequality, gender and family, urban sociology, quantitative methods, and computational social sciences.

Jonas Bergmann is Consultant for the Global Knowledge Partnership on Migration and Development (KNOMAD) Working Group on Migration and Environmental Change, as well as for the Climate Analytics and Advisory Services Team at the World Bank. His research focuses on migration, human rights, and sustainable development.

Dr. Rachel S. Bergmans holds a PhD in epidemiology from the University of Wisconsin-Madison and is currently a postdoctoral research fellow at the University of Michigan School of Medicine. Her research focuses on the social and environmental determinants of health.

Julia Blocher is a Communications and Coordination Officer at the United Nations University and a Ph.D. candidate and Associate Member of the Hugo Observatory at the University of Liège (Belgium). She previously worked for the Internal Displacement Monitoring Centre (IDMC) and the UN High Commissioner for Refugees (UNHCR).

Bonnie Boyd is an Environmental Planner at the South Nation Conservation Authority, Ontario, Canada, and is a graduate of the University of Ottawa.

Dr. Robin Bronen is a human rights attorney and researches the climate-induced relocation of Alaska Native communities. She holds a PhD from the Resilience and Adaptation Program at the University of Alaska-Fairbanks and received her Juris Doctorate from the University of California at Davis. She is a senior research scientist at the University of Alaska-Fairbanks

Institute of Arctic Biology and is the executive director of the Alaska Institute for Justice, a non-profit agency.

Oli Brown coordinates UN Environment's work on the environmental causes and consequences of natural disasters, industrial accidents and armed conflicts. Based at UN Environment's Nairobi headquarters, he holds degrees in Social Anthropology and International Relations and has worked extensively on issues of environmental displacement over the past decade.

Dr. Dug Cubie is a Lecturer in the School of Law, University College Cork (Ireland). His research focuses on the intersections of law and policy regarding humanitarian action, disasters, climate justice and the protection of persons, drawing upon his professional experience with UNHCR, the International Organization for Migration (IOM), and the Irish Red Cross.

Dr. Katherine J. Curtis is Associate Professor of Community and Environmental Sociology at the University of Wisconsin-Madison. Curtis' research is centered in spatial and applied demography with a strong focus on the relationship between migration and environmental change.

Dr. Jack DeWaard is an Assistant Professor in the Department of Sociology and Graduate Faculty of Population Studies in the Minnesota Population Center at the University of Minnesota. His research focuses, in part, on migration and population displacement caused by environmental conditions and climate change.

Marine Franck is Program Officer at UNHCR where she leads the portfolio on climate change, disaster and displacement. An expert in international climate policy and law, she previously worked at Ecoressources Consultants in Montreal, providing technical support to Congo Basin countries in Africa on the UNFCCC process, and as a Climate and Energy Officer at the Munciich-based NGO Women Engage for a Common Future.

Dr. Elizabeth Fussell is an Associate Professor of Population Studies at Brown University. She was formerly Postdoctoral Fellow at the University of Pennsylvania Population Studies Center, Assistant Professor at Tulane University and Associate Professor at Washington State University. Her research focuses on from Mexico to the United States and on population change after disasters.

Dr. François Gemenne is Director of the Hugo Observatory at the University of Liège (Belgium), the first research centre dedicated to the interactions between environmental change and human migration. A political scientist by training, he is also the executive director of the research programme Politics of the Earth at Sciences Po in Paris, where he is a lecturer in environmental politics.

Dalila Gharbaoui is Research Fellow and PhD Candidate in Political and Social Sciences, at the Hugo Observatory, University of Liège (Belgium) and at the Macmillan Brown Center, University of Canterbury (New Zealand). Her research examines climate change, relocation and land governance in the Pacific region.

Dr. Giovanna Gioli is a Livelihood Adaptation Specialist with the International Centre for Integrated Mountain Development in Kathmandu, Nepal. She was previously a post-doctoral scientist at the Institute of Geography, University of Hamburg (Germany), where her research revolved around the migration, environment, and development nexus in Pakistan.

Dr. Lori M. Hunter is Professor of Sociology at the University of Colorado-Boulder and Director of the CU Population Center at the Institute of Behavioral Science. Her migration-environment research focuses on rural South Africa and Mexico, as well as small, rural communities in the US.

Dina Ionesco is the Head of the Migration, Environment and Climate Change (MECC) Division at the International Organization for Migration (IOM) in Geneva. Dina has led the expansion of IOM's environmental and climate portfolio, resulting in the establishment of the MECC Division that oversees IOM's policy and programme development.

Dr. Craig Johnson is Professor of Political Science at the University of Guelph (Canada). He has published widely in the field of environmental politics and international development, focusing primarily on questions of urbanization, sustainability transitions, and climate change.

Dr. Dominic Kniveton is Professor of Climate Change and Society at the University of Sussex (UK). Originally focusing on the science and modelling of climate change his work encompasses studies of impact, vulnerability, adaptation, and climate resilience.

Kanta Kumari Rigaud is a Lead Environmental Specialist at the World Bank and leads the Pilot Program for Climate Resilience. Her work focuses on the knowledge and policy agenda for resilience, and she is currently leading the Bank's flagship report on climate change and migration. She is the co-chair of the KNOMAD's Environmental Change and Migration Working Group.

Dr. Rachel Licker is a Senior Climate Scientist with the Union of Concerned Scientists. Her research focuses on the effects of climate change on human migration and agricultural production.

Bonny Boyd has been working as an Environmental Planner at South Nation Conservation, Ontario, Canada, since 2014. She holds a BA in Geography from the University of Ottawa.

Brittany Main began her PhD studies in physical geography at the University of Ottawa in September 2016. Besides her passion for studying glaciers, Brittany enjoys working with the First Nations Natural Resources Youth Employment Program of Ontario, Canada, and volunteering with the Human Rights Clinic at the University of Ottawa.

Dr. Julie K. Maldonado is Director of Research for the Livelihoods Knowledge Exchange Network, a link-tank for policy-relevant research toward post-carbon livelihoods and communities. She also works for the Institute for Tribal Environmental Professionals, supporting tribes in developing climate change adaptation plans, and teaches at University of California-Santa Barbara, Environmental Studies. Dr. Maldonado co-organizes Rising Voices: Collaborative Science with Indigenous Knowledge for Climate Solutions.

Dr. Susan F. Martin is the Donald G. Herzberg Professor Emerita of International Migration at Georgetown University. She chairs the KNOMAD Working Group on Migration and Environmental Change in the World Bank. Recent book publications include *International Migration: Evolving Trends from the Early Twentieth Century to the Present* and *Migration* and *Humanitarian Crises: Causes, Consequences and Responses*.

Dr. Marina Mastrorillo is a Consultant with the Migration, Agriculture and Food Security Programme at the Food and Agriculture Organization of the United Nations. Her research focuses on the linkages among climate change, agricultural land use, and human migration patterns.

Dr. Benoît Mayer is an Assistant Professor in the Faculty of Law of the Chinese University of Hong Kong. He was previously an Associate Professor in the International Law Institute and Research Institute in Environmental Law in the School of Law of Wuhan University (China). His research focuses on international law on climate change, with particular regard to human mobility, loss and damage, and adaptation.

Dr. Robert McLeman is a former foreign service officer specializing in migration management and is presently Associate Professor of Geography and Environmental Studies at Wilfrid Laurier University (Canada).

Dr. Andrea Milan is a Programme Analyst on Migration with the Economic Empowerment Section (Policy Division) of United Nations Women in New York City. In 2017, Dr. Milan was seconded to the Office of the Special Representative of the Secretary-General of the UN for International Migration, providing UN system-wide support to the development of a global compact for safe, orderly and regular migration.

Dr. Colette Mortreux is Associate Research Fellow in Geography, University of Exeter (UK). Her research is on adaptation to climate risks, migration, and on the political economy of resettlement.

Stern Mwakalimi Kita is a PhD student in the School of Global Studies at the University of Sussex (UK). His research focuses on climate change adaptation, disaster risk reduction and resettlement in the context of Malawi. He holds an MSc in Environment and Development from the University of Dublin, Trinity College (Ireland). Stern joined Malawi's Department of Disaster Management Affairs in 2009, and currently works as the Chief Mitigation Officer.

Dr. Raphael J. Nawrotzki works as Postdoctoral associate for the Minnesota Population Center. A social demographer, his research centers on the relationship between environment and society, with a focus on mobility and migration.

Reiko Obokata holds an MA in Human Geography from the University of Ottawa and works in the community sector in Canada. Her thesis investigated how environmental factors influenced the migration decisions and experiences of Filipino newcomers to Canada. Her research interests include environmental migration, transnationalism, and feminist approaches to mobility and migration.

Dr. Bimal Kanti Paul is a Professor of Geography at Kansas State University. He is a natural hazard geographer with interests in health and population geography, and quantitative analysis.

Dr. Tristan Pearce is a Senior Research Fellow in Geography with the Sustainability Research Centre at the University of the Sunshine Coast (Australia) and Adjunct Faculty in the Department of Geography at the University of Guelph (Canada). His research focuses on the human dimensions of global environmental change, in particular the vulnerability and adaptation of Indigenous communities in the Canadian Arctic, Pacific Islands, and Australia.

Nakia Pearson is a PhD Candidate at the Hugo Observatory of Environmental Migration at the University of Liège. Her research focuses on border politics and conceptualization within the framework of environmental migration.

Dr. Kristina Peterson is an applied social scientist and a co-founder of the Lowlander Center, Natural Hazards Mitigation Association, and the Gender and Disaster Network. She co-facilitates AmeriCorps VISTA tribal volunteers engaged with the First Peoples' Conservation Council, is an Advisory Board member of the American Geophysical Union's 'Thriving Earth Exchange', and is a fellow in the Society for Applied Anthropology.

Dr. Etienne Piguet is Professor at the Institute of Geography of the University of Neuchâtel (Switzerland). He chairs the Population Geography Commission of the International Geographical Union (IGU) and is vice-president of the Swiss federal commission for migration (CFM/EKM).

Erika Pires Ramos is co-founder of the South American Network for Environmental Migrations (RESAMA) and Researcher at the Environmentally Displaced Persons Study Centre (NEPDA/UEPB), Human Rights and Vulnerabilities Research Group (UNISANTOS), and Brazilian Institute for the Climate Change Law (IClima). Her research focuses are climate change, disasters, human rights, and environmental migration governance.

Platform on Disaster Displacement (PDD) is a state-led process addressing the protection needs of people displaced across borders in the context of disasters and climate change. The PDD consists of a Steering Group, an Envoy, an Advisory Committee, and a Coordination Unit. The Coordination Unit provides technical and coordination support.

Dr. Clionadh Raleigh is a Professor of Political Geography at the University of Sussex (UK) and the Director of the Armed Conflict Location and Event Data project (ACLED). Her work focuses on patterns of political violence and political elites across the developing world, with a concentration on African political geography.

Avantika Ramekar is a doctoral candidate at Kansas State University, and a Geographical Information Science engineer who graduated with a Master's Degree in from the University of Edinburgh (Scotland).

Mary Robinson is President of the Mary Robinson Foundation – Climate Justice. She served as President of Ireland from 1990–1997 and UN High Commissioner for Human Rights from 1997–2002. She is a member of the Elders and the Club of Madrid and the recipient of numerous honours and awards including the Presidential Medal of Freedom from former U.S. President Barack Obama. She sits on the advisory board of Sustainable Energy For All (SE4All) and is also a member of the Lead Group of the Scaling Up Nutrition (SUN) Movement. Between 2013 and 2016, Mary served as the UN Secretary General's Special Envoy in three roles: first for the Great Lakes region of Africa, then on Climate Change, and most recently as his Special Envoy on El Niño and Climate.

A former President of the International Commission of Jurists and former chair of the Council of Women World Leaders, she was President and founder of Realizing Rights: The Ethical Globalization Initiative from 2002–2010 and served as Honorary President of Oxfam International from 2002–2012.

Mary Robinson serves as Patron of the Board of the Institute of Human Rights and Business, is an honorary member of The B Team, in addition to being a board member of several organisations including the Mo Ibrahim Foundation and the European Climate Foundation. She serves as Chancellor of the University of Dublin since 1998. Mary's memoir, *Everybody Matters*, was published in September 2012.

Dr. Clemens Romankiewicz is a human geographer and research fellow at the Institute of African Studies and Department of Political Geography at the University of Bayreuth (Germany). His research interests involve population mobility, climate and environmental change in Mali and Senegal, data and research methodologies, migrant networks, and migration policies.

Dr. Ricardo Safra de Campos is Associate Research Fellow in Geography, University of Exeter (UK). His research is on mobility, and migration and environmental risks, including in drylands, deltas and cities.

Dr. Alex de Sherbinin is Associate Director for Science Applications at the Center for International Earth Science Information Network, the Earth Institute, Columbia University. His research focuses on the human aspects of global environmental change and geospatial data applications, integration, and dissemination.

Daniel H. Simon is a National Science Foundation Graduate Research Fellow and doctoral student in Sociology at the University of Colorado-Boulder and is affiliated with the Institute of Behavioral Science. His research focuses on population-environment and population-health interactions in Mexico and the United States.

Dr. Christopher D. Smith is a Research Fellow at the University of Sussex (UK). His research focuses on the interactions between environmental change, migration decision-making, and livelihoods in numerous contexts worldwide.

Dr. Yan Tan is Associate Professor of Geography, Environment and Population at the University of Adelaide (Australia). Her research focuses on environmental change, migration, and adaptation in China and Australia.

Mariam Traore Chazalnoel is the Thematic Specialist in Migration, Environment and Climate Change at the International Organization for Migration (IOM) Office to the United Nations in New York, where she manages IOM's work in relation to the global climate negotiations.

Dr. Kees van der Geest is a human geographer, working at United Nations University. He studies impacts of climate change, migration, livelihoods and environmental change with a people-centred perspective. He has extensive field research experience in Ghana, Burkina Faso, Vietnam, Bangladesh, Nepal, Marshall Islands, and Bolivia.

Dr. Victoria van der Land is a sociologist with a research focus on climate change and migration. She has extensive work and field experience in West African countries, such as Benin, Chad, Cote d'Ivoire, Mali, and Senegal. Currently, she works as a DAAD lecturer at the University of Bamako (Mali).

Dr. Luisa Veronis is Associate Professor of Geography, Environment and Geomatics at the University of Ottawa (Canada). Inspired by feminist and community-based approaches, her research examines the social and political geographies of (im)migration, settlement, belonging, and identity formation with a focus on migrant and minority groups in Canadian cities.

Sara Vigil is an FNRS (National Fund for Scientific Research) Research Fellow at the Hugo Observatory of the University of Liège (Belgium) and at the International Institute for Social Studies (ISS) of Erasmus University Rotterdam (Netherlands). Her research focuses on the links between climate change, land grabbing, and migration.

Brian Wittbold is Regional Humanitarian Affairs Officer for UN Environment in the West Asia Regional Office. He has managed programmes addressing forced migration and supported disaster and post-conflict relief operations in the Middle East, Africa and Asia Pacific region since 2010. He holds a Master's degree in International Relations and an LLM in the International Law of the Sea.

Hanspeter Wyss served as Senior Program Officer at the World Bank's Development Economics – Indicators Group (DECIG). In the Migration & Remittances team, his responsibilities include the contribution to the implementation of the Global Knowledge Partnership on Migration and Development (KNOMAD), primarily in the areas of environmental change and migration, migrants' rights and integration in host communities, and gender.

Dr. Lilian Yamamoto is a research member of the South American Network for Environmental Migrations (RESAMA). Her research focuses on climate migration, refugee law and law of the sea.

Dr. Caroline Zickgraf is Deputy Director of the Hugo Observatory, FNRS Postdoctoral Research Fellow in the Department of Geography at the University of Liège (Belgium), and adjunct lecturer at Sciences Po-Paris. Her research focuses on the migratory impacts of environmental degradation and climate change, transnationalism, and (im)mobility.

Part I
Existing knowledge, theories and methods

Environmental migration research

Evolution and current state of the science

Robert McLeman and François Gemenne

The timeliness of this volume

We are at a moment in time when concerns about environmental challenges, migration, and international security are becoming increasingly intertwined – in political debates, in policy-making discussions, in media reporting, and in scholarly research. Thirty years ago – perhaps as recently as fifteen years ago – the present volume would have been neither possible nor needed. It would have been impossible because there was very little reliable research of a theoretical or empirical nature to show any systematic connections between environmental changes, human population movements, and the wellbeing and security of individuals, households, and states. This does not mean the connections never existed, but simply that a lot of research had yet to be done. This book would not have been needed because the audience for it would have been tiny. Relatively few researchers and even fewer policymakers paid much attention to environmental migration on any sustained basis until the mid-1990s, and even then, interest in the topic advanced in fits and starts for another decade. Most likely, such a volume would not have been thought of, period.

What has happened in the last decade to create interest in the subject of environmental migration and displacement (EMD) (Box 1.1) and a demand for research? Three things, we would suggest.

The first is that a threshold has been crossed in terms of societal awareness of the extent and scale of human degradation of the environment and of the worrying implications for human wellbeing, especially the risks posed by anthropogenic climate change. It was only thirty years ago that the UN General Assembly tasked the UN Environmental Programme (UNEP) and the World Meteorological Organization (WMO) with creating what would eventually become the Intergovernmental Panel on Climate Change (IPCC). Only twenty-five years ago was the UN Framework Convention on Climate Change (UNFCCC) drafted, and only twenty years ago were the first concrete steps to tackle climate change agreed upon by the international community through the Kyoto Protocol, in 1997. In the decade that followed, there was a veritable explosion in media coverage of climate change, especially in countries that were most responsible for global carbon emissions (Schmidt et al. 2013). The IPCC and US Vice-President-turned-environmental-activist Al Gore were awarded the Nobel Peace Prize in 2007. Governments and institutions that fifteen years previously had had little knowledge or interest in climate science were being asked through UNFCCC processes and by media and interest groups in their home countries to assess their vulnerability to the impacts of climate change, and to explain their policies and programs for mitigating their greenhouse gas emissions. Climate change was no longer just an abstract, scientific concern, but was becoming a very concrete reality for millions. Demand for reliable research grew commensurately. In the meantime, climate science itself became increasingly sophisticated, continuously generating greater understanding of the teleconnections between the changing composition of the atmosphere and the resulting impacts on global and regional temperatures, precipitation patterns, biodiversity, ocean circulation, and so forth. Whilst the science continues to evolve rapidly, it has become increasingly evident what the physical changes are likely to be in coming decades if greenhouse gas emissions continue to grow unabated (IPCC 2013).

Box 1.1   What is EMD?

In this chapter, we use the acronym 'EMD' as a substitute for the phrase 'environmental migration and displacement', which forms part of the title of the present Handbook. In academic literature, many different terms have been used to describe the phenomenon of people moving for reasons related to events, conditions, and changes in the natural environment, some examples including ecomigrants, environmental refugees, and climate displacees. In selecting EMD, we have sought out a term that provides a broad but clearly delineated description of the phenomenon that is easily recognizable and does not carry any specific legal implications. It includes people who choose to migrate with full agency, those who have no choice but to migrate, and the full spectrum of possibilities in between. It reflects an oft-cited, widely accepted definition of what constitutes an environmental migrant put forth by the International Organization for Migration (IOM), which has considerable experience and expertise in working with such people:

> Environmental migrants are persons or groups of persons who, for compelling reasons of sudden or progressive changes in the environment that adversely affect their lives or living conditions, are obliged to leave their homes or choose to do so, either temporarily or permanently, and who move either within their country or abroad.
>
> *(IOM 2011)*

Second, there has been growing awareness that environmental degradation has far-reaching consequences for human wellbeing and, consequently, for human mobility and migration patterns. Beginning in the late 1800s, there has been in western scholarly traditions a general understanding that human population processes and patterns are influenced to some degree by environmental conditions, but for reasons described ahead, social scientists – who do the bulk of migration research – were slow to engage with the subject. It was not until the 1970s and 1980s, when a series of catastrophic famines and natural disaster events struck countries in Africa and Asia, that significant numbers of scholars began investigating the question of how environment and migration may be connected. Even then, most of the published research was carried out by researchers and NGOs not historically engaged in migration research, resulting in the emergence and popularization of terms like 'environmental refugees' that continue to be used by media, policymakers, and the general public, to the frustration of many social scientists. It was only with the emergence of the UNFCCC process and the sustained attention given to climate change impacts in successive Intergovernmental Panel on Climate Change (IPCC) reports that social scientists, legal scholars and others outside the traditional natural hazards research community began studying EMD systematically. The British government and the European Union (EU) played an important role in fostering a rapid expansion of EMD research in the early 2000s by funding large, multi-year research initiatives to provide policy-oriented research on the topic. Again, details follow.

Third, the end of the Cold War in 1991 meant that security agencies and security scholars began taking an interest in broader influences on international security, including environmental factors. Scholars such as political scientist Thomas Homer-Dixon (1991) and ecologist Norman Myers (1993) warned of environmental conflicts and environmental refugees to come in future decades. A story about environmental degradation, conflict, and refugees in West Africa published in the February, 1994, issue of the *Atlantic Monthly*, bearing the title "The Coming Anarchy", was required reading in Bill Clinton's White House (Dabelko and Dabelko 1995). By 2003, the US government was commissioning studies of the security implications of climate change (Schwartz and Randall 2003), and on two subsequent occasions the UN Security Council debated the international security implications of climate change. In 2007, civil conflict in Darfur among pastoral groups and sedentary farmers during a period of persistent drought was described by then-UN Secretary General Ban Ki-moon as being the first example of climate change-related conflict (on the basis of UNEP [2007]), although many researchers questioned the reliability of such claims (Brown and McLeman 2009). In the meantime, reporters began actively seeking out the world's first 'climate change refugees', finding examples in locations as disparate as coastal Alaska, the South Pacific, dryland areas around Lake Chad, Chesapeake Bay, and Louisiana. Security researchers today generally agree that climate change and other environmental factors can indeed act as 'threat multipliers' in countries and regions where political tensions and instability are already strong, but that the connections between environment, violence, conflict, and migration are nuanced and context-specific (Gemenne et al. 2014; Chapter 28, this volume).

An overarching theme has been that, to a significant extent, policymaking needs have driven EMD research. Whilst there are many researchers in the field who pursue EMD research from the scholarly tradition of curiosity-based inquiry, a net benefit to all researchers working in this specialty field is that policymakers have an active interest in what they have to say. The common complaint of researchers in other fields and disciplines, and particularly in migration studies – that their work goes unnoticed by governments, decision makers, the media and the general public – does not apply here. The high-quality research that has been done in the past decade or so has successfully persuaded policymakers and the concerned public that environmental change, mobility, migration patterns, and human security can no longer be thought of in isolation. Further, policymakers' need for high quality EMD research continues to grow. We see this in the evolution of the UNFCCC process, where the 2016 Paris Agreement set into motion, through Article 50, a process to recommend to signatory states how to proceed with respect to population displacements attributable to climate change. We also see it in the many other international policy arrangements being developed to respond to people displaced for environmental reasons, through initiatives such as the Platform on Disaster Displacement (Chapter 34, this volume) and the increasing engagement of multilateral organizations and agencies in EMD policymaking and programming (see chapters by UNHCR, IOM, UNEP, and World Bank, later this volume).

Although the volume of EMD research and the attention given to it have exploded in a relatively brief period of time, the ways in which we currently think about and represent EMD have a much longer history of development. Geographer David Livingstone (2000) has observed that western thinking about the human-environment relationship traces through the Enlightenment, Renaissance, and on back to the ancient Greeks; we will not here dig so far into the past. However, we do in the following pages wish to trace the more recent evolution in EMD research and thinking, describing briefly contributors and conceptual developments that are critical to what we today believe EMD to be and to how we came to such an understanding.[1] We also offer a brief synopsis of what we believe to be important current trends and questions of interest to researchers, recognizing that the following thirty-plus chapters in this book will unpack these in far greater detail.

Origins and evolution of EMD research and scholarship

Current views on the relationship between migration and the natural environment have been influenced by a much older scholarship. Although a complete book might be written on the subject, we here wish to highlight some of the more important factors and contributors to its longitudinal development. Readers wanting to read additional, more detailed treatments of the development of EMD research (and critiques of it) may wish to consult Bettini and Gioli (2016), Gemenne (2011a), McLeman (2014, 2016), and Piguet (2013), among others.

Ravenstein's laws of migration

Contemporary migration scholarship (of any type) in the western tradition traces its theoretical and methodological origins to the work of Georg Ravenstein and a series of publications he wrote between 1885 and 1889 under the title, "The Laws of Migration". Using British census data as his evidence base, Ravenstein (1889) described a number of generalized characteristics about migration which, after updating the language, can be summarized as follows:

- most migration takes place over relatively short distances
- migration tends to flow from rural areas to urban centres
- the longer the distance travelled, the more likely the migrant is destined to an urban center
- migration in one direction tends to generate return flows of migrants in the opposite direction
- there are gendered differences in migration, with men being more likely to undertake international migration than women
- longer distance migration is more likely to be undertaken by individuals than by entire households
- urban centres grow more by in-migration than by natural increase
- improvements in transportation technology and infrastructure facilitate greater amounts of migration
- most causes of migration are economic in nature

Despite the use of the term 'laws', none of these statements are universally accurate (nor were they even in Ravenstein's day), and with the passage of time, many of them are now recognized as being gross simplifications that are unreflective of the complex, multi-scale processes that influence migration patterns and behaviour. Nonetheless, Ravenstein's work remains influential today on migration scholarship in general and on EMD research in particular, in three important ways. First, Ravenstein's work represents the first systematic attempts to develop broad explanations of migration patterns and behavior on the basis of empirical evidence, an approach that stands in considerable contrast with many of his contemporaries (see ahead). In doing so, Ravenstein anticipated the 'grounded theory' approach to developing theory on the basis of empirical evidence that is widely used today by social scientists (Charmaz 2004), and established the practice of using census and similar statistical data in demographic and migration research, including EMD research (Fussell et al. 2014).

Second, although there are many obvious exceptions to Ravenstein's 'laws', a great many of his statements remain accurate more often than not. Most migration today does indeed flow from rural areas to urban centers (Samers 2010). Far more people migrate within countries than to international destinations, and more international migration flows between contiguous countries than between distant ones. Migration is often indeed heavily gendered (Chapter 11, this volume), a term Ravenstein did not himself use, but which he recognized in the differential statistics with respect to male and female migration within the United Kingdom in his day. What is perhaps more surprising than how often Ravenstein's 19th-century observations generalizations remain valid is how often they are overlooked in modern-day discussions of global migration patterns. For example, if one were to judge only by recent media reports and political debates, one would think that all of the world's refugees and most of the world's impoverished people were on the move to Europe and the US, or had already arrived. Whilst worldwide there are indeed hundreds of millions of migrants (UN DESA 2015) and an estimated 65 million forcibly displaced people (UNHCR 2017), few will ever make their way to western countries. For example, during the European migration 'crisis' of 2015–2016, 1.2 million people per year made asylum claims in EU countries (Eurostat 2017). By contrast, Uganda, Iran, and Lebanon each host approximately 1 million Convention Refugees, Turkey hosts nearly 3 million, and a single refugee camp in northern Kenya is home to nearly a quarter million people (UNHCR 2017).

Third, Ravenstein conceived migration as being driven by a variety of factors at the sending and destination locations – subsequently described by migration scholars as push and pull factors – some of them exogenous (i.e. beyond the control, influence, or knowledge of the migrant), and some of them endogenous. In Ravenstein's view, most influences on migration decisions, both endogenous and exogenous ones, were economic in nature, a view that would be heavily influential on migration scholarship well into the 1970s, and continues to be widely held today.

Malthus and Malthusianism

Another key influence on modern EMD scholarship has been Thomas Malthus and his 1798 *An Essay on the Principle of Population*, which he revised and updated several times over the following quarter-century (Malthus 1817). In his essay, Malthus considered the relationship between human populations and the productivity of arable land, available food supply, and similar types of what are today often referred to as critical ecosystem goods and services (Millennium Ecosystem Assessment 2005). Using statistics on population change in England and his own observations of the living conditions of the rapidly growing number of urban poor, Malthus concluded that human population numbers tend to grow until they outstrip the productive capacity of the land and water resources available to them. Lack of employment, falling wages, increased poverty, malnutrition, disease, famine, and conflict then begin to act as positive checks that reduce the population until an equilibrium between population and resource availability is regained – at which point the process repeats itself. Malthus used Christian theology and the historical example of the decline of the Roman Empire to support his arguments, and critiqued government provision of relief to the poor, believing that it perpetuated poverty and increased the likelihood of the onset of the aforementioned positive checks on population.

Migration was seen by later scholars as being a means of relieving Malthusian 'overpopulation' and maximizing the utilization of natural resources, with Gregory (1928: 19) arguing that "the spread of settlers subdues the waste spaces of the earth and enables each clime to produce its special products for the general service". The fact that the global human population has increased more than seven-fold since his Essay was published two hundred years ago reflects many phenomena Malthus would have not been able to anticipate, such as industrial agriculture, advances in health and sanitation, changing cultural attitudes toward the role of women and girls in society, and the advent of birth control.[2] Nevertheless, neo-Malthusian concerns about population growth, resource availability, and overpopulation are found in late-19th century social Darwinism and early-20th century environmental determinism. Warnings of Malthusian-style population crashes were rekindled by Stanford ecologist Paul Ehrlich in his 1968 book, *The Population Bomb* and the Club of Rome's 1972 *Limits to Growth* report (Meadows et al. 1972), which in turn had influence on environmental refugee and environmental conflict literature of the late 20th century.

Social Darwinism and environmental determinism

The revolution in natural sciences stimulated in the second half of the 19th century by Charles Darwin's theories of evolution and natural selection was quickly embraced by many social scientists, as well. British scholar Herbert Spencer became an early proponent of what would become described as 'social Darwinism', a theory that social behaviour and social processes evolve in a fashion similar to biological evolution, and are shaped by competition between groups for control of resources and an underlying predisposition of individuals to act in their own self-interest (Hofstadter 1944). Political theorists, economists, and geographers began using evolutionary theory to explain the historical social and economic trajectories of states and societies. German scholar Friedrich Ratzel (1902) developed the concept of *lebensraum*, suggesting that states must acquire larger areas of land and resources to support population growth and economic development, particularly where physical geography is a limit to growth. The implication of this concept is that conflict and colonial expansion are thus understandable, natural outcomes of socio-economic development.

One of Ratzel's students, the American scholar Ellen Churchill Semple (1903, 1911), further developed Ratzel's theories by arguing that the natural environment was a key determinant of the historical evolution of global population patterns and, more controversially, of the social and economic success of nations and of racial groups. Her contemporary Ellsworth Huntington (1913, 1924) argued that climate change was responsible for many historical migrations and the collapse of civilizations, and combined maps of global climate regions with selected industrial output data to suggest that temperate climates were more likely to produce industrious people than hot, tropical climates. In this context, migration was seen as being driven by the interplay of the availability of natural resources, changes in ecological conditions due to such things as shift in climate, and the competition for resources triggered by population growth.

Environment as one of many push-pull factors

By the late 1920s, environmental determinism was discredited by other scholars for its dubious theoretical presuppositions, uneven methodological rigour, racist undertones, and *de facto* legitimation of colonialism (Peet 1985). Gregory (1928), for example, disputed Huntington's theory that slight changes in average global temperatures stimulated large-scale migrations of the past, and Park (1928) expressed reservations about the normative assumptions being made about races and ethnicities. For most of the remainder of the 20th century, social science research on migration causes and behaviour would focus on the influence of economic, social, and cultural processes, with only occasional interest shown in environmental factors. One of the few exceptions was a brief flurry of research on interstate drought migration carried out by economists and rural sociologists during the 1930s Dust Bowl, which ebbed with the return of precipitation to the US Great Plains and the outbreak of the Second World War (Duncan 1935, Taylor and Vasey 1936, Holzschuh 1939; see Gregory 1989 for review).

Petersen's (1958) typology of migration captured the mainstream view of mid-century social scientists, that resource scarcity, population growth, and ecological pressure really only influence migration patterns in "primitive societies" (i.e. pastoralists, hunter-gatherers, and agrarian groups using simple technologies). With respect to environmental influences on migration more generally, the environmental determinist viewpoint had been replaced by much more subtle interpretations. For example, in the growing research literature on residential preferences in the US, urban environmental problems like air pollution, contaminated land, and noise – often described as "locational stressors" (Clark and Cadwallader 1973) – were recognized as being relevant considerations for some people when deciding where to live in a given city (Wolpert 1966, Seskin 1973, Speare 1974; see Hunter 2005 for review). Researchers also recognized that environmental amenities, such as a mild climate or access to open spaces, can be economic or quality-of-life factors that influence movements of people within the US and in other developed countries (Ullman 1954; Svart 1976; Dillman 1979; see Gutmann and Field 2010 for review). The overall tone was that environmental factors are among a large range of possible influences on migration decisions, and are usually secondary to social and economic considerations.

Environment as hazard

In the 1970s and 1980s, natural scientists began taking a greater interest in the economic, political and social dimensions of natural hazard and disaster events. Scientists had long known that losses of property and life due to floods, storms, droughts, and other hazards were influenced by social processes that determined where people lived,[3] but most mid-century hazards research focused on understanding the physical causes of such events. A series of severe famines in West Africa (1968–1972), Ethiopia (1972–1973 and 1984–1985), Bangladesh (1974), Cambodia (1975–1979), and Uganda (1980–1981), along with multiple, deadly tropical cyclones in the Bay of Bengal, prompted many hazards researchers to look more systematically at the human dimensions of disasters. Burton et al. (1978) investigated how socio-economic limits on the choices available to institutions and individuals explain why a given hazard event might cause large scale loss of life and population displacement in one country but not another. Blaikie (1985, and with Brookfield 1987) showed how the problems of soil erosion and land degradation – important elements in famines and drought-related population displacements in Sahelian Africa – were caused not by lack of knowledge on the part of farmers and pastoralists, but by exploitative economic systems that oblige users to mismanage the land. Concurrent research by Sen (1981) and Watts (1983) showed that hunger, famine, and consequent economic and physical displacements of people arise primarily in situations where conflicts, corruption, and exploitative political systems deny people access to food. The overarching conclusion of these and other scholars in the emergent 'political ecology' field was that, while poor people are most often those who experience loss or harm, and who are displaced as a consequence of environmental hazards, poverty alone is not the key reason. Rather, vulnerability – a condition of defencelessness, insecurity, and chronic exposure to physical hazards – is what distinguishes those who are most at risk (Chambers 1989; see Adger 2006 for review).

Environmental refugees and environmental security

Allusions to the potential for large numbers of people to be displaced by environmental degradation and thus requiring some form of refuge are found in many well-known neo-Malthusian works of the mid-twentieth century such as Vogt (1948) and Osborn (1953). In 1985, UNEP researcher Essam El-Hinnawi coined the explicit term 'environmental refugees', which continues to be used commonly in popular reporting on environmental migration and displacement, but is often avoided by scholars. El-Hinnawi's (1985) contention was that so many people were being displaced worldwide because of natural hazard events, desertification, deforestation, famines, food shortages, conservation actions, and forced relocations to make way for the construction of dams that they constituted a new and distinctive category of displaced people. The Worldwatch Institute (Jacobson 1988) and ecologist Norman Myers (1986) further argued that existing environmental risks and emergent ones like ozone depletion, climate change, sea level rise, and the depletion of fish stocks raised the specter in coming decades of Malthusian-type food scarcities and resource-related conflicts. Such predictions seemed to be borne out by civil violence in Rwanda and Mauritania, diagnosed by security scholars, most notably Homer-Dixon (1994), as being attributable to environmental causes. A popular article in *The Atlantic Monthly* with the foreboding title 'The Coming Anarchy' (Kaplan 1994) elevated concerns among policymakers and the general public about the prospect of environmental conflicts and displacement.

Most social scientists, legal scholars, and migration and refugee researchers have tended to avoid using the term 'environmental refugee' or variants like 'climate refugee' for several reasons. An important one is the difficulty in isolating environmental factors from other non-environmental factors in the causation of displacement; another is the fact that an internationally agreed-upon definition of what constitutes a 'refugee' has been in place since the 1951 adoption of the *UN Convention Relation to the Status of Refugees*, and it explicitly does not include people obliged to migrate for environmental reasons (Richmond 1995; Bates 2002; Chapter 25, this volume). Other authors have noted the difficulty in isolating environmental factors from non-environmental factors as proximate causes of migration and displacement, noting that only rarely do environmental factors act in isolation as drivers of migration (Foresight 2011). Other scholars noted that environmental problems and resource scarcity are more often the outcomes of conflicts than the triggers for them (Kibreab 1997). Nonetheless, the term 'environmental refugees' continued to be used by Myers (1993, 1997, 2002), and often appears in popular media stories to this day. The role that environmental events play in the cause and consequences of violence, conflict, and subsequent forced displacement continues to be debated (Chapter 28, this volume), with security researchers increasingly treating environmental problems as 'threat multipliers' that increase the risk of conflict in places that are already politically unstable (Brown et al. 2007; Gemenne et al. 2014).

Vulnerability and adaptation to climate change

As scientific evidence accumulated in the late 1980s of the extent and scale of anthropogenic climate change, concerns emerged about the potential human implications. In 1988, the United Nations General Assembly charged the UNEP and WMO with creating an advisory body – the

IPCC – to report to global policymakers on the current status of physical science research on climate change, its impacts, and opportunities for reducing greenhouse gases (GHG) and their consequent forcing effect on the climate (generally referred to as 'mitigation'). In 1990, the IPCC released its first synthesis report, in which the authors warned of the growing potential for migration and environmental refugees in the future. Specifically, the report suggested in Volume II that changes in temperature and precipitation could lead to human population displacements and migration due to: shifts in vector borne diseases; loss of houses due to hazard events like floods and mudslides; changes in availability of water, energy, food or employment; and disruptions to social networks (Tegart et al. 1990). The report further suggested that the most common types of climate-related migration will take place in developing countries, and will entail the movement of poor people from rural areas to urban centres and from coastal areas threatened by sea level rise to inland locations.

In 1992, the UNFCCC was negotiated and signed by most of the world's countries, committing to track their greenhouse gas (GHG) emissions and take action to reduce them, to manage forests sustainably, to cooperate on technical and scientific initiatives to address climate change, and to cooperate in adapting to the impacts of climate change. The subsequent Kyoto Protocol (1997) to the UNFCCC assigned specific targets for GHG emission reductions to most developed nations and former Soviet Union states, and established a variety of mechanisms to help people living in vulnerable countries adapt. One effect of the language used in the Convention and the Kyoto Protocol was that the impacts of climate change and any responses taken to them – including migration, relocation, and displacement – became framed in terms of vulnerability and adaptation. Such terms were familiar to natural scientists, hazards researchers, and others who use socio-ecological systems approaches to understanding the relationship between people and the environment, but were not commonly used in social science research on migration. Although discussions of the migration effects of climate change also appeared in the next two reports of the IPCC (in 1995 and 2001), they continued to be discussed in terms of involuntary displacements of people by rising sea levels and hazard events, using very simple push-pull and environmental refugee language.

Social science interest in the human impacts of climate change expanded rapidly following the 2001 IPCC report, with researchers examining more carefully the meanings of vulnerability and adaptation in this context (Smit and Wandel 2006). The relationship between climate change and migration in particular came under increasing scrutiny, first by independent researchers and then through concerted, government-funded projects that sought to document the environment-migration relationship through empirical evidence. Drawing upon more traditional social science theories, scholars began demonstrating that climate-related migration was not simply the result of vulnerable people being displaced by natural hazards; rather, migration was one of any numbers of strategies by which people experiencing the impacts of climate change – or who perceive themselves to be at risk – may seek to adjust and adapt (McLeman and Smit 2006; Tacoli 2009; Black 2011). Research projects funded by the EU (EACH-FOR) and the British government (Foresight) assembled empirical evidence through case studies and modelling efforts to show that environmental factors, including climatic variability and change, interact with cultural, demographic, economic, political, and social processes operating at scales from the global to the local to influence migration decisions at household and community levels (Figure 1.1). In this way, environmental migration began to look a lot less like a simple push-pull phenomenon that affects only poor people in poor countries, and a lot more like a continually changing, complex interplay of processes that generate context-specific, heterogeneous outcomes in countries rich and poor.

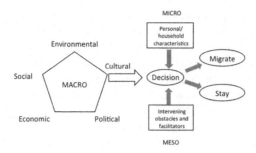

Figure 1.1 Conceptualization of the environmental migration process, simplified from final report of Foresight Report on Global Environmental Migration (Foresight 2011)

Current research: multidisciplinarity and (re)engagement with general migration scholarship

Environmental migration scholarship has evolved considerably from its 19th century origins, and is today best described by two key characteristics. First is an increasing and ongoing engagement between researchers specifically interested in the migration outcomes of environmental phenomena with the much larger and wider body of migration and refugee research that looks at the socio-economic causes and implications. This engagement – or re-engagement, if we account for the historical origins of current research – works in both directions: researchers coming from a natural hazards/socio-ecological systems/vulnerability background increasingly draw upon social science concepts in their work, and social science-grounded migration and refugee scholars are showing increasing interest in studying the environmental dimensions of migration. With this re-engagement, a much wider range of theories, conceptual approaches, and methodological tools are being brought to bear, many of which are described in the chapters that follow in the current volume.

A second characteristic is a broadening in the range of disciplines interested in environmental migration questions, bringing to EMD research many talented groups of people who historically were not represented. Environmental migration was once a relatively obscure corner of scholarship, primarily of interest to small numbers of demographers, economists, ecologists, geographers, and the occasional political scientist. The subject now engages researchers from an ever-widening spectrum of disciplines such as computer modelling, gender studies, history, human rights, international development, law, media studies, medicine, philosophy, and psychology; many of these are represented in the chapters that follow.

It is now widely accepted that EMD results from complex interplays of environmental and non-environmental issues, as was illustrated in Figure 1.1. Many who migrate and self-identify (or are identified by officials) as economic migrants or asylum seekers may be motivated by environmental reasons as well as political or economic ones. It is also accepted that EMD spans the spectrum from purely voluntary, opportunity-seeking migration to refugee-like flight from environmental hazards, with any number of variants between these extremes. Researchers are also increasingly interested in the inability to migrate and the desire to stay put in spite of environmental risks, a topic expanded upon by Zickgraf (Chapter 5, this volume).

EMD research continues to be highly policy-oriented and policy-responsive, and concern about the future impacts of climate change continues to be a key driver of much of the research presently being done. Policymakers are particularly interested in receiving information about how many people presently migrate for environmental reasons and how many will migrate or be displaced under various future climate scenarios, where these will occur, and what the social and economic implications will be. It is presently not possible to more than 'guess-timate' the number of people who currently migrate for environmental reasons, for reasons related to a lack of reliable global data on migration and challenges in defining what constitutes environmental migration – topics that are addressed in greater detail in the chapters that follow. We know that most migration – EMD or otherwise – takes place within national borders; we also know that in any given year, tens of thousands of people are displaced by environmental hazards, but that the number of people who migrate for other environment-related reasons is likely much larger (Gemenne 2011b).

To make more accurate measurements and predictions in the future, concerted research efforts using a range of methods will continue to be needed, in addition to better data and greater agreement on definitions. An emerging frontier in empirical EMD research is the generation of scalable models – quantitative and geospatial ones – that allow users to visualize potential future EMD patterns. Several chapters in Part I of this volume describe these in detail. At the same time, qualitative research is essential to 'ground truth' modelling efforts to better understand important non-environmental influences such as gender, perceptions, and behaviour, and to harness indigenous understandings of environment and human wellbeing. Again, Part I of this book provides the reader more details on the methodological and conceptual challenges and opportunities at hand, with Part II providing the reader with numerous regional examples of the application and results of research to date, and specific directions where more work is needed. Part III of this book summarizes key legal and policy developments that have been made to date and discussions that are still ongoing. It also provides insights from multilateral organizations at the centre of current policymaking discussions and debates relevant to EMD.

The conclusion Chapter 36 to this volume, by Professor Lori M. Hunter, offers a large number of prescient observations on the future directions and demands of EMD research, and we do not wish duplicate poorly here her excellent chapter. If we were to offer one specific critique of our own of current EMD research, it would be that there is a need to investigate more rigorously the many non-climate-change influences on migration and displacement. Efforts in this regard appear to have lagged behind. This is reflected in the content of this book; there is a heavy tendency in the following chapters to consider migration and displacement primarily in the context of climate change. That is fine, for it is an accurate reflection of where the field presently is. Were we to have expanded this book beyond its present thirty-six chapters – which might have given our publisher a figurative heart attack – we would have liked to include additional chapters on a wide range of topics that figure directly or indirectly on EMD writ large, such as food systems, desertification processes, water management, disaster preparedness, and population aging; but we had to draw the line somewhere. Perhaps these will find their way into a future edition.

Notes

1 For those who prefer more technically precise language, the epistemology and ontology of the field.
2 In Malthus's day, abstinence was the only reliable form of birth control. Although Malthus advocated strongly in favour of abstinence, he had little faith people could control their urges.
3 White's (1945) study of flood impacts in the US provides an early example.

References

Adger, W. N. (2006). Vulnerability. *Global Environmental Change*, 16(3), 268–281.

Bates, D. C. (2002). Environmental refugees? Classifying human migrations caused by environmental change. *Population and Environment*, 23(5), 465–477.

Bettini, G., & Gioli, G. (2016). Waltz with development: Insights on the developmentalization of climate-induced migration. *Migration and Development*, 5(2), 171–189.

Black, R. (2011). Climate change: Migration as adaptation. *Nature*, 478, 447–449.

Blaikie, P. (1985). *The political economy of soil erosion in developing countries*. London: Longman.

Blaikie, P., & Brookfield, H. (1987). *Land degradation and society*. London: Methuen.

Brown, O., Hammill, A., & McLeman, R. (2007). Climate change as the "new" security threat: implications for Africa. *International Affairs*, 83(6), 1141–1154.

Brown, O., & McLeman, R. (2009). A recurring anarchy? The emergence of climate change as a threat to international peace and security. *Conflict, Security and Development*, 9(3), 289–305.

Burton, I., Kates, R. W., & White, G. F. (1978). *The environment as hazard*. New York: Guilford Press.

Chambers, R. (1989). Editorial introduction: Vulnerability, coping and policy. *IDS Bulletin*, 20(2), 1–7.

Charmaz, K. (2004). Grounded theory. In S. N. Hesse-Biber & P. Leavy (Eds.), *Approaches to qualitative research: A readers on theory and practice* (pp. 496–521). New York: Oxford University Press.

Clark, W. A. V., & Cadwallader, M. (1973). Locational stress and residential mobility. *Environment and Behavior*, 5(1), 29.

Dabelko, G. D., & Dabelko, D. D. (1995). Environmental security: Issues of conflict and redefinition. Spring(1):3–13.

Dillman, D. A. (1979). Residential preferences, quality of life, and the population turnaround. *American Journal of Agricultural Economics*, 61(5), 960–966.

Duncan, O. D. (1935). *Population trends in Oklahoma*. Stillwater: Oklahoma Agricultural Experiment Station.

Ehrlich, P. (1968). *The population bomb*. New York: Ballantine Books.

El-Hinnawi, E. (1985). *Environmental refugees*. Nairobi: United Nations Environmental Program.

Eurostat. (2017). *Asylum statistics*. Retrieved from http://ec.europa.eu/eurostat/statistics-explained/index.php/Asylum_statistics

Foresight: Migration and global environmental change. (2011). Final Project Report. London: Government Office for Science.

Fussell, E., Hunter, L. M., & Gray, C. (2014). Measuring the environmental dimensions of human migration: The demographer's toolkit. *Global Environmental Change*, 28, 182–191.

Gemenne, F. (2011a). Why the numbers don't add up: A review of estimates and predictions of people displaced by environmental changes. *Global Environmental Change*, 21(S1), S41–S49.

Gemenne, F. (2011b). How they became the face of climate change: Research and policy interactions in the birth of the "environmental migration" concept. In E. Piguet, A. Pecoud, & P. de Guchteneire (Eds.), *Migration, environment and climate change* (pp. 225–259). Cambridge: Cambridge University Press.

Gemenne, F., Barnett, J., Adger, W. N., & Dabelko, G. D. (2014). Climate and security: Evidence, emerging risks, and a new agenda. *Climatic Change*, 123(1), 1–9.

Gregory, J. N. (1989). *American exodus: The Dust Bowl migration and Okie culture in California*. New York: Oxford University Press.

Gregory, J. W. (1928). *Human migration and the future*. London: Seeley, Service & Co.

Gutmann, M. P., & Field, V. (2010). Katrina in historical context: Environment and migration in the U.S. *Population and Environment*, 31(1–3), 3–19.

Hofstadter, R. (1944). *Social Darwinism in American thought*. Boston: Beacon Press.

Holzschuh, A. (1939). *A study of 6655 migrant households receiving emergency grants*. San Francisco: Farm Security Administration.

Homer-Dixon, T. (1991). On the threshold: Environmental changes as causes of acute conflict. *International Security*, 16(2), 76–116.

Homer-Dixon, T. (1994). Environmental scarcities and violent conflict: Evidence from cases. *International Security*, 19(1), 5–40.

Hunter, L. M. (2005). Migration and environmental hazards. *Population and Environment*, 26(4), 273–302.

Huntington, E. (1913). Changes of climate and history. *American Historical Review*, 18(2), 213–232.

Huntington, E. (1924). *Civilization and climate* (3rd ed.). New Haven: Yale University Press.

International Organization for Migration (IOM). (2011). *Glossary on migration* (2nd ed.). International Migration Law No. 25. Geneva.

IPCC. (2013). *Climate Change 2013: The Physical Science Basis. Contribution of Working Group I to the Fifth Assessment Report of the Intergovernmental Panel on Climate Change.* Cambridge: Cambridge University Press.

Jacobson, J. L. (1988). *Environmental refugees: A yardstick of habitability.* Washington, DC: Worldwatch Institute.

Kaplan, R. D. (1994). The coming anarchy. *The Atlantic Monthly*, February 1, 44–76.

Kibreab, G. (1997). Environmental causes and impact of refugee movements: A critique of the current debate. *Disasters*, 21(1), 20–38.

Livingstone, D. N. (2000). Environmental determinism. In R. J. Johnston, D. Gregory, G. Pratt, & M. Watts (Eds.), *The dictionary of human geography* (4th ed., pp. 212–215). Oxford: Blackwell.

Malthus, T. R. (1817). *An essay on the principle of population.* London: John Murray.

McLeman, R. A. (2014). *Climate and human migration: Past experiences, future challenges.* New York: Cambridge University Press.

McLeman, R. A. (2016). Migration as adaptation: Conceptual origins, recent developments, and future directions. In A. Milan, B. Schraven, K. Warner, & N. Cascone (Eds.), *Migration, risk management and climate change: Evidence and policy responses* (pp. 213–229). Dordrecht: Springer.

McLeman, R. A., & Smit, B. (2006). Migration as an adaptation to climate change. *Climatic Change*, 76(1–2), 31–53.

Meadows, D. H., Meadows, D. L., Randers, J., & Behrens, W. W. (1972). *The limits to growth: a report for the Club of Rome's Project on the Predicament of Mankind.* New York: Universe Books.

Millennium Ecosystem Assessment (2005). *Ecosystems and human well being: Synthesis.* Washington, DC: Island Press.

Myers, N. (1986). The environmental dimension to security issues. *Environmentalist*, 6(4), 251–257.

Myers, N. (1993). Environmental refugees in a globally warmed world. *BioScience*, 43(11), 752–761.

Myers, N. (1997). Environmental refugees. *Population and Environment*, 19(2), 167–182.

Myers, N. (2002). Environmental refugees: A growing phenomenon of the 21st century. *Philosophical Transactions of the Royal Society London: Biological Sciences: Series B*, 357(1420), 609–613.

Osborn, F. 1953. *The limits of the earth.* Boston: Little, Brown.

Park, R. E. (1928). Human migration and the marginal man. *American Journal of Sociology*, 33(6), 881–893.

Peet, R. (1985). The social origins of environmental determinism. *Annals of the Association of American Geographers*, 75(3), 309–333.

Petersen, W. (1958). A general typology of migration. *American Sociological Review*, 23(3), 256–266.

Piguet, E. (2013). From "Primitive Migration" to "Climate Refugees": The curious fate of the natural environment in migration studies. *Annals of the Association of American Geographers*, 103(1), 148–162.

Ratzel, F. (1902). *Die Erde und Das Leben.* Leipzig: Bibliographisches Institut.

Ravenstein, E. G. (1889). The laws of migration (second paper). *Journal of the Royal Statistical Society*, 52(2), 241–305.

Richmond, A. H. (1995). The environment and refugees: Theoretical and policy issues. *Population Bulletin of the United Nations*, 39, 1–17.

Samers, M. (2010). *Migration.* London: Routledge.

Schmidt, A., Ivanova, A., & Schafer, M. S. (2013). Media attention for climate change around the world: A comparative analysis of newspaper coverage in 27 countries. *Global Environmental Change*, 23(5), 1233–1248.

Schwartz, P., & Randall, D. (2003). *An abrupt climate change scenario and its implications for United States national security.* Emeryville, CA: Global Business Network.

Semple, E. C. (1903). *American history and its geographic conditions.* New York: Houghton Mifflin.

Semple, E. C. (1911). *Influences of geographic environment on the basis of Ratzel's system of anthropo-geography.* New York: Henry Holt and Company.

Sen, A. (1981). Ingredients of famine analysis: Availability and entitlements. *The Quarterly Journal of Economics*, 96(3), 433–464.

Seskin, E. P. (1973). Residential choice and air pollution: A general equilibrium model. *The American Economic Review*, 63(5), 960–967.

Smit, B., & Wandel, J. (2006). Adaptation, adaptive capacity and vulnerability. *Global Environmental Change*, 16(3), 282–292.

Speare, A. (1974). Residential satisfaction as an intervening variable in residential mobility. *Demography*, 11(2), 173–188.

Svart, L. M. (1976). Environmental preference migration: A review. *Geographical Review*, 66(3), 314–330.

Tacoli, C. (2009). Crisis or adaptation? Migration and climate change in a context of high mobility. *Environment and Urbanization*, 21(2), 513–525.

Taylor, P. S., & Vasey, T. (1936). Drought refugee and labor migration to California, June-December 1935. *Monthly Labor Review*, 42(2), 312–318.

Tegart, W. J. M., Sheldon, G. W., & Griffiths, D. C. (1990). *The IPCC impacts assessment: Report prepared for IPCC by working group II*. Canberra: Australian Government Publishing Service.

Ullman, E. L. (1954). Amenities as a factor in regional growth. *Geographical Review*, 44(1), 119–132.

UN Department of Economic and Social Affairs, Population Division. (2015). *World population prospects: The 2015 revision, key findings and advance tables*. Working Paper No. ESA/P/WP.241. New York.

UNEP. (2007). *Sudan: Post-conflict environmental assessment*. Nairobi. Retrieved from http://sudanreport. unep.ch/chapters/00_foreword_summary.pdf

UNHCR. (2017). *Figures at a glance*. Retrieved from www.unhcr.org/figures-at-a-glance.html

Vogt, W. (1948). *Road to survival*. New York: William Sloane Associates, Inc.

Watts, M. (1983). Hazards and crises: A political economy of drought and famine in Northern Nigeria. *Antipode*, 15(1), 24–34.

White, G. (1945). *Human Adjustment to Floods*. Chicago: University of Chicago, Research Paper No. 29.

Wolpert, J. (1966). Migration as an adjustment to environmental stress. *Journal of Social Issues*, 22(4), 92–102.

2

Theories of voluntary and forced migration

Etienne Piguet

Introduction

No clearcut delineation can be made between voluntary and forced migration, but it is fair to say that most attempts at theorizing migration – in the sense of suggesting general frameworks of understanding based on regularities[1] – address cases where potential migrants retain a fairly high level of agency and are not "forced" to move. On the contrary, as stated by Zolberg: "The most obvious thing about refugee flows is [for most social scientists] that they are unruly" (Zolberg 1983: 25), and thus hardly suitable for theorization. However, with the growing salience of concepts such as "mixed migration" (Van Hear, Brubaker, and Bessa 2009) and "survival migration" (Betts 2013), and calls to go beyond the structure versus agency dualism in migration studies (Bakewell 2010), a promising perspective of investigation opens up for re-embedding forced migration within a more general migration theory framework or within the even broader framework of a theory of social transformation, development and crisis (Castles 2003; Lubkemann 2008; Van Hear 2010; de Haas 2014). As I have argued elsewhere, such a move would also be fruitful in the specific case of environmentally driven migration studies (Piguet 2013), a subfield which developed to a large extent in isolation but is marked by a shift from monocausal environmental "push" theories toward "a greater integration of context, including micro-level, meso-level, and macro-level interactions" (Hunter, Luna, and Norton 2015: 377). Achieving a full reconciliation of these schools of thought is beyond the scope of this chapter, but I will try here to pave the way by giving a brief overview of some of the main theoretical directions suggested by researchers of both voluntary and forced migration.

Theories of voluntary migration

Why do people choose to migrate? For more than a century, the social sciences have been attempting to answer that question, which concerns geography as well as psychology, political economy and economics, sociology, anthropology and demography. As shown twenty years ago by Massey in his classic plea for theoretical pluralism in migration studies, one can consider each school of thought to have contributed valuable conceptual enlargements that are often complementary rather than antagonistic (Massey et al. 1994). These theories have led to unequal but often quite satisfactory results in terms of simulation and prediction where "there is little room for exclusive theoretical truth claim" (de Haas 2014: 11). They allow us to draw a reasonably coherent picture of the different factors and causal mechanisms that are at play in relation to migration. The recent history of migration studies can be understood, in that perspective, as a progressive enlargement of the spectrum of explanation mechanisms, although it is clear that no unified and specific theory of such a multifaceted phenomenon will ever exist (Brettell and Hollifield 2014; Castles, de Haas, and Miller 2014).

Among the most used, the neoclassical school – not to be confounded with the much broader push-pull approach – points to the central importance of economic factors and to the process of utility maximization by individual agents that underlies migration decisions. The expectation of higher wages and better employment leads those people who are not averse toward risk and can afford the cost of displacement to consider migration, whereas others discard it (Harris and Todaro 1970). Behaviourist geographers acknowledged this general framework but added – among other things – that actors have only limited access to information and that their rationality is thus bounded, leading them to pursue their satisfaction in an incremental way by seizing opportunities rather than by targeting the unique move that would maximize their utility in absolute terms (Wolpert 1965). Considering the ways in which people are aware of migration opportunities and risk, and the ways in which they process this information, thus appears paramount. Both the neoclassical and the behaviourist conceptions fit nicely into Everett Lee's famous, but very general, push-pull model (Figure 2.1), which mentions demographic, economic and political factors in the areas of departure and destinations, along with intervening opportunities and obstacles, as interacting to produce migrations:

> No matter how short or how long, how easy or how difficult, every act of migration involves an origin, a destination, and an intervening set of obstacles. We include the distance of the move as one that is always present.
>
> *(Lee 1966: 49)*

Although this has been forgotten by the many adherents and critics of the push-pull framework, one can note that Lee goes in the same subjectivist direction as Wolpert when he states that "it is not so much the actual factors at origin and destination as the perception of these factors which results in migration" (Lee 1966: 51).

Demographic approaches conceptualize the decision process as heavily influenced by the age (life-cycle) and family (life-course) status of the potential migrant: a young single student,

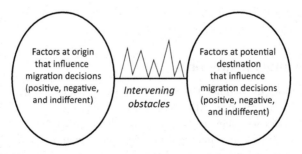

Figure 2.1 Origin and destination factors and intervening obstacles in migration, after Lee's (1966) model

a family whose children are not yet in school or a recently divorced person will have much stronger incentives to move than people in other situations (Leslie and Richardson 1961; Plane 1993; Wingens et al. 2011). In the same vein, the human capital approach (Sjaastad 1962) stresses that the propensity to migrate varies according to a person's level of education and skills, and that migration itself can bring a significant contribution to the accumulation of human capital by allowing the migrant to acquire valuable degrees and experience. Numerous authors use a framework inspired by Bourdieu's distinction between forms of capital (Bourdieu and Passeron 1978) and stress the importance of social and cultural capital as both a determinant for and a consequence of migration (Findlay 2011), and more specifically environmental migration (McLeman and Smit 2006). More recently, mobility studies (Urry 2007) have contributed to the conceptualization of migration in connection with various forms of capital by emphasizing that the very fact of moving and "knowing how to move" can be considered as an asset in itself, that facilitates subsequent moves (Tarrius 1989) and forms a component of spatial capital (Rérat and Lees 2011). Other researchers stressed that understanding migration could not be dissociated from understanding the reasons that prevent migration and thus foster voluntary or involuntary immobility (Fischer 1999; Hammar et al. 1997; Carling 2002) a credo that found some echo in forced migration studies (Lubkemann 2008) as well as in research on environmentally induced migration with the notion of "trapped populations" (Black et al. 2013. 355).

A significant conceptual improvement in migration theory can be associated with the "new economics of labour migration" (NELM) (Stark 1991). Central to this approach is the idea that the household, rather than the individual, should be considered as the decision-making unit regarding migration. Phenomena that might appear irrational through the lenses of the preceding schools of thought can be understood as rational when viewed this way. It is possible, for example, that while the departure of one member of a household brings no absolute increase in earnings, it nevertheless makes sense as a collective risk-diversification strategy. Another important concept brought to the fore by the NELM is the importance of relative deprivation: the decision to move can follow a degradation of the situation of a person or household relative to the rest of society, without any change in its absolute purchasing power. This is a central element that complicates the relationship between migration and economic development and explains a possible migration hump where migration increases rather than decrease with growth (de Haas 2007).

Theories rooted in social psychology and especially in theories of motivation and decision have also made a significant contribution to the understanding of migration intentions. Tartakovsky and Schwartz (2001) distinguish three types of motives for moving (preservation of the self and the quest for security, personal development and materialism), whereas De Jong and Fawcett (1981) point toward seven categories of improvement expectations: material life, status, comfort, stimulation, autonomy, affiliation and morality. These motivations interact with social and cultural norms as well as individual characteristics such as gender and personality. The propensity to take risks and the locus of control (the extent to which an individual believes himself or herself to be in control of events that affect his or her life) are often seen as central psychological dimensions in this regard (Winchie and Carment 1989; Chirkov et al. 2007; Boneva and Frieze 2001); they interact with the level of satisfaction or dissatisfaction and shape migration intentions (Stinner and Van Loon 1992).

Among recent contributions to migration theory, the network approach – rooted in older concepts such as chain migration and social capital – is of great relevance (Boyd 1989; Epstein 2008; Tilly 2007). Central here is the idea that contacts with already expatriated friends or members of one's close or distant family are significant assets that usually facilitate and encourage migration (De Jong 2000; Epstein and Gang 2006). According to Haug (2008), five mechanisms explain the impact of networks on migration:

- affinities (the existence of relatives and friends at the place of residence/destination reduces/increases the tendency to migrate),
- information (the more information channels, the more influential such information is on the decision to migrate),
- facilitation (relatives and friends promote migration to their own places of residence by facilitating adjustment to the new location),
- conflict (intra-familial conflicts within the community of origin cause migration), and
- support (families may encourage members to migrate for work, e.g., as a strategy to secure the household income).

In addition to affinities at home, networks might also discourage the move by providing dismal information about opportunities abroad or by putting additional constraints on the potential migrant (Faist 1997; Collyer 2005; de Haas 2010). An interesting and yet under-researched question in that context is the respective impact of weak versus strong, and family versus nonfamily, networks (Herman 2006). Another issue is the impact of new technologies of information and communication (NTIC) on networks and the way they might significantly facilitate migration and reduce distances (Dekker and Engbersen 2014), and also more broadly transform aspiration of potential migrants through the circulation of norms and values.

The line of thinking pioneered by network theory stresses the linkages between expatriates and potential migrants and can be associated with the general paradigmatic shift that has occurred in migration studies, from a conception of migration as a once-and-for-all movement between two geographical spaces, to the conception of a transnational space of flow within which migrants move without losing contact with their region of origin (Palloni et al. 2001; Faist 1997; Vertovec 1999; Portes 2001). This idea is also central in contemporary theories of globalization, often inspired by the neo-Marxist world system theory (Nikolinakos 1975; Massey et al. 1993: 444). Applied to migration, such theories point toward the connections between different kinds of flows and different segments of social and economic life often previously considered as isolated from one another but that contribute to keep peripheral states in a situation that provides a "reserve army" of cheap labor to the core of the capitalist economy. Sassen shows, for example, how a change in the world flow of goods implies new opportunities for work for women, which modify gender relations and ultimately increase the incentive for migration for men (Sassen 1988). In more recent work, the same author puts less weight on the function of reserve army assigned to international migrants, but continues to connect migration to wider globalization processes. She explicitly links recent migration crises, in the Mediterranean, in the Andaman see and at the Mexico-US border, with a "massive loss of habitat" due to inappropriate international development policies, processes of land grabbing and soil privatization by multinational companies (Sassen 2016). Finally, many authors have advocated a "return of the state" in migration theory. They contend that even in times of globalization, migrations remain highly constrained by nation-state policies. Recruitment agreements, political partnerships such as the EU or MERCOSUR, colonial links, political antagonisms, asylum policies, visa policies and border control imply power relations between political spaces that have to be understood as major drivers of migration (Hollifield 2000; Cornelius, Martin, and Hollifield 2004; Cornelius and Rosenblum 2005). This obviously points toward a link between the traditional migration theories on the one hand and forced migration on the other.

Theories of forced migration

What are the reasons which drive a person to flee his place of residence, and how does this person choose a destination? That simple question remained for a long time, and to a large extend still is, at the margin of forced migration studies. It seems obvious that, in a context of violence, emergency and danger, refugees are simply compelled to leave their home in hurry and move toward the first safe haven they encounter. The consequences for theory and empirical research are that the regularities necessary for theorization are lacking. Therefore, as stated by Zolberg:

> Social scientists who theorize about the causes and consequences of international migration generally exclude refugee *movements. (. . .). They do so because of an inherent distinction between the two types of population flows. Migration is generally viewed as an economic phenomenon. . . .). By* contrast, the most obvious thing about refugee flows is that they are unruly, in the sense that they result from events such as civil strife, abrupt changes of regime, arbitrary governmental decisions, or international war, all of which are generally considered singular and unpredictable occurrences.
>
> *(Zolberg 1983 :25)*

This central idea was already well illustrated by Kunz (1973: 131) for whom "[Refugee's] progress more often than not resembles the movement of the billiard ball: devoid of inner direction their path is governed by the kinetic factors of inertia, friction and the vectors of outside forces applied on them". As noted by Black (Black 1991: 281): "Existing work has tended to view refugee flows separately as temporary, unique, one-off events". In Lee's conceptual framework, one could say that the push factor "violence" – and hence the fate of the state as regulating violence – overdetermine the displacement and saturate the explanation of the flight. Apart of that overdetermination, random factors then govern the fate of the refugees. Attempts at theorizing refugee flows are therefore scarce, and focus strictly on the role of the state in "making" refugees (Marx 1990; Hein 1993). In the 27 papers selected by Robin Cohen for his influential reader *Theories of Migration* (1996), only five: Kunz (1973), Zolberg (Zolberg, Suhrke, and Arguayo 1986; Zolberg 1983), Beyer (1981) and Adelman (1988) are concerned with refugees, and only the first three make an attempt at theorizing refugee movements (see also Black [2001]). Twenty years later, forced migration seems even less present in theoretical review books and papers (Brettell and Hollifield 2014 ; Bakewell 2010; Piguet 2013; Smith and King 2012; Skeldon 2012; Favell 2007; Geyer 2002).

Two pioneers – reprinted in Cohen's reader – paved the way to theorize forced migration. The first, Egon F. Kunz, published papers in 1973 (Kunz 1973) and 1981 (Kunz 1981) which relied heavily on Lee's push-pull model. The former dealt with displacement, transit and arrival in the host society, whereas the second extended the analysis to aspects preceding and succeeding flight. The second, Anthony Richmond, published his thesis in 1969, several papers and an ambitious book – *Global Apartheid* – critically linking migrations flows with social theory, where he contested the dichotomy between 'voluntary' and 'involuntary' (or forced) migration (Richmond 1988, 1993, 1994, 2002).

One of the central contributions of Kunz is the distinction he made – along a continuum – between acute and anticipatory refugees: "The anticipatory refugee (. . .) leaves his home country before the deterioration of the military or political situation prevents his orderly departure. He arrives in the country of settlement prepared" (Kunz 1973: 131).

"Acute refugee movements arise from great political changes or movements of armies. The refugees flee either in mass or, if their flight is obstructed, in bursts of individual or group escapes, and their primary purpose is to reach safety in a neighbouring or nearby country which will grant them asylum. The emphasis is on the escape.

(Kunz 1973: 132)

The identification of an anticipatory component in refugee flight implies a more complex set of driving factors and justifies the attempt at theorizing. As stated by Johansson:

Pull factors are certainly more important for anticipatory than acute refugees as the former have more time to plan than the latter and are not immediately compelled to become refugees. In addition, anticipatory refugees typically have more information on possible countries of refuge and a clearer idea of their destination than acute refugees.

(Johansson 1990: 244)

Richmond goes in the same direction as he considers – relying on Anthony Giddens' structuration theory – that, even under heavy constraint, a certain margin of choice remains for most refugees. For him, "Human agency implies an element of choice and ensures that some degree of uncertainty is always present, even when the choices in question are severely constrained by external conditions" (Richmond 1993: 9). Even in the case of refugees:

Under certain conditions the decision to move may be made after due consideration of all relevant information, rationally calculated to maximize net advantage, including both material and symbolic rewards. At the other extreme, the decision to move may be made in a state of panic facing a crisis situation which leaves few alternatives but escape form intolerable threats.

(Richmond 1988: 17)

On the bases of these premises, attempts at theorizing refugee movements were made possible. A closer look is warranted at three important contributions to forced migration theorization.

The creation of nation-states as forced migration push factor

Relying on Hannah Arendt's *The Origins of Totalitarianism* (Arendt 1973 [1951], pp. 269–290), Aristide Zolberg underlined how the creation of new states could become a refugee-generating process (Zolberg 1983). The process is actually twofold. On the one hand, the creation of a new state is often associated with violence, revolution or annexation. On the other hand, the creation of a nation-state relies heavily on a process of exclusion which aims at creating a national identity (Geertz 1973; Wimmer 2002). As Zolberg explains:

Imperial government generally requires only minimal involvement on the part of the subject population; its demands upon them are limited to obedience and material tribute. Cultural diversity does not matter much because the system of rule is largely indirect, with traditional elites of the various groups acting as go-betweens. (. . .) The organizational imperatives of the nation-state are much more demanding in this respect, since the persistence of relatively autonomous sociocultural communities negates its very existence. In order for the nation to come into being, the population must be transformed into individuals who visibly share a common nationality; the process entails an actualization of the myth that they are quite literally "born together," that they constitute a natural community.

(Zolberg 1983: 36)

Consequently, "Massive refugee flows are most prominently concomitant of the secular transformation of a world of empires and of small self-sufficient communities or tribes into a world of national states" (p. 30). This early work of Zolberg mainly saw refugees as byproducts of an historical process that might ultimately end. In a subsequent work, Zolberg, Suhrke, and Aguayo (1986) developed this model in a less historicist way. They insist on the relevance of international power relations in refugee generating processes and challenge the "internalist" vision embodied in international law that "the reasons for flight should be traced to conflicts, or radical political, social, or economic changes in [refugees'] own country" (Goodwin-Gill 1983: 18). Especially following post-World War II decolonization, during the Cold War and, in recent times, refugee-generating crises are the products of transnational conflicts of interests between superpowers even if other processes such as development aid and, more controversially, humanitarian and peacekeeping interventions sometimes have a mitigating effect on the necessity to flee. Zolberg's insights were strikingly prescient when considering the refugee flows that followed the disintegration of Yugoslavia and recent attempts at creating new national entities such as South Sudan. They are also consistent with more recent attempts to link global processes to local displacement crisis as suggested by Sassen (see previous) and that of Stephen Castles.

The political economy of forced migration

Whereas Zolberg underlines through state formation a common feature of different historical episodes of flight, Stephen Castles considers the continuous growth of refugee flows, which characterized the end of the 20th century (Castles 2003). He sees this evolution in the framework of political economy, as the product of a general process of globalisation that created "a system of selective inclusion and exclusion of specific areas and groups, which maintains and exacerbates inequality" (p. 16). His statement that "Forced migration is not the result of a string of unconnected emergencies but rather an integral part of North-South relationships" (p. 17) leads to the necessity of considering a very general framework of explanations, loosely connected to world system theory, and which could be summarized with the label "social transformations". In simple terms, globalization increases economic inequalities around the world, undermines traditional regulation mechanisms and fosters conflicts and human rights abuse, even as it simultaneously increases the level of connexion between the different parts of the world through a process of transnationalisation. This in turn leads to a massive surge in various forms of migration which, to a certain extent, "blur[s] the distinction between forced and economic migration" (p. 17).

Exit instead of voice or loyalty

The previous two lines of argument explain forced migration on a macro scale, but do not consider the possible agency of refugees themselves. In this sense, they do not depart from the old assumption mentioned previously that refugees are merely passive victims. A third line of thought suggests that in certain circumstances the flight and the direction of the flight can be an autonomous choice. Albert O. Hirschman's "Exit, Voice and Loyalty" (1970) undertakes a study subtitled "responses to decline in firms, organizations and states" that considers the triad of Exit (i.e. emigration), Voice (protest) and Loyalty as mutually exclusive alternatives available to citizens of an unsatisfactory state. Hirschman provides insights into the conditions under which emigration becomes the response when individuals face violence, insecurity or persecution that undermine their loyalty, while the authoritative control of the state on freedom of speech and political association makes the "voice" option too dangerous.

Hirschman refined his theory after applying it to the disintegration of the German Democratic Republic and the sudden outflow of refugees it generated in 1989. In the case of East Germany, the relation between emigration and contestation at home (voice) appeared to be that of a tandem where both "reinforced each other, achieving jointly the collapse of the regime" (Hirschman 1993: 13 in the reprint version). Other recent studies relying on Hirschman's framework, such as Hoffmann (2004) on Cuban refugees, offer evidence that in other cases the inverse relationship suggested by Hirschman between exit and voice remains valid: some government have deliberately tolerated or even encouraged the exit of refugees in order to mitigate the contestation within the country.

In any case, although Hirschman's contribution remains more "a conceptual framework" than an operational model or a grand theory (Hoffmann 2004: 35), it is of great interest for forced migration theory building because it underlines the possible margin of action of certain refugees and call for a global analysis of the alternatives which are open to potential migrants. A second, even more important contribution is that Hirschman reintroduces the role of the state of origin in the analysis of refugee flows. By opening or closing its borders, by actively seeking to curb emigration or on the contrary by encouraging it, the state of origin plays a central role in shaping refugee flows. This role was often neglected, under the assumption that the country of origin of refugee would be, by definition, in turmoil and unable to control the movements of its citizens.

Toward an integrated theory of (forced) migration

Although conflicts and violence remain central features of refugee flows and differentiate them from other forms of migration, they all have to be understood in the context of a global political economy (Castles/Zolberg) which considers emigration as one option in the relations between a State and its citizens (Hirschman) and gives back to individuals a certain amount of autonomy in their migration choices (Richmond/Hirschman). As stated by Castles et al.: "Even among those who are fleeing violence or persecution and are therefore in need of protection, there is evidence that some, although not all, asylum seekers have a degree of control over where they go and how they travel" (Castles, Crawley, and Loughna 2003: 29).

The logical consequence is that a theory of forced migration flows would encompass a multiplicity of factors at various scales in the region of origin, along itineraries of flight, in the regions of destination as well as at global level, what Richmond called a "Multivariate Model of Reactive Migration" (Richmond 1993: 11). This is a clear improvement compared to the idea of refugees flights as untheorizable reactions to unsustainable thresholds of violence and persecution. An idea that has – as noted at the beginning of this chapter – largely prevented the theorization of forced migration. A second consequence of these conceptual improvements is that it seems less and less justified to treat forced migration as incompatible with migration theory in general. As stated by Carling (2014: 7): "there is no categorical analytical distinction between 'forced' and 'voluntary' migration, since all migration involves both choices and constraints". In the conclusion of this chapter we suggest a path to overcome this historical divide.

Conclusion

The chapter has summarized a well-developed and structured, if not fully coherent, corpus of theories of "voluntary" and mainly economic migration, along with a much less developed and patchy corpus of attempts at theorizing "forced" migration. Going further and re-embedding forced migration within the main stream of migration theories or within an even broader social theory is beyond the scope of this chapter, but I believe this is a promising avenue. Migrations linked to environmental change, a topic that was long forgotten, but witnessed a spectacular comeback in research since 2007 (Piguet and Laczko 2014) is an interesting case, where attempts are made at suggesting new conceptual models. In that context, environmental drivers are mediated by economic, political, social and cultural interactions that lead people to move or, on the contrary, voluntarily or involuntarily, stay put (EACH-FOR 2007; Black et al. 2011; Kniveton, Smith, and Wood 2011; McLeman 2013). Elaborating on that premises to include other compulsions than the natural environment is a first perspective.

A second one, at a broader conceptual level, is suggested by de Haas (2014) within an aspiration/capabilities framework. This framework has the advantage of convincingly conceptualizing virtually all forms of migration and non-migration. Refugees, for example, are characterized by a desire to stay in their place of origin but – contrary to trapped populations – do have the capabilities to react to violence by fleeing. These capabilities are simultaneously constrained by structures such as states, NGOs, family and networks, which determine the social, economic and human resources that potential migrants are able and willing to use.

These are only two avenues for bridging the gap between theories; others may exist or may yet be developed. All are well worth exploring because, as stated by the aforementioned author (de Haas 2014 : 6), the divide between the study of forced and voluntary migration is among the reasons for the lack of progress of migration theory as a whole.

Note

1 I define *theories* here, in Alejandro Portes's terms, as: narratives about how things got "from here to there" including the multiple contingencies and reversals encountered in the process. At this level of analysis, it is possible to delineate, at least partially, the structural constraints and other obstacles affecting a specific individual or collective pursuit (Portes 2000: 13).

Bibliography

Adelman, H. 1988. Refuge or asylum a philosophical perspective. *Journal of Refugee Studies* 1 (1):7–19.

Arendt, H. 1973 [1951]. *The Origins of Totalitarianism*. New York: Harcourt Brace Jovanovich.

Bakewell, O. 2010. Some reflections on structure and agency in migration theory. *Journal of Ethnic and Migration Studies* 36 (10):1689–1708.

Betts, A. 2013. *Survival Migration: Failed Governance and the Crisis of Displacement*. Ithaca, NY: Cornell University Press.

Beyer, G. 1981. The political refugee: 35 years later. *International Migration Review* 15 (1):26–34.

Black, R. 1991. Refugees and displaced persons: Geographical perspectives and research directions. *Progress in Human Geography* 15 (3):281–298.

———. 2001. Fifty years of refugee studies: From theory to policy. *International Migration Review* 35 (1):55–76.

Black, R., W. N. Adger, N. W. Arnell, S. Dercon, A. Geddes, and D. Thomas. 2011. Migration and global environmental change. *Global Environmental Change* 21, Supplement 1 (0):1–2.

Black, R., N. W. Arnell, W. N. Adger, D. Thomas, and A. Geddes. 2013. Migration, immobility and displacement outcomes following extreme events. *Environmental Science and Policy* 27 (Supplement 1):32–43.

Boneva, B., and I. Frieze. 2001. Toward a concept of migrant personality. *Journal of Social Issues* 57 (3):477–491.

Bourdieu, P., and J.-C. Passeron. 1978. *La reproduction: éléments pour une théorie du système d'enseignement*. Paris: Ed. de Minuit.

Boyd, M. 1989. Family and personal networks in international migration: recent developments and new agendas. *International Migration Review* 23 (3):638–670.

Brettell, C. B., and J. F. Hollifield eds. 2014. *Migration Theory: Talking Across Disciplines* (3rd ed.). London: Routledge.

Carling, J. 2002. Migration in the age of involuntary immobility: Theoretical reflections and Cape Verdean experiences. *Journal of Ethnic and Migration Studies* 28 (1):5–42.

———. 2014. The role of aspirations in migration. In *Determinants of International Migration 23–25 September 2014*, ed. P. R. I. Paper. Oxford: International Migration Institute.

Castles, S. 2003. Towards a Sociology of Forced Migration and Social Transformation. *Sociology* 37 (1):13–34.

Castles, S., H. Crawley, and S. Loughna. 2003. *States of Conflict: Causes and Patterns of Forced Migration to the EU and Policy Responses*. London: Institute of Public Policy Research.

Castles, S., H. De Haas, and M. J. Miller. 2014. Theories of Migration (chap. 2). In *The Age of Migration: International Population Movements in the Modern World* (5th ed.), eds. S. Castles, H. de Haas and M. J. Miller. Houndmills: Palgrave Macmillan.

Chirkov, V., M. Vansteenkiste, R. Tao, and M. Lynch. 2007. The role of self-determined motivation and goals for study abroad in the adaptation of international students. *International Journal of Intercultural Relations* 31 (2):199–222.

Cohen, R. ed. 1996. *Theories of Migration*. Cheltenham: E. Elgar.

Collyer, M. 2005. When do social networks fail to explain migration ? Accounting for the movement of Algerian asylum seekers to the UK. *Journal of Ethnic and Migration Studies* 31 (4):699–718.

Cornelius, W. A., P. L. Martin, and J. F. Hollifield eds. 2004. *Controlling Immigration: A Global Perspective*. Stanford: Stanford University Press.

Cornelius, W. A., and M. R. Rosenblum. 2005. Immigration and politics. *Annual Review of Political Science* 8:99–119.

de Haas, H. 2007. Turning the Tide? Why development will not stop migration. *Development and Change* 38 (5):819–841.

———. 2010. The internal dynamics of migration processes: A theoretical inquiry. *Journal of Ethnic and Migration Studies* 36 (10):1587–1617.

———. 2014. Migration theory — Quo Vadis? *International Migration Institute Working Papers*. November 2014 (100).

De Jong, G. F. 2000. Expectations, gender, and norms in migration decision-making. *Population Studies* 54 (3):307–319.

De Jong, G. F., and J. T. Fawcett. 1981. Motivations for migration: An assessment and a value-expectancy research model. In *Migration Decision Making: Multidisciplinary Approaches to Microlevel Studies in Developed and Developing Countries*, eds. G. F. De Jong and R. W. Gardner, 13–58. New York: Pergamon Press.

Dekker, R., and G. Engbersen. 2014. How social media transform migrant networks and facilitate migration. *Global Networks: A Journal of Transnational Affairs* 14 (4):401–418.

EACH-FOR. 2007. *Research Guidelines*. Bonn: Environmental Change and Forced Migration Scenarios Research Project.

Epstein, G. S. 2008. Herd and network effects in migration decision-making. *Journal of Ethnic and Migration Studies* 34 (4):567–583.

Epstein, G. S., and I. N. Gang. 2006. The influence of others on migration plans. *Review of Development Economics* 10 (4):652–665.

Faist, T. 1997. The crucial meso level. In *International Migration, Immobility and Development: Multidisciplinary Perspectives*, ed. T. Hammar, 47–64. Oxford: Berg.

Favell, A. 2007. Rebooting migration theory: Interdisciplinarity, globality and postdisciplinarity in migration studies. In *Migration Theory: Talking Across Disciplines*, eds. C. B. Brettell and J. F. Hollifield, 259–278. New York: Routledge.

Findlay, A. 2011. An assessment of supply and demand-side theorizations of international student mobility. *International Migration* 49 (2):169–190.

Fischer, P. A. 1999. *On the Economics of Immobility: Regional Development and Migration in the Age of Globalisation*. Bern: P. Haupt.

Geertz, C. 1973. *The Interpretation of Culture*. New York: Basic Books.

Geyer, H. S. 2002. An exploration in migration theory. In *International Handbook of Urban Systems: Studies of Urbanization and Migration in Advanced and Developing Countries*, ed. H. S. Geyer, 19–37. Cheltenham: E. Elgar.

Goodwin-Gill, G. S. 1983. *The Refugee in International Law*. 2nd ed. Oxford: Clarendon Press.

Hammar, T., G. Brochmann, K. Tamas, and T. Faist eds. 1997. *International Migration, Immobility and Development: Multidisciplinary Perspectives*. Oxford: Berg.

Harris, J., and M. P. Todaro. 1970. Migration, unemployment and development: A two-sector analysis. *American Economic Review* 60 (1):126–142.

Haug, S. 2008. Migration networks and migration decision-making. *Journal of Ethnic and Migration Studies* 34 (4):585–605.

Hein, J. 1993. Refugees, immigrants, and the state. *Annual Review of Sociology* 19:43–59.

Herman, E. 2006. Migration as a family business: The role of personal networks in the mobility phase of migration. *International Migration* 44 (4):191–230.

Hirschman, A. O. 1970. *Exit, Voice and Loyalty*. Cambridge (MA): Harvard University Press.

———. 1993. Exit, voice and the fate of the German democratic republic. *World Politics* (45):173–202 (reprint in A. O. Hirschman, A propensity to self-subversion, 1995, chap. 1).

Hoffmann, B. 2004. Exit, voice, and the lessons from the Cuban Case. Conceptual notes on the interaction of emigration and political transformation. *Institut für Iberoamerika-Kunde Working Papers* (19).

Hollifield, J. 2000. The Politics of International Migration: How Can We Bring the State Back In? In *Migration Theory: Talking Across Disciplines*, eds. C. B. Brettell and J. Hollifield, 183–237. New York: Routledge.

Hunter, L. M., J. K. Luna, and R. M. Norton. 2015. Environmental dimensions of migration. *Annual Review of Sociology* 41:377–397.

Johansson, R. 1990. The Refugee Experience in Europe After World War II: Some Theoretical and Empirical Considerations. In *The Uprooted: Forced Migration as an International Problem in the Post-War Era*, ed. R. Göran. Lund: Lund University Press.

Kniveton, D., C. Smith, and S. Wood. 2011. Agent-based model simulations of future changes in migration flows for Burkina Faso. *Global Environmental Change* 21, Supplement 1 (0):34–40.

Kunz, E. F. 1973. The refugee in flight: Kinetic models and forms of displacement. *International Migration Review* 7 (2):125–146.

———. 1981. Exile and resettlement: Refugee theory. *International Migration Review* 15 (1/2):42–51.

Lee, E. 1966. A theory of migration. *Demography* 3 (48):47–57.

Leslie, G. R., and A. H. Richardson. 1961. Life-cycle, career pattern, and the decision to move. *American Sociological Review* 26 (6):894–902.

Lubkemann, S. C. 2008. Involuntary immobility: On a theoretical invisibility in forced migration studies. *Journal of Refugee Studies* 21 (4):454–475.

Marx, E. 1990. The social world of refugees: A conceptual framework. *Journal of Refugee Studies* 3 (3):189–203.

Massey, D. S., J. Arango, G. Hugo, A. Kouaouci, A. Pellegrino, and J. E. Taylor. 1993. Theories of international migration: A review and appraisal. *Population and Development Review* 19 (3):431–466.

———. 1994. An evaluation of international migration theory: The North American case. *Population and Development Review* 20 (4):699–751.

McLeman, R. 2013. Developments in modelling of climate change-related migration. *Climatic Change* 117 (3):599–611.

McLeman, R., and B. Smit. 2006. Migration as an adaptation to climate change. *Climatic Change* 76 (1–2):31–53.

Nikolinakos, M. 1975. Notes towards a general theory of migration in late capitalism. *Race and Class* XVII (1):5–17.

Palloni, A., D. S. Massey, M. Ceballos, K. Espinosa, and M. Spittel. 2001. Social capital and international migration: A test using information on family networks. *American Journal of Sociology* 106 (5):1262–1298.

Piguet, E. 2013. Les théories des migrations—Synthèse de la prise de décision individuelle. *Revue européenne des migrations internationales* 29 (3):141–161.

Piguet, E., and F. Laczko eds. 2014. *People on the Move in a Changing Climate. The Regional Impact of Environmental Change on Migration.* Netherlands: Springer.

Plane, D. A. 1993. Demographic influences on migration. *Regional Studies* 27 (4):375–383.

Portes, A. 2000. The hidden abode: Sociology as analysis of the unexpected. *American Sociological Review* 65 (February):1–18.

———. 2001. Introduction: the debates and significance of immigrant transnationalism. *Global Networks* 1 (3):181–193.

Rérat, P., and L. Lees. 2011. Spatial capital, gentrification and mobility: Evidence from Swiss core cities. *Transactions of the Institute of British Geographers* 36 (1):126–142.

Richmond, A. H. 1988. Sociological theories of international migration: The case of refugees. *Current Sociology* 36 (2):7–25.

———. 1993. Reactive migration: Sociological perspectives on refugee movements. *Journal of Refugee Studies* 6 (1):7–24.

———. 1994. *Global apartheid. Refugees, racism, and the new world order.* Toronto: Oxford University Press.

———. 2002. Globalization: implications for immigrants and refugees. *Ethnic and Racial Studies* 25 (5):707–727.

Sassen, S. 1988. *The Mobility of Labour and Capital — a Study in International Investment and Labour Flow.* Cambridge: Cambridge University Press.

———. 2016. A massive loss of habitat — new drivers for migration. *Sociology of Development* 2 (2):204–233.

Sjaastad, L. A. 1962. The costs and returns of human migration. *Journal of Political Economy* 70 (5 [part 2 — Investment in Human Beings]):80–93.

Skeldon, R. 2012. Migration transitions revisited: Their continued relevance for the development of migration theory. *Population, Space and Place* 18 (2):154–166.

Smith, D. P., and R. King. 2012. Editorial introduction: Re-making migration theory. *Population, Space and Place* 18 (2):127–133.

Stark, O. 1991. *The Migration of Labor.* Cambridge, MA: Basil Blackwell.

Stinner, W. F., and M. Van Loon. 1992. Community size preference status, community satisfaction and migration intentions. *Population & Environment* 14 (2):177–195.

Tarrius, A. 1989. *Anthropologie du mouvement.* Caen: Paradigme.

Tartarovsky, E., and S. H. Schwartz. 2001. Motivation for emigration, values, wellbeing, and identification among young Russian Jews. *International Journal of Psychology* 36 (2):88–99.

Tilly, C. 2007. Trust networks in transnational migration. *Sociological Forum* 22 (1):3–24.

Urry, J. 2007. *Mobilities.* Cambridge: Polity Press.

Van Hear, N. 2010. Theories of migration and social change. *Journal of Ethnic and Migration Studies* 36 (10):1531–1536.

Van Hear, N., R. Brubaker, and T. Bessa. 2009. Managing mobility for human development: The growing salience of mixed migration. *UNDP – Human Development Research Paper* (20).

Vertovec, S. 1999. Conceiving and researching transnationalism. *Ethnic and Racial Studies* 22 (2):447–462.

Wimmer, A. 2002. *Nationalist Exclusion and Ethnic Conflict: Shadows of Modernity.* Cambridge: Cambridge University Press.

Winchie, D. B., and D. W. Carment. 1989. Migration and motivation: The migrant's perspective. *International Migration Review* 23 (1):96–104.

Wingens, M., M. Windzio, H. d. Valk, and C. Aybek. 2011. *A Life-Course Perspective on Migration and Integration.* Dordrecht: Springer.

Wolpert, J. 1965. Behavioral aspects of the decision to migrate. *Papers of the Regional Science Association* 15 (1):159–169.

Zolberg, A. R. 1983. The formation of new states as a refugee-generating process. *The Annals of the American Academy of Political and Social Science* 467:24–38.

Zolberg, A. R., A. Suhrke, and S. Arguayo. 1986. International factors in the formation of refugee movements. *International Migration Review* 20 (2):151–169.

3

Mobility, displacement and migration, and their interactions with vulnerability and adaptation to environmental risks

W. Neil Adger, Ricardo Safra de Campos and Colette Mortreux

Introduction

The world is changing, and changing fast. It is changing in both earth system processes and in cumulated social dynamics: we may even be approaching irreversible and profound changes to many environmental processes at the planetary scale. One of the principal changes is to the world's oceans and atmosphere that will bring about disrupted climates. Even with climate and ecosystem changes being well documented, it is always difficult to perceive them as significant, compared to where and how we live. As humans, it is easiest to perceive change in places and phenomena that are familiar to us. Often it is the growth of settlements, economic development and alteration of human-made and natural landscapes that catch our eye.

The human world is at the same time becoming more mobile, through both the movement of people and through the actual and virtual movement of people, goods, services and information (Adger, Eakin and Winkels 2009). The two phenomena, of mobility and systemic environmental change, are inextricably linked in both cause and effect. Hence, mobility should be a central element of all analysis of responses to climate change, for both mitigation of the causes of climate change through reducing greenhouse gas emissions to the atmosphere and for adapting to climatic changes and its cascading effect through ecosystems and the human world. This chapter therefore focuses on how climate change risks affect migration and displacement patterns, and how those are observed, researched and understood.

Mobility is multi-faceted. Migration and displacement are in effect two elements of vulnerability and adaptation to climate change. A large body of research has highlighted how people and places are vulnerable to the effects of climate change if they are exposed to such risks, are sensitive to such risks and lack the adaptive capacity to effectively deal with them (Füssel and Klein 2006). Individuals, communities and economic sectors adapt to climate change risks in a number of ways: through reinforcing and protecting the places and infrastructures that are exposed, or by reducing the risks, and sometimes by moving location. Places matter, because they are where we perceive change to occur and because they are the sites for investment in natural and built capital that makes them attractive for living. Places are also social constructs that imbue lives with meaning and security. Hence both migration (as a form of adaptation) and displacement (as a manifestation of vulnerability) are central to how climate change is to be experienced and adapted to in every region of the world.

Displacement is used here to focus on the involuntary and unforeseen movement of people from their place of residence due to weather-related impacts on property and infrastructure. Such movement is most often temporary and short-lived, but it is often highly disruptive and traumatic to those involved. Displacement from floods, droughts and wildfire is common throughout the world, with estimates of the number of people affected by weather-related extremes of over 20 million per year over the most recent decade (Internal Displacement Monitoring Center and Norwegian Refugee Council 2014). Importantly, all the climate phenomena that cause economic disruption and displacement – mainly drought, wildfire and floods – are projected to increase in intensity or frequency in many parts of the world as a result of climate change (Intergovernmental Panel on Climate Change 2014). Weather disasters are, in effect, how climate change will be experienced in place.

The term migration is used here to mean a permanent or semi-permanent movement of place of residence of an individual, recognising its economic and social dynamics. Climate change affects migration patterns by altering the landscape of economic incentives and options for individuals in both source and destination areas, and directly by altering the risks that people face. Displacement and migration are not discreet, but interrelated.

Vulnerability to environmental risks

Spatial and temporal continuum between displacement and migration

Mobility occurs along a spatiotemporal continuum which ranges from temporary moves to permanent relocation. Both displacement and migration are located within this continuum, and represent distinct facets of vulnerability to environmental risk (Hugo 1996). However, a clear distinction between the two is based on the voluntary nature of movement and the ability to exercise choice. In situations of displacement, people are forced to leave because their lives and livelihood are at risk to an extreme environmental hazard. Similarly, populations are involuntarily displaced because of land acquisition for development projects such as hydropower damming and mineral extraction, or from violent conflict (Cernea 1996; Barnett and Adger 2007; Wilmsen and Webber 2015).

Migration, in contrast to displacement, involves a conscious decision to change place of residence. The reasons may be numerous and interrelated, and may include minimising exposure to risks associated with water shortages or declining agricultural productivity or fisheries, or macro external factors such as volatility of markets or economic recession. Migration is also employed to reduce household consumption and maximise income opportunities through livelihood diversification (Stark and Taylor 1991; Ellis 2000).

Displacement and migration, as we define them here, interact in a number of ways with climate change at different spatial and temporal scales. Figure 3.1 portrays these relationships, showing that there is a spectrum of reactive movement and proactive movement, and part of the explanation for how migration unfolds may be the speed and duration of climate change events. The arrows in Figure 3.1 represent how mobility responses may change over time following climate events. Hence displacement is largely reactive and involuntary when associated with short-term weather events, leading to mainly temporary movements of relatively short distance.

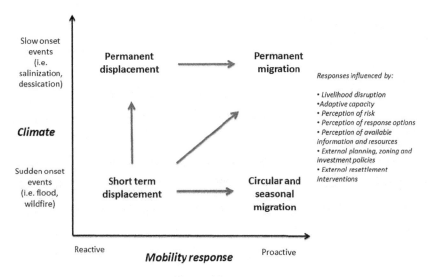

Figure 3.1 Migration and displacement interacting with sudden-onset and slow-onset climatic events

Displacement here is principally a short term unforeseen involuntary movement of populations from residence as a consequence of weather-related events. Migration involves deliberate and planned movement associated with changing attractiveness of places.

Conversely, slow-onset climate change events are more likely to lead to permanent migration. Mechanisms of regulation, markets and investment patterns can assist in shifting to more permanent settlement patterns – sending signals on the place utility and the attractiveness of places at risk such as exposed coastal zones or marginal agricultural areas.

Environmentally related displacement is often caused by sudden-onset events such as earthquakes and hurricanes, which combined with low levels of socioeconomic resilience of individuals and communities results in moves of unique spatiotemporal signature often involving return to place of origin. The 2010 earthquake in Haiti and the 2004 tsunami in Indonesia are examples of sudden-onset events that triggered the displacement of thousands of people across these two regions. Even when environmental hazards are concentrated in one specific location, impacts on migration outcomes can be significant. The impacts of Hurricane Katrina and Hurricane Rita on Louisiana in the US in 2005 produced significant temporary displacement. In addition, the temporary displacement has had major implications for long term movement and demographic patterns in the state. The large majority of residents of New Orleans evacuated the city before Katrina's landfall, and while a significant number of returnees have been recorded in census estimates, many people who left have not returned. Several studies have examined the spatial distribution of evacuees, the decision-making process behind the duration of relocation and choice of destination (McIntosh 2008; Fussell, Sastry and Van Landingham 2010; Groen and Polivka 2010). Those most severely impacted took longer to return to New Orleans or relocated permanently to other areas in the US. Long-term climatic risks like those in Louisiana can be managed through anticipatory planning, zoning and investment policies. Policy interventions might also bring about significant migration outcomes. For example, the Louisiana Comprehensive Master Plan for a Sustainable Coast released in 2012 involves recommendations on assisted migration of residents and compulsory purchase of land to be set aside (Barbier 2015: 287).

Discrete forms of migration – such as seasonal, circular, permanent movements – are widely recognised as key strategies to maintain livelihoods and adapt to the effects of climate variability, particularly in resource-based economies (Ellis 2000). Recent studies investigating the environment-migration nexus are beginning to construct a clearer picture of this relationship. Research has moved away from a linear connection to a multifaceted approach that acknowledges that factors driving migration go beyond climate change and other environmental hazards. Furthermore, current research seeks to expand on the notion of migration as adaptation to climate change by including cultural dimensions such as place attachment and community cohesion (Adger et al. 2013).

The body of knowledge on climate change impacts and options for adaptation is increasingly taking elements of demographic change and migration as adaptation into account. The IPCC's Fifth Assessment Report makes a strong case for the capacity of mobility responses to reduce vulnerability for populations exposed to extreme weather events and longer-term climate variability and change (Adger et al. 2014). This moves beyond seeking estimates of displacement as the only relevant interaction between migration and climate change.

Inverse relationships between vulnerability and mobility

The projected impacts of global environmental change are likely to be experienced worldwide. However, some areas are more vulnerable to impacts than others, and will be exposed to a different magnitude or rate of climate variation. Vulnerability can be broadly defined as the degree to which a system is susceptible to and is unable to cope with the adverse effects of environmental change. Therefore, vulnerability to climate change can be represented as a function of exposure, sensitivity and adaptive capacity (Füssel and Klein 2006). In other words, the greater the exposure or sensitivity, the greater is the vulnerability. However, adaptive capacity is inversely related to vulnerability. So, the greater the adaptive capacity, the lesser the vulnerability.

Thus, examining the concept of vulnerability of places becomes central to the study of the environment-migration nexus. Equally important is the notion that vulnerability to environmental change does not exist in isolation from the wider political economy of resource use and inadvertent or deliberate human interactions with natural variances of ecological systems (Adger 2006).

Inevitably, these factors suggest a complex relationship between vulnerability to climate change and mobility. Many studies of climate-related hazards indeed show complex causal relationships, with both increasing and decreasing migration outcomes associated with similar drivers. So drought, for example, in some circumstances appears to stimulate forms of migration, while in other instances reduced mobility and migration are observed. And the temporal and spatial dynamics of hazards also matter. Gray and Mueller (2012) show for Bangladesh, for example, that crop failure is positively associated with out-migration, while cyclones produce no discernible net out-migration.

Shocks and climate-related hazards reduce and disrupt income-generating activity, and also potentially destroy assets. Hence, such impacts affect the resources that facilitate mobility as well as defining vulnerability. Building on these insights, an emerging paradigm suggests that vulnerability and mobility are inversely related (Black et al. 2013). Parts of populations that are highly exposed also have low adaptive capacity are precisely those parts of the population that have the fewest options and fewest resources to allow them to move away and reduce exposure. Evidence from the Gulf States in the US over the past three decades, for example, shows segmented withdrawal of populations after hurricane damage: economically advantaged groups have left, while vulnerable populations have not had the resources to move (Logan, Issar and Xu 2016).

The implications of such a relationship are that climate change will in some sense trap vulnerable populations in exposed regions. Such circumstances will inevitably increase the demand for humanitarian interventions and assistance in vulnerable regions. It further demonstrates how migration needs to be incorporated into models and policies for adaptation to climate risks.

Vulnerability of places to environmental risks

As discussed in the previous section, the fundamental causes of vulnerability are structures in the economy and asymmetry of power in societies, behavioural and institutional phenomena, and the ability to respond to external stresses. While there are many ways to evaluate relative vulnerability of populations and places to climate change, one key lesson stands out: no place or no population is immune from the impacts of future climate change. This is because of the multiple direct and indirect means by which climate change impacts affect life and livelihood, as well as the constructed meaning of place. Hence, regions may be more vulnerable to climate change impacts through lack of adaptive capacity, through major direct health implications and liveability of their current places, or more indirectly through price and scarcity signals (Intergovernmental Panel on Climate Change 2014).

Despite this highly uneven landscape of risk, some studies have specifically highlighted potential areas where migration and displacement may be more immediate and apparent (see Afifi and Jäger 2010; Warner and Afifi 2014). De Sherbinin and colleagues (2012) showed that over the past recent decades net migration trends, when overlaid on ecological zones, have resulted in net in-migration to the world's coastal zones and net out-migration from drylands and mountain regions. Of course, these trends are explained through movement to cities. Nevertheless, coastal areas, drylands and mountain regions will continue to be critically vulnerable to climatic change impacts and will likely be the site of migration responses. Ahead, we summarise the likely effects of climate change on these geographical zones.

Low-elevation coastal zones are at risk from sea level rise and storm surges which may result in submergence of seafront settlements and increased flooding of coastal land, as well as saltwater intrusion of surface waters and groundwater (Nicholls and Cazenave 2010). Changes in the intensity and seasonality of cyclones and variance in rainfall regime are also likely to affect low-elevation coastal zones. Flooding in low-lying densely populated coastal areas is predominantly seasonal and usually short-lived, yet it can have significant impacts on vulnerable sections of society. For example, poor households living in high-risk areas might become displaced and forced to relocate to safer regions permanently. Alternatively, they might move temporarily seeking access to frontline services and alternative forms of income generation.

Climate projections for global drylands indicate a strong likelihood of amplified temperatures and reduced precipitation. Furthermore, the annual spatiotemporal distribution of precipitation is expected to change significantly, resulting in progressively long intervals without rain followed by short and highly unpredictable wet seasons in arid and semiarid regions with an increased likelihood of droughts (Stocker et al. 2014). Global drylands have been the focus of many studies investigating environmental signals to migration flows because of the high dependency on natural resources and progressive land degradation. Increasing populations, conflict over access to a diminishing natural resource base and recurrent drought are likely to intensify out-migration of persons from vulnerable places with limited capacity to cope or adapt to new conditions.

Mountain regions are projected to experience changes in precipitation regime, increased temperatures, reduced crop production, changes in glacier melt patterns and water scarcity in regions dependent on snowmelt (Foresight 2011). Nearly three-quarters of mountain populations living in rural areas in remote and fragile ecosystems are dependent on natural resources. The inhabitants of these areas are likely to become exposed to increased inaccessibility to these resources. This might result in out-migration responses, predominantly to urban areas, as a way of averting risk associated with gradual deteriorating conditions and amplified vulnerability.

Vulnerability of destination areas and the crucible of risk in cities

Displacement and migration are potential response strategies to the various impacts of global environmental change. These mobility responses obviously involve consequences for destination areas, with potential amplification of trends of inward migration of populations impacted by extreme climatic events or gradual deterioration of environmental conditions. Most studies on environmental dimensions of migration focus on the drivers of mobility, focusing on locations that are likely to be most affected by global environmental change. Hence, there is more limited research on where migrants might move in response to both sudden-onset and slow-onset environmental events (Findlay 2011).

There is an assumption that the majority of environmentally driven mobility, particularly in the world's most vulnerable nations, will be restricted to internal movements with projected flows originating from marginal regions (Tacoli 2009; Barnett and Webber 2010). Under such a scenario, it is highly plausible that urban areas will be the main destination for such moves, as has been the case in the past with the urbanisation transition by those seeking better economic opportunities or fleeing political persecution, armed conflict or regional economic inequality.

Urban areas are increasingly exposed to the impacts of global environmental change, particularly in the case of sea level rise in low-lying coastal cities. These cities are home to 18 per cent of the world's total urban population and growing rapidly. The occurrence of sudden-onset events like hurricanes and flash flooding already trigger large-scale evacuation and population displacement, which is generally to nearby areas and over a short period of time. Other impacts such as coastal erosion due to storm surges or increasing stress due to water scarcity are also likely to become a cause for concern in urban areas.

The potential movement of populations into cities is also likely to generate cultural and socioeconomic implications. The destinations of where people move to are often predictable: existing social networks and historical linkages between sending and destination areas are the main factors. But migration has the potential to affect social cohesion in destination settlements and communities (Benson and O'Reilly 2009; Skeldon 2014). New migrant populations can feel dislocated from norms and cultures in destination areas. Strong sense of attachment to communities of origin is shown to strengthen intra-community ties. But new populations and diversity are not universally positive: Putnam (2007) argued with data from the US that places with new populations often become more withdrawn. This finding spawned much research, which inevitably shows that whether new migrant populations can enhance the social cohesion of destination areas is contingent on many factors, many of which are amenable to social interventions (Portes and Vickstrom 2015).

Commonly, however, new migrant populations experience discrimination, seclusion and ghettoization in destination areas. This is observed in cities across the world, not least where resources and frontline services are not adequately provided by the public sector and employment opportunities are limited (McMichael, Barnett and McMichael 2012; Skeldon 2014).

In cases of deteriorating socioeconomic and environmental conditions in cities, the reduction of migrant inflows and the reversing of current flows or adoption of alternative forms of temporary mobility such as circular and short-term migration are alternatives to permanent relocation. This is because the size and directions of population movements respond quickly to changes in local conditions in destination areas.

Adaptation and resilience: bringing in mobility

Social and policy implications of migration in relation to environmental change

Given the centrality of place, home and identity to lived experience, migration movements – whether involuntary or seemingly more voluntary – involves significant social cost and may increase the vulnerability of social groups and other sectors of society (Barnett and O'Neill 2010). Migration could be regarded as an adaptation failure where policies and programmes fail to provide local people with the opportunity to adapt without resorting to moving location. Yet, evidence shows that migration flows may actually enhance aggregate exposure to environmental risk by moving to more hazardous areas, not least in the trends towards urban areas.

All forms of population movement and associated social and political challenges are reflected in and conditioned by governance systems in both migrant source and destination areas (Geddes et al. 2012). Populations facing climatic or other environmental risks might choose to move away from their original locations to reduce their exposure to risk. Evidence shows that upon relocation, these migrants face material and social problems of landlessness, unemployment, homelessness, social marginalization, food insecurity, reduced access to common-property resources and increased morbidity (Cernea and McDowell 2000). These consequences are complex, adaptive, interconnected and marked by stark uncertainty. For example, a migrant household's capacity to secure access to land and or commonly managed resources may be reduced in their new location, leading to a loss of income and food insecurity. These types of risks are well known, but intransigent.

Social risks resulting from migration are diverse and are equally intransigent for governance systems. Disruption of social cohesion and loss of place attachment have gained most attention by phycologists, geographers and sociologists. At the same time, continuity of place is an important component in maintaining or reinforcing identity and the sense of social cohesion within a community. Changes in identity represented by voluntary or involuntary change of locale are often associated with grief and strong sociocultural impacts related to loss. A study for returnees to Louisiana in the context of displacement from hurricanes by Simms (2017), for example, showed that the resilience of populations is significantly challenged by evacuation and return and positive place attachment may never recover for some individuals. Although the proactive choice to migrate to new places to diversify livelihoods and secure income can positively contribute to the adaptation process in the context of extreme climatic events and other environmental hazards, migration can also reduce these potential gains by increasing financial and emotional stress to both the migrant and persons left behind.

Much of the discussion about population movements associated with global environmental change has focused on exploring the drivers and conditions within which people voluntarily or involuntarily move. However, it is also important to recognise the negative outcomes of migration and displacement. Migrants face risks of further impoverishment as a result of moving, weakening socioeconomic structures in both source and destination communities. Table 3.1 highlights how both displacement and migration have significant implications for policy, planning and intervention. These include costs of urban planning and infrastructure in places that need to be protected (both potential sending and destination areas), through to overcoming social cohesion challenges in labour markets, housing and other sectors.

Table 3.1 Implications of migration and displacement for climate change adaptation strategies and their policy challenges

Type of movement	Adaptation response	Policy and social implications
Displacement (unforeseen and temporary)	Temporary displacement and return, rebuilding and recovery	Demand for humanitarian and public health assistance for internally and internationally displaced populations.
	Unplanned permanent migration	Impact on public services, labour markets and social cohesion in destination areas.
Migration	Investment to protect areas at risk from out-migration	Long term nature of protection, sunk costs, and impacts on insurance.
	Disinvestment in sending areas and planned resettlement	Impact on public services, labour markets and social cohesion in destination areas.

Under what circumstances does migration enhance system resilience?

Whilst much attention has been paid to migration as an involuntary imposition, or as a process with negative outcomes, migration has significant potential enhances the resilience of social and ecological systems. Migration can, for example, enhance resilience by supplementing incomes, diversifying livelihoods, spreading the exposure of people and their livelihoods to environmental risk, and building linkages between sending and receiving areas (Adger et al. 2002).

Rural households whose livelihoods are dependent on natural resources are highly vulnerable to environmental change. Migration allows such households to become more flexible and diversified in their livelihoods (Ellis 2003). In India, for example, seasonal migration for employment is a long-standing livelihood strategy for people in rural areas (Deshingkar and Start 2003). During off-peak seasons, migrants move temporarily to other areas, often migrating short distances, to engage in low-skilled jobs such as construction or rickshaw pulling and remit savings to support their family back home. By engaging in seasonal migration, these households reduce their dependency on a single livelihood, maintain their connection to their land without needing to migrate permanently, maintain social networks at home and build social networks away from home should they seek to migrate permanently in the future. Migration for the purposes of livelihood diversification will become increasingly important as households seek to adapt to climate change (Tacoli 2009).

Rural-urban migrants tend to have higher earning capacities compared to their place of origin. The increased income is beneficial for the resilience of the migrant but also, where remittances are sent, for the resilience of the sending area (Ackah and Medvedev 2012). Studies in Ghana demonstrate that remittance flows help to redistribute welfare and narrow the rural-urban welfare gap through migrant investments, including development projects in sending areas (Boakye-Yiadom 2008). Remittances act as a strategy for migrants to invest in assets for their family's wellbeing, and also act as a form of insurance should their migration experience prove unsuccessful and the migrant seeks to return (Amuedo-Dorantes and Pozo 2006). In this way, remittances build not only the resilience of the sending community, but also support migrants.

Migration enhances resilience by building linkages between sending and receiving areas (Levitt 1998). The movement of people between rural areas and urban areas helps increase the flow of ideas, goods and services to otherwise marginalised rural areas. Where migrants return home, sending areas can benefit from the skills and experiences of migrants. Whereas brain drain effects are often highlighted as an issue for sending areas with high rates of out-migration, the skills, ideas and investments of migrants are most often in circulation, benefitting both destination and sending communities (Khonje 2015).

Finally, migration can enhance the resilience of destination communities. Where urban areas have labour shortages in low-skilled employment sectors, such as construction and transport services, migrants can help fill these gaps in the economy and promote growth in those sectors (Foresight 2011). For example, in India many farmers from West Bengal are migrating to Kerala to fill the gap left by Kerala residents who have migrated to the Middle East for higher-paying construction work (Kumar 2011).

Planning for migration as adaptation

The centuries-long trend of rural-to-urban migration may well be intensified by environmental changes in particular regions of the world where major movements are currently observed. Hence, there is a challenge to governance processes to proactively plan for migration through creating favourable conditions for voluntary movement (Foresight 2011; Tacoli 2009). Broad policy approaches to enable adaptive migration include: facilitating people to stay, enhancing policies and infrastructure for voluntary migration away from environmental risks, and planning for relocation. The legitimacy of individual strategies depends, it is argued, on upholding the principle of respect for the autonomy of individuals and their decisions of where and how they live (Warner et al. 2013). But all government decisions, whether they involve active investment and regulation or whether they consist of an absence of action, in effect lead to social outcomes that affect long-term welfare. If governments plan for migration and displacement proactively, there are, it seems, more pathways to positive outcomes for those affected by environmental change.

Where governments have planned for relocation of whole settlements, for example, there is growing evidence that inclusive processes that are perceived to be equitable ameliorate many negative impacts and outcomes of the disruption associated with resettlement (Bronen and Chapin 2013). The challenge for fair process is compounded when new communities and locations become affected by environmental change over time. Decades of research on resettlement processes and impacts have revealed that resettled communities have often become further impoverished as a result of resettlement (Chakrabarti and Dhar 2009; Wilmsen and Webber 2015). Planning guidelines such as the "Impoverishment Risks and Reconstruction" model (Cernea 1997) most often identify risks that resettlement pose to communities: landlessness, joblessness, homelessness, marginalisation, food insecurity, loss of access to common property resources, increased morbidity and community disarticulation.

By facilitating voluntary migration, governments and institutions assist individuals and households to leave areas highly exposed to climate risk and reduce the emergence of trapped populations. People and communities are trapped when they wish to migrate but are unable to do so because they lack the capacity to leave, for reasons including poor health or social networks. Black and colleagues describe trapped populations as facing a double set of risks whereby they are exposed to environmental risks and are unable to move away from them due to their socio-economic vulnerability (Black et al. 2013). The vulnerability of trapped populations is further exacerbated as they can be difficult to identify by institutions to provide the necessary support (Lubkemann 2008). By providing basic welfare support to poor and marginalised communities in areas exposed to environmental risk, governments and other institutions can help avoid the emergence of trapped populations (Black and Collyer 2014).

Urban areas are a critical focus of anticipatory planning as the majority of migration flows to urban areas, even taking into account the short-distance temporary migrations often associated with sudden-onset environmental events (Adamo 2010). Urban areas face pressure to accommodate incoming migrants, with the most vulnerable communities facing disproportionate pressure. Social tensions and conflicts can arise from unforeseen migration in urban areas, such as labour market conflicts, housing disputes, competition over scarce resources and expansion of informal settlements. These tensions, however, can be anticipated and planned for. Both migrants and receiving communities benefit from collaborative and community-building approaches, investments in sustainable development and strengthening of social welfare provisions (Black et al. 2013).

Policies to protect the human rights of internal migrants in particular include removing restrictions on movement, giving access to health and education services, and supporting housing needs. Failing to support migrant populations can exacerbate social tensions, as shown for example in Kerala in India. The Kerala state government has been assessed to have failed to acknowledge the presence of internal migrants from other states in India, such that migrants have few rights protected. National policies in India set the framework for entitlements to national benefits and schemes for those moving across states, but require local recognition (Kumar 2011). If migrants from other states are not recognised, rice subsidies and ration cards are not made accessible. The lack of recognition of migrants into Kerala has not altered the aggregate flow of migrants, but the lack of state support has been associated with tensions between local Kerala residents and migrants (Kumar 2011).

At an international scale, the rights of migrants are guided by initiatives such as the Kampala Convention and even in the Cancun Adaptation Framework. The UNHCR's Guiding Principles on Internal Displacement, for example, proposes actions to protect and assist displaced persons, though does not have the strength of international law (Kälin 2008; McAdam 2012).

Conclusions

The causes and landscape of who and what is vulnerable to unforeseen environmental change now and in the future are well known: environmental risks tend to amplify social structures and inequality in society. In this chapter we have emphasized how mobility, displacement and migration are key elements of this landscape of vulnerability and also represent major opportunities to minimize and manage risk as well as overcoming underlying structural inequalities. Yet, this is a tall order. Climate change and indeed current weather and environmental hazards pose major risks throughout the world, and will continue to be one of the emerging and disruptive forces causing temporary displacement and affecting long term migration patterns.

Migration, displacement and resettlement are clearly part of any landscape of adaptation to these changes over the incoming decades: yet migration is not socially neutral or simple. The fundamental issue of freedom and choice that links human security to environmental risks, is also central to the issue of migration and to the politics of recognition. Societies and communities need to be able to plan and construct their own futures and trajectories. The principles and evidence outlined here show how limiting choice and mobility may in fact be one of the fundamental potential social costs and consequences of climate change.

Acknowledgements

We thank the UK Department for International Development and the International Development Research Centre, Canada for funding under the project Deltas, Vulnerability and Climate

Change: Migration and Adaptation, which is part of Collaborative Adaptation Research Initiative in Africa and Asia programme. We thank the editors and the anonymous reviewers for helpful steering and comments on this chapter. This version remains solely our responsibility.

References

Ackah, C. and Medvedev D., 2012. Internal migration in Ghana: determinants and welfare impacts. *International Journal of Social Economics* 39, 764–784.

Adamo, S. B., 2010. Environmental migration and cities in the context of global environmental change. *Current Opinion in Environmental Sustainability* 2, 161–165.

Adger, W.N., 2006. Vulnerability. *Global Environmental Change* 16, 268–281.

Adger, W.N., Barnett, J., Brown, K., Marshall, N. and O'Brien, K., 2013. Cultural dimensions of climate change impacts and adaptation. *Nature Climate Change* 3, 112–117.

Adger, W.N., Eakin, H. and Winkels, A., 2009. Nested and teleconnected vulnerabilities to environmental change. *Frontiers in Ecology and the Environment* 7, 150–157.

Adger, W.N., Kelly, P.M., Winkels, A., Huy, L.Q. and Locke, C., 2002. Migration, remittances, livelihood trajectories, and social resilience. *Ambio* 31, 358–366.

Adger, W.N., Pulhin, J.M., Barnett, J., Dabelko, G.D., Hovelsrud, G.K., Levy, M., Oswald Spring, U. and Vogel, C.H., 2014. Human security. In: *Climate Change 2014: Impacts, Adaptation, and Vulnerability.* Working Group II to the Fifth Assessment Report of the Intergovernmental Panel on Climate Change. Cambridge University Press: Cambridge, pp. 755–791.

Afifi, T. and Jäger, J. eds. 2010. *Environment, Forced Migration and Vulnerability.* Springer: Berlin.

Amuedo-Dorantes, C. and Pozo, S. 2006. Remittances as insurance: evidence from Mexican immigrants. *Journal of Population Economics* 19, 227–254.

Barbier, E.B., 2015. Hurricane Katrina's lessons for the world. *Nature* 524, 285–287.

Barnett, J. and Adger, W. N., 2007. Climate change, human security and violent conflict. *Political Geography* 26, 639–655.

Barnett, J. and O'Neill, S., 2010. Maladaptation. *Global Environmental Change* 20, 211–213.

Barnett, J.R. and Webber, M., 2010. *Accommodating migration to promote adaptation to climate change.* World Bank Policy Research Working Paper Series, World Bank: Washington, DC.

Benson, M. and O'Reilly, K., 2009. Migration and the search for a better way of life: A critical exploration of lifestyle migration. *Sociological Review* 57, 608–625.

Black, R., Arnell, N.W., Adger, W. N., Thomas, D. and Geddes, A. 2013. Migration, immobility and displacement outcomes following extreme events. *Environmental Science and Policy* 27, Supplement 1, S32–S43.

Black, R. and Collyer, M., 2014. Populations trapped at times of crisis. *Forced Migration Review* 45, 52.

Boakye-Yiadom, L. 2008. Rural-Urban linkages and welfare: The case of Ghana's migration and remittance flows. PhD Thesis, Department of Economics and International Development, University of Bath, Bath, UK.

Bronen, R. and Chapin III, F.S., 2013. Adaptive governance and institutional strategies for climate-induced community relocations in Alaska. *Proceedings of the National Academy of Sciences* 110, 9320–9325.

Cernea, M.M., 1996. Understanding and preventing impoverishment from displacement. In McDowell, C. ed. *Understanding Impoverishment: The Consequences of Development Induced Displacement.* Berghahn: Oxford, pp. 13–32.

Cernea, M.M., 1997. The risks and reconstruction model for resettling displaced populations. *World Development* 25, 1569–1587.

Cernea, M.M. and McDowell, C. eds., 2000. *Risks and Reconstruction: Experiences of Resettlers and Refugees.* World Bank: Washington, DC.

Chakrabarti, A. and Dhar, A.K., 2009. *Dislocation and Resettlement in Development: From Third World to the World of the Third.* Routledge: London.

de Sherbinin, A., Levy, M., Adamo, S., MacManus, K., Yetman, G., Mara, V., Razafindrazay, L., Goodrich, B., Srebotnjak, T., Aichele, C. and Pistolesi, L., 2012. Migration and risk: Net migration in marginal ecosystems and hazardous areas. *Environmental Research Letters* 7(4), 045602.

Deshingkar, P. and Start, D. 2003. *Seasonal Migration for Livelihoods in India: Coping, Accumulation and Exclusion.* Overseas Development Institute: London.

Ellis, F., 2000. *Rural Livelihoods and Diversity in Developing Countries.* Oxford University Press: Oxford.

Ellis, F. 2003. *A Livelihoods Approach to Migration and Poverty Reduction.* Department for International Development: London.

Findlay, A.M., 2011. Migrant destinations in an era of environmental change. *Global Environmental Change* 21 (Supplement 1), S50–S58.

Foresight, 2011. *Foresight: Migration and Global Environmental Change: Final Project Report.* Government Office for Science: London.

Füssel, H.M. and Klein, R.J., 2006. Climate change vulnerability assessments: an evolution of conceptual thinking. *Climatic Change* 75, 301–329.

Fussell, E., Sastry, N. and Van Landingham, M., 2010. Race, socioeconomic status, and return migration to New Orleans after Hurricane Katrina. *Population and Environment* 31, 20–42.

Geddes, A., Adger, W.N., Arnell, N.W., Black, R. and Thomas, D.S., 2012. Migration, environmental change, and the challenges of governance. *Environment and Planning C: Government and Policy* 30, 951–967.

Gray, C.L. and Mueller, V., 2012. Natural disasters and population mobility in Bangladesh. *Proceedings of the National Academy of Sciences* 109, 6000–6005.

Groen, J.A. and Polivka, A.E., 2010. Going home after Hurricane Katrina: determinants of return migration and changes in affected areas. *Demography* 47, 821–844.

Hugo, G., 1996. Environmental concerns and international migration. *International Migration Review* 30, 105–131.

Intergovernmental Panel on Climate Change. 2014. *Climate Change 2014: Impact, Adaptation, and Vulnerability.* Fifth Assessment Report, summary for policy maker. Cambridge University Press: Cambridge.

Internal Displacement Monitoring Center and Norwegian Refugee Council, 2014. *Global Estimates 2013: People Displaced by Disasters.* Geneva: Internal Displacement Monitoring Center. Retrieved online from www.internal-displacement. org/assets/publications/2014/201409--global-estimates2.pdf.

Kälin, W., 2008. Guiding principles on internal displacement. *Studies in Transnational Legal Policy* 38, 1.

Khonje, W.H. 2015. The dynamics of migration and development in small states. In Khonje, W. H. ed. *Migration and Development: Perspectives from Small States.* Commonwealth Secretariat: London, pp. 4–32.

Kumar, A.N., 2011. *Vulnerability of Migrants and Responsiveness of the State: The Case of Unskilled Migrant Workers in Kerala, India.* Working Paper 26, Centre for Socio-economic and Environmental Studies, Kochi.

Levitt, P., 1998. Social remittances: migration driven local-level forms of cultural diffusion. *International Migration Review* 32, 926–948.

Logan, J.R., Issar, S. and Xu, Z. 2016. Trapped in place? Segmented resilience to hurricanes in the Gulf Coast, 1970–2005. *Demography* 53, 1511–1534.

Lubkemann, S. C., 2008. Involuntary immobility: on a theoretical invisibility in forced migration studies. *Journal of Refugee Studies* 21, 454–475.

McAdam, J., 2012. *Climate Change, Forced Migration, and International Law.* Oxford University Press: Oxford.

McIntosh, M.F., 2008. Measuring the labor market impacts of Hurricane Katrina migration: evidence from Houston, Texas. *American Economic Review* 98, 54–57.

McMichael, C., Barnett, J. and McMichael, A.J., 2012. An Ill wind? Climate change, migration, and health. *Environmental Health Perspectives* 120, 646–654.

Nicholls, R.J. and Cazenave, A., 2010. Sea-level rise and its impact on coastal zones. *Science* 328, 1517–1520.

Portes, A. and Vickstrom, E., 2015. Diversity, social capital, and cohesion. In Dustmann, C. ed. *Migration: Economic Change, Social Challenge.* Oxford University Press: Oxford, pp. 461–479.

Putnam, R.D., 2007. E pluribus unum: Diversity and community in the twenty-first century. *Scandinavian Political Studies* 30, 137–174.

Simms, J.R., 2017. Why would I live any place else? Resilience, sense of place, and possibilities of migration in coastal Louisiana. *Journal of Coastal Research* 33, 408–420.

Skeldon, R., 2014. *Migration and Development: A Global Perspective.* Routledge: London.

Stark, O. and Taylor, J.E., 1991. Migration incentives, migration types: The role of relative deprivation. *Economic Journal* 101, 1163–1178.

Stocker, T.F., Qin, D., Plattner, G.K., Tignor, M., Allen, S.K., Boschung, J., Nauels, A., Xia, Y., Bex, V. and Midgley, P.M., eds. 2014. Climate Change 2013: The Physical Science Basis Working Group I contribution to the Fifth Assessment Report of the Intergovernmental Panel on Climate Change. Cambridge University Press: Cambridge.

Tacoli, C. 2009. Crisis or adaptation? Migration and climate change in a context of high mobility. *Environment and Urbanization* 21, 513–525.

Warner, K. and Afifi, T., 2014. Where the rain falls: evidence from eight countries on how vulnerable households use migration to manage the risk of rainfall variability and food insecurity. *Climate and Development* 6, 1–17.

Warner, K., Afifi, T., Kälin, W., Leckie, S., Ferris, B., Martin, S.F. and Wrathall, D., 2013. *Changing Climate, Moving People: Framing Migration, Displacement and Planned Relocation.* Policy Brief. Institute for Environment and Security, United Nations University, Bonn.

Wilmsen, B. and Webber, M. 2015. What can we learn from the practice of development-forced displacement and resettlement for organised resettlements in response to climate change? *Geoforum* 58, 76–85.

4

Environmental change and international migration

A review

Luisa Veronis, Bonnie Boyd, Reiko Obokata, and Brittany Main

Introduction

In this chapter, we review the growth and development of scholarly research on the relationship between environmental change and international migration over the last 25 or so years. As is reported in other chapters in this volume, most environmentally influenced migration takes place within national borders, and is most often undertaken by individuals and households moving relatively short distances, from rural areas to nearby urban centres, or to other rural areas with greater short-term economic opportunities. Although the scale of international migration for environmental reasons is believed to be relatively small in comparison, it tends to attract considerable attention among policymakers and decision makers. This may be because states have become increasingly preoccupied about issues of sovereignty and the integrity of national borders in the wake of violent civil conflicts, terrorist attacks, and other threats to international security; it may also be because the idea of large scale, cross border movements of environmental migrants:

> challenges the global community, not only because they are a growing phenomenon, not only because they lie outside the traditional framework that the world has developed to resolve refugee issues, but also because their plight and how it is dealt with ultimately affects us all.
>
> *(Nash 1999: 229)*

Discussions about environment and migration are riddled with debate and controversies, and can be polarized and polarizing, regardless of whether such discussions take place among policymakers, scholars, or the general public. While these debates are intellectually rich and informative (in terms of theory, empirics, methodologies, law, and policy), they can also be conceptually limiting and present an impediment to the development of progressive policy to address the complex practical concerns relating to the environment-migration nexus. Scholarly debates have arguably reinforced the status quo on the international stage, or at least done little to alter it, in terms of idleness of governments and major economic actors in the face of climate change. Furthermore, they can be seen as a hindrance to action when media coverage seizes on alarmist discourses and sensational claims, leaving policymakers and the general public unsure what to think or do. Our goal here is to trace the evolution of empirical, theoretical, legal, and policy scholarship on the subject of environmental change and international migration since the end of the Cold War, to summarize the key debates that have emerged and important trends that are likely to have influence in the near future, and to identify important areas needing further study. In doing so, we complement and set the stage for other chapters in this volume.

Methodology

We conducted a systematic literature review of English language peer-reviewed articles on international migration and environmental change published between 1989 and mid-2015 following the methodology of Berrang-Ford, Ford, and Paterson (2011) that has been used successfully by scholars working in the field of environmental migration (McLeman 2011; McLeman et al. 2014; Obokata, Veronis, and McLeman 2014). First, we completed a structured search of the peer-reviewed articles indexed in the ISI Web of Science database using a set of keywords pertaining to international migration and environmental pressures (Table 4.1). The results of each keyword search were recorded, including the number of results, and imported into an article inventory. The initial search yielded a total of 5,573 documents. The title and abstract of each article were then reviewed to determine whether to include it in the final inventory of articles. The references of these articles were also reviewed to identify additional articles not found in the initial searches; a number of articles were included in this way. This method resulted in a total of 183 articles that fit our main criteria – i.e., peer-reviewed articles that directly address the topic of international environmental migration in some meaningful capacity – and were thus included in our review. Of these, 108 articles (59%) have a primary focus on international migration or on both internal and international migration; the remaining 75 articles (41%) deal mainly with internal migration but also mention and/or are relevant to the study of international migration. Documents eliminated from consideration included such things as editorials, book reviews, commentaries, conference reports, duplicate entries, and articles dealing with non-human migration.

Next, we prepared a questionnaire with which to analyze each article, and to identify and code systematically:

- basic information such as authors, title, journal and year of publication, and type of article (empirical, theoretical, policy, legal, and literature review);
- the focus in terms of world regions, environmental pressures, and types of migration (internal/international; refugee flows, labour migration, etc.; rural-rural migration, rural-urban migration, etc.);
- main arguments and key points of discussion; and
- the specific nature of discussion of issues relating to definitions, methodology, structure/agency, class, gender, ethnicity, and so on.

Data about the articles were entered into a customized Microsoft Excel database, with short summaries and important sections of each article noted using standardized key words. The results were also recorded on paper, providing a summary of each article, and important sections of each article were noted for future coding. While this method is efficient and systematic, there are some limitations to it, which the reader should keep in mind when reading this chapter. For example, the findings reflect selections made by the authors about the keywords to be used

Table 4.1 Keywords used in the systematic review of English language peer-reviewed articles on environmental change and international migration

Environment	International	Migration
"Climate change"	International*	Migrant[s]
Deforestation		Refugee[s]
Desertification		Displace*
Disaster		
Drought		
El Niño		
Environment*		
Fire		
Flood*		
"Heat wave"		
Hurricane		
Landslide		
"Natural hazard"		
"Sea level rise"		
Tornado		
Tsunami		

Note: An asterisk following a word indicates a Boolean search for variants with the same root (e.g. flood, floods, flooding, etc.)

and how to interpret the work of others, and are limited to English language peer-reviewed scholarship for which digitized records could be found. While digitized back issues now exist for most significant scholarly publications, there is a chance older works that may be relevant are not yet online. We have deliberately focussed only on peer-reviewed publications, and in doing so we have by design excluded non-scholarly reports by NGOs, multilateral organizations, and other authors who have made meaningful contributions to the evolving understanding of the environmental dimensions of international migration. We further recognize that scholarly discussions will have further evolved between the cut-off date of our literature review and the final publication of the present volume, which is unavoidable in such a highly dynamic field of research. With these caveats, we now summarize our findings.

Findings

Trends in publication numbers and disciplinary orientation of research

Scholarly articles on environmental dimensions of migration have appeared throughout the period 1989–2015, but it is in the 2000s – and especially since 2010 – that we observe a rapid increase in the number of publications. We identified 21 papers published in the period 1990–1999, 27 papers from 2000–2009, and 136 papers since 2010 (Figure 4.1). We further organized the papers into five main categories according to the type of reporting being done, and found 63 (34%) to be articles that focused on reporting empirical findings, 51 (28%) to be principally theoretical or conceptual articles, 34 (18.5%) focusing on policy issues, 24 (13%) to be literature reviews, and 12 (6.5%) to be legal papers (Figure 4.2). We analyze articles in each of these categories in greater detail in later sections of this chapter.

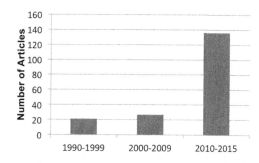

Figure 4.1 Scholarly articles published, by time period

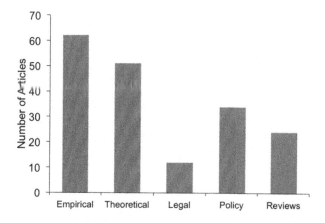

Figure 4.2 Distribution of articles by type of paper

We re-categorized journals into one of 11 disciplinary fields plus a twelfth category of "inter-disciplinary" (journals that by design publish from a wide range of scholarly fields in arts, science, and social science; Table 4.2). Almost one-quarter of all articles (45 in total) were published in interdisciplinary journals. The next largest grouping consists of articles published in geography journals (37 articles, or 20.2%), followed by journals explicitly dedicated to demography, migration, and population studies (22 articles, or 12%), international development journals, and general social science journals (14 each, or 7.6%) and law and policy journals (11, or 6%).

We identify three key trends in these publication statistics. First, there has been a gradual move away from environmental sciences as being the dominant source of scholarly reporting on the environmental international migration nexus (early examples include Roy and Connell 1991; Abbink 1993; Myers 1993; Ruitenbeek 1996; Döös 1997) toward a much larger and wider engagement of social scientists from multiple disciplines and backgrounds. Second, we see an expansion from primarily conceptual articles with modest amounts of empirical evidence and theoretical grounding to a much wider array of detailed studies with more developed methodological and/or theoretical grounding. A third, corresponding, trend is an increasing interdisciplinarity in research design, with growing numbers of scholars undertaking studies on environmental migration that deliberately straddle traditional disciplinary boundaries. In doing so, there is a visible broadening of the epistemological, theoretical, and methodological

Table 4.2 Selected articles by disciplinary journals

Journal Field	Empirical		Theoretical		Legal		Policy		Review		Total Articles
	Number	Percent	Number	Percent	Number	Percent	Number	Percent	Number	Percent	
Climate Change	0	0	4	7.8	0	0	0	0	2	8.6	6
Demography/migration/population studies	14	22.2	2	3.9	1	8.3	2	5.9	3	13	22
Ecology/Biology (excluding agricultural sciences)	0	0	3	5.9	0	0	0	0	0	0	3
Economics	4	6.3	1	2	0	0	1	2.9	0	0	6
Environmental Science (physical drivers of migration)	3	4.8	3	5.9	1	8.3	2	5.9	1	4.3	10
Geography	13	20.1	12	23.5	0	0	7	20.6	5	21.7	37
Health and Environment	0	0	0	0	0	0	0	0	2	8.6	2
Interdisciplinary	14	22.6	11	21.6	2	16.7	12	35.3	6	26	45
International Development	6	9.5	2	3.9	1	8.3	4	11.8	1	4.3	14
Law and Policy	0	0	2	3.9	6	50	2	5.9	1	4.3	11
Political science	1	1.6	1	2	0	0	0	0	0	0	2
Social Science	5	7.9	6	11.8	0	0	1	2.9	2	8.6	14
Other	3	4.8	4	7.8	1	8.3	3	8.8	0	0	11
Total	63	100	51	100	12	100	34	100	23	100	183

approaches being employed in research, and an increasing number of attempts to render more detailed and nuanced recommendations in the areas of policy and governance. This in turn suggests that coming years will see a further expansion of new dialogue, exchange, synergy, complementarity, and advancement in the field.

These trends mirror a concurrent expansion in reporting on migration within the context of IPCC reporting on impacts and adaptation of climate change, which grew from a few short sentences in the first IPCC report in 1990 to a large subsection in the human security chapter and multiple mentions elsewhere in the IPCC's most recent report in 2014 (see McLeman 2016 for a review; also Chapter 1, this volume). The trends also reflect the growing number of scholars involved in teaching and research in the field of environmental migration, evidenced by the increasing citation rates and impact factors of journals like *Population and Environment* and the establishment of research programs and centres at several European universities. It is likely not coincidental that geography has been from the early 1990s the discipline most represented in research on international environmental migration, given its inherent orientation toward human-environment interactions in general. The relatively recent influx of demographers and researchers in related population studies programs is in our view a welcome addition given the sophisticated numerical modelling techniques such researchers often employ (Fussell, Hunter, and Gray 2014). The growth in the number of legal and policy analyses being conducted by experts in such fields is reflective of the growing prominence of discussions of environmental migration in the UN Framework Convention on Climate Change (UNFCCC) process and in the context of international policymaking with respect to humanitarian and security issues, as is discussed in later chapters of this book.

Empirical studies

Our search identified 63 articles in which the authors reported findings from the collection and analysis of empirical data on international environmental migration, of which three-quarters (48 articles) were published in the period 2010–2015, suggesting that earlier calls for more empirical research were heeded. The most common journal categories for empirical research are demography and interdisciplinary journals (14 articles each) and geography (12 articles), followed by international development (7), social science (5), economics (4), and environmental science (3). In terms of methodologies and types of methods nearly half the articles rely on qualitative approaches such as interviews, questionnaires, case studies, collaborative action research, and participant observation, among others. Another 37% of articles employ quantitative approaches, with various modeling techniques being the most common, followed by surveys/questionnaires and statistical techniques applied to panel data. Roughly 13% of articles use a mixed-methods approach that combines quantitative and qualitative techniques.

The geographical orientation of empirical studies is shown in Figure 4.3. Most studies centre on countries and regions located in the Global South, with the detailed breakdown as follows: 22 in Africa, 20 in Asia, 14 in South America and the Caribbean, 12 in Oceania, and nine each in Europe and in North and Central America. The relatively high representation of Oceania reflects a sustained interest in the potential impacts of sea level rise on small island states (Chapter 24, this volume). In contrast, relatively few studies exist for South America and the Caribbean despite the much larger geographical area and population (some exceptions are Alscher 2011; Gray 2009; Wrathall 2012), and we found none investigating international environmental migration originating in the Middle East. The majority of studies focus on migration from the country or region of origin; relatively few investigate the migration experience from the

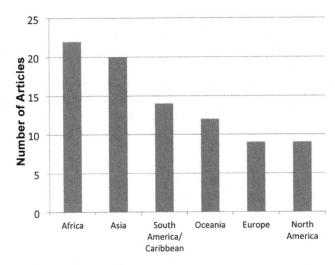

Figure 4.3 Articles by geographic region

Table 4.3 Types of environmental factors examined in the articles reviewed (main focus and mentioned), from most to least frequent

Factor	Articles (Main focus)	Articles (Mentioned)
General climate change (no specific factors)	40	40
Natural disaster	22	26
Drought	21	29
Land degradation	21	25
Rainfall	21	28
Food security	18	20
Water resources	16	18
Sea level rise	13	15
Flooding	12	22
Resource scarcity	9	11
Desertification	4	7
Landslides	2	2
Salinization	1	6
Fire	0	1

perspective of the destination country (some exceptions being Veronis and McLeman 2014) or consider both origin and destination.

Table 4.3 shows the types of environmental factors that are the main focus of each study, as well as additional ones that are mentioned. The most common factor discussed is global climate change in general (40 articles), followed by natural disasters (most often tropical cyclones; 26 articles), drought (29 articles) and rainfall (28 articles). In the period 1990–2010, studies that modelled future sea level rise scenarios were among the most common types of empirical studies, but their frequency has not increased, whereas the number of studies has grown for other aspects of climate change and associated issues such as land degradation (25 articles), flooding

(22), food security (20), scarcity of water (18) and other resources, and to a lesser extent desertification (7), salinization (6), and landslides (2). The vast majority of studies focus on how environmental factors affect rural populations and subsistence livelihoods (e.g., Afifi 2011; Alscher 2011; Dun 2011), with few empirical studies looking at international environmental migration originating in urban areas.

Taken together, the rapid growth in empirical reporting has significantly contributed to advancing debates in the field by providing grounded knowledge and more nuanced understandings of the dynamics between environmental change and international migration. A common theme throughout is the multicausality of migration drivers, with studies illustrating the multiple, complex ways in which specific environmental factors (e.g., drought, flooding, etc.) combine with economic, social, political and demographic factors in particular contexts to influence migration decisions (or not). For example, drought may contribute to increased migration in some cases (Feng, Krueger, and Oppenheimer 2010; Henry et al. 2004; Henry, Schoumaker, and Beauchemin 2004; Nawrotzki, Riosmena, and Hunter 2013), but not in others (Findley 1994).

Empirical studies reveal that many different migration outcomes are possible from a given environmental event or condition (i.e., no migration, internal migration, international migration, seasonal migration, circular migration) depending on the particular context; therefore, it is essential to consider the influence of non-environmental factors – economic, demographic, social, political, cultural – in these processes. For example, land ownership is associated with increased levels of international migration in Ecuador during times of drought (Gray 2009), but appears to be a disincentive to migration in response to floods in Vietnam's Mekong Delta (Dun 2011). By contrast, the landless are more mobile during floods in the Mekong Delta in Vietnam, but in Ecuador the associated lack of resources appears to make the rural landless less mobile. Gender and age are other important factors that can influence migration outcomes during times of environmental stress. For example, in rural Mali, it is mostly adult men who migrate away, leaving women, children, and the elderly to cope with deteriorating environmental conditions (Afifi 2011); in West Sahara, it is children, the elderly and those who are sick who are sent abroad on 'environmental holidays' (Gila, Zaratiegui, and Lopes de Maturana Dieguez 2011); while on Hispaniola, it is mostly women who travel abroad to work as domestics (Alscher 2011). Gioli and Milan discuss further the gender dimensions of environmental migration in Chapter 11, this volume. A small number of empirical studies focus on the role international environmental migration may play in the generation of conflict (Chapter 28, this volume).

An overarching theme of existing empirical studies is that the impacts of environmental change and the associated migration outcomes are contingent upon the unique environmental, economic, political, demographic, and social conditions of each place and region. This suggests that future research needs to pay increased attention to the dynamic interaction between environmental and non-environmental factors across and between multiple scales, from the local level of the individual, family, household, and community to the national, regional, and global levels. What is also evident is that environmental migration does not materialize out of nothing; in most empirical studies, there is an implied or explicit understanding that historically contingent factors – such as colonial histories and postcolonial relations – and ongoing macro-scale trends – such as the political and economic consequences of globalization and neoliberalism – help set the context within which international environmental migration occurs.

There are a number of gaps, shortfalls and ongoing discussions within the existing empirical research that are notable. For example, existing methodologies and research design tend to gravitate toward employing one particular type of method rather than mixing or combining multiple methods, which may limit the explanatory power of a study given the inherent complexity of the causal factors, interactions, and outcomes of the environmental migration process.

Where possible, increased numbers of studies should consider employing mixed methods. There is also an ongoing challenge in terms of longitudinal data availability; while individuals may undertake migration (or be confronted with decisions about whether to migrate) on multiple occasions throughout their life-course, and though the effects of an environmental event may linger for many years afterwards, most studies focus on migration over periods of at most a decade or two. A related consideration is that many empirical studies select study periods based on the dependent variable – periods when migration is known to have occurred in response to environmental factors – but are less likely to include periods when environmental changes have occurred but migration did not ensue.[1] We also suggest that research methods and approaches that include participation of local communities in study design and execution would be worthwhile, based on our own observations of the rich details about the migration decision process revealed in studies that have used such methods.

It is also evident that some environmental factors and some geographical regions have been the subject of much greater volume of study than others; while all factors and regions warrant additional attention, it is clear from Table 4.3 and Figure 4.3 that some are more lacking in attention than others. Moreover, we note the high concentration of studies on rural livelihoods, and suggest that future research attention should also be given to urban populations and the effects on migration patterns of urban ecological decline (such as waste management, air pollution, heat islands, access to safe water, overcrowding, lack of housing and infrastructure, etc.) and urban food (in)security. The lack of studies on cities represents a significant lacuna given extensive research suggesting that cities are highly vulnerable to climate change, especially in coastal and low lying areas, and the steady increase in urban population numbers worldwide.

As empirical evidence consolidates, we suggest this may be an opportune time to turn to the vast migration and mobility scholarship to assist with theorizing the complex linkages between environment and migration. In particular, critical and feminist approaches to migration may offer useful direction to move beyond binary thinking still pervasive in the field along the lines of environmental vs. economic migration, voluntary vs. forced migration, and mobility vs. immobility, among other examples (see Gill 2010; King 2012; Chapter 5, this volume). Existing studies already point to a need for more refined conceptualizations of the interplay between environmental and non-environmental factors in migration decisions; we consider such efforts essential to break loose from the grip of the nature/society binarism still dominating much of the literature. One promising way forward may be the adoption of transnational approaches to migration, whose aim is to move away from essentializing categories in order to grasp the fluidity and relationality of migration processes and experiences (Mitchell 2003; Chapter 21 this volume).

Further, more critical scrutiny of the multiscalar nature and dynamics of the processes involved will go a long way in terms of shedding light on the variety of scales involved in the linkages between environmental change and international migration, as well as how these scales are interconnected. Such an endeavor is especially significant to avoid privileging a given scale over others (e.g., national or global over local and regional) and to remain open to adopting the most adequate methodological scale in each specific case; put differently, attention to scale will help to reveal the social construction of scale as well as the politics of scale (see Gill 2010) that may be limiting further advancements in the field. Last, further consideration ought to be given to the relationship between migrants' agency as individuals occupying multiple subject positions and the structures that regulate their everyday lives in influencing migration decisions. It is essential to deepen understanding of how markers of difference (e.g., gender, class, ethnicity/race, age, family status, etc.) shape the complex "power geometries" (Massey 1994) of the environment-international migration nexus (see Obokata, Veronis, and McLeman 2014).

Theoretical and conceptual contributions

We identified 51 articles whose primary focus was to advance theoretical and conceptual under-standing of the environment-international migration nexus. This group represents the second fastest growing category of papers with 37 papers (72.5%) published in the period 2010–2015, and reflects an increasingly diverse range of theoretical perspectives, conceptual frameworks, and epistemological approaches being applied to the environment-international migration nexus. The largest number of papers were published in geography journals (12) followed closely by interdisciplinary journals (11), the social sciences (6), climate change (4), ecology (3) and environmental science (3).

Early theoretical discussions revolved around the so-called 'maximalists' vs. 'minimalists' debate – whereas the former tended to isolate environmental factors as primary migration driv-ers predicting alarming numbers of 'environmental refugees' in a not-so-distant future, the latter drew attention to the complexity of the matter by highlighting the multiple factors at play in migration processes (Suhrke 1994). Although a multiplicity of perspectives along the maximal-ist vs. minimalist debate can be found among the papers reviewed here, a notable shift toward the minimalist perspective and multicausality of factors in migration decisions is evident, con-firming that "at least in academia the minimalist argument has largely won the day" (Baldwin, Methmann, and Rothe 2014: 122).

These 51 theoretical/conceptual articles papers tend to fall within one of three general types:

- articles that seek to develop conceptual frameworks to be used in the study of environmen-tal change and migration;
- reflections on the relationship between climate, migration, and security; and
- critical discourse analyses on the study of environmental change and migration more broadly.

Each is now discussed in turn.

Conceptual frameworks, models, and typologies

Among articles that aim to develop conceptual frameworks for use in environmental migra-tion research, we identify seven different types of frameworks being proposed. These are not mutually exclusive, and a number of authors present frameworks that span or combine more than one type. The first and most common type of framework is to organize environmental migration knowledge according to specific categories of environmental factors, which range from identification of specific environmental factors (e.g., sea level rise, drought, flood, deser-tification, climate change, etc.: Myers 1993; Döös 1997; Connell 2015; Pryce and Chen 2011; Roy and Connell 1991; Westing 1994), to classifications with broader categories of environmen-tal causes (e.g., natural environmental disasters, expropriations due to industrial environmental damage, and gradual environmental degradation: Bates 2002), and more complex models that incorporate variables at various spatial scales (global climate change and its local effects with migration decisions involving the context of individuals/households, places, and communities: Perch-Nielsen, Bättig, and Imboden 2008).

A second type of framework organizes environmental migration research according to regional characteristics, where regions are defined in terms of:

- shared physical/environmental characteristics, such as drylands, mountainous regions, coastal regions, delta regions, low relief coral islands, etc. (Myers 1993; Döös 1997; Roy and Connell 1991; Westing 1994);
- a combination of environmental and non-environmental (i.e., structural, economic, political) characteristics – e.g., Pelling and Uitto (2001) and Julca and Paddison (2010) on Small Island Developing States (SIDS, a group sharing the environmental context of being small, low lying islands with also small developing states), and Team and Manderson (2011) on the countries of the '40 South' (which by lying below 40 degrees latitude south experience common environmental dynamics while also representing mostly settler societies with similar economic, political and social characteristics); and
- historical, economic, political, and demographic regional dynamics, with the environment being one factor among others, such as de Haas (2011) on migration dynamics in the Mediterranean and Connell (2012, 2015) on resettlement policies and history of migrations in the Pacific.

A third type of framework seeks to develop migrant typologies. The common rationale is that it is essential to distinguish between different types of 'environmental migrants' in order to develop effective policies, assist those in need, and gain (political/public) support. Recent authors attempt to provide more refined typologies that recognize the difficulty of classifying migrants based on degrees of voluntariness (i.e., along the forced/voluntary continuum). Neuteleers (2011) develops a classification with three types of migrants – disaster refugees, expropriation refugees, and deterioration refugees – that considers the severity of environmental factors (drawing from Bates [2002]). Similarly, Renaud et al. (2011) propose a decision framework based on different types of environmental factors: environmental emergency migrant, environmentally forced migrant, environmentally motivated migrant. Stojanov et al. (2014) develop a more general typology with three broad categories of migrants – environmental migrants, environmental displacees (rapid- or slow-onset), and development displacees – which they argue can be adapted to specific contexts.

A fourth approach is to develop frameworks that are based on contextualization of past and current migration movements in terms of migration drivers and systems, often done with an eye to predicting future migrations related to environmental change (e.g., Myers 1993; Döös 1997; Connell 2015; Kelman 2014). Black, Kniveton, and Schmidt-Verkerk (2011) develop a heuristic tool by assessing the main drivers of migration in specific contexts, and then consider the sensitivity of these drivers to climate change, an approach they believe could be useful to develop scenarios by integrating information relating to potential climate change drivers in the future. Others adopt a migration systems approach that considers economic, political, demographic, and environmental factors, and migration policies. For example, de Haas (2011) concludes from recent trends that economic and political factors will most likely play a more significant role than demographic and environmental factors in influencing migration patterns in the Mediterranean region. Findlay (2011) argues that examination of destination regions (in his case, Europe) can be productive to predict where environmental migrants go in the future, in part by shedding light on who does and who does not migrate (i.e., the issue of immobility in relation to environmental change). Harper (2012) takes a demographic approach to make a similar argument regarding the fact that Europe will become an increasingly attractive destination area for skilled workers from around the world, especially regions that face environmental change.

A fifth type of framework focuses on policy approaches to address migration and environmental change. Early on, Myers (2002) suggested that environmental migration needs to be understood under a broader framework of sustainable development. More recently, Kelman (2014) has suggested that we need to consider broader development context and policies to address challenges to climate change; further, he argues that a focus on climate change has depoliticized broader issues relating to the development challenges that small island developing states face (with migration being part of development strategies/responses). Connell (2012, 2015) discusses resettlement policy in the face of climate change by examining the case of the Pacific region, which has a long history of forced displacement and resettlement associated with colonialism and post-colonialism – thus past experiences of resettlement can teach us something; in this case, that resettlement will be difficult to accept. To a lesser extent, Pryce and Chen (2011) fall under this type of framework, but their focus is more specifically on the impacts of flood and flood risk on housing markets, real estate values, economies, and insurance. They recommend focusing on prevention and preparation through building physical resilience of communities, land planning, and market signals.

The studies grouped under the sixth type of framework draw attention to the dynamics between environmental and non-environmental factors at various scales. Pelling and Uitto (2001) argue that processes associated with globalization (economic flows, governance, migration, environmental change) need to be taken into account to understand the local experiences of climate change and migration responses in SIDS. Taking a different perspective, Black, Kniveton, and Schmidt-Verkerk (2011) argue that the focus of study should be on specific local contexts and their experiences of climate change in order to understand how migration drivers may change in the future, which can provide a useful tool to plan adaptation at larger scales.

The seventh and last type of framework aims to address (in part or in whole) the limitations of the frameworks discussed previously. Since the 1990s, a number of authors have raised the need to conceptualize the multicausality of migration drivers in relation to environmental change (e.g., Hugo 1996; Connell 2015; Kelman 2014; Kibreab 2010; Westing 1994). The best known of these is the framework generated as part of the Foresight (2011) study of global environmental migration, introduced in Figure 1.1 of Chapter 1 in this volume, which illustrates linkages and dynamic interactions between five main drivers of migration (economic, political, demographic, social, and environmental) and considers the role of factors at various scales in influencing migration decisions – including at the macro level (i.e., the aforementioned five main drivers), meso level (intervening factors such as political and legal frameworks, social networks, diasporic links), and micro level (individual and household characteristics).

Significant debate exists regarding the epistemological, ontological, and methodological shortcomings of migrant typologies (see King 2012), a critique that can be extended to the conceptual frameworks represented within these seven categories. They tend to be highly specific in terms of their focus on particular environmental factors, regions, types of migrants, migration systems, policy dimensions, and so forth, and it is often difficult to apply them outside the prescribed contexts. Further, these conceptual frameworks often represent idealized types of migration motivation and behaviour that do not fit empirical reality. Such frameworks also often shed no light on the complex dialectics between structure and agency in migration decisions made in the context of environmental change, and provide little guidance on how to conceptualize and articulate the interaction between multiple factors at various scales. The wide acceptance of the Foresight model likely reflects in part its attempt to address some of the challenges of structure versus agency and cross-scale interactions that are less satisfactorily accounted for in preceding conceptual models.

Scholars undertaking critical discourse analyses of the environmental migration literature often critique the ongoing concern with identification of the causal links, arguing that the pursuit of causality is futile, given the inherent complexity of the decision-making process and the myriad of factors interacting at multiple scales. Others have raised concerns about the potential impacts of research in terms of how it will be used by decision makers, the depoliticization of discussions about the impacts of climate change on migration, and that by attributing responsibility for adaptation and migration decisions to households, governments and institutions are let off the hook in terms of their own responsibility (Bettini 2014). Thus, according to some, it is a worthwhile exercise for environmental migration researchers to take time to think more critically not only about what is being studied, but also to what end or purpose.

Reflections on environment, migration, conflict, and security

A second important theme found in theoretical research relates to the linkages between international environmental migration, conflict, and security, a subject analyzed in greater detail in Chapter 28, this volume. While some authors focus more specifically on conflict and others on security/securitization, there is often some degree of overlap. Most articles published on the linkages between conflict, security, environmental change, and migration acknowledge the multicausality of factors, but differences emerge when it comes to conceptualizing the causal linkages between the processes, leading to the development of a variety of theoretical frameworks. One set of articles examines the role of environmental change (and/or climate change specifically) in contributing to migration and conflict in destination areas (Barnett and Adger 2007; Baum and Easterling 2010; Scheffran and Battaglini 2011; Weir and Virani 2011). These studies conclude that environmental factors and migration alone do not lead to conflict; rather, environment-induced migration may lead to conflict when it occurs concurrently with non-environmental factors that generate political instability or violence, such as pre-existing tensions among cultural groups or political factions, intense competition for scarce resources, endemic poverty, weak states, and persistent political and economic instability. In other words, conflict is invariably the outcome of a multiplicity of factors, one of which may be environmentally induced migration.

Other authors are concerned with how conflict may generate environmental change and migration. For example, using the case of the Horn of Africa, Kibreab (1997) sought to deconstruct the belief that environmental change and migration lead to conflict, advancing that conflict, war, and insecurity are sources of environmental degradation and in turn involuntary displacement. He argues that the problems of environmental degradation and migration need to be addressed together, rather than separately, in order to avoid falling into the trap of having to make binary choices of environmental protection over development needs, or vice versa. Selby and Hoffmann (2012) are critical of Malthusian views on how environmental stress can lead to migration and conflict, and use the example of water scarcity in Cyprus, Israel, the West Bank, and Gaza to argue that conflict combined with migration can cause environmental stress. In an earlier study on Rwanda, Uvin (1996) argued that political and environmental factors can contribute equally to conflict. In his assessment, the conflict in Rwanda, which caused multiple forms of displacement, led to further environmental degradation, and long-term solutions to the conflict would require the political and environmental crisis to be addressed simultaneously – an argument that to some extent aligns with Kibreab's views.

Studies on conflict-environment-migration linkages help advance environmental migration research more generally by shedding light on the multicausal factors involved in these processes and by underlying the many different causal pathways that may be identified depending on empirical focus. At the same time, scholars have pointed out that most attempts at understanding these causal linkages have been inconclusive, and that it may be more fruitful to consider cases where conflict is avoided and identify factors that contribute to peace development and cooperation (Gemenne et al. 2014; Scheffran and Battaglini 2011). We observe in the literature a recent shift away from an emphasis on conflict to a broader attention to questions of security (11 papers in all), including a special issue on "Securitizing 'climate refugees'" published in the journal *Critical Studies on Security* in 2014. Among these papers, a majority of authors recognize not only the multicausality of migration drivers – confirming the prominence of a minimalist perspective – but also a high degree of complexity in the security dimensions of climate change, especially given the unpredictability of future scenarios, what Baldwin, Methmann, and Rothe (2014) refer to as "futurology" (as in based on the future conditional tense).

Of the 11 papers on security, three address the climate change-security nexus more broadly (Barnett and Adger 2007; Scheffran and Battaglini 2011; Gemenne et al. 2014), where migration is examined as one variable in potential conflicts. The remainder scrutinize more specifically the climate change-migration-security nexus, with a majority of authors adopting critical approaches from a range of theoretical and epistemological streams. The papers can be organized in three groups based on their focus: (1) state security, (2) human security, and (3) discourse analysis. In the first case, Scheffran and Battaglini (2011) write that incidences of violence and conflict depend on context (environmental, economic, political) as well as national and regional capacity to cope with climate change. Gemenne et al. (2014) aim to shed light on the significance of unequal relations of power between states when it comes to policy responses to climate change; they argue that it is in cases of unequal power that risks arise and security and conflict become a concern. Trombetta (2014) analyzes the framing of climate-induced migration as a security issue and argues that it is caught between discourses of climate security and the securitization of migration. While the former may lead to proactive environmental initiatives and new forms of progressive governance, the latter involves practices of surveillance and policing aimed at increasing border control.

Among those concerned with human security, Barnett and Adger (2007) adopt a vulnerability approach and argue that climate change is increasingly threatening human security by reducing access to livelihoods and resources while undermining states' capacities to meet population needs; these conditions may directly or indirectly lead to violent conflict. Although their interest in migration is secondary, their multicausal and multiscalar approach is especially useful to address issues of agency and structure – i.e., how individuals or groups turn to violence and conflict, and the state's role in these processes. Detraz and Windsor's (2014) paper stands out for being the only one to explicitly adopt a gender analysis. They are critical of approaches that focus on state security and argue in favour of adopting a gender lens to understand the vulnerabilities of specific communities, groups, and individuals.

The third group consists of papers adopting critical discourse analysis to question and deconstruct the securitization turn of climate change and migration. Chaturvedy and Doyle (2010) take a critical geopolitics approach to examine the imaginative geographies of 'climate refugees' with a focus on Bangladesh. They show that the use of security rhetoric is reproducing imaginations of North-South geopolitics as being unequal, inducing fear in Northern countries, while rendering some social groups, places and territories (usually the South) invisible. The papers by Bettini (2014), Mehtman and Oels (2015) and Reid (2014) adopt Foucauldian approaches, including governmentality and biopolitics, to analyze the links between security discourses and climate-induced migration in the context of neoliberalism and neoliberal forms of governance. They demonstrate how the adoption of human security discourses tend to hold migrants responsible for their own security in the face of climate change, aligning with neoliberal ideologies of individualism, while also contributing to a depoliticization of climate change and climate-induced migration. Baldwin (2014b) also tackles the political dimensions of climate-induced migration by arguing that we cannot limit our interpretation of the debate as being solely secular. He argues we need to recognize theological imaginaries so that we may pose the right questions and consider new solidarities.

While seemingly opposed, we suggest that these three types of papers – on state security, human security, and critical discourse analysis of securitization – are complementary. They differ in their epistemological approaches and empirical foci, but together they allow us to better understand where and how conflict may arise and/or be prevented, as well as consider the types of solutions and policy responses that may be needed in different contexts and at different scales (from individual and community to state, regional, and global levels). In the future, more collaborative research may prove useful to further advance both theoretical and policy developments.

Critical discourse analyses

Last, we note an important shift among theoretical debates since around 2010 with a growing number of papers engaging in critical discourse analysis; we found 12 such articles representing over one-fifth of the theoretical papers with a majority (8) published since 2013, including papers from the special issue in *Critical Studies on Security* (2014) discussed previously. We note a majority of social scientists among the authors – including geographers (Baldwin, Bettini, Farbotko) and political scientists (Felli, Mehtman and Oels, Reid) – with a few authors contributing to multiple papers in this group (Baldwin, Bettini). This turn suggests increased critical introspection and maturation in the conceptual and theoretical developments of the field and appears to respond to Baldwin's (2014a) call for pluralizing the study of climate-induced migration. Indeed, the papers draw from a diversity of theoretical and epistemological approaches, including: critical education (Goulah 2010), critical geopolitics (Chaturvedy and Doyle 2010), political economy (Felli 2013), postcolonialism (Baldwin 2012, 2014a; Farbotko 2010), political philosophy (Baldwin 2014b), international development (Kelman 2014), and Foucauldian governmentality and biopolitics (Bettini 2014; Bettini and Andersson 2014; Mehtman and Oels 2015; Reid 2014).

Taken together, this group of papers makes two contributions to the field. First, they apply critical discourse analysis in diverse ways to illuminate ongoing Eurocentric epistemologies and imperialist discourses, policies, and practices that favour the Global North at the expense of the Global South and those communities and people most directly affected by climate change (e.g., the poor, those depending on subsistence livelihoods, small island states, etc.). Specifically, they reveal the reproduction of geographical imaginations and representations built on binary oppositions (us vs. them) that cast climate refugees/migrants as racialized others (Goulah 2010; Baldwin 2012; Reid 2014) and the South in negative light, usually as threatening and inferior (Chaturvedy and Doyle 2010; Farbotko 2010; Kelman 2014), thus justifying discourses and policies (e.g., securitization) that entrench the dominance of the North and protect its interests. Second, the papers – in spite of and through their diverse foci – shed light on the depoliticization of climate-induced migration, as well as of climate change more generally, and related issues such as the climate change-development-migration nexus (Kelman 2014) and the securitization of climate change and migration (discussed earlier) among others. These arguments are important for at least two reasons, the first being that epistemological approaches influence the production of knowledge, and thus shape the science of climate change and migration, and thus (often) also policy. Moreover, as these authors note, the framing and representation of climate change and migration (not only in academia, but also in political discourse and the media) bear tremendous political significance that may determine the course of future actions and thus ultimately the future of humanity and the planet itself.

Gaps and theoretical directions warranting future research

Since the early days of maximalist vs. minimalist debates, we note increasing sophistication and pluralism in the epistemological approaches adopted, as well as a critical turn. The latter provides useful tools for addressing a number of important issues that need further research, of which first and foremost is the depoliticization of the environment-migration relation, in addition to the depoliticization of climate change more generally. Critical approaches such as those reviewed above can help shed light on uneven power relations in the context of environmental change and migration that unfold at multiple scales – at regional and state levels (Global North and Global South, developed and developing states, etc.) and at community and individual levels (e.g. differences in class, ethnicity/race, gender, etc.). Equally important is the use of critical approaches to address the politics of representation – which also reflect and reproduce uneven power relations – and their implications for both theory and policy (Chapter 28, this volume).

Legal analyses

Our inventory contains 12 articles whose primary focus is legal analyses, although we should note that several articles described in the next section on policy analyses also contain some discussion of legal questions. The distribution of publications in this sub-area of the environment-international migration nexus is spread unevenly, with three articles dating from the 1990s, followed by a lack of publications until a spike of nine papers between 2009 and 2012. Six articles (or 50 percent) appear in journals specializing in law and policy, two are in interdisciplinary journals, and the remainder in journals of demography and international development, among others.

Papers in this category are primarily concerned with whether use of the term *refugee* is appropriate in the context of involuntary migration related to environmental change, and the legal implications of various possible frameworks to address the needs of people who move due to environmental factors (for more detailed review and discussion of this topic, see Chapter 25 and Chapter 26, this volume). The authors are almost equally split, with seven papers in favour of the term refugee (Collins-Chobanian, Comerford, and Kerlin 2010; Cooper 1998; Duong 2009; Marshall 2010; McCue 1993; Pourhashemi et al. 2012; Ramlogan 1996), and five papers against (Kolmannskog 2012; Myrstad and Kolmannskog 2009; McAnaney 2012; Moberg, 2009; Prieur, 2010). Authors in favour of using the term refugee argue that the current international refugee framework, the 1951 Convention Relating to the Status of Refugees, would provide adequate protection to those who are displaced by environmental factors. However, this would require an expansion (Cooper 1998; Duong 2009), amendment (Marshall 2010), or new drafting (Collins-Chobanian, Comerford, and Kerlin 2010; McCue 1993; Pourhashemi 2012; Ramlogan 1996) of the current international refugee framework, mostly by adopting a framework based on human rights (Cooper 1998; Duong 2009) and/or international environmental law (McCue 1993). Most authors advance a moral argument to justify protection and use of human rights lens as a basis for building on the existing regime. A general concern among these papers is the prospect that increases in environmental migration could incentivize the introduction of more restrictive international migration controls than those already in place (i.e., increased securitization of migration), further limiting movements of people from less developed countries to migrant recipient countries in Western Europe, North America, Australia, and New Zealand.

In contrast, the five articles opposed to the use of the term refugee point to the inadequacy and shortcomings of the current international framework. Most authors argue that the Refugee Convention is not the right tool (McAnaney 2012), often emphasizing the fact that the environment is explicitly not listed among the factors of persecution in the Convention (Prieur 2010). Further, it is noted that the existing framework does not help to protect internally displaced people (Kolmannskog 2012; McAnaney 2012), given its focus on international migration – refugees being international migrants by definition. Based on these arguments, the articles call for moving away from the current Convention.

Although the papers seemingly belong in opposite camps with regard to the use of the term refugee, we found that they actually share common views on a number of important issues. First, most articles take the perspective that environmental migration is a form of forced (vs. voluntary) migration, or at least as falling under the forced end of the spectrum. Second, all articles share a common concern for ensuring the best protection for people who are displaced by environmental factors, whether or not these are the direct cause of migration. Third, it is interesting to note that many authors from both camps side with the maximalist argument – i.e., they view the environment as the primary driver of migration. Among those in favour of the term refugee, only Cooper (1998) and McCue (1993) acknowledge the multicausality of migration; among those opposed to the use of the term refugee, more authors lean toward the minimalist perspective (Kolmannskog 2012; Myrstad and Kolmannskog 2009; McAnaney 2012). Last, the most significant similarity across the articles is that in spite of a clear division on the use of the term refugee, there is strong alignment in terms of the approaches and frameworks they recommend in practice. Most suggest revisiting the existing Refugee Convention and significantly expanding or amending it (as opposed to abandoning it altogether) by drawing on human rights and environmental law approaches. It emerges that the differences and variations in the proposed legal frameworks are a matter of degree rather than strict principles. A number of authors (all of them against the use of the term refugee) propose abandoning the Refugee Convention and developing a new regime (Kolmannskog 2012; Prieur 2010), using other international law tools (Moberg 2009), existing institutions such as UNFCCC (McAnaney 2012), or other frameworks (bilateral agreements: Myrstad and Kolmannskog 2009). Nevertheless, most papers agree on international responsibility and adopting a global approach – either the Convention or a UN body such as the UNFCCC, suggesting that the UN could be the basis or model for such a framework.

Subjects requiring additional research

Although consensus has not been reached on potential legal solutions and approaches, we interpret the decline in publication of legal articles as signalling an exhaustion of the debates in this area. Moreover, in a political context with little appetite for expanding the refugee definition, legal scholars may need to find more innovative approaches to addressing these issues. Yet the main conundrum remains that definitions are normative and prescriptive. We also note that political agendas and interests are shifting towards questions of governance and policy. There may thus be an avenue for legal scholars to work in this area of environmental migration and collaborate with policy researchers to develop pragmatic frameworks. Specifically, scholars in this sub-field may contribute strong arguments and useful legal tools to address the pressing issue of international responsibility in migration processes related to global environmental change. On this note, we now turn to policy articles.

Policy-oriented papers

We found 35 papers whose primary focus is on the policy dimensions of international migration related to environmental change. In contrast to the legal papers, we note that publication in this sub-area is more recent; four articles date from the 1990s and the remainder appeared since 2008, with a majority (27) published since 2010. Twelve articles were published in interdisciplinary journals, followed by seven papers in geography, with others appearing in international development (4), other journals (3), environmental science (2), and demography (2), as well as economics (1) and social science (1).

The majority of articles in this category focus on policy prescriptions that respond to migration stimulated by climate change, especially among those published recently. Across the complete sampling period, we found articles discussing policy dimensions with respect to a wide range of global environmental challenges, including desertification, drought, floods, food (in)security, land degradation, landslides, natural hazards (unspecified or multiple), rainfall variability, resource scarcity, sea level rise, soil salinization, water scarcity, and wildfires. These have been grouped together into general categories in Figure 4.4, showing how there is relatively broad coverage across categories, but that climate change and the linked phenomenon of sea level rise are mentioned more often than others. With the exception of papers published in the 1990s, authors generally take the perspective that migration is an adaptation undertaken by vulnerable people, and consequently approach migration as being a potential solution to be managed as opposed to being a problem to be solved, controlled, or prevented (Bardsley and Hugo 2010; Martin 2010, 2012; Warner 2010, 2012; Gemenne 2011; Geddes and Jordan 2012). This is particularly the case in articles addressing climate change, which typically call for proactive policies that increase resilience and adaptive capacity building in the present moment in order to limit

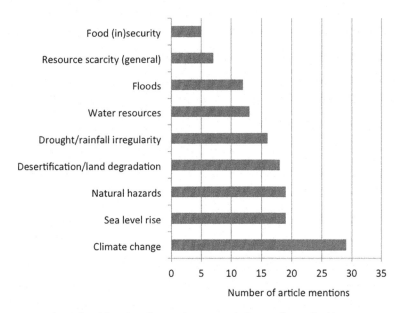

Figure 4.4 Number of publications by environmental change/hazard of interest.

Many articles in inventory mention multiple environmental phenomena, so sum of chart exceeds number of articles in inventory.

future impacts, rather than a 'wait and see' approach that may be more costly in the long-term. The overall tone of these articles tends to be 'pro-migration' (Tacoli 2009; Gemenne 2011; Omezeri and Gore 2014), advocating for a humanitarian approach to migration, rather than a security approach that would include stricter border controls and more selective and punitive immigration policies. The types of policy recommendations fall into one of two broad groups: some that make general calls for pro-migration policy and planning with limited specifics (e.g., Tacoli 2009; Warner 2010; Gemenne 2011; Martin 2010, 2012; Omezeri and Gore 2014), while others (e.g., Biermann and Boas 2008, 2010; Johnson and Krishnamurthy 2010; Geddes and Jordan 2012; Geddes and Somerville 2012; Gibb and Ford 2012; Fernández-Huertas Moraga and Rapoport 2014) offer specific and often detailed policy recommendations, including proposals for specific institutions or instruments.

Most articles highlight the significant level of uncertainty in the environment-migration nexus, including a lack of clear definitions in terminology, the limited amounts of reliable empirical data available, and the challenge of developing future models and scenarios due to the uncertainty, unpredictability, and complexity of environmental change processes and of human migration behaviour (McAdam 2011; Assan and Rosenfeld, 2012). As a result, most authors note that it is challenging to develop concrete policy provisions without detailed and specific information such as types and numbers of migrants, countries involved, types of environmental factors, and so on (Martin 2010). Nevertheless, authors such as Gibb and Ford (2012) take a pragmatic approach and argue that policy progress can be made in spite of these challenges.

When it comes to definitions, the papers can be divided into two subgroups. One includes authors who develop detailed and specific definitions, which they believe are necessary for the development of policies that can be implemented effectively. There are differences among such perspectives. For example, some (Akokpari 1998; Biermann and Boas 2008, 2010; Westing, 1994) believe that the term 'refugee' is an appropriate term to describe people who must move for environmental reasons, and suggest that the current Refugee Convention is inadequate and needs to be reconsidered, revised or expanded. Others such as Nash (1999) do not advocate revisiting the Convention, but adhere to a refugee terminology that reflects a broad concern with human rights and the protection of the people affected by environmental change – i.e., they side with a humanitarian approach and generally call for international responsibility (see Swain 1996; Locke 2009; Assan and Rosenfeld, 2012). Some authors, such as Biermann and Boas (2008, 2010), develop very precise definitions with a view to distinguish between forced/voluntary migrants, internal/international migration, environmental/other factors, etc., in order to include only the *real* environmental refugees. In the second sub-group are authors who favour more open definitions, rather than the restrictive term 'refugee', or question the ability to generate agreeable definitions altogether (Bardsley and Hugo 2010; Martin 2010, 2012; Gemenne 2011). This group generally adopts a migrant/migration terminology based on a mobility approach that recognizes the limitations of typologies and rigid categories, and the problematic nature of distinctions such as forced vs. voluntary migration or economic vs. environmental migration, among others. They tend to align with a minimalist perspective on the complexity of multicausality in migration, and thus opt for definitions that are more inclusive and flexible in their applicability (McAdam 2011).

Three key overarching themes can be summarized in terms of policy directions and recommendations. First is a debate between authors over whether to develop new institutions and mechanisms to govern and manage international environmental migration (e.g. Biermann and Boas 2008, 2010; Warner 2010; Fernández-Huertas Moraga and Rapoport 2014; Johnson and Krishnamurthy 2010) or to modify, expand, or revamp existing ones like the UNFCCC or the Guiding Principles on Internal Displacement, and/or alter the mandates of other UN agency mandates and initiatives (Martin 2010, 2012; Bardsley and Hugo 2010; Gibb and Ford 2012; Warner 2012; McDowell 2013; Westing 1994). McAdam (2011, 2014) makes a vocal case against the creation of any new 'universal' treaty to protect those who might be displaced by climate related factors not only due to the complexity of the process itself, but also because it would deter states from taking immediate responsibility and adopting a range of more timely measures. Moreover, she is concerned that such a treaty may trigger negative reactions or backlash against migrant protection, and argues that a blanket approach may not be adequate to respond to regional and more local, community needs. Tacoli (2009) argues that more attention needs to be paid to the role of national and local institutions, whilst Geddes and Jordan (2012) and Geddes and Somerville (2012) focus on Europe as a destination region and provide suggestions for EU policy changes.

A second common theme is the need to enhance local resiliency and adaptive capacity to provide greater options to people who might be at risk of displacement or involuntary migration (Tacoli 2009; Bardsley and Hugo 2010; Martin 2010; Hugo 2011; Gemenne 2011; Jennings 2013; Opeskin and MacDermott 2009; Tacoli 2009; Johnson and Krishnamurthy 2010; Geddes and Jordan 2012; Drolet et al. 2014). Examples include calls for a broad range of adaptive response policies across multiple sectors, including food security, trade, finance, environment, and development (Jennings 2013; Westing 1994; Swain 1996; Locke 2009).

A third theme is an ongoing discussion about the framing of environmental migration policy. A growing concern is the 'securitization' of policy discussions and the discourse of environmental refugees and migration 'control' that is used outside academia, in contrast with the 'migration-as-adaptation', humanitarian, and human rights perspectives more favoured by researchers (see Chapter 25, Chapter 26, and Chapter 28, this volume, for more detailed discussions; also Bettini 2014; Brown and McLeman 2009; Hartmann 2010; Geddes and Somerville 2012; Mayer et al. 2013). At issue here is how to mobilize multiple, often antagonistic, discourses representing different interests (science, politics, media, civil society) into effective and progressive policy in a timely fashion. In this regard, Mayer (2014) offers a useful analysis of how different frames may influence policy responses.

Directions for future research

In reviewing these articles, we found that the treatment of issues regularly encountered in migration policy research more generally – such as questions of structure and agency – tends to be oriented heavily towards modifying the structure of institutional arrangements, and relatively light in terms of engagement of the people affected. This seems to be particularly needed in discussions of planned resettlement of populations exposed to environmental risks (López-Carr and Marter-Kenyon 2015), although we would suggest that participatory governance in all aspects of environmental migration – an issue first raised by Westing (1994) – warrants a closer, more detailed look. There are also open questions as to how best to generate research combining empirical, theoretical and policy approaches, particularly those that bring together governance organizations and vulnerable communities (McAdam 2014). Moreover, there is room for further collaborative research on policy responses that take into account the multiscalar (temporal and spatial) dynamics of environmental change, of power relations and institutional jurisdictions at multiple levels (from local to global), with Drolet et al. (2014) calling for more attention to vulnerabilities at the group and individual level and for better dialogue between policymakers and communities.

Literature reviews

Our search identified 23 articles whose main purpose is to provide critical reviews of existing works. The earliest date from 1994 (McGregor 1994) and 1997 (O'Lear 1997), suggesting that there was by that time sufficient scholarship in the field to warrant such reviews. We notice a surge of such articles from 2010 onward with a total of 19 articles published since then. Most appear in interdisciplinary journals (6) and geography (5), followed by journals in demography (3), social science (2), climate change (2), and health and environment (2), among others (Table 4.2).

These literature reviews are diverse in purpose and scope, but can be loosely organized around six general themes. The first consists of six papers that provide general overviews of the literature, including main debates and arguments relating to definitions, terminology, and minimalist vs. maximalist approaches (Bailey 2010; O'Lear 1997; O'Neill and Balk 2001; Gill 2010; Gill, Calectrio, and Mason 2011; Krishnamurty 2012). Another seven articles focus on the empirical literature with a sustained interest in methodological issues (Piguet 2010; Gemenne 2011; Lilleør and Van Den Broeck 2011; Warner 2011; McLeman 2013; Fussell, Hunter, and Gray 2014; Obokata, Veronis, and McLeman 2014). All note the diversity of methodological approaches and the challenges this represents for the development of meaningful and coherent quantifications of environmentally related migration, with Fussell, Hunter, and Gray (2014) focussing on quantitative methodologies demographers use and offering suggestions on the development of global data on the environment-migration nexus. Obokata, Veronis, and McLeman (2014) put forward an exploratory framework to improve empirical approaches by taking into account the multiscalar nature of both environmental change and migration. Third, two authors provide historical reviews: McLeman (2011) discusses the role of past environmental events in migration and displacement, while Piguet (2013) provides a history and evolution of the study on the environment-migration nexus – explaining how the environment shifted from being central to becoming marginal in population and migration scholarship. A fourth set of three articles focusses on linkages between conflict, environment, and migration, and relate to the preceding section of this chapter (Bernauer, Böhmelt, and Koubi 2012; Jasparrro and Taylor 2008; Tertrais 2011), but predate the publication of more critical approaches in this area. Fifth, two papers focus on the health-environment-mobility nexus (Kistin et al. 2012; McMichael, Barnett, and McMichael 2012). Last, three papers have a more specific focus. McGregor (1994) reviews the literature on environment and migration with an interest in implications for food security. More recently, Morinière's (2012) article stands out for its unique focus on the linkages between urbanization, environment, and mobility. Through a systematic review, she found significant literature on the environmental impacts of urbanization, but much less on the effects of environmental change on urbanization (e.g., rural exodus due to environmental degradation). She argues that the latter issue merits further study, given growing urban populations and the environmental vulnerability of cities. Finally, Oliver-Smith (2012) reviews the debates on environmental migration in the context of climate change paying particular attention to the framing of the issues along the society-nature nexus.

Overall, most authors of review articles explicitly align with the minimalist perspective (Piguet 2010; Lilleør and Van Den Broeck 2011; Gemenne 2011; McLeman 2011; Warner 2011; Morinière 2012) or present the minimalist vs. maximalist debates (Gill 2010; Piguet 2013); few articles appear to lean towards a maximalist viewpoint (Bernauer et al. 2012; O'Lear 1997). With regard to terminology, Gill (2010) and O'Lear (1997) use *environmental refugee* as their descriptor, three authors rely on forced migration/displacement language (McGregor 1994; Gemenne

2011; Warner 2011), and most of the other authors adopt a migration and mobility framework (Piguet 2010; Morinière 2012; Obokata, Veronis, and McLeman 2014).

The increasing adoption of a mobility approach suggests an opening to migration scholarship that can present more complex conceptualizations of environmental migration, moving away from binary oppositions to understanding migration as a dynamic process along a continuum of forced-voluntary, temporary-permanent, and internal-international mobility. Such conceptualization is reflected among a number of review articles (e.g., Gill 2010; Gill, Caletrio, and Mason 2011; Warner 2011; Obokata, Veronis, and McLeman 2014), especially with attention to the linkages between internal-international migration and the difficulty in distinguishing between forced and voluntary migration. Yet, migration frameworks are not necessarily helpful to address the society/nature opposition; on the contrary, emphasis on the political dimensions of forced migration has served to entrench the separation between society and environment (Piguet 2013). We note that only two articles scrutinize the society/nature duality more closely (Gill 2010; Oliver-Smith 2012), both of which underline the conceptual, empirical, and political fallacy of separating the environment from other (social, economic, and political) factors. In light of these developments, we suggest that migration scholarship may provide a useful conceptual foundation to address the depoliticization of climate induced migration given its emphasis on the power/political dimensions of mobility; but this would require incorporating a more critical framing of the relationship between society and nature.

Future reviews could consider the policy dimensions of existing research, including the securitization of environmentally induced migration, to advance understanding of the differentiated outcomes resulting from distinct policy approaches, and thus inform policy design on the short, medium, and longer terms. Moreover, a review of the linkages between internal and international migration in relation to environmental change, with particular attention to the class, gender, and race dimensions of mobility, is much needed. In each instance, it may be fruitful to adopt critical approaches such as discourse analysis to shed light on the epistemological and political implications of existing research, considering how influential science has become in shaping policy today.

Conclusions

Based on the preceding review of research on international environmental migration, we suggest that a number of significant changes have emerged in the field in the past quarter-century. First, a degree of consensus seems to have been reached in recognizing the multicausal nature of migration in relation to environmental change. This simultaneously reflects a transition from increasing multidisciplinarity to greater interdisciplinarity, which we expect to continue into the foreseeable future. Discussions among authors are moving beyond the minimalist vs. maximalist debates of two decades ago (Bettini 2014, Baldwin, Methmann, and Rothe 2014) and exhibit increasing awareness of the national and international politics of migration, showing concerns about the securitization of both migration and climate change in popular and policymaking discourse.

Concomitantly, a language shift can be noted. Whereas earlier papers (in the 1990s) often use terms such as 'environmental refugees' with little discussion of definitions (e.g., Myers 1993, 1997; Döös 1997), most recent papers – especially since 2010 – provide critical reviews regarding terminology, definitions, and conceptualizations of migration, which suggest a degree of influence from migration and mobility studies. There is a noticeable move away from the term 'refugee' (in recognition of its limited meaning under the Convention), and a prevalence of broader terms such as 'migrants', 'migration', 'human mobility', and 'population movement' that avoid suggesting deterministic or causal linkages between environmental factors and migration (Baldwin 2014; Barnett and Adger 2007; Kelman 2014; Perch-Nielsen, Bättig, and Imboden 2008; Findlay 2011). The use of such broader terms aligns very much with the pro-migration perspective that many scholars in the field champion when it comes to general policy directions in the context of climate change (Tacoli 2009; Gemenne 2011; Omezeri and Gore 2014).

Further engagement in this field by scholars from migration and mobility studies, who until recently showed little interest in the environmental dimensions of migration, and the continued breaking of disciplinary silos by researchers, will benefit the field in the long run. The 'mobility turn' in the social sciences (Cresswell 2006, 2010; Sheller and Urry 2006) has been especially influential in bringing to the forefront the role of power structures and unequal power relations in mobility processes – embedding mobility and migration in broader political, economic, and social forces, and now also environmental conditions – thus in turn facilitating a move away from binary oppositions (forced/voluntary, permanent/temporary, labour/environmental, etc.) and a more explicit recognition that mobility and migration are situated along a continuum, between forced and voluntary, permanent and temporary, and so on (King 2012). Environmental migration literature shows a strong signal of a 'mobility turn', that will continue to be beneficial.

However, we note Baldwin's (2014a) call for further conceptual and epistemological diversification and expansion in the field. As has been commented in relation to other fields of research (e.g., Thrift 2000; Duncan and Duncan 2004; McDowell 2009), epistemological pluralism is to be celebrated for providing new avenues not only to understanding the world, but also to imagining possibilities and alternatives – and we clearly need more of both to address the complexities of climate change. Yet, while epistemological pluralism is a noble scientific endeavour, scholars need to be aware of how scientific debates and knowledge production – including epistemological pluralism and theoretical diversity – are received, perceived, and used by a broader audience. Pluralization and sophistication come with potential risks, such as a seeming lack of coherent message and loss of nuance as complex arguments become reduced and possibly even manipulated into simplified sound bites, that can be easily sold by decision makers and the media (see Mayer 2014 for such a discussion). Those who research environmental migration and displacement receive a significant amount of attention and interest from policymakers, the media, and the wider public; care must therefore be taken to ensure that findings from such research be communicated in a clear and accessible fashion while being reflected accurately in non-academic discussions.

Note

1 We owe this observation to Professor Myron Gutmann of the University of Colorado-Boulder.

References

Abbink J. (1993) "Famine, gold and guns: The Suri of southwestern Ethiopia, 1985–91" *Disasters*, 17(3) 218–225

Afifi T. (2011) "Economic or environmental migration? The push factors in Niger" *International Migration*, 49(S1) e95–e124

Akokpari J. K. (1998) "The state, refugees and migration in Sub-Saharan Africa" *International Migration*, 36(2) 211–234

Alscher S. (2011) "Environmental degradation and migration on Hispaniola Island" *International Migration*, 49(S1), e164–e188

Assan J. K. and Rosenfeld T. (2012) "Environmentally induced migration, vulnerability and human security: Consensus, controversies and conceptual gaps for policy analysis" *Journal of International Development*, 24(8) 1046–1057

Bailey A. J. (2010) "Population geographies and climate change" *Progress in Human Geography*, 35(5) 686–695

Baldwin A. (2012) "Orientalising environmental citizenship: climate change, migration and the potentiality of race" *Citizenship Studies*, 16(5–6) 625–640

Baldwin A. (2014a) "Pluralising climate change and migration: an argument in favour of open futures" *Geography Compass*, 8(8) 516–528

Baldwin A. (2014b) "The political theologies of climate change-induced migration" *Critical Studies on Security*, 2(2) 210–222

Baldwin A. Methmann C. and Rothe D. (2014) "Securitizing 'climate refugees': the futurology of climate-induced migration" *Critical Studies on Security*, 2(2) 121–130

Bardsley D. K. and Hugo G. J. (2010) "Migration and climate change: examining thresholds of change to guide effective adaptation decision-making" *Population and Environment*, 32, 238–262

Barnett J. and Adger W. N. (2007) "Climate change, human security and violent conflict" *Political Geography*, 26(6) 639–655

Bates D. C. (2002) "Environmental refugees? Classifying human migrations caused by environmental change" *Population and Environment*, 23(5) 465–477

Baum S. and Easterling W. (2010) "Space-time discounting in climate change adaptation" *Mitigation and Adaptation Strategies for Global Change* 15(6) 591–609

Bernauer T. Böhmelt T. and Koubi V. (2012) "Environmental changes and violent conflict" *Environmental Research Letters*, 7(1) 015601

Berrang-Ford L. Ford J. D. and Paterson J. (2011) "Are we adapting to climate change?" *Global Environmental Change*, 21 25–33

Bettini G. (2014) "Climate migration as an adaption strategy: de-securitizing climate-induced migration or making the unruly governable?" *Critical Studies on Security*, 2(2) 180–195

Bettini B. and Andersson E. (2014) "Sand waves and human tides: exploring environmental myths on desertification and climate-induced migration" *The Journal of Environment & Development*, 23(1) 160–185

Biermann F. and Boas I. (2008) "Protecting climate refugees: the case for a global protocol" *Environment: Science and Policy for Sustainable Development*, 50(6) 8–17

Biermann F. and Boas I. (2010) "Preparing for a warmer world: towards a global governance system to protect climate refugees" *Global Environmental Politics*, 10(1) 60–88

Black R. Kniveton D. and Schmidt-Verkerk K. (2011) "Migration and climate change: towards an integrated assessment of sensitivity" *Environment and Planning A*, 43(2) 431–450

Brown O. and McLeman R. (2009). "A recurring anarchy? The emergence of climate change as a threat to international peace and security" *Conflict, Security and Development*, 9(3) 289–305

Chaturvedy S. and Doyle T. (2010) "Geopolitics of fear and the emergence of 'climate refugees': imaginative geographies of climate change and displacements in Bangladesh" *Journal of the Indian Ocean Region*, 6(2) 206–222

Collins-Chobanian S. Comerford E. and Kerlin C. (2010) "Twenty million environmental refugees and counting: a call for recognition or a new convention" *Environmental Ethics*, 32(2) 149(16)

Connell J. (2012) "Population resettlement in the Pacific: lessons from a hazardous history?" *Australian Geographer*, 43(2) 127–142

Connell J. (2015) "Vulnerable Islands: climate change, tectonic change, and changing livelihoods in the Western Pacific" *The Contemporary Pacific*, 27(1) 1–36

Cooper J. B. (1998) "Environmental refugees: meeting the requirements of the refugee definition" *New York University Environmental Law Journal*, 6(2) 480–529

Cresswell T. (2006) *On the move: mobility in the modern Western world* Routledge, New York

Cresswell T. (2010) "Towards a politics of mobility" *Environment and Planning D: Society and Space*, 28(1) 17–31

Critical Studies on Security (2014) "Securitizing 'climate refugees': the futurology of climate-induced migration" 2(2)

de Haas H. (2011) "Mediterranean migration futures: patterns, drivers and scenarios" *Global Environmental Change*, 21 S59–S69

Detraz N. and Windsor L. (2014) "Evaluating climate migration: population movement, insecurity and gender" *International Feminist Journal of Politics*, 16(1) 127–146

Döös B. R. (1997) "Can large-scale environmental migrations be predicted?" *Global Environmental Change*, 7(1) 41–61

Drolet J. Sampson T. Jebaraj D. P. and Richard L. (2014) "Social work and environmentally induced displacement: a commentary" *Refuge*, 29(2) 55(8)

Dun O. (2011) "Migration and displacement triggered by floods in the Mekong delta" *International Migration*, 49(S1) e200–e223

Duncan J. S. and Duncan N. G. (2004) "Culture unbound" *Environment and Planning A*, 36 391–403

Duong T. T.V. (2009) "When islands drown: the plight of 'climate change refugees' and recourse to international human rights law" *University of Pennsylvania Journal of International Law*, 31(4) 1239–1266

Farbotko C. (2010) "Wishful sinking: disappearing islands, climate refugees and cosmopolitan experimentation" *Asia Pacific Viewpoint*, 51(1) 47–60

Felli R. (2013) "Managing climate insecurity by ensuring continuous capital accumulation: 'climate refugees' and 'climate migrants'" *New Political Economy*, 18(3) 337–363

Feng S. Krueger A. B. and Oppenheimer M. (2010) "Linkages among climate change, crop yields and Mexico-US border migration" *PNAS*, 107(32) 14257–14262

Fernández-Huertas Moraga J. and Rapoport H. (2014) "Tradable immigration quotas" *Journal of Public Economics*, 115 94–108

Findlay A. M. (2011) "Migrant destinations in an era of environmental change" *Global Environmental Change*, 21 S50–S58

Findley S. E. (1994) "Does drought increase migration? A study of migration from rural Mali during the 1983–1985 drought" *International Migration Review*, 28(3) 539–553

Foresight: Migration and Global Environmental Change (2011) *Final Project Report* The Government Office for Science, London

Fussell E. Hunter L. M. and Gray C. L. (2014) "Measuring the environmental dimensions of human migration: the demographer's toolkit" *Global Environmental Change*, 28 182–191

Geddes A. and Jordan A. (2012) "Migration as adaptation? Exploring the scope for coordinating environmental and migration policies in the European Union" *Environment and Planning C: Government and Policy*, 30(6) 1029–1044

Geddes A. and Somerville W. (2012) "Migration and environmental change in international governance: the case of the European Union" *Environment and Planning C: Government and Policy*, 30(6) 1015–1028

Gemenne F. (2011) "Climate-induced population displacements in a 4 C world" *Philosophical Transactions of the Royal Society A*, 369(1934) 182–195

Gemenne F. Barnett J. Adger W. and Dabelko G. (2014) "Climate and security: evidence, emerging risks, and a new agenda" *Climatic Change*, 123(1) 1–9

Gibb C. and Ford J. (2012) "Should the United Nations framework convention on climate change recognize climate migrants?" *Environmental Research Letters*, 7(4) 045601. doi:10.1088/1748–9326/7/4/045601

Gila O. A. Zaratiegui A. U. and Lopes de Maturana Dieguez V. (2011). "Western Sahara: Migration, exile and environment" *International Migration*, 49(S1), e146–e163

Gill N. (2010) "'Environmental refugees': key debates and the contributions of geographers" *Geography Compass*, 4(7) 861–871

Gill N. Caletrío J. and Mason V. (2011) "Introduction: mobilities and forced migration" *Mobilities*, 6(3) 301–316

Goulah J. (2010) "Conceptualizing environmental refugees in education: a transformative language-learning framework" *Diaspora, Indigenous, and Minority Education*, 4(3) 192–207

Gray C. L. (2009) "Environment, land, and rural out-migration in the southern Ecuadorian Andes" *World Development*, 37(2) 457–468

Harper S. (2012) "Environment, migration and the European demographic deficit" *Environmental Research Letters*, 7(1) 015605

Hartman B. (2010) "Rethinking climate refugees and climate conflict: rhetoric, reality and the politics of policy discourse" *Journal of International Development*, 22(2) 233–246

Henry S. Piché V. Ouédraogo D. and Lambin E. F. (2004) "Descriptive analysis of the individual migratory pathways according to environmental typologies" *Population and Environment*, 25(5) 397–422

Henry S. Schoumaker B. and Beauchemin C. (2004) "The impact of rainfall on the first out-migration: a multi-level event-history analysis in Burkina Faso" *Population and Environment*, 25(5) 423–460

Hugo G. (1996) "Environmental concerns and international migration" *International Migration Review*, 30(1) 105–131

Hugo G. (2011) "Future demographic change and its interactions with migration and climate change" *Global Environmental Change*, 21(S1) S21–S33

Jasparrro C. and Taylor J. (2008) "Climate change and regional vulnerability to transnational security threats in Southeast Asia" *Geopolitics*, 13(2) 232–256

Jennings M. (2013) "Climate disruption: are we beyond the worst case scenario?" *Global Policy*, 4(1) 32–42

Johnson C. A. and Krishnamurthy K. (2010) "Dealing with displacement: can "social protection" facilitate long-term adaptation to climate change?" *Global Environmental Change*, 20(4) 648–656

Julca A. and Paddison O. (2010) "Vulnerabilities and migration in Small Island developing states in the context of climate change" *Natural Hazards*, 55(3) 717–728

Kelman I. (2014) "No change from climate change: vulnerability and small island developing states" *Geographical Journal*, 180(2) 120–129

Kibreab G. (1997) "Environmental causes and impact of refugee movements: a critique of the current debate" *Disasters*, 21(1) 20–38

Kibreab G. (2010) "Climate change and human migration: a tenuous relationship?" *Fordham Environmental Law Review*, 20(2–3) 357–401

King R. (2012) "Geography and migration studies: retrospect and prospect" *Population, Space and Place*, 18 134–153

Kistin E. J. Fogarty J. Pokrasso R. S. Mccally M. and Mccornick P. G. (2012) "Climate change, water resources and child health" *Archives of Disease in Childhood*, 95(7) 545

Kolmannskog V. (2012) "Climate change, environmental displacement and international law" *Journal of International Development*, 24(8) 1071–1081

Krishnamurty P. K. (2012) "Disaster-induced migration: assessing the impact of extreme weather events on livelihoods" *Environmental Hazards*, 11(2) 96–111

Lilleør H. B. and Van Den Broeck K. (2011) "Economic drivers of migration and climate change in LDCs" *Global Environmental Change*, 21 S70–S81

Locke J. T. (2009) "Climate change-induced migration in the Pacific region: sudden crisis and long-term developments" *The Geographical Journal*, 175(3) 171–181

López-Carr D. and Marter-Kenyon J. (2015) "Manage climate-induced resettlement: governments need research and guidelines to help them to move towns and villages threatened by global warming" *Nature*, 517(7534) 265–68

Massey D. (1994) *Space, place and gender* University of Minnesota Press, Minneapolis

Marshall L. (2010) "Toward a new definition of 'refugee': is the 1951 convention out of date?" *European Journal of Trauma and Emergency Surgery*, 37(1) 61–66

Martin S. F. (2010) "Climate change, migration, and governance" *Global Governance*, 16(3) 397–415

Martin S. F. (2012) "Environmental change and migration: legal and political frameworks" *Environment and Planning C: Government and Policy*, 30(6) 1045–1060

Mayer B. (2014) "'Environmental migration' as advocacy: is it going to work?" *Refuge*, 29(2) 27–42

Mayer B. I. Boas J. J. Ewing A. Baillat and U. K. Das (2013) "Governing environmentally-related migration in Bangladesh: responsibilities, security and the causality problem" *Asian and Pacific Migration Journal*, 22(2) 177-198

McAdam J. (2011) "Swimming against the tide: why a climate change displacement treaty is not the answer" *International Journal of Refugee Law*, 23(1) 2–27

McAdam J. (2014) "Creating new norms on climate change, natural disasters and displacement: international developments 2010–2013" *Refuge*, 29(2) 11(16)

McAnaney S. C. (2012) "Sinking islands? Formulating a realistic solution to climate change displacement" *New York University Law Review*, 87(4) 1172–1209

McCue G. S. (1993) "Environmental refugees: applying international environmental law to involuntary migration" *Georgetown International Environmental Law Review*, 6(1) 151–190

McDowell L. (2009) "Understanding diversity: the problem of/for 'Theory'" In R. J. Johnston, P. J. Taylor, and M. J. Watts (Eds.), *Geographies of global change. Remapping the world*. Blackwell, Malden (MA)

McDowell C. (2013) "Climate-change adaptation and mitigation: implications for land acquisition and population relocation" *Development Policy Review*, 31(6) 677–695

McGregor J. (1994) "Climate change and involuntary migration: implications for food security" *Food Policy*, 19(2) 120–132

McLeman R. A. (2011) "Settlement abandonment in the context of global environmental change" *Global Environmental Change*, 21 S108–S120

McLeman R. (2013) "Developments in modeling of climate change-related migration" *Climatic Change*, 117 599–611

McLeman, R. (2016) "Migration as adaptation: conceptual origins, recent developments, and future directions" In A. Milan, B. Schraven, K. Warner, and N. Cascone (Eds.), *Migration, risk management and climate change: evidence and policy responses* (pp. 213–229) Springer, Dordrecht

McLeman R. A. Dupre J. Berrang Ford L. Ford J. Gajewski K. and Marchildon G. (2014) "What we learned from the Dust Bowl: lessons in science, policy, and adaptation" *Population and Environment*, 35 417–440

McMichael C. Barnett J. and McMichael A. J. (2012) "An ill wind? Climate change, migration, and health" *Environmental Health Perspectives*, 120(5) 646–654

Mehtman C. and Oels A. (2015) "From 'fearing' to 'empowering' climate refugees: governing climate-induced migration in the name of resilience" *Security Dialogue*, 46(1) 51–68

Mitchell K. (2003) "Cultural geographies of transnationality" In K. Anderson, M. Domosh, S. Pile and N. Thrift (Eds.), *Handbook of cultural geography* Sage, London 74–87

Moberg K. K. (2009) "Extending refugee definitions to cover environmentally displaced persons displaces necessary protection" *Iowa Law Review*, 94(3) 1107–1136

Morinière L. (2012) "Environmentally influenced urbanisation: footprints bound for town?" *Urban Studies*, 49(2) 435–450

Myers N. (1993) "Environmental refugees in a globally warmed world" *BioScience*, 43(11) 752–761

Myers N. (1997) "Environmental refugees" *Population and Environment*, 19(2) 167–182

Myers N. (2002) "Environmental refugees: a growing phenomenon of the 21st century" *Philosophical Transactions: Biological Science*, 357(1420), 609–613

Myrstad F. and Kolmannskog V. (2009) "Environmental displacement in European asylum law" *European Journal of Migration and Law*, 11(4) 313–326

Nash A. E. (1999) "Environmental refugees: consequences and policies from a western perspective" *Discrete Dynamics in Nature and Society*, 3(2) 227–238

Nawrotzki R. J. Riosmena F. and Hunter L. M. (2013) "Do rainfall deficits predict U.S.-bound migration from rural Mexico? Evidence from the Mexican census" *Populations Research and Policy Review*, 32 129–158

Neuteleers S. (2011) "Environmental refugees: a misleading notion for a genuine problem" *Ethical Perspectives*, 18(2) 229–248

Obokata R. Veronis L. and McLeman R. (2014) "Empirical research on international environmental migration: a systematic review" *Population and Environment*, 36(1) 111–135

O'Lear S. (1997) "Migration and the environment: a review of recent literature" *Social Science Quarterly*, 78(2) 606–618

Oliver-Smith A. (2012) "Debating environmental migration: society, nature and population displacement in climate change" *Journal of International Development*, 24(8) 1058–1070

Omezeri E. and Gore C. (2014) "Temporary measures: Canadian refugee policy and environmental migration" *Refuge*, 29(2) 43(11)

O'Neill B. and Balk D. (2001) "World population futures" *Population Bulletin*, 56(3) 3–40

Opeskin B. and MacDermott T. (2009) "Resources, population and migration in the Pacific: connecting islands and rim" *Asia Pacific Viewpoint*, 50(3) 353–373

Pelling M. and Uitto J. I. (2001) "Small island developing states: natural disaster vulnerability and global change" *Environmental Hazards*, 3(2) 49–62

Perch-Nielsen S. Bättig M. and Imboden D. (2008) "Exploring the link between climate change and migration" *Climatic Change*, 91(3) 375–393

Piguet E. (2010) "Linking climate change, environmental degradation, and migration: a methodological overview" *Wiley Interdisciplinary Reviews: Climate Change*, 1 517–524

Piguet E. (2013) "From 'primitive migration' to 'climate refugees': the curious fate of the natural environment in migration studies" *Annals of the Association of American Geographers*, 103(1) 148–162

Pourhashemi S. Khoshmaneshzadeh B. Soltanieh M. and Hermidasbavand D. (2012) "Analyzing the individual and social rights condition of climate refugees from the international environmental law perspective" *International Journal of Environmental Science and Technology*, 9(1) 57–67

Prieur M. (2010) "Draft convention on the international status of environmentally-displaced persons" *Urban Lawyer*, 42–43(4–1) 247–257

Pryce G. and Chen Y. (2011) "Flood risk and the consequences for housing of a changing climate: an international perspective" *Risk Management*, 13(4) 228–246

Ramlogan R. (1996) "Environmental refugees: a review" *Environmental Conservation*, 23(1) 81–88

Reid J. (2014) "Climate, migration, and sex: the biopolitics of climate-induced migration" *Critical Studies on Security*, 2(2) 196–209

Rénaud F. G. Dun O. Warner K. and Bogardi J. (2011) "A decision framework for environmentally induced migration" *International Migration*, 49(Supp.1) 5–29

Roy P. and Connell J. (1991) "Climatic change and the future of atoll states" *Journal of Coastal Research*, 7(4) 1057–1075

Ruitenbeek H. J. (1996) "Distribution of ecological entitlements: implications for economic security and population movement" *Ecological Economics*, 17(1) 49–64

Scheffran J. and Battaglini A. (2011) "Climate and conflicts: the security risks of global warming" *Regional Environmental Change*, 11(Supp 1) 27–39

Selby J. and Hoffmann C. (2012) "Water scarcity, conflict, and migration: a comparative analysis and reappraisal" *Environment and Planning C: Government and Policy*, 30(6) 997–1014

Sheller M. and Urry J. (2006) "The new mobilities paradigm" *Environment and Planning A*, 38(2) 207–226

Stojanov R. Kelman I. Shen S. Duží B. Upadhyay H. Vikhrov D. Lingaraj G. J. and Mishra A. (2014) "Contextualising typologies of environmentally induced population movement" *Disaster Prevention and Management*, 23(5) 508–523

Suhrke A. (1994) "Environmental degradation and population flows" *Journal of International Affairs*, 47(2) 473–496

Swain A. (1996) "Environmental migration and conflict dynamics: focus on developing regions" *Third World Quarterly*, 17(5) 959–974

Tacoli C. (2009) "Crisis or adaptation? Migration and climate change in a context of high mobility" *Environment and Urbanization*, 21(2) 513–525

Team V. and Manderson L. (2011) "Social and public health effects of climate change in the '40 South'" *WIREs Clim Change*, 2 902–918

Tertrais B. (2011) "The climate wars myth" *The Washington Quarterly*, 34(3) 17–29

Thrift, N. (2000) "Afterwords" *Environment and Planning D: Society and Space*, 18 213–255

Trombetta M. J. (2014) "Linking climate-induced migration and security within the EU: insights from the securitization debate" *Critical Studies on Security*, 2(2) 131–147

Uvin P. (1996) "Tragedy in Rwanda: the political ecology of conflict" *Environment: Science and Policy for Sustainable Development*, 38(3) 7–29

Veronis L. and McLeman R. (2014) "Environmental influences on African migration to Canada: focus group findings from Ottawa-Gatineau" *Population and Environment*, 36(2) 234–251

Warner K. (2010) "Global environmental change and migration: governance challenges" *Global Environmental Change*, 20 402–413

Warner K. (2011) "Environmental change and migration: methodological considerations from ground-breaking global survey" *Population and Environment*, 33 3–27

Warner K. (2012) "Human migration and displacement in the context of adaptation to climate change: the Cancun adaptation framework and potential for future action" *Environment and Planning C: Government and Policy*, 30(6) 1061–1077

Weir T. and Virani Z. (2011) "Three linked risks for development in the Pacific Islands: climate change, disasters and conflict" *Climate and Development*, 3(3) 193–208

Westing A. H. (1994) "Population, desertification, and migration" *Environmental Conservation*, 21(2) 110–114

Wrathall D. J. (2012) "Migration amidst social-ecological regime shift: the search for stability in Garifuna villages of northern Honduras" *Human Ecology*, 40 583–596

5

Immobility

Caroline Zickgraf

Introduction

Despite the great deal of attention currently accorded to migration in its various forms, the world remains a fairly sedentary place. Simply put, most of the world's population is not migrants (Hammar et al. 1997; Carling 2002). That is true on a general level, but also in the specific context of environmental disruption. Admittedly, a chapter dedicated to immobility may strike the reader of a handbook on migration as odd. At first glance, people who *do not move* when affected by environmental changes seem to fall outside the scope of interest. However, immobility is inextricably, albeit often invisibly, linked to our understandings of human mobility. Whenever we seek to understand the drivers or outcomes of migration, we are, in fact, asking why people *don't* stay and what that means for them, their families and for affected societies. Migration and non-migration can thus be seen as two sides of the same coin. Moreover, migration is given social meaning in its very relationship to immobility. Thus I will often refer in this chapter to a spectrum of *(im)mobility*, in order to acknowledge the relational dynamics of mobility (Adey 2006).[1]

One rather fundamental explanation for the general lack of interest in this type of research comes from the underlying sedentary bias that underpins many of the ways that we frame modern society and its norms (Castles 2011; Jònsson 2011). We tend to think that if given a choice, most people will choose to remain in one place. That is what creates the 'problem' of environmental migration: it is considered an abnormal human behaviour that responds to crisis. The fallibility of this assumption is demonstrated by such 'voluntary' migration motives as love or 'wanderlust' (which can occur alongside environmental drivers) and the traditional mobility of herders, borderlanders and other nomadic lifestyles. Yet despite the evidence of non-sedentary baselines, and the push *towards* mobility in world regions such as West Africa's ECOWAS and Europe's Schengen area,[2] sedentary assumptions continue to drive our understandings of migration. We are lulled into the false assumption that those who do not become 'environmental migrants' or 'climate refugees' are unproblematic, and thus unworthy of our collective academic or policy attention. The ensuing research then perpetuates this thinking (albeit unintentionally), further normalizing immobility.

However, research clearly refutes a simplistic storyline starring the 'climate refugee'. Empirical and theoretical research on environmental migration emanating from academia and grey literature continues to grow in complexity and variety, as demonstrated by this very Handbook. For example, in the context of an environmental disruption that adversely affects a given population, there has been a relatively recent shift from a singular focus on negative aspects, or the victimhood of migrants towards the recognition of migration as an adaptation strategy (Tacoli 2009; Warner 2009; Johnson & Krishnamurthy 2010; Afifi et al. 2016). The migrant, rather than a passive, anonymous victim, is an active agent who uses his or her mobility to escape danger. This can then increase the adaptive capacity of the migrant as well as her or his family in response to climate change through, for example, remittance mechanisms. In this more positive framing of migration, the immobile belong to two categories: 1) the receivers of remittances, helped by the migration of some so that they may stay in place; and 2) the 'left behind', those who are unable to migrate or to benefit from the mobility of household members. Regardless of whether migration is posed as a solution to or the symptom of environmental changes, those who do not move fall off the academic radar. Researchers effectively sample on the bias by isolating people on the move for subjects of study. We are left seeing the world of 'environmental migrants', whose experiences are privileged over their counterparts and in which we only examine successful movements (even in displacement scenarios). The inability to migrate, failed migration or a lack of migration aspirations are excluded from our narratives on the environment-mobility nexus.

This neglects the possibility that we may be facing a world in which *fewer* people are able to move as a result of climate change. As Black et al. (2011) point out, the literature is conflicting on the impacts that climate change will have on human migration: some say substantial impacts will occur (ADB 2011), others minor (Tacoli 2011). Indeed, the only consensus regarding climate change's effect on human migration is that there is no consensus. A variety of scenarios are possible dealing with the volume but also character of migration. Although there seems to be an almost *de facto* tendency to claim that climate change will increase human migration in the future, it may be just as likely that more people will be stuck in place, at risk of displacement or death because of the erosion of their resources resulting from climate change, land degradation and water mismanagement, or because governments (sending and receiving) are keen to prevent migration. This overlooks the essential role of peoples' actual abilities to migrate. Without some level of resources, for one, the possibility to move even across relatively short distances is drastically hindered. Thus, one argument for studying immobility is that, in fact, those left behind may be equally if not more vulnerable than the people who are able to leave environmental risk zones, becoming what has been termed 'trapped populations' (Foresight 2011).

However immobility is not only important because it represents the absence of migration, a counternarrative, an alternative to mobility, or a looming threat. The immobile (whether an individual, household or community) are wrapped up in the fabric of mobility. Particularly in 'migration cultures', they are embedded in the same social networks and spaces as the mobile. When research elevates the migrant and ignores the non-migrant, we blur the picture of migration. For one, it minimizes the importance of the immobile in motivating migration, despite migration theories such as the New Economics of Labour Migration (NELM) that acknowledge the importance of the household in the migration decision-making process (Stark & Bloom 1985; Taylor 1999). Even after migration is undertaken, international and internal migrants often operate in transnational social fields that are simultaneously occupied by non-migrants (Glick Schiller & Levitt 2006). We often speak of the potential of migration to act as adaptation for those who remain through remittances and livelihood diversification, yet the 'other side' of these remittances remain vague, passive counterparts in these narratives. The immobile are essential in stimulating and allocating both material and social remittances, and thus who these people are, the selection process and their roles in migration networks, etc., cannot be underestimated (Zickgraf 2016). Thus, researching immobility can elucidate the transnational and translocal relationships that link sending and receiving societies and their subsequent impacts (on adaptation).

With this rationale in mind, this chapter explores the evidence and current state-of-play regarding immobility in the study of environmental migration. The goals are the following: 1) to review the origins of immobility within and outside of environmental migration research; 2) to distill the empirical evidence on immobility in studies of environmental migration; 3) to further conceptualise immobility and 'trapped populations'; 4) to outline the relevance of immobility for environment and migration policy; and 5) to postulate certain future research avenues.

Origins of immobility studies

This chapter focuses specifically on immobility in environmental contexts, but that is certainly not to say it is the only relevant context. In fact, most of what we know empirically and theoretically about immobility (elsewhere called non-migration)[3] comes from outside the environmental scholarship (Hammar et al. 1997; Carling 2002; Lubkemann 2008; de Haas 2014). In one of the first contemporary studies to explicitly study immobility, Hammar et al. (1997) tackled the complicated relationship between migration, immobility and development. In an innovative push, they asked not just why some people go but also why some people stay, from a variety of levels and perspectives (gender, social networks, etc.). In doing so, they called into question the generally accepted sedentary preference rather than assuming it *a priori*.

In another seminal study coming from 'mainstream' migration literature,[4] Jorgen Carling incorporated immobility into his 2002 study of Cape Verdean migration, in which he noted that many of the people 'left behind' in Cape Verde wanted to leave the country, yet lacked the ability to do so. The primary constraint inhibiting migration was poverty, amidst a variety of micro-, meso- and macro-level forces. Carling, noting this 'involuntary immobility', incorporated his findings into a model of migration that balanced people's migration aspirations with their abilities. Crucially, Carling recognizes the dynamism of mobility status in that mobile people may become immobile and immobile populations may become mobile.

Lubkemann (2008), for his part, pushed for a complete theoretical reorientation of forced migration/refugee studies predicated on the case of 'involuntary immobilitization' in wartime Mozambique. He focused on the impacts of conflict on 'baseline' mobility patterns in Mozambique, demonstrating how men's transnational wartime mobility – a continuation of their pre-war life – in fact afforded them opportunities to limit the detrimental impact of conflict on their life projects. Women, however, saw their small-scale pre-war mobility strategies interrupted by the effects of war. Unlike their male counterparts, these women suffered 'displacement *in situ*' and suffered the most social disruption and disempowerment as they simultaneously suffered from the effects of drought and civil war without the ability to move away from them. Theoretically and empirically, environmental migrationists have much to gain from his arguments, including the fact that by focusing on movement, we may effectively be rendering an entire category of people invisible as well as distorting the experience of environmental migrants themselves.

Although the natural environment sometimes appeared in aforementioned work (c.f. Lubkemann 2008), the explicit environmental connection to immobility only really emerged in the 2010s. Under the heading of 'trapped populations', immobility first took precedent in the

2011 Foresight report, commissioned by the UK government. Although the report focused on climate change and migration, the threat posed by trapped populations was, in fact, one of its key findings. The report used evidence from various study sites such as Somalia and Bangladesh. In the latter, migration was only a coping strategy for some, while others facing disaster stayed in place because of increasing labour needs and decreased resources with which to migrate. Its authors proclaimed, "People who are trapped may become more prone to humanitarian emergencies and possibly even displacement if their situation worsens, or if extreme events occur. In such cases, human survival may depend upon unplanned and problematic displacement" (Foresight 2011: 16).

A small, but growing, movement to incorporate immobile populations has emerged within environmental migration scholarship (c.f. Foresight 2011; Black et al. 2011; Black et al., 2013; Black & Collyer 2014; Murphy 2014, Zickgraf et al., 2016; Adams 2016; Nawrotski & Bakhtsiyarava 2016). Unlike previous work that nearly exclusively referenced migration or displacement under the 'mobility umbrella', this body of literature integrates immobility within the mobility paradigm, as a mobility outcome in the wake of an extreme environmental event (Black et al. 2013; Hasegawa 2013) or slow-onset changes (Black et al. 2011; Adams 2016; Nawrotski & Bakhtsiyarava 2016). Unfortunately, the growing interest has not been matched by empirical production: data and explicit analysis of immobility in environmental contexts remains negligble. Many examples come from 'hindsight' reflections on past natural disasters or slow-onset events rather than case studies that directly and intentionally incorporated immobility in their research design. For reasons previously mentioned, this hardly comes as a shock, but it does hamper efforts to conceptualize and typologize immobility while directing policy based on sound empirical evidence.

Conceptual grounding

Alongside the lack of empirical studies specifically targeting or at least including the explicit examination of immobile populations, we still struggle with the conceptualization of immobility within environmental contexts. At the moment, academics are wont to use the term 'trapped populations' to indicate involuntary immobility. The Foresight report used the term trapped primarily as an adjective, without explicitly putting it forward as a concept in itself. As such, no definition is provided in the report. Black and Collyer (2014: 52) initially lay out a litmus test more than a definition: "To be 'trapped', individuals must not only lack the ability to move but also want or need to move." However, they then suggest all three criteria are essential to qualify as trapped: "Trapped populations are those people who not only aspire but also need to move for their own protection but who nevertheless lack the ability."

These three criteria – desire to move (+), need to move (+) and ability to move (−) – seem rather straightforward, but as currently defined it makes a better heuristic device than a concept. The emic/etic debate certainly seems pertinent. Who has the 'right' to define a need/desire/capacity to move? The need to migrate 'for their own protection' is, even in dire immediate circumstances, a relatively slippery notion. What the external researcher assesses as a physical threat may not align with the perceived risk of the affected individual, household or population.[5] Similarly, the ability and aspiration to migrate are also rather subjective notions. Distinguishing those who wish to move (or need to do so in times of crisis) but remain *in situ* from those who do not wish to move is extremely difficult, not least because people's judgment about whether it is necessary to move is likely to change over even quite short periods of time. One solution is to default to the perception of the participant as to whether he, she or they meet these criteria.

One must then accept that there will undoubtedly be a segment of affected populations that will not self-identify as trapped, even if external observers might disagree. Even those who do identify themselves as trapped may not see the environment as their main threat, just as the occurrence of environmental disruption does not mean it is a key player in migration motives for all those affected. Moreover, we know that households are not necessarily harmonious units, thus interviewing the head of household versus another member may give conflicting answers when mobility aspirations or self-assessments of need/capacity are considered. This implies that we are better off speaking of trapped individuals and households rather than entire communities or populations with homogenous characteristics.

One resulting question is then how do we address the people who do not identify as trapped and yet live in the same environmental risk areas, whether because they have the ability to migrate or because they do not aspire or feel a need to do so? Agency in immobility has been a rather gray area thus far that has hindered the development of a trapped population concept, yet "distinguishing between those who choose to stay and those who are forced to stay is essential if the notion of trapped populations is to have anything other than a very broad conceptual application" (Black & Collyer 2014: 54). Presumably using a similar set of criteria as Black and Collyer, the Foresight report distinguished between the *involuntarily* immobile (trapped) and the *voluntarily* immobile (immobile) and then exclusively focuses on those who are trapped. Both seem to cast aside the voluntarily immobile, even in recognizing that many people will choose to stay despite extreme environmental disaster. Black and Collyer go as far as to assert that trapped populations are the only population of concern among the immobile: "The justification for a concern with the immobile is that particularly vulnerable populations will be trapped. Yet the potentially extreme vulnerability of the involuntarily immobile justifies greater attention to this group anyway" (Black & Collyer 2014: 52). Unfortunately, this overlooks the threats posed to the voluntarily immobile in assuming that they are less vulnerable to environmental changes than their trapped counterparts and that they are fully aware and informed about the threats posed. Some people do not understand the severity or irreversibility of the risk, and thus have no intention of leaving their homes, lands or assets. These populations do not qualify as trapped, and yet their refusal to move pre-emptively (planned or not) can place them at great danger for health risks, fatality, immediate or protracted displacement, such was the case in the wake of the Fukushima nuclear reactor incident in Japan in 2011.

Conceptually and empirically speaking, the currently asserted line between trapped and immobile is blurry at best (after all, aren't the trapped immobile?). Immobility should rather be employed as an umbrella term covering the array of reasons and relative agency categorizing the people who do not move (whether they moved previously or move in the future). Within immobility, we can then consider a spectrum of agency ranging from the voluntarily immobile to the involuntarily immobile, or 'trapped populations', even if all immobility involves both choices and constraints as is often recognized in broader migration literature (Fischer et al. 1997; Lubkemann 2008). Ideally, these two spectrums will be integrated into one (im)mobility spectrum able to encompass agency and mobility potential. This move away from the binary then allows us to focus more on what underlies the (im)mobility decision and its resulting outcomes while also capturing a broader range of at-risk populations, including those immobilized after initial migration. This discussion also raises important ethical questions about how researchers, policy makers and other key actors in the field, such as humanitarian agencies and international organisations, understand and eventually act in relation to people who voluntarily choose to remain in the face of certain harm.[6]

Immobility and the environment

Setting aside the conceptual challenges, what has been firmly established empirically is that an environmental change (slow or sudden) does not necessarily lead to human migration, an overly deterministic assumption (Gemenne 2011). Migration is the result of a decision (albeit one that may be forced) in which not everyone will partake; it is never a 'foregone conclusion' (Lubkemann 2008). If we agree that there is logic behind migration – be it survival, improvement of wellbeing, livelihood diversification, income maximization, etc. – it goes to reason that there are also logics behind *non*-migration. One might then ask, in areas where people's livelihoods and residences, and/or very lives are threatened by environmental degradation, why would people stay? The answer to that question is far from simple. Just as there is no singular explanation for migration, there is no one explanation for immobility. Evidence shows a variety of micro-, meso- and macro-level factors influence (im)mobility decisions. Far from claiming comprehensive coverage, this section covers a range of (im)mobility drivers that interact based on the current state of knowledge. We posit that the most useful way to proceed in this endeavor is by covering drivers of immobility as they affect and are affected by: 1) abilities; and 2) aspirations.

Abilities

The conditions that contribute to immobility range from macro-structural migration barriers, including legal or administrative barriers, lack of transportation networks and the absence of migration infrastructure[7] (Black et al. 2011) to personal (e.g. gender, age, education, skills) and household characteristics (financial resources, social networks, human capital). By far, the most commonly cited constraint on the ability to migrate is a lack of financial resources (Foresight 2011). Accordingly, it is typically the poor who become 'trapped' in the event of environmental disasters, such as Hurricane Katrina (Masquelier 2006), Fukushima (Hasegawa 2013), and the Flint Water Crisis (Sim 2016). As such, "vulnerability to extreme environmental events is widely recognised to be inversely correlated with wealth, such that poorer people face a double risk: they are more vulnerable to disasters, but less able to move away from them" (Black et al. 2013: S36).

A lack of financial resources also has demonstrated impacts on immobility in slow-onset cases of environmental changes, primarily through agricultural pathways[8] (Müller et al. 2014; Nawrotzki & Bakhtsiyarava 2016). For example, in the case of drought there is evidence that dwindling resources are allocated to basic needs such as food and shelter rather than out-migration (Findley 1994). Studies in Ghana and Burkina Faso found that severe droughts in fact limited people's ability to invest their financial capital in migration as an adaptation strategy (Henry et al. 2004; van der Geest 2009). Gray and Wise found that:

> Across the continent in Burkina Faso, temperature has a consistently negative effect on all migration streams including international migration. [. . .] International migration from Burkina Faso also declines with precipitation, likely reflecting negative effects of precipitation on agricultural output in this context.
>
> *(Gray & Wise 2016: 566)*

Thus, while environmental change can increase the need to migrate, it may simultaneously inhibit migration. As environmental changes deplete or degrade natural resources, people who sustain themselves on those resources see their capacities to migrate dwindle, as well. This, of course, has major implications for countries and regions primarily dependent on agricultural livelihoods.

Other kinds of capital have been acknowledged in limiting populations' abilities to migrate, but to a much lesser degree. In our deference to material resources, the lack of them, and the pursuit of them as they fund or are generated by migration, we tend to overlook the other aspects that influence immobility. The lack of social networks that extend outside of the place of origin, for instance, can have a strong influence on the (im)mobility decision. Historically, McLeman & Smit (2006) noted the relative geographical expanse of social networks among migrants to California during the American Dust Bowl era of the 1930s in comparison to those who remained in eastern Oklahoma, whose social networks were largely local. In my work in the Mekong Delta of Viet Nam, for example, not knowing anyone, or, more precisely, not knowing anyone who could provide accommodation and potential employment contacts in a potential destination, played a major role in keeping people in place – more so than the financial costs of the move itself. A lack of contacts outside of New Orleans was one of the reasons why people could not evacuate before Hurricane Katrina, simply having no place else to go (Chapter 22, this volume). Moreover, even if a community is strongly embedded in a transnational social network, we should not assume that extensive social networks facilitate migration: social networks can act as migration facilitators or inhibitors through a series of negative feedback mechanisms (de Haas 2011).

In addition to financial and social resources limiting migration abilities, demographic variables are often cited in explanations of *who* goes or stays within a given household or community. The current knowledge aligns with mainstream migration literature in that, generally speaking, poor(er) groups, the low-skilled, women, the elderly and children are less likely to migrate, and, in the event of displacement, they are more likely to become trapped in transit. Age structure is influential in that older cohorts are less likely to be mobile than their younger counterparts (Belot & Ederveen 2012). The physical ability to move certainly plays a role, as does the capacity to work (and to be hired), since much of environmental migration, particularly in slow-onset situations, is simultaneously economic including rural-urban dynamics. Women are often 'left behind' to manage households and child socialization when their male counterparts migrate for economic opportunities, as documented in Bangladesh (Penning-Rowsell et al. 2013).

More often than not, it is a combination of the previously mentioned personal and household characteristics that affect (im)mobility outcomes in a given environmental situation. Just as we cannot isolate the environment from other migration drivers, we cannot separate social, demographic, economic, political and environmental factors as they induce immobility. One example of this blend was the immobilized populations during Hurricane Katrina. Those with resources and means of transportation evacuated New Orleans prior to the hurricane; those with friends and family elsewhere were also more likely to evacuate. On the flipside, those without resources (largely the poor, African-American, elderly or residents without cars) remained stuck in place or displaced within the city during the storm and in its devastating aftermath (Masquelier 2006; Chapter 22, this volume). In Fukushima, alongside poverty, age, strong social networks giving access to job opportunities, tech literacy strongly influenced (im)mobility outcomes in providing information on access to disaster relief and evacuation assistance (Hasegawa 2013).[9] Across a sample of eight case studies affected by rainfall variability, Afifi et al. (2016: 257–258) found that while the most affluent residents had no need to migrate, trapped populations were "forced to cope locally with rainfall variability as they neither have adult male family members who could work as labour migrants, nor resources to facilitate migration, nor access to the necessary migration networks."

These barriers to migration, however, are too often boiled down to personal and household characteristics. As Lindley (2014: 41) pointed out in her discussion of the displacement of Ethiopian pastoralists: "We often focus on proximate causes and immediate triggers but less on the structural factors and processes of deprivation, vulnerability and disempowerment that underlie displacement". Immobility is just as much a result of the meso- and macro-level factors at play as the individual and household features that shape migrant selectivity. After all, micro-level conditions such as household poverty are often produced, or at least reinforced, by macro-level inequalities, structural opportunities and constraints. Migration regimes have the power to halt migration just as much as they may facilitate it. Local land and resource management and bilateral agreements act in a similar fashion. For example, Senegal's agreement with Mauritania grants only 400 cross-border fishing licenses each year, enabling the (legal) circular migration of only a relative few. Those unable to obtain the coveted license must choose: either migrate and stay in Mauritania or remain behind, immobile, and find other means of adaptation to depleted fish stocks. Other legislation is more explicit in its ambition to deter 'environmental' migration: decreasing rural migration to urban centres (from drought-prone areas such as Rajasthan) is one of the central objectives of India's Mahatma Gandhi National Rural Employment Guarantee Act (MGNREGA). Such acts often rely on the aforementioned sedentary bias that assumes migration is an abnormal, undesirable behavioral response to external stressors.

Migration aspirations

By and large, literature on environmental immobility focuses on why people *cannot* move. The emphasis on migration abilities (in this case, the lack thereof) has the unfortunate consequence of minimising people's (im)mobility desires – or *aspirations* – as they influence decision-making. Part of the reason for this empirical and conceptual gap is the aforementioned concern over 'trapped populations', who by definition want to leave: "choosing to remain is obviously substantially different from being unable to move" (Black & Collyer 2014: 55). This starting point then justifies the research emphasis on why people can't move, rather than why they might not want to.[10]

So why when facing slow-onset environmental degradation or an extreme sudden-onset event would people *choose* to stay? Admittedly, because the few studies addressing immobility privilege involuntary immobility, we are lacking detailed data on (im)mobility aspirations in areas affected by environmental changes, including the choice to stay. Nonetheless, similar to abilities, (im)mobility aspirations can be analysed at various scales. On a macro and meso scale, we ask why a given population wish to migrate (regardless of geographic or temporal scale) within a particular *(im)mobility environment*, or the social, economic, environmental, demographic and political context that is largely common to all members of a given community and forms the basis for aspirations to migrate *or* to stay in place.[11] This includes the social meaning (and attached positive and negative attributes) of migration and immobility. The (im)mobility environment may be especially influenced by environmental changes, or it may be more profoundly shaped by other factors that may 'override' the environmental migration driver, e.g. cultural place attachment, gender roles, conflict or the social status accorded to successful migrants. A community may, for example, aspire for its women and children to remain behind while men are expected, and more valued, as migrants in the face of slow-onset change. Even in extreme circumstances, migration may be seen as a last resort response to environmental threats and communities and governments have actively resisted relocation. The backlash of Pacific Island states against the climate refugee discourse demonstrates that not all communities wish to migrate, even if the ability were afforded (McNamara & Gibson 2009).

Once the (im)mobility environment is assessed, variations within the community can be examined at the individual and household level. Why do some people in a given community wish to stay while others wish to go? One of the more simple answers comes from differentiated vulnerability: even in the same communities, not everyone suffers equally from environmental changes. People dependent on the natural environment for livelihoods are typically more vulnerable to progressive climate variability and environmental disruption than their counterparts (at least in the short term). Their vulnerability can, in turn, lead to greater out-migration, such as rural–urban patterns commonly witnessed (although these are not unique to environmental changes). Those whose livelihoods are not as vulnerable, or who have a great deal of resources with which they can adapt *in situ*, may not feel the same pressure to migrate. Similarly, people living on the 'front lines' of coastal erosion will face higher and more immediate impacts. In the Mekong Delta, those affected by landslides and mudslides living along the riverbank were clearly more desperate to move than their village counterparts. Linked to differentiated vulnerability is the importance of perception as it influences migration aspirations. Those who do not perceive a risk to their livelihoods, residences or lives are often more inclined to stay on in spite of environmental changes. Crucially, the perceptions of environmental changes that influence migration aspirations are not always aligned with externally observed climate data (Zickgraf et al. 2016). From this perspective, succinctly put, some people feel they *need to migrate* more than others.

However, variations in (im)mobility outcomes are also reflective of household and personal differentiations in place attachment, affective ties, local social status, etc. Even in cases of dissatisfaction with the place of residence, people choose to stay. Place attachment (both positive and negative) is perhaps the most underestimated in influencing (im)mobility aspirations.[12] Adams (2016: 430) rightly noted, "explanations for populations persisting in the face of difficult environmental conditions have focused on financial barriers to migration, and not socio-psychological or affective aspects of the decision to migrate." Affective ties, comfort in familiarity and reluctance to leave behind family members and friends represent positive forms of place attachment resulting in the choice to stay. A fear of the unknown, risk aversion and family obligations can also keep people in place (Adams 2016). One example of positive and negative place attachment acting in combination comes from Senegal, where many Guet Ndarians – regardless of ability – insist that their identities and values as 'Guet Ndarians' and obligations to their ancestral land, burial sites and traditional livelihoods outweighs the threat of coastal erosion, flooding and sea level rise (Zickgraf et al. 2016).[13]

So while involuntary immobility typically takes centre stage in studies of environmental (im)mobility – that is to say people who are 'stuck', 'left behind' or 'trapped' despite their wishes to leave a perceived undesirable circumstance – we should not underestimate the aspirations to stay in recognising community, household and individual variations. We can assert that combining immobility aspirations with abilities provides greater insight into (im)mobility decision-making processes and outcomes. Having said that, we should take neither aspirations nor abilities as a prerequisite: one can aspire to stay, but then be pushed into migration either because the opportunity presents itself or because of a household decision (Carling 2002). Similarly, ability can affect the aspiration to migrate when migration is not considered within the 'realm of possibility'.

Protection issues

Migration has, rightfully, moved into the environmental agenda, particularly when it comes to its links to climate change. Its relative success in gaining the attention of policy makers and the public has perhaps had the unintended consequence of minimizing the risks facing immobile populations (involuntary or otherwise), by implying that not migrating is unproblematic. Unfortunately, efforts to halt displacement and forced migration through privileging adaptation *in situ* risk the formation of policies that increase involuntary immobility: "[t]he greatest risks will be borne by those who are unable or unwilling to relocate, and may be exacerbated by maladaptive policies designed to prevent migration" (Black et al. 2011: 447). Inhibiting migration can, in fact, limit the ability of individuals, households and communities to adapt *in situ* because migration has the potential to produce financial and social remittances that benefit those who go *and* who stay. Incentivising such remittances, moreover, can facilitate further migration and enable the choice to remain.

Policies addressing abilities to migrate (or rather the lack thereof) must concomitantly address (im)mobility aspirations rather than assuming them *a priori*. The voluntarily immobile can be a more vulnerable population than those who are immobile against their will.[14] (Im)mobility aspirations are not always based on sound risk assessments, while other risks associated to leaving may outweigh those of staying behind. For instance, planned relocation is only effective insofar as people are willing participants, which has serious ethical and normative implications for the implementation of such programmes by governments, humanitarian agencies, international organisations, etc. (Marino 2012; Adams 2016). Those who are unconvinced that they will be 'better off' in the destination than in their present living conditions may be at serious risk of displacement or even death if they refuse to relocate or return after initial resettlement. Thus, following the Nansen Initiative principles, more efforts must be made by local and national governments implement relocation projects "on the basis of non-discrimination, consent, empowerment, participation and partnerships with those directly affected . . . without neglecting those who may choose to remain" (Nansen Initiative 2011: 5).

As will come to no surprise to the student of migration, there is no one-size-fits all solution to environmental (im)mobility. Avoiding or at least minimizing the risks associated with immobility requires simultaneous protection mechanisms safeguarding the 'right' to move *and* to stay at all points in the (im)mobility spectrum. This policy direction requires complex measures that by nature must involve consultation with affected populations to ascertain the limitations on both abilities and aspirations to leave areas adversely affected by environmental changes.

Into the future

Environmental immobility literature remains in its infancy, with much conceptual and empirical work to be done. Nonetheless, it is one of the most exciting and quickly evolving elements of current environmental migration scholarship at present, for one because it expands our notions of the environment-migration nexus. A previously invisible population now has the potential to reshape the ways we think about human migration in a world increasingly affected by environmental changes. Thus, I propose several directions for future research, which are in no way exhaustive. First, trapped populations must be further conceptualised, with a clear eye to promote methodologies of investigation. Precision in the conceptualization of trapped populations and of the more encompassing immobility spectrum must be accompanied, or rather guided, by an increase in empirical research specifically targeted at incorporating immobility into the mobility paradigm. As with out-migration, the relative influence of the drivers of immobility and their outcomes are highly context-dependent. That is not to say that we should abandon any attempts to extrapolate based on case studies, but rather that we collect data that covers a range of contexts in order to typologize immobility, with its many forms and functions. We might thus be able to locate certain 'immobility trends' that arise across case studies, and pursue policy objectives targeted at limiting the trapping aspects.

Second, establishing immobility trends requires a historical perspective that acknowledges migration as a social phenomenon. One useful way forward is to use (im)mobility histories, including migration events and their character, and then seek to establish if and how those baseline (im)mobilities are interrupted by an environmental event (correlation is sought more than direct causation) through mixed-methods investigation at the individual, household and community level. If we assume a sedentary life predated mobility rather than investigate it, we will understand the effects of environment much differently (Black et al. 2011a). Here insight can be gained from other 'crisis' migration research such as conflict: "the need to first understand the role that migration played in Mozambican social life before the war in order to make any sense of the meaning of mobility, as well as the impact of immobility, during the war" (Lubkemann 2008: 455).

A third route into the study of immobility entails the explicit investigation of who becomes immobile with more detailed explanations involving, for example, intersectional approaches. If women are immobile, how do gender norms (e.g. male and female) push people into mobility or immobility by interacting with other characteristics?[15] Attached to this suggested research pathway is the investigation of the outlier case. We know that broadly some groups are less mobile than others – women, the elderly, children, the poor – but research should consider why someone expected to migrate according to demographic variables, or, in other words, for whom migration could be considered a 'normal' response, remains in place. Why would a young, male Senegalese fisherman *not migrate*? What 'traps' them as opposed to their cohort?[16]

These research directions offer just a few pathways towards a more in-depth understanding of the vulnerability and resilience of the immobile, and will undoubtedly improve our knowledge regarding (im)mobility responses to environmental changes, their differentiated outcomes (including the impact of migration on the immobile) and the broader relational dynamics of environmental migration and immobility.

Notes

1 After all, "Mobility, like power, is a relational thing" (Adey 2006: 83).
2 Economic Community of West African States (ECOWAS) and the Schengen Area (European free movement protocol).
3 Cf. Jònsson 2011.
4 I personally reject the notion of environmental migration literature as a 'niche'. Its isolation from so-called 'mainstream' migration scholarship, while useful in some respects, seems to hinder our cross-theoretical development. For the purposes of this chapter, however, I set aside such arguments.
5 Nor is it clear how imminent the need to migrate must be for individuals to be considered trapped. In my work in West Africa, people facing coastal erosion knew that they (or future generations) would have to move *at some point*, but the actual timeline varied greatly.
6 This is relevant in the case of resettlement and relocation programs related to climate change, but the implications of such normative questions reach far beyond climate change or other environmental concerns including, but not limited to, situations of conflict or the ramifications of development projects on human settlements.
7 Including transnational and translocal social networks, recruitment agencies, migrant traffickers, etc.
8 Agriculture here includes fishing, livestock and crop production.
9 Accurate information on the severity of the nuclear accident through these social networks also played a large part. Among the first to evacuate were people who had friends and relatives working for Tokyo Electric Power Company (TEPCO) (Hasegawa 2013).
10 It is difficult to distinguish between those who want to leave and those who do not:

> The notion of a 'trapped' population is not a straightforward one, in scientific terms, not least because it is as difficult to distinguish, either conceptually or in practice, between those who stay where they are because they choose to, and those whose immobility is in some way involuntary.

(Black et al. 2013: S36) However, the persistence of 'trapped populations' seems to indicate it is indeed possible.

11 The definition of (im)mobility environment draws upon Carling's concept of the "emigration environment" (2002: 13) in his study of Cape Verdean involuntary immobility as it relates to international emigration. Notably, Carling excludes demographic and environmental attributes of a given community.

12 However, community aspirations and relative environmental influence are subject to change, e.g. becoming more important in a sudden-onset event or as the danger of sea level rise becomes increasingly apparent.

13 Many residents do aspire to migrate, in which case abilities to move internally are actually more constrained than international moves.

14 Of course, that is not the case for those who are able to stay in a risk zone because they have the resources to adapt *in situ*.

15 It is true in my own fieldwork that women are less likely to migrate to Mauritania than their male counterparts. However, this is not only related to their household responsibilities resulting from traditional gender roles. It is perhaps even more so driven by the fact that their jobs in the fishing sector, processing or selling fish, are land-based and less mobile than those of fishermen. Their equipment, networks, and infrastructure are land-based and much more difficult to transfer elsewhere (although some do indeed migrate with their spouses and engage in small-scale fish vending). These less-obvious explanations tend to slip through the cracks.

16 Thank you to Beth Fussell for her instrumental insights on this matter.

References

Adams, Helen. 2016. "Why Populations Persist: Mobility, Place Attachment and Climate Change." *Population and Environment* 37 (4): 429–48.

Adey, Peter. 2006. "If Mobility Is Everything Then It Is Nothing: Towards a Relational Politics of (Im) mobilities." *Mobilities* 1 (1): 75–94.

Afifi, Tamer, Andrea Milan, Benjamin Etzold, Benjamin Schraven, Christina Rademacher-Schulz, Patrick Sakdapolrak, Alexander Reif, Kees van der Geest, and Koko Warner. 2016. "Human Mobility in Response to Rainfall Variability: Opportunities for Migration as a Successful Adaptation Strategy in Eight Case Studies." *Migration and Development* 5 (2): 254–74.

Asian Development Bank (ADB). n.d. *Climate Change and Migration in Asia and the Pacific*. Manila: Asian Development Bank.

Belot, Michèle, and Sjef Ederveen. 2012. "Cultural Barriers in Migration Between OECD Countries." *Journal of Population Economics* 25 (3): 1077–1105.

Black, Richard, W. Neil Adger, Nigel W. Arnell, Stefan Dercon, Andrew Geddes, and David Thomas. 2011. "The Effect of Environmental Change on Human Migration." *Global Environmental Change* 21 (Supplement 1):S3–11. https://doi.org/10.1016/j.gloenvcha.2011.10.001.

Black, Richard, Nigel W. Arnell, W. Neil Adger, David Thomas, and Andrew Geddes. 2013. 3. "Migration, Immobility and Displacement Outcomes Following Extreme Events." *Environmental Science & Policy* 27, Supplement 1 (0): S32–43. doi:10.1016/j.envsci.2012.09.001.

Black, Richard, and Michael Collyer. 2014. "Populations 'Trapped' at Times of Crisis." *Forced Migration Review* 45: 52–56.

Carling, Jørgen. 2002. "Migration in the Age of Involuntary Immobility: Theoretical Reflections and Cape Verdean Experiences." *Journal of Ethnic and Migration Studies* 28 (1): 5–42.

Castles, Stephen. 2011. "Understanding Global Migration: A Social Transformation Perspective." *Journal of Ethnic & Migration Studies* 36 (10): 1565–1586. https://doi.org/10.1080/1369183x.2010.489381

de Haas, Hein. 2011. "The Internal Dynamics of Migration Processes: A Theoretical Inquiry." *Journal of Ethnic & Migration Studies* 36 (10): 1587–1617.

de Haas, Hein. 2014. "Migration Theory: Quo Vadis?" Oxford: The International Migration Institute WP-100–2014/DEMIG Project Paper 24.

Findley, Sally E. 1994. "Does Drought Increase Migration? A Study of Migration from Rural Mali During the 1983–1985 Drought." *International Migration Review*, 539–53.

Fischer, Peter A, Reiner, Martin, and Straubhaar, Thomas. 1997. "Should I Stay or Should I Go?" In *International Migration, Immobility and Development.*, edited by Hammar, Tomas, Brochmann, Grete, Tamas, Kristof, and Faist, Thomas. Oxford: Berg Press, 49–90.

Foresight. 2011. *Foresight: Migration and Global Environmental Change Final Project Report.* London: The Government Office for Science.

Gemenne, François. 2011. "Why the Numbers Don't Add Up: A Review of Estimates and Predictions of People Displaced by Environmental Changes." *Global Environmental Change* 21, Supplement 1 (0): S41–49.

Glick Schiller, Nina, and Peggy Levitt. 2006. "Haven't We Heard This Somewhere Before? A Substantive View of Transnational Migration Studies by Way of a Reply to Waldinger and Fitzgerald." CMD Working Paper #06–01. The Center for Migration and Development, Princeton University.

Gray, Clark, and Erika Wise. 2016. "Country-Specific Effects of Climate Variability on Human Migration." *Climatic Change* 135 (3): 555–68.

Hammar, Tomas, Grete Brochmann, Kristof Tamas, and Thomas Faist, eds. 1997. *International Migration, Immobility and Development: Multidisciplinary Perspectives.* Oxford and New York: Berg.

Hasegawa, Reiko. 2013. "Disaster Evacuation from Japan's 2011 Tsunami Disaster and the Fukushima Nuclear Accident." *IDDRI, Sciences Po Re Port*, no. 5: 1–54.

Henry, Sabine, Bruno Schoumaker, and Cris Beauchemin. 2004. "The Impact of Rainfall on the First Out-Migration: A Multi-Level Event-History Analysis in Burkina Faso." *Population and Environment* 25 (5): 423–60.

Johnson, Craig A., and Krishna Krishnamurthy. 2010. "Dealing with Displacement: Can 'social Protection' Facilitate Long-Term Adaptation to Climate Change?" *Global Environmental Change* 20 (4): 648–55.

Jónsson, Gunvor. 2011. *Non-migrant, sedentary, immobile, or "left behind"? Reflections on the absence of migration.* Working Paper 39. Oxford: The International Migration Institute (IMI), Oxford Department of International Development.

Lindley, Anna. 2014. "Questioning 'Drought Displacement': Environment, Politics and Migration in Somalia." *Forced Migration Review* 45: 39–43.

Lubkemann, Stephen C. 2008. "Involuntary Immobility: On a Theoretical Invisibility in Forced Migration Studies." *Journal of Refugee Studies* 21 (4): 454–75.

Marino, Elizabeth. 2012. "The Long History of Environmental Migration: Assessing Vulnerability Construction and Obstacles to Successful Relocation in Shishmaref, Alaska." *Adding Insult to Injury: Climate Change, Social Stratification, and the Inequities of Intervention* 22 (2): 374–81.

Masquelier, Adeline. 2006. "Why Katrina's Victims Aren't Refugees: Musings on a 'Dirty' Word." *American Anthropologist* 108 (4): 735–43.

McLeman, Robert, and Smit, Barry. 2006. Migration as an Adaptation to Climate Change. *Climatic Change*, 76 (1), 31–53. https://doi.org/10.1007/s10584-005-9000-7

McNamara, Karen Elizabeth, and Chris Gibson. 2009. "'We Do Not Want to Leave Our Land': Pacific Ambassadors at the United Nations Resist the Category of 'climate Refugees.'" *Themed Issue: Gramscian Political Ecologies Themed Issue: Understanding Networks at the Science-Policy Interface* 40 (3): 475–83.

Müller, Christoph, Katharina Waha, Alberte Bondeau, and Jens Heinke 2014. "Hotspots of Climate Change Impacts in Sub-Saharan Africa and Implications for Adaptation and Development." *Global Change Biology* 20:2505–17. https://doi.org/10.1111/gcb.12586.

Murphy, Daniel W.A. 2014. "Theorizing Climate Change, (Im)mobility and Socio-Ecological Systems Resilience in Low-Elevation Coastal Zones." *Climate and Development* 7 (4): 380–97. doi:10.1080/175 65529.2014.953904.

Nansen Iniative. 2011. *The Nansen Conference: Climate Change and Displacement in the 21st Century.* Oslo: The Nansen Initative.

Nawrotzki, Raphael J., and Maryia Bakhtsiyarava. 2016. "International Climate Migration: Evidence for the Climate Inhibitor Mechanism and the Agricultural Pathway." *Population, Space and Place*, January, n/a–n/a.

Penning-Rowsell, Edmund C., Parvin Sultana, and Paul M. Thompson. 2013. "The 'last Resort'? Population Movement in Response to Climate-Related Hazards in Bangladesh." *Global Environmental Change,*

Extreme Environmental Events and "Environmental Migration": Exploring the Connections 27, Supplement 1 (March): S44–59.

Sim, Bérengère. 2016. "Poor and African American in Flint: The Water Crisis and Its Trapped Population." In *State of Environmental Migration 2016: A Review of 2015*, edited by Gemenne, François, Zickgraf, Caroline, and Ionesco, Dina. Liège: Presse universitaires de Liège.

Stark, Oded, and David E. Bloom. 1985. "The New Economics of Labor Migration." *The American Economic Review* 75 (2): 173–78.

Tacoli, Cecilia. 2009. "Crisis or Adaptation? Migration and Climate Change in a Context of High Mobility." *Environment and Urbanization* 21 (2): 513–25.

———. 2011. *Not Only Climate Change: Mobility, Vulnerability and Socio-Economic Transformations in Environmentally Fragile Areas in Bolivia, Senegal and Tanzania.* Vol. 28. London: IIED Human Settlements Working Paper Series.

Taylor, J. Edward. 1999. "The New Economics of Labour Migration and the Role of Remittance in the Migration Process." *International Migration* 37: 63–88.

van der Geest, Kees. 2009. *Migration and Natural Resources Scarcity in Ghana* (Case Study Report for the Environmental Change and Forced Migration Scenarios Project). Brussels: EACH-FOR Project, European Commission.

Warner, Koko. 2009. "Global Environmental Change and Migration: Governance Challenges." *Global Environmental Change* 20 (3): 402–13.

Zickgraf, Caroline. 2016. "Transnational Ageing and the 'Zero Generation': The Role of Moroccan Migrants' Parents in Transnational Family Life." *Journal of Ethnic & Migration Studies* 43 (2): 321–337.

Zickgraf, Caroline, Sara Vigil Diaz Telenti, Florence De Longueville, Pierre Ozer, and François Gemenne. 2016. "The Impact of Vulnerability and Resilience to Environmental Changes on Mobility Patterns in West Africa." *Global Knowledge Partnership on Migration and Development (KNOMAD) Series.*

6

Geospatial modeling and mapping

Alex de Sherbinin and Ling Bai

Mapping efforts

Mapping of drivers and so-called hotspots of vulnerability can help to identify regions that, in the absence of *in situ* resilience building or adaptation efforts, either have already or may in the future become source areas for out-migration. They can also help to identify potential destination areas where migration may result in environmental pressures or populations may be at risk from climate or other stressors.

We start with a number of studies that have explicitly sought to make the link between various biophysical (especially climatic) drivers and human migration. In the past decade, there have been three studies that used maps to illustrate the impact of climate or other environmental factors on migration and displacement. UNEP (2007) produced a report on climate change, conflict and migration in the Sahel. Maps featured prominently in this report, showing a combination of drivers (changes to climate), regions affected by conflict events, and migration streams. Warner et al. (2009) used maps to illustrate key issues related to climate change and migration and displacement in several regions. Among other case studies, they explored glacier loss in the Himalaya region and its impact on downstream regions, rainfall variability and trends in West Africa, climate extremes and declining rainfall in Meso-America, and sea level rise and small island states, in each case tying the maps to findings from the Environmental Change and Forced Migration Project (EACH-FOR). Finally, Warner et al. (2012) used a similar approach to map rainfall variability and extremes as factors leading to migration. These maps also included migration pathways from affected regions as documented through field research. IOM will soon publish an *Atlas of Environmental Migration*, which combines cartography with text to describe the importance of geography and environmental change as factors affecting migration.

In conducting these kinds of mapping studies, there are a number of commonly used spatial data sets that describe climatic and environmental stresses that may contribute to migration. For climatic extremes such as floods, droughts, cyclones, storm surge and precipitation-triggered landslides, the most commonly used data layers are compiled by the Global Assessment Report on Disaster Risk Reduction (UNISDR 2015). These include the hazard layers provided via the UNEP PREVIEW Global Risk Data Platform.[1] Earlier assessments also used the World Bank Natural Disasters Hotspots data collection.[2] There is no single standard data set used for climate status and trends, but commonly used data sets include data from the Climate Research Unit (CRU 2013; New et al. 2002) and from the US National Oceanic and Atmospheric Administration (NOAA n.d.a, n.d.b). A helpful guide for social scientists to available climate data can be found in Auffhammer et al. (2013).

For current status and change in other environmental factors, researchers are often interested in the relationship between land, natural resources and migration. Data on crop and pasture lands have commonly been used (Ramankutty et al. 2010a, 2010b), and land cover maps may be useful for putting migration in context (e.g., Arino et al. 2007, and see Tchuenté et al. 2011 for a comparison of products). A number of efforts have been made to assess land degradation. While there is as yet no commonly accepted metric that comprehensively measures all aspects of land degradation, Bai et al. (2013) have developed one approach that has wide spatial coverage and which may be useful for broad area studies. Deforestation data produced by Hansen et al. (2013) and available via the Global Forest Watch portal may also be relevant for migration research.

Climate vulnerability mapping efforts represent another strand of this research. While vulnerability maps are not necessarily predictive of where migration may occur, they can point to regions where existing or future climate variability and change or sea level rise impacts may cause populations to move (de Sherbinin 2013; McLeman 2013). However, these maps are generally silent on the specific dynamics that may result in displacement or migration, as well as the timing and volume of those population movements. It is very difficult to anticipate what proportion of a population will migrate in response to an environmental or climate stress in the absence of more detailed household-level understandings of population-environment dynamics (Kniveton et al. 2011, de Sherbinin et al. 2008). Studies may also come to the wrong conclusions owing to the gaps in climate and socioeconomic data, inappropriate analysis of climatic data and mismatches in spatial and temporal scales (de Sherbinin et al. 2014).

Modeling efforts

In an effort to move beyond broad brush and largely conjectural mapping of drivers and vulnerability, there is incipient work to model environmental migration and displacement spatially. This work builds on empirical evidence from a growing number of studies that employ statistical models of migration as it relates to environmental phenomena (e.g., Backhaus et al. 2015; Nawrotzki et al. 2013; Feng et al. 2010; Massey et al. 2010; Afifi and Warner 2008; Henry et al. 2004). These studies provide a strong empirical foundation for understanding what kinds of environmental and climatic factors may, when controlling for known determinants of migration, contribute to migration of various types (internal, international, circular, etc.). Some also delve into household decision-making, which can illuminate perceptions of environmental change and the appropriateness of migration as a response that lead to a decision to migrate (or not).

While this field is expanding, it must be acknowledged that it is in its infancy. There are few spatially explicit models of environmental displacement and migration that take into account the location of source and destination areas and the linkages between environmental factors and migration. This may be due to the complexity of the linkages, the interdisciplinary nature of the subject area (McLeman 2013), gaps in theory and empirical evidence, data constraints and spatial and temporal scale mismatches (de Sherbinin 2016), among other factors. Here we explore two approaches that have a demonstrated ability to incorporate spatial aspects of the environment-migration dynamic: gravity modeling and agent based modeling. A third approach, systems dynamics modeling, is generally carried out outside a spatial framework, and therefore is not included here.

Derived from Newton's law of gravity, gravity models are used to predict the degree of interaction between two places. When used geographically, 'bodies' and 'masses' in Newton's law are replaced by 'locations' and 'importance', respectively, where importance can be measured in terms of population numbers, gross domestic product, or other appropriate variables. The gravity model of migration is therefore based upon the idea that as the importance of one or both of the location increases, there will also be an increase in movement between them. The farther apart the two locations are, however, the less movement there will be between them. This phenomenon is known as distance decay.

Bierwagen et al. (2010) developed a county-level spatial interaction model (i.e., gravity model) for the United States to represent domestic migration within the context of a cohort-component population-growth model. Their analyses are based on land-use change scenarios for the conterminous United States forecast for each decade from 2000–2100. The goal was to create national and consistent land-use change scenarios in a transparent modeling framework that could be integrated with assessments of climate change effects on environmental endpoints. Population movements derived from the gravity model were incidental to this goal. The study found significant differences in patterns of habitat loss and the distribution of potentially impaired watersheds among scenarios, indicating that compact development patterns can reduce habitat loss and the number of impaired watersheds. These scenarios are also associated with lower global greenhouse gas emissions and, consequently, the potential to reduce both the drivers of anthropogenic climate change and the impacts of changing conditions.

Jones and O'Neill (2016) produced scenario-based global population projections to 2100 by downscaling national-level projections of urban and rural population change to a 7.5 arc-minute grid framework using a gravity-type model. The population projections include explicit international and domestic migration modules. For domestic migration, they downscaled projected national-level urban and rural population change using the NCAR gravity-based approach (Jones and O'Neill 2013). Beginning with a gridded distribution of the base-year population (2010) the model consists of five steps: (1) calculate an urban population potential surface (a distribution of values reflecting the relative attractiveness of each grid cell), (2) calculate a rural population potential surface, (3) allocate projected urban population change to grid-cells proportionally according to their respective urban potentials, and (4) allocate projected rural population change to grid-cells proportionally according to rural potential. Population potential surfaces, both urban and rural, are continuous across all cells, and as such each cell may contain urban and rural population. Because the allocation procedure can lead to some redefinition of population from rural to urban (e.g., rural population allocated to cells with an entirely urban population is redefined as urban), a final step is to redefine population as urban or rural as a function of density and contiguity with fully urban/rural cells to match projected national-level totals.

McKee et al. (2015) project US population to 2030 and 2050 using a spatial population projection model that incorporates gravity and multivariate methods. Their model takes into account factors that affect population distribution such as land cover, slope, distances to larger cities and a moving average of current population. A novelty of their model is the inclusion of population projections, variables and weights that are adapted to address local characteristics of each of the 3,109 counties in the United States. Furthermore, the model has the ability to accommodate scenario-driven events, for example, accounting for 'what if' scenarios such as significant economic decline or climate impacts.

Gravity model approaches, predicated as they are on understandings of aggregate demographic behavior, are largely silent on the question of motivations for migration, relying rather on assumptions of relative attractiveness of locations. As demonstrated by McKee et al. (2015), it is possible to introduce environmental factors into the models in such a way that they affect, positively or negatively, the relative attractiveness of locations, and by extension, the implicit migration that contributes to population distribution. These models can also help to illuminate the relative importance of push (i.e., environmental or economic factors at origin influencing a decision to migrate) versus pull (i.e., factors at destination such as higher wages) factors influencing the desire to migrate, since modeling the attractiveness of locations in terms of economic or demographic agglomeration factors fits with existing theory.

By contrast, agent-based models (ABMs) explicitly seek to model the behavior of autonomous decision makers when confronted with environmental, economic or other changes. The Theory of Planned Behavior provides a basis that can be used to effectively break down the reasoning process relating to the development of a behavioral intention. Kniveton et al. (2011) developed an ABM of migration for Burkina Faso to investigate the role of the environment in the decision to migrate using scenarios of future demographic, economic, social, political and climate change in a dryland context. The paper replicates 1970–2000 climate migration in Burkina Faso and projects migration flows to 2060. ABMs consider the migration decision in terms of the rules of behavior that govern the response of individuals to complex combinations of multi-level stimuli. Their ABM was developed using theoretical developments in the fields of human migration and climate change adaptation, and was based on empirical evidence from detailed migration studies that have been carried out in Burkina Faso as well as prior research (Henry et al. 2004). These theoretical foundations were combined with advances in the field of social psychology to develop a conceptual basis for agent cognition in the model. Agents in the modeled environment of Burkina Faso interact with one another and their environment to develop intentions to adapt to changes in rainfall through migration. The likelihood of an agent migrating is affected by both their individual attributes and their placement in a social network within which changes in rainfall are discussed. The study, which incorporated climate scenarios along with different demographic, economic and governance scerios, finds that gradual drying produces the largest total and international migration fluxes when combined with changes to social systems and governance.

Walsh et al. (2013) use an ABM model to study the population-environment interactions in Nang Rong District, which is an agricultural area at northeastern Thailand. Their ABM has landscape and social modules. The social modules simulate changes in human population and social networks, including migration and household assets, whereas the land use modules simulate changes in land use and suitability, as well as crop yields. The social modules simulate transformation at three levels (individuals, households and village) via an aggregated multi-level social network. The model is supported by time series satellite land cover data and panel data (1984, 1994, 2000) that cover about 10,000 households. Based on the satellite imagery of land usage, their landscape module captures how the geographical settings (such as the local climate and landscape factors) affect agricultural production that further determine household income. In the ABM, individual agents have unique IDs, age, gender, migration status, marriage status and education. Since the researchers focused on the interactions between population and environment, they also evaluate how human activities affect the ecological system. Given high climate variability and extremes, with attendant impacts on crop yields, farmers in Nang Rong adopt a portfolio diversification strategy that includes cultivation of lands with different characteristics, as well as reliance on migration and remittances.

A significant strength of ABMs when compared to gravity models is the explicit modeling of micro-level demographic behavior based on theory and empirical evidence. This is a strength for local analyses that have sufficient data, as shown by the Burkina Faso and Nang Rong studies, but is a limitation for all those regions where the empirical evidence concerning migration and migration intention are scarce. Another limitation of ABMs is the limited spatial definition (or resolution) of the migration pathways. Models typically produce volumes of flows out of one location, and may identify flows into to alternative locations (usually administrative units; e.g., Kniveton et al. [2011] have four potential internal zones and "international" as possible destinations), but beyond this they do not situate the migrants in space. This makes it difficult to map changes in population that may result from the migration decision-making of individual actors.

Conclusion

As can be seen from the mapping and modeling efforts, while there has been important progress, there remains considerable room for further methodological refinement. It is important to understand modeling as a heuristic device; researchers learn about complex systems and their dynamics by seeking to model them. So the benefit is generally not so much in the projected number of migrants according to different scenarios as in understanding how the system behaves.

There is no one best modeling approach, but we may expect that modeling will improve as underlying data, methods, theory and empirical evidence improve. As McLeman (2013) addresses in some depth, gaps in data are particularly noteworthy and represent a barrier to progress; in all likelihood, we will continue to see relatively rich but localized data for small areas, with a much bigger gaps at regional to international scales. Such data are vital for model parameterization and validation. Moving forward, researchers should continue to seek improved understanding of the causal mechanisms linking migration flows to environmental status and change, and to understand geographical trajectories. For climate-migration modeling, it will be important to incorporate reliable assumptions about the potential for adaptation that may permit greater proportions of the existing population to remain in place (McLeman 2013).

An effort to model past net migration on a global scale using indirect estimation methods (de Sherbinin et al. 2012) found that out-migration was highest out of marginal environments such as dryland and mountain regions, and in-migration was highest in coastal zones that benefit from trade-related economic activities. This suggests a combination of push and pull factors influence environmental migration, and that environmental conditions in source areas do indeed play a role. By the same token, it speaks to the need to understand likely future flows into coastal areas, given their greater exposure to climate hazards such as cyclones, high winds and storm surge. In other words, the vulnerability in destination areas may be just as important a consideration as vulnerability in source areas.

Notes

1 See UNEP Global Risk Data Platform, available at http://preview.grid.unep.ch/
2 See NASA Socioeconomic Data and Applications Center (SEDAC) Natural Disaster Hotspots Data Collection, available at http://sedac.ciesin.columbia.edu/data/collection/ndh

References

Afifi, T. and Warner, K. 2008. The impact of environmental degradation on migration flows across countries. UNU-EHS Working Paper. UNU-EHS.

Arino, O., D. Gross, F. Ranera, M. Leroy, et al. 2007. *GlobCover: ESA service for global land cover from MERIS*. Paper presented at the 2007 IEEE International Geoscience and Remote Sensing Symposium, Barcelona Spain. DOI:10.1109/IGARSS.2007.4423328

Auffhammer, M., S.M. Hsiang, W. Schlenker and A. Sobel. 2013. Using weather data and climate model output in economic analyses of climate change. *Rev Environ Econ Policy*, Summer, 7(2): 181–198. doi:10.1093/reep/ret016

Backhaus, A., I. Martinez-Zarzoso, and C. Muris. 2015. Do climate variations explain bilateral migration? A gravity model analysis. *IZA Journal of Migration*, 4(3).

Bai, Z., D. Dent, Y. Wu, and R. de Jong. 2013. Land degradation and ecosystem services, in *Ecosystem Services and Carbon Sequestration in the Biosphere*, R. Lal, et al., eds. Netherlands: Springer. pp. 357–381.

Bierwagen, B.G., D.M. Theobald, C.R. Pyke, et al., 2010. National housing and impervious surface scenarios for integrated climate impact assessments. *Proceedings of the National Academy of Sciences of the United States of America*, 107(49), 20887–20892.

Climatic Research Unit (CRU), University of East Anglia. 2013. *CRU Time Series (TS) high resolution gridded datasets 3.2*. NCAS British Atmospheric Data Centre. http://badc.nerc.ac.uk/view/badc.nerc.ac.uk__ATOM__dataent_1256223773328276.

de Sherbinin, A. 2016. Remote sensing and socioeconomic data integration: Lessons from the NASA socioeconomic data and applications center. In: *Integrating Scale in Remote Sensing and GIS*, D.A. Quattrochi, E.A. Wentz, N. Lam, and C. Emerson (eds). Boca Raton FL: CRC Press.

de Sherbinin, A., M.F.A.M. van Maarseveen, and R.V. Sliuzas. 2014. *Mapping the Unmeasurable? Spatial Analysis of Vulnerability to Climate Change and Climate Variability*. PhD Thesis. Enschede, Netherlands: ITC-University of Twente.

de Sherbinin, A. 2013. Climate Change Hotspots Mapping: What Have We Learned? *Climatic Change*, 123(1): 23–37. http://dx.doi.org/10.1007/s10584-013-0900-7.

de Sherbinin, A., M. Levy, S.B. Adamo, K. MacManus, G. Yetman, V. Mara, L. Razafindrazay, B. Goodrich, T. Srebotnjak, C. Aichele, and L. Pistolesi. 2012. Migration and risk: Net migration in marginal ecosystems and hazardous areas. *Environmental Research Letters*, 7, 045602. http://dx.doi.org/10.1088/1748-9326/7/4/045602.

de Sherbinin, A., L. VanWey, K. McSweeney, R. Aggarwal, A. Barbieri, S. Henry, L. Hunter, W. Twine, and R. Walker. 2008. "Household Demographics, Livelihoods and the Environment." *Global Environmental Change*, 18(1): 38–53. http://dx.doi.org/10.1016/j.gloenvcha.2007.05.005

Feng, S., A.B. Krueger, and M. Oppenheimer. 2010. Linkages among climate change, crop yields and Mexico–US cross-border migration. *Proceedings of the National Academy of Sciences*, 107(32):14257–14262. www.pnas.org/cgi/doi/10.1073/pnas.1002632107

Hansen, M.C., P.V. Potapov, R. Moore, M. Hancher, et al. 2013. High-resolution global maps of 21st-century forest cover change. *Science*, 342: 850. doi: 10.1126/science.1244693

Henry, S., Schoumaker, B., and Beauchemin, C. (2004). The impact of rainfall on the first out-migration: a multi-level event-history analysis in Burkina Faso. *Population and Environment* 25 (5), 423–460.

Jones, B., and B.C. O'Neill. 2016. Spatially explicit global population scenarios consistent with the shared socioeconomic pathways. *Environmental Research Letters*, 11(8).

Jones, B., and B.C. O'Neill. 2013. Historically grounded spatial population projections for the continental United States. *Environmental Research Letters*, 8, 044021. doi: 10.1088/1748-9326/8/4/044021

Kniveton, D., C. Smith, and S. Wood. (2011). Agent-based model simulations of future changes in migration flows for Burkina Faso. *Global Environmental Change* 21S, S34–S40.

Massey, D.S., W.G. Axinn and D.J. Ghimire. 2010. Environmental change and out-migration: evidence from Nepal. *Population and Environment* 32(2/3): 109–136.

McKee, J.J., et al., 2015. Locally adaptive, spatially explicit projection of US population for 2030 and 2050. *Proceedings of the National Academy of Sciences of the United States of America*, 112(5): 1344–1349.

McLeman, R. 2013. Developments in modelling of climate change-related migration. *Climatic Change*, 117:599–611.

Nawrotzki, R., F. Riosmena, and L.M. Hunter. 2013. Do rainfall deficits predict U.S.-bound migration from rural Mexico? Evidence from the Mexican census. *Population Research Policy Review* 32:129–158.

New, M., D. Lister, M. Hulme, and I. Makin. 2002. A high-resolution data set of surface climate over global land areas. *Climate Research*, 21:1–25.

NOAA n.d.a. National Centers for Environmental Prediction (NCEP) Climate Prediction Center (CPC): CPC Unified Precipitation gauge based global data set.

NOAA n.d.b. National Centers for Environmental Prediction (NCEP) Climate Prediction Center (CPC): CPC Merged Analysis of Precipitation (CMAP).

Ramankutty, N., A.T. Evan, C. Monfreda, and J.A. Foley. 2010a. *Global Agricultural Lands: Croplands, 2000*. Palisades, NY: NASA Socioeconomic Data and Applications Center (SEDAC). http://dx.doi.org/10.7927/H4C8276G.

Ramankutty, N., A.T. Evan, C. Monfreda, and J.A. Foley. 2010b. *Global Agricultural Lands: Pastures, 2000*. Palisades, NY: NASA Socioeconomic Data and Applications Center (SEDAC). http://dx.doi.org/10.7927/H47H1GGR.

Tchuenté, A.T.K., J.-L. Roujean, S.M. De Jong. 2011. Comparison and relative quality assessment of the GLC2000, GLOBCOVER, MODIS and ECOCLIMAP land cover data sets at the African continental scale. *International Journal of Applied Earth Observation and Geoinformation*, 13(2): 207–219.

UNEP. 2007. *Climate Change, Conflict and Migration in the Sahel*. Nairobi, Kenya: United Nations Environment Programme (UNEP).

UNISDR. 2015. *Making Development Sustainable: The Future of Disaster Risk Management. Global Assessment Report on Disaster Risk Reduction*. Geneva, Switzerland: United Nations Office for Disaster Risk Reduction (UNISDR).

Walsh, S.J., G.P. Malanson, B. Entwisle, R.R. Rindfuss, P.J. Mucha, B.W. Heumann, et al. 2013. Design of an agent-based model to examine population–environment interactions in Nang Rong District Thailand. *Applied Geography*, 39: 183–198.

Warner, K., T. Afifi, K. Henry, T. Rawe, C. Smith, and A. de Sherbinin. 2012. *Where the Rain Falls: Climate Change, Food and Livelihood Security, and Migration*. Bonn, Germany: United Nations University and CARE.

Warner, K., C. Erhart, A. de Sherbinin, S.B. Adamo, T. Chai-Onn. 2009. *In Search of Shelter: Mapping the Effects of Climate Change on Human Migration and Displacement*. Bonn, Germany: United Nations University, CARE, and CIESIN-Columbia University.

7

Modeling migration and population displacement in response to environmental and climate change

Multilevel event history models

Jack DeWaard and Raphael J. Nawrotzki

Introduction

Claims that environmental and climate change (ECC) may lead to mass migration and population displacement (MPD) have helped to motivate research on the ECC-MPD relationship (Myers 2002; Stern 2007). In this chapter, we summarize an important part of these efforts by providing a brief, but targeted review of the motivations for and uses of multilevel event history models. Our work builds on earlier reviews that highlighted the importance of multilevel approaches (Hunter et al. 2015; Kniveton et al. 2008; McLeman 2013; Piguet 2010), including some of the tools (e.g., event history models) that demographers use to study migration (Fussell et al. 2014). One tool that received only limited attention in these reviews is that of multilevel event history models. As we later discuss, these models are characterized by several hallmarks that are particularly important in research on the ECC-MPD relationship.

This chapter is organized as follows. First, in an effort to accommodate readers from different training and disciplinary backgrounds, we (re)introduce event history models. We then describe two problems that complicate efforts to use event history models to study the ECC-MPD relationship. Following a discussion of three overlapping approaches that are commonly used to mitigate these problems, we detail their use in current empirical research. Specifically, we inventory and assess 20 studies published since the early 2000s in which the author(s) used multilevel event history models to study the ECC-MPD relationship. Particular attention is paid to the levels of analysis considered, the measure(s) of ECC used, and model specification(s). Given the targeted nature of this chapter, interested readers are encouraged to pursue more extended and advanced treatments of event history models (Allison 1982, 1984; Cox 1972; Singer and Willet 2003; Yamaguchi 1991), multilevel models (Gelman 2006; Kreft and De Leeuw 1998; Luke 2004; Rabe-Hesketh and Skrondol 2012; Raudenbush and Bryk 2002; Snijders and Bosker 2011), and multilevel event history models (Barber et al. 2000; Duchateau and Janssen 2010).

Event history models

Hallmarks

Event history models of MPD are characterized by at least four hallmarks (Allison 1982, 1984; Singer and Willet 2003; Yamaguchi 1991). First, MPD is treated as an event, whether one-time or repeat. MPD events include physical acts of crossing borders and/or defined boundaries; they also include associated status changes (from non-migrant to migrant, etc.) that can be classified as events. Second, event history models incorporate duration dependence, or the time to MPD events. This is an important feature given that the risk of out-migration tends to decline with the amount of time that is lived in a given locale (McGinnis 1968; Morrison 1967). Third, event history models are well-equipped to deal with censoring, which is the idea that MPD events can occur outside of (i.e., before and/or after) the observation window in a given study. Finally, in modeling the risk of MPD events in relation to a set of predictor variables, including those tapping ECC, event history models permit the inclusion of both time-constant and time-varying predictors.

Discrete-time models

Although MPD is clearly a continuous process such that MPD events can occur at any time (Willekens 2008), it is often the case that the time intervals in MPD data are very coarse. For example, consistent with the recommendations of the United Nations (1998), some data sources use a one-year timing criteria to distinguish MPD events from more temporary moves. In these sorts of cases, discrete- (versus continuous-) time event history models are often used (Allison 1982).

One common discrete-time event history model is the complementary log-log model, written as follows:

$$\log\left[-\log\left(1-P_{it}\right)\right]=\alpha+\beta_1\left(Time\right)+\beta_m\left(X_{mit}\right) \tag{1}$$

where:

$$P_{it}=\Pr[T_i=t\,|\,T_i\geq t] \tag{2}$$

Here, the hazard, or instantaneous rate, of MPD for actor i (an actor might be an individual, family, household, etc.) at time t is approximated by the conditional probability that i migrates/ is displaced at t given that i had not migrated/was displaced prior to t, α is the intercept term, $Time$ is the baseline hazard and β_1 is the associated parameter estimate,[1] and X_{mit} is a vector of time-constant and time-varying predictor variables for actor i, with β_m being the associated vector of parameter estimates. A key benefit of the complementary log-log model is that the parameter estimates for the predictor variables are identical to those from some continuous-time models, meaning that the complementary log-log model assumes that the data are generated by a continuous-time process (Allison 1982, 1984).

The above said, perhaps due to both familiarity and interpretability, another commonly used discrete-time event history model is the logit model, written as follows:

$$\text{logit}\left(P_{it}\right)=\log\left[\frac{P_{it}}{\left(1-P_{it}\right)}\right]=\alpha+\beta_1\left(Time\right)+\beta_m\left(X_{mit}\right) \tag{3}$$

This model is identical to the complementary log-log model on the right-hand side of the equation; however, given the logit specification on the left-hand side of the equation, the parameter estimates for the predictor variables take the very intuitive and interpretable form of changes in the log odds of migration, which are usually converted to and reported as odd ratios and/or predicted probabilities.

Extensions

The models previously described can be extended in many ways (Allison 1982, 1984; Barber et al. 2000; Cox 1972; Singer and Willet 2003; Yamaguchi 1991). To provide just a few examples, specifications other than those shown above can be used, including different specifications of the baseline hazard (Gompertz, Weibull, etc.). Going beyond MPD as a dichotomous event, another common extension is to use a multinomial logit model to model different types of MPD events, e.g., international versus internal migration, each relative to not migrating (Lindstrom and Lauster 2001). Finally, given the often cyclical nature of MPD (McHugh et al. 1995), the models can be extended to accommodate repeat, versus one-time, MPD events.

Problems

In empirical research on the ECC-MPD relationship, the object of interest is often with the effect(s) of one or more ECC predictors on the risk of MPD. As detailed in the previous section, MPD is usually measured at the level of actors. In contrast, ECC is usually, but not always (Gray 2011; Massey et al. 2010), measured at the level of places (communities, regions, etc.), which we might add to the model in (3) as follows:

$$\text{logit}\left(P_{ijt}\right) = \alpha + \beta_1\left(Time\right) + \beta_m\left(X_{mijt}\right) + \beta_n\left(Y_{njt}\right) \tag{4}$$

Here, Y_{njt} is a vector of time-constant and time-varying predictor variables, including measures of ECC, for place j, with β_n being the associated vector of parameter estimates. Note that we have added the subscript, j, to the probability of MPD and to the predictor variables for actor i to denote the clustering of actors within places.

Although the model in (4) is estimable, there are two significant problems that ultimately motivate the use of multilevel event history models in empirical research on the ECC-MPD relationship. First, because actors are clustered within places, the standard errors that accompany the parameter estimates tend to be artificially low, which, in turn, increases the risk of committing Type I errors (i.e., rejecting the true null hypothesis) (Angeles et al. 2005; see also Huber 1967; White 1980). Second, the model in (4) does not take into account that the probability of MPD has the potential to vary, perhaps even substantially, across places (for statistical treatments of this issue, see Barber et al. 2000 and Duchateau and Janssen 2010; for substantive discussions of this issue, see Hunter et al. 2015 and Opatowski and Borova 2016).

Multilevel event history models

Approaches

In current empirical research on the ECC-MPD relationship, one or more of three approaches are commonly used to mitigate the two problems described previously. First, cluster-adjusted (hereafter, clustered) standard errors to accompany the parameter estimates of interest are estimated and reported (Beauchemin and Schoumaker 2005; Ezra and Kiros 2001; Fussell et al. 2010; Gray 2009, 2010; Henry et al. 2004). While clustered standard errors do not address the problem of variation across places, they do reduce the risk of committing Type I errors (Angeles et al. 2005; see also Cameron and Miller 2015; Huber 1967; White 1980).

Second, in addition to using clustered standard errors, place fixed effects (hereafter, fixed effects) are sometimes included in the model to account for variation across places. This is achieved most parsimoniously by replacing the intercept, α, with a place-specific intercept, α_j:

$$\text{logit}\left(P_{ijt}\right) = \alpha_j + \beta_1\left(Time\right) + \beta_m\left(X_{mijt}\right) + \beta_n\left(Y_{njt}\right) \tag{5}$$

Despite the fairly common use of fixed effects in empirical research on the ECC-MPD relationship (Donato et al. 2016; Gray and Bilsborrow 2013; Gray and Mueller 2012a, 2012b; Hunter et al. 2013; Jennings and Gray 2015; Mueller et al. 2014), concerns have been raised about several "serious drawbacks such as less efficient estimation of the parameters and a less natural model interpretation" (Duchateau and Janssen 2010:78; see also Allison and Christakis 2006). The reduction in efficiency stems from the inclusion of a sometimes large number of dummy variables – one for each place – in the model when many places are represented in the data, thereby using up considerable degrees of freedom. With respect to model interpretation, the inclusion of fixed effects means that one cannot generalize their findings beyond the particular set of places considered in a given study. The fixed effects approach therefore has advantages for internal (versus external) validity.

If the aim is to generalize beyond the set of places considered in a given study, then random (versus fixed) effects are required (Rabe-Hesketh and Skrondol 2012). This entails specifying the model in (5) somewhat differently:

$$\text{logit}\left(P_{ijt}\right) = \gamma + \beta_1\left(Time\right) + \beta_m\left(X_{mijt}\right) + \beta_n\left(Y_{njt}\right) + \zeta_j \tag{6}$$

Here, the original intercept, α, is permitted to vary randomly, ζ_j, around an average probability of MPD, γ, while controlling for the characteristics of place j, Y_{njt}. This part of the model is sometimes called the level-2, or "contextual," model (Kreft and De Leeuw 1998: 8), and can be written as follows:

$$\alpha = \gamma + \beta_n\left(Y_{njt}\right) + \zeta_j \tag{7}$$

The random effects term, ζ_j, is a level-2 error term that quantifies unobserved variation in the average probability of MPD across places, and effectively accounts for the clustering of actors within places (Luke 2004). In contrast to models that only use clustered standard errors and/or fixed effects, the model in (6) is properly considered a multilevel event history model (Barber et al. 2000; see also Duchateau and Janssen 2010; Rabe-Hesketh and Skrondol 2012). That said, we do not use such a narrow definition in this chapter and consider each of the three approaches, discussed previously, that adjust for the clustering of actors within places as "multilevel" event history models.

Extensions

The previous models can be extended in many ways (Barber et al. 2000; Duchateau and Janssen 2010; Rabe-Hesketh and Skrondol 2012). To provide just a few examples, first, multinomial versions of multilevel event history models can be estimated. Second, in addition to random intercepts, one can extend the model in (6) to include random slopes; this involves developing equations similar to the one in (7) for any of the actor-level parameter estimates, β_m, of interest. Third, one can estimate and assess cross-level interactions between actor- and place-level predictor variables in order to see if the effect of one is conditioned by the other. Fourth, one can add additional levels of analysis to the model (individuals clustered within households, clustered within communities, etc.).

In current research on the ECC-MPD relationship

In Table 7.1, we present a fairly exhaustive list of 20 papers published since the early 2000s in which the author(s) used multilevel event history models to study the ECC-MPD relationship. Given limited space in this chapter, it is not possible to provide a detailed review of each and every one of these studies. It is also not necessary to do so, as some of these studies (e.g., Fussell et al. 2010; Gray and Mueller 2012b; Henry et al. 2004) have been reviewed elsewhere (see Fussell et al. 2014; Hunter et al. 2015; Piguet 2010). Given the focus of this chapter, we therefore organize our review of these studies thematically, focusing on the levels of analysis considered, the measure(s) of ECC used, and model specification(s). Additionally, where needed and to the extent possible, we have tried to provide examples from more recent studies (e.g., Donato et al. 2016; Jennings and Gray 2015; Meijer-Irons 2016; Mueller et al. 2014; Nawrotzki et al. 2015a, 2015b, 2015c; Nawrotzki and DeWaard 2016) that have not been previously reviewed elsewhere.[2]

We begin by discussing the levels of analysis considered in the studies listed in Table 7.1. This is an important starting point because doing so helps to locate, or source, the clustering of actors within places, described earlier. The levels of analysis considered in these studies reflect both the substantive interests of the author(s) and data availability and/or constraints. With respect to the former issue, most of the studies listed in Table 7.1 include the household as a level of analysis. Substantively, this makes sense when one considers that in many – especially rural and agriculturally-dependent – contexts, migration decisions are not (merely) those of solitary rational actors (Sjaastad 1962; Todaro 1976), but, rather, are part of coordinated strategies by households to mitigate uncertainty and risk (Ellis 2000; Scoones 1998; Stark and Bloom 1985), a point that was strongly emphasized during a panel convened by the International Organization for Migration (IOM) during the 2015 climate talks in Paris (DeWaard and Nawrotzki 2016).[3] Similar arguments can be and have been made for villages, communities, etc., (Massey et al. 1994; McLeman 2011).

With respect to data availability and/or constraints, Piguet (2010: 520; see also Entwisle 2007) noted that multilevel approaches run the risk of imposing a "predefined hierarchy of spatial units (usually the administrative units at which level the data [are] collected) that might not reflect the spatial distribution of the phenomenon." This criticism is perhaps warranted in the case of some of the studies listed in Table 7.1. For example, relative to communities in the Southern Ecuadorian Andes, is not clear why "census sectors" are also a meaningful spatial unit, despite the fact that they are represented in Gray's (2009: 459) data. Although similar arguments might be made for other spatial units like regions in Burkina Faso (Henry et al. 2004) or provinces in the Netherlands (Jennings and Gray 2015), ultimately, the substantive importance of these units depends on whether and to what extent they help to organize economic, political, and social life in ways that might be relevant for the ECC-MPD relationship. For example, in a recent paper by Donato et al. (2016) on internal migration within and international migration from Bangladesh following abnormally dry/wet and hot/cool years between 1973 and 2012, they included fixed

Table 7.1 Recent studies of the ECC-MPD relationship using multilevel event history models

Study	Study Area(s)	Period	Levels of Analysis	Measure(s) of Environment & Climate Change	Measure(s) of Migration & Population Displacement	Clustering & Place/Unit Effects
Beauchemin & Schoumaker (2005)	Burkina Faso: Rural	1980–1997	Individual; community	Avg. annual rainfall; local development (15 variables)	Individual out-migration (migrate vs. no)	Clustered SEs only
Donato et al. (2016)	Bangladesh	1973–2012	Individual (HH heads); mouza/region	Precipitation (drought year/ wet year vs. no); temperature (hot/ cool year vs. no)	Individual out-migration (internal/international vs. no)	Clustered SEs & Fixed Effects
Ezra & Kiros (2001)	Ethiopia: Shoa, Wello, & Tigray regions	1984–1994	Individual; household; community	Community vulnerability to food crisis	Individual out-migration (migrate vs. no)	Clustered SEs only
Fussell et al. (2010)	United States: New Orleans	2005–2006	Individual; household	Housing damage due to Hurricane Katrina	Individual return migration to New Orleans among those displaced by Hurricane Katrina (migrate vs. no)	Clustered SEs only
Gray (2009)	Ecuador: Southern Ecuadorian Andes	1996–2006	Individual; household; community; census sector	Flat land; land slope; precipitation; unusual harvest fluctuation	Individual out-migration (local/internal/ international vs. no)	Clustered SEs only
Gray (2010)	Ecuador: Southern Ecuadorian Andes	1996–2006	Individual; household; community	Soil erosion/ depletion; land slope; precipitation	Individual out-migration (internal/international vs. no)	Clustered SEs only
Gray (2011)	Kenya & Uganda: Rural	1 year in early 2000s (varies by country)	Individual; household; region	Soil quality index (seven variables); high soil carbon	Individual out-migration (temporary labor/ non-labor vs. no; permanent labor/ non-labor vs. no)	Clustered SEs & Random Effects

(Continued)

Table 7.1 (Continued)

Study	Study Area(s)	Period	Levels of Analysis	Measure(s) of Environmental & Climate Change	Measure(s) of Migration & Population Displacement	Clustering & Place/Unit Effects
Gray & Bilsborrow (2013)	Ecuador: Rural	2000–2008	Individual; household; community; parish	Irrigation; land quality, land slope; avg. annual rainfall; avg. rainfall seasonality; yearly rainfall deviation	Individual out-migration (local/internal/international vs. no)	Clustered SEs & Fixed Effects
Gray & Mueller (2012a)	Ethiopia: Rural	1999–2009	Individual; household; community	Reported drought; rainfall deficit; predicted drought	Individual out-migration (migrate vs. no; in/out of district vs. no; labor/marriage vs. no)	Clustered SEs & Fixed Effects
Gray & Mueller (2012b)	Bangladesh: Rural	1994–2010	Individual; household; community/village; subdistrict	Flood exposure; crop loss; livestock death; health shock	Individual out-migration (migrate vs. no; in/out of district vs. no)	Clustered SEs & Fixed Effects
Henry et al. (2004)	Burkina Faso: Rural	1970–1998	Individual; community/village; region/department	Avg. annual precipitation; three-year rainfall variability	Individual out-migration (migrate vs. no; rural/urban/abroad vs. no; long-term/short-term vs. no)	Clustered SEs only
Hunter et al. (2013)	Mexico: Western & Central regions	1987–2005	Household; community; state	Drought; severe drought; wet; severe wet	Household international out-migration (sent migrant vs. no)	Clustered SEs & Fixed Effects
Jennings & Gray (2015)	The Netherlands	1865–1937	Individual; household; station; municipality; province	Temperature; hot days; cold days; rainfall; coastal flooding; riverine flooding	Individual out-migration (short/long international vs. no)	Clustered SEs & Fixed Effects

Study	Location	Years	Level of analysis	Environmental measures	Migration outcome	Method
Massey et al. (2010)	Nepal: Western Chitwan	1997–1999	Individual; neighborhood	Productivity; % neighborhood covered in flora; minutes to gather firewood & fodder; pop. density	Individual out-migration (local/distant vs. no)	Clustered SEs & Random Effects
Meijer-Irons (2016)	Thailand: Rural	1997–2006	Household; village; amphoe/district	Vegetation index (NDVI); subjective perceptions of environment (2 measures)	Household out-migration (migrate vs. no)	Clustered SEs & Random Effects
Mueller et al. (2014)	Pakistan: Rural	1991–2012	Individual; household; village; province	Cum. rainfall over monsoon season, avg. temperature; flood intensity; moisture index	Individual out-migration (migrate vs. no; in/out of village vs. no)	Clustered SEs & Fixed Effects
Nawrotzki & DeWaard (2016)	Mexico: Western & Central regions	1986–1999	Household; community/ municipality	Warm spell duration index; no. days heavy precip.	Household international out-migration (sent migrant vs. no)	Clustered SEs & Random Effects
Nawrotzki et al. (2015a)	Mexico: Western & Central regions	1986–1999	Household; community/ municipality	Warm spell duration index; wet spell duration index	Household international out-migration (sent migrant vs. no)	Clustered SEs & Random Effects
Nawrotzki et al. (2015b)	Mexico: Western & Central regions	1986–1999	Household; community/ municipality	Temperature & precipitation (15 variables)	First and last international out-migration by household (sent migrant vs. no)	Clustered SEs & Random Effects
Nawrotzki et al. (2015c)	Mexico: Western & Central regions	1986–1999	Household; community/ municipality	Warm spell duration index; precip. on extremely wet days	Household international out-migration (documented/ undocumented vs. no)	Clustered SEs & Random Effects

effects for administrative districts called *mouzas*, or "revenue village[s]," which, historically, were established for purposes that included taxation (van Schendel 2005: 80).

Concerning the measurement of ECC, Hunter et al. (2015: 384) rightly pointed out that "environmental measures themselves [have] varied widely." This variability is clearly evident in the studies listed in Table 7.1, and can be traced to at least two sources. First, there is very little agreement on which measure(s) of ECC to use (Hunter et al. 2015; Meijer-Irons 2016). While most of the studies listed in Table 7.1 include measures of changes in both temperature and precipitation, two key dimensions of ECC (Bindoff et al. 2013), some studies do not include measures of one (e.g., Gray 2011) or both (e.g., Massey et al. 2010). Other studies have sought to go beyond measures of changes in temperature and precipitation to examine exactly what it is about these changes that matter for MPD. For example, Mueller et al. (2014) showed that MPD in rural Pakistan between 1991 and 2012 was driven by a negative income shock that, in turn, was produced by heat stress and extreme precipitation. Gray (2009) likewise documented a positive association between unusual harvest fluctuations and MPD in rural Ecuador, which might be explained, in part, by how ECC affects soil quality (Gray 2010; see also Gray 2011). Finally, in addition to the work of Mueller et al. (2014), other studies have focused on the role of flooding for MPD (Gray and Mueller 2012b; Jennings and Gray 2015), as well as related damages to housing and other structures (Fussell et al. 2010). Ultimately, discrepancies in the measurement of ECC informed the choices of Nawrotzki et al. (2015a, 2015b, 2015c) and Nawrotzki and DeWaard (2016) to choose from 27 standardized measures of ECC developed and made available by the Expert Team on Climate Change Detection and Indices (ETCCDI)[4] as part of the Third Assessment Report for the Intergovernmental Panel on Climate Change (IPCC) (Peterson 2005; Peterson et al. 2001; Peterson and Manton 2008).

In addition, a second issue has to do with the measurement of *change* in ECC. While a number of the studies listed in Table 7.1 use very short time windows of only one to several years for baselines (e.g., see Donato et al. 2016; Gray and Mueller 2012a; Jennings and Gray 2015), Hunter et al. (2013: 887) noted that "a large body of climate science . . . use[s] a 30-year mean as 'climate normal' for variability." A longer-term baseline is reflected in the work of Hunter et al. (2013), Nawrotzki et al. (2015a, 2015b, 2015c), and Nawrotzki and DeWaard (2016) in their assessments of the relationship between ECC in rural Mexico and Mexico-U.S. migration. Importantly, a longer baseline also makes it possible to measure and assess the effects of environmental and climatic changes that begin and materialize slowly (versus rapidly) over time (Leighton 2009). Of course, as we discussed earlier, issues of data availability and/or constraints increasingly play a role here. Several of the studies listed in Table 7.1 provide discussions of these sorts of data issues and potential solutions, e.g., interpolation (see Nawrotzki and DeWaard 2016).

Finally, with respect to model specification(s), in most of the studies listed in Table 7.1, multinominal logit models were estimated, in many cases after standard logit models were estimated (e.g., see Mueller et al. 2014). The former models are important because actors often have multiple MPD options available to them, each with a different set of costs (economic, psychic, etc.) attached. For example, many studies draw a distinction between short- and long-distance MPD. Short-distance MPD might include local or internal migration (e.g., see Gray and Bilsborrow 2013), whereas long-distance MPD might include international migration (e.g., see Hunter et al. 2013). In addition to the costs of MPD, given that most actors prefer to avoid MPD (Nawrotzki and DeWaard 2016) and, in the case of MPD, to relocate nearby (versus far away from) their previous place of residence (Findlay 2011), it therefore makes sense that the effect of ECC depends on the type of destination under consideration. Nawrotzki et al. (2013c) further extended this logic to examine the competing risks of documented and undocumented migration from Mexico to the United States. They showed that the ECC-MPD relationship was only evident in the case of undocumented migration, which adds another important compositional layer to current knowledge of the ECC-MPD relationship.

Of the 20 studies listed in Table 7.1, six studies used only clustered standard errors, seven studies used clustered standard errors and fixed (but not random) effects, and seven studies used clustered standard errors and random effects, in some cases while also including fixed effects at different (higher) levels of analysis (see Gray 2011; Meijer-Irons 2016). As we noted earlier, the use of fixed effects means that one cannot generalize their findings beyond the particular set of places considered in a given study. The parameter estimates are properly considered *within*-estimates, such that they must "be interpreted as comparing two [actors] who are exposed to the same" place (Gray and Mueller 2012a: 140). While the use of fixed effects has some additional practical advantages, e.g., alleviating the need to statistically control for time-constant place-level characteristics (Allison and Christakis 2006) and computational speed, ultimately, the aims of the study and the data used must dictate the specific modeling strategy employed. For example, one reason that Nawrotzki et al. (2015a, 2015b, 2015c) and Nawrotzki and DeWaard (2016) used random effects in their models was because the migration data come from the Mexican Migration Project, which, despite efforts to validate these data (Massey and Zenteno 2000), are not representative of all communities in Mexico and likely suffer from significant recall bias (Hamilton and Savinar 2015).

Discussion and conclusion

At the outset of this chapter, we noted that our review of the motivations for and uses of multilevel event history models in current research on the ECC-MPD relationship follows several earlier reviews that highlighted the importance of multilevel approaches more generally (Fussell et al. 2014; Hunter et al. 2015; Kniveton 2008; McLeman 2013; Piguet 2010). A consistent theme in these reviews is that of *variability*. The ECC-MPD relationship clearly varies across study areas and time periods (Hunter et al. 2015; Opatowski and Borova 2016).

Echoing this theme, in this chapter, we discussed several of the ways in which multilevel event history models can be and have been used to profitably attend to different sources of variability. Although the ECC-MPD relationship evident in most of the 20 studies listed in Table 7.1, it is borne out in different ways depending, in part, on the levels of analysis considered, the measure(s) of ECC used, and model specification(s). It is also influenced by other factors such as gender (e.g., see Henry et al. 2004 and Mueller et al. 2014), urbanization level (Nawrotzki et al. 2015a), and established social networks (Hunter et al. 2013; Nawrotzki et al. 2015b), that we did not discuss in this chapter. Recalling Tobler's (1970: 236) "first law of geography" that "everything is related to everything else, but near things are more related than distant things," multilevel approaches explicitly incorporate this idea, as well as extend it by considering other forms of clustering (e.g., individuals within households) that are not exactly spatial.

In closing, given the role that ECC is already playing and will continue to play in many economic, political, and social processes, including MPD, we hope that our review will provide a useful point of reference that will help to stimulate further research on the ECC-MPD relationship, including in the areas of data collection and sources (e.g., see Donato et al. 2016), new study areas and time periods, and modeling strategies.

Acknowledgements

This research is supported by center grant #P2C HD041023 awarded to the Minnesota Population Center at the University of Minnesota by the Eunice Kennedy Shriver National Institute of Child Health and Human Development. DeWaard and Nawrotzki are grateful to the Institute on the Environment at the University of Minnesota for the opportunity to attend the 2015 climate talks in Paris as official observers. Nawrotzki further acknowledges support from the National Science Foundation funded Terra Populus project (NSF Award ACI-0940818). DeWaard is also grateful for the opportunity and support to attend the Laurier/U.S. Embassy Workshop on Environmental Migration and Displacement at the Balsillie School of International Affairs in Waterloo, Ontario, on January 21–22, 2016.

Notes

1 For simplicity, we have specified the baseline hazard in (1) using a linear term for time. More flexible specifications include, for example, adding a squared time term (Barber et al. 2000) or using a set of dummy variables for each time period (Singer and Willet 2003).
2 In the interest of full disclosure, Nawrotzki is one of the authors of this chapter.
3 The IOM panel "Human Mobility and Climate Change" was convened on December 10, 2015.
4 The expert team is jointly sponsored by the World Meteorological Organization (WMO) Commission for Climatology (CCl), the World Climate Research Programme (WCRP) project on Climate Variability and Predictability (CLIVAR), and the Joint WMO-Intergovernmental Oceanographic Commission (IOC) of the United Nations Educational, Scientific and Cultural Organization (UNESCO) Technical Commission for Oceanography and Marine Meteorology (JCOMM).

References

Allison, P.D. (1982). Discrete-time methods for the analysis of event histories. *Sociological Methodology*, 13, 61–98.
Allison, P.D. (1984). *Event history analysis.* Thousand Oaks, CA: Sage Publications.
Allison, P.D., & Christakis, N.A. (2006). Fixed-effects methods for the analysis of nonrepeated events. *Sociological Methodology*, 36(1), 155–172.
Angeles, G., Guilkey, D.K., & Mroz, T.A. (2005). The impact of community-level variables on individual-level outcomes: Theoretical results and applications. *Sociological Methods and Research*, 34(1), 76–121.
Barber, J.S., Murphy, S.A., Axinn, W.G., & Maples, J. (2000). Discrete-time multilevel hazard analysis. *Sociological Methodology*, 30(1), 201–235.
Beauchemin, C., & Shoumaker, B. (2005). Migration to cities in Burkina Faso: Does the level of development in sending areas matter? *World Development*, 33(7), 1129–1152.
Bindoff, N.L., Stott, P.A., Achutarao, K.M., Allen, M.R., Gillett, N., Gutzler, D., . . . Zhang, X. (2013). Detection and attribution of climate change: from global to regional. In T.F. Stocker, D. Qin, G.K. Plattner, M. Tignor, S.K. Allen, J. Boschung, . . . P.M. Midgley (Eds.), *Climate change 2013: The physical science basis*. Contribution of working group 1 to the fifth assessment report of the Intergovernmental Panel on Climate Change. New York: Cambridge University Press.
Cameron, A.C., & Miller, D.L. (2015). A practitioner's guide to cluster-robust inference. *Journal of Human Resources*, 50(2), 317–372.
Cox, D.R. (1972). Regression models and life tables. *Journal of the Royal Statistical Society*, 34, 187–220.
DeWaard, J., & Nawrotzki, R.J. (2016). Migration is a climate change issue. *MPC News*, Minnesota Population Center, University of Minnesota. Spring.
Donato, K.M., Carrico, A., Sisk, B., & Piya, B. (2016). Migration, social capital and the environment in Bangladesh. Paper presented at the annual meeting of the Population Association of America. April 1.
Duchateau, L., & Janssen, P. (2010). *The Frailty Model*. New York, NY: Springer.
Ellis, F. (2000). *Rural livelihoods and diversity in developing countries*. Oxford: Oxford University Press.
Entwisle, B. (2007). Putting people into place. *Demography*, 44(4), 687–703.
Ezra, M., & Kiros, G.E. (2001). Rural out-migration in the drought prone areas of Ethiopia: A multilevel analysis. *International Migration Review*, 35(3), 749–771.

Findlay, A.M. (2011). Migration destinations in an era of environmental change. *Global Environmental Change*, 21S, S50–S58.

Fussell, E., Hunter, L.M., & Gray, C.L. (2014). Measuring the environmental dimensions of human migration: The demographer's toolkit. *Global Environmental Change*, 28, 182–191.

Fussell, E., Sastry, N., & VanLandingham, M. (2010). Race, socioeconomic status, and return migration to New Orleans after Hurricane Katrina. *Population and Environment*, 31, 20–42.

Gelman. A. (2006). Multilevel (hierarchical) modeling: What it can and cannot do. *Technometrics*, 48(3), 432–435.

Gray, C.L. (2009). Environment, land, and rural out-migration in Southern Ecuadorian Andes. *World Development*, 37(2), 457–468.

Gray, C.L. (2010). Gender, natural capital, and migration in the southern Ecuadorian Andes. *Environment and Planning A*, 42, 678–696.

Gray, C.L. (2011). Soil quality and human migration in Kenya and Uganda. *Global Environmental Change*, 21(2), 421–430.

Gray, C.L. & Bilsborrow, C. (2013). Environmental influences on human migration in rural Ecuador. *Demography*, 50, 1217–1241.

Gray, C.L. & Mueller, V. (2012a). Drought and population mobility in rural Ethiopia. *World Development*, 40(1), 134–145.

Gray, C.L. & Mueller, V. (2012b). Natural disasters and population mobility in Bangladesh. *Proceedings of the National Academy of Science*, 109(16), 6000–6005.

Hamilton, E.R. & Savinar, R. (2015). Two sources of error in data on migration from Mexico to the United States in Mexican household-based surveys. *Demography*, 52(4), 1345–1355.

Henry, S., Shoumaker, B., & Beauchemin, C. (2004). The impact of rainfall on the first out-migration: A multi-level event history analysis in Burkina Faso. *Population and Environment*, 25(5), 423–460.

Huber, P.J. (1967). The behavior of maximum likelihood estimates under non-standard conditions. In L.M. LeCam & J. Neyman (Eds.), *Proceedings of the Firth Berkeley symposium on mathematical statistics and probability* (pp. 221–223). Berkeley, CA: UC Press.

Hunter, L.M., Luna, J.K., & Norton, R.M. (2015). Environmental dimensions of migration. *Annual Review of Sociology*, 41, 377–397.

Hunter, L.M., Murray, S., & Riosmena, F. (2013). Rainfall patterns and U.S. migration from rural Mexico. *International Migration Review*, 47(4), 874–909.

Jennings, J.A., & Gray, C.L. (2015). Climate variability and human migration in the Netherlands, 1865–1937. *Population and Environment*, 36, 255–278.

Kniveton, D., Schmidt-Verkerk, Smith, C., & Black, R. (2008). Climate change and migration: Improving methodologies to estimate flows. Paper No. 33, IOM Research Series, International Organization for Migration, Geneva, Switzerland.

Kreft, I., & De Leeuw, J. (1998). *Introducing multilevel modeling*. Thousand Oaks, CA: Sage Publications.

Leighton, M. (2009). Migration and slow-onset disasters: Desertification and drought. In F. Laczko & C. Aghazarm (Eds.), *Migration, environment, and climate change: Assessing the evidence* (pp. 319–351). Geneva: International Organization for Migration.

Lindstrom, D.P., & Lauster, N. (2001). Local economic opportunity and the competing risks of internal and U.S. migration in Zacatecas, Mexico. *International Migration Review*, 35(4), 1232–1256.

Luke, D. A. (2004). *Multilevel modeling*. Sage university papers series: Quantitative applications in the social sciences 143. Thousand Oaks, CA: Sage Publications, Inc.

Massey, D.S., Axinn, W.G., & Ghimire, D.J. (2010). Environmental change and out-migration: Evidence from Nepal. *Population and Environment*, 32, 109–136.

Massey, D.S., Goldring, L., & Durand, J. (1994). Continuities in transnational migration: An analysis of nineteen Mexican communities. *American Journal of Sociology*, 99(6), 1492–1533.

Massey, D.S., & Zenteno, R. (2000). A validation of the ethnosurvey: The case of Mexico-US migration. *International Migration Review*, 34(3), 766–793.

McGinnis, R. (1968). A stochastic model of social mobility. *American Sociological Review*, 33(5), 712–722.

McHugh, K.E., Hogan, T.D., & Happel, S.K. (1995). Multiple residence and cyclical migration: A life course perspective. *The Professional Geographer*, 47(3), 251–267.

McLeman, R.A. (2011). Settlement abandonment in the context of global environmental change. *Global Environmental Change*, 21, S108–S120.

McLeman, R.A. (2013). Developments in modelling of climate change-related migration. *Climatic Change*, 117, 599–611.

Meijer-Irons, J. (2016). The role of proximate and cumulative subjective and objective environmental measures in migration decisions in rural Thailand. Paper presented at the annual meeting of the Population Association of America. April 1.

Morrison, P.A. (1967). Duration of residence and prospective migration: The evaluation of a stochastic model. *Demography*, 4(2), 553–561.

Mueller, V., Gray, C.L., & Kosec, K. (2014). Heat stress increases long-term human migration in rural Pakistan. *Nature Climate Change*, 4, 182–185.

Myers, N. (2002). Environmental refugees: A growing phenomenon of the 21st century. *Philosophical Transactions of the Royal Society of London Series B-Biological Sciences*, 357(1420), 609–613.

Nawrotzki, R.J., & DeWaard, J. (2016). Climate shocks and the timing of migration from Mexico. *Population and Environment*, 38, 72–100. doi 10.1007/s11111–016–0255-x.

Nawrotzki, R.J., Hunter, L.M., Runfola, D.M., & Riosmena, F. (2015a). Climate change as a migration driver from rural and urban Mexico. *Environmental Research Letters*, 10(11), 1–9.

Nawrotzki, R.J., Riosmena, F., Hunter, L.M., & Runfola, D.M. (2015b). Amplification or suppression: Social networks and the climate change-migration association in rural Mexico. *Global Environmental Change*, 35, 463–474.

Nawrotzki, R.J., Riosmena, F., Hunter, L.M., & Runfola, D.M. (2015c). Undocumented migration in response to climate change. *International Journal of Population Studies*, 1(1), 60–74.

Opatowski, M., & Borova, B. (2016). Rapporteurs' final report. Laurier/U.S. Embassy Workshop on Environmental Migration and Displacement, Balsillie School of International Affairs, Waterloo, Ontario. January 21–22.

Peterson, T.C. (2005). Climate change indices. *World Meteorological Organization Bulletin*, 54(2), 83–86.

Peterson, T.C., Folland, C., Gruza, G., Hogg, W., Mokssit, A., & Plummer, N. (2001). *Report of the activities of the working group on climate change detection and related rapporteurs*. Geneva: World Meteorological Organization.

Peterson, T.C., & Manton, M.J. (2008). Monitoring changes in climate extremes — a tale of international collaboration. *Bulletin of the American Meteorological Society*, 89(9), 1266–1271.

Piguet, E. (2010). Linking climate change, environmental degradation, and migration: A methodological overview. *Climate Change*, 1, 517–524.

Rabe-Hesketh, S., & Skrondal, A. (2012). *Multilevel and longitudinal modeling using Stata* (3rd ed.). College Station, TX: Stata Press.

Raudenbush, S.W. & Bryk, A.S. (2002). *Hierarchical linear models: Applications and data analysis methods*. Thousand Oaks, CA: Sage Publications.

Scoones, I. (1998) Sustainable rural livelihoods: A framework for analysis. IDS Working Paper No.72. Brighton: IDS.

Singer, J.D., & Willett, J.B. (2003). *Applied longitudinal data analysis: Modeling change and event occurrence*. Oxford and New York: Oxford University Press.

Sjaastad, L. (1962). The costs and returns of human migration. *Journal of Political Economy*, 70, 80–93.

Snijders, T.A.B., & Bosker, R.J. (2011). *Multilevel analysis: An introduction to basic and advanced multilevel modeling*. Thousand Oaks, CA: Sage Publications.

Stark, O., & Bloom, D.E. (1985). The new economics of labor migration. *American Economic Review*, 75(2), 173–178.

Stern, N. (2007). *Economics of climate change: The Stern review*. Cambridge: Cambridge University Press.

Tobler, W.R. (1970). A computer movie simulating urban growth in the Detroit region. *Economic Geography*, 46, 234–240.

Todaro, M.P. 1976. *Internal migration in developing countries*. Geneva: International Labour Office.

United Nations. (1998). Recommendations on statistics of international migration. Statistical Papers Series M, No. 58, Rev. 1. Statistics Division, Department of Economic and Social Affairs, United Nations, New York, NY.

van Schendel, W. (2005). *The Bengal Borderland: Beyond State and Nation in South Asia*. London: Anthem Press.

White, H. (1980). Heteroskedasticity-consistent covariance matrix estimator as a direct test for heteroskedasticity. *Econometrica*, 48, 817–838.

Willekens, F. (2008). Models of migration: Observations and judgements. In J. Raymer & F. Willekens (Eds.), *International migration in Europe: Data, models, and estimates* (pp. 117–147). Chichester: Wiley.

Yamaguchi, K. (1991). *Event history analysis*. Thousand Oaks, CA: Sage Publications.

8

Estimating the population impacts of sea level rise

Katherine J. Curtis and Rachel S. Bergmans

Sea level rise: what is it, and why is it of concern to population scientists?

Sea level rise is a growing concern to human populations. Small island and coastal populations are at the greatest risk of shouldering the impacts of sea level rise, which include an increase in the frequency and severity of flooding, associated storm surges, shoreline erosion and salt water contamination of fresh water supplies. Such impacts have the potential to shape demographic events and processes. Consequently, contemporary population scientists have an obvious interest in articulating the population impacts of sea level rise, and confront a unique set of conceptual and technical challenges in pursuing such investigations.

The most recent Intergovernmental Panel on Climate Change (IPCC) scenarios show that global average sea level will continue to rise, with estimated rates ranging from 26–55 cm to 45–82 cm by 2100 depending on the emissions scenario (Church et al. 2013). Many factors contribute to local sea level rise and subsequent weather events, not all of which are linked to human activity. Global sea level change unrelated to anthropogenic global warming, natural variability in atmospheric dynamics, ongoing response to the last ice age and local land motion are among such drivers (Strauss et al. 2016). Although not human-caused, these factors compound the effects of sea level rise and related weather events that ultimately impact human populations.

The frequency of coastal floods has risen along with sea levels, most especially recurrent "nuisance" floods which can occur even during periods of severe drought and are economically burdensome (Ezer and Atkinson 2014; Moftakhari et al. 2015; Strauss et al. 2016; Sweet and Park 2014). Additionally, there is some evidence that the severity of weather events (i.e., flooding, hurricanes and typhoons) that impact coastal populations will increase in coming decades (Webster et al. 2005). In 2005, the storm surge from Hurricane Katrina caused severe flooding from the levy breach on Lake Pontchartrain, resulted in more than 1,000 deaths, generated an extraordinary resorting of the Gulf of Mexico's population through migration and, consequently, has become an exemplar of why sea level rise is relevant to population science. Across the globe, there are a growing number of extreme weather events and severe conditions linked to sea level rise that are of a magnitude on par with Hurricane Katrina. The small island nation Tuvalu confronts mounting challenges in living conditions due to sea level rise and natural disasters (Hunter and

Nawrotzki 2016; Shen and Gemenne 2011). In 2004, a tsunami in the Indian Ocean resulted in 220,000 deaths and missing persons in the region (Ishiguro and Yano 2015), and in 2011, north-east Japan suffered nearly 20,000 deaths from a massive tsunami (Nakahara and Ichikawa 2013). There are less direct, although equally severe, impacts of sea level rise including infant mortality from water salinity caused by sea level rise in coastal Bangladesh (Dasgupta et al. 2015), and changes in human settlement patterns in the aftermath of Katrina (Curtis et al. 2015).

Population density in coastal areas is on average three times the global mean (McGranahan et al. 2007; Small and Nicholls 2003), thus putting a large number of people and assets at risk of exposure to coastal flooding and other impacts of sea level rise. Indeed, 13 of the top 20 most populated cities in the world are major port cities and house more than one million residents each (Bosello and De Cian 2014). Further, more than 10% of the world's total population lives in low-elevation coastal zones with a higher concentration of coastal populations (14%) in developing countries (McGranahan et al. 2007). As a result, concerns about the impacts of climate change are largely centered on coastal areas and cities (Handmer et al. 2012). However, connections between places via migration makes sea level rise relevant to coastal and inland populations alike (Curtis et al. 2015; DeWaard et al. 2015; Fussell et al. 2014; Hauer 2017).

Identifying at-risk populations

Sea level rise is disruptive for human populations, yet societies have the capacity to mitigate impacts through adaptation and planning. Accurate population estimates are needed for effective planning. Consequently, just as identifying specific locations at risk of the impacts of sea level rise is a high priority in climate change science (Wu et al. 2002), understanding specific populations at risk must become a high priority in population science.

Researchers investigating the population-environment nexus grapple with data analytical challenges along the temporal dimension. To properly identify which populations are at-risk, scientists must first understand how the forces posing the environmental risk operate. Environmental changes can occur suddenly (e.g., flood, hurricane, tsunami) or they can occur gradually (e.g., climate change, land degradation, sea level rise). Both fast-onset and slow-onset environmental changes have the potential to impact human populations. However, slow-onset changes are generally less well understood since they are conceptually more complex and data requirements are more demanding (Neumann and Hilderink 2015). For instance, interactions and mechanisms that cause a fast-onset event to impact migration are clearer than processes that unfold over a longer period and eventually lead to migration in response to a slow-onset change. The temporal reach of slow-onset change requires consistent time series data, sometimes spanning decades, which are often rarely available.

Environmental change affects populations within places in which the environmental change occurs. It follows that while population scientists are interested in studying the at-risk population, the object of study necessarily incorporates the at-risk land area. Accordingly, researchers must consider the spatial dimension of the population-environment link. There are recent advancements in spatial modeling that build from hazard vulnerability research and can inform future approaches (McLeman 2013). For example, by combining county-level data for the United States with spatial estimates of sea level rise, Curtis and Schneider (2011) demonstrate the scale of coastal population vulnerability, estimating that over 20 million residents of low-elevation coastal areas will be affected by sea level rise by 2030. By linking geographically referenced household data with satellite imagery, Leyk et al. (2012) show that the effect of household-level natural resource availability on migration in rural South Africa varies according to the spatial unit analyzed (i.e., region, village or subvillage).

In demographic research, the typical spatial unit of analysis represents an administrative boundary because population data are conveniently available for such units, and often are consistently measured over time. At a minimum, researchers would be wise to reflect on the spatial extent of the environmental change (i.e., sea level rise), and how well it aligns with the geographic unit for which population data are available. Given that most questions about the impact of sea level rise on human populations centers on vulnerability, mitigation and adaptation, the spatial unit must reasonably reflect social, economic and political forces that influence the population's level of vulnerability and its capacity to mitigate and adapt to an environmental impact.

Vulnerable populations and places are expected to be at risk of bearing disproportionate impacts of sea level rise. Therefore, assessing the size of potential vulnerable populations is critical for research aiming to address equity and environmental justice. There is an impressive body of regional- and country-level probabilistic projections of total population, age and life expectancy, and total fertility rates for 2008–2100 that bracket the upper and lower bounds of future population developments generated at the Institute of International Applied Systems Analysis (IIASA) (Grübler et al. 2007; Lutz et al. 2007). The estimates are limited to large-scale geographies and aggregate population groups. Thus, a challenge researchers confront is how to effectively develop meaningful subnational and subregional population projections that include information on age, sex, race and other dimensions relevant to population vulnerability. Vulnerability indices at the subnational level are an increasingly common approach to understand how environmental stressors will impact populations of various socioeconomic and demographic characteristics, and are used in research on numerous countries including the United States (Clark et al. 1998; Cutter et al. 2003; Chakraborty et al. 2005; Kleinosky et al. 2007; Olfert et al. 2006; Rygel et al. 2006; Wu et al. 2002; Yarnal 2007), the United Kingdom (Tapsell et al. 2002), Spain (Weichselgartner 2002), Germany (Fekete 2009), India (O'Brien et al. 2004), Latin America (Cardona 2005; Hahn et al. 2009), Australia (Dwyer et al. 2004), the Philippines (Acosta-Michlik and Espaldon 2008) and Africa (Vincent 2004), as well as for regions worldwide (Nakamura et al. 2001).

Today, population scientists researching the impacts of sea level rise have available to them a number of future environmental change scenarios. Sea level rise scenarios do not predict future change, but instead describe qualitative and quantitative information under a variety of plausible futures given potential anthropogenic activity and adaptation strategies (Moss et al. 2010; Parris et al. 2012). A principal source of scenario uncertainty is the dynamics of large ice sheets in Greenland and west Antarctica, which in the event of their collapse could contribute an additional 10–20 m to sea level rise projections (Bamber et al. 2009; Gardner et al. 2013; Bosello and De Cian 2014; DeConto and Pollard 2016). Incorporating a range of scenarios into sea level rise research also helps account for interactions between average sea level, extreme water levels and storm characteristics (Seneviratne et al. 2012). Given high climate variability at smaller scales, currently there is no widely accepted method for producing probabilistic projections of sea level rise at regional or local areas.

Scenarios from the IPCC and the National Oceanic and Atmospheric Administration (NOAA) are most widely circulated and commonly used for global and US coastal areas, respectively. IPCC AR5 global sea level rise estimates are based on representative concentration pathway (RCP) climate change trajectories, which supersede the Special Report on Emissions Scenarios (SRES) projections used in previous reports. RCP trajectories do not rely on unique socioeconomic or emissions scenarios, but instead rely on a combination of different demographic, economic, and policy futures (Moss et al. 2010). NOAA global SLR scenarios have been developed using semi-empirical models and a combination of the SRES estimates for ocean warming, potential ranges for ice sheet loss, and historical global sea level change. Researchers must keep in mind any assumptions or limitations when relying on various sources of global scenarios. A disclaimer about NOAA data is that the specific amount of sea level change in any single location will vary depending on regional and local vertical land movement, ocean dynamics and future land use change (Parris et al. 2012).

Select examples in population research

Several recent studies have made important analytical advances in assessing the population impacts of sea level rise. Lam et al. (2009) used four published datasets and GIS methods to analyze coastal states in the contiguous United States. Their study provides a detailed outline of how researchers can overlay various spatial datasets to identify the people and areas that are most likely to carry a disproportionate burden of sea level rise. The authors processed elevation data (DEM), moving from pixel to polygon data, which were subsequently overlaid with LandScan data to generate zonal statistics (e.g., population size). This approach yielded estimates of upwards of 19 million people residing within 1 km from the shoreline in the conterminous United States, whereas about 11.6 million people were estimated to live below the 3 m elevation threshold. State-specific estimates demonstrate that Florida has the highest percentage of population living in areas below 3 meters, at 32.5% of the total, approximating 5.9 million people. Louisiana was second with 27.6% of the total population, or 1.2 million people living below 3 meters.

Curtis and Schneider (2011) take a new approach by harmonizing data to the same temporal and spatial scale to generate estimates of future populations at risk of future sea level rise. Instead of relying on current population estimates, their research utilizes the classical cohort-component method to project populations that are at risk of future sea level rise for selected cases in the United States. This strategy reveals a dramatic difference between approaches using current versus future population estimates. For example, in Florida, 6.4 million people were estimated to be at risk in 2008, whereas the estimates of the projected population at the expected time of sea level rise in 2030 is 9.9 million, marking a 35% difference in the estimated at-risk population. In addition, the authors advance the idea of a "ripple effect" based on the connectedness of places through human migration (see Curtis et al. 2015; Fussell et al. 2014; DeWaard et al. 2015). The authors argue that there will be possibly new and/or overburdened counties receiving migrants if catastrophic sea level rise, storm surges or hurricane-induced flooding occurs and dislocates large populations. Moreover, the authors suggest that the specific structure of the network of migration flows will inform the extent of the impact on receiving counties; at-risk places with strong ties to other places expected to experience sea level rise will need to re-route migrants to other, viable destinations.

Using a computationally sophisticated agent-based modeling (ABM) approach, Hassani-Mahmooei and Parris (2012) develop a novel model of population redistribution in Bangladesh in response to sea level rise that directly incorporates migration. Bangladesh is among the countries most vulnerable to climate change due to its low-lying topography, high population density and prevalence of poverty. ABMs have great potential for research on the human impacts of environment change since the approach can accommodate the complexity of adaptive systems. Migration dynamics are a key feature of the human adaptive system and, further contributing to the complexity, are informed by multiple causal pathways. In considering the impacts of sea level rise, the authors integrate into their model the influence of socioeconomic aspects, demographic trends, and historical climatic dimensions (i.e., drought, cyclone, flood patterns). The model demonstrates that patterns are dramatically different across the regions of the country, with anticipated changes in population densities due to migration from the drought-prone western and southern areas susceptible to cyclones and floods, towards the less environmentally vulnerable northern and eastern regions. Depending on the severity of the environmental hazards, the authors estimate that there will be 3–10 million internal migrants between 2001 and 2050, representing 1.0 to 3.4% of the total estimated population.

Although not focusing on future populations, Runfola et al. (2016) utilize household-level data to gain insight on the interacting roles of household-scale migration decisions and economic and urban growth policy in climate change mitigation. Approximately 6% of Mexico's population (6.3 million people) migrated between 2005 and 2010, the specific patterns of which have potential implications for exposure to natural disasters. Overall, internal migration patterns decreased exposure, whereas migration increased exposure in key urban areas, including coastal municipalities. As with Hassani-Mahmooei and Parris' (2012) and Leyk et al.'s (2012) research, Runfola and colleagues demonstrate heterogeneous patterns at the subnational level, thereby signaling to population researchers the importance of reevaluating universal or global analytical approaches in favor of methods that permit subregional variation.

Hauer et al. (2016) innovatively use household-level data to predict future populations at risk of sea level rise. They couple small-area population projections with select sea level rise vulnerability assessments for all US coastal counties, demonstrating a potential range in the size of the at-risk population depending on the magnitude of the sea level rise. The authors find that under a sea level rise scenario of 0.9 m by 2100, 4.2 million people are estimated to be at risk of inundation, whereas the 1.8 m scenario is estimated to affect 13.1 million people. In an earlier study, Haer et al. (2013) assessed the potential range of human impacts in terms of Gross Domestic Product (GDP), reporting that the nation could suffer a decline of 70–289 billion USD depending on the magnitude of sea level rise. This research approach highlights the significant variability in the estimated extent of human impacts due to the specific sea level rise scenario.

Recent studies in the physical sciences also have made important headway in generating models of potential human impacts of future sea level rise. One notable difference across the sciences is the scale at which analyses are conducted. Larger scales used in the physical sciences are useful for grasping the overall magnitude of the problem, whereas local scales more common in population sciences are necessary for effective adaptation planning and implementation. In their analysis of global regions, Neumann et al. (2015) derive scenario-driven projections of coastal populations to identify areas with the greatest human risk of exposure to sea level rise in 2030 and 2060. Asia currently has and is estimated to have the highest future total coastal population exposure, yet Africa is expected to experience the highest rate of growth in the number of people exposed to sea level rise; thus, highlighting the continued and growing risk of exposure in certain regions and the associated need for adaptive planning. Although they do not integrate projections for future populations, Strauss et al. (2012) advance knowledge by incorporating the influence of tidal elevation to estimate areas most at risk of disruptions from sea level rise. Through this approach, which incorporates the National Elevation Dataset (NED) and NOAA's Vertical Datum Transformation (VDatum) with information on elevations for different modeled tidal datums, the authors find a larger number of communities of varying population sizes at risk of exposure than were previously identified. Hinkel et al. (2014) put the magnitude of potential human impacts of sea level rise on a financial scale. The authors estimate model uncertainty from four climate models, each incorporating the possible influence of ice sheets and glaciers, and use population estimates from the Global Rural-Urban Mapping Project (GRUMP) and LandScan. Model results suggest that 0.2–4.6% of the global population can expect to be flooded annually by 2100 with an accompanying annual loss of 0.3–9.3% of global gross domestic product, and highlight the potentially substantial offsetting impacts of adaptive policies and planning (e.g., dikes).

Existing challenges and promising opportunities

Population scientists have grown increasingly interested in the human impacts of sea level rise and, in their explorations, have made significant progress. However, the area remains in its infancy and much more work needs to be done. Existing limitations provide a roadmap for future researchers to continue to overcome challenges in the area.

A first set of opportunities for future work concerns the integration and utilization of current and more comprehensive data inputs. Building on efforts to identify at-risk populations, research will benefit from considering how sea level rise will impact specific subgroups including, for example, populations by employment status, housing status, and particular race/ethnic and age groups. Detailed information on specific vulnerable populations can be powerful for policy decisions and planning purposes (Lam et al. 2009). Similarly, more detailed input data on areas in which populations reside (i.e., land use/land cover) would improve estimates on which places and the populations within them are mostly likely to be affected. Additionally, integrating more complete information on populations and places can be subsequently modeled as a feedback process for improved development and evaluation of adaptation strategies. Finally, and perhaps most obviously, population scientists must incorporate the most recent environmental and sea level rise projections generated by environmental scientists as work on the environmental side of the relationship continues to progress. For example, DeConto and Pollard (2016) highlight the significance of the Antarctic ice sheet in generating viable sea level rise scenarios and develop a model that couples ice sheet and climate dynamics, and calibrates estimates against past sea level estimates (i.e., Pliocene Epoch of about 3 million years ago, and last interglacial period dating 130,000–115,000 years ago). Given the role of ice sheets, the authors stress that Antarctica could potentially contribute more than a meter of sea level rise by 2100 and more than 15 meters by 2500 if current emissions persist (see also Nicholls and Cazenave 2010). Similarly, by incorporating ice melt into sea level rise scenarios as an exponential function as opposed to a linear dynamic, Hansen et al. (2016) estimate a potential 5 m increase in sea level by 2100, as well as increasingly powerful storms and changes in ocean temperatures and overturning circulation.

A second area of opportunity for advances in the study of complex relationships between environmental change and human populations is in new analytical approaches. Most model-output alone is not enough to inform complex decisions involved in adaptation planning (Miller and Morisette 2014). Simulation models are well-positioned to add rigor to scenario planning approaches that otherwise lack quantitative modeling and validation procedures, while also offering researchers the ability to model complex system dynamics. Comparative studies are another approach to advance the study of complex causal population-environment relationships (Neumann and Hilderink 2015). Large-scale projects that move beyond specific field studies are currently rare given the large data costs, most central among them standardized measures across time and location. Ongoing efforts by key organizations, such as the Center for International Earth Science Information Network and Terra Populus, will permit researchers to more readily conduct comparative research in the future (Warner et al. 2012). Finally, a combination of methods might help overcome limitations associated with individual approaches. Mixed-methods research can integrate qualitative and quantitative approaches independently or sequentially to improve the identification and understanding of mechanisms, and to improve research conclusions and their application (Tashakkori and Teddlie 2008).

A third area for future development is germane to population projections in general: uncertainty. Researchers examining the human impacts of sea level rise must tackle the issue of uncertainty surrounding population projections. Existing population projections are highly controversial because many lack sound documentation of underlying assumptions and potential errors (Gemenne 2011). Uncertainty can be due to problems with the data (e.g., measurement error), assumptions about environmental processes and/or population dynamics, or the way in which the population-environment relationship is conceptualized. At present, uncertainty estimates are especially underreported in qualitative and simulation studies even though frameworks for assessing uncertainty exist (Walker et al. 2003). Sensitivity analyses, inverse modeling, scenario analysis, Monte Carlo simulation or Bayesian modeling are all potential options for assessing uncertainty (Refsgaard et al. 2007). Traditionally, uncertainty in population projections has been addressed by "uncertainty variants," generally labeled high, medium and 1low (Wilson and Rees 2005). Most users adopt the "medium" projection, considering it the most conservative and, it follows, the "high" and "low" as the upper and lower bounds. Yet the likelihood of whether the population will follow the high or low, or even the medium path, is unknown.

A variety of methods to assess probabilities have been advanced since it is vital for planners and decisions makers to have information on whether the estimated population at-risk of sea level rise impacts is an over- or under-estimate. Bayesian models have the advantage of providing probabilistic projections, in essence quantifying the extent of uncertainty in the population estimates (Raftery et al. 2012). Recent efforts have begun to consider how probabilistic methods might be extended to dimensions other than age and sex, including, for example, households (Leiwen and O'Neill 2004) and subnational areas (Wilson and Rees 2005). Back casting estimates can be used as a sensitivity analysis of projections and models. Back casts have the potential to offer relevant insights for population scientists by demonstrating the accuracy of the approach through comparing estimated to observed values. Less common approaches such as dating methods using quartz and feldspar optically stimulated luminescence used to reconstruct landscape evolution processes might also prove useful (Neumann and Hilderink 2015).

Perhaps the greatest uncertainty in any population projection models stems from the migration component. Even at the national scale, international migration estimates are plagued with error, and at the regional level, estimates lack consistent time or geographical coverage, calling attention to the need for better migration data (Wilson and Rees 2005; Willekens et al. 2016). Moreover, the bulk of research examines net migration rather than gross migration (Rogers 1990) with few exceptions (De Beer 1997; Wilson and Bell 2004), and thus restricts migration to a non-dynamic dimension of population change. Consequently, scholarship is limited in the depth and breadth of understanding how sea level rise and other environmental changes impact human populations directly and indirectly. Forecasting migration networks and identifying factors influencing changes in migration signals, including institutional forces and/or policy changes, is a promising direction.

Conclusion

What population scientists do know is that past trends do not guarantee future trends. The task for future research is to identify and model empirically demonstrated and theoretically identified social and environmental forces that work together to generate a different future. Within each challenge is an opportunity for continued advancement. Population scientists have much cause to tackle these obstacles given the state of knowledge in the environmental sciences; a growing number of people and areas are at an increasing risk of bearing the effects of environmental changes and events. By building on classic tools of the field and incorporating innovative approaches originated in others, demographers are uniquely positioned to understand and to mitigate the human impacts of sea level rise.

References

Acosta-Michlik, Lilibeth, and Victoria Espaldon. 2008. "Assessing Vulnerability of Selected Farming Communities in the Philippines Based on a Behavioural Model of Agent's Adaptation to Global Environmental Change." *Global Environmental Change* 18 (4): 554–63.

Bamber, Jonathan L., Riccardo E.M. Riva, Bert LA Vermeersen, and Anne M. LeBrocq. 2009. "Reassessment of the Potential Sea-Level Rise from a Collapse of the West Antarctic Ice Sheet." *Science* 324 (5929): 901–3.

Bosello, Francesco, and Enrica De Cian. 2014. "Climate Change, Sea Level Rise, and Coastal Disasters. A Review of Modeling Practices." *Energy Economics* 46: 593–605. doi:10.1016/j.eneco.2013.09.002.

Cardona, Omar D. 2005. "Indicators of Disaster Risk and Risk Management: Program for Latin America and the Caribbean: Summary Report." Inter-American Development Bank. https://publications.iadb.org/handle/11319/4801.

Chakraborty, Jayajit, Graham A. Tobin, and Burrell E. Montz. 2005. "Population Evacuation: Assessing Spatial Variability in Geophysical Risk and Social Vulnerability to Natural Hazards." *Natural Hazards Review* 6 (1): 23–33.

Church, J.A., P.U. Clark, A. Cazenave, J.M. Gregory, S. Jevrejeva, A. Levermann, M.A. Merrifield, et al. 2013. "Sea Level Change." In *Climate Change 2013: The Physical Science Basis. Contribution of Working Group I to the Fifth Assessment Report of the Intergovernmental Panel on Climate Change*, edited by T.F. Stocker, D. Qin, G.-K. Plattner, M. Tignor, S.K. Allen, J. Boschung, A. Nauels, Y. Xia, V. Bex, and P.M. Midgley. Cambridge, United Kingdom and New York, NY, USA: Cambridge University Press. www.ipcc.ch/pdf/assessment-report/ar5/wg1/WG1AR5_Chapter13_FINAL.pdf.

Clark, George E., Susanne C. Moser, Samuel J. Ratick, Kirstin Dow, William B. Meyer, Srinivas Emani, Weigen Jin, et al. 1998. "Assessing the Vulnerability of Coastal Communities to Extreme Storms: The Case of Revere, MA., USA." *Mitigation and Adaptation Strategies for Global Change* 3 (1): 59–82.

Curtis, Katherine J., Elizabeth Fussell, and Jack DeWaard. 2015. "Recovery Migration After Hurricanes Katrina and Rita: Spatial Concentration and Intensification in the Migration System." *Demography* 52 (4): 1269–93. doi:10.1007/s13524-015-0400-7.

Curtis, Katherine, and Annemarie Schneider. 2011. "Understanding the Demographic Implications of Climate Change: Estimates of Localized Population Predictions under Future Scenarios of Sea-Level Rise." *Population & Environment* 33 (1): 28–54. doi:10.1007/s11111-011-0136-2.

Cutter, Susan L., Bryan J. Boruff, and W. Lynn Shirley. 2003. "Social Vulnerability to Environmental Hazards." *Social Science Quarterly* 84 (2): 242–61. doi:10.1111/1540–6237.8402002.

Dasgupta, Susmita, Mainul Huq, and David Wheeler. 2015. "Drinking Water Salinity and Infant Mortality in Coastal Bangladesh." SSRN Scholarly Paper ID 2569459. Rochester, NY: Social Science Research Network. http://papers.ssrn.com/abstract=2569459.

De Beer, Joop. 1997. "The Effect of Uncertainty of Migration on National Population Forecasts: The Case of the Netherlands." *Journal of Official Statistics-Stockholm* 13: 227–44.

DeConto, Robert M., and David Pollard. 2016. "Contribution of Antarctica to Past and Future Sea-Level Rise." *Nature* 531 (7596): 591–97. doi:10.1038/nature17145.

DeWaard, Jack, Katherine J. Curtis, and Elizabeth Fussell. 2015. "Population Recovery in New Orleans after Hurricane Katrina: Exploring the Potential Role of Stage Migration in Migration Systems." *Population and Environment* 37 (4): 449–63. doi:10.1007/s11111-015-0250-7.

Dwyer, Anita, Christopher Zoppou, Ole Nielsen, Susan Day, and Stephen Roberts. 2004. *Quantifying Social Vulnerability: A Methodology for Identifying Those at Risk to Natural Hazards.* Citeseer. http://citeseerx.ist.psu.edu/viewdoc/download?doi=10.1.1.616.6484&rep=rep1&type=pdf.

Ezer, Tal, and Larry P. Atkinson. 2014. "Accelerated Flooding along the U.S. East Coast: On the Impact of Sea-Level Rise, Tides, Storms, the Gulf Stream, and the North Atlantic Oscillations." *Earth's Future* 2 (8): 2014EF000252. doi:10.1002/2014EF000252.

Fekete, Alexander. 2009. "Validation of a Social Vulnerability Index in Context to River-Floods in Germany." *Natural Hazards and Earth System Science* 9 (2): 393–403.

Fussell, Elizabeth, Katherine J. Curtis, and Jack DeWaard. 2014. "Recovery Migration to the City of New Orleans after Hurricane Katrina: A Migration Systems Approach." *Population and Environment* 35 (3): 305–22. doi:10.1007/s11111-014-0204-5.

Gardner, Alex S., Geir Moholdt, J. Graham Cogley, Bert Wouters, Anthony A. Arendt, John Wahr, Etienne Berthier, et al. 2013. "A Reconciled Estimate of Glacier Contributions to Sea Level Rise: 2003 to 2009." *Science* 340 (6134): 852–57. doi:10.1126/science.1234532.

Gemenne, François. 2011. "Why the Numbers Don't Add Up: A Review of Estimates and Predictions of People Displaced by Environmental Changes." *Global Environmental Change* 21: S41–49.

Grübler, Arnulf, Brian O'Neill, Keywan Riahi, Vadim Chirkov, Anne Goujon, Peter Kolp, Isolde Prommer, et al. 2007. "Regional, National, and Spatially Explicit Scenarios of Demographic and Economic Change Based on SRES." *Technological Forecasting and Social Change* 74 (7): 980–1029.

Haer, Toon, Eugenia Kalnay, Michael Kearney, and Henk Moll. 2013. "Relative Sea-Level Rise and the Conterminous United States: Consequences of Potential Land Inundation in Terms of Population at Risk and GDP Loss." *Global Environmental Change* 23 (6): 1627–36. doi:10.1016/j.gloenvcha.2013.09.005.

Hahn, Micah B., Anne M. Riederer, and Stanley O. Foster. 2009. "The Livelihood Vulnerability Index: A Pragmatic Approach to Assessing Risks from Climate Variability and change—A Case Study in Mozambique." *Global Environmental Change* 19 (1): 74–88.

Handmer, J.Y., Y. Honda, Z.W. Kundzewicz, N. Arnell, G. Benito, J. Hatfield, I.F. Mohamed, et al. 2012. "Chapter 4 Changes in Impacts of Climate Extremes: Human Systems and Ecosystems." In *Managing the Risks of Extreme Events and Disasters to Advance Climate Change Adaptation*, edited by C.B. Field, V. Barros, T.F. Stocker, D. Qin, D.J. Dokken, K.L. Ebi, M.D. Mastrandrea, et al., 231–90. A Special Report of Working Groups I and II of the Intergovernmental Panel on Climate Change (IPCC). Cambridge, UK, and New York, NY, USA: Cambridge University Press.

Hansen, James, Makiko Sato, Paul Hearty, Reto Ruedy, Maxwell Kelley, Valerie Masson-Delmotte, Gary Russell, et al. 2016. "Ice Melt, Sea Level Rise and Superstorms: Evidence from Paleoclimate Data, Climate Modeling, and Modern Observations That 2 C Global Warming Could Be Dangerous." *Atmospheric Chemistry and Physics* 16 (6): 3761–3812.

Hassani-Mahmooei, Behrooz, and Brett W. Parris. 2012. "Climate Change and Internal Migration Patterns in Bangladesh: An Agent-Based Model." *Environment and Development Economics* 17 (06): 763–80.

Hauer, Mathew E. 2017. "Migration Induced by Sea-Level Rise Could Reshape the US Population Landscape." *Nature Climate Change*. doi:10.1038/nclimate3271.

Hauer, Mathew E., Jason M. Evans, and Deepak R. Mishra. 2016. "Millions Projected to Be at Risk from Sea-Level Rise in the Continental United States." *Nature Climate Change* [advance online publication]. doi:10.1038/nclimate2961.

Hinkel, Jochen, Daniel Lincke, Athanasios T. Vafeidis, Mahé Perrette, Robert James Nicholls, Richard S.J. Tol, Ben Marzeion, et al. 2014. "Coastal Flood Damage and Adaptation Costs Under 21st Century Sea-Level Rise." *Proceedings of the National Academy of Sciences* 111 (9): 3292–97.

Hunter, Lori M., and Raphael Nawrotzki. 2016. "Migration and the Environment." In *International Handbook of Migration and Population Distribution*, edited by Michael J. White, 465–84. International Handbooks of Population 6. Springer, Netherlands. http://link.springer.com/chapter/10.1007/978-94-017-7282-2_21.

Ishiguro, A., and E. Yano. 2015. "Tsunami Inundation After the Great East Japan Earthquake and Mortality of Affected Communities." *Public Health* 129 (10): 1390–97. doi:10.1016/j.puhe.2015.06.016.

Kleinosky, Lisa R., Brent Yarnal, and Ann Fisher. 2007. "Vulnerability of Hampton Roads, Virginia to Storm-Surge Flooding and Sea-Level Rise." *Natural Hazards* 40 (1): 43–70.

Lam, N.S.-N., H. Arenas, Z. Li, and K.-B. Liu. 2009. "An Estimate of Population Impacted by Climate Change Along the U.S. Coast." *Journal of Coastal Research*, Proceedings of the 10th International Coastal Symposium ICS 2009, 2 (56): 1522–26.

Leiwen, Jiang, and Brian C. O'Neill. 2004. "Toward a New Model for Probabilistic Household Forecasts." *International Statistical Review* 72 (1): 51–64.

Leyk, Stefan, Galen J. Maclaurin, Lori M. Hunter, Raphael Nawrotzki, Wayne Twine, Mark Collinson, and Barend Erasmus. 2012. "Spatially and Temporally Varying Associations Between Temporary Outmigration and Natural Resource Availability in Resource-Dependent Rural Communities in South Africa: A Modeling Framework." *Applied Geography* 34: 559–68.

Lutz, Wolfgang, Sergei Scherbov, Gui Ying Cao, Qiang Ren, and Xiaoying Zheng. 2007. "China's Uncertain Demographic Present and Future." *Vienna Yearbook of Population Research* 5: 37–59.

McGranahan, Gordon, Deborah Balk, and Bridget Anderson. 2007. "The Rising Tide: Assessing the Risks of Climate Change and Human Settlements in Low Elevation Coastal Zones." *Environment and Urbanization* 19 (1): 17–37. doi:10.1177/0956247807076960.

McLeman, Robert A. 2013. *Climate and Human Migration: Past Experiences, Future Challenges.* Cambridge: Cambridge University Press. https://books.google.com/books?hl=en&lr=&id=99gaAgAAQBAJ&oi=fnd&pg=PR17&dq=+(McLeman+2013).&ots=PltjmIvkl2&sig=XK7tDLYuBYgZaJWVH0-NwPff1_4.

Miller, Brian W., and Jeffrey T. Morisette. 2014. "Integrating Research Tools to Support the Management of Social-Ecological Systems Under Climate Change." *Ecology and Society* 19 (3): 41.

Moftakhari, Hamed R., Amir AghaKouchak, Brett F. Sanders, David L. Feldman, William Sweet, Richard A. Matthew, and Adam Luke. 2015. "Increased Nuisance Flooding Along the Coasts of the United States Due to Sea Level Rise: Past and Future." *Geophysical Research Letters* 42 (22): 2015GL066072. doi:10.1002/2015GL066072.

Moss, Richard H., Jae A. Edmonds, Kathy A. Hibbard, Martin R. Manning, Steven K. Rose, Detlef P. van Vuuren, Timothy R. Carter, et al. 2010. "The Next Generation of Scenarios for Climate Change Research and Assessment." *Nature* 463 (7282): 747–56. doi:10.1038/nature08823.

Nakahara, Shinji, and Masao Ichikawa. 2013. "Mortality in the 2011 Tsunami in Japan." *Journal of Epidemiology* 23 (1): 70–73,

Nakamura, Takehiro, Chris Hutton, Xia Kunbao, and Jorge Gavidia. 2001. "Assessment of Vulnerability to Flood Impacts and Damages." In *Assessment of Vulnerability to Flood Impacts and Damages.* UN. Centre for Human Settlements (Habitat). Disaster Management Programme. http://bases.bireme.br/cgi-bin/wxislind.exe/iah/online/?IsisScript=iah/iah.xis&src=google&base=DESASTRES&lang=p&nextAction=lnk&exprSearch=14385&indexSearch=ID.

Neumann, Barbara, Athanasios T. Vafeidis, Juliane Zimmermann, and Robert J. Nicholls. 2015. "Future Coastal Population Growth and Exposure to Sea-Level Rise and Coastal Flooding — A Global Assessment." *PLOS ONE* 10 (3): e0118571. doi:10.1371/journal.pone.0118571.

Neumann, Kathleen, and Henk Hilderink. 2015. "Opportunities and Challenges for Investigating the Environment-Migration Nexus." *Human Ecology* 43 (2): 309–22.

Nicholls, Robert J., and Anny Cazenave. 2010. "Sea-Level Rise and Its Impact on Coastal Zones." *Science* 328 (5985): 1517–20.

O'Brien, Karen, Robin Leichenko, Ulka Kelkar, Henry Venema, Guro Aandahl, Heather Tompkins, Akram Javed, et al. 2004. "Mapping Vulnerability to Multiple Stressors: Climate Change and Globalization in India." *Global Environmental Change* 14 (4): 303–13.

Olfert, Alfred, Stefan Greiving, and Maria João Batista. 2006. "Regional Multi-Risk Review, Hazard Weighting and Spatial Planning Response to Risk-Results from European Case Studies." *Special Paper-Geological Survey of Finland* 42: 125.

Parris, A., P. Bromirski, V. Burkett, D. Cayan, J. Culver, J. Hall, R. Horton, et al. 2012. "Global Sea Level Rise Scenarios for the US National Climate Assessment." NOAA Tech Memo OAR CPO-1.

Raftery, Adrian E., Nan Li, Hana Ševčíková, Patrick Gerland, and Gerhard K. Heilig. 2012. "Bayesian Probabilistic Population Projections for All Countries." *Proceedings of the National Academy of Sciences* 109 (35): 13915–21. doi:10.1073/pnas.1211452109.

Refsgaard, Jens Christian, Jeroen P. van der Sluijs, Anker Lajer Højberg, and Peter A. Vanrolleghem. 2007. "Uncertainty in the Environmental Modelling Process–a Framework and Guidance." *Environmental Modelling & Software* 22 (11): 1543–56.

Rogers, Andrei. 1990. "Requiem for the Net Migrant." *Geographical Analysis* 22 (4): 283–300.

Runfola, Daniel Miller, Patricia Romero-Lankao, Leiwen Jiang, Lori M. Hunter, Raphael Nawrotzki, and Landy Sanchez. 2016. "The Influence of Internal Migration on Exposure to Extreme Weather Events in Mexico." *Society & Natural Resources* 29 (6): 750–54. doi:10.1080/08941920.2015.1076918.

Rygel, Lisa, David O'Sullivan, and Brent Yarnal. 2006. "A Method for Constructing a Social Vulnerability Index: An Application to Hurricane Storm Surges in a Developed Country." *Mitigation and Adaptation Strategies for Global Change* 11 (3): 741–64.

Seneviratne, Sonia I., Neville Nicholls, David Easterling, Clare M. Goodess, Shinjiro Kanae, James Kossin, Yali Luo, et al. 2012. "Changes in Climate Extremes and Their Impacts on the Natural Physical Environment." *Managing the Risks of Extreme Events and Disasters to Advance Climate Change Adaptation*, 109–230.

Shen, Shawn, and François Gemenne. 2011. "Contrasted Views on Environmental Change and Migration: The Case of Tuvaluan Migration to New Zealand." *International Migration* 49 (June): e224–42. doi:10.1111/j.1468-2435.2010.00635.x.

Small, Christopher, and Robert J. Nicholls. 2003. "A Global Analysis of Human Settlement in Coastal Zones." *Journal of Coastal Research* 19 (3): 584–99.

Strauss, Benjamin H., Remik Ziemlinski, Jeremy L. Weiss, and Jonathan T. Overpeck. 2012. "Tidally Adjusted Estimates of Topographic Vulnerability to Sea Level Rise and Flooding for the Contiguous United States." *Environmental Research Letters* 7 (1): 014033. doi:10.1088/1748-9326/7/1/014033.

Strauss, B.H., R.E. Kopp, W.V. Sweet, and K. Bittermann. 2016. "Unnatural Coastal Floods: Sea Level Rise and the Human Fingerprint on U.S. Floods Since 1950." Climate Central Research Report.

Sweet, William V., and Joseph Park. 2014. "From the Extreme to the Mean: Acceleration and Tipping Points of Coastal Inundation from Sea Level Rise." *Earth's Future* 2 (12): 2014EF000272. doi:10.1002/2014EF000272.

Tapsell, Sue M., Edmund C. Penning-Rowsell, Sylvia M. Tunstall, and T. L. Wilson. 2002. "Vulnerability to Flooding: Health and Social Dimensions." *Philosophical Transactions of the Royal Society of London A: Mathematical, Physical and Engineering Sciences* 360 (1796): 1511–25.

Tashakkori, Abbas, and Charles Teddlie. 2008. "Quality of Inferences in Mixed Methods Research: Calling for an Integrative Framework." *Advances in Mixed Methods Research*, 101–19.

Vincent, Katharine. 2004. "Creating an Index of Social Vulnerability to Climate Change for Africa." *Tyndall Center for Climate Change Research*. Working Paper 56: 41.

Walker, Warren E., Poul Harremoës, Jan Rotmans, Jeroen P. van der Sluijs, Marjolein BA van Asselt, Peter Janssen, and Martin P. Krayer von Krauss. 2003. "Defining Uncertainty: A Conceptual Basis for Uncertainty Management in Model-Based Decision Support." *Integrated Assessment* 4 (1): 5–17.

Warner, Koko, Kees van der Geest, Sönke Kreft, Saleemul Huq, Sven Harmeling, Koen Kusters, and Alex De Sherbinin. 2012. *Evidence from the Frontlines of Climate Change: Loss and Damage to Communities despite Coping and Adapation*. UNU-EHS. https://collections.unu.edu/view/UNU:1847.

Webster, P. J., G. J. Holland, J. A. Curry, and H.-R. Chang. 2005. "Changes in Tropical Cyclone Number, Duration, and Intensity in a Warming Environment." *Science* 309 (5742): 1844–46. doi:10.1126/science.1116448.

Weichselgartner, Jürgen. 2002. "About the Capacity to Be Wounded: The Need to Link Disaster Mitigation and Sustainable Development." *Extreme Naturereignisse–Folgen, Vorsorge, Werkzeuge, DKKV, Bonn*, 150–58.

Willekens, Frans, Douglas Massey, James Raymer, and Cris Beauchemin. 2016. "International Migration Under the Microscope." *Science* 352 (6288): 897–99.

Wilson, Tom, and Martin Bell. 2004. "Comparative Empirical Evaluations of Internal Migration Models in Subnational Population Projections." *Journal of Population Research* 21 (2): 127–60.

Wilson, Tom, and Phil Rees. 2005. "Recent Developments in Population Projection Methodology: A Review." *Population, Space and Place* 11 (5): 337–60. doi:10.1002/psp.389.

Wu, Shuang-Ye, Brent Yarnal, and Ann Fisher. 2002. "Vulnerability of Coastal Communities to Sea-Level Rise: A Case Study of Cape May County, New Jersey, USA." *Climate Research* 22 (3): 255–70. doi:10.3354/cr022255.

Yarnal, Brent. 2007. "Vulnerability and All That Jazz: Addressing Vulnerability in New Orleans After Hurricane Katrina." *Technology in Society* 29 (2): 249–55.

9

Qualitative research techniques

It's a case-studies world

François Gemenne

Introduction

Though recent years have witnessed a significant push for more robust quantitative studies (Kniveton et al. 2008, Gemenne 2011), the vast majority of work conducted on environmental migration and displacement remains rooted in qualitative studies. Most of our knowledge on the subject is derived from case-studies that were seeking to understand to what extent environmental changes were drivers of migration and displacement.

Some major collaborative research projects, which contributed much to the structuration of this emerging research field, were primarily collections of case-studies, compared with each other in order to identify explanatory patterns. This is for example the case of the EACH-FOR project, a pioneer European project that gathered 23 case-studies across the world between 2007 and 2009 (Jäger et al. 2009), and the *Where the Rain Falls* project, which looked at the influence of rainfall on food security and migration in eight case-studies from 2010–2012 (Warner and Afifi 2014).

Piguet (Chapter 2, this volume) and his team at the University of Neuchâtel (Switzerland) have conducted an impressive effort to document the development of research on environmental migration, through the compilation of the research database CliMig. They found that of studies published between 1980 and 2013, empirical case-studies represented about half the total of all publications on environmental migration and displacement, and a majority throughout the 2010s (Figure 9.1).

Though there is undeniably some geographical diversity in the case-studies covered, some countries have quickly become darlings of researchers, as they epitomised the challenges brought upon by environmental changes, and global warming in particular, on migration (Figure 9.2). This has been the case of Bangladesh, of course, but also of some Pacific island countries such as Tuvalu. A review of empirical studies conducted by Obokata et al. (2014) reached similar conclusions.

What explains this proliferation of case studies? Two factors can provide the beginning of an explanation. First, most of the initial research on the subject was devoted to the environmental causes of migration. Such research was also, albeit sometimes unknowingly, a militant research: one needed to show the very real human impacts of climate change for governments and others

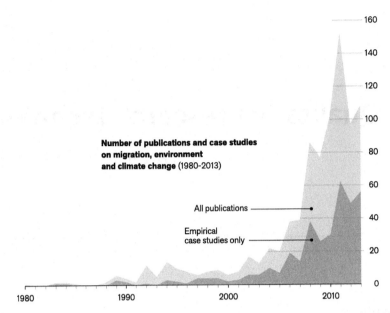

Number of publications and case studies
on migration, environment
and climate change (1980-2013)

All publications

Empirical
case studies only

Figure 9.1 Publications and case studies on migration, environment and climate change (1980–2013)

Source: Ionesco et al. 2016

to take it seriously. Case-studies provided the ideal vehicles for this objective. Second, the development of this emerging research field was largely driven by young and enthusiastic researchers, many of whom were doctoral students and postdoctoral fellows. Many of them had no spouse nor children, as well as limited teaching and administrative duties, and could therefore afford to spend several months on the field. This, combined with a sense of adventure and an aspirational desire to connect with people on the frontline of climate change, made it a favourable soil for the proliferation of case-studies.

Yet most case-studies focused on the causes of migration – other research questions appeared more recently, including critical research lead by scholars such as Baldwin (2013) and Bettini (2013). Therefore, though empirical case-studies have achieved a lot when it came to widening the geographical scope of research, there is now a growing perception that research needs to go beyond the environmental causes of migration and explore deeper, more complex questions (Piguet 2009). This chapter tries to situate how qualitative techniques can be instrumental in this endeavour.

Descriptive techniques

All qualitative techniques have in common that they focus on a small number of objects that are studied in detail in order to try and understand a larger, more complex reality. Within these, two families of qualitative techniques may be distinguished, following the classification of Piguet (2010): descriptive techniques and analytical techniques. Both will need to be combined if one is to fully understand this reality.

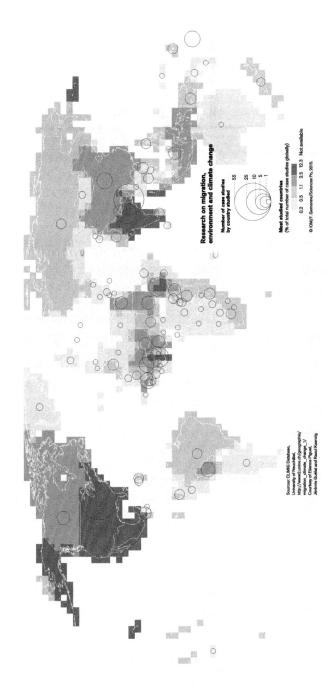

Figure 9.2 Publications and case studies on migration, environment and climate change, by country

Source: Ionesco et al. 2016

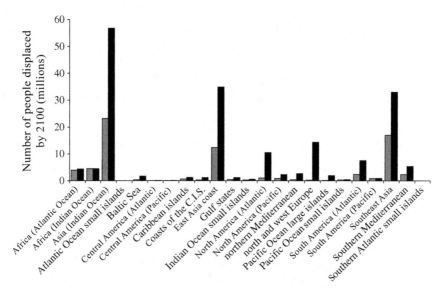

Figure 9.3 Projections of number of people to be displaced by sea level rise by 2100, by region
Source: Nicholls et al. (2011)

Descriptive techniques are often related to those used in natural sciences, and seek not just to describe a situation, but also to extrapolate and assess how it could evolve in the future. Such techniques will often try to map the regions of the world, or of a given country, that are at risk of environmental disruptions, often combining environmental and population data in some way (e.g. Cutter et al. 2000, O'Brien et al. 2004, Ishemo 2009). In that vein, such techniques have allowed for the production of vulnerability maps or indices, ranking countries or regions according to their level of vulnerability to environmental changes – often climate impacts (e.g. CARE International 2009). Though such maps or indices can provide useful tool to assess the vulnerability of a specific population or region and inform policymakers, they are also often rooted in a deterministic perspective, especially when they try to assess the number of potential migrants as a result of environmental disruptions. When employed in this fashion, the technique assumes that migration will be determined first and foremost by the extent of environmental disruptions, without necessarily considering other drivers and obstacles. For example, Figure 9.3 comes from a study that forecasts the number of people who would be displaced for different levels of sea level rise in various regions; such forecasts are made without accounting for the possibility of adaptation by means other than migration or relocation. Consequently, descriptive techniques are highly useful for identifying current patterns and processes of environmental migration and displacement, but alone often do not provide sufficient information to make future forecasts and predictions.

Analytical techniques

Analytical techniques, on the other hand, do not seek to describe a situation, but rather to answer a question. Most often, the question is related to the causes of migration, but other questions can also be addressed (though this has been the case only lately). Two categories of analytical techniques can be distinguished, those that rely on secondary data and those in which the researcher engages in direct data collection.

First are those studies that do not involve direct interactions with the populations under study: these can be described as *desk studies* that seek to infer individual and social behaviours from the observation and analysis of climate and population data, which can include remotely sensed data such as satellite imagery (e.g. Leyk et al. 2017), and other secondary sources. The technique of ecological inference (King 1997) is often implicit or explicitly embedded in such studies, which seek to reproduce individual behaviours on the basis of collective observations, relying on the idea that there is a correlation between a region's environmental, socio-economic, and migration patterns. Examples span a wide range of studies, from those that seek to identify the various dimensions of pastoralist mobility (Davies and Hatfield 2007) and those that have sought to identify linkages between environmental change, migration, and conflict in Africa (Brown et al. 2007). Systematic literature reviews, with or without accompanying statistical meta-analyses, have also been used to analyse environment-migration connections from secondary data, such as in the North American Great Plains (McLeman et al. 2013) and Sahelian Africa (Neumann and Hermans 2015); McLeman (2011) used this technique to identify environmental drivers of settlement abandonment from historical examples.

Time series or longitudinal studies offer opportunities further refinement, by seeking to understand the evolution of the environment-migration nexus over time, using different iterations of similar or comparable data.[1] Examples include studies of 1980s drought migration in Mali (Findley 1994) and of the linkages between migration, livelihoods, migration, and sustainability in coastal in Vietnam (Adger et al. 2002). Though such techniques can provide a useful way to objectify the relationship between environmental changes and migration, they typically require data that are often scarce and/or incomplete. Migration data, in particular, are often unreliable and patchy, as many developing countries simply lack the statistical apparatus that would allow them to monitor the movements of their population. However, researchers have shown the ability to use data collected for other purposes to opportunistically reanalyse and use in investigating environmental migration; Gray has been at the forefront of such techniques in recent years (Gray 2011; Gray and Mueller 2012). Such techniques are also often compounded by practical limitations: for example, provided they exist and are reliable, environment data are often difficult to study in conjunction with migration data, for the simple reason that they do not use the same spatial or temporal units of analysis. While migration data are collected using administrative boundaries, environmental data know no such boundaries. Weather records that are used for climate-migration research are often collected at specific points, and must in such cases be smoothed using various geomatic techniques before they can be used in conjunction with population data. The interoperability of the datasets is thus a crucial issue for inference techniques. The Mexican Migration Project (MMP) operated out of Princeton University is an example of a large dataset that includes environmental and population data that have been successfully mined and re-analysed by researchers interested in environmental migration patterns within Mexico and from Mexico to the US (Hunter et al. 2013, Nawrotzki et al. 2015).

Other techniques will involve direct interactions with the population under study, typically done through fieldwork using various data collection methods. The most commonly used are ethnographic techniques, entailing interviews with migrants and experts. The interviewing techniques can be diverse, from structured individual interviews with a common interview template to informal collective focus groups that allow for collective reactions to be observed. Mortreux and Barnett (2009) used the former method to investigate how climate change influences international migration from Tuvalu, whilst Veronis and McLeman (2014) used the latter method to assess environmental influences on the migration from Francophone countries in sub-Saharan Africa to Canada. Many researchers combine interviews and focus groups, potentially in conjunction with other qualitative, quantitative, and geomatic methods. For example, Wolf and Moser (2011) aggregated in-depth, mixed method studies from a variety of countries to analyse perceptions, attitudes, and the potential for engagement in adaptation to climate change, finding there exists considerable variation across social, cultural, and economic groups. Herrmann et al. (2014) merged focus group data with geospatial data to identify the impacts of changing vegetation patterns on livelihoods in Sahelian Africa, whilst Mertz et al. (2009) combined interviews with household surveys to assess agricultural adaptation to climate change in that same region. Systematic observation – be it participatory or passive observation – is also a widely used ethnographic technique that allows for a refined understanding of ongoing processes, though it typically does not allow for predictions or the collection of quantitative data. Participant observation was an important component of research done by Shen and Gemenne (2011) on how climate may influence migration from Tuvalu to New Zealand, and Nielsen and Reenberg's (2010) analysis of environmental drivers of rural change in Burkina Faso. An important reason for ethnographic techniques being used so frequently, including in multi-sited projects such as EACH-FOR and *When the Rain Falls*, is that they are inexpensive, and the research can be conducted by a lone researcher. Another form of direct data collection, household surveys, allow for the capture of data from a much larger sample of a given population than the aforementioned methds, usually using a standardised questionnaire. Though surveying is often considered a quantitative technique, it can also provide qualitative results, especially if some questions of the survey are open-ended. Studies by Meze-Hausken (2000) of drought migration in Ethiopia and Ng'ang'a et al.'s (2016) study of mobility and climate adaptation in Kenya offer useful examples of household survey-based research.

There is wide agreement, however, that there is no ideal qualitative research technique, and that each one has its own contingencies and is best suited to some particular context. Ideally, different techniques should be used together, so that each would offset the shortcomings of the other. This is the idea behind multi-level analysis, which is often considered an ideal approach that combines many of the aforementioned techniques. Such multi-level analyses, as good as they are, remain however difficult to perform: they require both significant funding, time, and the ability to access and process large volumes of data. Although multi-level analyses are often used in studies on demographic patterns and on the impacts of land use on the environment, they have to date rarely been employed in environmental migration research directly. One of the few, oft-cited examples of multi-level analysis of environmental migration was conducted by Henry et al. (2004) in Burkina Faso, the researchers having correlated data and surveys over a period of 40 years (1960–1999), and concluding that migration there was more influenced by slow-onset changes – such as desertification – rather than by sudden-onset, extreme events.

Conclusion

There is no perfect or ideal methodological technique: what is of greater interest is the research question. Until fairly recently, the principal research question that accompanied qualitative research on environmental migration was, why do people move (see Chapter 1, this volume). Ethnographic techniques were used to accumulate large inventories of case studies, answering the same question in different context. The considerable expansion of research on environmental migration in recent years means that new questions need to be explored, perhaps with a more critical look. The research challenge in the field in coming years is thus not simply exploring new places and developing new case studies, but is also about exploring new questions. To do this, combinations of qualitative and quantitative techniques, through mixed methods of analysis, should prove helpful. Until recently, these two types of techniques were used by different groups of environmental migration researchers working in relative isolation from one another. Combining both in more integrated approaches to research will prove instrumental in advancing knowledge in the field.

Note

1 Note that here the line becomes blurred between qualitative and quantitative methodologies, and the present chapter thus dovetails with Chapters 6 and 7 of this volume.

References

Adger, W. N., Kelly, P. M., Winkels, A., Huy, L. Q., & Locke, C. (2002). Migration, remittances, livelihood trajectories and social resilience. *Ambio, 31*(4), 358–366.

Baldwin, A. (2013). Racialisation and the figure of the climate-change migrant. *Environment and Planning A, 45*(6), 1474–1490. doi:10.1068/a45388

Bettini, G. (2013). Climate Barbarians at the gate? A critique of apocalyptic narratives on "climate refugees." *GeoForum, 45,* 63–72.

Brown, O., Hammill, A., & McLeman, R. (2007). Climate change as the "new" security threat: Implications for Africa. *International Affairs, 83*(6), 1141–1154.

CARE International. (2009). *In Search of Shelter: Mapping the Effects of Climate Change on Human Migration and Displacement.* Washington, DC: CARE International.

Cutter, S., Mitchell, J. T., & Scott, M. S. (2000). Revealing the vulnerability of people and places: A case study of Georgetown County, South Carolina. *Annals of the Association of American Geographers, 90*(4), 713–737.

Davies, J., & Hatfield, R. (2007). The economics of mobile pastoralism: A global summary. *Nomadic Peoples, 11*(1), 91–116.

Findley, S. E. (1994). Does drought increase migration? A study of migration from rural Mali during the 1983–1985 drought. *International Migration Review, 28*(3), 539–553.

Gemenne, F. (2011). Why the numbers don't add up: A review of estimates and predictions of people displaced by environmental changes. *Global Environmental Change, 21,* S41–S49. doi:10.1016/j.gloenvcha.2011.09.005

Gray, C. L. (2011). Soil quality and human migration in Kenya and Uganda. *Global Environmental Change, 21*(2), 421–430.

Gray, C., & Mueller, V. (2012). Drought and population mobility in rural ethiopia. *World Development, 40*(1), 134–145.

Henry, S., Piché, V., Ouédraogo, D., & Lambin, E. F. (2004). Descriptive analysis of the individual migratory pathways according to environmental typologies. *Population and Environment, 25*(5), 397–422.

Herrmann, S. M., Sall, I., & Sy, O. (2014). People and pixels in the Sahel: A study linking coarse-resolution remote sensing observations to land users' perceptions of their changing environment in Senegal. *Ecology and Society, 19*(3), 23.

Hunter, L. M., Murray, S., & Riosmena, F. (2013). Rainfall variation and U.S. migration from Rural Mexico. *International Migration Review, 47*(3), 874–909.

Ionesco, D., Mokhnacheva, D., & Gemenne, F. (2016). *The Atlas of Environmental Migration.* London: Routledge.

Ishemo, A. (2009). Vulnerability of coastal urban settlements in Jamaica. *Management of Environmental Quality, 20*(4), 451–459.

Jäger, J., Frühmann, J., Grünberger, S., & Vag, A. (2009). *EACH-FOR Synthesis Report.* Budapest: EACH-FOR.

King, G. (1997). *A Solution to the Ecological Inference Problem: Reconstructing Individual Behavior from Aggregate Data.* Princeton NJ: Princeton University Press.

Kniveton, D., Schmidt-Verkerk, K., Smith, C., Black, R., & IOM. (2008). *Climate Change and Migration: Improving Methodologies to Estimate Flows. IOM Migration Research Series* (Vol. 33). Geneva: IOM.

Leyk, S., Runfola, D., Nawrotzki, R. J., Hunter, L. M., & Riosmena, F. (2017). Internal and international mobility as adaptation to climatic variability in contemporary Mexico: Evidence from the integration of census and satellite data. *Population, Space and Place.* https://doi.org/10.1002/psp.2047

McLeman, R. A. (2011). Settlement abandonment in the context of global environmental change. *Global Environmental Change, 21*(supp), S108–S120.

McLeman, R. A., Dupre, J., Ford, L. B., Ford, J., Gajewski, K., & Marchildon, G. (2013). What we learned from the Dust Bowl: Lessons in science, policy, and adaptation. *Population and Environment, 35*(4), 417–440.

Mertz, O., Mbow, C., Reenberg, A., & Diouf, A. (2009). Farmers' perceptions of climate change and agricultural adaptation strategies in rural Sahel. *Environmental Management, 43*(3), 804–816.

Meze-Hausken, E. (2000). Migration caused by climate change: How vulnerable are people in dryland areas? *Mitigation and Adaptation Strategies for Global Change, 5*(4), 379–406.

Mortreux, C., & Barnett, J. (2009). Climate change, migration and adaptation in Funafuti, Tuvalu. *Global Environmental Change, 19*(1), 105–112.

Nawrotzki, R. J., Hunter, L. M., Runfola, D. M., & Riosmena, F. (2015). Climate change as a migration driver from rural and urban Mexico. *Environmental Research Letters, 10*, 114023.

Neumann, K., & Hermans, F. (2015). What drives human migration in Sahelian countries? A meta-analysis. *Population, Space and Place.* https://doi.org/10.1002/psp.1962

Nicholls, R. J., Marinova, N., Lowe, J. A., Brown, S., Vellinga, P., de Gusmao, D., . . . Tol, R. S. J. (2011). Sea-level rise and its possible impacts given a "beyond 4°C world" in the twenty-first century. *Philosophical Transactions of the Royal Society A, 369*(1934), 161–181.

Nielsen, J. Ø., & Reenberg, A. (2010). Temporality and the problem with singling out climate as a current driver of change in a small West African village. *Journal of Arid Environments, 74*, 464–474.

Ng'ang'a, S. K., Bulte, E. H., Giller, K. E., McIntire, J. M., & Rufino, M. C. (2016). Migration and self-protection against climate change: A case study of Samburu County, Kenya. *World Development, 84*, 55–68.

O'Brien, K. L., Leichenko, R., Kelkar, U., Venema, H., Aandahl, G., Tompkins, H., . . . West, J. (2004). Mapping vulnerability to multiple stressors: Climate change and globalization in India. *Global Environmental Change, 14*, 303–313.

Obokata, R., Veronis, L., & McLeman, R. (2014). Empirical research on international environmental migration: a systematic review. *Population and Environment.* doi:10.1007/s11111-014-0210-7

Piguet, E. (2009). Re-embedding the environment into migration theory. In *Conference: Remaking migration into migration theory: Intersections and cross-fertilisations.* University of Brighton and University of Sussex.

Piguet, E. (2010). Linking climate change, environmental degradation, and migration: A methodological overview. *Wiley Interdisciplinary Reviews: Climate Change, 1*(4), 517–524. doi:10.1002/wcc.54

Shen, S., & Gemenne, F. (2011). Contrasted views on environmental change and migration: The case of Tuvaluan migration to New Zealand. *International Migration, 49*(S1), e224–e242.

Veronis, L., & McLeman, R. (2014). Environmental influences on African migration to Canada: Focus group findings from Ottawa-Gatineau. *Population and Environment, 36*(2), 234–251.

Warner, K., & Afifi, T. (2014) Where the rain falls: Evidence from 8 countries on how vulnerable households use migration to manage the risk of rainfall variability and food insecurity. *Climate and Development, 6*, 1–17.

Wolf, J., & Moser, S. C. (2011). Individual understandings, perceptions, and engagement with climate change: insights from in-depth studies across the world. *Wiley Interdisciplinary Reviews: Climate Change, 2*(4), 547–569.

10

Incorporating Indigenous knowledge in research

Tristan Pearce

Introduction

Indigenous peoples are particularly sensitive to the effects of climate change due to their close association with, and dependence on, the natural environment for their lives and livelihoods (Ford 2012; Nakashima et al. 2012). Research on climate change impacts and adaptations has documented numerous examples of how Indigenous peoples are experiencing and responding to climate change, including among Inuit in the Canadian Arctic (Pearce et al. 2011; Ford et al. 2012), Sami reindeer herders in Norway (Forbes et al. 2016), Indigenous peoples in the South Pacific Islands (McCubbin et al. 2015), Aboriginal and Torres Strait Islanders in Australia (Petheram et al. 2010; Leonard et al. 2013), small-scale farmers in India (Rakshit and Bhowmick 2012) and pastoralists in Ethiopia (Debela et al. 2015). Some positive effects of climate change have been recorded, such as longer growing seasons for agriculture in some areas, but the overall effects of climate change for Indigenous peoples are believed to be negative.

Indigenous peoples are not passive victims of climate change, but are rather active players in both stabilizing the climate and adapting to adverse effects. Several studies conducted with Indigenous peoples suggest that Indigenous knowledge allows them to account for and deal with a large number of variations in the biophysical environment, including recent climate change (Nakashima et al. 2012; Pearce et al. 2015). In Paris in 2015, after twenty-three years of international meetings, the Conference of the Parties (COP) – the supreme decision-making body of the United Nations Framework Convention on Climate Change (UNFCCC) – officially recognized for the first time the important roles that Indigenous peoples, their rights and their traditional knowledge have in climate governance, setting the stage for serious conversations on how to include Indigenous peoples and their knowledge in climate change research and decision-making.

The 2015 Paris Agreement and implementing decisions included five explicit references to Indigenous peoples, their rights and their traditional knowledge. Notably, the agreement states:

> [P]arties acknowledge that adaptation action should follow a country-driven, gender-responsive, participatory and fully transparent approach, taking into consideration vulnerable groups, communities and ecosystems, and should be based on and guided by the

best available science and, as appropriate, traditional knowledge, knowledge of Indigenous peoples and local knowledge systems, with a view to integrating adaptation into relevant socioeconomic and environmental policies and actions, where appropriate.

Paris Agreement 2015: Article 7, paragraph 5 (UNFCCC 2015)

The Paris Agreement established a platform for the exchange of experiences and sharing of best practices on mitigation and adaptation between Indigenous and non-Indigenous peoples in a holistic and integrated manner. The creation of the platform recognizes that Indigenous peoples will need access to more western knowledge to support their own Indigenous knowledge about how to adapt to climate change and that Indigenous traditional knowledge is an asset for helping themselves, and other Indigenous and non-Indigenous peoples adapt to climate change (Paris Agreement 2015: Decision V, paragraph 135).

The Paris Agreement recognizes the role of Indigenous knowledge in climate governance but falls short on explaining how to operationalize it. Key discussions at COP22 and COP23 focused on how we move beyond recognition to operationalize Indigenous knowledge in climate change research and decision-making but with no concrete outcomes. This chapter explores this question and examines opportunities for the greater inclusion of Indigenous knowledge in climate change and other environmental change research.

What is Indigenous knowledge?

Achieving greater inclusion of Indigenous knowledge in research starts with understanding what Indigenous knowledge is and how it relates to other types of knowledge. Several, often complimentary, terms have been used to describe the knowledge of Indigenous peoples, including, but not limited to: *traditional knowledge (TK), traditional ecological knowledge (TEK), Indigenous knowledge (IK)* and *local knowledge (LK)*.

The term "traditional knowledge" (TK) is broadly defined as a cumulative body of knowledge, practice and values which have been acquired through experience, observation from the land or from spiritual teachings, and handed down from one generation to another (Huntington 1998; Noongwook et al. 2007; Cruikshank 1998). TK is built on personal experience and interaction with peers, including people from other communities (Huntington 1998; Berkes 1999) and passed on through stories, apprenticeship and practice (Condon 1996; Noongwook et al. 2007; Oskal et al. 2009). Some academics interpret the term traditional to imply "old" knowledge that, while interesting, does not necessarily have a role in modern society (Stevenson 1996). This perspective may be an interpretation of the vernacular definition of "tradition" – "a long-established custom or belief that has been passed on from one generation to another" (Oxford Dictionaries 2017). However, Bell (2002, p. 3) and others, in the context of *Inuit Qaujimajatuqangit (IQ)* – a term used in Nunavut, Canada to describe Inuit traditional knowledge – maintain that the term "traditional" is properly defined as "the Inuit way of doing things," and includes the past, present and future knowledge of Inuit society (IQ TaskForce 2002; Simpson 2004). In a practical sense, TK can thus be understood as knowledge and skills that are fluid, dynamic, flexible, adaptable and continually updated and revised in light of new observations and experiences, and the incorporation of new technologies alongside the traditional (Stevenson 1996; Berkes 1999; Usher 2000; Takano 2005; Bravo 2009).

The term "traditional ecological knowledge" (TEK) has been used by various commentators as a synonym for TK and/or referring specifically to those aspects of TK about the relationships of living beings (including humans) with one another and with their environment (Berkes et al.

1995; Wenzel 1999). Usher (2000) defines TEK as "all types of knowledge about the environment derived from the experience and traditions of a particular group of people." Usher (2000) uses the term TEK in the same way as Wenzel (1999), in preference to TK, because it is more specific. However, TEK is nonetheless also a problematic descriptor of Indigenous knowledge. As is the case with the use of traditional knowledge, by using the term traditional, there is a risk of implying a static or archaic form of knowledge that is inherently non-adaptive, when in fact the knowledge depicted by TEK is both evolving and current (Usher 2000). TEK does not appear to be treated as static or archaic in COP proceedings, but such attitudes toward Indigenous knowledge may subtly reside with some non-Indigenous actors (Nadasdy 1999). This is cause for concern, as the politicization of language could lead to the misinterpretation and/or dismissal of Indigenous knowledge in contemporary policy debates on account of its historical foundations. Irniq and Tester (2006) argue that definitions of Indigenous knowledge, referring specifically to Inuit knowledge, reflect what the dominant society sees as important. For example, the use of TEK emphasizes the ecological component of Indigenous knowledge rather than its spiritual foundations. TEK is often reduced to a source of "data" or factual information rather than being seen as a worldview and system of values and processes. This has been described as a process of "scientizing" Indigenous knowledge for use in and the consumption of Euro-Canadian society (Simpson 2004).

The terms TK and TEK are often interchanged with "aboriginal knowledge" or "Indigenous knowledge" (IK) (Stevenson 1996); however, TEK is not restricted by genetics or heritage to Aboriginal/Indigenous persons (Usher 2000). Usher (2000) suggests that "TEK could be characterized as the knowledge claims of those who have a lifetime of observation and experience of a particular environment and as a result function very effectively in that environment, but who are untutored in the conventional scientific paradigm" (186). The term "local knowledge" is sometimes used consistent with TEK to refer to community member's knowledge of the environment regardless of their intergenerational history (Neis et al. 1999). For the purposes of this chapter, we consider the term Indigenous knowledge to be synonyms and interchangeable with TK and TEK.

Bridging Indigenous knowledge and western science

Unlike the holism of Indigenous knowledge, western science tends to be reductionist and often focuses on understanding a single part of a larger complex system. This is the case for most climate change impact and adaptation research, which tends to focus on the direct relationships between individual climatic changes and human activities. A key question then becomes whether we should call for greater inclusion of Indigenous knowledge in research, which is for the most part driven by a western science paradigm, or should we call for a paradigm shift under which Indigenous knowledge and western science are on a more equal footing? To date, research and policy efforts have focused on the former, largely because western science is the dominant ontology that drives "academic" research but in doing so we may be missing critical insights held by Indigenous knowledge by reducing it to its parts and only including what fits within a western science construct.

Here I examine a case study that combined Indigenous knowledge and western science to examine environmental change in a river ecosystem. I use the case study to highlight the unique contributions Indigenous knowledge can make to research and discuss opportunities to facilitate greater inclusion of Indigenous knowledge in research, including expanding the research agenda to include Indigenous ontologies.

Case study of Indigenous knowledge in research

The study combined remotely sensed satellite imagery with TEK of Kabi Kabi Traditional Owners to document changes in mangrove extent over time, drivers of change and implications for ecosystem services on the Maroochy River, Sunshine Coast, Queensland, Australia (Brown 2016). Mangrove forests support a variety of ecosystem functions and services important for ecosystem health including filtering and removing toxins, cycling nutrients, preventing erosion, providing coastal defense and supporting valuable habitat for aquatic and terrestrial organisms. Despite the importance of mangroves for ecosystem health, however, mangrove forests world-wide are under serious threat from human development and climate change. Until now, most research on mangrove extent in Australia has drawn on approximately 40 years of remotely sensed imagery, a fraction of the time period needed to assess longitudinal change. This study extended the breadth and time scale of previous studies by combining remotely sensed satellite imagery with TEK of Kabi Kabi Traditional Owners. Data were collected using remotely sensed satellite imagery and participatory mapping together with semi-structured interviews using open-ended questions. The results show that mangrove extent in the lower Maroochy River has changed significantly since European colonization in the mid- to late 1800s, and has continued to decline in recent decades. The key drivers of past change were land clearing for cattle grazing and sugar cane production, and present drivers include agricultural activities, population growth, large-scale urbanization and discharge of pollutants and sewage. These changes have resulted in negative effects on ecological functions and ecosystem services, including compromising coastal protection, water purification, biodiversity and cultural services.

Considerations for the inclusion of Indigenous knowledge in research

The case study has important insights for how Indigenous knowledge can advance our understanding of environmental change. In this section, some challenges to including Indigenous peoples and their knowledge in research are discussed, followed by examples of how Indigenous knowledge can advance understanding of environmental changes, including climate change.

First, at the onset of the study, senior university academics in the biological sciences contested that TEK no longer existed for the study location as a result of colonization and the forced relocation of Indigenous peoples. They considered the Traditional Owners living on country[1] today to be disconnected with the TEK of their ancestors because their definition of TEK is rooted in the vernacular of "traditional" meaning old, historic knowledge, rather than dynamic, living knowledge that is constantly evolving with new experiences, observations and the advent of new technologies. This view, like many legislative definitions of what constitutes "traditional" or "cultural" is problematic for Indigenous peoples, particularly those living in peri-urban and urban areas such as the study site. This stereotype deprives people perceived as "non-traditional" or "disconnected" from country or culture, such as those living in urban areas, from due consideration to have their knowledge and experience included in research relevant to their lands. The case study research is testament to the resilience of Indigenous peoples and Indigenous knowledge systems despite undergoing widespread socio-economic-political and environmental changes.

Second, the research was initially designed based on western scientific principles, in which the system of interest, the Maroochy River, was reduced to its parts – the research foci was mangroves and specifically mangrove stands in three defined locations on the river. During pre-research consultations with Kabi Kabi Traditional Owners, it became evident that Traditional

Owners viewed mangroves as part of a larger complex interconnected system that includes other biological (e.g. salt marsh) and human features and behaviors (e.g. housing, infrastructure, use of the river) that are part of the river system, which itself is part of a larger ecosystem. For them, mangroves could not be isolated from these other parts, nor could the spiritual connection they have with the river be separated from the research. The spiritual connections the Kabi Kabi have with the Maroochy River is rooted in stories of their ancestors, which are brought to life through oral traditions, visiting culturally important sites on the river, and daily interactions with the ecosystem. It is this broader ontology of human-environment relations, including both empirical and non-empirical ways of knowing, that governs how Traditional Owners interact with the river and how they perceive river ecosystem health. The case study research recognized the spiritual components of TEK but did not explicitly include it in the research, a shortcoming of the research and something that is symptomatic of most efforts to include Indigenous knowledge in research.

Third, monitoring spatial changes in mangrove extent with Landsat satellite imagery is restricted in terms of data availability and sensor capabilities. Satellite imagery data showed general changes in mangrove extent over a short period of time (approximately forty years), leaving questions as to what mangrove extent was prior to European colonization. Moreover, course spatial resolution reduces the accuracy of land cover interpretation, which was particularly evident where small mangrove stands exist. The course resolution of the satellite images creates a high level of uncertainty and in many instances it is difficult to differentiate mangroves from other vegetation types, let alone identify specific mangrove species or the health of mangrove stands. Given the limitations of satellite imagery, Indigenous knowledge was invaluable for extending the time period over which change in mangroves could be assessed. Kabi Kabi Traditional Owners continue to live in close association with the Maroochy River ecosystem and hold a cumulative body of knowledge about ecosystem components and processes, including mangroves and salt marshes. This includes past knowledge of mangroves and salt marshes, passed down between generations through oral transmission, and contemporary understanding of ecosystem processes and change accrued through daily observations and interactions with the environment. Taken together, this knowledge provided longer-term data on changes in mangrove extent that pre-dated European colonization and the advent of satellite imagery.

Fourth, Traditional Owners identified and described key drivers of change in mangrove extent and provide detailed observations of changes in ecosystem function and services. The contributions to the research is twofold: relying on western scientific methods to identify drivers of change in mangrove extent is limited to making assumptions based on available data, whereas Traditional Owners were able to identify drivers of change not readily captured by satellite imagery, and Traditional Owners' knowledge of ecosystem change was highly detailed and rooted in personal observations and experiences. Key drivers of change in mangrove extent evident in satellite imagery and real-time assessment of the sites included mass deforestation and land clearing practices employed by early settlers for cattle grazing and sugar cane production, and more recent suburban development along the river. Other drivers of change that were not captured by these western scientific techniques but were identified by Traditional Owners included the removal of salt marshes for housing development and the negative effects on mangroves, run-off from agriculture, suburban development and sewage treatment plants entering the waterway resulting in widespread dieback of mangroves, and human activities such as wakeboarding and high-speed watercraft causing bank erosion and negative effects on mangroves. Traditional Owners provided highly detailed descriptions of individual storm events and resulting run-off entering the river, including the time and speed of onset, the effects of the events on mangroves and river health, and the longer-term response and sometimes recovery of the system. Western science tell us that these run-off events typically result in gross nitrogen, potassium and phosphorous absorption, which promotes above ground biomass production including new shoots and foliage but stunts the production of below-ground biomass such as complex root systems (Lovelock et al. 2015). Consequently, mangroves become more sensitive to saline conditions and periods of low rainfall and are highly compromised by erosional processes. Indigenous knowledge provides the context for these processes and extends understanding beyond cause-and-effect relationships to include descriptions of highly localized impacts and the resulting consequences for ecosystem services, such as the quality of fishing and crabbing.

Fifth, data from instrumental measurements of river health showed marginal changes in river health over time, but Traditional Owners described significant changes in river health over time, highlighting a difference between the two knowledge systems' approaches to monitoring and measuring ecosystem health. Instrumental measurements focus on single attributes in the environment (e.g. pH levels, electrical conductivity, turbidity, dissolved oxygen temperature and salinity), and samples are taken at certain locations on the river at specific times. Unless multiple samples are taken over an extended period of time and at different locations in the river, the data is limited spatially and temporally. For example, samples may be taken upstream of a point source of pollution or before a run-off event. In contrast, Indigenous knowledge held by Traditional Owners is cumulative and is based on repeated observations and experiences in the environment over time. Here, Traditional Owners described, in detail, changes in river health. Overall, these changes have been negative, and the current river health is heavily compromised compared to historic conditions. Traditional Owners described the clarity and taste of the water, the size and distribution of fish, the presence of wildlife and the visual health of mangroves, notably which species of mangroves were doing better than others under changing conditions. Interestingly, the baseline assessment of river health used by the local council is based on instrumental measurements taken after European colonization (after mass deforestation and intensive agriculture and cattle grazing along the river), whereas Traditional Owners' baseline assessment of river health is derived from oral traditions describing pre-European colonization and their current assessment is founded in first-hand observations and experiences on the river.

Moving forward

How do we move beyond the recognition of Indigenous peoples, their rights and their traditional knowledge to include Indigenous knowledge in climate change and other environmental change research and decision-making? It would have been a straightforward task to review how Indigenous knowledge has been included in research to date and highlighted the inadequacies of many of these attempts. This exercise, however, would have done little for advancing the current research agenda beyond adding to the growing body of critical geography. Instead, I have tried to highlight some key points to consider when including Indigenous knowledge in research and provided examples of the potential contributions of Indigenous knowledge to environmental change research. I offer these insights as suggestions and recognize that if, and how, Indigenous knowledge is included in research depends on the nature of the research question and the availability of Indigenous knowledge for the topic of interest.

While there is no one prescription or set of methods for including Indigenous knowledge in research, there are some universal principles that should generally guide the engagement of Indigenous peoples and knowledge in research. Notably, if the focus of the research is Indigenous peoples or their lands, there needs to be a commitment to research by, with and for Indigenous peoples. It makes practical and ethical sense to meaningfully engage the people who are the focus of the research and draw on all possible sources of information, including

Indigenous knowledge, to answer the research question. The next question is how should we engage Indigenous peoples in research and facilitate the sharing of Indigenous knowledge? This question has been the focus of anthropologists and geographers for generations and several approaches, methods and anecdotes have been offered (e.g. Smith 1999; Nickels et al. 2006; Pearce et al. 2009; Castleden et al. 2012). Noting research regulations, ethical responsibilities and cultural protocols specific to different peoples and regions, some universal guiding principles may start here: imagine that a team of researchers is interested in interviewing your mother, father, grandparents, siblings, spouse and/or children about their knowledge of the environment and places that are important to them. What courtesies would you like the researchers to take when approaching your family members to participate in the research, when entering their homes and when speaking with them? What courtesies would you like the researchers to take when collecting and storing the information your family members share, how would you like your family members to be acknowledged in the research and how would you like the researchers to return the research findings to your family? We can ask ourselves these questions and then apply the answers to how we approach working with Indigenous peoples and knowledge, and bestow the same courtesies we would expect other researchers to give members of our family to the people and knowledge that is the focus of our research. It may sounds simple, perhaps pedantic, but it is these basic human decencies that lay the foundation for more equitable and mutually beneficial relationships among researchers and Indigenous peoples.

The case study highlights important insights for the inclusion of Indigenous knowledge in climate and environmental change research. First, Indigenous knowledge is too often discussed in a way that it is disembodied from its ontological framing and there is a risk of instrumentalizing and misinterpreting Indigenous knowledge if ontology is ignored. Second, the term "traditional" when used as "traditional knowledge" or "traditional ecological knowledge" risks implying a static or archaic form of knowledge that is inherently non-adaptive, when in fact Indigenous knowledge is constantly evolving. Perhaps the term "cultural knowledge" would be a more appropriate term, to remove the ambiguity of "traditional" being interpreted as "old" knowledge or practices, and not restricting knowledge by genetics or heritage to Aboriginal/Indigenous persons recognizing that some non-Indigenous peoples also hold deep knowledge of the environment and place. Last, Indigenous knowledge should be collected and analyzed with the same level of rigor as other sources of knowledge, including western science. Indigenous knowledge is not synonymous with Indigeneity, nor do all people hold the same depth of knowledge about all things, and it is the responsibility of researchers to identify knowledge holders most relevant to their research question. In other words, inviting a person who identifies as Indigenous to be part of a research project or a policy discussion does not suffice for the inclusion of Indigenous knowledge. Moreover, different people hold different depths of knowledge. Some people may have detailed knowledge of fishing, others weather forecasting or traditional medicines, and so on. Empirical aspects of Indigenous knowledge such as that related to knowledge and use of the environment should be held up to the same standards of analysis as other sources of information. This means that single observations should be substantiated with interviews with other knowledge holders and narrative descriptions corroborated with other relevant sources of information (triangulation).

There continues to be persistent calls for greater inclusion of Indigenous knowledge alongside scientific knowledge in research and decision-making about climate change and environmental management. Most efforts have been limited to co-management agreements, structured on western scientific ideals, and the inclusion of Indigenous peoples at policy making tables, with less focus on Indigenous ontologies and ways of knowing. In the context of climate change, at the time of writing there have been twenty-three meetings of COP and twenty years of negotiations following the Kyoto Protocol (UNFCCC 1997) and little has been done to mitigate the climate crisis. It is time to consider other approaches and sources of knowledge for stabilizing climate change and adapting to its effects. This chapter offers some insights for the inclusion of Indigenous knowledge in climate and environmental change research, which may be useful for advancing the climate change research agenda from recognition of Indigenous knowledge to the operationalization of Indigenous knowledge in research and decision-making.

Acknowledgements

I respectfully acknowledge the Kabi Kabi peoples and their elders both past and present, who are the Traditional Owners and custodians of the country on which the case study research was conducted. I thank those members and friends of Bunya Bunya Country Aboriginal Corporation who generously contributed to the research. I respectfully acknowledge Inuit in the Canadian Arctic, specifically in Ulukhaktok, Northwest Territories whose knowledge and experiences contributed to the ideas shared in this chapter. Thank you also to members of the Environmental Change Research Group (ECRG) for intellectual input, notably Mathew Brown, Eric Lede and Rachele Wilson.

Note

1 "Country" meaning the family origins and associations between Aboriginal and Torres Strait Islander peoples and particular areas of Australia (Rose 1996).

References

Bell, M. 2002. Nunavut literacy development in the context of Inuit Qaujimajatuqanginnut (IQ) (Inuit Traditional Knowledge): A discussion paper. Inukshuk Management Consultants, Yellowknife.

Berkes, F., Folke, C., and Gadgil, M. 1995. Traditional ecological knowledge, biodiversity, resilience, and sustainability. In: Perrings, C., Mahler, K., Folke, C., Holling, C., Jansson, B., (Eds.), *Biodiversity conservation: problems and policies*. Kluwer Academic, Dordrecht (The Netherlands), pp. 281–299.

Berkes, F. 1999. *Sacred ecology: traditional ecological knowledge and management systems*. Taylor & Francis, Philadelphia and London.

Bravo, M.T. 2009. Voices from the sea ice: the reception of climate impact narratives. *Journal of Historical Geography* 35, 256–278.

Brown, M. 2016. *How times change: the use of traditional ecological knowledge and science to understand changes in mangrove extent and implications for ecosystem services*. B.Sc. Environmental Science Honours Thesis, Sustainability Research Centre, University of the Sunshine Coast, Queensland, Australia, 68p.

Castleden, H., Morgan, V.S. and Lamb, C. 2012. "I spent the first year drinking tea": Exploring Canadian university researchers' perspectives on community-based participatory research involving Indigenous peoples. *The Canadian Geographer/Le Géographe canadien* 56(2), 160–179.

Cruikshank, J. 1998. *The social life of stories: narrative and knowledge in the Yukon Territory*. UBC Press, Vancouver.

Condon, R.G., 1996. *The Northern Copper Inuit: A history*. University of Toronto, Toronto.

Debela, N., Mohammed, C., Bridle, K., Corkrey, R. and McNeil, D. 2015. Perception of climate change and its impact by smallholders in pastoral/agropastoral systems of Borana, South Ethiopia. *SpringerPlus* 4, 236.

Forbes, B., Kumpula, T., Meschtyb, N., Laptander, R., Macias-Fauria, M., Zetterberg, P., Verdonen, M., Skarin, A., Kim, K.Y., Boisvert, L.N., Stroeve, J.C. and Bartsch, A. 2016. Sea ice, rain-on-snow and tundra reindeer nomadism in Arctic Russia. *Biology Letters* 12, 20160466.

Ford, J. 2012. Indigenous health and climate change. *American Journal of Public Health* 102(7), 1260–1266.

Ford, J.D., Bolton, K.C., Shirley, J., Pearce, T., Tremblay, M. and Westlake, M. 2012. Research on the human dimensions of climate change research in Nunavut, Nunavik, and Nunatsiavut: A literature review and gap analysis. *Arctic* 65(3), 289–304.

Huntington, H., 1998. Observations on the utility of the semi-directive interview for documenting traditional ecological knowledge. *Arctic* 51 (3), 237–242.

IQ TaskForce. 2002. *First annual report.* Government of Nunavut. Iqaluit, Nunavut.

Irniq, P. and Tester, F. Inuit Qaujimajatunqangit: community history, politics and the practice of resistance. *Coastal Zone Canada 2006 Conference*, Tuktoyaktuk, NWT, 21p. 2006.

Leonard, S., Parsons, M., Olawsky, K. and Kofod, F. 2013. The role of culture and traditional knowledge in climate change adaptation: insights from East Kimberley, Australia. *Global Environmental Change* 23, 623–632.

Lovelock, C.E., Cahoon, D.R., Friess, D.A., Guntenspergen, G.R., Krauss, K.W., Reef, R., ... Saintilan, N. 2015. The vulnerability of Indo-Pacific mangrove forests to sea-level rise. *Nature* 22; 526(7574): 559–63.

McCubbin, S., Smit, B. and Pearce, T. 2015. Where does climate fit? Vulnerability to climate change in the context of multiple stressors in Funafuti, Tuvalu. *Global Environmental Change* 30, 43–55.

Nadasdy, P. 1999. The politics of TEK: Power and the "integration" of knowledge. *Arctic Anthropology*, 1–18.

Nakashima, D.J., Galloway McLean, K., Thulstrup, H.D., Ramos Castillo, A., and Rubis, J.T. 2012. *Weathering uncertainty: traditional knowledge for climate change assessment and adaptation.* UNESCO; Darwin: United Nations University, Paris. 120p.

Neis, B., Schneider, D.C., Felt, L., Haedrich, R. I., Fischer, J. and Hutchinon, J.A. 1999. Fisheries assessment: what can be learned from interviewing resource users? *Canadian Journal of Fisheries and Aquatic Sciences* 56(10), 1949–1963.

Nickels, S., Shirley, J., and Laidler, G. 2006. *Negotiating research relationships with Inuit communities: a guide for researchers.* Inuit Tapiriit Kanatami, Nunavut Research Institute, Ottawa.

Noongwook, G., The Native Village of Savoonga, The Native Village of Gambell, Huntington, H., George, J., 2007. Traditional knowledge of the bowhead whale (Balaena mysticetus) around St. Lawrence Island, Alaska. *Arctic* 60(1), 47–54.

Oskal, A., Turi, J.M., Mathiesen, S.D. and Burgess, P. (Eds.), 2009. *EALAT Reindeer herders' voice: reindeer herding, traditional knowledge and adaptation to climate change and loss of grazing land.* Report, 135p.

Oxford Dictionaries 2017. Definition of *tradition* in English, https://en.oxforddictionaries.com/definition/tradition

Pearce, T., Ford, J.D., Laidler, G.J., Smit, B., Duerden, F., Allarut, M., Andrachuk, M., Baryluk, S., Dialla, A., Elee, P. and Goose, A. 2009. Community collaboration and climate change research in the Canadian Arctic. *Polar Research* 28(1), 10–27.

Pearce, T., Ford, J.D., Duerden, F., Smit, B., Andrachuk, M., Berrang-Ford, L., and Smith, T. 2011. Advancing adaptation planning for climate change in the Inuvialuit Settlement Region (ISR): a review and critique. *Regional Environmental Change* 11(1), 1–17.

Pearce, T., Ford, J., Willox, A.C., and Smit, B. 2015. Inuit traditional ecological knowledge (TEK), subsistence hunting and adaptation to climate change in the Canadian Arctic. *Arctic* 68(2), 233.

Petheram, L., Zander, K.K., Campbell, B.M., High, C. and Stacey, N. 2010. 'Strange changes': indigenous perspectives of climate change and adaptation in NE Arnhem Land (Australia). *Global Environmental Change* 20, 681–692.

Rakshit, A., and Bhowmick, M.K. 2012. Unrealized potential of traditional knowledge in combating climate change. *SATSA Mukhapatra Annual Technical Issue* 16, 68–73.

Rose, D. B. 1996. *Australian aboriginal views of landscape and wilderness.* Australian Heritage Commission, Canberra.

Simpson, L., 2004. An Inuit way of knowing and the making of Nunavut. *Policy Options*, 1–12.

Smith, L.T. 1999. *Decolonizing methodologies: research and indigenous peoples.* Zed Books, London & New York.

Stevenson, M.G. 1996. Indigenous knowledge in environmental assessment. *Arctic* 49(3), 278–291.

Takano, T. 2005. Connections with the land: land-skills courses in Igloolik, Nunavut. *Ethnography* 6(4), 463–486.

UNFCCC 1997. Kyoto Protocol to the United Nations Framework Convention on Climate Change adopted at COP3 in Kyoto, Japan, on 11 December 1997.

UNFCCC 2015. *Adoption of the Paris Agreement.* Report No. FCCC/CP/2015/L.9/Rev.1, http://unfccc. int/resource/docs/2015/cop21/eng/l09r01.pdf

Usher, P. 2000. Traditional ecological knowledge in environmental assessment and management. *Arctic* 53(2), 183–193.

Wenzel, G. 1999. Traditional ecological knowledge and Inuit: reflections on TEK research and ethics. *Arctic* 52(2), 113–124.

11

Gender, migration and (global) environmental change

Giovanna Gioli and Andrea Milan

Introduction: (en)gendering migration and global environmental change

Most studies in the field of migration and global environmental change tend to neglect or underestimate the importance of gender in explaining drivers, processes and outcomes of migration. The integration of a gender dimension, if any, tends to be confined to the analysis of sex-disaggregated data, at times combined with an analysis of the specific needs and vulnerabilities of women and girls.

However, thinking about sex differences as a dichotomous variable is different from integrating more complex gender analysis and theory (Nawyn 2010:749). Gender refers to the identities, social attributes and opportunities associated with being male and female and the relationships between women, men, girls, boys, trans and intersex persons (modified from OSAGI 2001). These social attributes, identities, opportunities and relationships are socially constructed and they are context/time-specific and changeable. This means that there is no universal definition or description of women's or men's social attributes, identities, opportunities and relationships. This conception of gender also widens the field of inquiry beyond women to also consider men, LGBTI communities and the gendered dimensions of institutions, policies and other relevant structures. In most societies, there are differences and inequalities between women and men, girls and boys, and gender minorities in responsibilities assigned, activities undertaken, access to and control over resources, as well as decision-making opportunities. Gender is part of the broader socio-cultural context, and is used alongside other important criteria for socio-cultural analysis such as class, race, poverty level, ethnic group and age (OSAGI 2001).

Gender is an organizing principle in migration (Fitzpatrick 1997:23). However, relatively few studies on migration and global environmental change have explicitly looked at human mobility in the context of environmental change through gender lenses (e.g. Tacoli 2011; Hunter and David 2011; van der Land and Hummel 2013; Gioli et al. 2014; Tiwari and Joshi 2016; Bhatta et al. 2015; Velan & Mohanty 2015).

The majority of those that do have a regional focus on South Asia, where most of the early studies on gender and the environment emerged, from those that developed the ecofeminism perspective, arguing that women are eminently closer to and have a deeper understanding of nature and its protection than men (Mies and Shiva 1993), to those that critiqued ecofeminism's essentialist underpinning from a feminist political ecology perspective (e.g. Agarwal 1992; Rocheleau et al. 1996; Schroeder and Suryanata 1996; Gururani 2002; Sultana 2009).[1] Some of the few examples of empirical, longitudinal studies that conduct gender analyses as part of environmental migration dynamics also come from that part of the world. They highlight, for example, how in Nepal the effects of environmental change vary by gender and ethnicity, with women being more affected by changes in the time required to gather fodder, men by changes in the time gathering firewood, and high-caste Hindus generally being less affected than others by environmental change (Massey et al. 2010; see also Bohra-Mishra and Massey 2011; Shrestha and Bhandari 2007).

The role of gender in explaining determinants and impacts of migration in the context of global environmental change appears generally under-theorized and marginal at best. In fact, the few empirical studies available to date tend to use qualitative analyses deemed incompatible with theory building by scholars that employ more quantitative methods, on the grounds that they yield less generalizable and reliable data (Denzin and Lincoln 2000; Mahler and Pessar 2006: 31). This is reflected in a problematic lack of conceptualisation and suitably developed theoretical frameworks. First attempts at discussing gender in relation to the migration and climate change nexus in the policy literature (e.g. IOM 2014) rely on the small number of case studies that deal explicitly with the topic, and thus run the risk of over-generalising from a few, context-specific findings for the sake of providing policy recommendations.

This chapter provides an overview of existing literature that links gender to the migration and environmental change nexus (and highlights some of its shortcomings), whilst situating it in relation to literature from other germane areas of research, such as gender and environmental hazards/climate change, gender and development, as well as the broader migration scholarship. Following Hunter and David (2009), we identify two pathways through which global environmental change's gendered impacts on human mobility may manifest:

1) Increases in severity and/or frequency of extreme weather events.
2) Shifts in proximate natural resources and agricultural potential, i.e. changes in natural capital's availability, that push households to make adjustments in the use of other assets (financial, human, social capitals).

We delve into what we describe as the 'developmentalisation' of migration and climate; that is, the replication within this strand of literature of themes previously developed in the broader 'migration and development' scholarship (see Bettini and Gioli 2016). The increasing convergence of adaptation and development (the 'migration-as-adaptation' narrative) is analysed as a gendered discourse, one that articulates differentially through the lived experience of labour and remittance economies.

Gender and global environmental change: putting migration into the picture

The integration of gender concerns in the literature on global environmental change gained momentum in the early 2000s, with a special issue of the journal *Gender and Development* in 2002 providing some of the first seminal works on the topic that have since become key references for subsequent scholarship and policy analysis (e.g. Denton 2002; Nelson et al. 2002; Dankelman 2002). This early work led to the establishment of the transnational network "GenderCC (Women for Climate Justice)"[2] and, eventually, to a more coherent and strategic call for gender justice in international climate change negotiations, symbolized by the slogan "No climate justice without gender justice" introduced at the 2007 meeting of the Conference of Parties (COP13) to the UNFCCC (Terry 2009). The emergent 'gender and climate change' movement, encompassing academics, activists and grassroots organizations, has drawn heavily on earlier scholarly work in the environmental hazards tradition, as well as from the experience of the Gender and Disaster Network, established in 1997.[3] This body of work has brought to the fore the need for understanding ways in which gender relations are (re)negotiated and (re)produced vis-à-vis natural hazards and disasters (see Sultana 2010).

The hazard literature has considered how gender determines social spaces and availability or non-availability of opportunities to women and men, thereby influencing their vulnerability, as well as their ability to prepare, respond and recover in the wake of an environmental hazard. Existing vulnerabilities (often, but not always, overlapping with poverty) are further complicated by gendered power relations. In a nutshell, the key message of the hazard literature is that existing inequalities multiply vulnerability, and are exacerbated through disaster processes (e.g. Enarson and Morrow 1998; Enarson and Fordham 2001; Cannon 2002; Seager 2006, 2009; Ray-Bennett 2009). Feminists and political ecologists have long warned against the danger of essentialising the relation between gender and the environment without a relational and contextual understanding of gender as a power relation (e.g. Rocheleau et al. 1996; Sultana 2009; Elmhirst 2011).

The implication is that gender should not be conceived as simply being synonymous with 'women'. If gender is not understood and implemented as a relational, intersectional category, it is at risk of becoming reified in what could easily be translated as biological sex (see e.g. Batilwal and Dhanrah 2004; Froehlich and Gioli 2015). Equating gender to women might be strategically important in terms of advocating and lobbying for women's rights, but "it also has the potential to limit the attention to the complex ways that masculinities and femininities are constructed, negotiated, altered, and transformed through climate change processes" (Sultana 2014: 374). Neither women nor men are a homogenous category with the same needs and possibilities. Rather, gender needs to be seen in conjunction with other social identity markers, such as social class, age, sexual orientation, marital status, disability, urban/rural location and ethnic or religious background.

On top of this, reducing gender to a binary opposition of male and female obscures gender minorities. For instance, the literature on hazards and vulnerability largely ignores gender minorities with few notable exceptions (Cianfarani 2012; Dominey-Howes et al. 2014). Mustafa et al. (2015) have showed how in Pakistan, the transsexual, transgender and intersex population (known as *hijra*) of the twin cities of Islamabad and Rawalpindi are particularly vulnerable to flood, and less likely to be reached by the early warning system at place, or to be compensated for the loss.

This is why an intersectional or relational approach is needed in order to understand the complex interplay between gender and other identity markers (Myrttinen et al. 2014). Empirically, in gender-blind quantitative studies on the determinants and impacts of migration, the previously mentioned markers are very often considered 'control variables'. This implies on the one hand ignoring the gendered power relations in society that determine who moves, why and how, as well as their support networks when they move, their legal status and their subsequent economic, social and political opportunities; and on the other hand, missing the gender dimension of migration and its variations over space and time.

Clearly, when it comes to the first pathway identified by Hunter and David (2009), 'increases in severity and/or frequency of extreme weather events' triggering displacement and forced mobility, there is a lot to harvest from the hazard literature mentioned previously. Gender considerations and analysis shall be integrated in all the phases of the migratory process (before, during and after displacement).

The understanding of differentiated vulnerability is key to making sense of the availability (or not) of mobility options vis-à-vis environmental hazards. Who is able to move, how, when and where are crucial questions, but gendered differentiations in access to mobility are often overlooked in current research on the impacts and outcomes of natural hazards. For example, during the displacement phase immediately after a natural disaster event, certain sectors of the affected population are more likely to undergo deprivation or experience violence. By comparison, literature on conflict-related displacement and Internally Displaced Persons (IDPs) offers valuable methods and insights that might be utilised in the context of environmental displacements. Few studies have addressed the issue of Gender Based Violence (GBV) in the context of disasters, mostly coming from the community of practitioners (e.g. WEDO 2008; Le Masson et al. 2016), and focusing solely on women and girls.

Chindarkar (2012) has made a welcome first attempt to apply knowledge gathered in the gender and climate change literature to analysing the links between gender, migration and climate change. As illustrated in Table 11.1, the author follows the IPCC trinity of Sensitivity, Exposure and Adaptive Capacity, and draws examples from the vulnerability literature, highlighting the gender dimension, as well as the phase of migration in which gendered vulnerability seemed to play a role. In doing so, the author reveals many of the shortcomings and contradictions that are inherent to the case studies or descend from overgeneralising and oversimplifying their results. First, all the case studies highlight women-specific vulnerabilities and use gender as a synonym for women. This essentialises women as a fictitious monolithic category, ignoring questions of scale (see Massey 1994), context-specificity, generational processes (Tacoli and Mabala 2010), power relations, belonging and membership (Donato et al. 2006), which are necessary for gender analysis. The outcome of the "women-only" narrative is a binary, contradictory narrative that portrays women simultaneously as victims and as solution providers (Sultana 2014). As Chindarkar observes: "migration outcomes of climate change are also gendered. On the one hand they may seem to be empowering women, while on the other they may actually exacerbate their socio-economic status and make them worse off" (Chindarkar 2012: 6). Women (as a homogenous category) are simultaneously portrayed as "agents of adaptation" and as "most vulnerable to climate change". This collapsing of gender-as-women has been common in the wider gender and climate change literature, and is here acritically reproduced in relation to human mobility. One consequence is the emergence and reproduction of overly simplistic storylines in policy circles and the popular media, such as "women will be disproportionately affected by climate change", that are ultimately counter-productive for addressing real gendered vulnerabilities and the power structures that (re)produce them.

Gender and the migration-as-adaptation discourse

The second pathway that we have identified, i.e. "shifts in proximate natural resources and agricultural potential" (Hunter and David 2009: 3), builds on the Sustainable Livelihood Approach (SLA) and assumes that changes in natural capital's availability will push households to make adjustments in the use of other assets (financial, human, social, etc.).

Labour migration is a livelihood diversification option overwhelmingly undertaken in LDCs where households whose members cannot afford formal insurance, social security and other risk-mitigation mechanisms need to diversify their income and mitigate the risk (economic, environmental) they are exposed to.

Table 11.1 Framework to operationalise and examine vulnerability to climate change-induced migration and their gender dimensions

Vulnerability component	Indicators	Gender dimensions or differential impacts on women	Phase of migration	Case example (where available)
Exposure	Climate, Variability, Frequency of environmental hazards	Due to cultural constraints on women's mobility, there is evidence that women are more likely than men to die during environmental disasters or during the process of migration.	Pre- or during migration	Women in Bangladesh were found to be more vulnerable to cyclones because cultural norms prevented them from leaving their homes on time and learning to swim (Nelson et al. 2002).
Sensitivity	Water sensitivity,	Due to women's distinct roles in water collection and use, water stress would result in increased burden on women due to increase in time spent and distance travelled to collect water before and after migration.	Pre- or during migration,	Water stress due to climate change is expected to cause further difficulties for women in West Africa (Denton 2002).
	Land sensitivity,	Women's informal rights to resources could decrease or disappear as access to land and natural resources dwindle due to climate change-induced migration.	Post-migration,	Many women were permanently displaced post-Hurricane Katrina due to lack of housing ownerships (Willinger 2008).
	Food sensitivity,	Due to household level differences in food distribution, low productivity due to climate change may result in further deterioration in nutritional status for women post-migration.	Post-migration	Women's pre-disaster low nutritional status in Bangladesh was found to have worsened post-disaster (Cannon 2002).
	Economic sensitivity,	Due to women's low economic freedom, they have fewer resources to cope with the adverse impact of climate change, or engage in migration.	Pre-migration,	Post-Hurricane Andrew, poor female-headed households were less able to provide immediate relief to their families (Enarson and Morrow 1998).
	Perceived sensitivity,	Women tend to perceive migration risks more seriously because of their engagement in caregiving and preparedness activities.	Pre- or during migration	Post-Hurricane Bonnie, women were found to be more likely to feel threatened and evacuate due to their caregiving roles (Bateman and Edwards 2002).

(Continued)

Table 11.1 (Continued)

Vulnerability component	Indicators	Gender dimensions or differential impacts on women	Phase of migration	Case example (where available)
Adaptive Capacity	Education,	Women are generally less educated than men and have fewer vocational skills, which would make it difficult for them to find formal employment after being forced to migrate.	Post-migration,	Post-cyclones and floods, displaced women in Bangladesh were forced into labour-intensive and low-paying jobs due to the low levels of education (Kakissis 2010).
	Health,	Women's low nutritional status may put them at high health risk both following the environmental disaster as well as after migrating to a new place.	During and post-migration,	Post- El Niño, displaced women in Peru were found to be disproportionately exposed to epidemics and health risks such as peri- and post-partum illnesses (Reyes 2002).
	Livelihood diversification,	Women primarily engaged in agricultural labour have limited fallback options to spread their risks and therefore lack the adaptive capacity to cope with climate change-induced migration.	Post-migration,	Women from the fishing community in the Philippines facing climate disasters were forced to work as domestic helps due to lack of skills (UNFPA 2009).
	Safety net and social safeguard,	Communities where women effectively engage in natural resources management may also have better adaptive capacity to recover from the climate disaster and avoid migration.	Pre-migration,	Mama Watoto Women's Group in Kenya has successfully addressed issues of loss of biodiversity and scarcity of fuelwood through collective participation and cooperation (Aguilar 2009).
		Strong social networks of women with extended family members or neighbours may prevent individuals and families from seeking shelter elsewhere.	Pre-migration,	
	Technological capacity	Women having access to agricultural technology such as new crop varieties, may be better able to adapt to climate change and avoid migration.	Pre-migration,	Positive effects of technological capacity on climate change adaptation were found among women in the Ganga basin in Bangladesh, India and Nepal (Mitchell et al. 2007).
		Women having access to TV, radio or mobile phones may be able to forewarn their families and the larger community of the impending climate risks and consequently avoid migration or relocate to safer locations.	Pre- or during migration	Providing mobile phones to vulnerable communities in the Lower Mekong Basin in Vietnam was found to increase the effectiveness of response to the 2008 flood season (Ospina and Heeks 2010).

Source: Chindarkar (2012: 4)

Since the late 2000s, the merging of the Sustainable Livelihood Approach (SLA) with the New Economic of Labour Migration (NELM) has provided the theoretical base for a new generation of studies within the migration and climate change research area (see Kniveton et al. 2008). In fact, "both approaches can be easily integrated if we see internal as well as international migration as part of a broader household livelihood strategy to diversify income and overcome development constraints in the place of origin" (de Haas 2010: 245).

The emergent 'migration-as-adaptation' approach was first developed in McLeman and Smit (2006), then developed further by Tacoli (2009) and popularized by the influential Foresight Report (2011) on migration and global environmental change. This approach frames human mobility as a livelihood strategy undertaken by households to diversify their income sources and mitigate the risks associated with a range of potential stressors, including climatic stressors (that may have an influence, for instance, on agricultural productivity and cause losses of livestock) (Warner and Afifi 2014). Proactive labour migration can be used as a self-insurance mechanism, providing vulnerable households with a source of income (remittance) which is not threatened by local stressors and risks (Yang and Choi 2007). Labour migration, including short-term and short-distance mobility (Milan and Ho 2014), is hence understood as a potential adaptation strategy aimed at reducing the vulnerability of populations at risk (Black et al. 2011). Remittances are seen as something to be leveraged and invested at household and community levels in order to build resilience (Warner and Afifi 2014), and mobility thus becomes a mechanism for fostering development and reducing vulnerability.

By emphasizing the importance of labour migration and remittances, the migration-as-adaptation approach mimics many of the arguments developed within the broader 'migration and development' field that emerged in the 1990s and boomed following Ratha's (2003) article "Workers' Remittances: An Important and Stable Source of External Development Finance". It is therefore possible to speak of a 'developmentalisation' of the discourse on global environmental change and migration (Bettini and Gioli 2016). In a nutshell, the argument goes, since international remittances dwarf official development assistance and are rising faster, they should be leveraged for both development and climate adaptation purposes. Migrants are thus depicted in policy circles as 'champions of development' and 'agents of adaptation' simultaneously. However, common critiques levelled at both NELM and SLA put forward by political ecologists and critical geographers have not been taken into full consideration by the proponents of the 'migration-as-adaptation' thesis, and scholars have warned against 'remittances euphoria' and its neoliberal underpinnings that put the burden of development (and adaptation) on the shoulder of migrants rather than governments (Kapur 2005; de Haas 2012; Gamlen 2014).

Both NELM and SLA have been criticized for overlooking unequal gendered power relations between and within communities, including between migrants and non-migrants in areas of destination (Arango 2000; de Haas 2010; Kunz 2011; Lindley 2009). The attention to the household as decision-making unit has also been criticized, as it ignores intra-household and inter-generational dynamics that shape migration decision-making and processes (Thieme 2011), and are crucial for gender analysis.

In line with other mainstream approaches to migration, NELM scholars often gives for granted that migrants are 'men', completing ignoring the fact that almost 50% of the world's international migrants are women (United Nations 2015a), the copious literature on feminization of migration (e.g. Piper 2008; Silvey 2004), and the long established fact that 'birds of passage' are also women (Gabaccia and Donato 2015; Morokvasic 1984). Research on international migration and transnationalism also often lacks detailed gender analysis (Pessar and Mahler 2003). A gender-relational perspective is completing missing from these approaches, hence the intersection of gender with other crucial identity markers such as race, is completely overlooked.

These critiques hold true for the 'remittances for adaptation' literature, which is mostly gender-blind and ignores the racial underpinning of the climate change and migration debate and its new racial vocabulary that distinguishes would-be migrants on the basis of their adaptive and maladaptive capacities (Baldwin 2017).

In the global South, circular labour migration as a livelihood diversification strategy is often a highly gendered process, with male out-migration and the concomitant 'feminization of agri-culture' and agrarian transition. In the 'Gender and Development' literature, a significant number of scholars have considered the gender dimensions of agrarian transformation, especially in rela-tion to land rights and land grabbing issues (e.g. Agarwal 1994), but migration literature has been slow in taking advantage of this, and still a relatively small number of studies have addressed the nexus between gender, migration, and agrarian transition in the global South (e.g. Kelly 2011).

Environmental change is indubitably a key factor in shaping (gendered) labour migration fluxes in the global South. Much work is needed in order to unpack the relations between migra-tion, environmental change and other drivers of change like fast-paced urbanisation and glo-balisation that are transforming developing countries, beyond the narrow focus on remittances.

The global remittances trend and its gendered blindspots

Whilst remittances are nothing new, Kunz (2011) identifies a recent Global Remittances Trend (GRT), that signifies a change in "the way in which remittances have become a global object of knowledge, and migration and development have become linked in theoretical and practical ways" (Kunz 2011: 1). Kunz highlights how the GRT discourse and its conceptual apparatus are not gender-neutral, but rather gender-blind. The remittances-as-development perspectives tend to either ignore or underestimate the gender dimension of migration and the labour market both at origin and destination, where horizontal and vertical occupational sex segregation and gender pay gaps persist. Moreover, women tend to be overrepresented in the informal economy, precarious work and in low-paid jobs (e.g. in agriculture, homework, care work and domestic work), and may have a harder time accessing job opportunities.

Kunz identifies the key elements which make the GRT discourse appear gender-neutral, i.e. the narrow financial definition of remittances as a sum of money, the level of abstraction at which the GRT is generally framed and the exclusive choices of actors deemed relevant and legitimate within the GRT (Kunz 2011). Elements of the GRT discourse are embedded in key current global policy processes. For instance, the exclusive focus on reducing transaction costs for remittances in the 2030 Agenda for Sustainable Development (SDG target 10.c) and the Addis Ababa Action Agenda (paragraph 40) comes at the expense of financial inclusion, which is an extremely important problem for those women left behind who cannot access and/or use remittances (Deere et al. 2015).

Another issue associated with the GRT and remittances-centred literature from a gender perspective is that it tends to generalize time- and context-specific conclusions based on sex-disaggregated data, with scant gender analysis and lack of longitudinal data. For example, state-ments such as "a frequent finding is that women are the more consistent remitters; they send larger amounts, and they do so more regularly than men" (Rahman 2012: 4), essentialise a context-specific finding that holds true in certain cases (see, e.g. Collinson et al. 2006 on South Africa or Curran and Saguy 2001 on Thailand, or Orozco et al. 2006), but it's not true in many other cases where 'men remit more than women' (see e.g. Semyonov and Gorodzeisky 2005 on the Philippines). In addition, whilst the collection of sex-disaggregated data is crucial, gender analysis cannot be reduced to an allegedly higher propensity of 'women' to remit, which just (re)produces stereotypes on the alleged instinctive 'caregiving nature' of women, understood as a homogeneous, monolithic category. Women are also often depicted as more 'altruist', sacrificing for the family rather than for their own individual interest (see e.g. Barbieri and Carr 2005). Without proper analysis of power relations at several scales, such findings make very little sense. Similarly, slogans such as 'women spend remittances better than men' are frequent in both the academic and policy literature. Hence, scientific studies on the gender-migration-environment nexus shall bring sound empirical evidence, beyond misleading slogans. On the one hand, the collection of sex-disaggregated data on remittances must be encouraged and supported; on the other hand, gender analysis must go beyond this, and use a relational approach (see previous) in order to understand what intersection with other social markers plays a role in creating vulnerability or agency, and hence provide robust evidence to the policy community.

Policy processes, gaps and ways forward

Research on gender in relation to the migration and environmental change nexus is still in its infancy. Because the number of empirical studies on migration and global environmental change that take into account gender concerns is limited, there has been repeated reproduction of a limited number of findings that are oversimplified and de-contextualised, sometimes making their way into policy recommendations. Scholars should be conscious to avoid simplistic descriptions of women in heteronormative, universal and static terms. At the same time, progress has been made in related areas of study such as gender and migration, gender and environmental hazards/climate change, and gender and development. Despite clear overlap between these study areas and related approaches, there has been so far scant cross-fertilizing across disciplines.

Particularly in 2015 and 2016, global leaders have recognized at the United Nations that collecting gender-disaggregated data is a necessary first step for achieving sustainable development leaving no one behind, including migrant women and men. In fact, target 17.18 of the 2030 Agenda for Sustainable Development on "enhancing capacity-building support to developing countries to increase significantly the availability of high-quality, timely and reliable data" highlights that such data should be disaggregated by a number of factors, including age, sex and migratory status (United Nations 2015b: 23). Yet, data collection is challenging in many ways. The 2013 report of the Statistical Commission of the United Nations on the state of gender statistics across national platform shows the percentage of countries regularly producing sex-disaggregated statistics by topic (Table 11.2). It is worth noting that sex-disaggregated water statistics are amongst the least available, whereas they are a necessary prerequisite for researchers working on the environment-migration nexus. In the 1980s, sex-disaggregated data started to be collected in relation to human mobility. However, recent UNDESA data from 1990–2010 shows that the number of countries with sex-disaggregated migration data has actually decreased (Hovy 2013, cited in Fleury 2016).

The increasing focus on data disaggregation by sex in global policy debates offers an entry point for scholars working on gender and migration in the context of global environmental change to integrate a gender perspective in such debates. In order for this to happen, qualitative migration research – more typically adopted by feminist migration scholars – needs to be better integrated within traditional quantitative migration research.

From an empirical point of view, recent multi-country literature on migration in the context of global environmental change tends to take the household as the main unit of analysis, hindering the analysis of power relations within communities and within households that shape migration patterns and outcomes (Tacoli and Mabala 2010; Warner and Afifi 2014). Gender analyses must move beyond the 'add women, mix and stir' or the 'sex as a variable' approach and integrate a broader gender analysis, which involves an intersectional approach to gender in

Table 11.2 Percentage of countries "regularly" producing gender-disaggregated statistics on selected topics

Topic	Percentage
Mortality	85% *(highest)*
Labour force	83%
Education & training	81%
Poverty	71%
Agriculture	44%
Access to sanitation	39%
Access to clean water	37%
Informal employment	37%
Media	15%

Source: Fletcher (2014)

conversation with elements such as race, class, generation and sexuality that migrants experience (Hondagneu-Sotelo 2000; Indra 1999). Data disaggregation by sex, including disaggregation of households by the sex of its head, is a necessary yet insufficient basis for the integration of a gender perspective, because it overlooks the social dynamics and inequalities hidden behind the data. Moreover, any analysis based on a binary comparison of men and women implies that the situation of LGBTI is completely neglected.

The next generation of research on migration and global environmental change must integrate a strong relational gender perspective in order to bridge the gaps we have identified in this chapter, and harvest the benefit of more contamination across discipline and inter-disciplinary research.

Going back to the classification put forward by Hunter and David (2009), the two most common lenses with which we can look at the gender-global environmental change-migration nexus are extreme weather events, and changes in natural capital as proximate cause influencing decision-making at the household levels. We suggest a set of methods and issues for each of the two in the context of key ongoing policy processes.

Pathway 1: extreme weather events, hazards and displacement

The current international policy context is conducive to the integration of a strong gender perspective into debates around forced migration scenarios in the context of global environmental change.

The integration of a gender perspective is included in the task force on climate-related displacement, which was agreed upon at the 21st Conference of the Parties to the UNFCCC (COP21) in Paris in December 2015. This task force aims at developing recommendations for integrated approaches to avert, minimize and address displacement related to the adverse impacts of climate change.

Another ongoing process offering avenues for better gender integration is the Platform on Disaster Displacement, launched in May 2016 at the World Humanitarian Summit, which aims to implement the recommendations of the Nansen Agenda for the Protection of Cross-Border Displaced Persons in the Context of Disasters and Climate Change that was endorsed by 109 governmental delegations at a Global Consultation in October 2015. The Platform started its work on July 2016 and it will play a key role in bridging the current legal gaps for persons displaced across borders by natural disasters and the adverse impacts of climate change.

In order to integrate a gender perspective in environmental displacement, there is much to learn from both the environmental hazards and conflict research on the way in which femininities and masculinities play a role and are negotiated and contested in various phases of environmental displacement (before, during and after displacement occurs). Research on migration and global environmental change tends to ignore important issues related to forced movement, including sexual and gender-based violence (that is not restricted to girl and women, see e.g. Myrttinen et al. 2014), and access to justice. For instance, the issue of the links between environmental displacement and trafficking is completely unexplored.

Pathway 2: changes in natural capital and the 'developmentalised' narrative

As illustrated previously, the migration and global environmental change literature has adopted narratives and conceptual tools belonging to the 'migration and development' scholarship.

Scientific debates increasingly recognize the interconnectedness of climate change adaptation and sustainable development (Denton et al. 2014), and this recognition is reflected in global policy debates. For example, targets associated with Sustainable Development Goal (SDG) 13 "Taking urgent action to combat climate change and its impacts" focus on building adaptive capacity and resilience (13.1), as well as integrating climate change considerations into national policies, strategies, and planning (13.2) (United Nations 2015b: 20). In this respect, SDG 13 has similar objectives to the National Adaptation Plan (NAP) process to be undertaken by both least developed countries (LDC) and non-LDC countries in accordance with the United Nations Framework Convention on Climate Change (UNFCCC), the goals of which are to identify medium- and long-term adaptation needs and to generate and implement strategies and programmes to address those needs.

From this perspective, there is a need to move beyond remittances and SLA and NELM approaches that are gender-blind and do not account for broader dynamics and intergenerational dynamics. More integration with the literature on gender and development, and agrarian transition, is needed. A feminist political ecology framework proves particularly useful in allowing a nuanced analysis of the complex intersections of knowledge, power and practice in nature-society struggles. It allows seeing that "what happens on the ground is far from simple binaries of 'women' losing or winning" (Joshi 2015: 166) and unpacking what makes for "women", "household" or the "poor" (Rocheleau 2008: 7) through a relational analysis that understand gender as a set of socially constructed and situated identities and practices embedded in power structures.

Moreover, there is need for longitudinal studies that are better suited for capturing the complex dynamics of environmental change – for instance, in relation to land use and access over resources, agrarian transition, and intergenerational dynamics. Gender must be integrated in the picture.

While many studies mention the problematic access for women and girls to opportunities associated with human mobility, past research in this field has not paid sufficient attention to the differentiated access for women and men to formal and informal social networks and migrant support systems. A gender analysis of these networks and systems would deepen our understanding of migration in the context of global environmental change.

Last but not least, future research should shed light on the often neglected voice and leadership of women migrant workers, rather than just on their specific needs and vulnerabilities.

Notes

1 For an overview on the evolution of the debate on gender and the environment see Nightingale 2006.
2 The network began to take shape at the 2003 UNFCCC COP9 in Milan, Italy. See www.gendercc. net/home.html
3 The Gender and Disaster Network is an educational and advocacy project was initiated in 1997 by women and men interested in gender relations in disaster contexts www.gdnonline.org/who_are_we.php

References

Agarwal, B. (1992). The gender and environment debate: lessons from India. *Feminist Studies*, 119–158.

Agarwal, B. (1994). *A field of one's own: gender and land rights in South Asia*. Cambridge, UK and New York, NY: Cambridge University Press.

Aguilar, L. (2009). *Training Manual on Gender and Climate Change*. New York: UNDP.

Arango, J. (2000). Explaining migration: a critical view. *International Social Science Journal*, 52, 283–296.

Baldwin, A. (2017). Resilience and race, or climate change and the uninsurable migrant: towards an anthroporacial reading of 'race'. *Resilience*, 5(2), 129–143.doi:10.1080/21693293.2016.1241473

Barbieri, A. F., and Carr, D. L. 2005. Gender-specific out-migration, deforestation and urbanization in the Ecuadorian Amazon. *Global and Planetary Change*, 47(2), 99–110.

Bateman, J. M., and Edwards, B. (2002). Gender and evacuation: A closer look at why women are more likely to evacuate for hurricanes. *Natural Hazards Review*, 3(3), 107–117.

Batilwal, S., and Dhanrah, D. (2004). Gender myths that instrumentalise women: a view from the Indian frontline. *IDS Bulletin*, 35, 11–18.

Bettini, G., and Gioli, G. (2016). Waltz with development: insights on the developmentalization of climate-induced migration. *Migration and Development* (5), 171189.

Bhatta, G.D, Aggarwal, P.K., Poudel, S., and Belgrave, D.A. (2015). Climate-induced migration in South Asia: migration decisions and the gender dimensions of adverse climatic events. *The Journal of Rural and Community Development*, 10(4), 1–23.

Black, R., Bennett, S., Thomas, S., and Beddington, J. (2011). Climate change: migration as adaptation. *Nature*, 478, 447–449.

Bohra-Mishra, P., and Massey, D.S. (2011). Environmental degradation and out-migration: evidence from Nepal. In: Piguet, E., Pécoud, A. and De Guchteneire, P. (eds.) *Migration and climate change*. Cambridge: Cambridge University Press/UNESCO.

Cannon, T. (2002). Gender and climate hazards in Bangladesh. *Gender and Development*, 10(2), 45–50.

Chindarkar, N. (2012). Gender and climate change-induced migration: proposing a framework for analysis. *Environmental Research Letters*, 7, 1–8.

Cianfarani, M. (2012). Integrating diversity into Disaster Risk Reduction (DRR): a literature review. *International Association of Emergency Managers Bulletin*, 29, 26–27.

Collinson, M. A., S. M. Tollman, K. Kahn, S. J. Clark and M. Garenne. (2006). "Highly Prevalent Circular Migration: Households, Mobility and Economic Status in Rural South Africa." In: M. Tienda, S. E. Findley, S. M. Tollman and E. Preston-Whyte (eds.), *Africa on the move: African migration and urbanisation in comparative perspective*. Johannesburg, South Africa: Wits University Press.

Curran, S. (1995). *Gender roles and migration: 'Good Sons' vs. Daughters in rural Thailand*. Seattle Population Research Center Working Paper 95-11, University of Washington, Seattle.

Curran, S. R., and Saguy, A. C. (2001). Migration and cultural change: a role for gender and social networks? *Journal of International Women's Studies*, 2(3), 54–77.

Dankelman, I. (2002) Climate change: learning from gender analysis and women's experiences of organizing for sustainable development. *Gender & Development*, 10: 21–29

Dankelman, I. (Ed.). (2010). *Gender and climate change: an introduction*. Washington, DC: Earthscan.

de Haas, H. (2010). Migration and development: a theoretical perspective. *International Migration Review*, 44, 227–264.

de Haas, H. (2012). The migration and development pendulum: a critical view on research and policy. *International Migration*, 50, 8–25.

Deere, C.D., Alvarado, G., Oduro, A.D., and Boayke-Yiadom, L. (2015). *Gender, remittances and asset accumulation in Ecuador and Ghana.* UN Women Discussion Paper. New York City: UN Women.

Denton, F. (2002). Climate change vulnerability, impacts, and adaptation: why does gender matter? *Gender and Development*, 10, 10–20.

Denton, F., Wilbanks, T.J., Abeysinghe, A.C., Burton, I., Gao, Q., Lemos, M.C., Masui, T., O'Brien, K.L., and Warner, K. (2014). Climate-resilient pathways: adaptation, mitigation, and sustainable development. In: Field, C.B., V.R. Barros, D.J. Dokken, K.J. Mach, M.D. Mastrandrea, T.E. Bilir, M. Chatterjee, K.L. Ebi, Y.O. Estrada, R.C. Genova, B. Girma, E.S. Kissel, A.N. Levy, S. MacCracken, P.R. Mastrandrea, and L.L. White (eds.), *Climate change 2014: impacts, adaptation, and vulnerability. Part A: Global and sectoral aspects.* Contribution of Working Group II to the Fifth Assessment Report of the Intergovernmental Panel on Climate Change. Cambridge, UK and New York, NY: Cambridge University Press, pp. 1101–1131.

Denzin, N.K., and Lincoln, Y.S. (2000). The discipline and practice of qualitative research. *Handbook of Qualitative Research*, 2, 1–28.

Dominey-Howes, D., Gorman-Murray, A., and McKinnon, S. (2014). Queering disasters: on the need to account for LGBTI experiences in natural disaster contexts. *Gender, Place and Culture*, 21, 905–918.

Donato, K.M., Gabaccia, D., Holdaway, J., and Pessar, P.R. (2006). A glass half full? Gender in migration studies. *International Migration Review*, 40(1), 3–26.

Elmhirst, R. (2011). Introducing new feminist political ecologies. *Geoforum*, 42, 129–132.

Enarson, E., and Morrow, B. (1998) *The gendered terrain of disaster: through women's eyes.* Westport, CT, Praeger.

Enarson, E., and Fordham, M. (2001). From women's needs to women's rights in disasters. *Environmental Hazards*, 3:, 133–136.

Fitzpatrick, J. (1997). The gender dimension of U.S. immigration policy. *Yale Journal of Law & Feminism*, 9(1), Article 5.

Fletcher, A. (2014) *Background document on water and gender: state of the art of gender-disaggregated indicators: Overview and Assessment of Major Sources.* United Nations World Water Assessment Programme. Paris: UNESCO.

Fleury, A. (2016) *Understanding women and migration: a literature review.* KNOMAD Working Paper 8.

Fordham, M. (1999). The intersection of gender and social class in disaster: balancing resilience and vulnerability. *International Journal of Mass Emergencies and Disasters*, 17(1): 15–36.

Fordham, M. (2003). Gender, disaster and development: the necessity for integration. In: M. Pelling (eds.), *Natural disasters and development in a globalizing world.* London and New York: Routledge, 57–74.

Foresight Report. (2011). *Final project report – foresight: Migration and global environmental change.* London: Government Office for Science.

Froehlich, C., and Gioli, G. (2015). Gender, conflict, and global environmental change. *Peace Review: A Journal of Social Justice*, 27, 137–146.

Gabaccia, D. and Donato, K.M. (2015). *Gender and international migration.* New York: Russell Sage Foundation.

Gamlen, A. (2014). The new migration-and-development pessimism. *Progress in Human Geography*, 38, 581–597.

Gioli, G., Khan, T., Bisht, S., and Scheffran, J. (2014). Migration as an adaptation strategy and its gendered implications: a case study from the Upper Indus Basin. Special issue "Gender and Sustainable Development in Mountains: Innovative Transformations, Tenacious Resistances", *Mountain Research and Development*, 34(3), 255–265.

Gururani, S. (2002). Forests of pleasure and pain: gendered practices of labor and livelihood in the forests of Kumaon Himalayas, India. *Gender, Place and Culture*, 9, 229–243.

Hawkins, R., and Ojeda, D. (2011). Gender and environment: critical tradition and new challenges. *Environment and Planning D: Society and Space*, 29(2), 237–253.

Hemmati, M., and Rohr, U. (2009). Engendering the climate change negotiations: experiences, challenges, and steps forward. *Gender & Development*, 17(1), 19–32.

Hondagneu-Sotelo, P. (2000). Feminism and migration. *The Annals of the American Academy of Political and Social Science*, 571(1), 107–120.

Hunter, L., and David, E. (2009). *Climate change and migration: Considering the gender dimensions.* Working paper of the Institute of Behavioral Science, University of Colorado at Boulder. Migration & Climate. UNESCO.

Hunter, L.M., and David, E. (2011). Displacement, climate change and gender. In: E. Piguet et al. (ed.), *Migration and climate change.* Cambridge: Cambridge University Press.

Indra, D.M. (1999). *Engendering forced migration: theory and practice* (Vol. 5). Ann Arbor, Michigan: Berghahn Books.

IOM. (2014). *IOM outlook on migration, environment and climate change.* Geneva: IOM.

Joshi, D. (2015). Gender change in the globalization of agriculture? *Peace Review: A Journal of Social Justice,* 27(2), 165–174. DOI:10.1080/10402659.2015.1037620

Kakissis, J. (2010). Environmental refugees unable to return home. New York Times, 3.

Kapur, D. (2005). Remittances: the new development mantra? In: S.M. Maimbo and D. Ratha (eds.), *Remittances: Development impact and future prospects.* Washington, DC: The World Bank, pp. 19–51.

Kelly, P. (Ed.). (2011). Special issue, Migration, agrarian transition, and rural change in Southeast Asia. *Critical Asian Studies,* 43(201).

King, R., Dalipaj, M., and Mai, N. (2006). Gendering migration and remittances: evidence from London and Northern Albania. *Population Space and Place,* 12, 409–434.

Kniveton, D., Schmidt-Verkerk, K., Smith, C., and Black, R. (2008). Climate change and migration: improving methodologies to estimate flows. IOM Migration Research Series, 33. Geneva, Switzerland: International Organization for Migration

Kunz, R. (2011). *The political economy of global remittances. Gender, governmentality and neoliberalism.* Abingdon: Routledge.

Le Masson, V., Lim, S., Budimir, M., and Podboj, J.S. (2016). *Disasters and violence against women and girls: can disasters shake social norms and power relations?* ODI Working Paper, London: Overseas Development Institute.

Lindley, A. (2009). Remittances and conflict: some conceptual issues. *Jahrbücher für National Ökonomie und Statistik/ Journal of Economics and Statistics,* 229, 774–786.

Mahler, S.J., and Pessar, P.R. (2006). Gender matters: ethnographers bring gender from the periphery toward the core of migration studies. *International Migration Review,* 40(1), 27.

Massey, D.S., Axinn, W.G., and Ghimire, D.J. (2010). Environmental change and out-migration: evidence from Nepal. *Population and Environment,* 32, 109–136.

Massey, D.S. (1994). *Space, place and gender.* Minneapolis, MN: University of Minnesota Press.

McLeman, R., and Smit, B. (2006). Migration as an adaptation to climate change. *Climatic Change,* 76(1–2), 31–53.

Mies, M., and Shiva, V. (1993). *Ecofeminism.* London: Kali for Women.

Milan, A., and Ho, R. (2014). Livelihood and migration patterns at different altitudes in the Central Highlands of Peru. *Climate and Development,* 6, 69–76.

Mitchell, T., Tanner, T., and Lussier, K. (2007). *We Know What We Need: South Asian Women Speak Out on Climate Change Adaptation.* Brighton: ActionAid and Institute of Development Studies (IDS) at the University of Sussex.

Morokvasic, M. (1984). Birds of Passage are also Women . . . *The International Migration Review,* 18(4), 886–907.

Mustafa, D., Gioli, G., Qazi, S., Rehman, A., and Zahoor, R. (2015). Gendering flood early warning systems: the case of Pakistan. *Environmental Hazards.* DOI:10.1080/17477891.2015.1075859

Myrttinen, H., El-Bushra, J., and Naujoks, J. (2014). *Re-thinking gender in peacebuilding.* London: International Alert.

Nawyn, S.J. (2010). Gender and migration: integrating feminist theory into migration studies. *Sociology Compass,* 4/9, 749–765.

Nelson V., Meadows, K., Cannon, T., Morton, J., and Martin, A. (2002) Uncertain predictions, invisible impacts, and the need to mainstream gender in climate change adaptation. *Gender & Development* 10, 51–59. Nightingale, A. (2006). The nature of gender: work, gender, and environment. Environment and Planning D: Society and Space, 24, 165–185.

Office of the Special Adviser on Gender Issues and the Advancement of Women, United Nations. (2001). *Important concepts underlying gender mainstreaming*. www.un.org/womenwatch/osagi/conceptsandefinitions.htm (accessed June 2016).

Orozco, M., Lindsay Lowell, B., and Schneider, J. (2006). Gender-specific determinants of remittances: differences in structure and motivation. Report to the World Bank Group www.remesasydesarrollo.org/uploads/media/GenderSpecific_Determinants_of_Remittances.pdf (accessed June 2016).

Ospina, A., & Heeks, R. (2010). *Unveiling the Links between ICTs & Climate Change in Developing Countries: A Scoping Study*. Manchester: Centre for Development Informatics Institute for Development Policy and Management, SED, University of Manchester.

Pessar, P.R., and Mahler, S.J. (2003). Transnational migration: bringing gender in. *International Migration Review*, 37, 812–846.

Piper, N. (2008). Feminisation of Migration and the Social Dimensions of Development: The Asian Case. *Third World Quarterly*, 29(7): 1287–303.

Rahman, M.M. (2012). Gendering migrant remittances: evidence from Bangladesh and the United Arab Emirates. *International Migration*, 51 (s1), 159–178.

Ratha, D. (2003). Workers' remittances: an important and stable source of development finance. In: The World Bank (ed.), *Global development finance*. Washington, DC: The World Bank.

Ray-Bennett, N. (2009). The influence of caste, class and gender in surviving multiple disasters: a case study from Orissa, India. *Environmental Hazards – Human and Policy Dimensions*, 8, 5–22.

Reyes, R. R. (2002). Gendering responses to El Niño in rural Peru. *Gender & Development*, 10(2), 60–69.

Rocheleau, D., Thomas-Slayter, B., and Wangari, E. (Eds.). (1996). *Feminist political ecology: global issues and local experience*. New York: Routledge.

Rocheleau, D.E. (2008). Political ecology in the key of policy: from chains of explanation to webs of relation. *Geoforum*, 39, 716–727.

Schroeder, R., and Suryanata, K. (1996). Case studies from Indonesia and West Africa. *Liberation ecologies: Environment, development, social movements*, 188–204.

Seager, J. (2006). Noticing gender (or not) in disasters. *Geoforum*, 37(1), 2–3.

Seager, J. (2009). Death by degrees: taking a feminist hard look at the 2° climate policy. *Kvinder, Køn & Forskning*, 34, 11–21.

Semyonov, M., and Gorodzeisky, A. (2005). Labor, migration, remittances, and household income: A comparison between Filipino and Filipina overseas workers. *International Migration Review*, 39(1), 45–68.

Shrestha, S., and Bhandari, P.B. (2007). Environmental security and labour migration in Nepal. *Population and Environment*, 29, 25–38.

Silvey, R. (2004). Power, difference and mobility: feminist advances in migration studies. *Progress in Human Geography*, 28(4), 490–506.

Sultana, F. (2009). Fluid lives: subjectivity, gender and water management in Bangladesh. *Gender, Place, and Culture*, 16(4), 427–444.

Sultana, F. (2010). Living in hazardous waterscapes: gendered vulnerabilities and experiences of floods and disasters. *Environmental Hazards – Human and Policy Dimensions*, 9, 43–53.

Sultana, F. (2014). Gendering climate change: geographical insights. *The Professional Geographer*, 6, 372–381.

Tacoli, C. (2009). Crisis or adaptation? Migration and climate change in a context of high mobility. *Environment and Urbanization*, 21(2), 513–525.

Tacoli, C., and Mabala, R. (2010). "Exploring mobility and migration in the context of rural-urban linkages: why gender and generation matter." *Environment and Urbanization*, 22, 389–396.

Tacoli, C. (2011). *Not only climate change: mobility, vulnerability and socio-economic transformations in environmentally fragile areas of Bolivia, Senegal and Tanzania*. Human Settlements Working Paper Series. Rural-Urban Interactions and Livelihood Strategies 28. London: IIED.

Taylor, M.J., Moran-Taylor, M.J., and Ruiz, D.R. (2006). Land, ethnic, and gender change: transnational migration and its effects on Guatemalan lives and landscapes. *Geoforum*, 37, 41–61.

Terry, G. (2009). No climate justice without gender justice: an overview of the issues. *Gender and Development*, 17(1), 5–18.

Thieme, S. (2011). Sustaining a multi-local life: possible theoretical foundations for livelihood and transnational migration studies. In U. Wiesmann and H. Hurni (eds.), *Research for sustainable development: foundations, experiences, and perspectives*. Bern: Universität Bern, pp. 331–341.

Tiwari, P.C., and Joshi, B. (2016). Gender processes in rural out-migration and socio-economic development in the Himalaya. In G. Gioli, G. Hugo, J. Scheffran, and M. Manez-Costa (eds.), Special issue Human Mobility, Climate Adaptation and Development, *Migration and Development*, 5(2), 330–350.

UNFPA (2009). State of World Population 2009—Facing a Changing World: Women, Population, and Climate. New York: United Nations Population Fund.

United Nations (2015a). *International migrant stock 2015*. New York City: United Nations.

United Nations (2015b). *Transforming our world: the 2030 agenda for sustainable development*. New York: United Nations.

van der Land, V., and Hummel, D. (2013). Vulnerability and the role of education in environmentally induced migration in Mali and Senegal. *Ecology and Society*, 18(4), 14.

Velan, N., and Mohanty, R.K. (2015). Gender-wise rural-to-urban migration in Orissa, India: an adaptation strategy to climate change. In: G.G. Delgado-Ramos (ed.), *Inequality and climate change: perspectives from the Global South*. Dakar: CORDESIA.

Warner, K., and Afifi, T. (2014). Where the rain falls: evidence from 8 countries on how vulnerable households use migration to manage the risk of rainfall variability and food insecurity. *Climate and Development*, 6(1), 1–17.

WEDO (Women's Environment and Development Organization). (2008). Climate change and displacement: what it means for women. *Forced Migration Review*, 31, 56.

Willinger, B. (Ed.) (2008). *Katrina and the Women of New Orleans*. New Orleans, LA: Newcomb College Center for Research on Women.

Wisner, B., Blaikie, P.M., Cannon, T., and Davis, I. (2004). *At risk: natural hazards, people's vulnerability and disasters*, 2nd ed. New York: Routledge.

Yang, D., and Choi, H.J. (2007). Are remittances insurance? Evidence from rainfall shocks in the Philippines. *World Bank Economic Review*, 21, 219–248.

12

Environmental migrants, climate 'refugees' and sun-seeking expats

Capturing the larger context of migration in a changing climate through appropriate and effective behavioural research

Dominic Kniveton, Sonja Ayeb-Karlsson and Christopher D. Smith

Climate and migration narratives

The last 10–20 years have seen an explosion of interest in academia and policy around how migration patterns might evolve with environmental and climatic change (e.g. Foresight 2011; Graeme et al. 2012). This interest begs the question 'why environmental change and migration should be of particular concern?' – especially given the widespread recognition of the overriding importance of other non-environmental factors in determining migration flows, such as economic disparity and relationships with other global transformations such as development.

One supposition around the popularity of the environmental change and migration discourse is that the issue combines two societal preoccupations: climate change and migration. Alternatively, at a deeper political level, it may be that both migration and environmental change speak to tensions around state control, power (or lack thereof), and an inherent fear of exogenous influences. More likely it relates to the mainstreaming of fears of the estimated hundreds of millions of 'environmental refugees' predicted to occur by 2050 as far back as the 1980s and 1990s (El Hinnawi 1985; Jacobsen 1988; Myers 1993; Myers and Kent 1995).

While there is currently no refugee status for those forced to move across borders[1] due to environmental or climatically[2] related events (Gemenne and Brücker 2015), a repeated, and thus reinforced, narrative has emerged that sees climate change as likely to result in the mass displacement of populations. Further development of this narrative supposes that displaced people will gravitate up environment gradients to countries and places of relative prosperity and environmental safety. Against this supposition is the observation that past empirical work (e.g. Lu et al. 2016a; Ayeb-Karlsson et al. 2016) suggests that, rather than travelling large distances and across borders, those displaced by natural hazards tend to move short distances and for short periods of time, and even to locations of greater environmental exposure and sensitivity.

There are, however, notable exceptions to this general rule. One oft-quoted example in this regard is the narrative around the European manifestation of the Syrian crisis in 2015 (Kelley et al. 2015), although this is not without its critiques (Selby and Tadros 2016). In this example, it has been argued that the mass migration from the Syrian countryside to cities was linked to an exceptional five-year drought, statistically attributable to anthropogenic global climate change (Kelley et al. 2015). In turn, the Syrian government's failure to adequately provide for those internally displaced people then led to conflict and mass displacement internationally, triggering the European element of the crisis. Ignoring whether conflict is associated with climate extremes, there remains the issue that environmental threats are unlikely to calm any conflict related movements of people and future research might focus on where future environmental hazards spatially co–exist with regions prone to conflict and containing vulnerable populations.

Another issue to bear in mind is the power of language when talking about sudden 'mass' movements of populations. In particular, one needs to think critically about the origins and meanings of phrases used to describe migrants and mass migration. For example, who is described as a migrant? In many policy and media circles, 'mass migration' is not necessarily defined by the number of people moving, but rather who is moving and where they are moving to. When, for example, 300,000 British 'expat citizens' move to Spain, commentators do not describe them as 'migrants' or their movement as a 'mass migration'.[3] In contrast, when around 300,000 people from Syria applied for asylum in the UK in 2015, references were made to a 'migrant crisis' and 'uncontrolled mass migration'.[4] Baldwin (2016) argues that climate change and migration discourses are currently reproduced in a manner where: (1) climate change induced migration is proposed to be not yet taking place but will occur in a distant future; and (2) post-colonial framings shape ideas relating to the nature of the locations and the individuals that will be affected by climate change or will migrate due to climate change.

Another argument against those positing that the world is likely to be swamped by millions of environmental refugees is that the very foundation of this argument relies on an unsubstantiated assumption of immutable limits of adaptation being breached forcing migration. This is despite the acknowledgment of the socially constructed nature of limits to adaptation which is supposed to be driving migration. For example, it has been argued that limits to adaptation are as much a function of ethics, knowledge, attitudes to risk, and culture as they are defined by immutable biological, environmental or technological thresholds (Adger et al. 2009).

Reflecting on the question of why there is so much modern interest in environment and migration suggests to us that future research within this arena should probably ask: (1) what (or who) is driving the interest in the interaction between environmental change and migration; and (2) how has this shaped the way that we think about the terminology used and the ways we define, theorise, facilitate and problematise the movement of people in the context of a changing climate?

Coping with seemingly insurmountable uncertainty

Uncertainty is a key characteristic of the environment and migration nexus, in terms of both our understanding of the interactions between environmental change and migration now and how we anticipate they will evolve in the future. Uncertainty is endemic to our understanding of future climate change in terms of unknowns around natural variability, climate processes, greenhouse gas and aerosol emission pathways, and model uncertainties. For example, in terms of natural variability, we have a decided lack of ability to predict volcanoes or solar variability (both of which influence the climate) with any accuracy at long lead times. Indeed, differentiating current knowledge claims around climate change is best summarised according to whether they may be classified as 'known-knowns'; 'known-unknowns' or 'unknown-unknowns' (e.g. Donald Rumsfeld).[5] The 'known-knowns' of climate change for many parts of the world are limited to the generalities that temperatures, rain intensities, atmospheric carbon dioxide levels, ocean acidification and sea levels will all increase. By contrast, for much of the world the jury is still out on whether the future will see an anthropogenic climate change induced increase or decrease in rainfall.

If our knowledge of future climate change is uncertain, then our understanding of human responses to environmental pressures on livelihoods and lives is at best superficial. The interactions between climate change and socio-ecological systems include considerable uncertainty with regard to how people perceive and respond to climate change impacts (Streets and Glantz 2000), or how they find safety and certainty within the uncertainty they face (Fox et al. 2017). There is a general assumption within academia and policy that people will try to escape or move away from environmental stressors and shocks as long as they have the ability to do so. However, this supposedly 'rational' response to stresses and shocks has been shown to not always determine a person's behaviour (e.g. Mitchell 2010; Stephens et al. 2013; Oakes 2014; Morrison et al. 2015). Increasingly, the assumptions of economic and bounded rationality are being challenged (e.g. World Bank 2015). As stated previously, risk perceptions are known to be heavily influenced by social and cultural values that may impede limits to adaptation for different reasons. For example, religious beliefs and social attitudes strongly influence people's mobility and immobility, so that praying more may serve as a more rational response for some individuals if they believe that the disaster befalling them is God's punishment (Krüger et al. 2015; Ayeb-Karlsson et al. 2017).

Understanding the many manifestations of (im)mobility

The concept of 'Trapped Populations' was brought into contemporary thinking by the UK government's Foresight: Migration and Global Environmental Change (MGEC) Report (Foresight 2011; Black et al. 2011). Trapped Populations are proposed to be those impoverished people that face a "double set of risks" (Foresight 2011: 14) by being both unable to move away from environmental threats and especially vulnerable to their impacts, especially in "urban areas [of low-income countries] that are particularly vulnerable to environmental change" (Foresight 2011: 201).

However, despite its conceptual importance as an opportunity to protect those people most affected by environmental change, it should be recognised that it has emerged from an already complex and disputed body of literature on the role of the environment in human mobility. To date, there has been little in the way of critical analysis on the potential existence of people 'trapped' in vulnerable locations. For example, should the category of 'trapped' people also include those neither explicitly recognising an environmental threat nor seeing that migration is an appropriate solution for them? Even if it does not (yet) serve to protect the rights of severely affected people, the concept of being 'trapped' at least highlights the non-linear relationship between migration and environmental change. In some ways, the general relationship can be thought of as mirroring the inverted 'U' relationship between migration and development where the axis of increasing economic development is replaced by increasing environmental damage (McLeman et al. 2015).

Rationalising seemingly irrational behaviour

Migration scholars have long recognised the cultural, social, emotional, psychological and powered factors influencing migration decision-making by individuals, households and societies (e.g.

Massey et al. 1993; Lu 1999). Indeed, recent work from cognitive anthropology and social neuroscience over the way in which people make decisions in complex and uncertain environments (typical of those in which people face environmental risks) has largely rejected rational models of behaviour in favour of placing more emphasis on how the human brain actually functions (Beratan 2007). In these revised understandings, rather than viewing decision-making as a linear process involving problem definition, the delineation of alternatives and a choice of responses, they indicate that the decision-making process involves a pathway emerging from non-conscious/preconscious and cognitive processing. In such a way, the first steps of decision-making involve an idea of a desired outcome (or avoidance of outcome) arising from the priming of past experiential learning and social discourse. Here, priming arises from a variety of sensory input, including verbal and nonverbal communication and environmental events. For example, a narrative around the benefits of migration might be primed in one area from concern over a climate threat but be ignored or contradicted in another where experiences of migration have been more negative (Schmidt-Verkerk 2012). The decision to migrate in these cases is not simply a rational summing up of benefits versus costs, but is based on previous personal and societal associations of migration and climate hazard outcomes and is subject to a number of biases.

Alternative framings of the decision-making process argue that instead of being purely rational or irrational it is of 'in between' nature, making use of judgments of prior knowledge and experience based on emotions, issues of trust and intuition (Zinn 2008). The use of these judgment criteria is posited to reduce the uncertainty that can arise in many decision-making situations from a lack of knowledge about a situation, a lack of time to make decisions or from the inherent complexity of conceiving how reality will play itself out. For example, in terms of migration, there remains a high level of uncertainty and non-linearity in the future employment and living environment of a would-be migrant and how the absence of a household member will affect the wellbeing of those left behind. Emotion-based judgements can be favoured in overly complex situations because of the speed at which they occur (Zinn 2008), or because they overcome the inability to analytically work out what might happen in the future (e.g. Damasio 1994).

Modelling the decision to migrate

If we put together these framings of the decision-making process, the relationship between migration and climate change is highly unlikely to be uniform across different locations, genders, cultures, experiences and environments. Rational decision models have long been applied to debates around migration and the environment to imply the relevance of classical 'push-pull' type theories of migration (e.g. Lee 1966) to situations of environmental stress. However, the variation in strength and direction of migration-environment relationships observed by numerous past empirical studies can be taken as evidence to support the rejection of the concept of rational decision models of such behaviour. In an effort to move beyond these classical theories of migration and towards an understanding from which each individual is afforded their own context-dependent 'agency', agent-based models (ABMs) have been used to a small extent to test the conditions under which large scale movements (longer distance, longer duration, larger numbers of people) are more likely to occur (Kniveton et al. 2011, 2012). However, their use represents a conflict between the ideals of social science and the accepted wisdom of the computational background of such a simulation-based approach. Finding an acceptable middle ground presents something of a challenge. So too does collecting, or gaining access to, the sort and scale of data needed to develop verified and validated simulation models.

Recently, discussions around the value and use of 'Big Data', such as anonymised mobile-phone data to track down population movements after disasters, have arisen (Lu et al. 2016a, 2016b). One way to effectively use the sort of spatial and social data that may be accessed from mobile phones is the development of agent-based models. As computational models that simulate the actions and interactions of autonomous agents (in this case, virtual versions of potential migrants), agent-based models offer the greatest potential to contribute to our understanding of real-world situations when they are parameterised using data relating to real individuals. However, the breadth of data required to parameterise a model that can offer insight on a scale that is useful to policymakers, or the depth of data necessary to inform a model that can provide insight at a resolution that could be used in a humanitarian context is likely to be both costly to collect and laden with issues relating to personal privacy.

If the challenges of collecting and appropriately storing and handling data relating to the movement of people in areas affected by changes to the environment can be overcome, agent-based models may offer a means of operationalising our understanding of the complex and multifaceted nature of migration decision-making. Efforts made in this regard to date offer insight into the potential contribution that agent-based models can make to environmental migration studies in the near future (Kniveton et al. 2011, 2012; Smith 2014; Entwisle et al. 2016). Although such models should not be expected to *predict* future flows of migrants, the simulation capacity enabled by such an approach permits a rigorous scientific method to be used to undertake comparative projections of possible future scenarios and their likely (im)mobility outcomes. In such a way, scholars working this arena can aid in the development of our understanding of how migration decision-making might be manifest in the future given our understanding of the complex interactions between environment and agent that are occurring now or have occurred in the past.

Despite the promise offered by agent-based models informed by Big Data, their potential is presently limited by difficulties associated with the collection of and access to large amounts of detailed data relating to population movements. Such data will be necessary to develop well informed, and thus policy/practice-relevant, models. However, the sensitive nature of such information and the ethical implications of its collection and use must be adequately accounted for. As such, academic progress in this regard must be paired with protection measures that do not inadvertently impose external ideals relating to mobility upon populations affected by environmental change. Before such research initiatives can realise their true potential therefore, interdisciplinary and international collaborations and agreements on the collection, management and sharing of high quality relevant data and the development of appropriate simulation structures will be necessary.

Interdisciplinary approaches to assessing the depth of environmental migration

The subject of environment and migration is characterised by a high degree of uncertainty and complexity. As a result, a wide array of methods and data have been developed to expand our understanding of the dynamics of socio-ecological systems. These techniques range from questionnaires, Q methodology, and Critical Discourse Analysis (CDA) to regressions and Bayesian network analyses. Through these different methodological approaches, additional aspects of the nexus between the environment and migration have been revealed, including issues of emergence, the role of power at multiple levels and the influence of culture, psychology and perception on migration futures.

Critical Discourse Analysis (CDA), for example, is one way to better understand the decision-making of people in a socio-psychological context. Discourses can be described as the process people engage in to reason ideas in a social space and thereby create order and meaning (Morinière and Hamza 2012). The negotiating process takes place within discourses, e.g. a collectively space of shared reality or a 'general domain of statements' (Foucault 1972, 1981). Q methodology can be used to identify such discourse groups in relation to a specific subject matter.

Q methodology was originally born out of psychology (Stephenson 1935), but is now gaining ground within social science and beyond. Q is the 'science of subjectivity' (Stephenson 1953). The method groups people's subjective responses in relation to a specific topic, such as climate policy and fire management, environmental migration or hurricane evacuation (e.g. Ockwell 2008; Morinière and Hamza 2012; Oakes 2014). These insights reflect the broader discourses in the study area or participant group. People's behaviour and decision-making process are strongly influenced by current discourses and existing social norms. This is why Q and CDA shed light on social and psychological elements of (im)mobility that other research methods may not be able to capture.

A set of Q-statement cards are sorted by participants on an agree, neutral and disagree scale. There are a few important advantages with this methodology: (1) the method does not require a large sample size; there are even single participant Q-studies identifying multiple viewpoints on a discourse of a specific issue (Watts and Stenner 2012; Morinière and Hamza 2012); (2) the Q-sorting activity depends on feelings around agreement and disagreement; the risk for assumptions around what are the 'right' or 'wrong' answers are therefore lower (Watts and Stenner 2005); and (3) the Q-sorting activity is participant-led and seeks to understand the attitudes, views and subjective reality of the participant rather than 'test' researcher's pre-conceived ideas.

The sorting values are entered in a software program (for example, PQ Method) to identify the discourse groups, referred to as factor groups, or subjectivity groups in Q-terminology. The post-sorting interview around statement extremes (e.g. most agree, most disagree and neutral statements), support the understanding of each discourse group. To ensure even richer qualitative research data, the Q-sort activity can be combined with in-depth open interviews and Critical Discourse Analysis of the interview transcripts.

Inter-disciplinary methods such as Q and CDA aim to explore the complex and multifaceted depth of im(mobility) or people's reasoning around staying and going. The methods explain the 'unexplainable'. For example, why people decide not to evacuate, escape or move away from environmental shocks that are a direct threat to their lives. The research methods also explore how much of people's immobility is linked to fear, emotions or feelings of doing the 'right' thing, e.g. taking social norms and power relation into account.

Exploring the meanings behind different perceptions of mobility

Central to the 'new' understandings of migration decision-making that have emerged in recent years is the role that discourse and social networks play. In terms of discourse, one can imagine a variety of socially constructed storylines around migration and the climate interacting with an individual's past and present experience, being mediated via priming effects and heuristics to produce a preferred behavioural choice to achieve (or avoid) a particular outcome. When asked to explain a decision, an individual may then construct a logical rationale for the decision and consciously reflect on their perceived ability to achieve this behaviour.

Despite the apparent repetition by some in policy and media of an environmental determinism narrative around the subject, migration is not just dependent on environmental factors but also on a complex interplay between multi-scale social, economic, political and demographic factors and contexts impacting livelihoods and wellbeing. As the Foresight project (Foresight 2011) posited, these drivers of migration are sensitive to the spatially and temporally differentiated impacts of global environmental change in both origin and destination locations. Less investigated, however, has been how macro, meso and micro changes (both due to global environmental change and other global transformations) in these determinants might interact with each other. Similarly, little focus has been placed on how attempts to mitigate, adapt or build resilience to the impacts of climate change may influence migration more indirectly. For example, it is not difficult to imagine that a major impact of future climate change in terms of population displacement may be the resettlement of populations from large hydropower schemes. However, it will be of paramount importance to consider who will be being resettled, by whom and for what purpose. Justifications proffered in such circumstances may include clearance of land to allow the building of climate change mitigation-related projects such as the production of biofuels, or the removal of those deemed by governments to be liable to be 'trapped' (unable to move) in the future. Again the 'trapped' narrative is increasingly taking a hold in policy circles with legitimate fears that it may be used as part of government climate change rhetoric to forcibly resettle populations (de Sherbinin et al. 2011) deemed to be at risk from future climate related hazards and appropriate the origin lands to other uses.

In contexts such as these, it is important to understand how language and power interact with one another and what the consequences may be of reducing migrating people to an anonymous moving mass, flow or stream. It is also crucial to acknowledge the dangers of shifting the responsibility of 'how' to adapt, build resilience or adaptive capacity to an individual level (Bettini 2014). There are intrinsic dangers to reproducing normative language around resilience and adaptive agency, or right and wrong adaptive pathways.

Migration is not the end

As the previous discussion has shown, predictions of the exact numbers of people whose mobility pathways can be attributable to environmental change are inherently uncertain, and thus unreliable. Yet, past empirical evidence (e.g. Foresight 2011) still strongly indicates that future environmental change is likely both to reduce migration by trapping impoverished and vulnerable populations in exposed contexts, as well encourage those that can to migrate in order to build their financial, and in some cases their other, capitals.

As a corollary to the opposite impacts of environmental change that are anticipated to both increase and decrease migration, it is likely that those who are the first to migrate (the canaries down the coal mine) in response to environmental change will not be the worst off (see Cai et al. 2016 and Cattaneo and Peri 2016). It is also important to acknowledge that early- or late-arriving migrants may benefit differently from the circumstances of their arrival. On the one hand, people arriving 'last' might be better off due to having a strong social network in the migration destination and thus a greater chance to build up a new and better future or secure a new livelihood and housing through their social networks. However, on the other hand, people arriving first could face even more fruitful social circumstances than those arriving last as social stigmas and stereotypes around 'new arrivals or immigrants' are yet not in place. People in the settlement may therefore be more welcoming and supportive of new arrivals when there are fewer of them. Large urban settlements containing 'outsiders' such as urban slums or migrant neighbourhoods generally face social stigmas that make it more difficult for people to achieve better housing, better jobs or better education.

Conclusion

Research efforts around emotional wellbeing, mental and physical health, as well as a stronger psychological aspect of environmental migration, seem to these authors as a profitable endeavour to further the understanding of migration in the context of climate change. So too is a better inclusion of empirical social studies from other research areas, such as identity studies, diaspora communities and non-environmental migration studies. Interdisciplinary collaborations such as these can provide us with more complex insights that may better enable future environmental migration research to move beyond an academic pursuit of those whose migration is in some way driven by the environment towards the development of actions and initiatives that may serve to protect and benefit affected people.

Despite certain methodological advances, it is crucial that future research and policy within this arena considers the loaded nature of language and the ways in which terms such as 'climate change' and 'migration' are interpreted. Care should thus be taken not only by thinking critically about the ways these terms are used in academia, media and politics, but also in terms of what the results and consequences will be of the ways they are being used.

Notes

1 See the Nansen Initiative's work on moving 'Towards a protection agenda for people displaced across borders in the context of disasters and the effects of climate change' at www.nanseninitiative.org/ and the subsequent Platform on Disaster Displacement, a follow-up to the Nansen Initiative, at http://disasterdisplacement.org/

2 While clearly the 'climate' as in related to the atmosphere is a subset of the '[physical/natural] environment', here we follow the Intergovernmental Panel on Climate Change in referring to the climate system as including the atmosphere, the hydrosphere, the cryosphere, the land surface and the biosphere, and so will use the terms interchangeably.

3 For example, see The Guardian, Carroll, L.O. (2017) 'Hundreds of thousands of retired Britons in EU 'may be forced to return' www.theguardian.com/politics/2017/jan/18/retired-britons-eu-return-campaigners-pensioners-spain-healthcare and BBC, Kovacevic, T. (2017) 'Reality Check: How many Brits live in the rest of the EU?' www.bbc.co.uk/news/uk-politics-eu-referendum-36046900

4 See for example BBC (2016) 'Migrant crisis: Migration to Europe explained in seven charts' www.bbc.co.uk/news/world-europe-34131911 and The Guardian, Mason, R. (2016) 'Theresa May to warn UN of dangers of uncontrolled mass migration' www.theguardian.com/world/2016/sep/19/theresa-may-to-warn-un-of-dangers-of-uncontrolled-mass-migration

5 Defense.gov News Transcript: DoD News Briefing – Secretary Rumsfeld and Gen. Myers, United States Department of Defense (defense.gov), 2002.

References

Adger, W. N., Dessai, S., Goulden, M., Hulme, M., Lorenzoni, I., Nelson, D. R., . . . Wreford, A. (2009). Are there social limits to adaptation to climate change? *Climatic change*, *93*(3–4), 335–354.

Ayeb-Karlsson, S., van der Geest, K., Ahmed, I., Huq, S., & Warner, K. (2016). A people-centred perspective on climate change, environmental stress, and livelihood resilience in Bangladesh. *Sustainability Science*, *11*(4), 1–16.

Ayeb-Karlsson S., Kniveton D., Cannon T., van der Geest K., Ahmed I., Derrington E.M., Florano E., & Opoyo D. (2017). *I wont go. I cannot go: Cultural and social constraints to disaster preparedness in Asia, Africa and Oceania*. Working Paper.

Baldwin, A. (2016). Premediation and white affect: Climate change and migration in critical perspective. *Transactions of the Institute of British Geographers*, *41*(1), 78–90. doi: 10.1111/tran.12106

Black, R., Adger, W. N., Arnell, N. W., Dercon, S., Geddes, A., & Thomas, D. (2011). The effect of environmental change on human migration. *Global Environmental Change*, *21*, S3–S11.

Beratan, K. (2007). A cognition-based view of decision processes in complex social–ecological systems. *Ecology and Society*, 12(1).

Bettini, G. (2014). Climate migration as an adaptation strategy: De-securitizing climate-induced migration or making the unruly governable? *Critical Studies on Security*, 2(2), 180–195.

Cai, R., Feng, S., Oppenheimer, M., & Pytlikova, M. (2016). Climate variability and international migration: The importance of the agricultural linkage. *Journal of Environmental Economics and Management, 79*, 135–151.

Cattaneo, C., & Peri, G. (2016). The migration response to increasing temperatures. *Journal of Development Economics, 122*, 127–146.

Damasio, A. R. (1994). *Descartes' error: Emotion, rationality and the human brain.* Vintage, New York.

de Sherbinin, A., Castro, M., Gemenne, F., Cernea, M. M., Adamo, S., Fearnside, P. M., . . . Pankhurst, A. (2011). Preparing for resettlement associated with climate change. *Science, 334*(6055), 456–457.

El-Hinnawi, E. (1985). *Environmental refugees.* UNEP, Nairobi.

Entwisle, B., Williams, N. E., Verdery, A. M., Rindfuss, R.R., Walsh, S.J., Malanson, G.P., Mucha, P.J., Frizelle, B.G., McDaniel, P.M., Yao, X. & Heumann, B.W. (2016). Climate shocks and migration: An agent-based modeling approach. *Population and Environment, 38*, 47.

Foucault, M. (1972). *The archaeology of knowledge.* London: Routledge.

Foucault, M. (1981). The order of discourse (I. McLeod, Trans.) *Untying the text: A post-structuralist reader.* London: Routledge.

Foresight, (2011), *Migration and global environmental change: Future challenges and opportunities.* Final Project Report. London: The Government Office of Science.

Fox, G., Ayeb-Karlsson, S., Tall, L., and Kniveton, D. (2017). A discursive approach to developing pathways for adaptation to the impacts of climate change. *Regional Environmental Change.* Working paper.

Gemenne, F., and Brücker, P. (2015). From the guiding principles on internal displacement to the Nansen initiative: What the governance of environmental migration can learn from the governance of internal displacement. *International Journal of Refugee Law, 27*(2), 245–263.

Graeme, H., Bardsley, D., Sharma, V., Tan, Y., Williams M & Bedford R. (2012). *Addressing Climate Change and Migration in Asia and the Pacific.* Mandaluyong City: Asian Development Bank.

Jacobson, J. L. (1988). *Environmental refugees: A yardstick of habitability.* Worldwatch Institute, Washington.

Kelley, C. P., Mohtadi, S., Cane, M. A., Seager, R., & Kushnir, Y. (2015). Climate change in the Fertile Crescent and implications of the recent Syrian drought. *Proceedings of the National Academy of Sciences, 112*(11), 3241–3246.

Kniveton, D., Smith, C., & Wood, S. (2011). Agent-based model simulations of future changes in migration flows for Burkina Faso. *Global Environmental Change, 21*, S34–S40.

Kniveton, D. R., Smith, C. D., & Black, R. (2012). Emerging migration flows in a changing climate in dryland Africa. *Nature Climate Change, 2*(6), 444–447.

Krüger, F., Bankoff, G., Cannon, T., Orlowski, B., & Schipper, E. L. F. (2015). *Cultures and disasters: Understanding cultural framing in disaster risk reduction.* London: Routledge.

Lee, E. S. (1966). A theory of migration. *Demography, 3*(1), 47–57.

Lu, M. (1999). Do people move when they say they will? Inconsistencies in individual migration behavior. *Population and Environment, 20*(5), 467–488.

Lu, X., Wrathall, D. J., Sundsøy, P. R., Nadiruzzaman, M., Wetter, E., Iqbal, A., Qureshi, T., Tatem, A., Canright, G., Engø-Monsen, K. & Bengtsson, L. (2016a). Unveiling hidden migration and mobility patterns in climate stressed regions: A longitudinal study of six million anonymous mobile phone users in Bangladesh. *Global Environmental Change, 38*, 1–7. doi: https://doi.org/10.1016/j.gloenvcha.2016.02.002

Lu, X., Wrathall, D. J., Sundsøy, P. R., Nadiruzzaman, M., Wetter, E., Iqbal, A., . . . Bengtsson, L. (2016b). Detecting climate adaptation with mobile network data in Bangladesh: Anomalies in communication, mobility and consumption patterns during cyclone Mahasen. *Climatic change, 138*(3), 505–519. doi: 10.1007/s10584-016-1753-7

Massey, D. S., Arango, J., Hugo, G., Kouaouci, A., Pellegrino, A., & Taylor, J. E. (1993). Theories of international migration: A review and appraisal. *Population and Development Review*, 431–466.

McLeman, R., Faist, T., & Schade, J. (2015). Environment, migration, and inequality — a complex dynamic. In R. McLeman, J. Schade, & T. Faist (Eds.), *Environmental migration and social inequality*. Dordrecht: Springer, pp. 3–26.

Mitchell, J. T. (2010). The hazards of one's faith: Hazard perceptions of South Carolina Christian clergy. *Global Environmental Change Part B: Environmental Hazards*, 2(1), 25–41.

Morinière, L. C. E., & Hamza, M. (2012). Environment and mobility: A view from four discourses. *Ambio*, 41(8), 795–807.

Morrison, M., Duncan, R., & Parton, K. (2015). Religion does matter for climate change attitudes and behavior. *PloS One*, 10(8), 1–16.

Myers, N. (1993). Environmental refugees in a globally warmed world. *BioScience*, 43(11), 752–761. doi: 10.2307/1312319

Myers, N., & Kent, J. (1995). *Environmental exodus: An emergent crisis in the global arena*. Climate Institute, Washington.

Oakes, R. D. (2014). *Using Q method and agent based modelling to understand hurricane evacuation decisions*. Doctoral thesis DPhil., University of Sussex, Brighton.

Ockwell, D. G. (2008). 'Opening up' policy to reflexive appraisal: A role for Q Methodology? A case study of fire management in Cape York, Australia. *Policy Sciences*, 41(4), 263–292.

Schmidt-Verkerk, K. (2012). The potential influence of climate change on migratory behaviour – a study of drought, hurricanes and migration in Mexico. Doctoral dissertation, University of Sussex.

Selby, J., & Tadros, M. (2016). Introduction: Eight myths of conflict and development in the Middle East. *IDS Bulletin*, 47(3). doi: http://dx.doi.org/10.19088/1968-2016.141

Smith, C. D. (2014). Modelling migration futures: Development and testing of the Rainfalls Agent-Based Migration Model–Tanzania. *Climate and Development*, 6(1), 77–91.

Stephens, N. M., Fryberg, S. A., Markus, H. R., & Hamedani, G. M. (2013). Who explains Hurricane Katrina and the Chilean earthquake as an act of God? The experience of extreme hardship predicts religious meaning-making. *Journal of Cross-Cultural Psychology*, 44(4), 606–619.

Stephenson, W. (1935). Technique of factor analysis. *Nature, 136*, 297. doi:10.1038/136297b0

Stephenson, W. (1953). *The study of behavior; Q-technique and its methodology*. Chicago: University of Chicago.

Streets, D. G., & Glantz, M. H. (2000). Exploring the concept of climate surprise. *Global Environmental Change, 10*(2), 97–107.

Watts, S., & Stenner, P. (2005). Doing Q methodology: Theory, method and interpretation. *Qualitative Research in Psychology, 2*, 67–91. doi:10.1191/1478088705qp022oa.

Watts, S., & Stenner, P. (2012). *Doing Q methodological research: Theory, method and interpretation*. Los Angeles, London, New Delhi, Singapore, and Washington: Sage.

World Bank. (2015). *World development report 2015: Mind, society, and behavior*. Washington, DC: World Bank. doi: 10.1596/978-1-4648-0342-0.

Zinn, J. O. (2008). Heading into the unknown: Everyday strategies for managing risk and uncertainty. *Health Risk and Society, 10*, 439–450.

Part II
Empirical evidence from regions

13

Environmental change and migration

A review of West African case studies

Victoria van der Land, Clemens Romankiewicz
and Kees van der Geest

Introduction

West Africa is considered one of the world's regions that is presumed to be highly affected by climate and environmental changes in the future (IPCC 2007). The majority of the rural population in the region depends on small-scale agriculture, crop production and livestock farming, and therefore on the natural environment. Environmental changes can thus constitute a severe threat to people's livelihoods. Mobility in West Africa has a long tradition and the seasonality of rainfall influences mobility patterns. Agricultural activities depend on only one rainy season, during which the workload in agriculture is high. The seasonal movements of pastoralists with their animals to pasture grounds or the labour migration of farmers during the dry season are well-established patterns of migration (Davies 1996; Ellis 1998; Rain 1999). Main destinations are urban areas or more productive rural areas, either within the country or in neighbouring countries. The most established inter-regional mobility pattern in West Africa was and still is the north-south movement from the Sahelian landlocked countries of Burkina Faso, Mali and Niger to coastal states, particularly to the economically strong Côte d'Ivoire. These patterns date back at least to the colonial area in the 19th century, when plantation economies (e.g. cocoa, coffee, cotton, groundnut) attracted labour migrants from neighbouring countries and cities as Dakar, Abidjan, Lome and Accra benefited from investments for the export of goods to Europe (Hummel et al. 2012; Bakewell and de Haas 2007). Dryland West Africa has harsh environmental conditions and long established mobility patterns, but that does not necessarily mean that the two are related.

This review analyses 15 empirical case studies that focus explicitly on the complex linkages between environmental factors and human mobility in West African drylands – in the semi-arid Sahel zone and the savannah (Table 13.1). This includes studies conducted in Senegal, Mali, Burkina Faso, Niger and (Northern) Nigeria, Ghana and Benin. In contrast to existing reviews on African case studies (e.g. Jónsson 2010; Morrissey 2014), the present chapter focuses specifically on West African drylands with relatively homogenous climatic and cultural conditions compared to other regions. Environmental parameters investigated in the case studies comprise slow-onset changes such as rising temperature, increasing rainfall variability and land degradation, as well as the severe droughts of the 1970s and 1980s. In addition, the review provides a systematic analysis

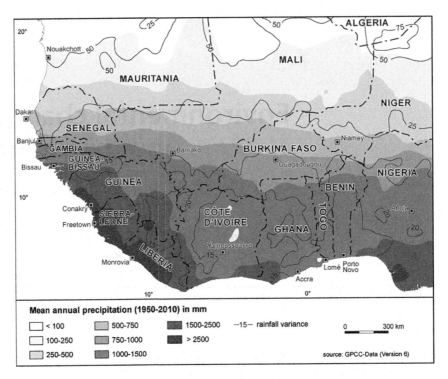

Figure 13.1   Map of West Africa with mean annual precipitation

Source: Modified by authors based on: Martin Brandt, Heiko Paeth, Cyrus Samimi (2013): Vegetationsveränderungen in Westafrika – Spiegel von Klimawandel und Landnutzung. Georaphische Rundschau 9: 36

on the similarities and differences of concepts, methods and results of the most relevant case studies on the environment-migration nexus, aiming at drawing conclusions and identifying future directions for research on the environment-migration nexus in the region.

Approaching the environment and migration nexus in West African drylands – concepts and theories

The great Sahel droughts of the 1970s and 1980s and the assumed direct effects of climate and environmental change on human migration have shaped the image of the entire Sahel region as being a serious hotspot of environmental displacement. Contemporary political concerns of (uncontrollable) large-scale population movements as a consequence of unbearable environmental conditions in dryland West Africa influence and dominate the focus in research, as well as conceptual approaches applied in empirical investigations on the linkages between migration and environmental change. Empirical studies can basically be classified into two conceptual categories (Suhrke 1994; Jónsson 2010): a) a push-pull framework (maximalist view) derived from the approach of neoclassical economics in migration theory that assumes (unidirectional) migration to be a result of economic-spatial differences, or analogously here, driven by spatial differences in environmental conditions; and (b) approaches that regard the environment as a contextual component and emphasize and elucidate the multiple dimensions and levels, complexity and multicausality of population movements (minimalist view). Even though authors of

Table 13.1 Overview of the reviewed case studies

Author(s)	Title	Publication year	Study country
Henry, S., Boyle, P. and Lambin, E.F.	Modelling inter-provincial migration in Burkina Faso, West Africa: the role of socio-demographic and environmental factors	2003	Burkina Faso
Henry, S., Piché, V., Ouédraogo, D. and Lambin, E.F.	Descriptive analysis of the individual migratory pathways according to environmental typologies	2004	Burkina Faso
Henry, S.; Schoumaker, B. and Beauchemin, C.	The importance of rainfall on the first out-migration: a multi-level event-history analysis in Burkina Faso	2004	Burkina Faso
Kniveton, D.; Smith, C. and Wood, S.	Agent-based model simulations of future changes in migration flows for Burkina Faso	2011	Burkina Faso
Findley, S.E.	Does drought increase migration? A study of migration from rural Mali during the 1983–1985 drought	1994	Mali
Pederson, J.	Drought, migration and population growth in the Sahel: The case of the Malian Gourma: 1900–1991	1995	Mali
van der Land, V.	The environment-migration nexus reconsidered: Why capabilities and aspirations matter	2015	Mali, Senegal
Romankiewicz, C.; Doevenspeck, M.; Brandt, M. and Samimi, C.	Adaptation as by-product: migration and environmental change in Nguith, Senegal	2016	Mali, Senegal
Bleibaum, F.	Senegal. Case study report	2009	Senegal
Afifi, T.	Economic or environmental migration? The push factors in Niger	2011	Niger

(Continued)

Table 13.1 (Continued)

Author(s)	Title	Publication year	Study country
Mounkaïla, H.	De la migration circulaire à l'abandon du territoire local dans le Zarmaganda (Niger)	2002	Niger
van der Geest, K.	North-South migration in Ghana: What role for the environment?	2011	Ghana
Rademacher-Schulz, C.; Mahama, S.	"Where the rain falls" project. Case study: Ghana. Results from Nadowli District, Upper West Region	2012	Ghana
Doevenspeck, M.	The thin line between choice and flight: environment and migration in rural Benin	2011	Benin
Dillon, A.; Mueller, V. and Salau, S.	Migratory responses to agricultural risk in Northern Nigeria	2011	Nigeria

recent empirical investigations widely acknowledge the complexity and mulicausality of migration, this classification can be useful "to illustrate how conceptual frameworks shape the kinds of data and analyses researchers produce" (Jónsson 2010: 8). The theoretical-conceptual approaches and research designs applied in most of the reviewed West African case studies are framed to a greater or lesser extent by plausible basic assumptions of environmental push and pull factors of migration. The following exemplary quote illustrates the underlying premises in the investigations: "Since rain-fed agriculture is the main source of livelihood in rural Burkina Faso, intuitively it makes sense that environmental factors (e.g. rainfall and land degradation) will influence socio-economic conditions and may lead people to emigrate" (Henry et al. 2004b: 424).

Several studies do not specify the theoretical-conceptual approach that guided their research (e.g. Mounkaïla 2002; Bleibaum 2009; Afifi 2011), however, implicitly they mainly follow the push-pull idea. In the case studies of Henry et al. (2003, 2004a, 2004b) and van der Geest (2011), even though considering a variety of demographic, socio-economic and environmental parameters in their statistical model/analysis, the respective approaches basically involve testing the explanatory power of environmental and socio-economic area characteristics as push or pull factors for migration. Whereas Pedersen (1995) looked at the demographic effects of exceptional droughts in Mali, of which migration is only one parameter, Findley's (1994) analysis frames migrants as social and economic members of a larger household, and presents socially and spatially differentiated movements as drought coping strategies. In contrast, both Doevenspeck (2011) and Romankiewicz et al. (2016) stress the importance of making use of the multiple approaches contemporary migration theory offers, and put the environmental dimension in the context of migration shaped by social capital and migration networks. Three case studies (Dillon et al. 2011; Rademacher-Schulz and Salifu Mahama 2012; van der Land 2015) use the

Sustainable Livelihood Approach (SLA) to analyse the importance of migration as a household's survival, risk reducing, or adaptation strategy in the face of climatic or environmental stress. Van der Land (2015) combines the SLA and a capability approach and thus, in contrast to other studies, not only considers the household level, but also highlights individual aspirations and preferences in migration decisions. Kniveton et al.'s (2011) Agent Migration Adaptation to Rainfall Change model, which incorporates the theory of planned behaviour, involves multiple sets of migration drivers and the assumption that migration away from affected areas is an adaptation strategy.

Apart from the variety of theoretical-conceptual approaches applied in the reviewed papers, the empirical studies rely on different definitions and classifications of human mobility. They depend on the type of analysis (quantitative/qualitative) or the availability and quality of data sources. Studies referring to migration information from censuses usually use a migration definition of an absence of at least 12 months (Pedersen 1995; Henry et al. 2003; van der Geest 2011). Other studies that use survey data differentiate for instance between seasonal/circular (less than 6 months) and temporary/permanent migration (more than 6 months) (Findley 1994; Rademacher-Schulz and Salifu Mahama 2012), or short-term (3–10 months), temporary (10 months–5 years), and permanent migration (more than 5 years) (van der Land 2015). Henry et al. (2004) exclusively look at the first out-migration from the village after age 15. Romankiewicz et al. (2016) follow the IOM definition of migration (IOM 2004) that encompasses any kind of population movement irrespective of length, boundaries crossed or causes. Moreover, the environmental parameters considered vary among the case studies. Almost all studies refer to respective rainfall variability in time and space. Rademacher-Schulz and Mahama (2012) and Dillon et al. (2011) also include temperature as a variable. Authors who go beyond a general description of so-called environmental stressors, and thus quantify environmental parameters in their study, include a combination of explanatory factors. Such factors are rainfall, land degradation (soil fertility) and crop yields (Henry et al. 2003; Henry and Schoumaker et al. 2004), annual rainfall and land use change (Romankiewicz et al. 2016), and vegetation cover (NDVI), crop yields and rainfall (van der Geest 2011).

The analysis of theoretical-conceptual approaches shows that most empirical case studies on West African drylands are still guided and entrenched in traditional push-pull frameworks. Only a few authors point out and apply alternative approaches in order to make sense of observed contemporary migration phenomena in West Africa beyond an interpretation of environmental displacement. Moreover, the variety of migration definitions and combination of environmental parameters applied in the studies make it difficult to compare the results.

Methods: Diversity, trends, challenges and opportunities

The studies use an impressive variety of methods to analyse the relation between environmental change and migration in dryland West Africa. All six types of research methods that Piguet (2010) distinguishes have been applied in the region: a) ecological inference based on area characteristics; b) sample surveys; c) time series; d) multilevel analysis; e) agent-based modelling (ABM); and f) qualitative and ethnographic work. Some of Piguet's categories include several different research tools. For example, qualitative research methods might include individual interviews, focus groups, expert interviews and participatory research approaches.

Table 13.2 indicates the methodological approach and the spatial and temporal dimensions applied in the reviewed case studies. The table shows that most studies combined two or more methods that complement each other, helping to validate or triangulate findings. A particularly

Table 13.2 Overview of methods and spatio-temporal dimensions

Author(s)	Publication year	Study country	1 Ecological inference	2 Surveys	3 Time series	4 Multi-level	5 ABM	6 Qualitative research	Source area	Destination area	Past or present	Future
Henry et al.	2003/2004a/2004b	Burkina Faso	X	X	X	X			X	X	X	
Kniveton et al.	2011	Burkina Faso					X					X
Findley	1994	Mali		X					X		X	
Pederson	1995	Mali		X					X		X	
van der Land	2015	Mali, Senegal		X				X	X	X	X	
Romankiewicz et al.	2016	Mali, Senegal	X					X	X	X	X	
Bleibaum	2009	Senegal		X				X	X	X	X	
Afifi	2011	Niger		X				X	X	X	X	
Mounkaila	2002	Niger		X				X	X		X	
van der Geest	2011	Ghana	X	X	X	X			X	X	X	
Rademacher-Schulz & Mahama	2012	Ghana		X				X	X		X	
Doevenspeck	2011	Benin		X				X	X	X	X	
Dillon et al.	2011	Nigeria		X	X	X			X		X	
Total			**3**	**12**	**3**	**3**	**1**	**9**	**13**	**7**	**13**	**1**

Notes:

- Kniveton et al. (2011) use survey and time series data from Henry et al. (2003, 2004) to construct their agent based model.
- Pederson's (1995) work is based on a literature review and statistical data from demographic and nutrition surveys. These were not designed to study migration-environment linkages specifically.
- The surveys in the EACH-FOR studies (Bleibaum 2009; Afifi 2011) had a low sample size (N = approximately 30) and contained several open-ended questions yielding qualitative data. The other qualitative work in these two studies consisted of expert interviews. Most of the findings seem to be based on a desk study and, following Piguet's (2010) description of research approaches, are categorized under qualitative research. Mounkaila has also conducted a survey in two 'source area' villages.
- The study by Mounkaila (2002) has no methods section.
- In the work by Rademacher & Salifu Mahama (2012), PRA tools play a central role. These are classified under qualitative methods here.

common mix has been the combination of a sample survey and qualitative research tools. Table 13.1 also shows that the focus is mostly on past and current population movements; few studies have extrapolated into the future, which is a challenging exercise (Brown 2008; Gemenne 2011; McLeman 2013). With regards to the spatial dimension, the table shows that almost all studies are based on data from migrant source areas, where the environmental push factors were at play. About half the studies under review also included data from migrants' destination areas.

Jónsson's (2010) review of African case studies on environmental migration identifies several methodological challenges. The scholarly work reviewed in this chapter also faces these challenges to varying degrees. First, many studies are too narrowly focused on environmental drivers. This is especially the case for studies that use a macro-level push-pull framework that fails to take into account micro- and meso-level contextual factors that were highlighted in the previous section of this review. Several studies (e.g. Bleibaum 2009; Afifi 2011) asked directly for the impact of environmental drivers on migration while others (e.g. van der Geest 2011; Rademacher-Schulz and Salifu Mahama 2012; van der Land 2015; Romankie-wicz et al. 2016) followed a broader approach by inquiring a wide variety of potential reasons for people to migrate, including environmental factors. A second challenge or weakness is that many studies lack a longitudinal perspective: they provide snapshots that fail to grasp the historical context of migration and longer-term dynamics of the environment. Third, there is an issue with the reliability and validity of data. This is particularly the case for interview data about migration reasons. It also applies, however, to secondary data about mobility (e.g. population census data and people's recall of migration years) and the environment (e.g. rainfall data). There is a general paucity of reliable migration data in West Africa, especially at sub-national level. National census data often includes – if at all – only limited information about migration. In addition to the challenges Jónsson identified, several reviewed studies chose to interview the head of the households (e.g. Bleibaum 2009; Doevenspeck 2011; van der Geest 2011). Most of the household heads, however are men, which can cause gender imbalances in the results, especially with regard to questions about perceptions and migration reasons. Rademacher-Schulz & Mahama (2012) address this challenge by interviewing wives of male household heads in approximately half the sample. The seemingly simple, but potentially complicated question 'who to interview?' is crucial in migration research. Household heads may not know or want to reveal the migration motives of the different household members. It often depends on the research focus whether the choice should fall on individual migrants, their household heads or others. Another challenge is that the results of case studies are hard to compare due to the different research approaches, including methods used, scale levels, sample sizes and amount of time spent in the field. Therefore, a systematic analysis of research findings on the environment-migration nexus, as is attempted in this chapter, has its limitations.

Besides challenges, there are also opportunities that have not yet been fully exploited. For example, increasingly granular datasets depicting environmental change have become freely available in the past years. For dryland West Africa, where drought and desertification are key issues, a more thorough analysis of these datasets can help to better understand the environmental drivers of migration. Moreover, methods for studying migration-environment linkages in dryland West Africa have improved considerably since the first studies on this topic appeared in the 1990s. Particularly there is a move towards more mixed-method research that produces more robust findings. Several challenges remain, and new opportunities for analysis arise.

Ambiguous findings on the impact of environmental factors on migration behaviour

The agreed aspects on the linkages between the environment and migration

The reviewed case studies focus on different aspects of the relationship between the environment and migration and apply different concepts, data and methods. This makes it difficult to compare and to draw consistent conclusions even from case studies that focus on the same region. Nevertheless, all studies agree at least on three relevant aspects for the research on environment and migration in the region: a) environmental conditions and changes favour temporary migration; b) migration is a well-established activity to diversify income; and c) migration is multi-causal.

Climatic conditions in the region, such as the long dry season and highly variable inter- and intra-annual rainfalls, favour temporary migration from the rural areas. For many people in the region, seasonal or temporary labour migration from rural areas is a common activity and well-established strategy to diversify income. Particularly, migration during the dry season is often an economic activity complemental to agriculture and crucial to ensure the household's food security, as has been widely acknowledged in literature on West African drylands (e.g. Mortimore 1989; Davies 1996; Ellis 1998; de Haan 1999; Breusers 1999; Mortimore and Adams 1999; Rain 1999; de Haan et al. 2002; Ellis 2003; McLeman 2014). Nevertheless, the studies agree that migration in the region is multi-causal. Environmental factors are usually not the only driver of migration, but cultural, economic, environmental, political and social aspects also influence the migration decision. While the studies agree on these basic aspects, there is little consensus on the role and weight of environmental change and stress as a driver of migration compared to other aspects, on the necessity or the degree of urgency to migrate and on the impact of environmental factors on the duration and destination of migration.

The multi-causality of migration as a major challenge

Economic and environmental factors as main reasons for migration

The studies on the environment-migration nexus in West Africa acknowledge that a variety of variables influences the migration decision and that migration is complex and context-dependent. However, this complexity of migration seems to be a major conceptual and methodological obstacle to research on the environment-migration nexus. Afifi, for instance, recognises that "it is hard to link migration to the environment" (Afifi 2009: 17), and Doevenspeck notes that it is very difficult to achieve a clear differentiation between the different impact factors (Doevenspeck 2011: e61). Concluding that migration is complex and context-dependent is a very unsatisfying result (Nicholson 2014; van der Land 2015, 2018; Romankiewicz et al. 2016). The relationship between environmental and economic drivers of migration seems to be particularly complex. This is because environmental stress may be an indirect driver of migration through economic needs. Often it is not environmental factors themselves which influence the migration decision but rather their consequences or related structural constraints, such as reduced productivity or food insecurity (Mounkaïla 2002; Afifi 2011; Rademacher-Schulz and Salifu Mahama 2012). At the same time, labour migration in West African drylands not only ensures food security but is also a means to increase assets and improve economic wellbeing and livelihoods (Ellis 2003). Nevertheless, some of the reviewed studies assume environmental problems as a driver of economic motivated migration, while the migrants themselves do not relate their migration to environmental problems. Interviewees in Afifi's EACH-FOR study on Niger state economic factors, such as poverty and unemployment, as main causes of migration. Afifi reckons that the underlying causes of the economic motives were declining crop yield or death of animals due to the droughts and water shortage. He even suggests the term "environmentally induced economic migration" (Afifi 2011: e116). In Findley's (1994) study on the effect of the 1980s drought in Mali, surprisingly few of the household heads explicitly reported drought or famine as the reason for migration. Instead, economic reasons, marriage or other family reasons were the main migration motives. Other studies show that better economic prospects in other regions influence the migration decision and patterns. In the EACH-FOR study on Northern Ghana, people mentioned better agro-ecological conditions in the destination area more often as reasons for migration than the unfavourable conditions for farming at home (van der Geest 2011: e85). Henry and colleagues relativize the role of the environmental conditions by stating that "Burkinabe migrants are not likely pulled by rainfall conditions in Cote d'Ivoire but are rather attracted by job opportunities in plantations of cafe and cacao" (Henry et al. 2004a: 414). The research project "MICLE: migration, climate change and environment" (http://www. micle-project.net/) finds that economic motives are the main migration motives for both Senegalese and Malian migrants. Environmental reasons played a role as underlying causes for 71% of the Senegalese, while this applies only to 13% of the Malians. Malians relate their economic motivated migration rather to consumption, like buying clothes or dowry (Hummel 2015; van der Land 2015). The "Where the rain falls" project (https://wheretherainfalls.org/) finds for Ghana that people migrated mainly for economic and food security reasons. The most common reasons for migration were the decline in crop production for own consumption, shifts in the rainy season, unemployment, longer drought periods followed by unreliable harvest and increase in drought frequency (Rademacher-Schulz and Salifu Mahama 2012). With respect to gender, earlier studies showed that male migration was dominated by economic motives and women rather migrated for marriage and family reasons (Findley 1994; Petit 1997). While this tendency is still valid, women also seem to migrate increasingly for economic reasons (de Haan et al. 2002; Sieveking and Fauser 2009; van der Land 2015). It is, however, not clear if this is due to deteriorating environmental conditions or due to an increasing acceptance of women migrating for economic reasons.

Economic motives for migration include different levels of voluntariness or necessity. Rademacher-Schulz and Mahama show in their Ghana study that 75% of their survey participants perceive migration as a normal income-generating strategy, whereas 36% perceive and use it as a strategy only in times of crisis (Rademacher-Schulz and Salifu Mahama 2012). Van der Geest (2011) suggests for Northern Ghana that only 24% of the migrants in his sample moved for reasons that indicate a high level of urgency and distress, citing "food insecurity" or "hunger" as migration reasons. For most migrants, the level of urgency was lower and their migration rather attempts to improve their livelihoods (van der Geest 2011). He concludes that "[t]he picture that emerges for northern Ghana is not one of distress migration in the face of environmental disaster but rather of migration as a way of dealing with structural environmental scarcity" (van der Geest 2011: e69). The reviewed studies suggest that this conclusion applies for the whole region. The underlying motives for people's economic migration are manifold and migration is often a voluntary decision, which goes beyond risk prevention and adaptation to environmental stress. Better income opportunities and the desire for progress and prosperity – inspired by the prestige and economic achievements of previous migrants – as well as the aspirations for a better life and a different lifestyle are important motives for economic migration (van der Land 2015, 2018; Romankiewicz et al. 2016).

The importance of individual characteristics, structural conditions and social determinants for migration in environmentally fragile areas

Studies that consider multiple variables as drivers of migration find that environmental factors are often not the main driver of migration in the region. Instead, they show that individual characteristics (e.g. level of education, religion, ethnicity and the economic activity), structural conditions (e.g. infrastructure and lacking [non-farm] income opportunities on site, and better income opportunities elsewhere) or social determinants (e.g. conflict, envy, migration tradition and relative deprivation) strongly influence migration.

For Burkina Faso, Henry et al. (2004b) find no evidence of a general effect of rainfall conditions on people's first out-migration from rural areas. Instead, they find that migration mostly depends on individual characteristics such as the educational level, the type of economic activity or the ethnic group to which the individual belongs (Henry et al. 2004b: 454). In an earlier study on inter-provincial migration in Burkina Faso in the 1980s, Henry et al. (2003) also show that socio-demographic variables, such as literacy and economic activity, have more power to explain migration than environmental factors, such as rainfall variability, drought frequency and soil degradation (Henry et al. 2003: 134). Individual characteristics not only determine the migration propensity, but also the migration motives. The MICLE project, for instance, shows that individual characteristics, such as gender, age, economic activity and educational level, strongly influence people's reasons to migrate (van der Land and Hummel 2013; Hummel 2015; van der Land 2015). Environmental factors predominantly influence the migration of middle-aged male farmers with no or a low formal education (van der Land 2015).

Van der Geest and colleagues (2009; 2010; 2011) find in their studies on Ghana that migration propensities tend to be higher in districts that experience more resource scarcity – depending on annual rainfall, vegetation cover, crop yields and, to a lesser extent, rural population density. However, van der Geest (2011: e80) suggests that religion and a higher level of education, migration tradition and poorly developed infrastructure could be important influencing variables to explain the higher out-migration from the Upper West region compared to the Upper East, two regions with similar resource scarcity. Similarly, Doevenspeck (2011) finds for the northwest of Benin that environmental problems, such as soil degradation, poor harvests and food security, are not necessarily the main migration determinants, but that economic reasons, envy, and conflicts influence migration (Doevenspeck 2011: e63).

Moreover, several studies on migration in West Africa show that social networks, social capital and identity play a role in the migration decision (Hampshire 2002; de Haan et al. 2002; Doevenspeck 2011; van der Land 2015; Romankiewicz et al. 2016). Particularly, recent studies suggest that environmental stress might have been the principal cause for migration during the 1970s and 1980s, and that these migrations still influence current migration behaviour (Gonin and Lassailly-Jacob 2002; Doevenspeck 2011; van der Land 2015; Romankiewicz and Doevenspeck 2015; Romankiewicz et al. 2016). Established networks facilitate migration and lead to social prestige and relative wealth of the migrants and their families. This in turn encourages other member to migrate and leads to a perpetuating effect, even if the initial causes of migration do not remain (Massey et al. 1993; de Haas 2010). Some studies even suggest that men and women use unfavourable environmental conditions as excuses for other more delicate or less accepted migration reasons, such as sorcery or to escape traditional norms in the village, to be economically independent and to postpone or avoid arranged marriages (Gonin and Lassailly-Jacob 2002; Doevenspeck 2011; van der Land 2015, 2018).

The impact of environmental factors on spatial and temporal migration patterns

Only a few studies consider the impact of environmental stress on migration patterns. The use of different definitions with respect to duration and destination of migrations makes it difficult to compare the findings. The impact of environmental factors on migration patterns is controversial. Several studies suggest that factors such as economic opportunities, social networks or the person's life phase, education and professional prospects, and the type of residence permits and/or labour contract influence the duration and destination of migrations (Henry et al. 2004a; Doevenspeck 2011; van der Geest 2011; van der Land 2015; Romankiewicz et al. 2016). In general, migration in the region is mainly temporary, often seasonal, and takes mainly place within the country or to neighbouring countries (Adepoju 2005, 2008; Bakewell and de Haas 2007; Afifi 2011; van der Geest 2011; Rademacher-Schulz and Salifu Mahama 2012; Mueller and Romankiewicz 2013; van der Land 2015).

Studies which investigated the changes in migration flows during the severe droughts in the beginning of the 1970s and 1980s found that droughts tended to limit migration flows. Studies on northern Ghana and Mali found, for instance, that migration flows had been lower during the severe droughts during in the 1970s and 1980s compared to the years before 1970 and after 1984 (Gonin and Lassailly-Jacob 2002; van der Geest 2011). Two further studies on Mali show that migration at least did not increase during the drought period in the 1980s (Findley 1994; Pedersen 1995). Particularly, these earlier studies tended to find that environmental stress favours short-term and short-distance migration. Findley finds for the region of Kayes in Mali that short-cycle migrations more than doubled during the droughts in the 1980s. Migration during that time shifted from permanent (more than 6 months absent) to short-term migration (less than 6 months absent) and destinations shifted from intercontinental destinations to destinations in Mali and other African countries (Findley 1994: 544). In contrast, Henry et al. (2004b) find for migration during the 1970–1998 period that short-term migration did not rise following a severe rainfall deficit. They, however, define short-term migration as up to two years. Recent studies find that acute or anticipated stress changes the usual temporal migration patterns. Studies in Ghana (Rademacher-Schulz and Salifu Mahama 2012; Rademacher-Schulz et al. 2014) observe an accelerated migrant departure rate during the rainy season in 2011, and not during the dry season as is usually the case for short-term seasonal migration. The assumption is that people leave earlier due to acute food shortages and/or in anticipation of a poor harvest. Similarly, interviewees in van der Land's study on Mali and Senegal indicate they leave earlier and stay longer in migration in years with (expected) poor yields (van der Land 2015). With respect to gender, Dillon and colleagues find in their model for northern Nigeria that households are more inclined to send men out of the village to reduce the risk and retain women in the household in response to ex post covariate shocks, thus as risk management (Dillon et al. 2011). Similarly, Henry and colleagues find that women are less likely to move after bad rainfall conditions (Henry et al. 2004b). The short-term increase of numbers of migrating male household members seems to be a common strategy to respond to environmental stressors.

Today, studies on the region agree that rural households generally consists of two groups: members who stay and members who migrate (de Haan et al. 2002; Mounkaïla 2002; van der Land 2015). They often take turns of migrating and staying with other family members. The long-term migration of some members to urban areas and neighbouring countries seems to become increasingly common (e.g. Rademacher-Schulz et al. 2014; van der Land 2015). Several studies suggest that temporary long-term migration may become the main livelihood activity and end up marginalising agricultural activity (Hampshire 2002; Mounkaïla 2002; Afifi 2011; van der Land 2015; Romankiewicz et al. 2016). Studies, however, disagree on whether a change from seasonal to long-term migration is a consequence of more and more deteriorating environmental conditions (Mounkaïla 2002; Afifi 2011; Rademacher-Schulz et al. 2014) or a consequence of economic development, social transformation processes and changes in lifestyle (van der Land 2015, 2018; Romankiewicz et al. 2016). Permanent out-migration of entire households seems to be rare in the region (Mortimore 1989; Hampshire 2002; van der Land 2015).

Migration usually moves from the north to the south or to coastal and urban areas, and thus to areas with higher soil fertility and rainfall as well as better economic prospects. Many studies find that the economically attractive Cote d'Ivoire is often a main destination for people from Mali, Burkina Faso and Ghana (Hampshire 2002; Henry et al. 2004a; Afifi 2011; Rademacher-Schulz and Salifu Mahama 2012; van der Land 2015). International migration to destinations beyond the African continent is less common and considered as prestige migration rather than a consequence of deteriorating environmental conditions (Afifi 2011; Tacoli 2011; van der Land 2015). The entry costs for international migration to Europe or North America are high, and therefore it seems unlikely that people would migrate to non-African destinations because of worsening climate conditions (Henry et al. 2003; Afifi 2011; van der Geest 2011; van der Land 2015; Romankiewicz et al. 2016). With respect to migration within the country and to neighbouring countries, the impact of environmental factors is less clear. Afifi suggests that migration within the country and to neighbouring countries is "a matter of survival" and determined by the search for better livelihoods, (Afifi 2011: e111). With respect to the migration destination, Henry et al. (2004b) show for Burkina Faso, in line with Findley's findings on drought in Mali (Findley 1994), that temporary migration to other countries was less common among males after periods with low rainfall levels. In contrast, other studies (including those that use model simulations) suggest that migration during times of stress is directed to neighbouring countries, particularly when considering migration from urban centres and the South of the Sahel (Pedersen 1995; Kniveton et al. 2011). Overall, most studies suggest that people choose their destination for factors other than environmental ones, such as social networks, employment options, better educational or economic prospects, etc. (e.g. Henry et al. 2004b; Doevenspeck 2011; van der Geest 2011; van der Land 2015; Romankiewicz et al. 2016).

Conclusion

Our review of case studies on the linkages of the environment and migration in West African drylands shows that these studies use different concepts of mobility and environmental factors, and apply a broad variety of different methods. This influences the results and makes it difficult to compare the findings, even when focussing on a region with relatively similar climatic and environmental conditions. Population mobility has a long tradition in the region, and the seasonality of rainfall has been shaping the mobility patterns for generations. Temporary migration is a well-established activity to diversify income and to cope with the harsh environmental conditions in the region. Permanent out-migration of entire households, however, seems to be rare. Although the financial support of the migrants is crucial for most households in rural areas, people have many different reasons to migrate. These reasons often go beyond risk prevention and adaptation to environmental stress. Several studies suggest that environmental factors are often not the main driver of migration in the region. Instead, individual characteristics (e.g. level of education, religion, ethnicity and the economic activity), structural conditions (e.g. infrastructure and lacking [non-farm] income opportunities on site, and better income opportunities elsewhere), social determinants (e.g. conflict, envy, migration tradition and relative deprivation) or individual aspirations (e.g. for progress, prosperity and a different lifestyle) strongly influence the migration decision.

Despite these findings, many studies on the environment-migration nexus still use simplistic push/pull frameworks assuming that environmental stressors are the main determinants of migration. Future research on the environment-migration nexus will have to pursue a broader approach, which considers the variety of people's migration motives and drivers of migration in environmental fragile environments. This is important in order to assess the role of environmental factors in the migration decision as well as the level of urgency, necessity, usefulness and/or normality of human mobility in West African contexts.

References

Adepoju, A. 2005 *Migration in West Africa*. A paper prepared for the Policy Analysis and Research Programme of the Global Commission on International Migration. Available at https://www.iom.int/jahia/webdav/site/myjahiasite/shared/shared/mainsite/policy_and_research/gcim/rs/RS8.pdf

Adepoju, A. 2008 Migration in sub-Saharan Africa. *Current African Issues*, Accessed November 22, 2013.

Afifi, T. 2009 *Niger. Case Study Report*. Environmental Change and Forced Migration Scenarios (EACH-FOR) Project. Bonn: United Nations University Institute for Environment and Human Security (UNU-EHS). Available at http://www.ccema-portal.org/article/read/each-for-project-publications

Afifi, T. 2011 "Economic or Environmental Migration? The Push Factors in Niger" *International Migration*, 49, e95.

Bakewell, O. and de Haas, H. 2007 "African Migration: Continuities, Discontinuities and Recent Transformation", in Chabal, P., Engel, U. and de Haan, L. eds. *African Alternatives*, Leiden: Brill, 95–118.

Bleibaum, F. 2009 *Senegal. Case Study Report*.

Brandt, M., Paeth, H. and Samimi, C. 2013 "Vegetationsveränderungen in Westafrika: Spiegel von Klimawandel und Landnutzung." *Geographische Rundschau*, 9, 36–42.

Breusers, M. 1999 *On the move. Mobility, Land Use and Livelihod Practices on the Central Plateau in Burkina Faso (Anthropology and development, 3)*. Hamburg: Lit.

Brown, O. 2008 "The Numbers Game" *Forced Migration Review*, 31, 8–9.

Davies, S. 1996 *Adaptable Livelihoods. Coping with Food Insecurity in the Malian Sahel*. New York: St. Martin's Press; Macmillan Press.

de Haan, A. 1999 "Livelihoods and Poverty: The Role of Migration – a Critical Review of the Migration Literature" *Journal of Development Studies*, 36(2), 1–47.

de Haan, A., Brock, K. and Coulibaly, N. 2002 "Migration, Livelihoods and Institutions: Contrasting Patterns of Migration in Mali" *Journal of Development Studies*, 38(5), 37–58.

de Haas, H. 2010 "Migration and Development: A Theoretical Perspective" *International Migration Review*, 44(1), 227–264.

Dillon, A., Mueller, V. and Salau, S. 2011 "Migratory Responses to Agricultural Risk in Northern Nigeria" *American Journal of Agricultural Economics*, 93(4), 1048–1061.

Doevenspeck, M. 2011 "The Thin Line Between Choice and Flight: Environment and Migration in Rural Benin" *International Migration*, 49, e50–e68.

Ellis, F. 1998 "Household Strategies and Rural Livelihood Diversification" *The Journal of Development Studies*, 35(1), 1–38.

Ellis, F. 2003 *A Livelihood Approach to Migration and Poverty Reduction*. UK Department for International Development (DFID). Available at http://citeseerx.ist.psu.edu/viewdoc/download?doi=10.1.1.553.5678&rep=rep1&type=pdf

Findley, S.E. 1994 "Does Drought Increase Migration? A Study of Migration from Rural Mali During the 1983–1985 Drought" *International Migration Review*, 28(3), 539–553.

Gemenne, F. 2011 "Why the Numbers Don't Add Up: A Review of Estimates and Predictions of People Displaced by Environmental Changes" *Global Environmental Change*, 21, S41–S49.

Gonin, P. and Lassailly-Jacob, V. 2002 "Les réfugiés de l'environnement" Revue européenne des migrations internationales, 18(2), 139–160.

Hampshire, K. 2002 "Fulani on the Move: Seasonal Economic Migration in the Sahel as a Social Process" *Journal of Development Studies*, 38(5), 15–36.

Henry, S., Boyle, P. and Lambin, E.F. 2003 "Modelling Inter-Provincial Migration in Burkina Faso, West Africa: The Role of Socio-Demographic and Environmental Factors" *Applied Geography*, 23(2–3), 115–136.

Henry, S., Piché, V., Ouédraogo, D. and Lambin, E.F. 2004a. "Descriptive Analysis of the Individual Migratory Pathways According to Environmental Typologies" *Population and Environment*, 25(2), 397–422.

Henry, S., Schoumaker, B. and Beauchemin, C. 2004b. "The Impact of Rainfall on the First Out-Migration: A Multi-Level Event-History Analysis in Burkina Faso" *Population and Environment*, 25(5), 423–460.

Hummel, D. 2015 "Climate Change, Land Degradation and Migration in Mali and Senegal – Some Policy Implications" *Migration and Development*, 5(2), 211–233.

Hummel, D., Doevenspeck, M. and Samimi, C. 2012 Climate Change, Environment and Migration in the Sahel. Selected Issues with a Focus on Mali and Senegal (micle — Working Paper 1), Frankfurt am Main.

IOM 2004 *International Migration Law. Glossary on Migration*. International Organization for Migration. Geneva. Available at http://www.iomvienna.at/sites/default/files/IML_1_EN.pdf

IPCC 2007 *Climate Change 2007: The Physical Science Basis*. Contribution of Working Group I to the Fourth Assessment Report of the Intergovernmental Panel on Climate Change, Cambridge University Press, Cambridge, United Kingdom and New York, NY, USA.

Jónsson, G. 2010 *The Environmental Factor in Migration Dynamics – a Review of African Case Studies* (Working papers 21). Oxford: International Migration Institute, James Martin 21st Century School, University of Oxford.

Kniveton, D., Smith, C. and Wood, S. 2011 "Agent-Based Model Simulations of Future Changes in Migration Flows for Burkina Faso" *Global Environmental Change*, 21, S34–S40.

Massey, D.S., Arango, J., Hugo, G., Kouaouci, A., Pellegrino, A. and Taylor, J.E. 1993 "Theories of International Migration: A Review and Appraisal" *Population and Development Review*, 19(3), 431–466.

McLeman, R. 2013 "Developments in Modelling of Climate Change-Related Migration" *Climatic Change*, 117(3), 599–611.

McLeman, R.A. 2014 *Climate and Human Migration. Past Experiences, Future Challenges*. New York, NY: Cambridge University Press.

Morrissey, J. 2014 "Environmental Change and Human Migration in Sub-Saharan Africa", in Piguet, E. and Laczko, F. eds. *People on the Move in a Changing Climate. The Regional Impact of Environmental Change on Migration*. (2), Dordrecht: Springer Netherlands, 81–109.

Mortimore, M. 1989 *Adapting to Drought. Farmers, Famines and Desertification in West Africa*. Cambridge: Cambridge University Press.

Mortimore, M. and Adams, W. M. 1999 *Working the Sahel. Environment and Society in northern Nigeria* (Routledge Research Global Environmental Change Series, 2). London and New York: Routledge.

Mounkaïla, H. 2002 "De la migration circulaire à l'abandon du territoire local dans le Zarmaganda (Niger)" *Revue européenne des migrations internationales*, 18(2), 161–187.

Mueller, A. and Romankiewicz, C. 2013 "Mobilität zwischen westafrikanischer Freizügigkeit und europäischer Grenzziehung" *Geographische Rundschau*, 9, 12–18.

Nicholson, C.T.M. 2014 "Climate Change and the Politics of Causal Reasoning: The Case of Climate Change and Migration" *The Geographical Journal*, 180(2), 151–160.

Pedersen, J. 1995 "Drought, Migration and Population Growth in the Sahel: The Case of the Malian Gourma: 1900–1991" *Population Studies*, 49(1).

Petit, V. 1997 "Société d'origine et logiques migratoires. Les Dogon de Sangha (Mali)" *Population (French Edition)*, 52(3), 515–543.

Piguet, E. 2010 "Linking Climate Change, Environmental Degradation, and Migration: A Methodological Overview" *WIREs Climate Change*, 1.

Rademacher-Schulz, C. and Salifu Mahama, E. 2012 *"Where the Rain Falls" project. Case study: Ghana.* Results from Nadowli District, Upper West Region (Report 3), Bonn.

Rademacher-Schulz, C., Schraven, B. and Mahama, E.S. 2014 "Time Matters: Shifting Seasonal Migration in Northern Ghana in Response to Rainfall Variability and Food Insecurity" *Climate and Development,* 6(1), 46–52.

Rain, D. 1999 *Eaters of the Dry Season. Circular Labor Migration in the West African Sahel.* Boulder: Westview Press.

Romankiewicz, C. and Doevenspeck, M. 2015 "Climate and Mobility in the West African Sahel: Conceptualising the Local Dimensions of the Environment and Migration Nexus", in Greschke, H. and Tischler, J. eds. *Grounding Global Climate Change.* Dordrecht: Springer Netherlands, 79–100.

Romankiewicz, C., Doevenspeck, M., Brandt, M. and Samimi, C. 2016 "Adaptation as By-Product: Migration and Environmental Change in Nguith, Senegal" *Die Erde,* 147(2), 95–108.

Sieveking, N. and Fauser, M. 2009 *Migrationsdynamiken und Entwicklung in Westafrika: Untersuchungen zur entwicklungspolitischen Bedeutung von Migration in und aus Ghana und Mali* (COMCAD Working Papers 68). Bielefeld: COMCAD (Center on Migration, Citizenship and Development), Bielefeld University. Available at https://pub.uni-bielefeld.de/publication/1857026

Suhrke, A. 1994 "Environmental Degradation and Population Flows" *Journal of International Affairs,* 47(2), 473–496.

Tacoli, C. 2011 *Not Only Climate Change: Mobility, Vulnerability and Socio-Economic Transformation in Environmentally Fragile Areas of Bolivia, Senegal and Tanzania* (Human Settlements Working Paper Series Rural-Urban Interactions and Livelihood Strategies). London: International Institute for Environment and Development (IIED). Available at http://pubs.iied.org/10590IIED.html

van der Geest, K. 2011 "North-South Migration in Ghana: What Role for the Environment?" *International Migration,* 49, e69–e94.

van der Geest, K., Vrieling, A. and Dietz, T. 2010 "Migration and Environment in Ghana: A Cross-District Analysis of Human Mobility and Vegetation Dynamics" *Environment and Urbanization,* 22(1), 107–123.

van der Geest, K. 2009 *Ghana: Case Study Report.* Bonn: Environmental Change and Forced Migration Scenarios (EACH-FOR) Project.

van der Land, V. 2018 Migration and Environmental Change in the West African Sahel. Why Capabilities and Aspirations matter. Routledge Studies in Environmental Migration, Displacement and Resettlement, London: Routledge.

van der Land, V. 2015 *The Environment-Migration Nexus Reconsidered: Why Capabilities and Aspirations Matter* (Dissertation), Frankfurt am Main. Available at: http://publikationen.ub.uni-frankfurt.de/frontdoor/index/index/docId/39825.

van der Land, V. and Hummel, D. 2013 "Vulnerability and the Role of Education in Environmentally Induced Migration in Mali and Senegal" *Ecology and Society,* 18(4).

14

Burkina Faso

The adaptation-migration policy nexus in a drying climate

Nakia Pearson

Introduction

Forty-seven percent of Burkina Faso's land is degraded, while 37% is at high risk of degradation (UNCCD 2008). Such extensive environmental degradation has been linked to a series of major Sahelian droughts that began in the 1960s, and from which the region has yet to fully recover. While rainfall recovery and increased vegetation have been observed in the Sahel since the 1990s, leading some to suggest that the drought may have ended then (Ozer et al. 2003), long-term analysis of rainfall and temperature in Burkina Faso (1950–2013) shows a decrease of total annual precipitation, with rainfall levels in 2013 still far from what they were before the great droughts (De Longueville et al. 2016). Furthermore, analysis of vegetation trends using low resolution remote sensing data from 1982–1999 points to ongoing desertification processes in Burkina Faso (Hountondji et al. 2006).

Such environmental stresses have wreaked havoc on the livelihoods of rural Burkinabés, leading to large scale rural-rural migration as populations, particularly from northern and central regions, have sought more fertile land to cultivate as a survival response in the face of drought and rainfall-induced crop failures. While scholars have found it insufficient to explain environmental migration through a linear 'push' factor model that draws a direct causal link between environmental conditions and migration (Jonssen 2010), loss and damage studies have identified food insecurity as a serious vulnerability that often prompts distress migration (Afifi et al. 2013). Indeed, with 80% of its livelihood linked to rain-fed subsistence farming, Burkina Faso was considered one of the most seriously affected countries of the 2012 Sahel droughts in terms of loss in cereal production (FAO 2012).

Migration in response to environmental pressures is not new to Burkina Faso. For decades, Malian and Burkinabé farmers have alternated between their cocoa fields in what is now Ghana and Côte d'Ivoire, while cultivating cereals at home during the Sahelian rainy season from July–September (De Haan et al. 2002, Konseiga 2007). This chapter explains the relationship between drought and migration in Burkina Faso, highlighting past and present episodes, and considering policy implications for the future.

Explaining Burkina Faso's drying climate

Rainfall and temperature increase

A UNEP (2011) study of the nine country members of the Permanent Interstate Committee for Drought Control in the Sahel (CILSS) shows an overall rise in average seasonal temperature from 1970–2006 of approximately 1°C. In southern and central Burkina Faso, rises are between 0.5°C and 1.0°C, while less remarkable increases of up to 0.5°C have been observed in northern and western Burkina Faso (UNEP 2011). Both minimum and maximum temperature increases have been observed, with a significant increase in annual occurrence of hot days and nights (De Longueville et al. 2016).

An intertropical country marked by a Sudano-Sahelian climate, Burkina Faso experiences a mean annual rainfall ranging from 350mm in the northern Sahelian region to more than 1000 mm in the south.[1] The country has two distinct cycles of humidity: a rainy season that typically occurs through the months of June–September, while the rest of the year is dry.

Weather station observations of the country show that since 1902, the dry zone has been gradually spreading southward. These observations are corroborated with studies showing annual rainfall decrease, particularly in Bobo Dioulasso in the West, and along the Burkina Faso and Ghana borders where decline of seasonal rainfall between 1970–2006 exceed 50mm (UNEP 2011). Studies have related this decrease in rainfall in the last few decades to a reduced number of rainy days in August and September and thus, a premature cessation of the rainy season (Lodoun et al. 2013; Zorom et al. 2013). Furthermore, the warming of the Atlantic Ocean has been weakening the West African monsoon, causing the southward shift of isohyets, and displacing agro-ecological zones further south (Epule et al. 2014).

Although there is a general perception that average annual rainfall has been increasing since the 1990s, De Longueville et al.'s (2016) study suggests a more nuanced interpretation is in order. The study reveals various changes in Burkina Faso's long-term rainfall patterns, showing a decrease in overall rainfall, an increase in average rainfall for wet days, an increase in the maximum of consecutive dry days, and a decrease in maximum wet days (idem). Such climate variability seems to support other observations since 1993 that reveal longer successions of dry years, interspersed with single humid years, particularly 1994, 1999, and 2003 (Ali 2010).

It is expected that rainfall decline will continue throughout the 21st century, with a further 7.3% reduction in total rainfall by 2050 (Government of Burkina Faso 2007). Likewise, IPCC models predict more frequent and intense drought events in the future, with increasing atmospheric dust loadings and continued deforestation and land cover change (Boko et al. 2007), exacerbated by rainfall decline and increasing evapotranspiration rates in line with temperature rises (Nicholson 2000; IPCC 2012).

Desertification and drought processes

The United Nations Convention to Combat Desertification (UNCCD) defines desertification as "land degradation in arid, semi-arid and dry sub-humid areas resulting from various factors, including climatic variations and human activities" (UNCCD 1994, Article 1). A natural feature of the climate of regions affected by desertification, droughts have been defined as multi-year events when rainfall drops below a mean, as opposed to gradual climatic warming and drying (Warren & Khogali 1992). The relationship between desertification and drought are complex and largely debated. Stringer et al (2009) distinguish between drought, desertification, and climate change by delineating drought as a consequence of human-induced climate change, which could then cause desertification. IOM, on the other hand, considers desertification a slow-onset natural disaster comparable to drought, which is intensified by climate change (IOM 2009). Human-induced climate change is seen as a major cause of drought as it is linked to air and sea surface temperature rise, vegetation degradation, and dust feedbacks, all contributing factors of drought (Epule et al. 2014).

As in most West African countries, Burkina Faso's intensively weathered, arid soils inherently suffer from poor fertility, exhibiting limited water retention capacity, limited nutrient value, and reduced depth for root extension due to chemical and physical limitations such as laterite hardpans or severe acidity (Lahmar et al. 2012). The acceleration of water evaporation from free surfaces due to temperature rise has further reduced the capacity in soils to retain water and absorb aquifers (Government of Burkina Faso 1999). When erosive crusts or *zipelle* develop, they block infiltration, initiating a vicious cycle of desertification (Valentin 1992).

Such soils, having lost their physical and chemical integrity, are more easily swept away in the dust storms or violent rains that occur during the later part of rainy season. Indeed, large amounts of soil erosion have been attributed to wind erosion (windstorms) in the Burkinabé Sahelian climatic zone that comprises the Sahel, parts of the north and central north regions of the country. Dust feedbacks from the storms further suppress rainfall by promoting the formation of small cloud droplets not big enough to form rain drops (Lohmann & Feichter 2005), while at the same time contributing to surface heating by reflecting incoming solar radiation (Li et al. 1996). Both of these effects feed into a loop that leads to drier soils.

Exacerbating these processes are destructive agricultural practices and large-scale deforestation. Indeed, most degradation in Burkina Faso has occurred in the densely populated Central Plateau where land scarcity and declining yields have led farmers to drastically reduce fallow periods and expand cultivation onto marginal lands, both on less moisture-retentive gravelly soils in 'borrowed' plots and "richer, but difficult to work and sometimes waterlogged valley-bottoms" (Batterbury 1998: 889). Cambrézy and Sangli (2011) show that new land cultivation has led to a reduction of Burkina Faso's savannahs from 93,113 km^2 to 83,801 km^2 between 1992 and 2002. The chemical depletion of soils caused by such overcultivation reduces organic material through oxidation and the leaching of unused nutrients, accounting for soil degradation in both the Sahelian and Soudano-Sahelian zones of the country (Government of Burkina Faso 1999).

Studies have often emphasized the relationship between the rate of increase of cultivated surfaces (40.8% in 2007) and the 35.6% rate of rural population growth (Cambrézy & Sangli 2011). Ouedgraogo et al's (2010) analysis of land cover change and population dynamics in Burkina Faso's southern province of Sissili revealed a positive correlation between population size and deforestation, explaining for the conversion of forest land to cropland at an annual rate of 0.96% at the same time that population density in the south central Burkina almost doubled from 17 inhabitants/km^2 in 1986 to 30/km^2 in 2006. Often, this population growth is linked to the north-south migration of farmers and herders escaping drought and desertification in the northern parts of the country. Interestingly, while migration likely contribute to negative environmental changes in destination areas, such outflows from the northern ecologically marginal provinces of northern Burkina Faso have helped to reduce pressure in these regions (Lambin et al. 2001).

Environmentally-induced migration in Burkina Faso

During the years of the first major Sahelian droughts, out of the 700,000 Burkinabés who migrated, 336,000 went abroad, mostly originating from rural areas (52.2%)[2] and settling in neighboring countries like the Ivory Coast (53%)[3] (Coulibaly et al. 1975). Notably, internal rural-rural migration was also an important option: rural zones constituted 68% of departures and 41% of destinations between 1969 and 1973 (idem). Since then, the preference for rural destinations has fluctuated, with census figures showing a rise in migrants settled in rural zones to 75.3% in 1985 before descending to 70.4% in 1996. Despite large returns from Ivory Coast following xenophobic tenure politics in the 1990s and the internal conflict of the previous decade, current estimates of Burkinabés still living in Ivory Coast vary from 1.5–3.5 million, while the remaining international migrants reside in other member states of the Economic Community of West African States (ECOWAS) such as Ghana, Mali, Niger, and Benin, with a very low number living beyond those states or in countries belonging to the Organisation for Economic Co-operation and Development (OECD).

Migration from northern regions of Burkina Faso is positively correlated to soil degradation, rainfall anomalies within the season, and drought frequency. Certainly, "longer dry seasons are driving farmers to migrate from northern and central parts of the country into the fertile east and west" (Brown & Crawford 2008: 52). Henry et al. (2003) found that while statistical evidence showed drought to be significant in explaining migration patterns in Burkina Faso, sociodemographic factors were equally or slightly more important. Population growth, ill-equipped infrastructures, political instability, and weak crop reserves are all factors that may increase vulnerability in West Africa (Crétat et al. 2014).

Henry (2006) shows that economic and environmental factors are interconnected as destination areas are considered more attractive when natural resources are economically valorized (cash crops), and when development initiatives such as hydro-agricultural installations and the organization of a production system are present. The areas around the Kompienga and the Bagré dams in the East Region that became centers of diversified activities resulting from new farming hamlets, the development of horticulture, tree plantations, etc attracted waves of 'spontaneous' migrants who were initially reluctant to move under the Development of the Volta Valleys (AVV) resettlement scheme (Marchal and Quesnel 1996). This state-led scheme was developed in the aftermath of the severe Sahelian droughts of 1970–1972, in an attempt to resettle families from the densely populated Mossi Plateau to the under-populated valleys of the three Volta rivers that had been cleared of the onchocercose cattle disease (FAO 1987). Despite its ambitious goals of settling 55,000 families and increasing cotton and cereal production by 10%, the AVV program facilitated the movement of only 2,500 families by 1982 (idem). Populations had initially failed to migrate, limited by high costs, cohabitation problems, and land problems between natives and migrants.

Henry et al.'s (2004) findings suggest that people from drier regions are more likely than those from wetter areas to engage in both temporary and permanent migrations to other rural areas, thereby corroborating suggestions that out-migration may reduce population pressures on ecologically fragile areas. Jonsson (2010: 12) posits that "permanent abandonment of an environmentally degraded area is rather a solution, and immobility would indeed be a major constraint, in some cases certainly resulting in continuing degradation and death from starvation". Moreover, as exposure to such shocks increases people's vulnerability, their ability to migrate may be hindered, resulting in immobility (Black et al. 2011) and them becoming 'trapped'(Foresight 2011). Studies show that migration did in fact decrease during the severe drought years of the 1970s and 1980s in Burkina Faso (Henry et al 2004), indicating that the financial resources needed for migration may be difficult to obtain in times of severe drought. By limiting people's ability to rely on well-tested strategic mechanisms like *temporary migration* to diversify their livelihoods, such environmental events become 'precipitating events' (Tacoli 2011;Jonssen 2010) that greatly increase vulnerability.

Wouterse and Taylor (2008) demonstrated the importance of migration in the face of severe scarcity of natural resources in Burkina Faso. Like others living in fragile climatic conditions, Burkinabé rural communities have long used seasonal migration as a strategy to insure against the risk of climate variability. Studies show that urban or international remittances make up to 22% of rural household income in the drought-prone areas of Burkina Faso (Zahonogo 2011). Such remittances go to purchasing animals as an insurance investment (Wouterse 2008), and for animal traction which can increase labor output (Zahonogo 2011).

While the increasing frequency of droughts and unsteady rainfall patterns have undoubtedly increased households' dependence on extra-farm activity such as seasonal migration to diversify risks of bad harvests, famine, and scarce revenues (Peyraut 2012), environmental migration is increasingly becoming a permanent response to an increasingly variable climate (UNEP 2011). Traditional coping strategies like seasonal and circular migration that occur during extended periods of droughts and loss of agricultural production may evolve into permanent migration as a survival strategy when food security becomes problematic (IOM 2009).Henry et al.'s (2004) findings suggest that short-term rainfall deficits tend to increase the risk of long-term migration to rural areas and decrease the risk of short-term moves to distant destinations. It has been suggested that severe, irreversible forms of slow-onset events, often taking the form of repetitive droughts, have a lasting impact on resources and may lead to permanent moves, while sudden natural disasters spur more temporary migration (IOM 2011;Tacoli 2011).

Policy implications

Adaptation without migration

Since the state-led AVV resettlement project was launched in the 1970s, there has been no direct policy action to facilitate the movement or protect the livelihoods of environmental migrants in Burkina Faso. Keeping in line with the policy climate of the 1970s in which NGOs and donors emphasized sustainable agricultural techniques and natural resource management, the country's climate policy has rather focused on decentralization, reducing desertification, climate adaptation, and rural development.

The government has placed major emphasis on "the sustainable management of water, soils, and land use security in the countryside [which] constitute major challenges for Burkina Faso" (Government of Burkina Faso, 2012). Soil and water conservation techniques (Tacko et al. 2006), such as zaï and contour stone bunds, have been used on up to 300,000 hectares in Burkina Faso (Ouedraogo 2005), resulting in higher productivity, sustainable development, and increased growth rates, as well as evidence of reduced rural-rural and rural-urban migration (Reij 2005). Pearson (2013) observed that migrant farmers, often unable to afford chemical inputs, overwhelmingly implement these techniques in order to increase yields on their limited parcels of borrowed or rented land.

In order to better implement Burkina Faso's National Action Plan to Combat Climate Change (Government of Burkina Faso 1999), signed in conjunction with the 1994 UNCCD Convention, the government has made concerted efforts to decentralize decision-making power and democratize rural development, through the election of the Village Council for Development (CVD) (Mathieu & Yilmaz 2010). Such decentralization efforts have led to the implementation of tenure charts, in which local authorities and village members participate in elaborating legal conventions to fix rules and principles on natural resource use (Hôchet & Sanou 2012). Such an initiative is crucial in recognizing customary tenure law, which has a major stake in ensuring migrants' access to land, and may affect their likelihood to invest in sustainable farming practices on that land (Gray & Kevane 2001).

Legal context for environmental migration

Burkina Faso's migration policy lacks a comprehensive legal apparatus. The current institutional framework deals mainly with immigration management, foreign labor migration, and trafficking, each element managed by a distinct ministry and public institution with little consultation or cooperation between them. Such a decentralized framework might facilitate the addition of environment displacement through other managing institutions concerned with climate adaptation or risks and disaster such as the National Emergency Relief and Rehabilitation Council (CONASUR). Unfortunately, migration is regarded as one of the main sources of environmental degradation in the CONASUR framework (Government of Burkina Faso 2009). Furthermore, the National Action Plan on Combating Desertification, while classifying migration as a survival and livelihood diversification strategy, focuses on the need to control migration, which it also links to environmental degradation in destination areas (Pearson & Niaufre 2013).

While Burkina Faso is a ratifying member of the 2009 African Union Convention for the Protection and Assistance of Internally Displaced Persons in Africa (also known as the Kampala Convention), which explicitly recognizes the environment as a potential cause for forced displacement, it is unclear how the country's drought-induced migrants would benefit from the convention's singular focus on displacement in cases of 'natural disasters' without much attention dedicated to slow onset events.[4] It is essential that any policy concerned with the protection of displaced persons in the context of environmental change addresses not only movement precipitated by disasters, but also migration that is used to cope with or to avoid gradual environmental degradation that have the potential to evolve into humanitarian crises that prompt forced displacement.

Burkina Faso applies a tolerant immigration policy, particularly in regards to the reception of migrants who are nationals of ECOWAS member states, as outlined in the ECOWAS Protocol Relating To Free Movement Of Persons, Residence And Establishment.[5] But while the Protocol promotes the removal of obstacles to mobility, it provides no specific provisions for humanitarian aid to migrants. How people internationally displaced for environmental reasons might be assisted in terms of policies and programs is very unclear. One possible analogous example, albeit one that was used to integrate refugees from conflict, is that of the UNHCR's local integration initiative for Sierra Leonean and Liberian refugees in ECOWAS nations (Boulton 2009).

Conclusion

There exist several opportunities for the Burkina Faso government to adapt its institutions more directly towards recognizing migration as a strategy for adaptation to environmental degradation and climate change. Its AVV resettlement project in the past, though it may not have immediately succeeded, developed rural areas for migrants experiencing the protracted effects of repeated droughts, allowing them to re-establish their livelihoods. The country's commitment to decentralization and participation in local natural resource management puts it on track to more effectively deal with potential conflict between internal migrants and local communities competing for scarce land resources. The guidelines of international mandates to which Burkina Faso is currently held are, however, insufficient in tackling the particularities of slow-onset event-induced migration in the context of drought. Still, examples from ECOWAS provide clues for how to manage integration for those displaced by conflict in member states. What seems key to generating concrete policy action for the protection of environmentally-induced migrants in Burkina Faso is a willingness for the government – and many other governments, for that matter – to recognize the potential for migration to be used as an adaptive strategy that relieves pressures on ecologically stressed areas, provides opportunities for remittances which can be used to invest in sustainable agricultural techniques that increase productivity, fuels the recovery of desertified lands, and provides a means of sustenance for people whose livelihoods have been destroyed, among many other benefits. This would be a first step towards harmonizing the policy nexus between migration and the adaptation.

Notes

1 World Bank Dashboard Climate Baseline Overview Burkina Faso, retrieved May 2013, http://sdwebx. worldbank.org/climateportalb/home.cfm?page=country_profile&CCode=BFA
2 Percentage represents portion of international migrants originating from rural areas. Calculated using data from Coulibaly, S., Gregory J., Lavoie, A., &Piché, V. 1975. "Tome III mesure de la migration, 1969–73," *Les migrations voltaiques*, Centre Voltaïque de la Recherche Scientifique, Institut National de la Statistique et de la Démographie, Ouagadougou 1975, pp. 1–57.
3 Percentage refers to portion of international migrants who went to Ivory Coast. Calculated using data from Coulibaly, S., Gregory J., Lavoie, A., &Piché, V. 1975. "Tome III mesure de la migration, 1969–73." *Les migrations voltaiques*, Centre Voltaïque de la Recherche Scientifique, Institut National de la Statistique et de la Démographie, Ouagadougou 1975, pp. 1–57.
4 In article 4.2 of the Convention, states commit to prevent internal displacement related to environment issues by:

> devis[ing] early warning systems, in the context of the continental early warning system, in areas of potential displacement, establish[ing] and implement[ing] disaster risk reduction strategies, emergency and disaster preparedness and management measures and, where necessary, provid[ing] immediate protection and assistance to internally displaced persons.

5 Protocol A/P.1/5/79 Relating To Free Movement Of Persons, Residence And Establishment, ECOWAS, www.comm.ecowas.int/sec/index.php?id=ap010579&lang=en

Bibliography

Afifi, T., Liwenga, E., & Kwezi, L. (2013). Rainfall-induced crop failure, food insecurity and out-migration in Same Kilimanjaro, Tanzania. *Climate and Development*, 6 (1): 53-60.doi:10.1080/17565529.2013.82 6128

AfricanUnion 2009. Convention for the Protection and Assistance of Internally Displaced Persons in Africa (Kampala Convention).

Ali, A. 2010. "La variabilité et les changements climatiques au Sahel: Comprendre la situation actuelle de part l'observation," Le Sahel face aux changements climatiques: Enjeux pour un développement durable, Centre Régional AGRHYMET, Bulletin Mensuel, Comité permanent Inter-Etats de Lutte Contre la Sécheresse dans le Sahel.

Awumbila, M., Manuh, T., Quartey, P., Addoquaye Tagoe, C., &Antwi Bosiakoh, T. 2008. "Country Paper: Ghana," prepared for African Perspectives on Human Mobility Programme, MacArthur Foundation, Centre for Migration Studies, University of Ghana.

Batterbury, S. 1998. "Local Environmental Management, Land Degradation and the 'Gestion Des Terroirs' Approach in West Africa: Policies and Pitfalls." *Journal of International Development*, 10 (7): 871-898.

Black, R., Ammassari, S., Mouillesseaux, S., &Rajkotia, R. 2004. "Migration and Pro-Poor Policy in West Africa," Working Paper, C8, Sussex Centre for Migration Research, November 2004.

Black, R., Adger, W.N., Arnell, N.W., Dercon, S., Geddes, A., &Thomas, D. 2011. "The Effect of Environmental Change on Human Migration." *Global Environmental Change* 21 (Supp), S3–S11. http://dx.doi.org/10.1016/j.gloenvcha.2011.10.001

Boko, M., Niang, I., Nyong, A., Vogel, C., Githeko, A., Medany, M., Osman-Elasha, B., Tabo, R., Yanda, P.2007.*Africa. Climate Change 2007: Impacts, Adaptation and Vulnerability*. Contribution of Working Group II to the Fourth Assessment Report of the Intergovernmental Panel on Climate Change, M.L.

Parry, O.F. Canziani, J.P. Palutikof, P.J. van der Linden and C.E. Hanson, Eds., Cambridge University Press, Cambridge UK, 433–467.

Boulton, A., 2009. "Local Integration in West Africa." *Forced Migration Review*, 33, 32–34.

Brown, O. and Crawford, A. 2008. "Climate Change: A New Threat to Stability in West Africa? Evidence from Ghana and Burkina Faso." *African Security Review*, 17(3), September.

Cambrézy, L., &Sangli, G. 2011. "Les effets géographiques de l'accroissement de la population en milieu rural africain : l'exemple du Sud-ouest du Burkina Faso ", CFC, N°207.

Coulibaly, S., Gregory, J., Lavoie, A., &Piché, V. 1975. "Tome III mesure de la migration, 1969–73, " *Les migrations voltaïques*, Centre Voltaïque de la Recherche Scientifique, Institut National de la Statistique et de la Démographie, Ouagadougou 1975, pp. 1–57.

Crétat, J., Vizy, E. K., and Cook, K. H. 2014. "How Well Are Daily Intense Rainfall Events Captured by Current Climate Models Over Africa?" *Climate Dynamics* 42(9–10): 2691–2711.

De Longueville, F., Hountondji, Y-C., Kindo, I., Gemenne, F., &Ozer, P. 2016. Long-Term Analysis of Rainfall and Temperature Data in Burkina Faso (1950–2013)." *International Journal of Climatology*. DOI: 10.1002/joc.4640

De Haan, A., Brock, K., &Coulibaly, N. 2002. "Migration, Livelihoods and Institutions: Contrasting Patterns of Migration in Mali." *Journal of Development Studies*, 38(5), 37–58.

ECOWAS 1979. Protocol A/P.1/5/79 Relating to Free Movement of Persons, Residence and Establishment

Epule, T.E., Peng, C., Lepage, L., & Chen, Z. 2014. "The Causes, Effects and Challenges of Sahelian Droughts: A Critical Review" *Regional Environmental Change*, 14:145, DOI: 10.1007/s10113-013-0473-z

FAO Executive Brief, The Sahel crisis 2012, 27 April 2012, http://reliefweb.int/node/493556

FAO 1987. *Effets des migrations sur les structures agraires et l'emploi rural au Burkina Faso: Rapport préparé par la société africaine d'Etudes et de Développement.*

Foresight: Migration and Global Environmental Change 2011. Final Project Report, The Government Office for Science, London.

Government of Burkina Faso 1999. "Programme d'Action National de Lutte Contre la Désertification (PAN/LCD)," Adopted by the decree n°2000-160/PM/MEE on 28 April 2000. Ministère de l'Environnement et de l'Eau, Secrétariat Permanent du Conseil National Pour la Gestion de l'Environnement.

Government of Burkina Faso 2007. "Programme d'Action National d'Adaptation à la Variabilité et aux Changements Climatiques (PANA du Burkina Faso)," Ministère de l'Environnement et du Cadre de Vie, Secrétariat Permanent du Conseil National Pour l'Environnement et le Developpement Durable.

Government of Burkina Faso 2009. "Plan National Multi Risque de Préparation et de Réponse aux Catastrophes, " Plan de Contigence Burkina Faso, Conseil National de Secours d'Urgence et de Réhabilitation (CONASUR).

Government of Burkina Faso 2012. Programme natonal du secteur rural (PNSR) 2011-2015. October 2012, Ouagadougou. Gray, L. C., &Kevane, M. 2001. "Evolving Tenure Rights and Agricultural Intensification in Southwestern Burkina Faso." *World Development*, 29(4), 573–587, Elsevier Science Ltd.

Hampshire, K. 2010. "Fulani on the Move: Seasonal Economic Migration in the Sahel as a Social Process." *Journal of Development Studies*, 38 (5) :15-36.

Henry, S., Boyle, P. J., & Lambin, E. F. 2003. "Modelling Inter-Provincial Migration in Burkina Faso, West Africa: The Role of Socio-Demographic and Environmental Factors." *Applied Geography*, 23 (2-3): 115–136. doi:10.1016/j.apgeog.2002.08.001

Henry, S., Schoumaker, B., &Beauchemin, C. 2004. "The Impact of Rainfall on the First Out-Migration: A Multi-Level Event-History Analysis in Burkina Faso." *Population and Environment*, 25(5): 423–460.

Henry, S. 2003. *The Influence of the Natural Environment on Migration in Burkina Faso.* Louvain-la-Neuve: UCL, p. 190.

Henry, S. 2006. "Panel Contribution to the Population-Environment Research Network Cyberseminar on Rural Household Micro-Demographics, Livelihoods and the Environment", 2006. www.populationenvironmentresearch.org/seminars.jsp. Retrieved on 14 March 2013.

Hountondji, Y-C., Sokpon, N., &Ozer, P. 2006. "Analysis of the Vegetation Trends Using Low Resolution Remote Sensing Data in Burkina Faso (1982–1999) for the Monitoring of Desertification." *International Journal of Remote Sensing*, 27(5), 871–884.

Iliffe, J. 2007. *Africans: The History of a Continent*. New York, NY: Cambridge University Press, p. 66.

Intergovernmental Panel on Climate Change. 2012. *Managing the Risks of Extreme Events and Disasters to Advance Climate Change Adaptation*. A Special Report of Working Groups I and II of the Intergovernmental Panel on Climate Change [Field, C.B., V. Barros, T.F. Stocker, D. Qin, D.J. Dokken, K.L. Ebi, M.D. Mastrandrea, K.J. Mach, G.-K. Plattner, S.K. Allen, M. Tignor, and P.M. Midgley (eds.)]. Cambridge, UK and New York, NY: Cambridge University Press, 582 pp.

International Organization for Migration (IOM) 2009. "Migration, Environment and Climate Change: Assessing The Evidence," 72–73. https://publications.iom.int/system/files/pdf/migration_and_environment.pdf. Retrieved on 4 May 2012.

International Organization for Migration (IOM) 2011. "Climate Change, Environmental Degradation and Migration," Background Paper, International Dialogue on Migration Intersessional Workshop, 29-30 March 2011.Jonssen, G. 2010. "The Environmental Factor in Migration Dynamics – a Review of African Case Studies," Paper 21, Working Papers, International Migration Institute, James Martin 21st Century School, University of Oxford.

Konseiga, A. 2007. "Household Migration Decisions as Survival Strategy: The Case of Burkina Faso." *Journal of African Economies*, Centre for the Study of African Economies (CSAE), 16(2), 198–233.

Lahmar, R., Bationo, A.B., Lamso, N.D., Guéro, Y., & Tittonell, P. 2012. "Tailoring Conservation Agriculture Technologies to West Africa Semi-Arid Zones: Building on Traditional Local Practices for Soil Restoration. *Field Crop Res.*, 132, 158–167.

Lambin, E., Turner, B., Geist, H., Agbola, S., Angelsen, A., Bruce, J., Coomes, O., Dirzo, G., Fischer, R., and Folke, C. 2001. "The Causes of Land-Use and Land-Cover Change: Moving Beyond the Myths." *Global Environmental Change*, 11(4), 261–269.

Li, X., Maring, H., Savoie, D., Voss, K., and Prospero, J.M. 1996. "Dominance of Mineral Dust in Aerosol Light Scattering in the North Atlantic Trade Winds." *Nature*, 380, 416–419.

Lodoun, T., Giannini, A., Traoré, P.S., Somé, L., Sanon, M., Vaksmann, M., & Rasolodimby, J.M. 2013. "Changes in Seasonal Descriptors of Precipitation in Burkina Faso Associated with the Late 20th Century Drought and Recovery in West Africa." *Environmental Development*, 5, 96–108.

Lohmann, U., & Feichter, J. 2005. "Global Indirect Aerosol Effects: A Review." *Atmospheric Chemistry and Physics*, 5, 715–737, www.atmos-chem-phys.org/acp/5/715/ SRef-ID: 1680–7324/acp/2005–5–715

Marchal, J-Y., & Quesnel, A. 1996. "Dans les vallées du Burkina Faso, l'installation de la mobilité. " *La ruralité dans les pays du Sud à la fin du vingtième siècle*. Gastellu Jean-Marc (ed.). Paris : ORSTOM, 1997, p. 595–614. (Colloques et Séminaires). Atelier sur la Ruralité dans les Pays du Sud à la Fin du Vingtième Siècle, Montpellier (FRA), 1996/04/02–03. ISBN 2-7099-1369-0

Mathieu, S., & Yilmaz, S. 2010. "Local Government Discretion and Accountability in Burkina Faso." *World Bank, USA Public Administration and Development Public Admin. Dev.*, 30, 329–344. Published Online in Wiley Online Library (Wileyonlinelibrary.Com) Doi: 10.1002/Pad.579

McIntyre, S. "The Impact of Drought on Burkina Faso's Agricultural Sector: Implications for Food-Security Related Human Health." Uploaded on Academia: www.academia.edu/13386793/The_impact_of_drought_on_Burkina_Fasos_agricultural_sector_and_its_implications_for_food-security_related_human_health

Nicholson, S. 2000. "Land Surface Processes and Sahel Climate." *Reviews of Geophysics*, 38(1), 117–139.

Ouedraogo, S 2005. "Intensification de l'agriculture dans le Plateau Central du Burkina Faso. Une analyse des possibilités à partir des nouvelles technologies, " Doctoral Thesis, 322.p

Ouedraogo, T., Savadogo, C., & Oden, O. 2010. "Land Cover Change and Its Relation with Population Dynamics in Burkina Faso, West Africa." *Land Degradation & Development*, 21, 453–462. Published online 17 March 2010 in Wiley Online Library (wileyonlinelibrary.com) DOI: 10.1002/ldr.981

Ouedraogo, I., Ouattara, K., Kaboré' S., Séraphine, P., & Souleymane, B.J. 2011. "Permanent Internal Migration as Response to Food Shortage: Implication to Ecosystem Services in Southern Burkina Faso." *Food Production – Approaches, Challenges and Tasks*, Prof. Anna Aladjadjiyan (Ed.), InTech, DOI: 10.5772/33857. Available from http///www.intechopen.com/books/food-production-approaches-challenges-and-tasks/permanent-internal-migration-as-response-to-food-shortage-implications-to-ecosystems-services-in-south

Ozer, P., Erpicum, M., Demarée, G., &Vandiepenbeeck, M. 2003. "The Sahelian Drought May Have Ended During the 1990s." *Hydrological Sciences Journal*, 48(3), 489–492.doi: 10.1623/hysj.48.3.489.45285

Pearson, N. 2013. "Burkina Faso: The Effects of Environmental Migration on the Implementation of Agro-Ecological Methods, Exchanges and Cooperation," Unpublished Masters Thesis, Sciences Po.

Pearson, N., & Niaufre, C. 2013. "Desertification and Drought Related Migrations in the Sahel – The Cases of Mali and Burkina Faso," *The State of Environmental Migration 2013: A Review of 2012*, François Gemenne, Pauline Brücker, Dina Ionesco (eds.), pp. 79–98.

Hochet, P., & Sanou, S. 2012. Reconnaissance des droits fonciers locaux – Enjeux opérationnels de l'établissement des accords de prêt prévus par la loi burkinabè portant régime foncier rural. *Les Notes de politique de Negos-GRN*, N°16., www.foncier-developpement.fr/wp-content/uploads/Note-politique-Negos_16.pdf

Peyraut, M. 2012. "Gérer les déplacements des populations dus aux phénomènes climatiques extrêmes," Field Report-Burkina Faso (Nov 6–26,2011), Projet EXCLIM: Exil Climatique., 21p.

Pretty, J., Toulmin, C., Williams, S. 2011. "Sustainable Intensification in African Agriculture." *International Journal of Agriculture*, 9(1), 5–24.

Reij, C. 2005. "Investment in Africa's Dry Lands: Impacts on Agriculture, Environment and Poverty Reduction." *Rural Development in Sub-Saharan Africa: Policy Perspectives for Agriculture, Sustainable Resource Management and Poverty Reduction*. Ruerd Ruben and Bart de Steenhuijsen Piters (eds.), Royal Tropical Institute (KIT) – Amsterdam KIT Development, Policy and Practice.

Remy, G. 1972. "Donsin: les structures agraires d'un village mossi de la région de Nohoro, " Collège de France, Laboratoire d'anthropologie sociale.

Stringer, L. C., Dyer, J. C., Reed, M. S., Dougill, A. J., Twyman, C., &Mkwambisi, D.2009. "Adaptations to Climate Change, Drought and Desertification: Local Insights to Enhance Policy in Southern Africa." *Environmental Science & Policy*,12(7), 748–765.

Tacko, K.S.,Verchot, L.,& Mackensen, J. 2006. *Climate Change and Variability in the Sahel Region: Impacts and Adaptation Strategies in the Agricultural Sector*. Nairobi, Kenya: World Agroforestry Center and United Nations Environment Program.

Tacoli, C. 2011.*Not Only Climate Change: Mobility, Vulnerability and Socio-Economic Transformations in Environmentally Fragile Areas of Bolivia, Senegal and Tanzania*. London: International Institute for Environment and Development (IIED) 28.

Thieba, D. 2003. "Enjeux fonciers et développement durable dans les zones libérées de l'onchocerose au Burkina Faso, "Groupe de Recherche et d'Action sur le Foncier (GRAF).

UNCCD 1994. United Nations Convention to Combat Desertification in Countries Experiencing Serious Drought and/or Desertification, Particularly in Africa, New York, 12 September 1994. http://www.unccd.int/Lists/SiteDocumentLibrary/conventionText/conv-eng.pdf

UNCCD 2008. "International Experts' Consultation: Desertification, Migration & Local Development," The Global Mechanism of the United Nations Convention to Combat Desertification. http://www.migration4development.org/sites/default/files/migration_desertification.pdfUnited Nations Environment Programme (UNEP) 2011. *Livelihood Security: Climate Change, Migration and Conflict in the Sahel*. Châtelaine, Geneva: United Nations Environment Programme.

Valentin, C. 1992. "Surface Crusting in the Sahel: Assessment, Causes and Control." *Erosion, Conservation and Small-Scale Farming*. Hans Hurni and Kebede Tato (eds.). Marceline, Missouri: Walsworth Publ. Comp., pp. 63–74.

Warren, A.,& Khogali, M. 1992. *Desertification and Drought in the Sudano-Sahelian Region 1985–1991*. New York, NY: United Nations Sudano-Sahelian Office (UNSO), 102 pp.

Wouterse, F., &Taylor, J. E. 2008. "Migration and Income Diversification: Evidence from Burkina Faso." *World Development*, 36, 625–640.

Zahonongo, P. 2011. "Migration and Agricultural Production in Burkina Faso." *African Journal of Agricultural Research*, 6(7), 1844–1852.

Zorom, M., Barbier, B., Mertz, O., & Servat, E. 2013. "Diversification and Adaptation Strategies to Climate Variability: A Farm Typology for the Sahel." *Agricultural System*s, 116, 7–15.

15

Fleeing from arid lands

Pastoralism in the context of climate change

Julia Blocher[1]

Introduction

The negative impacts of gradual climate change and natural hazards most directly and disproportionately affect the livelihoods of rural, natural resource-reliant households (Obokata et al. 2014). Pastoralists around the world are uniquely affected by the growing prevalence of natural hazards and negative effects of climate change (Galaty and Johnson 1990). In the savannahs and the highlands of the world, enhancing livelihoods while preserving natural resources is a high-wire act. It is expected that with increased frequency and severity of droughts, pastoralists will continue to be among the most vulnerable to climatic changes. For some, water and pasture scarcity will prompt not only more frequent but also more prolonged movements. For others, as is already observed among semi-pastoralist groups such as the Fulani of West Africa, environmental pressures may lead to increased sedentarisation, intensification of livestock-raising techniques, or abandonment of livestock production (Jabbar et al. 1995). While mobility has been a traditional adaptive response to change for millennia, this chapter argues more emphasis is needed on how these 'normal' nomadic movements are influenced by climate change, in a way that considers pastoralist agency.

The body of literature on pastoral systems and cultures is historically and empirically rich, and many studies take an ecological approach to relating mobility cycles to the environment. Johnson (1969) offered nuanced models of 'nomadism' and 'semi-nomadism', suggesting that the adjustment of any group to environmental conditions is a dynamic adjustment, moving the group towards a more sedentary mode of life or to a more nomadic way of life. This approach to framing the human-environment relationship has been updated by more recent authors, consistent with wider developments in environmental migration research. Today, this area of study increasingly considers the potential impacts of unprecedented anthropogenic environmental degradation and climate destabilisation on the delicate balance struck by pastoralist livelihoods. This chapter provides an overview of the current state of knowledge on complex pastoral responses to environmental and climate change, and offers insights into how pastoralist peoples negotiate a changing climate, taking into account the historical, socio-cultural, and political processes in which pastoral communities develop their livelihood strategies.

Two important points of departure underlie the findings in this chapter. The first is that pastoral movements are regular and orderly, governed by the seasonal regimes of rainfall, temperature, and pasture availability, as well as by the social arrangements of different groups on their territories or traditional pastures (Johnson 1969). The second is that the predictability and reliability of those regimes are all increasingly at threat by anthropogenic climate change (Nelson et al. 2007; Parry et al. 2007). Pastoralist societies' deeply-entrenched flexibility and adaptability will be key assets as they confront the challenges presented by rapidly changing environmental conditions.

Pastoralism defined

Pastoralism is a lifestyle and livelihood marked by the shepherding of livestock on open pastures: it is both process and praxis. While 'pure' nomadic pastoralism, in which whole communities and their livestock move regularly, does exist, most pastoralist groups diversify their livelihoods by practicing varying degrees of sedentary agricultural production. Agro-pastoralists are often described as being largely subsistence agriculturalists who also maintain considerably sized mobile herds (Brandström et al. 1979). Transhumant livestock management typically involves part of the household or community in migratory herd management between summer and winter points – usually the young males herd the more robust animals – while elders, women, and children may remain in a semi-permanent settlement (Devereux 2006; McPeak et al. 2011). For the sake of simplicity, 'pastoralist' and 'agro-pastoralist' are used in this chapter as crude shorthand to describe all the complexity of groups predominantly engaged in pastoral and semi-pastoral lifestyles.

Because pastoralist and agro-pastoralist communities exist on a continuum between a purely sedentary society and a hypothetical 'pure' nomadism (Johnson 1969), they are not easily defined as static 'types'. Many pastoralist groups in the Sahel, for example, are increasingly relying on sedentary agricultural production and thus are increasingly agro-pastoralist (Niamir-Fuller 1998). Using fourteen case studies, Johnson (1969) nevertheless attempts a flexible classification of 'nomadism', distinguishing between 'horizontal' nomadism (moving between dry season water points and wet season pastures, also frequently referred to as transhumant livestock management), 'vertical' nomadism (oscillating up and down slopes), and a number of sub-classifications, based on the groups' political and social organization, length of migratory route, kinds of animals herded, types of seasonal location, the role of agriculture, and methods of trading. Galaty and Johnson (1990) offer three categories of pastoralists: pastoralists of the plains (such as the Fulbe/Fula, Maasai, Samburu, and India), of the desert and tundra (mainly the Taureg, Bedu, Middle Eastern Hima system, Botswana, and reindeer herders of the Arctic), and mountain pastoralism (including the Lakenkhel, camelid herders of the Andes, Mediterranean semi-pastoral livestock producers, and agro-pastoral communities of eastern North Africa [e.g. Berbers in Morocco]). Pastoralists may be in some ways compared to people practicing other nomadic and semi-nomadic lifestyles (e.g. the Aka and Twa ['pygmies'] of Central Africa, the San of Southern Africa) in terms of the similarity of challenges they face in today's globalised world, but this will not be a focus of this chapter.

A disproportionate share of research on pastoral and semi-pastoral communities is focused on the Sahel and the Horn of Africa, regions that are the main foci of this chapter. Nonetheless, pastoralism is a global phenomenon. The livelihoods and lifestyles of pastoralists vary across regions, but they share three common characteristics: some degree of mobility, a livelihood based principally on the keeping of livestock, and a special attachment to land resources (IDMC 2014).

Pastoral livelihoods may be best understood not as *embodying* the roles and qualities characterised as distinctively pastoralist, but rather as *performing* the activities that are reflective of this state (Galaty and Johnson 1990: 65–66).

While climate change demonstrably affects the resources on which pastoralist groups sustain themselves, the premise of this chapter is that pastoral communities are meeting the challenge of climate change with resilience and self-determination, and by using traditional knowledge. The cultural values, history, and practices of pastoralists are important for understanding the meanings and consequences of climate-induced migration – which is both a discursive and material phenomenon. This chapter does not present a one-size-fits-all or static view of pastoralism as a phenomenon. Pastoralism is not simply an occupation, even when it is practiced in combination with more sedentary forms of agriculture (Johnson 1969); it is a way of life intrinsically linked to the identity of the communities and individuals that practise it. Individual pastoralist groups and pastoralists have their own perceptions of and responses to changing ecological and climatological patterns, and their own experiences of mobility.

Evolving western views of pastoralism

The impressions and interpretations held by outsiders of pastoralist lifestyles have evolved considerably in the last half-century. Beginning in the 1950s and 1960s, the ecologist movement and concurrent boon in anthropological research[2] was accompanied by an increased attention to preservation of Indigenous communities' lands, art, practices, and cultures. Colourful images of exotic tribesmen and bare-breasted women from Samburu, Maasai, Turkana, and other pastoralist and semi-pastoralist groups splashed across the covers of western magazines, mainly. *Time Magazine's* September 1959 issue exemplifies this, describing the Maasai as:

> fierce, sensual warriors who used dung and ochre for hair oil and drank cattle blood laced with urine. In periodic sport they swooped down on their Bantu neighbours, ramming seven-foot spears through the males and carrying off their women, who often did not seem to mind.
>
> *(Time 1959: n.p.)*

The overt sexual overtones in the representation of both women and warriors form a recurrent theme in western photographs of pastoralists, consistent with other representations of 'the savage' throughout history (Kasfir 2007: 282). Fascination for the exotic – akin to a nostalgia for the virility of one's youth, but tainted with a bit more than a hint of voyeurism – is exemplified by what Alloula (1986: 130–131) characterises as the "colonial postcard" featuring familiar images of young Samburu, Masaai and Turkana women with beaming smiles. Such images situate the colonized in a helpless passivity and objectification, on the other side of the 'tourist gaze', prey to a non-physical form of violence (Urry 1992). Indeed, colonial era historians and onlookers admired the Maasai for their impressive 'breeding' (Cameron 1955: 45).

Romantic fascination with pastoralists ebbed in the face of severe droughts and famines in Sahelian Africa in the 1970s and 1980s. In both popular media and scholarly research, pastoralists have become more often described as the poorest and most vulnerable members of society, given their exposure to multiple hazards, their minority status or perceived political marginalisation, and their relatively low income per capita (UN 2013). Those who move to urban centres to seek employment, support from relatives, or emergency aid are frequently labelled by external parties as 'pastoralist dropouts' (Adow 2008; Desta et al. 2008; Headey et al. 2014).

The view that traditional pastoral livelihoods were under siege in the face of a rapidly changing environment came to a head in 2007, with UN Secretary-General Ban Ki-moon explaining in the *Washington Post* that climate pressures were pitting pastoralist herders against agriculturalists for control over a shrinking resource base, causing conflict in Sudan (Ban 2007). "It is no accident that the violence in Darfur erupted during the drought," he wrote; "Until then, Arab nomadic herders had lived amicably with settled farmers" (Ban 2007: n.p.). This claim is probably inaccurate, since longstanding pre-existing animosity between these groups is well documented. The Nilotic peoples of South Sudan (especially the Dinka and Nuer) and the Nubian peoples of central Sudan mistrust Arab herders due to the latter's long-time targeting of the former for enslavement. The practice was 'revived' in 1983 by the Bagarra cattle herders, a group which fought for the government of Khartoum against the Sudan People's Liberation Army (SPLA) (De Waal 1998: 135; Jok 2010: viii–x). Concurrently, drought in the Darfur region in 1983–1985 and desertification in the northern Sahara led many cattle herders to lose their livestock, prompting them to seek resources by encroaching on southern farmers' land and, for some, by conducting raids (Grawert 1998; Jok 2010).

For many, the Darfur example suggests that prolonged droughts of the type expected to become more frequent and severe under climate change can put pastoral groups into increased contact and competition with each other and with their agriculturalist neighbours, contributing to localised flare-ups of violence and ultimately to larger civil conflict, a dynamic described in greater detail later in this chapter (Ahmed et al. 2002). On the other hand, such claims that attempt to draw reductive links between climate change and conflict can obscure important socio-political factors. While feuds and cattle raiding among pastoralist groups do indeed occur, inter-group dynamics are very complex and driven by a host of socio-economic factors. Cattle theft is also driven by entrenched cultural practices, and is often mutually authorised by the elders of the groups involved (Halderman et al. 2002; Meier et al. 2007).

The linkages between climate, conflict, and pastoral livelihoods under threat are made in good faith, and generate a useful discussion of how potentially serious the impacts of climate change will be in terms of migration and involuntary displacement. Accounts from the mid-2000s of pastoralists provoking conflict both across group lines and with their settled neighbours, apparently emboldened by drought- and famine-induced desperation, typify the conventional wisdom of the broader climate refugee discourse (e.g. Myers 2002) that has characterized many public discussions. Activists, policymakers, the media, and many scholars continue to repeat the underlying assumptions and implications of this logic, echoing the Malthusian idea that ecological stresses foment migration and conflict in a mutually reinforcing process (Bettini 2013).

In the arenas where battles for post-colonial justice are fought, in which criticisms of ecological destruction, securitisation of borders, and notions of citizenship are debated, the example of pastoralists is often invoked. Critical scholars draw attention to the agency of migrants, often overlooked in the climate displacement narrative. For example, Farbotko and Lazrus (2012: 1) observe: "those identified as imminent climate refugees are being held up like ventriloquists to present a particular (western) 'crisis of nature'", and that global narratives like 'climate refugee' discourses can "entrench vulnerable communities in inequitable power relations, redirecting their fate from their hands" (Farbotko and Lazrus 2012: 382). Continued exploitation of vulnerable communities is made possible through the commodification of the 'victims', which enables political point-scoring, greater newsworthiness, and selective presentation of 'evidence' to justify western attention to their subjects (Hingley 2017).

The humanitarian representation of 'pastoralist dropout', which nicely echoes the victimisation narrative, is, however, generally inaccurate in terms of the motivations why some pastoralists opt for some degree of settlement, and overlooks how mobility (and immobility) cuts across the dynamic life-courses of people (c.f. Findlay et al. 2015). In particular, it overlooks the time horizons and processes of adaptation relevant to pastoralist societies. In climate change research, adaptation usually refers to how systems or processes manage or adjust to changing conditions, stresses, hazards, risks, and opportunities. Adaptations can occur at multiple scales, in anticipatory or reactive fashion, and what may be adaptive today may not be tomorrow (Nelson et al. 2007; Gemenne and Blocher 2017). As is detailed ahead, processes of adaptation in pastoral societies are distinctive relative to others, with migration and mobility playing an important role. The natural state of pastoral systems is one of continuous change, making it difficult or unhelpful to attempt to assess its state of adaptation at any point in time (Galvin 2009). Because pastoralism is itself an inherently adaptive livelihood practice, the representation of pastoralists as victims is flawed. While there are indeed limits on the adaptability of pastoralists in the face of climate change, many such limits are the result of external pressures than on the adaptability of the pastoralist way of life.

Pastoralist livelihoods today

Today, estimates suggest there are between 30–40 million nomadic pastoralists worldwide (Hampshire 2002). Pastoral production systems support a much larger number of people, including household members not directly involved in herding. The estimates vary widely, largely depending on how pastoralism is defined. More inclusive estimates count between 120 million (Rass 2006) to 200 million[3] (IFAD 2009; Galvin et al. 2008) in total. Pastoral production provides an estimated 10 per cent of meat consumed by people worldwide, and non-exclusively occupies between 25 per cent (Blench 2001; Boto et al. 2012) and 45 per cent (Herrero et al. 2009) of the world's land. Pastoral livelihoods are common in the arid and semi-arid areas of Africa, the Arabian peninsula, the highlands of Latin America and in central Asian countries such as Afghanistan and Mongolia. Pastoral livelihoods are mostly found in arid and semi-arid lands (ASALs).

Pastoralist livelihoods are common in the ASALs of Djibouti, Eritrea, Ethiopia, Kenya, Uganda, Somalia, South Sudan, and Sudan (see REGLAP 2012). In Kenya, for example, the ASALs constitute about 80 per cent of the total land mass and are home to about three million people who are directly employed in pastoralist livestock production or, to a lesser extent, wild game preservation for tourism, an occupation that requires similar aptitudes (IOM 2010). People living in these fragile environments necessarily maintain a delicate balance of consumption and conservation, and cash income is scarce. In Kenya's ASALs of Kenya, over 60 per cent of inhabitants subsist on less than one dollar per day (IOM 2010).

Pastoralist livelihoods can be quite diversified. Whilst men and older boys are occupied primarily with the management of livestock, more sedentary members of the community, especially women, engage in crop production, rearing of livestock, petty trade of dairy and leather products, making and selling handmade items (like jewellery), firewood collection, and/or charcoal production (Coppock et al. 2011). In a study of the Somali region of Ethiopia, for example, Devereux (2006) found that almost 70 per cent of households engage in livestock rearing, but large numbers also engage in cereal crop production (43.4 per cent), firewood collection (17 per cent), and charcoal production (14.7 per cent), while smaller numbers of households engage in various petty trade, services, crafts (for example, 6.3 per cent were engaged in mat making), or higher value crop production (Devereux 2006; Desta et al. 2014).

Scholarly work on the effects of environmental changes and climate change on pastoralist livelihoods and mobility is complex and nuanced. Researchers have provided insights into how pastoralists' adaptive nomadism has and will respond to steady and irreversible climate changes (Galvin et al. 2008; Galvin 2009; Homewood et al. 1984; 2001, 2004). Such studies usually consider not only the direct impacts of climate, but also of other long-term factors that interact to drive land degradation, such as population growth, globalization, institutional dynamics (such as changes to land tenure and governance regimes), government policies (such as conservation policies), and socio-economic and cultural factors (e.g. filial parcelling of territories) that lead to fragmentation of pastoralist land.[4] In this context, climate change is understood as accelerating and exacerbating the many non-climatic challenges facing mobile peoples (Gemenne and Blocher 2017), with the climate 'signal' being strong for pastoralists given the particular nature of their resource-based livelihoods. Scholarly research in this area is complemented by a significant body of 'grey' literature from NGOs and humanitarian organizations (see Adow 2008; Oxfam 2008; IOM 2010; IDMC 2014).

Pressures on pastoralism

Thirty-four peer-reviewed academic studies on pastoralism found in the University of Neuchatel CliMig database[5] and through Google scholar were reviewed in preparation for this chapter and to identify key challenges facing modern day pastoralists. Roughly two-thirds of the studies reviewed consider pastoralism in East and West Africa (in roughly even proportions), the remaining studies coming from the Middle East, North Africa, Asia, and montane regions of South America. In parallel with the wider field of environmental migration research, the effects on pastoralist mobility of climate change has been a growing area of concern, and is addressed in more than half the articles studied. Other common areas of interest include conflict and security; pastoralists' perceptions of and migration responses to environmental changes; and the health, fertility, and impact on ecological conservation of pastoralist groups and their herds. Additional details now follow.

Migratory pressures and opportunities

Climatic variability and change

Given the strong connection between climate and livelihoods, pastoralists are especially affected by the growing prevalence of natural hazards and of the negative effects of climate change. Climate change is expected to accelerate the already shrinking resource base of pasture, cropland, and water, and is likely to compromise agriculture and food security across Africa (Niang et al. 2014). Lands are becoming drier and temperatures are rising in many areas, as rainfall is less plentiful and less predictable. Arid and semiarid areas are expected to increase by 5–8% by 2080 (Solomon et al. 2007). Climate change may also affect El Niño events, which significantly influence climate and rainfall variability in east Africa (Schreck and Semazii 2004). The increased severity of dryness and drought adds to other migratory pressures and causes of herd depletion (which can itself prompt herders to move, as explained ahead), including flash floods, conflict and localised violence, cattle rustling, population growth, the privatisation of grazing lands, and exploitation of natural resources.

Droughts have been known to force pastoralists to move across ecological systems that span multiple countries in search of water and pastures, where they face diverse policy environments, creating significant political challenges. Indeed, pastoralists in Kenya reported the search for pasture was the main 'pull factor' for cross-border migration, cited by 79 per cent of respondents in North Eastern region, 98 per cent of Turkana and 94 per cent of Maasai surveyed (IOM

2010). Drought is considered by Kenyan pastoralists to create the strongest trigger for increased movement (77 per cent in the North Eastern area, 88 per cent in Turkana and 92 per cent in the Maasai clusters), because of its effect on pastureland and thus on livestock.

Erratic rainfall is a frequently cited concern among pastoralists. For example, Turkana and Wajir elders report that the dry season is becoming longer, and the rains fail more often than in the past, creating an environment less habitable for people and livestock (IOM 2010: 28). Elders expressed their perception that in previous years the failure of either the short or the long rainy seasons resulted in droughts, and in recent years it was increasingly common for both seasons to fail. Some suggest that what was once an eight-year drought cycle two decades ago has become a two-year cycle (IOM 2010). Eritrean, Somali, and Sudanese refugees in Ethiopia and Uganda have similarly reported that discernible shifts in weather patterns had negatively impacted agro-pastoralist livelihoods and food security, and reduced their resilience to the concurrent effects of conflict (Afifi et al. 2012). Individuals not directly involved in pastoralist production have the perception that they have also been negatively affected by rising food prices, declining profits, and decreased turnover amongst traders, which was partly a consequence of declined output (*idem*).

Drought is a chronic and growing problem in the Greater Horn of Africa; from 1971–2006, there was a significant decrease in the number of rainy season days and an increase in warm extremes, particularly at night (Omondi et al. 2014). Vegetative cover is expected to decrease significantly in the Horn should such trends continue (Hoscilo et al. 2015), with an observed reduction in water storage from 2002–2010 suggesting such changes are already occurring (Omondi et al. 2014). Droughts are likely to be more frequent and prolonged in East Africa and the Sahel in the future, as they have been in the past three decades (Niang et al. 2014). For example, in the ASALs of northern Kenya, the frequency of droughts has increased from once in every ten years in the 1970s, to once in every five years in the 1980s, to once in every two to three years in the 1990s, and now annually since the year 2000 (Kosonei et al. 2017).

Disease and pests

Outbreak of diseases and pests, which is among the top three most cited causes of loss of live-stock among pastoralists (IOM 2010), is likely to be exacerbated by climate change (Niang et al. 2014). With warming temperatures, livestock pests and lack of adequate nutrition from less pro-ductive pasturelands weaken cattle physically, reducing their resilience. Female cattle become less fertile and produce less milk for their offspring. In addition, warmer average annual temperatures enable the expansion of the geographical range of vector-borne diseases, plant pathogens, and crop-damaging insect pests (Rosenzweig et al. 2001).

In Ethiopia, additional pasture-related stresses relate to previous governments having banned pastoralists from burning off bushland, with the result that the bushlands encroached on tra-ditional grassland grazing areas, something that is not easily reversed. Invasive bush and plants pest, such as the toxic *Prosopis Juliflora* that has invaded parts of Ethiopia, can be harmful to herd animals and prevent their access to water (Little et al. 2010; Desta et al. 2014).

Insecurity and conflict

Pastoralists in the Turkana and Maasai regions of Kenya cite security reasons among their main causes for changing migration routes, particularly across borders (IOM 2010; HRW 2015). The main form of insecurity is cattle theft, which is more common in times of climate stress (*idem*). This is because herders cluster their livestock around fewer, more easily identified water sources, where they are more vulnerable to cattle rustlers and their transnational cartel backers (Hendrickson et al. 1996: 191).

Accounts of violence among pastoralists during times of drought are often anecdotal and underreported to the authorities. Meier et al. (2007) tested the veracity of the 'climate conflict' narrative by collecting incident and situation reports from more than two dozen areas along the borders of Ethiopia, Kenya, and Uganda, and compared the results to indicators of the availability of precipitation, vegetation, and forage. Their preliminary analyses suggest that availability of these resources, while not being the sole factor, may be sufficient to prompt increased herd mobility and competitive behaviour between pastoral groups (Meier et al. 2007). Competitiveness between pastoral groups may turn to opportunistic violence and cattle raiding when herds are already depleted and tensions with opposing groups are flaring (Hendrickson 1996; Meier et al. 2007). Fragmentation of traditional grazing areas increases the likelihood that herders trespass on commercial or privately owned land, which can lead to localised violence with sedentary ranchers and agriculturalists. In a study by Blocher (2016), an expatriate landholder outside of Morogoro in central Tanzania described the potential for disputes with Maasai pastoralists: "The Maasai have a funny idea that all cattle belong to them, which is a convenient excuse to raid cattle from local landholders.[6] They have little respect for my property lines, which used to be within their traditional grazing lands."[7]

There is little evidence to support claims that the increased mobility of agro-pastoralists increases the likelihood of conflicts on scales any larger than local level, intergroup violence. None of the refugees interviewed in Ethiopia and Uganda for a relevant study described the impacts of climatic variability as a *direct* catalyst for violent conflict (Afifi et al. 2012). Researchers, however, have characterised resource scarcity exacerbated by worsening weather conditions as a multiplier or magnifier of pre-existing conflicts (Afifi et al. 2012; Raleigh and Kniveton 2012).

Land fragmentation and sedentarisation

The resilience of pastoralists is closely linked to herd size and health (ILRI 2010; Little et al. 2010). By necessity, pastoralist culture and practices encourage the sustainable use of pasture and water resources. Particularly in semi-arid areas, certain grazing areas are put aside in periods of drought in order to keep them in good condition. Nonexclusive land tenure and reciprocal relationships among pastoral communities also help to ensure that land is not overused. Among the Maasai, access to various territorial units called *orosho* is negotiated during times of environmental stress (Mwangi 2003). The Maasai and other African pastoralists commonly redistribute portions of their herds to poorer friends or family in greater need, or to friends and relatives who have better access to productive lands (BurnSilver 2007; Galvin 2009). Such cohesive and flexible arrangements, which help maintain the balance of the region's socio-ecological systems, are assured by reciprocal land use rights, social practices, ritual, and ceremony (Mwangi 2003).

Filial inheritance, formal tenure recognition, and government-supported development projects lead to land subdivision and/or re-classification. Effective barriers (physical and non-physical) created by land subdivision can limit mobility,[8] accelerating the need for pastoralists to intensify livestock raising or to diversify livelihoods. This accounts in part for trends towards increased sedentarisation and increasingly agro-pastoralist livelihoods (Niamir-Fuller 1998). BurnSilver et al. (2008) compared mobility of pastoralists in areas that were subdivided and areas that were not, and found that those living in subdivided areas are more likely to be sedentarized and less mobile in years with normal precipitation levels. During drought, households living in subdivided areas, including those that are typically sedentary, become mobile. Mobility therefore appears to be a key factor differentiating households' overall vulnerability to drought (McPeak and Little 2005).

Institutional frameworks can also contribute to the subdivision and fragmentation of pastoral lands. Many governments actively seek to deter mobility as a means of consolidating political and economic control in pastoralist territories. This may be done tacitly, by promoting policies that incentivize the privatization of pastureland, or explicitly, by enclosing and selling pasture land with or without the users' consent. In Ethiopia, Kenya, and Tanzania, pastoralists have been relocated from land intended for tourism or development projects (IOM 2016). In Kenya and Tanzania, the Greater Maasai Mara has been designated as a wildlife reserve since the 1970s and is gradually being enclosed and fenced, generating conflicts between pastoralists and the wildlife tourism industry (Løvschal et al. 2017; Chatty and Colester 2002).

Most grasslands in East Africa are under *du jure* or *de facto* communal governance (Behnke and Scoones 1993). However, governments selling off pastoralist and reserve land to private companies (both foreign and domestic) for agricultural purposes has removed large areas of pastureland in parts of East Africa (Desta et al. 2014). In some areas, pastoralists themselves are also fencing off land without the authority to do so (Devereux 2006; Flintan 2011). Private land ownership takes various forms, from privately owned individual parcels to group-owned ranches, and it is in areas where land is individually-owned lands that the greatest alienation of pastoralists from their land occurs (Gebre 2001). Some land tenure regime changes are supported by the pastoralists themselves, who have the goal of preventing agriculturalists, conservation organizations, and other powerful groups from gaining title to their traditional lands (e.g., BurnSilver et al. 2008; Galvin et al. 2008). In Kajiado District, Kenya, the conversion to group ranches of what was previously communal land occupied by Maasai is a key manifestation of the rapid privatization of land (Galvin 2009). While the Maasai supported the establishment of group ranches decades ago (Kimani and Pickard 1998), the subsequent parcelling and privatization of land has led to fragmented pastoral rangelands and contributed to sedentarisation (Thornton et al. 2006). The breakdown of traditional land management systems creates pressure for other pastoralists to do the same, reducing the overall land area available for pasture, creating disconnected fragments of grazing, and diminishing the overall scale and healthy functioning of the socio-ecological system (Galvin 2009; Galvin et al. 2008). There are important implications for the integrity of pastoral culture, as well. Maasai elders interviewed for a 1992 study, for example, regard private landownership as an 'alien concept', and express fears that subdividing existing pasture land may lead to an irreversible change in the Maasai lifestyle (World Bank 1992). These views are changing.

Population pressures

Growing human populations place additional stress on pastoralist resources. In Djibouti, Eritrea, Ethiopia, Kenya, Somalia, South Sudan, and Sudan, between 70 and 75 per cent of the total population is under 30 years of age (World Population Review 2017). In Uganda and Tanzania, between 77 and 80 per cent of people are under age 30. Population growth rates are especially high in pastoral areas. In the Maasai Mara, the population has more than doubled in less than thirty years (Murphy 2016). Populations in pastoralist areas of Ethiopia are doubling at a similar rate (Desta et al. 2014), in a country where the share of the total population in rural areas has remained relatively high, at approximately 81 per cent (World Population Review 2017). As pastoral populations grow and availability of grazing land declines, pastoralists must diversify their income sources in order to cope (Galvin et al. 2002; Galvin 2009; Ng'ang'a et al. 2016). Systems models that simulate the combined effects of population growth, drought, declining access to pastureland, and conflict-induced displacement on pastoralists in Kenya, Ethiopia, and Somalia show that current population trends generate a particularly high likelihood of pastoralist livelihood failure (Ginnetti and Franck 2014).

Cultural resilience in the face of change

The combined effects of the aforementioned factors place considerable pressure on the cultural importance of pastoral lifestyle and on community cohesion. Land fragmentation and privatization generate inter-group inequality and poverty (BurnSilver 2007; Galvin 2009; Thornton et al. 2006). As pastoral livelihoods fail, people adopt more sedentary lifestyles, and many young people migrate to cities in search of employment. While migration and 'pastoralist dropout' is seen by some communities as a livelihood failure and abandonment of their 'traditional' ways of life, others have embraced new strategies, including technologies to communicate and share resources (see Ng'ang'a et al. 2016), which enable some traditional institutions to survive as others evolve. The adoption of cultivated agriculture presents an opportunity to receive technical and economic assistance from African governments, which have traditionally not similarly invested as much in livestock production. The Maasai stand out as one example of a population that has often been successful at diversifying livelihoods as changing conditions seriously threaten their livelihoods. In 2002, it was estimated that 88 per cent of Tanzanian Maasai and 46 per cent of Kenyan Maasai were involved in some degree of rain-fed or irrigated agriculture, with cultivation becoming a proportionately larger source of income over time (Coast 2002; BurnSilver et al. 2007). The Maasai have also become more actively involved in mainstream politics. Saning'o ole Telele, Tanzania's Deputy Minister Livestock and Fisheries Development is one in a line of Members of Parliament for the Maasai constituency in Ngorongoro in northern Tanzania (GoT 2017). Kenya also saw the first ever election to parliament of a Maasai woman, Peris Pesi Tobiko, in 2013 (IPU 2014).

Many socio-cultural values of pastoralists appear able to persist despite migration to urban areas. Maasai youth in Dar es Salaam, Tanzania, for example, remain connected amongst themselves and with their home community via cell phones and with groups on messaging services like Whatsapp. They use this form of network communication to keep in touch, rapidly distribute information, organize, and rally together in times of need.[9] For the hierarchical and patriarchal Maasai, maintaining fealty to this network serves as a proxy for the tight-knit tribal relationships they are known for. There is anecdotal evidence that they and other urban migrants send significant internal remittances through cell phones, bolstering the health of their home communities. Furthermore, while they have yet to catch up to the general population in terms of education, both settled (sedentarised) and unsettled Maasai and Samburu people have lower rates of licit and illicit substance use (Othieno et al. 2000).

Political, legal, and normative frameworks

The potential increased mobility of pastoralists is a source of interest for governments and researchers for a few main reasons. Rural-urban migration and the movement of pastoralists across internal and international boundaries have political implications. Pastoralists are in the minority in most countries, and tend to identify with their community before they identify with a nation-state (IDMC 2014; IRIN News 2012). In Kenya, for example, pastoralists voted overwhelmingly against unification with the rest of country in a 1962 referendum (Goldsmith 2013), and some still do not consider themselves as Kenyans. Pastoralists' concept of citizenship and state loyalty has been shaped historically by issues of taxation, confrontation with state-supported nationalist movements, and accusations of disloyalty due to states' shifting post-colonial borders (Markakis 2004).

In order for pastoralists to achieve full enjoyment of rights and citizenship, their ability to choose their livelihood options and to use mobility to its full advantage must be protected by national governments – though this is not always the case. At the international level, the UN Declaration on the Rights of Persons belonging to National or Ethnic, Religious and Linguistic Minorities (the Minority Declaration), ILO Convention 169 (articles 13–19 on land and natural resource rights), and the UN Declaration on the Rights of Indigenous Peoples (articles 25–30) go to some length to protect pastoralists' economic, political, and social rights. The Guiding Principles on Internal Displacement are an internationally recognised, but not binding, framework for the assistance and protection of internally displaced people (IDPs), including pastoralists affected by slow- or sudden-onset natural hazard induced disasters (Kälin 2010). These principles have been domesticated into national law via the Great Lakes Pact and its protocols, to which Kenya, Uganda, and Sudan are signatories. Also, Djibouti, Eritrea, Ethiopia, Kenya, Somalia, and South Sudan are among the signatories to the African Union Convention for the Protection and Assistance of Internally Displaced Persons in Africa (Kampala Convention), a continental instrument that legally binds governments to protect the rights and wellbeing of people forced to flee their homes due to "natural or human made disasters, including climate change" (African Union 2009: Art. 5.4). Some countries have additional provisions, such as Kenya, which developed a policy on IDPs in 2012 and passed the Prevention, Protection and Assistance to Internally Displaced Persons and Affected Communities Act of 2012 (IDMC 2014).

A conceptual and legal study produced by the Internal Displacement Monitoring Centre (IDMC), the Norwegian Refugee Council (NRC), and the Nansen Initiative was among the first to challenge the conceptualisation of 'pastoralist dropout' described previously. The authors reframed disarticulation of traditional pastoralists from the pastoral lifestyle, understood as 'pastoralist dropout', as a form of displacement that leads to the disenfranchisement of rights, marginalisation and neglect (IDMC 2014: 7). IDMC proposes that there is a 'tipping point' at which pastoralists fall from voluntary migration into forced displacement, which is observed as reduced resilience and livelihood failure (Ginnetti and Franck 2014).

Directions for future research

East Africa and the Horn of Africa have been the major focus of scholarly research on the effect of environmental change on pastoralist mobility and adaptation; a wider geographical representation in the literature is needed. More longitudinal studies would also be helpful, as what may appear to be adaptive in the short term for some may prove to be maladaptive over longer time horizons, or for others (Gemenne and Blocher 2017). Galvin (2009) points out that if the resilience of pastoralists is based on flexibility and the capacity to adapt, when one or both of these appear to be dwindling in the short term, it may also indicate just another adjustment to changing circumstances in the long term. Connected to this, a useful lens for researchers could be to take a rights-based approach to Indigenous pastoralist groups most affected by climate change, and consider their changing access to social, political and economic rights over time.

A one-size-fits-all prescription approach to research will not succeed in highly diverse, complex, and networked pastoralist communities, especially research that aims to support policymaking. As outlined earlier in this chapter, pastoralist societies are not homogenous, and not easily reduced to a singular caricature. Diversity exists within and among pastoralist and agro-pastoralist groups. The degree of vulnerability to future risks such as climate change, between and within pastoral groups, varies greatly according to various factors such as age, sex, ownership of different livestock species, and geographical location. Research considering pastoralists' adaptation to climate change must continue to be conducted in a heterogeneous manner, with consideration to different age and demographic groups. Also, while a small number of studies on pastoralist groups consider gender roles and gender relations (e.g. Hodgson 1999; Thebaud and Batterbury 2001), there is a need to mainstream gender considerations more deliberately in future research, given the very different roles men and women occupy in pastoralist cultures (for further reflection on the lack of gender considerations in environmental migration research see Chapter 11, this volume).

Research on pastoralist mobility is helpful not only for humanitarian and development actors working with pastoralists, but also to understand the nature of displacement in slow and sudden-onset disaster contexts in regions with large pastoral populations (see Ginnetti and Franck 2014). The special risks faced by pastoralists should be considered in current efforts to build a protection agenda for people displaced across international borders in the context of disasters (e.g. the Platform on Disaster Displacement [PDD], described in Chapter 34, this volume).

Conclusion: pastoralism at a tipping point?

Migration is commonly presented in public debates as the result of a failure to adapt (Gemenne and Blocher 2017), and the 'pastoralist dropout' label is an example of this. Ongoing efforts to privatize pastoral grasslands reflect a questionable belief that individual ownership leads to better development and better land stewardship than the practices of customary user groups (Little 1996; Peters 1994; Lesorogol 2003; Galvin et al. 2008). Pastoralism has often been characterized as an unsophisticated, unorganised manner of using pasture resources, and is often unfairly identified as being counter to conservation goals (Goldman 2011), further justifying government restrictions on pastoralist land use and mobility. Such views are contrary to a significant body of research that demonstrates that pastoralist-managed lands are as – if not better – conserved than officially conserved or protected lands, and that pastoral production is as efficient as large ranches (Goldman 2011; Mapinduzi et al. 2003; Homewood et al. 1984, 2004).

Pastoralism is a livelihood defined by organised, fluid, and reciprocal land governance and use arrangements. There is no single style of pastoralism, and many 'pastoral' groups commonly engage in varying levels of settled cultivation. The sedentarisation of some pastoral community members does not necessarily indicate a full-time or permanent departure from the pastoralist livelihood, nor does it indicate a reduction or abandonment of pastoral production (McPeak and Little 2005). While pastoralist groups face serious and mounting challenges to their lifestyle, a more rigorous, nuanced view of their responses to adversity is required to devise appropriate means of support.

Human mobility is a complex and multi-dimensional phenomenon. The premise of this chapter is that pastoralists groups are themselves diverse and complex, employing a range of livelihood strategies both successfully and, at times, unsuccessfully. Flexible mobility is the most critical ingredient for resilient pastoralist societies. If pastoral livelihood systems are to be sustained, mobility combined with adequate pasture land and water resources security, and legal and political authorisation for movement, must be maintained. Climate change will test the adaptive capacity of pastoralists. In spite of this, pastoralist communities could have a sustainable and productive future, if their lifestyle practices are given the appropriate support and legal protection.

Notes

1 The author would like to express sincere thanks to the editors and an anonymous reviewer for their very helpful suggestions.
2 Anthropological research in the United States and Britain, in particular, received considerable funding from governments and the Rockefeller Foundation after the Second World War, mirroring an overall increase in social and economic research (see Drackle et al. 2003).
3 UN bodies the Food and Agriculture Organization (FAO) and the International Fund for Agricultural Development (IFAD) cite the higher figures, defining pastoralists as "people who derive more than 50 per cent of their incomes from livestock and livestock products". The figure includes agropastoralists, defined as "people who derive less than 50 per cent of their incomes from livestock and livestock products, and most of the remaining income from cultivation" (IFAD 2009).
4 The fragmentation and acquisition of traditional pastoral lands by outside interests is discussed further in Chapter 29, this volume.
5 CliMig database is a collection of academic resources that focuses on migration, the environment and climate change: www.unine.ch/geographie/home/recherche/migration_climate_change_1/bibliographic-database.html
6 This point refers, in short, to the belief of the Maasai that God (Enkai/Ngai) has bestowed trusteeship of all the world's cattle to them for safekeeping. This is one reason why cattle are treated like family members, and rarely sold or slaughtered, except in times of need. It is also why sedentary agriculture is traditionally looked down upon; it makes the land unsuitable for grazing.
7 Personal communication with the author, February 2015.
8 It is noteworthy that some governments, like Kenya and the ECOWAS states, have sought to mediate the resulting concerns by testing 'social tenure' models.
9 Personal communication with Emmanuel Ole Kileli, Coordinator, Ereto Maasai Youth (EMAYO), January 2016.

References

Adow M. (2008). Pastoralists in Kenya. In a conference on Climate Change and Forced Migration, the Institute for Public Policy Research, London.

Afifi, T., Govil, R., Sakdapolrak, P. and Warner, K. (2012). Climate change, vulnerability and human mobility: Perspectives of refugees from the East and Horn of Africa. United Nations University, Institute for Environment and Human Security (UNU-EHS).

African Union (2009). The African Union Convention for the Protection and Assistance of Internally Displaced Persons in Africa (Kampala Convention). Available: www.peaceau.org/uploads/au-convention-for-the-protection-and-assistance-of-idps-in-africa-kampala-convention-.pdf [Accessed 2 February 2017]

Ahmed, A. G. M., Azeze, A., Babiker, M., & Tsegaye, D. (2002). The post-drought recovery strategies among the pastoral households in the Horn of Africa: A review. Addis Ababa: Development Research Report Series, 3.

Alloula M. (1986) The colonial harem (Vol. 21). Minneapolis: University of Minnesota Press.

Ban K. (2007) A climate culprit in Darfur. Washington Post. Available: www.washingtonpost.com/wp-dyn/content/article/2007/06/15/AR2007061501857.html) [Accessed 12 February 2017].

Behnke, R. H., & Scoones, I. (1993). Rethinking range ecology: implications for rangeland management in Africa. In Range Ecology at Disequilibrium: New Models of Natural Variability and Pastoral Adaptation in African Savannas, ed. R. H. Behnke, I. Scoones, & C. Kerven. London: Overseas Dev. Inst., pp. 153–172.

Bettini, G. (2013). Climate barbarians at the gate? A critique of apocalyptic narratives on 'climate refugees'. Geoforum, 45, 63–72.

Blench, R. (2001). 'You Can't Go Home Again': Pastoralism in the New Millennium. London: Overseas Development Institute.

Blocher, J. (2016). Water always Flows Downhill: A case for Participatory Forest Management (PFM) and decentralization of Forest Governance in REDD+ implementation. In: Climatic and Environmental

Challenges: Learning from the Horn of Africa. Addis-Abeba: Centre français des études éthiopiennes. Available http://books.openedition.org/cfee/449 [Accessed 29 July 2016].

Boto, I., Edeme, J., & Lopes, I. (2012). Resources on new challenges and opportunities for pastoralism in the context of African countries, Briefing No. 26, Brussels 4.

Brandström, P., Hultin, J., & Lindström, J. (1979). *Aspects of agro-pastoralism in East Africa*. Nordiska Afrikainstitutet.

BurnSilver, S. B. (2007). Pathways of continuity and change: Diversification, intensification and mobility in Maasai. PhD diss. Grad. Degree Program Ecol., Colo. State Univ., Fort Collins, CO.

BurnSilver, S. B., Worden, J., & Boone, R. B. (2008). Processes of fragmentation in the Amboseli ecosystem, southern Kajiado District, Kenya. See Galvin et al. 2008, pp. 225–253.

Cameron R. (1955). *Equator farm*. London: Heinemann.

Chatty, D., & Colester, M, eds. (2002). *Displacement, forced settlement and conservation*. Oxford: Berghahn.

Coast E. (2002). Maasai socioeconomic conditions: A cross-border comparison. *Human. Ecology*, 30(1), 79–105.

Coppock, D. L., Desta, S., Tezera, S., & Gebru, G. (2011). Capacity building helps pastoral women transform impoverished communities in Ethiopia. *Science*, 334(6061), 1394–1398.

Desta, S., Berhanu, W., Gebru, G., & Amosha, D. (2008). Pastoral drop out study in selected Weredas of Borana Sone Oromia Regional State. *Care International Ethiopia and USAID*. Available at www.celep. info/wp-content/uploads/2012/07/Solomon-et-al-2008-Borana-Zone-pastoral-dropout-study.pdf

Desta, S., Mungai, C., & Muchaba, T. (2014). *Rangeland enclosures could help pastoralist cope with climate variability*. Climate Change, Agriculture and Food Security (CCAFS). Available at https://ccafs.cgiar. org/blog/rangeland-enclosures-could-help-pastoralists-cope-climate-variability#.WX-nM62ZMUE [Accessed 31 July 2017].

Devereux, S. (2006). *Vulnerable livelihoods in Somali Region, Ethiopia*. ODI Research Report No. 57. Sussex, UK: Overseas, Development Institute.

de Waal A. (1998). Exploiting slavery: Human rights and political agendas in Sudan. *New Left Review*, 227, 135.

Drackle, D., Edgar, I., & Schippers, T., eds (2003). *Learning fields: Educational histories of European social anthropology* (Vol. 1). Oxford: Berghahn Books.

Farbotko, C., and Lazrus, H. (2012). First climate refugees? Contesting global narratives of climate change in Tuvalu. *Global Environmental Change*, 22(2), 382–390.

Findlay, A., McCollum, D., Coulter, R., and Gayle, V. (2015). New mobilities across the life course: A framework for analysing demographically linked drivers of migration. *Population Space Place*, 21, 390–402.

Flintan F. (2011). *Broken lands: Broken lives? Causes, processes and impacts of land fragmentation in the rangelands of Ethiopia, Kenya and Uganda*. Research report. Nairobi, Kenya: Regional Learning and Advocacy Programme (REGLAP).

Galaty, J. G., & Johnson, D. L., eds. (1990). *The world of pastoralism: Herding systems in comparative perspective*. New York: Guilford Press, 436.

Galvin K. A. (2009). Transitions: Pastoralists living with change. *Annual Review of Anthropology*, 38, 185–198.

Galvin, K. A., Ellis, J., Boone, R. B., Magennis, A. L., & Smith, N. M. (2002). Compatibility of pastoralism and conservation? A test case using integrated assessment in the Ngorongoro Conservation Area, Tanzania.

Galvin, K. A., Reid, R. S., Behnke, R. H., Jr., & Hobbs. N. T., eds. (2008). *Fragmentation of semi-arid and arid landscapes. Consequences for human and natural systems*. Dordrecht, The Netherlands: Springer.

Gebre A. (2001). *Pastoralism under pressure: Land alienation and Pastoral transformations among the Karayu of Eastern Ethiopia, 1944 to the present*. Maastricht: Shaker. 441.

Gemenne, F., & Blocher, J. (2017). How can migration serve adaptation to climate change? Challenges to fleshing out a policy ideal. *The Geographical Journal*, 183(4), 336–347.

Ginnetti, J., and Franck, T. (2014). *Assessing drought displacement risk for Kenyan, Ethiopian and Somali pastoralists*. Geneva: the Internal Displacement Monitoring Centre.

Goldman, M. (2011). Introduction: Circulation of environmental knowledge: Networks, expertise, and science in practice. In: Goldman, M. J., Nadasdy, P., & Turner, M. D. (Eds.), *Knowing nature: Conversations at the intersection of political ecology and science studies*. Chicago: University of Chicago Press.

Goldsmith, P. (2013). The future of Pastoralist Conflict in the Horn of Africa. In Catley/Lind/Scoones (eds) *Pathways to sustainability, pastoralism and development in Africa: Dynamic change at the margins*. New York: Routledge, 141–142.

Government of Tanzania (GoT). (2017). Website of the Ministry of Agriculture, Livestock and Fisheries. Available at www.mifugouvuvi.go.tz [Accessed 2 February 2017].

Grawert E. (1998). *Impact of food insecurity on peasant livelihood: Making a living in rural Sudan*. London: Palgrave Macmillan, 57–83.

Halderman, M., Jenner, H., Karuru, N., Ong'ayo, M., Smith, S., Smith Z. with assistance from Carter L. (2002). Assessment and Programmatic Recommendations: Addressing Pastoralist Conflict in the Karamoja Cluster of Kenya, Uganda and Sudan. Greater Horn of Africa Peacebuilding Project. Written for the S.O. 6 Conflict Strategy Team USAID/REDSO, March.

Hampshire, K. (2002). Networks of nomads: Negotiating access to health resources among pastoralist women in Chad. *Social Science & Medicine*, 54(7), 1025–1037.

Headey, D., Taffesse, A. S., & You, L. (2014). Diversification and development in pastoralist Ethiopia. *World Development*, 56, 200–213.

Hendrickson, D., Mearns, R., & Armon, J. (1996). Livestock raiding among the pastoral Turkana of Kenya: Redistribution, predation and the links to famine. *IDS Bulletin*, 27(3), 17–30.

Herrero, M., Thornton, P. K., Gerber, P., & Reid, R. S. (2009). Livestock, livelihoods and the environment: understanding the trade-offs. *Current Opinion in Environmental Sustainability*, 1(2), 111–120.

Hingley, R. (2017). 'Climate Refugees': An oceanic perspective. *Asia & the Pacific Policy Studies*, 4(1), 158–165.

Hodgson, D. L. (1999). Pastoralism, patriarchy and history: Changing gender relations among Maasai in Tanganyika, 1890–1940. *The Journal of African History*, 40(01), 41–65.

Homewood, K. M., & Rodgers, W. A. (1984). Pastoralism and conservation. *Human Ecology*, 12(4), 431–441.

Homewood, K., Lambin, E. F., Coast, E., Kariuki, A., Kikula, I., Kivelia, J., & Thompson, M. (2001). Long-term changes in Serengeti-Mara wildebeest and land cover: Pastoralism, population, or policies? *Proceedings of the National Academy of Sciences*, 98(22), 12544–12549.

Homewood, K. M., Rodgers, W. A., & Homewood, K. (2004). *Maasailand ecology: pastoralist development and wildlife conservation in Ngorongoro, Tanzania*. Cambridge: Cambridge University Press.

Hoscilo, A., Balzter, H., Bartholomé, E., Boschetti, M., Brivio, P. A., Brink, A., Clerici, M., & Pekel, J. F. (2015). A conceptual model for assessing rainfall and vegetation trends in sub-Saharan Africa from satellite data. *International Journal of Climatology*, 35(12), 3582–3592.

Human Rights Watch (HRW). (2015). *"There is No Time Left": Climate change, environmental threats, and human rights in Turkana County, Kenya*. Amsterdam: HRW.

Internal Displacement Monitoring Centre (IDMC). (2014). *On the margin: Kenya's pastoralists*. Geneva: IDMC. Available at www.internal-displacement.org/library/publications/2014/on-the-margin-kenyas-pastoralists/ [Accessed 31 July 2017].

International Fund for Agricultural Development (IFAD). (2009). *Livestock and pastoralists*. Rome: IFAD Livestock Thematic Papers, 1–8.

International Organization for Migration (IOM). (2010). *Pastoralism at the edge: Effects of drought, climate change and migration on livelihood systems of pastoralist and mobile communities in Kenya (North Eastern, Turkana, and the Maasai Regions)*. Nairobi: IOM.

International Organization for Migration (IOM). (2016). *Assessing the evidence: Migration, environment and climate change in Kenya*. Available at https://publications.iom.int/system/files/assessing_the_evidence_kenya.pdf [Accessed 19 February 2017].

Inter-Parliamentary Union (IPU). (4 March 2014). *Gender parity in parliament possible within 20 years, new trends show*. Available at www.ipu.org/press-e/pressnote201403041.htm [Accessed 2 February 2017].

ILRI (International Livestock Research Institute). (2010). *An assessment of the response to the 2008–2009 drought in Kenya*. Report commissioned by the European Delegation to the Republic of Kenya. Nairobi, Kenya: International Livestock Research Institute.

IRIN News. (2012). *Disquiet over Lamu port project*. Available at www.irinnews.org/report/96675/kenya-disquiet-over-lamu-port-project [Accessed 2 February 2017].

Jabbar, M. A., Reynolds, L., & Francis, P. A. (1995). Sedentarisation of cattle farmers in the derived savannah region of south-west Nigeria: Results of a survey. *Tropical Animal Health and Production*, 27(1), 55–64.

Johnson, D. L. (1969). *The nature of nomadism: A comparative study of pastoral migrations in Southwestern Asia and Northern Africa (No. 118)*. Dept. of Geography, University of Chicago.

Jok, J. M. (2010). *War and slavery in Sudan*. Philadelphia: University of Pennsylvania Press.

Kälin W. (2010). *Conceptualising climate-induced displacement. Climate change and displacement: Multidisciplinary perspectives*. Oxford: Hart Publishing.

Kasfir, S. L. (2007). *African art and the colonial encounter: Inventing a global commodity*. Bloomington: Indiana University Press.

Kimani, K., & Pickard, J. (1998). Recent trends and implications of group ranch subdivision and fragmentation in Kajiado District, Kenya. *Geographic Journal*, 164, 202–213.

Kosonei, R. C., Abuom, P. O., Bosire, E., and Huho, J. M. (2017). Effects of drought dynamics on vegetation cover in Marigat Sub-County, Baringo County, Kenya. *International Journal of Scientific and Research Publications*, 7(5), 89.

Lesorogol, C. K. (2003). Transforming institutions among pastoralists: Inequality and land privatization. *American Anthropologist*, 105(3), 531–541.

Little, P. D. (1996). Pastoralism, biodiversity, and the shaping of savanna landscapes in East Africa. *Africa*, 66(1), 37–51.

Little, P. D., Behnke, R., McPeak, J., & Gebru, G. (2010). *Future scenarios for pastoral development in Ethiopia, 2010–2025*. Pastoral economic growth and development policy assessment, Ethiopia, Report Number 2. London: Department for International Development.

Løvschal, M., Bøcher, P. K., Pilgaard, J., Amoke, I., Odingo, A., Thuo, A., Svenning, J. C. (2017). Fencing bodes a rapid collapse of the unique Greater Mara ecosystem. *Scientific Reports*, 7, 41450.

Mapinduzi, A. L., Oba, G., Weladji, R. B., & Colman, J. E. (2003). Use of indigenous ecological knowledge of the Maasai pastoralists for assessing rangeland biodiversity in Tanzania. *African Journal of Ecology*, 41(4), 329–336.

Markakis, J. (2004). *Pastoralism on the margin*. London: Minority Rights Group International, 2–37.

McPeak, J., & Little, P. D. (2005). Cursed if you do, cursed if you don't: The contradictory processes of pastoral sedentarization in northern Kenya. In: *As Pastoralists Settle: Social Health and Economic Consequences of Pastoral Sedentarization in Marsabit District, Kenya*, ed. E. Fratkin and E. A. Roth, pp. 87–104. New York: Kluwer Academy.

McPeak, J., Little, P. D., & Doss, C. R. (2011). *Risk and social change in an African rural economy: Livelihoods in pastoralist communities*. New York: Routledge.

Meier, P., Bond, D., & Bond, J. (2007). Environmental influences on pastoral conflict in the Horn of Africa. *Political Geography*, 26(6), 716–735.

Murphy, D. (2016). *Preserving the Masai 'Way of Life' in Tanzania*. Dublin: The Irish Times. Available at www.irishtimes.com/news/world/africa/preserving-the-masai-way-of-life-in-tanzania-1.2603374 [Accessed 29 July 2016].

Mwangi, E. (2003). *Institutional change and politics: The transformation of property rights in Kenya's Maasailand*. PhD diss., Bloomington, Indiana University.

Myers, N. (2002). Environmental refugees: A growing phenomenon of the 21st century. *Philosophical Transactions of the Royal Society of London B: Biological Sciences*, 357(1420), 609–613.

Nelson, D. R., Adger, W. N., & Brown, K. (2007). Adaptation to environmental change: Contributions of a resilience framework. *Annual Review of Environmental Resources*, 32, 395–419.

Ng'ang'a, S. K., Bulte, E., Giller, K. E., McIntire, J. M., & Rufino, M. C. (2016). Migration and self-protection against climate change: A case study of Samburu district, Kenya. *World Development*, 84, 55–68.

Niamir-Fuller, M. (1998). The resilience of pastoral herding in Sahelian Africa. See Berkes et al. 1998, 250–284.

Niang, I., Ruppel, O. C., Abdrabo, M. A., Essel, A., Lennard, C., Padgham, J., and Urquhart, P. (2014). Africa. In: Climate Change 2014: Impacts, Adaptation, and Vulnerability. Part B: Regional Aspects. Contribution of Working Group II to the Fifth Assessment Report of the Intergovernmental Panel on Climate Change [Barros, V.R., C.B. Field, D.J. Dokken, M.D. Mastrandrea, K.J. Mach, T.E. Bilir, M. Chatterjee,

K.L. Ebi,Y.O. Estrada, R.C. Genova, B. Girma, E.S. Kissel, A.N. Levy, S. MacCracken, P.R. Mastrandrea, and L.L. White (eds.)]. Cambridge, United Kingdom and New York, NY: Cambridge University Press, 1199–1265.

Obokata, R.,Veronis, L., and McLeman, R. A. (2014). Empirical research on international environmental migration: A systematic review. *Population and Environment*, 36, 111–135.

Omondi, P.A. O.,Awange, J. L., Forootan, E., Ogallo, L. A., Barakiza, R., Girmaw, G. B., Fesseha, I., Kululetera,V., Kilembe, C., Mbati, M. M., and Kilavi, M. (2014). Changes in temperature and precipitation extremes over the Greater Horn of Africa region from 1961 to 2010. *International Journal of Climatology*, 34(4), 1262–1277.

Othieno, C. J., Kathuku, D. M., & Ndetei, D. M. (2000). Substance abuse in outpatients attending rural and urban health centres in Kenya. *East African Medical Journal*, 77(11).

Oxfam. (2008). Survival of the Fittest: Pastoralism and climate change in East Africa. Available at www.oxfam.org.hk/content/98/content_3534tc.pdf

Parry, M. L., Canziani, O. F., Palutikof, J. P.,Van Der Linden, J. P., & Hanson, C. E. eds. (2007). *Climate change 2007: Impact, adaptation and vulnerability. contribution of working group II to the fourth assessment report of the intergovernmental panel on climate change*. Cambridge, UK: Cambridge University Press.

Peters, P. E. (1994). *Dividing the commons: Politics, policy, and culture in Botswana*. Charlottesville: University Press of Virginia.

Platform for Disaster Displacement (PDD). (2017). *Our response*. Available at http://disasterdisplacement.org/the-platform/our-response/ [Accessed 12 February 2017].

Raleigh, C., & Kniveton, D. (2012). Come rain or shine: An analysis of conflict and climate variability in East Africa. *Journal of Peace Research*, 49(1), 51–64.

Rass, N. (2006). *Policies and strategies to address the vulnerability of pastoralists in sub-Saharan Africa*. Rome: FAO, Pro-poor Livestock Policy Initiative (PPLPI) Working Paper Series, 37

Regional Learning & Advocacy Programme for Vulnerable Dryland Communities (REGLAP). (2012). *Key statistics on the drylands of Kenya, Uganda and Ethiopia*. Nairobi: REGLAP Secretariat.

Rosenzweig, C., Iglesias, A.,Yang, X. B., Epstein, P. R., & Chivian, E. (2001). Climate change and extreme weather events; implications for food production, plant diseases, and pests. *Global Change and Human Health*, 2(2), 90–104.

Schreck, C. J. III, & Semazii, F. M. (2004). Variability of the recent climate of east Africa. *International Journal of Climatology*., 24, 681–701.

Solomon, S., Qin, D., Manning, M., Chen, Z., Marquis, M., et al. eds. (2007). *Climate change 2007: The physical science basis. Contribution of working group I to the fourth assessment report of the intergovernmental panel on climate change*. Cambridge, UK: Cambridge University Press.

Thebaud, B., & Batterbury, S. (2001). Sahel pastoralists: opportunism, struggle, conflict and negotiation. A case study from Niger. *Global. Environmental Change*, 11, 69–78.

Thornton, P. K., BurnSilver, S. B., Boone, R. B., & Galvin, K. A. (2006). Modelling the impacts of group ranch subdivision on agro-pastoral households in Kajiado, Kenya. *Agricultural Systems*, 87(3), 331–356.

Time Magazine (1959) U.S. Edition, September 7, 1959 Vol. LXXIV No. 10

Urry, J. (1992). The tourist gaze "revisited". *American Behavioral Scientist*, 36(2), 172–186.

United Nations. (2013). Chronic Marginalization, Fragmentation, Encroachment, Lack of Land Rights Make Pastoralists in Africa among Poorest in World, Indigenous Forum Told, Meeting of the Twelfth Session of the UN Economic and Social Council Permanent Forum on Indigenous Issues. Available at www.un.org/press/en/2013/hr5135.doc.htm [Accessed 12 May 2017].

World Bank. (1992). *World development report 1992*. Oxford: Oxford University Press.

World Population Review. (2017). Country statistics available at worldpopulationreview.com/countries [Accessed 2 February 2017].

16

Climate and risk of migration in South Africa

Rachel Licker and Marina Mastrorillo

Introduction

As the twenty-first century progresses, South Africa is projected to experience significant levels of warming as a result of anthropogenic climate change (DEA, 2013a). Such changes will expose the country's large number of vulnerable individuals to unprecedented temperature regimes and potentially large shifts in precipitation patterns (DEA, 2013a). These projections raise questions of the measures that South Africa's diverse communities may take to adapt.

It is well established that migration is one of the possible adaptation strategies individuals may use to cope with adverse changes in climate (IOM, 2009). Initial evidence suggests that South Africa's population movements are already responsive to climate variability (Mastrorillo et al., 2016), indicating the possibility that future changes in climate may amplify migration flows within the country. However, migration might be not available to all individuals, and the inability of the most vulnerable individuals (e.g. the poorest) to migrate may expose a large number of people to the risk of being trapped in the face of climate change (Clarke and Eyal, 2014). Given South Africa's already strong culture of mobility, the large proportion of the country living in conditions of extreme poverty, and the effects that changing mobility patterns might have for sending and receiving regions, it is important to develop understanding of whether a changing climate may create a risk of increased migration for some portions of the population. Furthermore, due to the wide range of living standards represented within the country – the country has one of the highest Gini coefficients (a measure of wealth inequality) in the world (World Bank, 2012) – relationships between climate and migration garnered from the South African case study may be relevant to a variety of other countries both within and off of the African continent.

In this chapter, we examine the sources of vulnerability within South Africa that may interact with climate to influence future migration flows. We focus on climate as an environmental driver of migration, though other environmental drivers (e.g. the availability of natural resources) have been identified in South Africa, as well (Leyk et al., 2012; Hunter et al., 2014). Finally, we focus on internal migration dynamics, as within-country migration accounts for the large majority of population movements in South Africa (Polzer Ngwato, 2010).

Historical and contemporary migration dynamics

South Africa is home to a highly mobile population. Between 2007 and 2011, approximately 12% of the South African population moved (Statistics South Africa, 2011a). Of that, 0.3% moved internationally, while the remaining 11.7% moved internally between municipalities (within or between provinces). Most internal migrants are absorbed by five metropolitan districts, three of them belonging to the Gauteng province (Johannesburg, Tshwane/Pretoria and Ekurhuleni), the city of Cape Town in the Western Cape province, and the city of Durban (eThekwini metropolitan municipality) in the KwaZulu-Natal province. The provinces of Limpopo and Eastern Cape, which are the two poorest provinces in South Africa, exhibit a preponderance of emigration over immigration.

The previously mentioned migration flows hint to the importance of economic factors in explaining internal migration patterns in South Africa. A study of non-environmental determinants of South African migration performed by Kok et al. (2003), which used data from the 1996 census, found that the probability of an individual migrating increases with income and education (and is higher if they are living in urban areas), while the probability decreases with age. Similarly, Clarke and Eyal (2014) found that the probability of an individual migrating in South Africa increases non-linearly with income. The authors found evidence of the inverse U-shaped relationship with income that is found in other regions, in which low-income individuals do not have the capital to migrate whilst high-income individuals do not necessarily have reasons to move. Kok et al. (2003) also describe province-to-province migration flows from 1992–1996, exploring the importance of variables such as relative origin-destination income, unemployment, ethnic dominance (as proxied by the size of the largest ethnic group at destination), and security (as proxied by reported crimes). Education and economic factors were important for assessing the migration preferences of black males to alternative locations. Using the same data, Choe and Chrite (2014) show that individuals exhibit a tendency to move to higher-wage districts. Furthermore, they suggest that black, highly educated South Africans tend to migrate to districts with a high share of highly educated people. Conversely, low-educated South Africans tend to migrate to districts with a low share of highly educated individuals. Indeed, Clarke and Eyal (2014) found significant differences in the key drivers of migration in South Africa depending on the race and gender of an individual, whether they were from a high, middle, or low-income household, and whether they were migrating permanently or were labor migrants. However, the authors found that in general, South Africans in rural areas are less likely to move, that individuals between 18–30 years of age are more likely to move, and that receiving housing assistance decreased the likelihood of a move.

Stepping back from microeconomic migration determinants, the country's contemporary movement patterns are heavily influenced by the policies of the apartheid era. During the apartheid regime, through a series of "influx control" acts, rural-to-urban movements of black South Africans were heavily constrained – black South Africans were largely required to live outside of metropolitan areas on rural reserves known as homelands (Collinson et al., 2003). Furthermore, black South Africans were not allowed to bring their spouses and families with them if they moved for work (Posel, 2004). Similar rules applied to foreign African contract laborers. This, in addition to a lack of economic opportunity in the former homelands, forced black males to engage in temporary migration to urban areas in search of work. This culture of temporary labor migration within the black community has generally persisted (Wentzel and Tlabela, 2006; Collinson et al., 2003), though there are signs that it might be on the decline (Posel, 2010). Temporary labor migration is further amplified by South Africa's mining sector, which draws large numbers of labor migrants each year (Collinson et al., 2003).

While internal migration accounts for the majority of movements made in South Africa, the country is one of the most attractive destinations for migrant workers originating in Sub-Saharan Africa countries, particularly Zimbabwe, Lesotho, Mozambique, and Swaziland (Adepoju, 2006). Labor immigration has traditionally been comprised of highly regulated, temporary migration of workers employed in the mining industry, combined with informal and unregulated movements of people across borders to work in the agricultural sector (IOM, 2014). Irregular migration has increased in recent years, with estimates ranging from 1–8 million people (IOM, 2014). Furthermore, permanent emigration from South Africa to developed countries (such as the UK, the US, Canada, Australia, and New Zealand) increased in the late 1990s. According to Myburgh (2004), in 1999, permanent emigration amounted to 58,000 individuals, which was about three times the emigration rate in year 1995. Statistics South Africa (2011b) suggests that the number of South African individuals migrating outside the country has continued to grow during the 2000s. Most of the emigrants are highly skilled graduates looking for a better life and employment conditions.

Sources of vulnerability and risk exposure

Poverty, race, and inequality

South Africa is one of the largest economies in Africa and is the only African G-20 member (World Bank, 2012). Since the early 1990s, economic growth has been driven mainly by the tertiary sector, i.e. finance and services, which in year 2011 accounted for approximately 68.3% of total Gross Domestic Product (GDP) (statssa.gov.za).[1] Although South Africa saw a more than twofold increase in its GDP from 1996–2013 (databank.worldbank.org), per-capita GDP growth has been limited, and is lower than the world average (World Bank, 2012). Economic growth has been unequal across the population, with poverty and inequality persisting for many despite some improvement. Indeed, the country has one of the highest levels of inequality of the world, with an income Gini coefficient of approximately 0.70 and a consumption Gini coefficient of approximately 0.63, respectively, in 2008 and 2009. In 2000, the share of population living on less than 1.90 US$ a day (PPP),[2] the international poverty line, was 35.2%, whereas in 2011 this share was 16.6%, cf. povertydata.worldbank.org/poverty/country/ZAF. The share of population living on less than 3.10 US$ a day (PPP) in 2000, a slightly higher poverty line, was 35.2%, whereas in 2011 this share was 34.7%. Bhorat and van der Westhuizen (2011) argue that, in spite of persistent, high levels of poverty, the poverty reduction displayed over the period 1995–2005 is more significant at a lower poverty line, suggesting a faster income improvement for the poorest.

It follows that income inequality is highly correlated with race in South Africa – an enduring legacy of the apartheid system. Of the country's 51.8 million inhabitants, 79.2% are "black Africans", 8.9% are "white", and the remaining part of individuals are "coloured" or "Indian/Asian" ethnicity (Statistics South Africa, 2012). White South Africans earn approximately 11 times more per year than their black South African counterparts, although income differences across racial lines have shown some improvements since the end of apartheid (Leibbrandt et al., 2012).

The lack of large-scale job creation has been another important source of inequality in South Africa. According to the World Bank (2012), in 2012, the unemployment rate reached 25% (excluding "discouraged" workers, or those who are unemployed and not looking for work). However, unemployment is extremely high among youth (ages 15–24). In the fourth quarter of 2012, 51% of this age group was unemployed compared with 22% of adults (ages 25–54) and less than 8% for senior workers (ages 55–64). Differences among ethnic groups are also high, with the unemployment rate at 28.5% among black South Africans compared to 5.5% for white South Africans (OECD, 2013). Even those who are employed display huge disparities in wages based on education, ethnicity, gender, and location (urban township, informal settlement, or rural area).

In order to better understand how unequal South African society is with respect to specific services, and which demographic and socio-economic factors contribute the most in explaining this inequality, the World Bank (2012) performed an analysis based on the Human Opportunity Index[3] (HOI) across different types of services. This analysis revealed that some services, such as school attendance for children under age 16 and access to telecommunications, are almost universal in South Africa, with an HOI index above 90%. Other services are instead highly unequal: finishing primary school (13–15-year-olds), having health insurance, access to safe water on site and improved sanitation, as well as access to adequate space without overcrowding are well below universal, showing a HOI of about 60% or below. Furthermore, results suggested that ethnicity explains part of inequality in all opportunities. The location of the household (informal settlements or rural areas as opposed to urban areas) and the household head's education were the strongest determinants of the aforementioned inequalities – especially, respectively, those concerning the access to safe water on site – improved sanitation and electricity, and those related to having health insurance and finishing primary school on time.

Climate hazards

South Africa forms the tip of the African continent, occupying 1.2 million km² of land and bordering Namibia, Botswana, Zimbabwe, Mozambique, Lesotho, and Swaziland. While most of the country's borders are formed by rivers or coastline, South Africa has no significant lakes or any commercially navigable bodies of water in its interior (Byrnes, 1996; Tibane and Honwane, 2015).

Much of South Africa's climate is arid or semi-arid, with small sections of land experiencing Mediterranean and subtropical conditions (DEA, 2013b). Using monthly timeseries data from the Climate Research Unit (Harris et al., 2014), average annual temperatures in South Africa between 1981–2010 ranged from 14.3–22.4°C across the country's 52 district councils, while annual precipitation totals ranged from 158–1072 mm. A study by Kruger and Sekele (2013) identified six distinct thermal regimes, or regions with generally similar annual temperature conditions: the western, Mediterranean-climate coastline that borders the Atlantic Ocean; the eastern, subtropical coastline along the Indian Ocean; the low-altitude lowveld region lining the eastern border of South Africa; a region in the western interior portion of the country that is marked by relatively dry conditions, hot summers, and cold winters; a region in the southeastern interior with a relatively small diurnal range that is influenced by the Indian Ocean; and a region in the northernmost part of the country with relatively warmer winters and fewer temperature extremes.

Analyses of long-term trends in southern Africa's climate reveal significant changes in temperature regimes attributable to anthropogenic greenhouse gas (GHG) emissions (Knutson et al., 2013). In South Africa, temperatures have increased across much of the country in recent history (DEA, 2013a). In a comprehensive analysis of monthly climate data over the 1960–2010 period, it was found that South Africa's mean annual temperature has increased faster than the global average temperature (DEA, 2013a). An exception is in the central interior of the country, where significant trends in annual temperature were not detected. The frequency of days with positive (warm) temperature extremes has generally increased across South Africa, while the frequency of days with negative (cold) temperature extremes has generally declined (Kruger and Sekele, 2013). The magnitude of change in temperature extremes observed by Kruger and Sekele (2013) over the 1960–2009 time period varied across the country, with temperature extremes increasing most dramatically in the western, northeastern, and far eastern portions of South Africa. Changes in precipitation have been less clear in recent history. The report by the Department of Environmental Affairs (DEA, 2013a) did not observe trends in annual total precipitation, although the study did identify a decrease in the number of days receiving precipitation, indicating that the magnitude of precipitation received in a single event is increasing. Furthermore, the authors observed a small decline in autumn precipitation across the country.

In addition to anthropogenic influences, South Africa's climate is also subject to variations in temperature and precipitation that are tied to the El Niño-Southern Oscillation (ENSO), as well as sea-surface temperature (SST) anomalies in the Indian Ocean (DEA, 2013a).

Beyond the long-term trends and regular modes of variation observed in South Africa's climate record, significant changes in temperature and precipitation are projected to occur over the course of the twenty-first century. Such changes will create unprecedented conditions that the population will have to cope with and adapt to. Under high GHG emission scenarios (Relative Concentration Pathway 8.5, or RCP8.5) (van Vuuren et al., 2011), annual temperatures are projected to increase over interior South Africa by as much as 5–8°C (over a 1971–2005 baseline) by the end of the twenty-first century, with lower levels of warming along the coastline (DEA, 2013a). Under high emission scenarios, temperatures are projected to increase outside the range of normal even in the near term (2015–2035). Similar to the observed records, the certainty surrounding precipitation projections is lower than that of temperature projections (DEA, 2013a). In general, the DEA study projects a risk of drier conditions in the western and southern portions of the country, and a risk of wetter conditions in the east. South Africa's climate is extremely sensitive to the international greenhouse gas mitigation efforts – levels of warming are reduced by approximately 50% in many locations under RCP4.5, and precipitation changes in many instances are undetectable.

Climate and agriculture

Arid conditions and a thin topsoil layer limit the suitability of some portions of South Africa for crop cultivation (Byrnes, 1996). Indeed, only an estimated 11% of South Africa's surface is available for crop production, of which only 22% is high-potential arable land (Johnston et al., 2013). Nevertheless, the agricultural sector is still critical for the development of the country, because of the economic importance of its commercial sector and the ubiquity of subsistence smallholder farming, informally involving approximately 20% (approximately 2.9 million) of South African households (Statistics South Africa, 2011a). Commercial agriculture accounts for an estimated 80% of the country's agricultural production (Johnston et al., 2013), and makes South Africa among the world's top producers of many agricultural products, e.g., maize, sugarcane, grapefruits, dairy, and poultry, in terms of both quantity and value (FAOSTAT, 2017). Although the country harbors southern Africa's most intensive irrigation system and the highest rates of fertilizer application (Frenken, 2005; Mueller et al., 2012), a high proportion of South African agriculture is still rainfed, with only about 1.5% of the total agricultural land (1.3 million hectares) under irrigation (Johnston et al., 2013). Nevertheless, more than 50% of South Africa's available surface water is used for agriculture, making water scarcity one of the main concerns in agricultural production.

Several studies suggest that climate change is likely to have a negative influence on output and performance in African countries (Lobell et al., 2008). In the case of South Africa, Turpie and Visser (2012) conclude that a simultaneous decrease in rainfall and increase in temperature will reduce net revenue for both subsistence farmers and commercial farmers by the end of the century. Benhin (2006) investigated the role of temperature and precipitation on agricultural GDP and planted and harvested area of major crops in South Africa (maize, wheat, and sorghum) in the 2002–2003 time period. The author found, unexpectedly, that increasing temperature has had a positive impact on annual crop net revenues for all farms except those that are dryland (rainfed), and that increasing precipitation has positively influenced annual net revenue, except for small-scale farms. However, there are significant seasonal differences in the sign of the impacts, which farmers should be aware of in order to more easily cope with adverse climatic conditions.

The changes in climate that South Africa has already experienced, coupled with the changes in climate projected, raise concerns for the livelihood of individuals dependent on rainfed agriculture, in addition to the possible increase in the percentage of people suffering from hunger and undernourishment. Gbetibouo and Ringler (2009) state that South African agriculture is characterized by a medium-level risk of exposure to climate change, but the high levels of social inequality and poverty, and the socio-economic disparity in access to infrastructure and resources, are critical factors that increase the vulnerability of its agricultural population to climate change. Turpie and Visser (2012) also raise this point, highlighting a concern for the negative consequences that climate change might have on the agricultural sector, and for the already-marginal farming communities that could become even further impoverished.

Climate and water resources

In addition to effects on agricultural systems, climate change will have effects on the South African population through a variety of other channels. For example, climate change impacts on water resources are of particular concern in South Africa given the already dry baseline conditions (DEA, 2013b). As precipitation projections are relatively uncertain for the country, projected impacts on the water sector are also uncertain. However, given the possibility of drying for some regions (and wetting in others), the possibility of precipitation occurring in more concentrated time periods, and the projected increase in demand for water resources following population increases and development, there are concerns about the availability of water resources for water-intensive sectors such as agriculture and energy, as well as the ability of these sectors to plan for necessary adaptation measures (DEA, 2013b).

Migration effects on sending and receiving regions

Depending on the circumstances, migration can have a complex set of benefits and/or adverse consequences for both sending and receiving regions (Licker and Oppenheimer, 2013). For example, the receipt of remittances is typically a benefit for sending households. In South Africa, Lu and Treiman (2007) found that among black South Africans, households receiving remittances from labor migrants increased the probability that children present would be enrolled in school. However, children were at a disadvantage if they had a parent engaged in labor migration that did not send remittances. Similarly, in an analysis of the KwaZulu-Natal Income Dynamics Study data, Nagarajan (2009) found that remittances allowed households to access better-quality healthcare. However, migration can also burden sending households in South Africa. A study of a rural community in northeastern South Africa found that labor migrants are contracting diseases at an increasing rate in urban parts of the country, and are returning home at the end of their lives – a dynamic that places a burden on the households and healthcare systems in rural sending regions (Clark et al., 2007).

Receiving regions similarly face a mixture of benefits and adverse impacts as a result of immigration. In Gauteng – the most popular destination for migrants in South Africa – immigration poses a number of challenges for the regional government (Oosthuizen and Naidoo, 2004). Large levels of migration place an added demand on infrastructure, housing, and the healthcare sector and the services it provides. At the same time, migrants have been an integral part of the economic growth of the province, with large numbers of highly skilled workers moving to the province and contributing to its economic activity (Oosthuizen and Naidoo, 2004). Facchini et al. (2013) study the effects of immigration in South Africa on natives' employment rates and incomes. The authors perform a district-level analysis, finding that increased foreign migration negatively affects natives' employment rates, but not total income. A corresponding analysis at the national level suggests instead that increased immigration has a negative effect on natives' total income, but not on their employment rates. These national results are consistent with outflows of natives across districts (from high-immigration to low-immigration districts) as a consequence of immigration, as in Borjas (2006).

While the impacts on sending and receiving regions discussed here are not comprehensive, they highlight the potential for the action to both benefit and negatively affect sending and receiving regions depending on the circumstances of the move and the policies of the local governments.

Impacts of climate variability and change on migration

The interplay of factors reviewed in the previous sections of this chapter were illustrated in a recent study by Mastrorillo et al. (2016), which explored the role of climate variability in South African inter-district migration flows in the periods 1997–2001 and 2007–2011, along with a number of geographic, socio-economic, and demographic factors traditionally identified as potential drivers of migration. The authors found that an increase in positive temperature extremes, as well as positive and negative excess rainfall at the origin, act as a push effect and amplify out-migration. Also, the significance of the effect of climate on migration greatly varies by migrant characteristics. Particularly, flows of black and low-income South African migrants are strongly influenced by climatic variables, whereas those of white and high-income migrants exhibit a weak impact. This supports the hypothesis that black and poor migrants tend to be more vulnerable to climate variability and may be forced to use migration as an adaptation strategy. However, this finding only concerns migrants by definition, and does not necessarily apply to non-migrants. In other words, among non-migrants it is possible that there are individuals who are even more vulnerable to climate variability who cannot afford to migrate, and therefore remain trapped despite their migration intentions. Furthermore, agriculture – specifically agricultural employment – is found to be a possible channel through which climate shocks may trigger population mobility. Since agriculture is one of the sectors most affected by climate variations – and is a sector that is vulnerable to future climate change – it is plausible that reductions in agricultural output could induce individuals involved in agriculture activities, especially in marginal or less productive zones, to emigrate looking for better employment opportunities.

Additionally, a study by Dinkelman (2013) suggests that migrant networks in poor communities represent one channel through which households may mitigate the negative impacts of a local environmental shock. The authors documented that early life exposure to drought has had long-run effects on health among black South Africans confined to homelands during Apartheid. Specifically, drought exposure significantly raises later life male disability rates by 4%

and reduces cohort size. Also, the analysis performed on a subset of homelands reveals that in the areas of Transkei, Bophuthatswana, Venda, and Ciskei (the so-called TBVC areas), the disability effects are double and negative cohort effects are significantly larger, possibly due to particular restrictions in spatial mobility across TBVC as compared to non-TBVC areas.

Conclusion

This chapter has examined the patterns of migration in South Africa, and has critically discussed the sources of vulnerability and risk exposure that may contribute to increases or decreases in migration flows within the country. We have focused on climatic factors, and a number of socio-economic and demographic components (e.g. poverty, racial inequality, and unemployment, among others), which interact with one another and may increase the vulnerability of some groups within South Africa.

Initial evidence suggests that increasing temperatures projected across South Africa and the possibility of changing precipitation patterns throughout the twenty-first century could amplify the country's already high levels of internal migration. On the one hand, such changing temperature regimes may disproportionately amplify the migration of black and lower-income, highly vulnerable South Africans. On the other hand, given the evidence that the probability of migration is lower for lower-income individuals (Clarke and Eyal, 2014), there is also a risk of some low-income individuals being unable to move in response to climate hazards.

Further research is therefore needed to increase and consolidate the lines of evidence regarding the climate-migration link in South Africa. First, the relationship between climate variability and immobility, and the potential constraints to individual migration, need to be more deeply investigated and understood. A second line of inquiry to be pursued in the future would be achieving a better comprehension of how climatic factors influence different types of migration, including rural-to-urban, internal vs. international, and temporary vs. permanent. Third, projections of future migration flows using alternative climatic scenarios would allow for the assessment of the effects of climate on total population mobility, as well as the evaluation of how the marginal impact of climate is distributed across different regions. Since in South Africa (and elsewhere), population movements present both benefits and challenges to the migrants, their sending regions, and the regions receiving them, such analyses would be highly relevant to design effective policy measures to help populations cope with and adapt to a changing climate.

Finally, given the limits of South African data sources that are currently available, especially concerning the paucity of information on historical movements and the socio-economic status of individuals prior to and following migration, future research would benefit from the design of new ad-hoc surveys. This would be extremely helpful in exploring the aforementioned lines of research, as well as in investigating further issues regarding the complex nexus between climate and migration in South Africa.

Notes

1 The primary sector (i.e., agriculture and mining) and the secondary sector (i.e., manufacturing and construction) respectively accounted for 12.3% and 19.4% in year 2011 (statssa.gov.za).
2 Purchasing Power Parity.
3 This is an indicator of the coverage rate of a particular service (for instance, primary school enrollment), adjusted by how equitable that service is among children belonging to different population groups. The index runs from 0–100. The lower the value of HOI for a certain service, the more unequal a society is in distributing that service among children of different circumstances.

References

Adepoju, A. (2006). Internal and international migration within Africa, in Kok, P., Gelderblom, D., Oucho J. O. and van Zyl, J. (eds.), *Migration in South and Southern Africa, Dynamics and Determinants* (pp. 26–45). Cape Town, South Africa: Human Sciences Research Council.

Benhin, J. K. A. (2006). Climate Change and South African Agriculture: Impacts and Adaptation Options. CEEPA Discussion Paper No. 21. Centre for Environmental Economics and Policy in Africa (CEEPA), University of Pretoria, South Africa.

Bhorat, H. and van der Westhuizen, C. (2011). *Pro-Poor Growth and Social Protection in South Africa: Exploring the Interactions*. Input paper prepared for the National Planning Commission.

Borjas, G. J. (2006). Native international migration and the labor market impact of immigration. *Journal of Human Resources*, 41:221–258.

Byrnes, R. M., ed. (1996). *Geography, in South Africa: A Country Study*. Washington, DC: GPO for the Library of Congress.

Choe, C. and Chrite, L. (2014). Internal migration of Blacks in South Africa: An application of the Roy Model. *South African Journal of Economics*, 81(1): 81–98.

Clarke, R. and Eyal, K. (2014). Microeconomic determinants of spatial mobility in post-apartheid South Africa: Longitudinal evidence from the National Income Dynamics Study. *Development Southern Africa*, 31(1):168–194.

Clark, S. J., Collinson, M. A., Kahn, K., Drullinger, K. and Tollman, S. M. (2007). Returning home to die: Circular labour migration and mortality in South Africa. *Scandinavian Journal of Public Health*, 35(Suppl 69):35–44.

Collinson, M., Tollman, S., Kahn, K. and Clark, S. (2003). Highly prevalent circular migration: Households, mobility and economic status in rural South Africa. Paper prepared for Conference on African Migration in Comparative Perspective, Johannesberg, South Africa, 4–7 June, 2003. Accessed 05/22/2016 from www.queensu.ca/samp/migrationresources/Documents/Collinson_highly.pdf

DEA (Department of Environmental Affairs) (2013a). *Long-Term Adaptation Scenarios Flagship Research Programme (LTAS) for South Africa. Climate Trends and Scenarios for South Africa*. Pretoria, South Africa.

DEA (Department of Environmental Affairs) (2013b). *Long-Term Adaptation Scenarios Flagship Research Programme (LTAS) for South Africa. Climate Change Implications for the Water Sector in South Africa*. Pretoria, South Africa.

Dinkelman, T. (2013). *Mitigating Long-run Health Effects of Drought: Evidence from South Africa*. NBER Working Papers 19756, National Bureau of Economic Research, Inc.

Facchini, G., Mayda, A. M. and Mendola, M. (2013). *South-South Migration and the Labor Market: Evidence from South Africa*. IZA DP No. 7362, Forschungsinstitut zur Zukunft der Arbeit Institute for the Study of Labor.

Food and Agriculture Organization of the United Nations (2017). FAOSTAT. Accessed 11/27/2017 from www.fao.org/faostat

Frenken, K., ed. (2005). *Irrigation in Africa in figures: AQUASTAT Survey — 2005*. Rome: Food and Agriculture Organization of the United Nations.

Gbetibouo, G. A. and Ringler, C. (2009). *Mapping South African Farming Sector Vulnerability to Climate Change and Variability: A Sub-national Assessment*. IFPRI Discussion Paper 00885. Washington, DC: International Food Policy Research Institute.

Harris, I., Jones, P. D., Osborn, T. J., and Lister, D. H. (2014). Updated high-resolution grids of monthly climatic observations — the CRU TS3.10 Dataset. *International Journal of Climatology*, 34(3):623–642.

Hunter, L. M., Nawrotzki, R., Leyk, S., Maclaurin, G. J., Twine, W., Collinson, M. and Erasmus, B. (2014). Rural outmigration, natural capital, and livelihoods in South Africa. *Population, Space and Place*, 20:402–420.

IOM (International Organization for Migration) (2009). *Migration, Environment and Climate Change: Assessing the Evidence*. Edited by Laczko, F. and Aghazarm, C. Geneva: International Organization for Migration.

IOM (International Organization for Migration) (2014). Data Assessment of Labour Migration Statistics in the SADC Region: South Africa, Zambia and Zimbabwe. Pretoria 0083, South Africa: International Organization for Migration.

Johnston, P., Thomas, T. S., Hachigonta, S. and Majele Sibanda, L. (2013). South Africa, in Hachigonta, S., Nelson, G. C., Thomas, T. S. and Majele Sibanda, L. (eds.) *Southern African Agriculture and Climate Change: A Comprehensive Analysis* (pp. 175–212). Washington, DC: International Food Policy Research Institute.

Kok, P., Rural, H. S. R. C. I., and Programme, R. D. R. (2003). *Post-Apartheid Patterns of Internal Migration in South Africa*. Cape Town, South Africa: HSRC Publishers.

Knutson, T. R., Zeng, F., and Wittenberg, A. T. (2013). Multimodel assessment of regional surface temperature trends: CMIP3 and CMIP5 twentieth-century simulations. *Journal of Climate*, 26: 8709–8743.

Kruger, A. C. and Sekele, S. S. (2013). Trends in extreme temperature indices in South Africa: 1962–2009. *International Journal of Climatology*, 33: 661–676.

Leibbrandt, M., Finn, A. and Woolard, I. (2012). Describing and decomposing post-apartheid income inequality in South Africa. *Development South Africa*, 29(1): 19–34.

Leyk, S., Maclaurin, G. J., Hunter, L. M., Nawrotzki, R., Twine, W., Collinson, M. and Erasmus, B. (2012). Spatially and temporally varying associations between temporary outmigration and natural resource availability in resource-dependent rural communities in South Africa: A modeling framework. *Applied Geography*, 34:559–568.

Licker, R. and Oppenheimer, M. (2013). Climate-induced human migration: A review of impacts on receiving regions. Paper prepared for the Impacts World 2013 International Conference on Climate Change Effects, Potsdam, Germany.

Lobell, D. B., Burke, M. B., Tebaldi, C., Mastrandrea, M. D., Falcon, W. P., and Naylor, R. L. (2008). Prioritizing climate change adaptation needs for food security in 2030. *Science*, 319(5863): 607–610.

Lu, Y. and Treiman, D. K. (2007). *The Effect of Labor Migration and Remittances on Children's Education among Blacks in South Africa*. California Center for Population Research On-Line Working Paper Series, CCPR-001–08. Accessed 05/22/2016 from http://papers.ccpr.ucla.edu/papers/PWP-CCPR-2007-001/PWP-CCPR-2007-001.pdf

Mastrorillo, M., Licker, R., Bohra-Mishra, P., Fagiolo, G., Estes, L. D. and Oppenheimer, M. (2016). The influence of climate variability on internal migration flows in South Africa. *Global Environmental Change*, 39: 155–169.

Mueller, N. D., Gerber, J. S., Johnston, M., Ray, D. K., Ramankutty, N. and Foley, J. A. (2012). Closing yield gaps through nutrient and water management. *Nature*, 490: 254–257.

Myburgh, A. (2004). Explaining emigration from South Africa. *The South African Journal of Economics*, 72(1): 122–148.

Nagarajan, S. (2009). Migration, Remittances, and Household Health: Evidence from South Africa. Dissertation, The George Washington University, 183 pp. Accessed 05/22/2016 from http://pqdtopen.proquest.com/doc/304889079.html?FMT=ABS

OECD (2013). OECD Economic Surveys: South Africa 2013, OECD Publishing.

Oosthuizen, M. and Naidoo, P. (2004). Internal Migration to the Gauteng Province. Development Policy Research Unit Working Paper 04/88. Accessed 05/22/2016 from www.queensu.ca/samp/migration-resources/Documents/Oosthuizen_internal.pdf

Polzer Ngwato, T. (2010), Population Movements in and to South Africa, Migration Fact Sheet 1, Forced Migration Studies Programme, University of Witwatersrand, Johannesburg, South Africa.

Posel, D. (2004). Have migration patterns in post-Apartheid South Africa changed? *Journal of Interdisciplinary Economics*, 15:277–292.

Posel, D. (2010). Households and labour migration in post-Apartheid South Africa. *Journal for Studies in Economics and Econometrics*, 34(3):129–141.

Statistics South Africa (2011a). *Census 2011 Agricultural Households*. Report No. 03–11–01. Accessed 05/22/2016 from www.statssa.gov.za/census/census_2011/census_products/Agricultural_Households.pdf

Statistics South Africa (2011b). *Tourism and Migration*. Report No. 03–51–02. Accessed 05/02/2017 from: www.statssa.gov.za/publications/Report-03-51-02/Report-03-51-022011.pdf

Statistics South Africa (2012). *Census 2011 Statistical release — P0301.4*. Accessed 05/22/2016 from www. statssa.gov.za/publications/P03014/P030142011.pdf

Tibane, E. and Honwane, E., eds. (2015). *Land and Its People, in South Africa Yearbook 2014/15*. Accessed 05/22/2016 from www.gcis.gov.za/content/resourcecentre/sa-info/yearbook2014-15

Turpie, J. and Visser, M. (2012). *The Impact of Climate Change on South Africa's Rural Areas*. Chapter 4, in Financial and Fiscal Commission: Submission for the 2013/2014 Division of Revenue, Johannesburg, South Africa.

van Vuuren, D.P., Edmonds, J., Kainuma, M., Riahi, K., Thomson, A., Hibbard, K., Hurtt, G. C., Kram, T., Krey, V., Lamarque, J.-F., Masui, T., Meinshausen, M., Nakicenovic, N., Smith, S. J., and Rose, S. K. (2011). The representative concentration pathways: an overview. *Climatic Change*, 109: 5–31.

Wentzel, M. and Tlabela, K. (2006). Historical background to South African migration, in Kok, P., Gelderblom, D., Oucho, J.O., and van Zyl, J. (eds.) *Migration in South and Southern Africa: Dynamics and Determinants*. Cape Town: HSRC Press, 376 pp.

World Bank (2012). *South Africa Economic Update Focus on Inequality of Opportunity*. Washington, DC: The International Bank for Reconstruction and Development.

17

Deforestation, drought and environmental migration in Brazil

An overview

Erika Pires Ramos and Lilian Yamamoto

Introduction

The Brazilian Panel on Climate Change has found that the Legal Amazon and Northeast regions are the parts of the country most likely to suffer severe, adverse consequences of climate change. Rainfall is expected to decrease across most of the North and Northeast regions (PBMC 2016). Temperatures in Amazon are expected to increase by 1–1.5°C, while temperatures in the Northeast region, particularly in the biome called Caatinga, are expected to increase between 0.5–1°C through the year 2040. The Fifth Assessment Report of the Intergovernmental Panel on Climate Change (IPCC AR5 2013) projects significant, adverse impacts on water availability for agriculture, with subsequent economic consequences that could potentially stimulate large-scale migrations from the Northeast region. The same IPCC report expects a decrease in precipitation of 20–30% in Central and Eastern Amazon, with increases in precipitation in Western Amazon; such outcomes would also have the potential to influence population movements in those regions.

One of the most important ecological systems in the world, the Legal Amazon Basin is the world's largest contiguous tropical forest and contains one of the greatest reservoirs of biological diversity (Foley et al. 2007), making it of critical importance to global ecosystem health more generally. It remained almost intact until the 1960s (Hirakuri 2003), when large-scale deforestation began with the 1958 construction of the Belém-Brasília Highway, which was intended to integrate the Northern and Western states into the rest of the country. In the following two decades, over 2 million people settled along this road (Moran 1993) and with their settlement, deforestation accelerated quickly. This trend continued until the mid-2000s, and was reversed beginning in 2004, when annual forest loss decreased by about 80%. This was made possible by the combination of increased law enforcement, satellite monitoring, pressure from environmentalists, creation of new protected areas and other private and public sector initiatives (Butler 2016).

The Northeast is considered to be the region in Brazil most vulnerable to the effects of global warming, whose effect is linked to declines in agricultural production and reduction of hydroelectric energy generation (CEDEPLAR/UFMG and FIOCRUZ 2008). The region is drought prone, with average of one drought every seven years. Rain falls during a 3–4-month rainy season, and in the remainder of the year agriculture is possible only with irrigation (Magal-hães and Martins 2011). Because of the inevitability of droughts in this region, out-migration to the Southeast and Southern regions has historically been high, although this trend reversed between 2000 and 2010, when this region received the highest number of returnees while compared to other regions in Brazil. This occurred due to various factors such as the decrease of population absorption capacity of the states of the Southeast region, the emergence of new economic activities and growth of medium-sized cities of the Northeast region. (Ojima and Nascimento 2015).

The combination of environmental factors such as drought, soil erosion, desertification and deforestation, combined with rapid population growth, can affect the capacity of people to maintain sustainable livelihoods and stimulate temporary or indefinite migration (Ginneken and Wiegers 2005; Myers 2002). Such interactions are clearly observable in migration patterns in Legal Amazon and in the Northeast region, where migration is driven by interactions of economics, social tensions and environmental conditions (Hoffman and Grigera 2013; CEDE-PLAR/UFMG and FIOCRUZ 2008). However, migration is not a universal outcome, and there are cases where residents of isolated communities cannot migrate even should they wish to do so (UNFPA 2015).

Deforestation and climate change in the Legal Amazon

The Legal Amazon region comprises 59% of Brazilian territory and is constituted by the states of Acre, Amapá, Amazonas, Mato Grosso, Pará, Rondônia, Roraima and Tocantins, as well as parts of the state of Maranhão (IPEA 2008). It is the world's largest intact tropical rain forest, covering approximately 5 million km^2 (Garcia 2011). Deforestation of the Amazon, as in other forests in Latin American countries, is the result of government policies that incentivized the conver-sion of forest to agriculture, cattle-ranching and other uses (Hirakuri 2003). Climate change and climate variability exacerbate such changes by stimulating increased droughts and flooding in the Amazon, and causing more frequent and intense fires, destructive storms and landslides (Hoffman and Grigera 2013).

The process of deforestation was implemented as part of the National Integration Plan (*Plano de Integração Nacional*) created during the military dictatorship of 1964–1985. It aimed to inte-grate the Amazon region with the rest of the country through the Transamazon and the North-ern Perimetral highways. During the same period, the government also promoted the migration to Amazon of peasants from the Northeast region, who arrived in organized settlements and spontaneously as well (NUPAUB 1997). In the 1970s, large scale development projects were established in the Amazon region, examples including the Carajás mining project, construction of dams at Tucuruí and Balbina and development of industrial centers in São Luís and Manaus, along with various agribusiness projects (NUPAUB 1997). The National Institute for Coloni-zation and Agrarian Reform (INCRA) estimated optimistically that 1 million families would settle in the Transamazon region, but by the mid-1970s, only 7% of that number had done so (Kohlhepp 2002). In the late 1970s, rampant deforestation and conversion of forest to cattle ranching caused irreparable damage to ecosystems, causing soil erosion, loss of nutrients by drainage and disturbances to water balances (Kohlhepp 2002).

In the 1970s and the 1980s, the states of Legal Amazon contributed less than 2% of national greenhouse gas emissions, but by 2015 this figure had increased to 9% (Observatório do Clima 2013). In the 1980s, the intensification of mining and agriculture activities encouraged migration into Legal Amazon, while hydropower dams led to displacement and deforestation. Currently, there are 74 dams under operation, 91 planned and 31 under construction in Legal Amazon (Dams in Amazon n.d.). A severe economic recession in the 1980s stimulated large numbers of unemployed people to migrate to the Northern Brazil as opposed to urbanized areas in the Southeast region of the country, the traditional destination of migration for many Brazilians (Young 1998).

Agricultural expansion of soybean plantations, uncontrolled cattle ranching and growing production of biofuel feedstock are main causes of deforestation today. In the Brazilian Amazon, the top cause of deforestation is cattle ranching (65–70%), followed by small-scale agriculture (20–25%), large-scale agriculture (5–10%), logging (2–3%) and mining, urbanization, road construction, dams and fires (1%) (Butler 2016).

However, due to integrated policies to control illegal deforestation, it declined to a much lower rate of 4,656 km^2 for the year 2012 (IPCC AR5 2013). During this same period, between 2008 and 2013, the Amazon was affected by multiple extreme events, such as serious droughts and floods. The record flooding in the Amazon in 2012 surpassed the previous record extreme of 2009, while river levels during the droughts of 2005 and 2010 were among the lowest during the last 40 years (Marengo et al. 2013).

Droughts in the Northeast region

The Northeast region of Brazil includes the states of Ceará, Piauí, Rio Grande do Norte, Paraíba, Pernambuco, Alagoas, Sergipe and Bahia. It is simultaneously the poorest and the second most populated region in the country, home to 28% of the national population (Barbieri et al. 2010). Droughts have affected semiarid parts of the Northeast region for a very long time, and it is the type of natural disaster that affects the highest number of people in Brazil (Ojima 2014). Beginning with the 1877 drought and continuing throughout the 20th century, the Northeast region was considered to be the nation's most problematic region. In the late half of the 1950s, there was a large out-migration from the Northeast region to the Southeast, caused by a severe drought (Fusco and Ojima 2014). Since then, any number of proposals for "solutions to drought" were put forward by powerful political and economic actors. A so-called "drought industry" has emerged, consisting of groups that benefit from development investments and bank credits granted to the region that rarely trickle down to ordinary residents. Droughts are consequently a source of economic wealth for powerful people who have little incentive to take effective actions to reduce the region's vulnerability to drought (FIOCRUZ 2010).

In the semiarid area of the Northeast region, the main economic activities are centered on small-scale livestock operations and subsistence agriculture, which are inherently limited by climatic conditions; they have also been pointed to as triggers of environmental degradation (Giongo 2011). It is forecasted that droughts may increase in frequency and intensity in the Northeast of Brazil as a result of climate change (World Bank 2013) placing intense pressure on freshwater resource availability. El Niño events are often associated with droughts in the Northern region of Brazil (Gutiérrez et al. 2014), aggravate the environmental challenges in this region and contribute to potential migration.

Deforestation, drought and environmental migration in the context of climate change

Although migration in Brazil has a strong environmental component, environmental factors such as drought and deforestation are rarely addressed in academic or government studies as compared with research on labour markets and economic influences on migration. Except for responses to sudden-onset natural disasters, there is no unified policy on internal displacement in Brazil (Muggah 2016). The Brazilian legal system does not take an integrated approach that makes links between migration, climate change and disasters, although it does have a system which considers prevention, mitigation and responses to disasters[1] (Ramos et al. 2016).

The National Plan on Climate Change, adopted in 2007, guides government responses to the impacts of global warming, but does not formally include environmental migration (Machado-Filho 2013). The Brazilian National Adaptation Plan (NAP) launched in May 2016 recognized, in general terms, that the increase of temperature will induce the rise of extreme events in different regions of Brazil – such as the modification of rainfall patterns, droughts and floods – and may trigger displacement of people in affected areas. It mentions "the possibility of new migratory flows in response to the negative consequences to climate change and as a "possible strategy of adaptation to climate change", but does not explain how migration could be considered an adaptation strategy (MMA, 2016, vol. II, p.223). Instead, it used a concept of Specific Traditional Population Groups (STPG)[2] to define groups which are highly vulnerable to climate change in Brazil according to their income, educational level and access to basic services. The NAP points out that most of these groups were concentrated in the Northeast arid area and Caatinga biomes (19.9%) and in the Amazon (60.3%) (MMA, 2016). The NAP foresees plans that would evaluate the vulnerability of groups that are exposed to the risks of climate change, including suggestions to improve the adaptative capacity in the Caatinga and Amazon biomes. Although it recognizes the need to include migration as a possible adaptation strategy, it predicts that the STPG in the Amazon region is unlikely to migrate in contrast to the Northeast region population that is expected to migrate to urban areas.

A study led by Marengo et. al. (2013) shows that the Brazilian government foresees short-term goals and lacks long-term planning for dealing with natural hazards. The study notes that, between 2003 and 2013, victims of droughts and floods in the Amazon were assisted by the government through provision of food supply and emergency care; but, as soon as the emergency phase ended, the populations remained without further assistance. This indicates that while efforts have been devoted to mitigation by reducing deforestation, long-term drought and flood recovery and adaptation policies have been overlooked in the Amazon region and are an example of institutional maladaptation. The NAP also is vague in promises of "measures to enhance understanding, coordination and cooperation with regard to climate change induced displacement, migration and planned relocation … at national, regional and international levels", as provided by paragraph 14 (f) of the Cancun Adaptation Framework (UNFCCC 2010).

Wellink (2013) studied the relationship between drought, land degradation and deforestation in inter-state migration in Brazil. The findings suggest that droughts in the state of origin increases out-migration, and that droughts in migrant destination states cause migration rates to that destination to fall. The results concerning the link between migration and deforestation were less strong, but concluded that forest clearance is associated with lower levels of out-migration due to increased availability of work opportunities in forestry. The study could find no effect of land degradation on migration. In a study that simulated scenarios of impacts of climate change on migration for Brazil's Northeast region up to 2050, Barbieri et al. (2010)

found that the agricultural sector would be adversely affected by climate change, consequently pushing people out of the region. Bastos et al. (2013) studied the long-term effect of drought on labor markets in Brazil, including patterns and linkages between agriculture and other sectors of activity, and found that in the long-term drought led to out-migration from impacted areas.

An innovative report, "*Mudanças climáticas, Migrações e Saúde: cenários para o nordeste, 2000–2050*" ("Migration, Climate Change and Public Health:scenarios for the Northeast, 2000–2050") (CEDEPLAR/UFMG, FIOCRUZ 2008), sought to evaluate the demographic and economic impacts of climate change and its consequences for public health in the Northeast region of Brazil.[3] The study pointed out that climate change may affect the whole economic system of the region, and reduce its Gross Domestic Product (GDP) by over 11%, which could in turn stimulate migration of about 500,000 people, motivated by a combination of severe drought periods and better economic opportunities outside the region (CEDEPLAR/UFMG, FIOCRUZ 2008). In the face of this result, Bolson (2013) points out that the Brazilian climate change law (no. 12.187/09) in its art. 5°, III, which refers to adaptation measures in order to reduce adverse effects of climate change, could provide a legal basis for the necessary migration policies in the Northeast region.

The Northeast region has a long history of migration to Legal Amazon. Between 1877 and 1879, one of the worst droughts in the Northeast region caused a massive migration to Amazon; similarly, between 1943 and 1945, another long drought caused the out-migration of about 50,000 people to Amazon. The arrival of migrants, farmers and companies put pressure on Indigenous and traditional populations, who were often faced with physical violence and were forcibly displaced to urban centres (UNFPA 2015). More recent conflicts in the region have been related to land and resources disputes, such as land grabbing, illegal logging and erosion of water courses due to mining on the rivers (Castro 2005).

Although population growth has been identified as one of the main root causes of deforestation (Allen and Barnes 1985), the role of migration in this dynamic is complicated by other factors. Although dramatic declines of forest-cover have occurred in Legal Amazon when there was a heavy in-migration (IOM 2009), Perz et al. (2005) attribute population growth in Legal Amazon as caused by high fertility rates and declining mortality rates as well as by in-migration. The population of the Amazon region is presently increasing at an annual rate of 2.8%, considerably higher than the national rate of 1.8%. Ten Amazonian cities have doubled in population over the past decade, and the region's population climbed 23% from 2000–2010 (IBGE 2010). The farm-forest frontier is continually extending toward the centre of Amazonia, driven by an increase of inter-regional migration, especially to the south of Roraima, north of Mato-Grosso and southern Amazonia. This migration seems to contribute directly to the deforestation rate in the south of Amazon (Carrero 2009). At the same time, the majority of inhabitants of the Amazon live in urban areas (71.8%), and even rural people tend to live close to the urban centres (Parry et al. 2010). Economic expansion has in some areas generated an increase in illegal deforestation, pollution and land conflicts, which in turn can result in displacement (Hoffman and Grigera 2013).

Protected areas affect population movements in Legal Amazon. About 44% of the Legal Amazon is protected, with 8% in integral areas, 14% in sustainable use and 22% in Indigenous lands. The integral areas do not allow consumption, extraction or destruction of natural resources and restrict the presence of people. In sustainable areas, extraction of natural resources is allowed. García (2015) carried out a study aimed at understanding how protected areas (PAs), which include Federal Conservation Units, State Conservation Units and Indigenous lands, affect internal migration in Legal Amazon region. The study found that in general, people who were employed in agriculture or resource extraction were less likely to migrate, but that areas close to protected areas had higher levels of out-migration, since the development of economic activities becomes limited.

Federal and state policies in the Amazon region focus mainly on providing incentives for traditional and Indigenous people to remain in their lands and do not encourage them to migrate; such policies do not consider that migration could diversify their income sources and encourage the sending of remittances back to family members, thereby increasing resilience in their places of origin (Ober, n.d). Government policies also create financing mechanisms such as the 2007 Forest Allowance Programme, which provides cash transfers to Indigenous and traditional people as long as they do not deforest primary forests areas in Amazonas state (Viana 2008). Its goal is to pay for environmental services and products provided by the traditional communities in order to promote the sustainable use of natural resources, conservation and environmental protection (Lucas 2013).

The overall theme is that climate change will put stress on basic livelihoods and fragile ecosystems, and while government policies recognize such potential, there are no specific mechanisms in the National Adaptation Plan that take into consideration the potential for adaptation through migration.

Conclusions

There is a growing literature on deforestation and drought in Brazil, and on the impacts of climate change on various regions of the country. In this chapter we focussed on two regions that are hotspots of environmental degradation and climate change risks and which also have highly dynamic migration patterns, finding that research has rarely made an explicit link between environment and migration in the Brazilian context.

Studies on the relationship between drought and migration in Brazil based on rainfall and population census data have found that states which suffer from drought experience out-migration from the impacted areas. Migration patterns in the Amazon have links to deforestation through historical government policies – dam construction, mining, cattle ranching and crop farming have since had significant influences on migration patterns in the region, and deserve greater attention from research. The influence of extreme weather events on mobility have not yet been explored with due attention.

Both in the Northeast and Legal Amazon regions, migration tends to flow toward larger cities, where major income and financial resources are available. State cash-transfer programmes such as the Forest Allowance, currently available in the Amazonas state (Fundação Amazonas Sustentável, n.d.), have potential to discourage the migration of vulnerable groups and may help with conservation and preservation of the forest.

Brazil has no specific policies on climate change-related migration, notwithstanding its mention in the National Adaptation Plan. New research approaches to migration that consider the influence of climate change would help decision- and policy-makers develop policies for the protection of vulnerable population in the context of extreme weather events in order to prevent future displacement and/or weigh the merits of migration as a climate change adaptation strategy.

Acknowledgements

The authors would like to thank Dr. Risélia Duarte Bezerra and Dr. Sofia Hirakuri for their comments that greatly improved this chapter.

Notes

1 1988 Brazilian Constitution, arts. 21, XVIII, 22, XXVIII e 136; Law n° 12.608 of 10 April 2012, National Policy of Protection and Civil Defence authorizes the creation of an information and disaster monitoring system; Law n° 12.340 of 1 December 2010 provides resource transfers for the execution of preventive actions in disaster risk areas, response and recovery in disaster affected areas; the National Fund for Public Calamities, Protection and Civil Defence, Decree n° 7.257 of 4 August 2010, establishes recognition of emergency situations and state of public calamity, resource transferring for relief actions, assistance to victims, re-establishment of essential services and reconstruction of disaster-affected areas; Interministerial Resolution n° 2 of 6 December 2012 sets forth a National Collective Protocol for the Integral Protection of Children and Teenagers, Elderly People and People with Disabilities in Situations of Risk of Disasters; and Normative Instruction n° 1 of 24 August 2012 (Ministry of National Integration) establishes procedures and criteria for the declaration of urgency situations and state of public calamity and the recognition of situations of abnormality declared by the Federation´s entities.
2 Extractivist, indigenous, quilombola communities (constituted by Afro-descendants of slaves who fled plantations), small-scale fishermen, riverside communities, family farmers and people settled by agrarian reform belong to these groups, according to the NAP.
3 The study used climatic scenarios were the A2 (most pessimistic, high emissions) and B2 (most optimistic, low emissions) of the INPE (Instituto Nacional de Pesquisas Espaciais). In the former, the increase in temperature would be between 2–5.4°C and in the later, the increase in temperature would be between 1.4–3.8°C, in the projection scenarios for the Northeast region in 2000–2050. Based on this, it was created a general model of a computer equation that simulated income, employment and consumption scenarios.

References

Allen, J. C., and Barnes, D. F. (1985) "The Causes of Deforestation in Developing Countries" *Annals of the Association of American Geographers* 75 163–184.
Barbieri, A., Domingues, E., Queiroz, B. L., Ruiz, R. M., Rigotti, J. I., Carvalho, J. A. M., and Resende, M. F. (2010) "Climate Change and Population Migration in Brazil's Northeast: Scenarios for 2025 to 2050" *Population and Environment* 31(5) 344–370.
Bastos, P., Busso, M., and Miller, S. (2013) "Adapting to Climate Change: Long Term Effects of Drought on Local Labor Markets." <www.webmeets.com/files/papers/lacea-lames/2013/659/BBM2013_full.pdf> Accessed 2 August 2016.
Bolson, S. H. (2013) "As mudanças climáticas e a política de adaptação de Anthony Giddens: em busca de um modelo preventivo no combate aos efeitos das alterações do clima na Região do Semiárido do Nordeste no Brasil" *Revista Direito Ambiental e Sociedade* 3(1) 221–240.
Butler, R. (2016) "Amazon Destruction." *Mongabay* <http://rainforests.mongabay.com/amazon/amazon_destruction.html> Accessed 27 May 2016.
Carrero, G. C. (2009) *Dinâmica do desmatamento e consolidação de propriedades rurais na fronteira de expansão agropecuária no sudeste do Amazonas.* Dissertação de mestrado, INPA. <http://bdtd.inpa.gov.br/bitstream/tede/750/1/Dissertacao_%20Gabriel_%20Carrero.pdf>. Accessed 1 August 2016.
Castro, E. (2005) "Dinâmica socioeconômica e desmatamento na Amazônia." *Novos Cadernos NAEA* 8(2) 5–39.
CEDEPLAR/UFMG, FIOCRUZ (2008) *Mudanças climáticas, Migrações e Saúde: cenários para o nordeste, 2000–2050.* CEDEPLAR, Belo Horizonte.
Dams in Amazon. n.d. <http://dams-info.org/en/about/us/> Accessed 27 May 2016.
FIOCRUZ (2010) Radis-comunicação em saúde, n. 94, jun. <http://www6.ensp.fiocruz.br/radis/sites/default/files/radis_94.pdf>. Accessed 13 August 2016.
Foley, J., Asner, G. P., Costa, M. H., Coe, M. T., De Fries, R., Gibbs, H. K., Howard, E. A., Olson, S., Patz, J., Ramankutty, N., and Snyder, P. (2007) "Amazonia Revealed: Forest Degradation and Loss of Ecosystem Goods and Services in the Amazon Basin." *The Ecological Society of America* 5(1) 25–32.

Fundação Amazonas Sustentável (n.d.) Programa Bolsa Floresta, <http://fas-amazonas.org/pbf/>. Accessed 21 November 2017.

Fusco, W. and Ojima, R. (2014) "Migrações e nordestinos pelo Brasil: uma breve contextualização" in Fusco, W. and Ojima, R. eds, *Migrações nordestinas no século 21*, um panorama recente Blucher, São Paulo 12–26.

Garcia, B. (2011) *The Amazon from in International Law Perspective*, Cambridge University Press, New York.

García, L. D. H. (2015) *Protected Areas' Deforestation Spillovers and Two Critical Underlying Mechanisms: An Empirical Exploration for the Brazilian Amazon*, PhD dissertation, Graduate School of Duke University.

Ginneken, J. and Wiegers, M. (2005) "Impact of Population Pressure on Armed Conflicts in Developing Countries" <http://iussp2005.princeton.edu/papers/51215>. Accessed 13 August 2016.

Giongo, V. (2011) "Balanço de carbono no semiárido brasileiro: perspectivas e desafios" in Lima, R. C. C., Cavalcante, A. M. B., and Marin, A. M. P. eds, *Desertificação e Mudanças Climáticas no Semiárido Brasileiro*, Instituto Nacional do Semiárido, Campina Grande, 115–130.

Gutiérrez, A. P., Nathan, L., Engle, A. N., Erwin, D. N., Molejón, C., and Martin, E. S. (2014) Drought preparedness in Brazil. *Weather and Climate Extremes* 3 95–106.

Hirakuri, S. (2003) "Can Law Save the Forests?" Center for International Forestry, Research, Jakarta.

Hoffman, M. and Grigera, A. (2013) Climate Change, Migration and Conflict in the Amazon and the Andes – Rising Tensions and Policy Options in South America, Center for American Progress, Washington.

IBGE (2010) Sinopse do Censo Demográfico <http://biblioteca.ibge.gov.br/visualizacao/livros/liv49230.pdf>. Accessed 13 August 2016.

IOM (2009) *Migration, Environment and Climate Change: Assessing the Evidence*, IOM, Geneva,

IPCC AR5 (2013) Climate Change 2013-The Physical Science Basis < http://www.climatechange2013.org/>. Accessed 21 November 2017.

IPEA (2008) O que é? Amazônia Legal. <www.ipea.gov.br/desafios/index.php?option=com_content&id=2154:catid=28&Itemid=23>. Accessed 29 July 2016.

Kohlhepp, G. (2002) "Conflitos de interesse no ordenamento territorial da Amazônia brasileira". *Estudos Avançados* 16 (45), 37–61.

Lucas, N. (2013) *Efficiency of Bolsa Floresta Program in the Brazilian Amazon*. Swedish University of Agricultural Sciences, Uppsala University. Master thesis.

Machado-Filho, H. (2013) "Climate Change Policy and Legislation in Brazil" in *Climate Change and the Law*, Hollo, E.J., Kulovesi, K. and Mehling, M. Springer, 639–651.

Marengo, J. A., Borma, L. S., Rodriguez, D. A., Pinho, P., Soares, W. R., and Alves, L. M. (2013) "Recent Extremes of Drought and Flooding in Amazonia: Vulnerabilities and Human Adaptation" *American Journal of Climate Change* 2 87–96.

Magalhães, A. R. and Martins, E. S. (2011) "Drought and Drought Policy in Brazil" in: Sivakumar, M. et al. Towards a Compendium on National Drought Policy- proceedings of an expert meeting, July 14–15, Washington, DC, World Meteorological Organization, 57–67.

Moran, E. F. (1993) "Deforestation and Land Use in the Brazilian Amazon" *Human Ecology* 21 (1) 1–21.

Ministério do Meio Ambiente do Brasil (MMA) (2016) Plano Nacional de Adaptação à Mudança do Clima –Volume II: Estratégias Setoriais e Temáticas, versão consulta pública, 2015. <http://hotsite.mma.gov.br/consultapublicapna/wp-content/uploads/sites/15/2015/08/PNA_-Volume-2-07.10.15_Consulta-P%C3%BAblica_texto-final.pdf>. Accessed 21 November 2017.

Myers, N. (2002) "Environmental Refugees: A Growing Phenomenon of the 21st Century" *Philosophical Transactions of the Royal Society B: Biological Sciences* 357 609–613.

Muggah, R. (2016) "The Invisible Displaced: A Unified Conceptualization of Population Displacement in Brazil" *Journal of Refugee Studies*. doi: 10.193/jrs/feu033.

NUPAUB Research Center on Human Population and Wetlands, University of São Paulo (1997) Deforestation and Livelihoods in the Brazilian Amazon, São Paulo <http://nupaub.fflch.usp.br/sites/nupaub.fflch.usp.br/files/deforestation.pdf>. Accessed 13 August 2016.

Ober, K. (n.d.) Migration as Adaptation-Exploring Mobility as a Coping Strategy for Climate Change. <http://climatemigration.org.uk/wp-content/uploads/2014/02/migration_adaptation_climate.pdf>. Accessed 1 August 2016.

Observatório do Clima (2013) Evolução das emissões de gases de efeito estufa no Brasil (1970–2013): setor agropecuário/Instituto de Manejo e Certificação Florestal e Agrícola (IMAFLORA), São Paulo.

Ojima, R. (2014) "Urbanização, dinâmica migratória e sustentabilidade no semiárido nordestino: o papel das cidades no processo de adaptação ambiental" in Fusco, W. and Ojima, R. eds., Migrações nordestinas no século 21, um panorama recente Blucher, São Paulo, 134–154.

Ojima, R. and Nascimento, T. C. L. (2015) "Nos caminhos para o nordeste: reflexões sobre os impactos diretos e indiretos da migração de retorno no período recente" *Redes* 20 (2) 48–62, maio-ago. <https://online.unisc.br/seer/index.php/redes/article/viewFile/4526/pdf>. Accessed 13 August 2016.

Painel Brasileiro de Mudança Climática (2016) Impactos, vulnerabilidades e adaptação às mudanças climáticas. vol. 2. <www.pbmc.coppe.ufrj.br/pt/publicacoes/documentos-publicos/item/impactos-vulnerabilidades-e-adaptacao-volume-2-completo?category_id=7>. Accessed 13 August 2016.

Parry, L., Peres, C. A., Day, B. and Amaral, S. (2010) "Rural-Urban Migration Brings Conservation Threats and Opportunities to Amazonian Watersheds". *Conservation Letters* 3 251–259.

Perz, S. G., Aramburú, C. and Bremner, J. (2005) "Population, Land Use and Deforestation in the Pan Amazon Basin: A Comparison of Brazil, Bolivia, Colombia, Ecuador, Perú and Venezuela" *Environment, Development and Sustainability* 7 23–49.

Ramos, E. P., Jubilut, L. L., Cavedon-Capdeville, F. S., and Claro, C. A. B. (2016) Environmental Migration in Brazil, Current Context and Systemic Challenges, Migration, Environment and Climate Change. Policy Brief Series, IOM, issue 5, n. 2. <https://publications.iom.int/system/files/pdf/policy_brief_series_vol2_issue5_en.pdf>. Accessed 13 August 2016.

UNFCCC (2010) Report of the Conference of the Parties on its sixteenth session, held in Cancun from 29 November to 10 December 2010. <https://unfccc.int/resource/docs/2010/cop16/eng/07a01.pdf>. Accessed 21 November 2017.

UNFPA — Fundo de População das Nações Unidas, (2015) "População e desenvolvimento sustentável na Amazônia", (Pesquisa texto de Donald Sawyer) Brasília.

Viana, V. M. (2008) "Bolsa Floresta: um instrumento inovador para a promoção de saúde em comunidades tradicionais do Amazonas". *Estudos Avançados* 22 143–153.

Wellink, L. C. (2013) "The Effect of Drought on Internal Migration: The Case of Brazil", master thesis, Erasmus School of Economics, Erasmus University Rotterdam.

World Bank (2013) Water Resources Planning and Adaptation to Climate Variability and Climate Change in Selected River Basins in Northeast Brazil. Final Report on a Non Lending Technical Assistance program. (P123869). World Bank, Washington, DC.

Young, C. E. F. (1998) "Public Policies and Deforestation in the Brazilian Amazon". *Planejamento e Políticas Públicas* 18 202–222.

18

Internal migration in Bangladesh

A comparative analysis of coastal, environmentally challenged, and other districts

Bimal Kanti Paul and Avantika Ramekar

Introduction

Bangladesh is one of the most vulnerable countries in the world to global climate change. According to the latest Climate Change Vulnerability Index (CCVI), the country ranks at the top and "most at risk" to climate change, followed by Nigeria, India, Myanmar, and the Philippines (Maplecroft 2015). Climate change will have devastating effects on the environment of the entire country, particularly its coastal region. According to the first report of the Intergovernmental Panel on Climate Change (IPCC) published in 1990, a substantial part of coastal Bangladesh is likely to be inundated before the middle of this century (Ericksen et al. 1993). Consequently, residents of the coastal region face potential mass displacement from their ancestral homes. Some (e.g., Shamsuddoha and Chowdhury 2007; Seltz 2010; Salauddin and Ashikuzzaman 2011; Mallick and Etzold 2015) have already observed evidence of rising sea levels in the country, contending that the process of forced relocation of coastal residents in Bangladesh has already started. In fact, two coastal districts of Barisal division have experienced negative population growth rate during the 2001–2011 intercensal period because people from these districts were living to inland districts (The Economist 2013).[1]

Others (e.g., Houghton 2004; Mehdi 2011; Rahaman 2012; Rashid and Paul 2014) have claimed that frequency and intensity of natural disasters across Bangladesh have increased remarkably in recent years. Two key documents (GoB 2005, 2009) of the Bangladesh government have provided evidence of climate change-induced migration in the country. Indeed, Walsham (2010) claims that environmental challenges and pressures are already the major driver of internal migratory movements in Bangladesh.

The implication is that migration rates in coastal areas, other environmentally challenged areas, and non-challenged and non-coastal areas in Bangladesh will differ significantly. The first two areas would receive a relatively lower proportion of migrants than the third area. Our study explores whether vulnerability induced by global climate change and consequent environmental degradation have any impact on migration in Bangladesh. More specifically, the primary objective of this study is to examine spatial patterns of contemporary internal migration in Bangladesh. We expect that the internal migration in recent years into environmentally challenged coastal and non-coastal areas will be significantly lower than the rest of Bangladesh. Please note that the purpose of this study is not to definitively ascribe causation, but to bring additional insight into migration in Bangladesh induced by climate change and environmental degradation.

Environmental threats and migration: a review

Published research has long noted that in developing countries, broader environmental degradation and climate change have a great effect on migration decisions (Hugo 1996; Mortreux and Barnett 2009; Bardsley and Hugo 2010; Massey et al. 2010; Gray and Mueller 2012; Warner and Afifi 2014). Many climate change researchers hold the view that environmental degradation and climate change deprive people of their livelihood and force them to migrate to places with better environmental attributes and better income opportunities (e.g., Jacobson 1988; Myers 1993, 1995, 1997, 2002, 2005; Conisbee and Simms 2003; Biermann and Boas 2008, 2010; Barnett and Webber 2009). This argument suggests that mobility is a direct, unidirectional, causal relationship between environmental degradation and migration, but fails to take into account that people may adapt to environmental change before they consider migration. Further, it disregards lack of economic resources and human capital as impediments to human movement (Black et al. 2011a) or cultural impediments like strong attachment to a place of residence (Mortreux and Barnett 2009; Adger et al. 2013).

The negative effects of slow-onset disasters like climate change provide opportunity to adopt *in situ* adaptation measures. Using micro-level data collected from migrants and non-migrants from 16 developing countries, Koubi et al. (2012) concluded that individuals tend to respond to long-term environmental problems with adaptation, not migration, particularly if they are socially bonded to their current residence. Adaptation measures can help vulnerable communities and households better cope with the adverse effects of slow-onset extreme natural events. Adaptation, in general, involves processes and actions undertaken to adjust to some changing condition, stress, risk, or hazard (Fankhauser et al. 1999; Smit and Skinner 2002; Brooks et al. 2005; Smit and Wandel 2006). It includes local strategies like livelihood diversification and participation in risk-sharing networks and temporary or permanent migration (Ellis 2000; Gray and Mueller 2012).

Evidence from developing countries suggests that the poor often find it impossible to move because they lack the necessary funds and other types of support in the destination (Gray and Mueller 2012). Even those who are not poor will be reluctant to migrate because they may have developed strong personal bonds and place attachment over their lives with their home location and its people (Kandel and Massey 2002; Koubi et al. 2012). Neoclassical economists maintain that potential migrants compare their current earnings in their place of origin with expected earnings in the place of destination (Sjaastad 1962; Todaro 1969). They also claim that migration decisions, as part of a household's survival strategy, are taken by a household as a whole, not by the prospective migrant alone. Thus, households may perceive migration as a way to minimize household risks and maximize the chances of survival under conditions of economic uncertainty through diversifying sources of income (Stark and Bloom 1985).

Some authors (e.g., Boano et al. 2008; Renaud et al. 2011) argue that people who move because of environmental factors are in fact unable to adapt – and thus have no option but to leave. This means migration is the worst-case scenario, and an option to avoid. But others posit (e.g., Barnett and Webber 2009; Tacoli 2009; Black et al. 2011a; Foresight 2011; ADB 2012; Banerjee et al. 2012) that migration is an effective adaptation strategy in itself; it should not be seen as intrinsically negative. Piguet et al. (2011) maintain that:

> [M]igration is not only a reactive, but also a proactive strategy; rather than being a last-resort option, it represents a coping mechanism and a way of adapting to climate change, for example through seasonal migration patterns or by arranging for one member of the family to leave (and thus enabling the other members to stay).
>
> *(p. 15)*

Similarly, Foresight (2011) considers that migration is not a part of the problem, but an important solution.

Thus many researchers (e.g., McGregor 1993; Kibreab 1997; Black 1998, 2001; Wood 2001; Castles 2002; Hulme 2008; Hugo 2012) maintain that the relationship between migration and environmental change is complex, and the decision to migrate is influenced by many interrelated factors; and to single out environmental factors as the only reason for migration is misleading, oversimplifying the causal relationship between environmental degradation and migration. Yet other researchers (e.g., Foresight 2011; Black et al. 2011b) view environmental change as one driver of migration in overlapping social, political, economic, environmental, and demographic spheres. Different factors in these spheres can often act together. They may increase the vulnerabilities of local people and work as triggers for migration (Piguet 2008). Foresight (2011) believes that migration is influenced by environmental change, while recognizing that even when this influence is strong, other factors are also often at play.

Research methods

This section provides information on the sources of data and description of the study area. The statistical technique applied to accomplish the study objective is also included in the section.

Sources of data

The data used in this study is derived from the latest Population and Housing Census of Bangladesh conducted in 2011 (BBS 2011). Through Module 4, this census collected data at household level on internal migration that occurred from 2006–2010, i.e., five years before the census year. Each household head was asked to provide the name of the district where one or more family members lived during the stated period. Coastal areas suffered two major tropical cyclones during the study period: Cyclone Sidr in 2007 and Cyclone Aila in 2009. The former was a Category 4 storm, caused 3,406 deaths, and made landfall in the southwestern coast of Bangladesh (Paul 2009). Aila was a Category 1 storm and killed 330 people (Mallick et al. 2011). The country also suffered two severe consecutive floods in 2007.

The Population and Housing Census of Bangladesh aggregated the household migration data at the district level. As indicated, concerns about the effects of climate change in Bangladesh surfaced in the late 1980s. However, these concerns were further reinforced by two back-to-back high-magnitude floods and one powerful cyclone that struck the country's coastal areas in 2007. The study period, thus, coincides with emerging public concerns over the damaging effects of climate change in Bangladesh.

The Population and Housing Census of Bangladesh defined migration as the movement of persons who change their place of residence, for reasons other than marriage, for a period of six months or more. Movement within district is not considered migration (BBS 2011). In this study, internal migration rate (IMR) is expressed as a percentage and calculated as follows:

$$IMR = \left(\text{Number of migrants of a district/Total population of the district}\right) \times 100$$

Study area

This research relies on census data at district level. All 64 districts of Bangladesh are not equally affected by environmental stresses (Marshall and Rahman 2013). The coastal districts and environmentally challenged districts are susceptible to environmental stress. Therefore, the districts of the country are divided into three categories: coastal districts, environmentally challenged districts, and other districts.

Although the Bangladesh government has initiated measures to address coastal problems since the 1960s, it formally defined the coastal boundary in 2005 when the government formulated the Coastal Zone Policy (CZPo) to develop an integrated coastal management plan (MoWR 2005). According to CZPo, the coastal zone of Bangladesh includes 19 of the 64 districts of the country (Figure 18.1). Three indicators determine the landward boundaries of the coastal zone: influence of tidal waters, salinity intrusion, and cyclones/storm surges (MoWR 2005).

The coastal zone, as defined in the CZPo, covers an area of 18,220 square miles (47,201 square km) land area, or 32 per cent of the total landmass of the country. According to the 2001 census, the population of the coastal zone was 34.8 million, or 27 per cent of the total population of Bangladesh. The population of coastal zone is projected to increase to 60.8 million by 2050 (Ahmad 2005). The population density of the coastal zone (754 per square km) is lower than the population density for Bangladesh (964 per square km) as a whole (MoA 2012).

The coastal zone extends 23–121 miles (37–195 km) from the shore inland. In the coastal zone, 62 per cent of the land has an elevation of up to 3 meters and 86 per cent up to 5 meters (Islam et al. 2006). According to official poverty indicators, a slightly higher proportion of the population lives below the absolute poverty line in the coastal zone as in the country as a whole (52 per cent versus 49 per cent (Islam et al. 2006).[2]

Similarly to the coastal zone, two other areas also face severe environmental challenges: the *Haor* area in the northeast and the *Monga*-affected districts in the northwest (Figure 18.1). The *Haor* area is challenged by seasonal flooding and waterlogging during the monsoon, as well as remoteness from the core of the country; these areas encompass four districts (Habiganj, Maulavibazar, Sunamganj, and Syslhet). Within this area, which are dominated by subsistence agriculture, workers have always moved to secure their livelihoods, albeit temporarily. This was initially to neighbouring agricultural localities, but in the last 20 years, this cycle has expanded to include working within the core urban centres. Some evidence has shown that these movements have become more permanent in nature (Marshall and Rahman 2013).

Monga-affected areas comprise five districts (Galibanda, Kurigram, Lalmonishat, Nilphamari, and Rangpur) and face seasonal drought that precludes agricultural activities for four months (September through December) of the year.[3] Many people in these districts face chronic poverty, seasonal food insecurity, and seasonal unemployment. Seasonal labor migration has become a normal livelihood strategy for many households in these districts (Sultana 2010; Marshall and Rahman 2013; Mallick and Etzold 2015). The remaining 36 non-coastal districts of Bangladesh are grouped as 'other districts'; they have fewer environmental challenges than the other two types of districts.

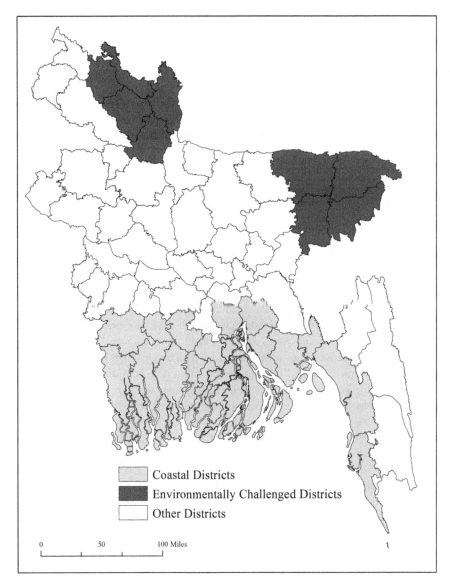

Figure 18.1 Districts of Bangladesh

Source: Compiled by the authors

Data analysis

In addition to descriptive statistics, one way analysis of variance (ANOVA) will be used to test the null hypothesis that there is no IMR difference among these three groups of districts. We expected that the IMR would not differ significantly between coastal and environmentally challenged districts. This can be tested using Scheffe's Test, a flexible and robust post hoc test in ANOVA. This test finds any critical difference between any two sample means that are necessary to reject the null hypothesis that their corresponding population means are equal (Sirkin 1999).

If the IMR of these three types of districts do not differ significantly, the Scheffe's Test would be unnecessary.

Results

Figure 18.2 shows internal migration rates from 2006 to 2010 for the 64 districts of Bangladesh. The migration rates differ remarkably by districts. The rates range from 0.2 per cent in Bhola to 20.3 per cent in Gazipur, with a mean of 2.26 per cent for the country as a whole. This means that of the 139.26 million people in 2011, 4.65 million moved from one district to another between 2006 and 2010 (BBS 2011). Only 13 districts, scattered all over the country, had migration rates higher than the national average rate (Figure 18.2). As expected, all of the coastal districts and several environmentally challenged districts had fewer internal migrants than the national average. Figure 18.2 suggests that above average migration rates are concentrated in the central part of the country around Dhaka, which had a population of 9.3 million in 2011. In the same year, the city and the outlying areas that formed the wider metropolitan area, was home to an estimated 17.2 million (BBS 2011).

The wide range in IMR among the districts of Bangladesh was not surprising. Bhola, which had the lowest IMR, is the only island district in Bangladesh. This island is formed from sediment deposition of three mighty rivers: the Padma, Meghna, and Brahmaputra. Its recent formation means the island is too unstable for settlement, as well as being exposed to tropical cyclones, storm surges, and coastal flooding. As an unstable island, Bhola has actually been losing land to erosion caused by destructive ocean waves associated with diurnal high tides, strong winds, and coastal hazards; although the island has also been gaining new land due to accretion (Krantz 1999; Brammer 2013). Despite the considerable risk of coastal disasters, the newly-formed land attracts many landless households from neighboring inland districts (Mallick and Vogt 2012), while internally displaced people either migrate to other districts or settle on the newly-formed land. This explains why Bhola had lowest migration rate during the study period.

Highest internal migration is recorded in Gazipur district, which is located just north of the capital city of Dhaka. Many people who work in Dhaka live in this district, which is well connected with Dhaka city both by roads and railways. Housing prices and rent, as well as cost of living, is cheaper in Gazipur than the capital city, and population density, pollution, and congestion are also less in Gazipur. In addition, several universities and many government offices and industries are located in this district. Moreover, the overwhelming majority of the garment industries of Bangladesh are located in this district. It is worthwhile to note that, in absolute terms, the Dhaka district attracted the most migrants (1.8 million) during the study period, while Gazipur district attracted only 650,000 migrants (BBS 2011). However, as a percentage, migration into the Gazipur district ranks higher because the Dhaka district had almost four times as many people in 2011 than the Gazipur district (BBS 2011).

> As the capital and largest city of Bangladesh, Dhaka attracts a large number of rural migrants every year. This migration is the dominant component of the continuing growth of Dhaka, contributing up to half of its total population increase (Marshall and Rahman 2013). Most rural migrants are poor and most of them live in some 3,399 slums and squatter settlements (BBS 2015). Slums dwellers and squatters account for about one-third of the total population of Dhaka (Angeles et al. 2009) and about 70% of slum residents faced some kind of environmental hardship in their place of origin (Mahajan 2010). Dhaka city accounts for 29% of all slum dwellers in the country.
>
> *(BBS 2015)*

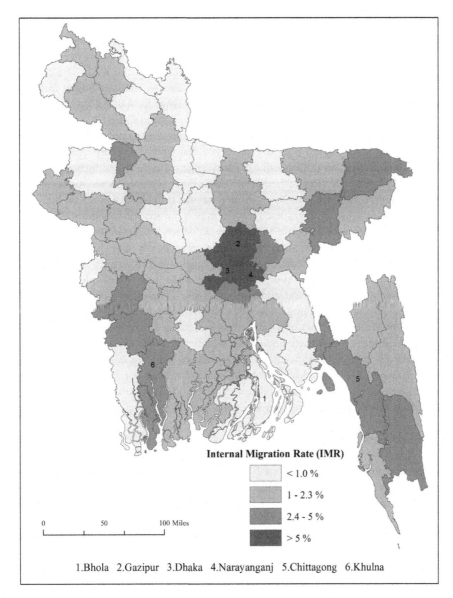

Figure 18.2 Internal migration rates (Bangladesh), 2006–2010
Source: BBS (2011)

Additionally, Dhaka is the major cultural, educational, and business center of the country, as well as containing many public and private offices. Because the city of Dhaka itself lies at the center of Dhaka district, the district recorded the second highest migration rate (15.9 per cent), followed by the Narayanganj district (10 per cent), which is adjacent to the Dhaka district and very close to the city of Dhaka. Many people of this district, particularly from the city of Narayanganj, commute to Dhaka for work and other reasons, like those mentioned earlier for Gazipur. Unlike the Dhaka district, Chittagong's migration rate was 3.5 per cent and Khulna's

231

migration rate was 2.5 per cent. The second largest city of Bangladesh (Chittagong) and third largest (Khulna) are in these two districts.

Table 18.1 presents the basic statistics associated with internal migration rates and test statistics for the three different categories of districts considered in this study. The table shows that environmentally challenged districts have the lowest average IMR, and other districts have higher average IMRs. The table further shows that IMRs range from 0.2–3.5 per cent in coastal districts, whereas minimum IMR for environmentally challenged districts are 0.6 per cent and maximum IMRs are 3.4 per cent. For other districts, the corresponding figures are 0.8 per cent and 20.3 per cent. This provides some evidence that environmentally challenged districts, including coastal districts, are not attracting as many migrants as the other districts. Therefore, an attempt is made here to determine whether the IMRs differ significantly among the three types of districts using ANOVA or F-test. The F-value presented in Table 18.1 confirms that the IMR of the three groups of districts considered in this study is not statistically significant.

The statistical difference among the three types of districts is insignificant for internal migration rates. This implies that migration is only one of many outcomes of climate and environmental change. Penning-Rowsell et al. (2011) believe that large-scale migration from an environmentally challenged region is unlikely because of the problems people encounter when they move. Based on their empirical study in Bangladesh, Penning-Rowsell et al. (2011) identified problems associated with migration destinations: hard physical labor relative to income, uncertainty, competition, conflict over opportunities, leaving family behind, homesickness and difficulty in adjusting to a new place, households with female heads, and inability to earn enough to maintain two households (also see Afsar 2003; Gray and Mueller 2012). In context of urban destinations, Tacoli (2009) added such problems as employment insecurity, high cost of living, and often unsafe and insecure accommodations. Kartiki (2011) maintains that resource scarcity, including lack of information, financial and social capital, and social protection, can prevent coastal households from considering migration.

Mallick and Etzold (2015) expressed a similar view in their recent book, *Environment, Migration and Adapotation: Evidence and Politics of Climate Change in Bangladesh*. they claim that migration is not uncommon for residents of Bangladesh's hazard-prone area, particularly seasonal migration. This migration is an important livelihood option that helps individual households gather resources from their destination while offsetting the resource pressure back home. Short-term migration for work as day labor is also common among many poor coastal households.

Although individuals can migrate for work, Mallick and Etzold (2015) claim that very few choose to move permanently to distant locations. People have a strong tendency to remain in their places of origin and avoid upheaval in their social network and social bonds (Koubi et al. 2012). Impoverished residents of coastal Bangladesh and environmentally challenged districts have lived for generations with a variety hazards using Indigenous coping strategies (Rashid and Paul 2014). Mehdi (2011) expressed a similar sentiment, claiming that many residents of

Table 18.1 Basic statistics associated with internal migration rate (IMR) by district

Category of District	Lowest IMR	Highest IMR	Average IMR
Coastal districts (N=19)	0.2	3.5	1.72
Environmentally challenged districts (N=9)	0.6	3.4	1.44
Other districts (N=36)	0.8	20.3	2.74
F-value=0.98 (p=0.381; d.f.=2, 61)			

environmentally challenged areas remain within their own community because of strong social networks, ancestral bonding and cultural commitment to their place of origin.

Conclusion

Based on aggregate data, our findings show no strong evidence of a causal link between environmental degradation and district level migration in Bangladesh. At this level, it seems that environmental factors have not yet become the dominant driver of population movement within the country. The evidence produced in this study show that the people of environmentally challenged areas – particularly residents of coastal zone – have not migrated in large numbers, and most seem content to stay in these environments.

The truth is that the coastal environment in Bangladesh has been deteriorating because of waterlogging, overexploitation of natural resources, and increased salinity in soil and water. These pose serious threats to agricultural productivity and food security. However, National Agricultural Research System (NARS) institutes have been consistently developing salt-tolerant crop varieties and fish species for the residents in the coastal zone. Additionally, these institutions modified an appreciable number of technologies suitable for the agriculture in the zone. Some of these innovative technologies include cultivation of vegetables in mounded or raised beds in waterlogged areas, floating gardens in permanently submerged areas, growing vegetables on hanging basket, and year round vegetables production on *gher* boundary (Paul and Rashid 2016; MoA 2012).[4]

Besides, the people of Bangladesh, including residents of coastal and environmentally challenged districts, have lived with extreme natural events for centuries. Available studies (Kartiki 2011, Mallick and Vogt 2012, Mallick and Etzold 2015, Marshall and Rahman 2013, Penning-Rowsell et al. 2011, Rahman et al. 2015, Rashid and Paul 2014, Walsham 2010) suggest that many coastal residents are reluctant to leave their homes permanently. This may change as environmental and climatic changes become more drastic.

However, the findings of this study should be interpreted cautiously. The district-level internal migration does not truly capture the extent of migration flows; a lower spatial unit, such as upazila, would be more appropriate.[5] It is important to mention that 22 of the 40 upazilas of Barisal division experienced negative population growth during the last intercensal period (BBS 2011). Our district level analysis failed to capture this trend. However, these upazilas are located in the poorest of all seven divisions of Bangladesh and are the traditional sources of migrants to large cities, including Dhaka. Nearly 23 per cent of the population in Dhaka slums moved from this division (Marshall and Rahman 2013). Ideally, disaggregated data at household level on motivation of the migration is necessary to examine the importance of environmental, economic, and other factors as determinants of migration.

Martin et al. (2013) posit that migration in Bangladesh often involves short-term movement (within a district) to neighboring places familiar to the migrants. They reported that disaster-related migration in Bangladesh is often short-term and involves short distances. Responses to cyclones showed similar trends. Such rapid-onset disasters lead to temporary displacement to nearby areas because people lack the resources to move farther, and many return to repair/rebuild their homes. People do, moreover, prefer to stay near family and friends, linked to social networks, and continue to live in ways familiar to them.

The five-year time frame used in this study also may be too short to show significant migration flows. Ideally, future research should consider a unit of study smaller than the district and a time frame longer than five years. Analysis of field data is also needed. This type of analysis will provide a useful link between climate change and migration as well as deeper insights into the specific ways in which households and their members assess and evaluate migration options compared to other adaption alternatives and the critical thresholds at which distress migration becomes the predominant adaptation option.

Notes

1 Administratively, Bangladesh is divided into seven divisions, and each contains several districts. A district is the top-tier official administrative unit of local governments in Bangladesh. On average, each district contains slightly more than 2 million people.
2 The poverty estimates are based on poverty lines developed by the Bangladesh Bureau of Statistics (BBS) jointly with World Bank by employing a Cost of Basic Needs (CBN) approach. Intuitively, CBN poverty lines represent the level of per capita expenditure at which a household can be expected to meet their basic needs (food and non-food). This is measured by: (i) estimating a food poverty line as the cost of a fixed food bundle (consisting of 11 key items), providing minimal nutritional requirements corresponding to 2,122 kcal/day/person; and (ii) adding an 'allowance' for non-food consumption to the food poverty line. For the *lower poverty line*, the non-food allowance is the average non-food expenditure of households whose *total* consumption is equal to the food poverty line; whereas for the *upper poverty line*, the non-food allowance is the average nonfood expenditure of households whose *food* consumption was equal to the food poverty line (World Bank 2008).
3 Monga districts account for 7 per cent of the total population in Bangladesh, and 55 per cent of residents of these districts live below the poverty line, which is much higher than the national average poverty level (Sultana 2010).
4 In *gher* farming, a pond is dug into a rice field to use primarily for shrimp farming. The dug-out soil used to create dikes around the pond for growing vegetables.
5 Upazila (sub-district) is a territorial unit nested within a district that is roughly equivalent to a US county.

References

ADB (Asian Development Bank) (2012) "Addressing Climate Change and Migration in Asia and the Pacific" Mandaluyong City, Philippines: ADB

Adger W. N., Barnett J., Brown K., O'Brien K., Marshall N. (2013) "Cultural dimensions of climate change impacts and adaptation" *Nature Climate Change*, 3(2), 112–117

Afsar R. (2003) "Internal Migration and the Development Nexus: The Case of Bangladesh" London: Department of International Development

Ahmad M. (2005) "Living in the Coast – People and Institution" Dhaka: WARPO, Ministry of Water Resources- Government of People's Republic of Bangladesh

Angeles G., Lance P., Barden-O'Fallon J., Islam N., Mahbub N., and Nazem N. (2009) "The 2005 Census and Mapping of Slums in Bangladesh: Design, Select Results and Application" *International Journal of Health Geographics*, 8 (32): 1–19

Banerjee S., Black R. and Kniveton D. (2012) "Migration as an Effective Mode of Adaptation to Climate Change: Policy Paper for the European Commission" Brighton: Sussex Centre for Migration Research, University of Sussex

Bardsley D.K. and Hugo G.J. (2010) "Migration and Climate Change: Examining Thresholds of Change to Guide Effective Adaptation Decision-Making" Population and Environment 32: 238–261

Barnett J. and Webber M. (2009) "Accommodating Migration to Promote Adaptation to Climate Change" Stockholm: Commission on Climate Change and Development

BBS (Bangladesh Bureau of Statistics) (2011) "Population and Housing Census 2011: Preliminary Result" Dhaka: Ministry of Planning

BBS (Bangladesh Bureau of Statistics) (2015) "Preliminary Report on Census of Slum Areas and Floating Population 2014" Dhaka

Biermann F. and Boas I. (2008) "Protecting Climate Refugees. The Case for a Global Protocol" *Environment*, 50(6), 8–16

Biermann F. and Boas I. (2010) "Preparing for a Warmer World: Towards a Global Governance" *Global Environmental Politics*, 10(1), 60–88

Black R. (1998) "Refugees, Environment and Development" New York: Addison Wesley Limited

Black R. (2001) "Environmental Refugees: Myth or Reality? UNHCR 'New Issues in Refugee Research'" Working Paper No. 34. Geneva: UNHCR

Black R., Adger W., Arnell N.W., Dercon S., Geddes A., and Thomas D. S. G. (2011a) "The Effect of Environmental Change on Human Migration" *Global Environmental Change*, 21S, S3–S11

Black R., Kniveton D., and Schmidt-Verkerk K. (2011b) "Migration and Climate Change: Towards an Integrated Assessment of Sensitivity" *Environment and Planning A* 43: 431–450

Boano C. R., Zetter R. and Morris T. (2008) "Environmentally Displaced People: Understanding the Linkages Between Environment Change, Livelihoods and Forced Migration" Oxford: Forced Migration Policy Briefing Refugee Studies Center, University of Oxford

Brammer H. (2013) "Bangladesh's Dynamic Coastal Regions and Sea-Level Rise" *Climate Risk Management*, 1, 51–62

Brooks N., Adger W. N. and Kelly P. M. (2005) "The Determinants of Vulnerability and Adaptive Capacity at the National Level and the Implications for Adaptation" *Global Environmental Change*, 15, 151–163

Castles S. (2002) "Environmental Change and Forced Migration: Making Sense of the Debate" UNHCR New Issues in Refugee Research Working Paper No. 70. Geneva: UNHCR.

Conisbee M. and Simms A. (2003) "Environmental Refugees. The Case for Recognition" London: New Economics Foundation

Ellis F. (2000) "Rural Livelihoods and Diversity in Developing Countries" Oxford: Oxford University Press

Ericksen N. J., Ahmad Q. K. and Chowdhury A. R. (1993) "Socio-Economic Implications of Climate Change in Bangladesh" Dhaka: BUP, CEARS, and CRU

Fankhauser S., Smith J. B. and Tol R. S. J. (1999) "Weathering Climate Change: Some Simple Rules to Guide Adaptation Decisions" *Ecological Economy*, 30(1), 67–78

Foresight (2011) "Migration and Global Environmental Change: Future Challenges and Opportunities" London: Government Office for Science

GoB (Government of Bangladesh) (2005) "National Adaptation Programme of Action (NAPA)" Dhaka: Ministry of Environment and Forest

GoB (Government of Bangladesh) (2009) "Bangladesh Climate Change Strategy and Action Plan 2009" Dhaka: Ministry of Environment and Forest

Gray C. L. and Mueller V. (2012) "Natural Disasters and Population Mobility in Bangladesh" *PNAS*, 109(16), 1–1–10

Houghton J. (2004) "Global Warming: The Complete Briefing" Third Edition. Cambridge: Cambridge University Press

Hugo G. (2012) "Environmental Change and Migration: Methods and Methodologies – a Research Note" Presented at the Environmental Change and Global Migration Futures Workshop held at University of Oxford, Oxford, UK, June 21–22, 2012.

Hugo G. (1996) "Environmental Concerns and International Migration" *International Migration Review*, 30(1), 105–131

Hulme M. (2008) "Climate Refugees: Cause for a New Agreement (Commentary)" *Environment*, 50(6), 50–52

Islam M. R., Ahmad M., Huq H. and Osman M. S. (2006) "State of the Coast 2006" Dhaka: University Press

Jacobson J. L. (1988) "Environmental Refugees: A Yardstick of Habitability" Worldwatch Paper 86. Worldwatch Institute: Washington, DC.

Kandel W. and Massey D. S. (2002) "The Culture of Mexican Migration: A Theoretical and Empirical Analysis" *Social Forces*, 80(3), 981–1004

Kartiki K. (2011) "Climate Change and Migration: A Case Study from Rural Bangladesh" *Gender & Development*, 19(1), 23–38

Kibreab G. (1997) "Environmental Causes and Impacts of Refugee Movements: A Critique of the Current Debate" *Disasters*, 21(1), 20–38

Koubi V., Schaffer L., Spilker G. and Bernauer T. (2012) "Environmental Degradation and Migration" Available at SSRN: http://ssrn.com/abstract=2107133

Krantz M. (1999) "Coastal Erosion on the Island of Bhola, Bangladesh" Gotenborg, Sweden: Gotenborg University

Mahajan D. (2010) "No Land's Man: Migration in a Changing Climate. In On the Move: Migration Challenges in the Indian Ocean Littoral" ed. by Laipson E., and Pandya A. Washington, DC: The Henry L. Stimson Center

Mallick B., Rahaman K. R. and Vogt J. (2011) "Coastal Livelihood and Physical Infrastructure in Bangladesh After Cyclone Aila" *Mitigation and Adaptation Strategies for Global Change*, 16(6), 629–648

Mallick B. and Vogt J. (2012) "Cyclone, Coastal Society and Migration: Empirical Evidence from Bangladesh" *International Development Planning Review*, 34(3), 217–240

Mallick B. and Etzold B. ed. (2015) "Environment, Migration and Adaptation: Evidence and Politics of Climate Change in Bangladesh" Dhaka: AHDPH

Maplecroft V. (2015) "Climate Change and Environmental Risk Atlas: Latest Products and Reports" Available at http://maplecroft.com/portfolio/new-analysis/2014/10/29/climate-change-and-lack-food-security-multiply-risks-conflict-and-civil-unrest-32-count — retrieved on 12 June 2016

Marshall R. and Rahman S. (2013) "Internal Migration in Bangladesh: Character, Drivers and Policy Issues" Dhaka: UNDP

Martin M., Kang Y. H., Billah M., Siddiqui T., Black R. and Kniveton D. (2013) "Policy Analyses: Climate Change and Migration Bangladesh" Dhaka: MMU and SCMR

Massey D. S., Axinn W. G. and Ghimire D. J. (2010) "Environmental Change and Out-Migration: Evidence from Nepal" *Population and Environment* 32: 109–136

McGregor J. (1993) "Refugees and the Environment. In Geography and Refugee: Patterns and Processes of Change" eds. by Black R. and Robinson V., McGregor, 157–170. Belhaven: London

Mehdi A. (2011) "Factors Driving Environmentally Induced Migration in the Coastal Regions of Bangladesh: An Exploratory Study" Master's Thesis, Albert-Ludwigs-Universitat. Freiburg, Germany

MoA (Ministry of Agriculture) (2012) "Master Plan for Agricultural Development in Southern Region of Bangladesh" Dhaka: Government of Bangladesh

Mortreux C. and Barnett J. (2009) "Climate Change, Migration and Adaptation in Funafuti, Tuvalu" *Global Environmental Change* 19:105–112

MoWR (Ministry of Water Resources) (2005) "Coastal Zone Policy" Dhaka: Government of Bangladesh

Myers N. (1993) "Environmental Refugees in a Globally Warned World" *Bioscience* 4(11): 752–761

Myers N. (1995) "Environmental Exodus: An Emergent Crisis in the Global Arena" Washington, DC: Climate Institute

Myers N. (1997) "Environmental Refugees" *Population and Environment* 19:167–182

Myers N. (2002) "Environmental Refugees: A Growing Phenomenon of the 21st Century" *Philosophical Transactions of the Royal Society B* 357: 609–613

Myers N. (2005) "Environmental Refugees: An Emergent Security Issue" Prague: Economic Forum

Paul B. K. (2009) "Why Relatively Fewer People Died? The Case of Bangladesh's Cyclone Sidr" *Natural Hazards* 50: 483–495

Paul B. K. and Rashid H. (2016) "Climatic Hazards in Coastal Bangladesh: Non-Structural and Structural Solutions" New York: Elsevier

Penning-Rowsell E., Sultana P. and Thompson P. (2011) "Migration and Global Environmental Change-CS4: Population Movement in Response to Climate-Related Hazards in Bangladesh: The 'Last Resort.'" London: Government Office for Science

Piguet E. (2008) "Climate Change and Forced Migration" Research Paper No. 153. Geneva: UNHCR Evaluation and Policy Analysis Unit

Piguet E., Pecoud A., and de Guchteneire, P. (2011) "Migration and Climate Change: An Overview" *Refugee Survey Quarterly*, 30(3), 1–23

Rahaman P. (2012) "A Briny Future for Bangladesh" *The Third Pole*, July 13 Available at www.thethirdpole.net/a-briny-future-for-bangladesh — retrieved on 25 July, 2014

Rahman M. K., Paul B. K., Curtis A., and Schmidlin T. W. (2015) "Linking Coastal Disasters and Migration: A Case Study of Kutubdia Island, Bangladesh" *The Professional Geographer*, 67(2), 218–228

Rashid H. and Paul B. K. (2014) "Climate Change in Bangladesh: Confronting Impending Disasters" Lanham: Lexington Books

Renaud F. G., Dun O., Warner K. and Bogard. J. (2011) "A Decision Framework for Environmentally Induced Migration" *International Migration*, 49(S1), e5–e29

Salauddin M., and Ashikuzzaman M. (2011) "Nature and Extent of Population Displacement Due to Climate Change-Triggered Disasters in the Southwestern Coastal Region of Bangladesh" *Management of Environmental Quality: An International Journal*, 22(5), 620–631

Seltz K. (2010) Preface. In "Climate Refugees" Beyond Copenhagen: Legal Concept, Political Implications, Normative Considerations, ed. by Bauer S, 5. Stuttgart, Germany: Brot fur die Welt

Shamsuddoha M. and Chowdhury R. K. (2007) "Climate Change Impact and Disaster Vulnerabilities in the Coastal Areas of Bangladesh" Dhaka: COAST Trust

Sirkin R. M. (1999) "Statistics for the Social Sciences" Thousand Oaks: SAGE

Sjaastad L. A. (1962) "The Costs and Returns of Human Migration" *Journal of Political Economy* 70(5): 80–93

Smit B. and Skinner M. (2002) "Adaptation Options in Agriculture to Climate Change: A Typology" *Mitigation and Adaptation Strategies for Global Change* 7: 85–114

Smit B. and Wandel J. (2006) "Adaptation, Adaptive Capacity, and Vulnerability" *Global Environmental Change* 16(3): 282–292

Stark O., and Bloom D. E. (1985) "The New Economics of Labor Migration" *The American Economic Review* 75(2): 173–178

Sultana Z. (2010) "Impact of Monga on Rural Urban Migration: Its Socio-Economic Consequences" *ASA University Review* 4(2): 151–167

Tacoli C. (2009) "Crisis or Adaptation? Migration and Climate Change in a Context of High Mobility" *Environment and Urbanization* 21: 513–525

The Economist (2013) "Bangladesh's Internal Migrations: Ebb and Flow," 16 May

Todaro M. P. (1969) "A Model of Labor Migration and Urban Unemployment in Less Developed Countries" *The American Economic Review* 59(1): 138–148

Walsham M. (2010) "Assessing the Evidence: Environment, Climate Change and Migration in Bangladesh" Dhaka: IOM

Warner K., and Afifi T. (2014) "Where the Rain Falls: Evidence from 8 Countries on How Vulnerable Households Use Migration to Manage the Risk of Rainfall Variability and Food Insecurity" *Climate Development* 6: 1–17

Wood W. B. (2001) "Ecomigration: Linkages Between Environmental Change and Migration" In *Global Migrants, Global Refugees*, ed. by Zolberg A R., and Benda P. M., pp. 42–61. Berghahn: New York and Oxford

World Bank (2008) "Poverty Assessment for Bangladesh: Creating Opportunities and Building the East-West Divide. Bangladesh Development Series, Paper No. 26" Dhaka

19

Environmental stressors and population mobility in China

Causes, approaches and consequences

Yan Tan

Introduction

The nexus between climate change (used in this chapter to encompass environmental change) and human migration is already one of the defining global issues of the 21st century. In many parts of China, climate change has presented major challenges to people's livelihoods and their living environment (Li, 2013; MEA, 2005; NDRC, 2007, 2013). As a response, over 7.7 million rural migrants, mostly in western China, absolutely poor and mostly displaced, were relocated and resettled largely in other rural communities by 2010 (SCC, 2011b). This figure is projected to be around 10 million by 2050 (Shi et al., 2007). 'Ecological migration' became an official policy of the Chinese government in 2001 to direct environment-related human resettlement (SCC, 2001). Yet, ecological (or environmental) migration is less studied, mostly because China's displacement and resettlement studies have focused overwhelmingly on cases induced by development projects such as the Three Gorges Project. There is limited understanding of how environmental stress relates to mobility, how policy-driven ecological migration is being implemented in the Chinese context and what environmental, economic and social consequences ecological migration has brought about to people and communities affected. These issues present a significant gap in knowledge which this chapter seeks to address. This chapter reviews the Chinese perspectives and practices to enrich the global discussion of human mobility (including displacement and resettlement) as a proactive adaptive response to, or even an 'effective adaptation' strategy for, rather than being only a problematic outcome of, environmental change. It shows that many aspects of environment-related displacement and resettlement make China a unique case, in terms of causes, approaches and consequences. This chapter also identifies critical research gaps that help to inform future research investments on environmental change and migration studies in China.

Relationships between climate change, poverty and human mobility

Climate change is rarely considered to be the only, or main, cause of human mobility. Human mobility is well recognised as a complex and multivariate process that involves a number of influences that are not only environmental, but economic, demographic, social and political (Black et al., 2011). However, climate change can shape and influence human migration and displacement – decisions and patterns, both directly and indirectly, the latter through its impact and influence on the other drivers.

Environmental stressors and ecological vulnerability

China is vulnerable because of its extensive exposure to climate change impact. Substantial parts of the country are classified as 'ecologically vulnerable zones' (EVZs) (MEP, 2008). The environments in EVZs have an intrinsically low environmental carrying capacity to support human settlement (Meng et al., 2010, Xu et al., 2006). Estimated climatic and other environmental changes in the coming decades will continue influencing the drivers of change in ecosystem services, with the most significant and extensive being climate change (J. Wang et al., 2012). In the eastern coastal region, sea level rise, storm surges and coastal flooding will contribute to land degradation, and the degradation of coastal, river-lake and marine ecosystems (Yang et al., 2011). In the western and northern regions, increasing occurrence and severity of drought will continue to accelerate land degradation (Tao et al., 2011). Water shortage, mostly triggered by climate variability (particularly drought), could be the biggest risk factor threatening rural livelihoods and food security in China (Li et al., 2013; Peng, 2011).

Western China, in particular, has experienced severe environmental deterioration associated with (the often interrelated factors of) climate change: desertification, water scarcity, soil erosion, deforestation, over-reclamation, overgrazing and the impact of resource and infrastructure development (Li et al., 2012, Liu et al., 2005, MAC, 2011, Wang et al., 2006, Zhang et al., 2007). Desertification and soil erosion have been two major environmental challenges in rural areas of west China (Kolas, 2014, Wang et al., 2006, Wang et al., 2008, Xu et al., 2003). Rock desertification, salinisation, glacier retreat and thawing permafrost, together with geological or mountain hazards (e.g. earthquakes and landslides) also remain fundamental problems in some areas. Climate change has particularly intensified the environmental risks of drought, desertification, land degradation and water shortage, worsening agricultural conditions in the region (Piao et al., 2010). Environmental change is also linked to China's land tenure policies, such as those implemented in Inner Mongolia, whereby the existing nomadic land tenure system (where land was common property) was transformed, first to a fixed communal rights system, and then to a pasture contracting system (in which use rights became fixed to households and to specific plots of grazing land) (Da and Zheng, 2010, Song, 2006). The contracting system resulted in the introduction of enclosures by those who could afford fences, undermining some effective traditional coping mechanisms, and increasing land degradation and reduced productivity on the remaining unfenced, and over-grazed, rangelands (Webber, 2012). The expansion of coal mining in Inner Mongolia has added to these problems by impacting the scale and quality of pastoral land and using up available water (Da and Zheng, 2010). The impact of market forces has further intensified the environmental problems because huge areas of agricultural land in the western and central regions of China have been taken over to meet the growing demand for minerals and energy created by the strong economic growth in the east.

Environmental degradation (e.g. grassland degradation and land desertification) leads to poverty, and in turn, poverty deepens environmental degradation in extensive rural areas of China (Song et al., 2015). The poorest areas are mostly located in mountainous and environmentally deteriorated areas. A study by Ouyang et al. (2009) estimated that 2.24 million km² (accounting for 23.3% of the land area of China) lie within the EVZs in western China. All twelve provinces in western China, including five ethnic autonomous regions (Inner Mongolia, Ningxia, Gansu,

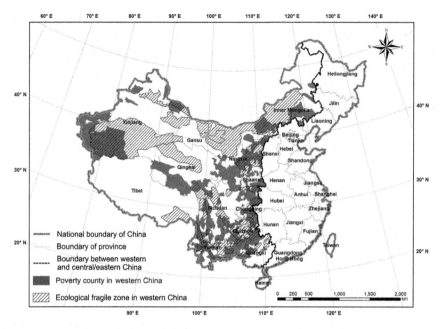

Figure 19.1 Distribution of ecologically vulnerable zones and national poverty-stricken counties in western China

Source: Author

Qinghai, Xinjiang, Tibet, Shaanxi, Sichuan, Chongqing, Guizhou, Yunnan, Guangxi) contain EVZs (Figure 19.1). Xinjiang and Inner Mongolia contain the largest of such areas while Guizhou and Inner Mongolia have the largest percentages of their land falling in the EVZs. Strikingly, the poor rural population in China's ethnic autonomous areas in 2011 accounted for a third of the nation's total poverty-stricken population (i.e. 39.17 million of 122 million) (SEACC, 2012).

Climate change and its impact on poverty

Climate change and associated severe environmental deterioration is found to be an important causal factor of a high rate of poverty in the EVZs (Li et al., 2013, Tu and Yuki, 2012, Xu and Ju, 2009). Dramatic population growth in western China, increasing from 175 million in 1950 to 367.3 million at the Chinese census of 2010, has intensified the pressure on land, water, energy and food supplies, by increasing population densities in areas that have experienced a decline in habitability and natural resources and adversely affected ecosystem functions, processes and services (MEA, 2005). One inevitable result has been prevalent poverty for those living in these vulnerable areas. Zhou et al. (2008) note that 92% of the counties, and 83% of the residents, in the typical EVZs are impoverished. Moreover, most of the poor counties in western China are situated in areas where ethnic minority groups are concentrated (210 counties). These minorities account for 47.4% of the local population and three-quarters of the total (113.8 million) ethnic minority population in China. Poverty reduction in the ethnic areas has thus been exceptionally challenging. Ethnicity thereby adds an extra dimension to the challenge of human resettlement and migration in the context of environmental change (Li et al., 2013).

Clearly, the need for an adaptive response to climate change is especially relevant to those living in rural areas in the western region, where millions of rural households are already impoverished and find their plight further exacerbated by this change. To rehabilitate the deteriorated ecosystems and eradicate prevalent rural poverty, a range of environmental and poverty-relief programs have been implemented by the Chinese central government since the mid-1980s, including the:

- 'Poverty Alleviation' (aimed to reduce the number of rural residents living under the national poverty line through capital investment by the government, to foster local economic development and to move some people out of environmentally unliveable areas);
- 'Grain for Green' (a program aiming to return cropping land with a gradient of 25 degrees or greater to forest or grassland);
- 'Water and Soil Conservation' (a program aiming to protect water and land resources, to prevent water and soil erosion, to reduce the occurrences and severity of floods, droughts and sandstorms, and to rehabilitate degraded ecosystems);
- 'National Forest Protection' and 'Protection of National-level Nature Reserves' (two programs aiming to prevent deforestation, especially in the upper reaches of major rivers such as the Yangzi, Yellow and Songhua; to reduce commercial timber extraction through commercial logging bans; and to establish nature reserves and parks to protect natural forests); and
- 'Building a New Socialist Countryside' (a program aiming to narrow disparities between China's rural and urban areas in the new millennium through enhancing agriculture, improving farmers' living standards and providing clean housing) (NDRC, 2012a).

Importantly, since 1994, the national 'Poverty Alleviation' scheme has focused on 592 poor counties in which 58.6 million were living below the absolute poverty line at that time. Of these counties, 375 are in western China and all are located within the EVZs (Figure 19.1).

Significance of ecological migration

Moving people out of extremely vulnerable environments is perceived by the Chinese governments from county to national levels (SCC, 2001) and researchers (e.g. Chen et al., 2013, Qin, 2004, Xu et al., 1996, Yan and He, 2014) as a vital tool for reducing population pressure on the environment, alleviating rural poverty, rehabilitating ecosystems and combating natural disasters (especially mountain hazards). Therefore, 'environmental migrants', either environmentally induced or environmentally displaced – a concept used internationally in environment-population research (e.g. IOM, 2007) – is often conceptualised by Chinese scholars (e.g. Bao, 2006, Zheng, 2013) as *ecological migrants* or *poverty-relieving migrants* in the Chinese context. *Ecological migration* has come into a national policy since 2001 (SCC, 2001). As a consequence, during China's 11th Five-Year Plan period (2006–2010), there was a relocation of 1.63 million rural residents from locales where environmental conditions were not conducive to human habitation (such as arid and desertified regions with no, or limited, access to basic infrastructure and social services, as well as areas prone to earthquakes or landslides). Out of the estimated total number of 10 million poverty-stricken population in China in 2010, 2.4 million people were planned to be relocated to relatively better-off places over the nation's 12th Five-Year Plan period (2011–2015) (NDRC, 2012b). Local residents have also undertaken various spontaneous adaptations including out-migration, but there is no statistic showing the magnitude of out-migrants who relocated voluntarily in response to environmental change (Chen et al., 2014).

Approaches to environmental (ecological) migration

Stages and scope

Environmental migration has experienced three stages since the mid-1980s: (1) 'poverty-alleviating migration' in some of the least viable and poorest mountainous areas of western China (especially in the provinces of Ningxia and Gansu) in 1983–1993 (Li et al., 2013, Wu et al., 2010); (2) 'development-oriented migration' which targeted extremely poor households and the poorest villages under the national 'Poverty Alleviation' program (started in 1986). The major scheme involved the '80/7 Plan to Combat Poverty (1994–2000)' that successfully helped some 80 million rural people living under the national poverty line to escape poverty over the seven-year period to 2000; and (3) 'environmental conservancy and poverty-alleviating resettlement' since 2000 (SCC, 2001, 2011a). At the current stage, environment-related relocation programs are being undertaken in three situations: (1) where people are attempting to live in conditions normally not conducive to human habitation or essential livelihoods (e.g. severely arid areas); (2) in pastoral areas that have suffered serious desertification, areas vulnerable to geological or mountain hazards and areas that suffer from severe soil erosion; and (3) in protected areas where the biodiversity and landscape are fundamental to the national or regional environmental sustainability, and thus need to be better conserved, or naturally regenerated, to adapt to climate change and reverse some processes of environmental degradation (e.g. desertification and soil erosion) (SCC, 2011a).

Population displacement and migration practiced in the Minqin oasis in Gansu provides an example. The oasis, located at the lower reach of the Shiyang River (the third largest inland river in China) and sandwiched by two large deserts (Badain Jaran Desert in the northwest and Tengger Desert in the northeast), is one of the most vulnerable arid oasis systems in the world (NDRC & MWR, 2007). Farmers living in the oasis have exploited groundwater for agricultural production to cope with the shortage of surface water since the late 1950s. Excessive extraction of groundwater has caused a severe groundwater budget deficit (Zhang et al., 2004) and consequently has led to natural vegetation degradation and soil salinisation, and has reinforced the process of land desertification in the oasis (Lee and Zhang, 2005). As a result, the Minqin area has become one of four origins for major dust storms across China (Kang et al., 2008). This situation has also caused 26,500 farmers to abandon, mostly voluntarily, their homes in the lake area of the oasis (i.e. the terminus of the Shiyang River) and to resettle elsewhere over the decade to 2007 (NDRC & MWR, 2007). The likely merger of the two large deserts would threaten the environmental security of the entire region of northwest China and the agricultural livelihoods of millions of farmers (Zhang et al., 2004). It is thus not surprising that, since 2002, the Chinese central government has repeatedly ranked the environmental issues of Minqin oasis among the most crucial environmental challenges in the country and the top policy concern of the provincial government of Gansu (CMA, 2013). To alleviate water scarcity in the Shiyang River Basin and prevent Minqin oasis from further desertification, the Chinese government has implemented the 'Governing Plan for Focal Issues in the Shiyang River Basin' since 2007 (NDRC & MWR, 2007). Among a suite of environmental and socio-economic policies, human resettlement by moving 10,500 rural residents out of the vulnerable lake area was carried out in 2007–2012 (NDRC & MWR, 2007). As a result, nearly 9,500 residents had been relocated by late June 2011 (MRR, 2011).

Governmental commitments: Planning and organising ecological migration

A distinctive feature of environmental migration in China is that it has been primarily led by the Chinese government, thereby adopting a top-down (i.e. a government-oriented policy for migration) process. Ecological migration is mostly permanent, and sometimes involuntary, involving the displacement and resettlement of poor rural residents (Bao, 2006, Zheng, 2013). Governments at all levels (central, provincial, county and township) have played a key role in the planning, organisation and financial support for this process. Ecological migration is supposed to be carried out in light of the following five principles: direction by the government, respect for the voluntary nature of relocation, actions must fit the capability of the people affected, subsidises are to be provided to those to be displaced, and suitable resettlement approaches must be adopted (NDRC, 2012b).

Financial support from the government covers approximately 80% of the total cost of displacement and resettlement, while another 20% of the total cost is borne by the displaced (Li et al., 2005). Government funding is invested mainly in the resettlement communities for building basic infrastructure, subsidising migrants to build new or purchase existing houses, equipping water conservancy infrastructure, improving the fertility of farmland and pastoral lands, and providing social services. This support, however, has not been enough for the displaced to reconstruct their livelihoods post-displacement in many cases. The cost becomes much greater when it comes to resettling people into communities located beyond their original county (Zeng and Zhu, 2006) Financial constraints not only delay the process of resettlement, but also affect people's capacity to re-establish their economic livelihood in their resettlement communities (Tan et al., 2013).

Near resettlement vs. distant resettlement

The destination of the relocated depends on the carrying capacity of the environment (especially the quantity of water and land available) where people are supposed to be resettled. Studies indicate that the eastern coastal provinces of China have a greater carrying capacity and thus settling migrants there would create greater opportunities for migrants to seek multiple livelihood sources and facilitate environmental rehabilitation in the areas from which they came (Fan and Zhao, 2003, Fang and Peng, 2002). However, only limited environmental resettlement has occurred to these provinces due to reasons including, but not limited to, the lack of national operational guidelines and policy on inter-provincial resettlement (Wuli, 2007). Indeed, most resettlement so far has been within western China and within their home county boundary, which is termed as *near resettlement*. Near resettlement is seen to foster local industrialisation and urbanisation, especially if people are resettled in peri-urban areas and township or country seats (Liu, 2011). Where enormous environmental stressors and constraints in natural resources are experienced, it is now becoming more common to resettle the displaced outside their counties via *government-organised distant resettlement* (GODR) schemes, but this is still within the boundary of their original province. For example, of 350,000 rural residents to be displaced from the mountainous region of southern Ningxia over 2011–2015, almost two-thirds (65%) were planned to be resettled in other relatively better-off counties, in terms of access to irrigation water, transportation and urban centres, in central and northern parts of Ningxia (Wu, 2011).

How to select host communities suited to resettle migrants is a major concern of researchers, policymakers and practitioners (Shi and Gai, 2006). Quantitative analysis, geographical information systems (GIS) and remote sensing (RS) techniques are used to analyse and model the environmental carrying capacity of the resettlement areas and to identify suitable resettlement sites. Taking Lushui county (located in a steep mountainous area of the Nu River in northwest Yunnan province) as a case study, Li (2010) applied GIS techniques to identify sites suited to resettlement. Using a fuzzy logic theory, Zhou et al. (2009) advanced methodologies for how to optimise the selection of resettlement areas. They constructed a 19-indicator system involving not only quantitative factors (which measure production conditions, basic infrastructure, accessibility of public services and environmental conditions), but also some qualitative factors (production modes, language, religion and culture), and employed an analytic hierarchy process (AHP) method to determine the weighting of each indicator. Based on a pressure-state-response (PSR) model, Shi (2010) built an indicator system, which captures the characteristics of population, water resource, quality of farmland, environmental pollution, economic development and education, to measure the sustainability of development in the resettlement areas.

Rural resettlement vs. urban resettlement

Rural resettlement has been the fundamental approach to settling relocated residents over the last three decades. However, it is now very difficult to secure viable arable or pastoral land which also has an adequate amount of irrigation water available. Rapid urbanisation and climate change impact further restrict the potential supply of agricultural land and water. Urbanisation affects land use and downgrades the quality of agricultural land. Over the past three decades, China has experienced massive rural-to-urban migration, rising from 6.57 million in 1982 to 221 million in 2010 (Duan et al., 2013). China's urbanisation has reached a critical point, with the government expecting the number of migrant workers to increase from 253 million in 2014 to 291 million by 2020, of which over three-quarters are rural-to-urban migrants (NHFPC, 2015). The urbanisation rate has climbed from 17.9% in 1978 to 50% by 2010, a share expected to rise to 70% by 2030 (World Bank, 2014). Land-use patterns have changed accordingly with an estimated 83,000 km² of cultivated land converted from agricultural to urban use from 1996–2007 (NDRC, 2008). This is particularly the case in the most rapidly urbanising regions, such as the Yangzi River Delta, where urbanisation has encroached upon a massive amount of cropland, forest and river-lake bodies over 2000–2010 (Xu et al., 2013). Waste disposal from extensive human and industrial activities in urban areas has significantly polluted soil and river-lake ecosystems, decreasing both the quantity and quality of agricultural land and thus of agricultural products (Chen, 2007). Competition for water resources between the industrial and agricultural sectors has also added exceptional pressure on water supply in mega-cities, including Shanghai, jeopardising agricultural productivity levels (Finlayson et al., 2013, Khan et al., 2009). Notably, average per capita cultivatable land (<0.1 ha) and renewable freshwater resources (2,083 m³ in 2013) in China is around half and one-quarter of the world's average, respectively (Liu and Diamond, 2005). Thus, any reduction to the already limited land and water resource availability will directly add enormous challenges to land-based resettlement in China for people to be displaced (or relocated).

Urban resettlement (i.e. resettling displaced people into non-agricultural sectors in urban areas) has been successfully tested in some provinces including Jiangxi (Huang, 2008), Chongqing (Song and He, 2014) and Guizhou (Wang et al., 2014). Resettling people in township or county seats facilitates them to find jobs in secondary and tertiary industry sectors, revitalises rural towns and fosters in-situ urbanisation processes in economically lagging, ethnic and rural areas. Resettlement which emphasises a combination of small industry creation, off-farm employment, self-employment, land consolidation and commercialised family or collective farms that yield value-added agricultural and livestock products could diversify the livelihood and income sources of the displaced people. It is likely that more environmentally displaced people will settle in urban and peri-urban areas in the future because accelerating urbanisation in established towns and small cities is gaining momentum, according to China's 'New-Style Urbanisation Plan (2014–20)' (SCC, 2014). However, empirical research also questions urban resettlement. Wu (2015) elaborates the urban resettlement process of ecological migration in Guizhou, one of

China's most multi-ethnic, poorest and environmentally harsh provinces. To combat karst rocky desertification and alleviate poverty, from 2012–2020 the provincial government has endeavoured to relocate 2.04 million villagers, many of which are ethnic minorities that are native to the region. Consequently, 0.67 million people were displaced in 2001–2014, over half of which were ethnic minority groups. The majority of the uprooted were resettled in newly designated industrial parks nearby townships, county seats or prefectural cities. These resettlers were expected to be transformed from farmers to factory workers and public employees. Yet such a rural-to-urban conversion has imposed enormous challenges for the resettlers, including high unemployment, a struggle to meet non-agricultural job requirements due to their low schooling, diverse cultural backgrounds and languages, difficulty in adapting to urban lifestyle and potential loss of their ethnic identity, traditional values and belief systems.

Consequences of ecological migration

Mixed outcomes of livelihood reconstruction and environmental rehabilitation

The consequences of ecological migration in China are highly debated among scholars. A case study in Alukeyiqi of Inner Mongolia (Dong, 2000) showed that migrants' living conditions, industrial structure (sifting from traditional animal husbandry before displacement to mixed farming and livestock production), income and quality of life improved after displacement. In the origin areas of migrants, intensive and large-scale agricultural use of pastoral land and natural recovery of grassland become possible. This was also the case in Yikezhaomeng of Inner Mongolia (Liu, 2002). Similarly, in Alashan of Inner Mongolia, relocation enabled the ecological rehabilitation in migrant sending areas as farmlands left by the relocated households were returned to forest or grassland (Jiao et al., 2008). Relocation facilitates poverty reduction via subsidising the displaced households at an annual rate of RMB 2–3 yuan per mu (1 ha=15 mu) of farmland if it was returned to forest or grassland. Relocation also fosters the integration of multi-ethnic groups (e.g. Mongolian, Hui and Han-Chinese) and economic development in the resettlement areas. Displacement practiced in the Sanjiangyuan region (i.e. the water-head area of three major rivers in Asia: the Yangzi, Yellow and Lancang) in Guoluo prefecture of Qinghai province curbed further desertification of the pastoral land through moving the scattered herding households in the region to other township or county seats. In some cases, human relocation increased migrants' income, fostered urbanisation, and produced a far-reaching influence on economic restructuring in resettlement communities (Tao, 2007). Both effective resettlement planning and a serious government 'commitment to settlement and not just resettlement' are indispensable to its relative success (Wilmsen and Wang, 2015: 612).

However, the strategy to resettle poor people to overcome poverty due to environmental pressures is not working in some resettlement areas. Various types of poverty (e.g. temporary, long-lasting) post-displacement are observed in southern Shaanxi province (Liu et al., 2015). Those households relocated involuntarily, those resettled in a scattered form (by which villagers from the same village were inserted into different communities) and those displaced in earlier time (before 2011, the government had less subsidies for human relocation than the amount offered after 2011) had greater propensity to slip into poverty after post-resettlement. Through analysing the livelihoods-based vulnerability in a drought-prone and poor county (Jixian) in China's Shanxi province, emerging research (Rogers and Xue, 2015) finds that resettlement adversely impacts on the household asset base (particularly financial and natural capital) and concludes that resettlement, as it is currently practiced, has the potential to intensify (acting as a driver of vulnerability) rather than lessen the vulnerability of rural households to climate change relative to non-resettled households.

Resettlement can involve hardships beyond the financial costs. Many environmentally displaced or relocated people have experienced enormous hardships in reconstructing their livelihoods, causing instability in the resettlement areas. This is especially the case for the displaced ethnic minority groups who often face fundamental changes in production activities, culture, language, lifestyle and health (Abliz and Gulisumu, 2006, Bao and Meng, 2005, Feng and Chen, 2009, Rogers and Wang, 2006, Zhou et al., 2010). For the Tibetan pastoralists displaced from the Sanjiangyuan region on the Qinghai-Tibetan plateau, their production methods and lifestyle have been shifted from previous nomadic pastoralism to non-agricultural activities (e.g. running small business, hospitality, transportation and earning wages as migrant workers) after being resettled in urban areas (Tian et al., 2012). Due to loss of their grassland and lack of skills to seek jobs in secondary or tertiary industries, social assistance and training in job skills are especially needed to support these Tibetan resettlers (Wang et al., 2010). Based on field surveys in the central and southern arid areas of Ningxia, He and Zhang (2014) analysed the continued depreciation of human capital of those displaced caused by prevalent droughts in the central and southern regions of Ningxia. Lack of new techniques and skills required for agricultural production in the new resettlement areas, or absence of adequate skills to pursue non-agricultural activities, malnutrition and infectious diseases have significantly hindered the livelihood reconstruction of some resettled groups.

From a sociological perspective, Xun and Bao (2007) provide an overview of the environmental migration policy and its implementation in Inner Mongolia. A study of Dong et al. (2012) in Inner Mongolia examined how well the relocated families have adapted to their new living conditions (e.g. incomes, ability to obtain employment, dependence on government policies and overall satisfaction with their lives) and factors influencing their willingness to remain in the new villages. They find that four factors – age of the household head, duration (years) the household has resided in the new village, proportion of government subsides against total income and level of fixed, durable and current assets – significantly affect their willingness to stay in their resettlement communities.

Triggering new environmental risks

Implementing ecological migration in some arid, and semi-arid, pastoral and cropping land areas is found to be ecologically and economically unsustainable, and could exacerbate local social and ecological problems. A study of Sun et al. (2016) in Hongsipu district, the largest resettlement area in semi-arid central region of Ningxia, tracked the impact of resettlement on change in land-use forms in this area in 1989–2008. The study finds that grassland and shrub land have almost disappeared due to resettling migrants and the development of irrigation-based agriculture, creating possible new ecological risk in the region. Xu (2001) argues that ecological migration is a short-term solution in relieving population pressure on pastoral land as ecological migration can lead to overconsumption of limited water resources. This is supported by a case study in Alxa League of Inner Mongolia, which shows that ecological migration can trigger more serious ecological damage (e.g. overtapping underground water in some already desertified oasis areas) and cause new socio-ecological feedbacks (e.g. water shortage and deteriorating water quality) in the resettlement areas (Jiao and Wang, 2008). Further research of Fan et al. (2015) in Alxa Left Banner of western Inner Mongolia evidently shows that resettlement greatly increased the usage of water resources, reduced the efficiency of water use and exacerbated regional water shortages. They argue that traditional livestock practices of herders should not be abandoned.

Some studies provide comprehensive evaluations of the effects of ecological migration on environmental rehabilitation and socio-economic development in both the origin and receiving areas of migrants, as in resettlement practices in Qinghai (Fei et al., 2011), Inner Mongolia (Jiao et al., 2008), and Ningxia (Li, 2001, Sun et al., 2013, Yang et al., 2013, Zhang, 2006). Their results show that ecological migration benefits the sending areas as it reverses some adverse environmental processes (e.g. soil erosion on the Loess Plateau). Yet ecological migration has aggravated some problems of those not relocated. Some households left behind (usually comprising the poorest who could not afford the costs for relocation) still remain in persistent poverty. Such villagers experience increased difficulties in access to schools and healthcare clinics, as such social services were removed from their local villages to township centres because of decreased population after relocation. Problems related to relocation of whole villages in a rural community to resettle in new, and/or distant, places are even greater (Zeng and Zhu, 2006): high costs for removals, lack of follow-up support, involuntary displacement and inadequate natural resource endowment (e.g. water and land) for sustainable livelihoods post-displacement.

Outcomes of migration due to environmental disasters

A large body of literature exists which critiques the policy options, processes and consequences of environmental disaster-induced displacement and resettlement, as reported in the case studies from provinces of Sichuan (He et al., 2012), Chongqing (Song and He, 2014), Shaanxi (He, 2014), and Jiangxi (Lai, 2009, Zheng and Wang, 2012). He et al. (2012) investigated the livelihood reconstruction problems of resettlers produced by a devastating mega-earthquake at magnitude 8.0 in Wenchuan of Sichuan province in 2008. Wang and Fei (2015) discussed the economic deprivations of villagers in the process of relocating their entire villages in Chongqing. Studying migration induced by flash floods in Zhouqu county of Gansu and droughts in central Ningxia, Zhou et al. (2014) suggest that the main policy options, from a disaster relief perspective, should integrate sudden and slow-onset hazards, combine top-down and bottom-up (i.e. a household-oriented policy for migration) methodology and encourage private enterprises to establish public-private partnerships to assist rebuilding livelihood. Transformation from re-active migration (i.e. an emergency measure in and after disasters) to pro-active migration (i.e. relocating people potentially affected by environmental hazards to safer places) is also recommended.

A number of studies have assessed the satisfaction in their social lives and livelihood reconstruction of mountain disaster-induced migrants in southern Shaanxi province (Liu and Li, 2015), and observed social exclusion (He and Dang, 2012) and issues of ecological compensation (i.e. a trade-off whereby loss of ecological values and natural resources in the context of development or resource use is offset by corresponding compensations for people affected) for the displaced (Zhan et al., 2007). Some plausible outcomes of resettlement (e.g. improved living environment and housing conditions and increased accessibility to schools, clinics and basic infrastructure such as water, roads and electricity) are also reported in case studies of Shaanxi (Li and Wu, 2014, Liu and Li, 2015), and Ningxia (Li, 2001, Zhang, 2006).

Social and cultural impacts of ecological migration

Social and cultural impacts on both migrant individuals and their resettlement communities are tremendous. Psychological factors (e.g. strong attachment to hometown, worries about uncertain life after relocation) are important barriers constraining the implementation of ecological migration schemes (Li and Han, 2012). Social exclusion is identified as a crucial issue in the process of relocating people whose life and livelihoods are threaten by natural hazards in the mountainous areas of southern Shaanxi (He and Dang, 2012). Social, cultural, psychological and health costs of displacement are important factors impacting the success of resettlement but are not easily or accurately quantifiable using available quantitative tools. Accordingly, displaced people are not compensated for such costs (or loss and damage). One consequence is an increased likelihood of social exclusion, which may aggravate pre-existing ethnic tensions. Of particular significance is people's sense of identity, which might be lost, in part, through the resettlement process. Cultural continuity (or cultural reconstruction) – which includes the availability of culturally relevant and accessible health programs, education and skills training schemes, religious places of worship, local governance and community centres (Feng, 2013, Wen et al., 2005, Xu, 2011, Foggin, 2011) – has a significant effect on people's sense of wellbeing. Social adaptation of ethnic minority groups is therefore a major challenge post-displacement (Wang and Dai, 2014, Wang et al., 2014). This is particularly the case for ethnic minority groups, as is the case with the Tibetan people displaced in provinces of Qinghai (Foggin, 2011) and Sichuan (Tan et al., 2013). A crucial question that needs to be considered in resettlement policy, planning and implementation is how the loss of social and cultural capital can be avoided or minimised in the first place so that it does not need to be re-established later at the resettlement destination. The potential for this loss, and the need for its re-establishment, must become an area of policy concern and be addressed in research and practice.

Factors influencing environmental migration behaviour

A few quantitative studies have examined how environmental factors combine with demographic, social, economic and political factors to influence people's migration behaviour. At the household level, Feng and Nie (2013) analysed key factors influencing the willingness to undertake ecological migration and the actual migration behaviour of farmers in Ningxia. They find that a small household size, poor quality of farmland, lack of irrigation water, poor environmental conditions, and poor accessibility to a well established mosque in the original villages are significant *push* factors stimulating both the willingness and the actual out-migration of people. Additional variables – experience (or years) of previous out-migration and annual household income – are, significantly and positively, associated with both the willingness of farmers to pursue migration and action of migrating. A case study in the Sangong River watershed of Xinjiang shows that household size, net income per capita, main source of income, the proportion of non-agricultural income, and farmers' participation in the 'Grain for Green' project significantly affect the willingness to undertake ecological migration (Tang et al., 2011). A study by Dong et al. (2012) in Inner Mongolia examined the factors that affected the willingness for those displaced households to stay in their new resettlement villages. They find that significant factors include the age of the household head, years post-resettlement, the ratio of the governmental subsidies against the household's total income, and the level of fixed, durable and current assets.

'Social inequality' has been identified as an important contributor to increasing the vulnerability of communities and people in the context of global climate change (e.g. Adger and Kelly, 1999, Paavola and Adger, 2006). Understanding the role of *social inequality* is crucial if we are to unravel the environmental (climate) impact, human adaption and migration nexus, but there is limited empirical evidence addressing it, especially in urban settings in China. Built on the theories of socio-spatial inequality (Sheppard, 2002) and social inequality (Goldthorpe, 2010), a study of Tan et al. (2015) considered social inequality from three major dimensions: *material inequality* (the economic), *social status inequality* (the social) and *power inequality* (the political). Taking the Yangzi River Delta as a case study area, their study provides new evidence that suggests urban households with low socio-economic status (characterised as renting housing, working on low-skill jobs, holding low-level educational attainment and having little social connection with their family and other people) exhibit a higher probability of experiencing more adverse climate impacts. All factors measuring social inequality exacerbate the adverse climate effects on already disadvantaged groups and impede their capacity, and decision, to move or integrate into urban centres.

Discussion

Ecological migration is an important approach to overcoming the limits of in-situ adaptation where vulnerable groups are unable to adjust adequately to stressors associated with climate and other environmental changes. Migration and planned relocation could also be an effective approach to diversifying livelihoods and building the future resilience of people and their communities to environmental change and poverty. However, the risks of impoverishment and socio-cultural impact after relocation are immense, and thus planning for environmental migration is essential. China has had more successes (in terms of livelihood reconstruction) in resettlement than any other developing country. Such successes are directly linked to measures such as the government's serious commitment to seeking the development of displaced people rather than simple relocation and restitution. Of course, China has also had many failures in the past, and policies resulting in adverse consequences in migration and resettlement, in ecological, economic and social terms, and in areas of both origin and destination, need to be built upon to ensure improved outcomes in the future. Some directions for future research are suggested as follows.

Addressing environmental change and migration in urban settings: Whilst there has been much research on human response (mainly displacement and resettlement) to environmental changes in rural areas, there has been little research attention paid to *urban* people's *migration* responses under the complex context of increasing urban environmental challenges. There is inadequate academic evidence and assessment of the impacts of climate change and other dimensions of environmental change on urban households in China (Li, 2013). Taking the Yangzi River Delta (YRD) as an example, this region has China's largest *concentration* of inter-provincial migrants, and is a *major climate change hotspot* that is highly susceptible to sea level rise and heatwaves (Gu et al., 2011, J. Wang et al., 2012). Dramatic industrialisation and urbanisation in the YRD since the early 1990s has caused widespread environmental degradation, especially air, water and soil pollution. Severe water pollution, as exemplified by the water crisis in Wuxi city of Jiangsu province in 2007 (Yang et al., 2011), worsening air pollution (T. Wang et al., 2012) and toxic heavy metal and organic pollutants in the soil (Zhao et al., 2010), and a tremendous degradation risk of ecosystem services in the core area of the delta from 1985–2020 (Xu et al., 2016), are a few examples of the environmental degradation threatening people's livelihood sources and liveability of affected areas in the region. Strikingly, the YRD has become one of China's most severely polluted regions in the last decade (Ma et al., 2012). Environmental pollution has posed great threats to public health and environmental security. Using a fuzzy discontinuity model, emerging research suggests that air quality influences people's migration choice (Xi and Liang, 2015). There is a knowledge gap in understanding how climate change, climate related hazards and other dimensions of environmental change (including pollution) impact on current migration behaviour (including in-migration to cities and out-migration from cities) in large urban areas such as the YRD. How environmental factors *interact* with economic, social, demographic and political factors is especially understudied. In areas clearly influenced by climate (environmental) change, like the YRD and the Pearl River Delta (Yang et al., 2014), such research is urgently needed to inform specific migration and adaptation policies and programs.

Advancing theoretical understanding of the nexus between environmental change, urbanisation, and human migration: As massive numbers of migrants continue to flow into mega- and large cities, new risks will almost certainly emerge, risks that are as much to do with the demands new migrants place on existing infrastructure and institutions as with changes to the social-ecological systems that sustain urban life, including climate. Whatever risks emerge at the interface of environmental change impacts, migration and rapid urbanisation, these are almost certain to be exacerbated by widening disparities between advantaged urbanites and disadvantaged groups, including migrants. A major challenge for Chinese policymakers today concerns how best to respond to these future challenges. Future research that advances theoretical understanding of the relationship between climate change, urbanisation, and human migration in urban areas will be of significance. It is necessary to combine socio-ecological theory, contemporary urban theory and complex systems theory in urban settings to understand how social inequality impacts on migration behaviour, to characterise urban contexts and to characterise urban risk in the context of environmental change. Innovative studies that deepen our understanding of migrant behaviours by simulating and analysing how people (including migrants) respond to future climate change using interdisciplinary and advanced methods (e.g. agent-based modelling) to address such challenges will be important. To date, few attempts have been made systematically to model and evaluate how migrants may adapt to future risks associated with climate (environmental) change, and how and with what effects such adaptive efforts intersect with urban citizenship, green urbanism, and widening social inequality between established urban citizens and migrants in rapidly urbanising cities in China.

Stressing environmental change and migration in the rural-urban interactions: The transformation of rural-urban interactions and the dynamics of human migration are poorly understood. Future research needs to address how the complex relationships between climate change, human migration and displacement, and associated resource flows influence the transformation of rural-urban interactions, including environmental degradation, natural hazards, livelihood changes and social stabilities.

Conclusion

This literature survey identifies four characteristics of ecological migration practised in China since the mid-1980s: complex and significant cause-effect links between environmental stresses, prevalent poverty and human resettlement; government-led and serving governmental (national) interests; mixed consequences of environmental rehabilitation in migrant sending areas and new environmental risks triggered by resettlement in migrant destinations; and enormous challenges in post-resettlement livelihood and socio-cultural reconstruction. This chapter also highlights issues of concern that has been little addressed, such as the need to embed the migration-climate (environment) nexus more convincingly within the framework of broader socio-ecological and contemporary urban theories.

References

Abliz, Y. & Gulisumu, A. 2006. On the relation between eco-culture of minorities and the eco-migration in Xinjiang. *Ecological Economy*, 12, 40–43.

Adger, N. & Kelly, M. 1999. Social vulnerability to climate change and the architecture of entitlements. *Mitigation and Adaptation Strategies for Global Change*, 4, 253–266.

Bao, Z. & Meng, L. 2005. Impacts of environmental migration on lifestyle and production modes of herdsmen (in Chinese). *NW Ethno-National Studies*, 45, 147–164.

Bao, Z. M. 2006. Definition, categorisation and some other issues of ecological migration (in Chinese). *Journal of the Central University for Nationalities*, 33, 27–31.

Black, R., Adger, W. N., Arnell, N. W., Dercon, S., Geddes, A. & Thomas, D. 2011. The effect of environmental change on human migration. *Global Environmental Change*, 21, S3–S11.

Chen, H., Wang, J. & Huang, J. 2014. Policy support, social capital, and farmers' adaptation to drought in China. *Global Environmental Change*, 24, 193–202.

Chen, J. 2007. Rapid urbanization in China: A real challenge to soil protections and food security. *CATENA*, 69, 1–15.

Chen, Y., Tan, Y. & Mao, C. 2013. Mountain hazards, risk management, disaster-preventive and poverty-alleviating resettlement (in Chinese). *Journal of Catastrophology*, 2, 136–142.

CMA (China Meteorological Adminitration). 2013. *Securing Minqin against Water Scarcity (in Chinese)* [Online]. Available: www.cma.gov.cn/2011xzt/2013zhuant/20131021/2013090404/201310/t20131021_229319.html.

Da, L. & Zheng, Y. 2010. *Pastoral Areas and Market: A Herder-Based Economics*, Beijing, Social Sciences Academic Press.

Dong, C., Liu, X. & Klein, K. K. 2012. Land degradation and population relocation in Northern China. *Asia Pacific Viewpoint*, 53, 163–177.

Dong, R. 2000. Practice of eco-migration and its implications for poverty alleviation (in Chinese). *China's Underdeveloped Regions*, 10, 37–40.

Duan, C. R., Lu, L. D. & Zou, X. J. 2013. Major challenges for China's floating population and policy suggestions: An analysis of the 2010 population census data. *Population Research*, 37, 17–24.

Fan, H. & Zhao, X. 2003. Eco-migration problems in west China and the roles of central and eastern regions of China (in Chinese). *Rural Economy*, 36–37.

Fan, M., Li, Y. & Li, W. 2015. Solving one problem by creating a bigger one: The consequences of ecological resettlement for grassland restoration and poverty alleviation in Northwestern China. *Land Use Policy*, 42, 124–130.

Fang, B. & Peng, Z. 2002. *Ecological Migration: New Ideas of Poverty Elimination and Eco-Environmental Protection in West China (in Chinese)*, Nanning, Guangxi People Publishing House.

Fei, J., Jai, S. & Zhu, W. 2011. Evaluating the effects of 'aid-the-poor' migration program in the Xiangride-Balong areas of Qinghai province on the origin of displaced people (in Chinese). *Research of Agricultural Modernization*, 6, 681–685.

Feng, W. 2013. The construction of ethnic culture among eco-migrants: A case study in Ningxia (in Chinese). *People's Tribune*, 11, 166–168.

Feng, X. & Nie, J. 2013. Migration intention and behavior of the ecological migrants among the Hui ethnic groups of Ningxia (in Chinese). *Journal of Lanzhou University(Social Sciences)*, 06, 53–59.

Feng, Y. & Chen, Y. 2009. Barriers of and countermeasures for environmental displacement and resettlement of Lisu ethnic people in Nujiang Lisu Autonomous Prefecture of Yunnan Province. *Inquiry into Economic Issues*, 3, 68–73.

Finlayson, B., Barnett, J., Wei, T., Webber, M., Li, M., Wang, M., Chen, J., Xu, H. & Chen, Z. 2013. The drivers of risk to water security in Shanghai. *Regional Environmental Change*, 13, 329–340.

Foggin, J. 2011. Rethinking 'ecological migration' and the value of cultural continuity. *AMBIO: A Journal of the Human Environment*, 1, 100–101.

Goldthorpe, J. H. 2010. Analysing social inequality: A critique of two recent contributions from economics and epidemiology. *European Sociological Review*, 26, 731–744.

Gu, C., Hu, L., Zhang, X., Wang, X. & Guo, J. 2011. Climate change and urbanization in the Yangtze River Delta. *Habitat International*, 35, 544–552.

He, D. 2014. Innovative management in resettlement communities produced by natural disasters and 'aid-the-poor' programs in the mountainous areas of west China: A case study in Ankang (in Chinese). *Journal of Chinese Academy of Governance*, 03, 97–101.

He, D. & Dang, G. 2012. Studying the mechanism for social exclusion in the process of natural disaster induced displacement and resettlement in south Shaanxi province (in Chinese). *Journal of Chinese Academy of Governance*, 6, 84–88.

He, L., Chen, Y., Mao, C. & Zhang, Q. 2012. Disaster-driven resettlement and sustainable livelihood: A case study of Qingping township in Sichuan province (in Chinese). *Northwest Population Journal*, 06, 45–49+54.

He, Z. & Zhang, M. 2014. Human capital loss and reconfiguration for climate migrants induced by climate change: Case study of the central and southern arid area in Ningxia (in Chinese). *China Population, Resources and Environment*, 12, 109–116.

Huang, Z. 2008. Combination of poverty elimination and balancing urban and rural development—a case study in Zixi County of Jaingxi Province (in Chinese). *Journal of Old Revolutionary Base Building*, 53–55.

IOM (international organization for migration). 2007. *Discussion Note: Migration and the Environment* [Online]. Available: www.iom/int/jahia/webdav/site/myjahiasite/shared/shared/ mainsite/microsites/ IDM/workshops/evolving_global_economy/2728112007/MC_INF_288_EN.pdf.

Jiao, K. & Wang, R. 2008. Investigating the effectiveness of eco-migration in ethnic areas: A case study in Luanjingzitan of Inner Mongolia (in Chinese). *Inner Mongolia Social Sciences*, 84–88.

Jiao, K., Wang, R. & Su, L. 2008. Effects of eco-migration in ethnic minority regions: Taking eco-migration in Alax of Inner Mongolia as example (in Chinese). *Northwest Population Journal*, 05, 64–68.

Kang, S., Su, X., Tong, L., Zhang, J., Zhang, L. & Davies, W. J. 2008. A warning from an ancient oasis: Intensive human activities are leading to potential ecological and social catastrophe. *International Journal of Sustainable Development and World Ecology*, 15, 440–447.

Khan, S., Hanjra, M. & Mu, J. 2009. Water management and crop production for food security in China: A review. *Agricultural Water Management*, 96, 349–360.

Kolas, A. 2014. Degradation discourse and green governmentality in the Xilinguole Grasslands of Inner Mongolia. *Development and Change*, 45, 308–328.

Lai, B. 2009. Studying the motivation of 'aid-the-poor' migration in the mountainous areas of northwest Jiangxi province (in Chinese). *Journal of Old Revolutionary Base Building*, 09, 30–34.

Lee, H. F. & Zhang, D. D. 2005. Perceiving land-degrading activities from the lay perspective in northern China. *Environmental management*, 36, 711–725.

Li, B. 2013. Governing urban climate change adaptation in China. *Environment and Urbanization*, 25, 413–427.

Li, J. & Wu, Z. 2014. Benefit of rural households displaced from the hazard prone mountainous areas in Hanyin county of Shaanxi province (in Chinese). *China State Finance*, 18, 64.

Li, N. 2001. 'Aid-the-poor' migration and development of Hui ethnic minority groups in Ningxia province (in Chinese). *Journal of Hui Muslim Minority Studies*, 03, 52–55.

Li, S. & Han, G. 2012. Psychological factors limiting the implementation of eco-migration strategy and countermeasures: A case study in Inner Mongolia (in Chinese). *Heilongjiang National Series*, 04, 39–44.

Li, S.Y., Verburg, P. H., Lv, S. H., Wu, J. L. & Li, X. B. 2012. Spatial analysis of the driving factors of grassland degradation under conditions of climate change and intensive use in Inner Mongolia, China. *Regional Environmental Change*, 12, 461–474.

Li, X., Zhu, Q., Zhao, X. & Tang, L. 2005. *Evaluation of the effects of voluntary migration on poverty and poverty reduction*, Beijing: College of Humanities and Development, China Agricultural University.

Li, Y. 2010. GIS-based selection of distant resettlement sites produced by poverty alleviation schemes in Lushui county (in Chinese). *Geomatics World*, 03, 59–63.

Li, Y., Conway, D., Wu, Y., Gao, Q., Rothausen, S., Xiong, W., Ju, H. & Lin, E. 2013. Rural livelihoods and climate variability in Ningxia, Northwest China. *Climatic Change*, 119, 891–904.

Liu, J. & Diamond, J. 2005. China's environment in a globalizing world. *Nature*, 435, 1179–1186.

Liu, J., Tian, H., Liu, M., Zhuang, D., Melillo, J. & Zhang, Z. 2005. China's changing landscape during the 1990s: Large-scale land transformations estimated with satellite data. *Geophysical Research Letters*, 32, 1–5.

Liu, S. & Li, S. 2015. Analysis of the survival status and satisfaction of disaster-induced poverty migration in southern Shannxi province: A case study of the resettlement site in Yungaisi town (in Chinese). *Urban Development Studies*, 01, 102–107.

Liu, W., Li, J., Li, C. & Li, S. 2015. Types of poverty and the factors of farmers displaced in Ankang of south Shaanxi province (in Chinese). *Journal of Zhongnan University of Economics and Law*, 06, 41–48.

Liu, X. 2002. Effects and problems of ecological migration in Northwest China (in Chinese). *Chinese Rural Economy*, 4, 47–52.

Liu, X. 2011. The Interaction Between the Government Authority and Civil Society in the Process of Ecological Migration (in Chinese). Doctoral dissertation, Beijing, Minzu University of China.

Ma, J., Xu, X., Zhao, C. & Yan, P. 2012. A review of atmospheric chemistry research in China: Photochemical smog, haze pollution, and gas-aerosol interactions. *Advances in Atmospheric Sciences*, 29, 1006–1026.

MAC (Ministry Of Agriculture Of China) 2011. *2010 National Grassland Monitoring Report*, Beijing: Ministry Publication.

MEA (Millennium Ecosystem Assessment) 2005. *Ecosystems and Human Well-Being*, Washington, DC: Island Press.

Meng, J., Zhang, Y. & Zhou, P. 2010. Ecological vulnerability assessment of the farming-pastoral transitional zone in Northern China: A case study of Ordos City. *Journal of Desert Research*, 30, 840–856.

MEP (Ministry of Environmental Protection). 2008. *Planning Outline of Protection of the Ecologically Vulnerable Areas in China* [Online], Beijing: Government document. Available: www.gov.cn/gongbao/content/2009/content_1250928.htm.

MRR (Minqin Resettlement Bureau). 2011. *Progress of human relocation and resettlement in Minqin county by late June 2011.* Minqin county, Gansu province, China.

NDRC (National Development And Reform Commission). 2007. *China's National Climate Change Program*, [Online]. Available: <www.china.org.cn/english/environment/213624.htm>.

NDRC (National Development and Reform Commission). 2008. *National Plan for Expansion of Grain Production Capacity (2008–2020)* [Online]. Available: www.gov.cn/jrzg/2008-11/13/content_1148414.htm.

NDRC (National Development and Reform Commission). 2012a. *The 12th Five-Year Plan of Grand Development of Western China* [Online]. Available: http://guoqing.china.com.cn/zwxx/2012-02/21/content_24691623.htm.

NDRC (National Development and Reform Commission). 2012b. *The 12th Five-Year Plan for Aid-the-poor through Displacement of the Poor* [Online]. Available: www.gov.cn/zwgk/2012-09/17/content_2226625.htm.

NDRC (National Development and Reform Commission). 2013 *China's National Strategies for Adapting to Climate Change* [Online]. Available: www.gov.cn/gzdt/att/att/site1/20131209/001e3741a2cc140f6a8701.pdf.

NDRC and MWR (National Development and Reform Committee & Ministry of Water Resources). 2007. *Governing Plan for Focal Issues in the Shiyang River Basin* [Online]. Available: www.sdpc.gov.cn/fzgggz/fzgh/ghwb/gjjgh/200806/P020150630514361951622.pdf.

NHFPCC (National Health and Family Planning Commission of China) 2015. *2015 Report on China's Floating Population Development Report*, Beijing: China Population Publishing House.

Ouyang, Z. Y., Zheng, H., Gao, J. X. & Huang, B. R. 2009. *Regional Ecological Assessment and Ecosystem Service Zoning*, Beijing: China Environmental Science Press.

Paavola, J. & Adger, N. 2006. Fair adaptation to climate change. *Ecological Economics*, 56, 594–609.

Peng, S. 2011. Water resources strategy and agricultural development in China. *Journal of Experimental Botany*, 62, 1709–1713.

Piao, S., Ciais, P., Huang, Y., Shen, Z., Peng, S., Li, J., Zhou, L., Liu, H., Ma, Y. & Ding, Y. 2010. The impacts of climate change on water resources and agriculture in China. *Nature*, 467, 43–51.

Qin, X. 2004. Research on voluntary migration in the process of poverty alleviation (in Chinese). *Seeker*, 09, 129–131.

Rogers, S. & Wang, M. 2006. Environmental resettlement and social dis/re-articulation in Inner Mongolia, China. *Population and Environment*, 28, 41–68.

Rogers, S. & Xue, T. 2015. Resettlement and climate change vulnerability: Evidence from rural China. *Global Environmental Change*, 35, 62–69.

SCC (State Council of China). 2001. *Outline of Development-Oriented Poverty Reduction Program for Rural China (2001–2010)* [Online]. Available: http://news.xinhuanet.com/zhengfu/2005-07/19/content_3239424.htm.

SCC (State Council of China). 2011a. *The Essentials of the Aid the Poor and Development in Rural China (2011–2020)* [Online]. Available: www.gov.cn/jrzg/2011-12/01/content_2008462.htm.

SCC (State Council of China). 2011b. *New Progress in Development-Oriented Poverty Reduction Program for Rural China* [Online]. Available: http://usa.chinadaily.com.cn/china/2011-11/16/content_14106364.htm.

SCC (State Council of China). 2014. *National New-Type Urbanization Plan 2014–2020*, Beijing: People's Publishing House.

SEACC (State Ethnic Affairs Commission of China). 2012. *Results of the Monitoring Data About Rural Poverty in the Ethnic Regions of China in 2011* [Online]. Available: www.gov.cn/gzdt/2012-11/28/content_2277545.htm.

Sheppard, E. 2002. The spaces and times of globalization: Place, scale, networks, and positionality. *Economic Geography*, 78, 307–330.

Shi, G., Zhou, J. & Li, J. 2007. Protection of rights and interests and government's responsibilities: A case study of the Tarim River ecological migration as an example. *Jilin University Journal Social Sciences Edition*, 47, 78–86.

Shi, J. 2010. Study on appraisal procedure and index system of sustainable development in resettlement areas of ecological migration based on a pressure-state-response model (in Chinese). *Northwest Population Journal*, 04, 31–35.

Shi, J. & Gai, Z. 2006. Resettlement site selection issues of eco-migrants in Inner Mongolia (in Chinese). *Inner Mongolia Agricultural Science and Technology*, 01, 1–4.

Song, H. 2006. *Research Report on Grassland Improvement and Pastoral Area Development*, Beijing: China Financial & Economic Publishing House.

Song, H. & He, W. 2014. Analysing the effects of 'aid-the-poor' migration under the ecological civilization ideology: Practice in mountainous areas of Chongqing municipality (in Chinese). *Chongqing Administration (Public Forum)*, 05, 22–24.

Song, Y., Li, C., Jiang, L. & Lu, L. 2015. Ecological indicators for immigrant relocation areas: a case in Luanjingtan, Alxa, Inner Mongolia. *International Journal of Sustainable Development & World Ecology*, 22, 445–451.

Sun, D., Yu, X., Liu, X. & Li, B. 2016. A new artificial oasis landscape dynamics in semi-arid Hongsipu region with decadal agricultural irrigation development in Ning Xia, China. *Earth Science Informatics*, 9, 21–33.

Sun, Y., Wang, Z., Liu, Y., Cui, L. & Han, J. 2013. Outcomes, problems and strategies of government organised eco-migration: Analysis based on the survey in the area of Xihaigu, Ningxia (in Chinese). *West Forum*, 02, 44–50.

Tan, Y., Liu, X. & Hugo, G. 2015. Exploring relationship between social inequality and adaptations to climate change: Evidence from urban household surveys in the Yangtze River Delta, China. *Population and Environment*, 36, 400–428.

Tan, Y., Zuo, A. & Hugo, G. 2013. Environment-related resettlement in China: A case study from the Ganzi Tibetan Autonomous Prefecture of Sichuan Province. *Asian and Pacific Migration Journal*, 22, 77–107.

Tang, H., Zhang, X. & Yang, D. 2011. Ecological migration willingness and its affecting factors: A case of Sangonghe River watershed, Xinjiang (in Chinese). *Journal of Natural Resources*, 10, 1658–1669.

Tao, F., Zhang, Z. & Yokozawa, M. 2011. Dangerous levels of climate change for agricultural production in China. *Regional Environmental Change*, 11, S41–S48.

Tao, Z. 2007. The far-reaching impact of eco-migration program on the economic development of Guoruo prefecture of Qinghai province (in Chinese). *Qinghai Statistics*, 22–26.

Tian, Z., Sun, R. & Zhang, K. 2012. Poverty and social assistance strategy of the ecological migrants from Sanjiangyuan region (in Chinese). *Ecological Economy*, 09, 169–172.

Tu, B. & Yuki, K. 2012. Implementation and challenges of ecological migration as environmental policy in China's Inner Mongolia. *Japanese Journal of Human Geography*, 64, 41–54.

Wang, C. & Fei, Z. 2015. Relative deprivation of the relocated farmer households in the process of whole-village advance: A case study in Dazhu village of Chongqing (in Chinese). *Journal of Southwest University (Natural Science Edition)*, 04, 41–46.

Wang, J., Gao, W., Xu, S. & Yu, L. 2012. Evaluation of the combined risk of sea level rise, land subsidence, and storm surges on the coastal areas of Shanghai, China. *Climatic Change*, 115, 537–558.

Wang, T., Jiang, F., Deng, J., Shen, Y., Fu, Q., Wang, Q., Fu, Y., Xu, J. & Zhang, D. 2012 Urban air quality and regional haze weather forecast for Yangtze River Delta region. *Atmospheric Environment*, 58, 70–83.

Wang, X., Chen, F. & Dong, Z. 2006. The relative role of climatic and human factors in desertification in semiarid China. *Global Environmental Change*, 16, 48–57.

Wang, X., Chen, F., Hasi, E. & Li, J. 2008. Desertification in China: An assessment. *Earth Science Reviews*, 88, 188–206.

Wang, Y. & Dai, B. 2014. Social adaptation of eco-migrants in ethnic regions: A case study in 'aid-the-poor' and eco-migration areas of Guizhou province (in Chinese). *Journal of Guiyang University(Social Sciences)*, 01, 31–34.

Wang, Y., Wu, X., Huang, H. & Zhou, P. 2014. Resettlement methods for ecological migration in the regions with scarce land resources: A case study of Guizhou province (in Chinese). *Ecological Economy*, 01, 66–69+82.

Wang, Z., Song, K. & Hu, L. 2010. China's largest scale ecological migration in the Three-River Headwater region. *Ambio*, 39, 443–446.

Webber, M. 2012. *Making Capitalism in Rural China*, Cheltenham UK, Edward Elgar.

Wen, B., Song, Y., Zhang, T. & Qiao, Z. 2005. Resettlement means of eco-migration: A case study in Manan village of Yongshan county (in Chinese). *Ecological Economy*, 01, 27–31.

Wilmsen, B. & Wang, M. 2015. Voluntary and involuntary resettlement in China: a false dichotomy? *Development in Practice*, 25, 612–627.

World Bank 2014. *Urban China: Toward efficient, inclusive, and sustainable urbanization*, Washington, DC: World Bank.

Wu, J. 2015. Running away is the best? Ecological resettlement of ethnic minorities in Guizhou, China. *Geography Research Forum*, 35, 95–112.

Wu, J., He, B., Lü, A., Zhou, L., Liu, M. & Zhao, L. 2010. Quantitative assessment and spatial characteristics analysis of agricultural drought vulnerability in China. *Natural Hazards*, 56, 785–801.

Wu, Z. 2011. Report on implementing the Plan for Environment-related Displacement in the Central and Southern Areas of Ningxia Hui Autonomous Region During the 12th Five-Year Period (2011–2015). *Report to the 27th session of the 10th Meeting of People's Representatives of Ningxia Hui Autonomous Region*. Yinchuan.

Wuli, G. 2007. Talking about the trans-provincial area arrangements for ecological migrants in the western minority area and the issue of programming the ecological depopulated zone. *Guizhou Ethnic Studies*, 27, 47–53.

Xi, P. & Liang, R. 2015. Air quality in urban areas and environmental migration—based on a fussy discontinuous model (in Chinese). *Economic Science*, 04, 30–43.

Xu, F., Guo, S. & Zhang, Z. 2003. The distribution of soil erosion in China at the end of the 20th Century. *Acta Geographica Sinica*, 58, 139–146.

Xu, H. 2001. Eeffectiveness of ecological migration policy on alleviating the ecological pressure of grassland (in Chinese). *Territory & Natural Resources Study*, 4, 24–27.

Xu, J. 2011. Leaving or attachment: Studying poverty-alleviation migration in Tibet and other Tibetan regions of Chian (in Chinese). *Journal of Tibet University*, 04, 12–19.

Xu, J., Ouyang, Z., Cheng, H. & Lin, Q. 1996. Environmental migration (in Chinese). *China Population, Resources and Environment*, 01, 12–16.

Xu, L., Yang, X., Wang, K., Li, X. & Zhang, M. 2006. Research progress in ecological carrying capacity. *Ecology and Environment*, 15, 1111–1116.

Xu, X., Tan, Y., Chen, S. & Yang, G. 2013. Changing patterns and determinants of natural capital in the Yangtze River Delta of China 2000–2010. *Science of the Total Environment*, 466–467, 326–337.

Xu, X., Yang, G., Tan, Y., Zhuang, Q., Li, H., Wan, R., Su, W. & Zhang, J. 2016. Ecological risk assessment of ecosystem services in the Taihu Lake Basin of China from 1985 to 2020. *Science of the Total Environment*, 554–555, 7–16.

Xu, Y. & Ju, H. 2009. Climate Change and Poverty – A Case Study of China. *Research report by Hong Kong Oxfam, Greenpeace China.*

Xun, L. & Bao, Z. 2007. Environmental policies based on government mobilization and their local implementation: A sociological analysis of ecological migration at S Banner in Inner Mongolia (in Chinese). *Social Sciences in China,* 05, 114–128+207.

Yan, W. & He, D. 2014. Resettlement issues of natural disaster induced migrants in mountainous areas from a sustainable livelihood point of view (in Chinese). *Forward Position,* Z1, 117–119.

Yang, G., Zhu, C. & Jiang, Q. 2011. *Yangtze Conservation and Development Report 2011,* Wuhan: Yangtze River Press.

Yang, L., Scheffran, J., Qin, H. & You, Q. 2014. Climate-related flood risks and urban responses in the Pearl River Delta, China. *Regional Environmental Change,* 15, 379–391.

Yang, X., Mi, W., Qi, T. & Cheng, Z. 2013. Evaluating ecological migration in Ningxia (in Chinese). *Journal of Arid Land Resources and Environment,* 04, 16–23.

Zeng, F. & Zhu, Q. 2006. Problems and countermeasures of the whole village migration for slleviating poverty (in Chinese). *Journal of Northwest A&F University(Social Science Edition),* 03, 9–13.

Zhan, X., Ma, Z., Huang, S., Hua, Y. & Zhu, X. 2007. Ecological compensation policy on Tibetan eco-migrants in the Sanjiangyuan region (in Chinese). *New Heights,* 06, 91–95.

Zhang, K., Qu, J. & Liu, Q. 2004. Environmental degradation in the Minqin oasis in northwest China during recent 50 years. *Journal of Environmental Systems,* 31, 357–365.

Zhang, K., Yu, Z., Li, X., Zhou, W. & Zhang, D. 2007. Land use change and land degradation in China from 1991 to 2001. *Land Degradation and Development* 18 209–219.

Zhang, M. 2006. Emperical research into the ecological transmigration in the southern mountainous area of Ningxia (in Chinese). *Social Sciences in Ningxia,* 05, 66–69.

Zhao, Y., Wang, Z., Sun, W., Huang, B., Shi, X. & Ji, J. 2010. Spatial interrelations and multi-scale sources of soil heavy metal variability in a typical urban–rural transition area in Yangtze River Delta region of China. *Geoderma,* 156, 216–227.

Zheng, R. & Wang, Y. 2012. Improving resettlement induced by natural disasters based on the feasibility analysis: A case study in Jiujiang city of Jiangxi province (in Chinese). *Journal of Socialist Theory Guide,* 07, 96–97+101.

Zheng, Y. 2013. Environmental migration: concepts, theoretical ground and policy implications (in Chinese). *China Population, Resources and Environment,* 23, 96–103.

Zhou, H., Zhang, W., Sun, Y. & Yuan, Y. 2014. Policy options to support climate-induced migration: Insights from disaster relief in China. *Mitigation and Adaptation Strategies for Global Change,* 19, 375–389.

Zhou, H., Zhao, X., Zhang, C., Xing, X., Zhu, B. & Du, F. 2010. The predicament of ecological migrants and sustainable development strategy in the source area of Three Rivers. *China Population, Resources and Development* 20 185–188.

Zhou, J., Shi, G. & Sun, Z. 2009. Optimizing selection of resettlement areas of ecological migrants based on fuzzy logic (in Chinese). *Ecological Economy,* 05, 33–36.

Zhou, Y., Li, X. & Zhao, J. 2008. Analysis of the correlation between the typical ecological fragile zones and poverty in China. *Transactions of Beijing Institute of Technology,* 28, 260–262.

20

Environmental migration in Mexico

Daniel H. Simon

Introduction

Over the last decade, research on the climate-migration connection has burgeoned. In the case of Mexico, research has only recently begun investigating environmental influences on human migration. This is particularly concerning given that Mexico will likely be at the forefront of climate-related migration in North America due to a strong tradition of migration and projected climatic change impacts. Historically, Mexico has experienced relatively stable climate patterns, but this stability has begun to change with the emergence of contemporary global warming (IPCC 2013). Between 1960 and 2003, Mexico experienced a 0.6 degree Celsius increase in the mean annual temperature, with 1.1–3.0 degree increases expected by 2060 (McSweeney et al. 2008). Further, temperature extremes are likely to increase in both frequency and intensity (Collins et al. 2013). Global climate models also project declines in precipitation across much of the country (Christensen et al. 2013). Therefore, it is possible that Mexico could continue to experience climate shocks like the severe drought that affected the country from 1994–1999.

These future environmental challenges will exacerbate existing climate vulnerabilities in Mexico. Rural Mexican households are particularly susceptible to climate change since agricultural production contributes as much as two-thirds of rural household incomes (de Janvry and Sadoulet 2001). Additionally, due to persistent poverty and a lack of available financial resources, much of the rural population is unable to secure technology such as irrigation to help guard against and mitigate environmental hazards. As such, most agricultural production in Mexico relies on rain-fed cropland and is highly vulnerable to climate impacts (Carr et al. 2009; Endfield 2007). For example, around 80 percent of all economic losses between 1980 and 2005 were estimated to be a result of climate change and extreme weather events (Saldana-Zorrilla and Sandberg 2009). Further, recent research suggests that reductions in crop yields as a result of climate variability increased emigration from rural states in Mexico (Feng and Oppenheimer 2012).

Given these climate vulnerabilities and dependence on agriculture in rural Mexico, previous research has focused on migration from rural sending areas. While internal moves are the most common response to environmental change (Black et al. 2011), international migration is also an option for many households or individuals – especially in places with strong migration networks and traditions (Bardsley and Hugo 2010; Fussell and Massey 2004). Mexico has a long history of labor migration to the United States, and this migrant stream represents one of the largest and most sustained flows of people in the world. Therefore, much of the work on the climate-migration relationship in Mexico has focused on international migration from rural origins. Previous findings suggest that the climate-migration relationship in Mexico is dependent on historical climate conditions (Nawrotzki et al. 2013), the history of migration in the community (Hunter et al. 2013), and the degree of urbanization (Feng and Oppenheimer 2012). While there have been sharp declines in the size of the migrant flow from Mexico to the United States in recent years (Gonzalez-Barrera 2015; Villarreal 2014), changing climatic conditions in rural Mexico, as well as potential future impacts in urban areas like Mexico City, could renew the attractiveness of international migration.

The review carried out in this chapter is not exhaustive, but highlights specific studies that illustrate the present state of the literature, and identifies important themes and new research directions. The chapter begins with background on the Mexican context to ground subsequent discussion of the climate-related influences on human migration. Included in this section is a brief overview of the history of Mexico-U.S. migration and a description of the rural Mexican context. The focus then turns to migration responses to climate variability such as precipitation deficits and temperature increases, which represents much of the existing literature. Due to the historical nature of Mexican migration, the chapter then reflects on the importance of social networks, with the last two sections in this chapter highlighting understudied, yet emerging, areas of research – the timing of movement and internal migration following climate shocks.

Background: The Mexican context

Mexico-U.S. migration

Mexico provides a unique context in which to study the relationship between the environment and migration given that Mexico-U.S. migration is one of the largest and most sustained flows of people in the world (Massey and Sana 2003). This historical migration stream dates to the early 1900s, when Mexicans began providing labor on farms and for railroad construction projects (Durand and Arias 2000). Migration increased drastically following the creation of the Bracero Program, a labor agreement forged between Mexico and the United States which aimed to address labor shortages on U.S. farms (Calavita 1992). The program began in 1942 and was discontinued in 1964 following changes to civil rights and immigration policy. Unintendedly, both legal and undocumented migration persisted after the Bracero Program (Cornelius 1992; Massey et al. 2002). Migration to the United States continued to rise well into the 1990s and the beginning of the 21st century (Martin and Midgley 2010; Passel and Cohn 2011). Legal migration grew in response to the 1986 Immigration Reform and Control Act (IRCA), which penalized the hiring of undocumented immigrants and increased border protections. However, contrary to the IRCA policy goals, undocumented migration also continued (Massey and Riosmena 2010), due in large part to the established migrant networks and continued labor demand in U.S. destinations (Kandel and Parrado 2005). However, recent research suggests that the migrant flow between Mexico and the United States is currently the smallest it has been since the 1990s, a result of sharp declines in the number of Mexican immigrants entering the United States (Gonzalez-Barrera 2015). The Great Recession and the slower-than-expected economic recovery provide one of the most common explanations for this recent net-negative migration flow. Moreover, the economic contractions related to the Great Recession decreased labor demand in sectors that employ large numbers of immigrants, such as construction. As such, migration among younger men with low levels of education has declined significantly (Villarreal 2014). In addition to the Great Recession explanation, scholars have pointed to family reunification, increased enforcement at the border, rising deportations since 2005, improved economic conditions in Mexico, and demographic changes in Mexico as a result of declining fertility (Gonzalez-Barrera 2015; Villarreal 2014). Despite these recent trends, Mexico is still one of the largest sources of new immigrants to the United States, so a better understanding of the forces behind this migration stream remains important.

U.S.-bound migrants come from nearly all areas of Mexico. Previous work has identified the central-western areas of Mexico as the key historical sending regions (Durand et al. 2001), while the south and east of Mexico City comprise less traditional sources of migration. Rural communities are particularly relevant in the Mexican context as they make up a significant proportion of the overall Mexico-U.S. migration flow (Riosmena and Massey 2012). Thus, to analyze the environmental correlates of migration in this context, it is important to begin with a background on rural Mexico.

Climate vulnerability in rural Mexico

To better understand the rural Mexican context, one must first begin with the history of *ejidos*, which are officially recognized communal agricultural lands. Following the Mexican Revolution in 1910, the ejido sector was created to allocate land to peasant communities, allowing residents to a plot of their own. Between 60 and 65 percent of rural Mexicans live in Ejido communities (de Janvry and Sadoulet 2001). Using a nationally representative survey of ejidos, de Janvry and Sadoulet (2001) found that 92 percent of male household heads report farming as their main occupation, and that anywhere between one-quarter and two-thirds of ejido household incomes come from agriculture. Farming is central to rural livelihoods more generally, as 78 percent of rural households – including those who do not live on ejidos – engage in farming of some sort (Wiggins et al. 2002). Agricultural production is often small-scale, with households lacking technological adaptations needed to mitigate the potential impacts of climate variability. For example, estimates suggest that less than 25 percent of cropped land is irrigated (Carr et al. 2009; Winters et al. 2002; World Bank 2009).

The high degree of dependence of rural livelihoods on rain-fed agriculture is problematic in the context of contemporary climate change, and this is already seen through the impacts of existing climate variability (Boyd and Ibarraran 2009; Eakin 2005; Koziell and Saunders 2001). For example, between 80 and 90 percent of crop losses between 1980 and 2000 were connected with weather related disasters (Appendini and Liverman 1994; Saldana-Zorrilla and Sandberg 2009). Feng et al. (2010) have found that lower levels of corn and wheat yields are associated with higher levels of emigration to the United States. While questions were raised about their methodology (see Auffhammer and Vincent 2012), Feng and Oppenheimer (2012) continue to argue that reduced crop yields lead to increased migration to the United States from rural states in Mexico. This is intuitive, as drought is particularly detrimental to crop yield in already dry areas of Mexico that depend on rainfall. For example, corn is one of the most important crops in Mexico (Eakin 2000), but recent studies suggest that rainfall patterns have changed such that annual farming cycles are less reliable, with the rainy season beginning later than usual. Farmers have increasingly struggled to complete the annual agricultural cycle and harvest before the start of the cold season (Schmidt-Verkerk 2010) and, as a result, the unpredictable nature of rainfall patterns provides more reasons for rural Mexicans to emigrate (Alscher 2010).

In settings with unreliable banking systems and limited or no crop insurance programs, such as Mexico, migration can serve as a proactive insurance strategy against potential crop failure, with households choosing to send a migrant to international destinations to seek remittances (Massey et al. 1993). However, a household might also send a migrant as an ex post form of adaptation to stabilize income and livelihoods following a climate shock such as drought (Meze-Hausken 2000). The historical nature of Mexico-U.S. migration and rural Mexico's vulnerability to climate variation suggests that future climate-related migration may well rise.

Climate variability and international migration: precipitation deficits and temperature increases

Much of the existing research on the climate-migration relationship in Mexico has focused on population movements associated with variation in precipitation (Barrios et al. 2016; Hunter et al. 2013; Nawrotzki et al. 2013) and temperature (Nawrotzki and DeWaard 2016; Nawrotzki et al. 2015c). Most of these studies have analyzed rural sending areas, which makes sense given rural Mexico's reliance on rain-fed agriculture. Since Mexican livelihood strategies are best represented as household processes (Hondagneu-Sotelo 1994), the New Economics of Labor Migration (NELM) framework has proved particularly useful as a theoretical framework in integrating environmental factors into household decisions to send a migrant to the United States to maximize household income and minimize risks associated with crop failures and market fluctuations (Massey et al. 1993; Stark and Bloom 1985). Through this selective migration process, households are able to diversify their income sources, which is an important strategy for poor rural families that have little access to formal insurance markets (Lucas and Stark 1985). Remittances from a migrant abroad can serve as an ex ante risk mitigation strategy or an ex post means of coping with environmental and economic stressors (Gray 2010; Halliday 2006).

In studying the size of international migration networks in rural areas and the impacts of networks on Mexican migrant wages in the United States, Munshi (2003) used precipitation as an instrumental variable. While not the primary focus of the study, Munshi (2003) provided some of the first evidence that precipitation increases were negatively associated with migration. Later work from Hunter et al. (2013) confirmed this finding, using Mexican Migration Project (MMP) data coupled with state-level rainfall measures to analyze how drought influenced migration from rural areas in 12 Mexican states. Their study measured precipitation deviations from a 30-year climate normal, defining drought as years below 1 standard deviation of the precipitation normal and severe drought as 2 standard deviations from the normal. Their results show the relationship between drought and migration is highly situated and context specific, and depends on the historical migration conditions in the community. Generally, emigration rates increase two years after a drought for households in communities with strong historical migration networks, whereas households in less historically strong migration sending areas exhibited reductions in out-migration after a drought. The authors attributed these differences to social networks, as the costs of emigration would be much greater for households in non-historical sending regions. For households and communities that lack access to social networks created through past migration, emigration rates increased only after a period of good environmental conditions.

Nawrotzki et al. (2013) also used state-level rainfall data in combination with the 2000 Mexican census to model international migration. The authors utilized 1988–1993 as a rainfall reference period to examine the influence of precipitation deficits on household emigration to the United States between 1994 and 1999, and further categorized states as being generally wet or dry using 64-year precipitation records. Results from this study added nuance to previous work, showing that international migration was only associated with rainfall deficits in dry states. In these dry areas, drought acted as a "push" to migrate; by contrast, in wet states out-migration was unrelated to precipitation, and social networks were the most important driver.

One limitation of the aforementioned studies are the coarse state-level measures of climate. More recent work investigating the degree to which precipitation influences international migration has begun to incorporate finer scale measurements of climate. For example, Barrios et al. (2016) draw on satellite data from NASA to examine migration from small Mexican communities. Consistent with previous work, they find that increased precipitation reduces Mexican migration to the United States, the authors observing a 10.3 percent reduction in emigration following rainfall that was 20 percent higher than normal.

Two other recent studies have significantly improved the existing explanations of international migration from Mexico following climate stress. While previous work focused on precipitation deficits, these more recent studies have included measures of temperature extremes, a necessary addition given their negative impact on agricultural production and profit (Mueller et al. 2014). Moreover, one of Mexico's primary crops, corn, is especially sensitive to high temperatures (Keleman et al. 2009) during the flowering and pollination stages of development (Schoper et al. 1987). Nawrotzki et al. (2015a) investigated the climatic influence on undocumented migration from rural Mexico to the United States (also an important advance, as earlier work did not distinguish between legal and undocumented movement) between 1986 and 1999, using precipitation and temperature data from the Global Historical Climate Network and the Mexican Migration Project (MMP). Above-average temperatures were found to be an important migration push, with a one standard deviation increase in warm spell duration leading to a 19 percent increase in undocumented migration to the United States. In line with prior work on precipitation deficits, increased rainfall was associated with lower levels of out-migration. A second study from Nawrotzki et al. (2015b) focused on migration from rural and urban sending locations. The study documents an overall increase in international migration following periods of increased temperature and excessive precipitation, but when results were disaggregated according to the level of urbanization in the state of origin, the authors found that temperature increases are associated exclusively with increased levels of migration from rural areas. While these studies confirm the importance of precipitation and migration patterns in rural sending areas, future studies should continue to include temperature variables and consider urban sending areas as well.

The importance of social networks

One common theme noted in many of the aforementioned studies was the importance of social networks. Social networks may play varying roles in climate-related migration. Social networks may influence the distance and type of movement (Massey and Riosmena 2010), particularly from rural sending areas (Fussell and Massey 2004). In the context of Mexico, social networks help migrants locate and succeed in labor markets in the United States (Fussell 2004; Massey and Riosmena 2010), and provide general information about the migration process itself. It has been suggested that "migration corridors" created by social networks that connect origin and destination communities could amplify climate-related international migration (Bardsley and Hugo 2010: 249). On the other hand, social networks might also help rural households adapt in place of origin, such as by channeling remittances to affected areas, and reduce the potential for climate-related migration (Adger 2003).

Nawrotzki et al. (2015c) provided the first formal test of social networks and their impacts on climate-migration in Mexico. Their study employed a novel set of 15 climate change indices derived from daily temperature and precipitation data gathered from weather stations in

Mexico, obtained from the Global Historical Climate Network-Daily dataset made publicly available by the National Oceanic and Atmospheric Administration (NOAA). Using geostatistical interpolation methods the authors linked these climate data to migration histories from the Mexican Migration Project (MMP) database, and examined the differences between first and last international migration trips. The first migration trip helps to establish social ties and capital flows between origin and destination (Massey and España 1987). Following the first trip, the probability of a later trip increases substantially (Curran and Rivero-Fuentes 2003), particularly for households in rural areas. Nawrotzki et al. (2015c) found that increased temperatures led to higher probabilities of a first international migration trip, while increased precipitation resulted in a reduction in the odds of a first migration from dry areas of Mexico. At the household level, climate measures were largely predictive of the first international migration trip, with 60 percent of the climate change indices significantly associated with the first trip, while only 13 percent were predictive of a later migration. This suggests that at the household level, climate shocks more strongly influence the original migration event. To investigate further, the authors used community-level international migration prevalence data. Results demonstrated that these community-level social network measures suppressed two of the temperature extreme predictors, warm spell duration and percentage of warm nights, when measuring the likelihood of a first international trip. Their study thus provided evidence that social networks suppress the likelihood that climate effects will stimulate migration.

It is also important to consider the unequal access to social networks in Mexico, since social networks appear to reduce inequality in communities with high levels of emigration (McKenzie and Rapoport 2007). Schmidt (2016) investigated this using data from two Mexican states, Zacatecas and Veracruz. Here, the author discussed how poverty, social inequality and lack of social networks can create "trapped" immobile populations unable to undertake an initial migration in the face of climatic stress. Migration is most common among those in the middle of the income distribution, as they have the means to migrate as well as the motivation to seek higher wages. The adverse impacts of climate change could strain the financial resources of middle-income households that would have migrated under normal environmental conditions, thereby increasing the vulnerability and immobility of those without access to social networks. In short, further research is needed to explore the wider effects of social networks on climate-related migration patterns between Mexico and the United States.

The timing of migration following climate shocks

Although rural Mexican migration patterns are sensitive to climate shocks such as increased temperature or precipitation declines, little is known about *when* individuals or households choose to migrate. On the one hand, migration following a natural disaster might lead to an immediate response (Gray and Mueller 2012), while migration following slow-onset environmental stressors such as drought could be a strategy of last resort (Findlay 2011; McLeman 2011). To assess this, Nawrotzki and DeWaard (2016) tested three scenario models to gauge the timing of migration in response to a climate shock. The first scenario posits an immediate migration response, with the risk of migration high following a climate shock and subsequently declining over time. The authors suggest a few examples of when this scenario might take place. First, the climate shock could be an extreme, rapid onset-natural disaster that displaces large numbers of people immediately. Second, individuals or households might choose to migrate immediately after a climate shock if in-situ adaptive options are not available. Finally, even in settings with available in-situ strategies, some cultural contexts or social networks may lead households to engage in migration regardless of other livelihood strategies (Massey and Espinosa 1997).

The second scenario posits a delayed migration response following a climate shock, which may be expected in situations with available and accessible in-situ strategies. For example, these might include tapping into formal capital and credit markets, informal borrowing, reducing household expenditures, liquidating assets, public assistance programs, and drawing on social networks. In this way, households experiencing environmental stress such as a drought would first attempt to adapt in-situ before sending a migrant (Findlay 2011). Yet, when households exploit and deplete their available resources, migration may become a more attractive strategy (Dow et al. 2013; McLeman 2011). The third scenario is similar, but instead of a continued rise in the risk of migration, it posits that households adapt in place. As such, the risk of migration is low following a climate shock, increases as households employ various in-situ strategies, but then declines as in-situ strategies prove to be successful in the end. The likelihood of migration therefore declines over time.

To test these three scenarios, Nawrotzki and DeWaard (2016) used socio-demographic data and detailed migration histories from the previously mentioned Mexican Migration Project (MMP) and climate data from the Global Historical Climate Network-Daily (GHCN-D) for the years 1986–1999. Using multilevel event-history models, the authors analyzed household migration from rural communities (i.e. fewer than 10,000 inhabitants) with the primary predictor variables being the warm spell duration index and the number of days of heavy precipitation, thereby focusing on extremes rather than average conditions. The study found the greatest support for the third scenario, such that migration following a climate shock exhibits a delayed response pattern. The initial risk of migration is initially quite low, then increases, with a peak around three years, followed by consistent declines after the third year. The authors argue that this provides evidence to suggest that households attempt to adapt in-situ first, but pursue migration as these strategies are exploited. The decline in the risk of migration after three years would then imply that households eventually are successful at adapting in place. However, it could also be that households are simply saving money to pursue migration later, as financial resources are likely to be limited in the short term.

Another interesting finding from this case study is that migration is more strongly influenced by temperature increases than precipitation declines. The authors suggest this is because farmers and rural households have more in-situ adaptive strategies to deal with precipitation declines, such as by using alternative tillage methods to retain soil moisture (Howden et al. 2007) or by installing irrigation systems. Conversely, there is little one can do about heat stress, which has many negative implications for corn yields, Mexico's primary staple crop (Lobell and Field 2007, Keleman et al. 2009).

Internal migration in Mexico

Many scholars expect climate change to increase internal migration, as people move within, rather than across, borders (Bardsley and Hugo 2010). Recent trends in Mexican migration also suggest that much of the migration in Mexico is now domestic (Aguayo-Tellez and Martinez-Navarro 2013). Previous work in Mexico has largely neglected these types of movements, which makes sense given that internal migration was historically uncommon throughout much of Mexico (Whetten and Burnight 1956). Since the end of World War II, two key policy changes have led to increased population redistribution within Mexico. First, shortly after the end of the war, the Mexican government enacted steep tariffs on imported goods. This led to increased national investment as large-scale industries developed along the urban centers of Mexico City, Guadalajara, and Monterrey, attracting rural migrants seeking wage labor (Fussell 2004; Kunz Bolanos et al. 1996; Partida Bush 1993). The second major change was the market liberalization reforms implemented following the economic crisis in the 1980s, which increased foreign investment in the export processing areas close to the Mexico-U.S. border and shifted internal migration in that direction (MacLachlan and Aguilar 1998; Robertson 2004; Villarreal and Hamilton 2012).

There has been little research on environmental influences on migration within Mexico. Of the few that have, Nawrotzki et al. (2016) found that international migration was more strongly influenced by climate during the period 1986–1999 compared to internal migration. A recent study from Leyk et al. (2017) that used more refined rainfall measures from NASA's Tropical Rainfall Measuring Mission satellite found that municipal-level rainfall deficits influence *both* international and internal migration, especially from communities that rely heavily on rain-fed agriculture. Interestingly, this study finds that the relationship between precipitation deficits and internal movement is stronger for communities with irrigation; the precise reasons are unclear.

Another study from Nawrotzki et al. (2017) adds further nuance. Using the 2000 and 2010 Mexican censuses and climate data from the Terra Populus database (www.terrapop.org), the authors measured internal migration following extreme heat events and droughts. The authors found that each additional drought month increases internal rural-urban migration by 3.6 percent, which is in line with studies on climate-related international migration. Second, each additional high heat month decreased the odds of rural-urban internal migration by 1.0 percent. However, the authors find important nonlinearities in this relationship. For example, there appears to be a decrease in the odds of migration following heat stress, but after 34 months the relationship becomes positive, with further increases in heat resulting in increased rural-urban migration.

The three studies described in this section suggest there is indeed a relationship between climate and internal migration in Mexico, that there are similarities and differences in internal and international environmental migration in Mexico, and that there is the potential for non-linearity in migration after extreme climate events. They highlight the need for more research, particularly in light of studies that suggest that local employment and social networks strongly influence migrants' choices between internal versus international destinations (Lindstrom and Lauster 2001).

Conclusion

This chapter has reviewed the existing state of the literature regarding climate-migration in Mexico. Given the long history of international migration from Mexico to the United States, it is no surprise that previous research on the climate-migration relationship in Mexico has focused almost exclusively on international migration, showing that rainfall deficits are associated with increased emigration (Munshi 2003), especially from dry areas (Nawrotzki et al. 2013) and states with longstanding migration networks (Hunter et al. 2013). Much of this scholarship has examined migration from rural sending areas, a logical place to begin due to rural Mexico's dependence on rain-fed agriculture. Migration appears to be highest 2–3 years following climate shocks, indicating that migration is a short-term adaptation strategy in response to environmental stress (Nawrotzki and DeWaard 2016). Yet, social networks and access to social capital appear to mediate the relationship between climate and migration, with increased social networks suppressing rural sensitivity to climate variability (Nawrotzki et al. 2015c).

Scholarship on the climate-related influences of human migration in Mexico has burgeoned in the last few years, but important gaps remain. For example, there is less work that considers internal migration following climate shocks. This is problematic since much of the contemporary migration in Mexico is domestic (Aguayo-Tellez and Martinez-Navarro 2013), and scholars have noted how most people prefer to remain in place, or move short distances to limit the economic and social costs (Bodvarsson and Van den Berg 2009; Findlay 2011). Recent work from Nawrotzki et al. (2017) finds that drought increased rural-urban migration across the years 2000–2010, but future work is needed to confirm these trends. The long-term role of climate in both origin and destination is another potential avenue for future research, as internal moves appear to have increased the number of people exposed to extreme weather events in several urban destinations in coastal municipalities in Mexico (Runfola et al. 2016).

Migration to, and from, urban areas represents another area ripe for investigation. While the relationship between climate and migration is more complex and indirect for urban residents, it is important nonetheless. For example, extreme weather events can result in flooding damage to transportation infrastructure, buildings, and wastewater systems (Revi et al. 2014). Urban residents might also participate in employment in agricultural industries near the city, or work in factories that process agricultural outputs. As such, crop failures due to climate-related stressors in rural areas can impact urban livelihoods directly, or indirectly through decreased food supply and higher prices. Further, urban agriculture and food production has become an important survival strategy for the poor (e.g. Ngome and Foeken 2012). In peri-urban Toluca, for example, maize production is used as a buffer against economic shocks to non-farm income (Lerner et al. 2013). Finally, climate change-related declines in precipitation could stress urban water resources, negatively affecting residents and businesses (Connolly 1999; Romero-Lankao 2010), while increased temperatures might exacerbate the urban heat island effect (Adachi et al. 2012). Such changes could make urban areas less livable and less desirable for tourism – one of Mexico's most important economic sectors. Thus, future work on the climate-migration connection in urban areas will be vital in the coming years.

Previous research has also failed to explicitly examine gender differences in the relationship between climate-migration, a shortcoming not unique to the Mexican setting. Yet, previous studies suggest gendered differences in livelihood strategies across varied settings are linked to migration patterns (de Sherbinin et al. 2008; Henry et al. 2004). Moreover, men and women likely respond to climate variability and strain in different ways. Prior work has largely just controlled for gender, with few studies integrating gender into the primary analyses (Hunter and David 2011). A notable exception is Gray (2010) in rural Ecuador, which finds that access to land resources are important for migration. There is no comparable examination of the relationship between climate-migration-gender in the context of Mexico, even though there are large gender disparities in the Mexico-U.S. migration flow (Hamilton 2015).

Finally, future research should also aim to develop and utilize more nuanced climate measures. In using more precise measures of the "climate signal," one could better pinpoint when and where climate variability matters. For example, climate stress might matter most during particular months of the year, such that growing season and crop productivity predictors might better isolate the relationship between climate and migration. Qualitative scholarship also has an important part to play in this literature, as data collection in origin communities could help us better understand the motivations behind migration, and the impacts of climate and climate-related migration on those left behind. Overall, scholars have made great strides in better understanding the environmental correlates of Mexican migration, but there is still so much yet to be done.

Acknowledgments

This research has benefited from research, administrative, and computing support provided by the University of Colorado Population Center (Project 2P2CHD066613–06), funded by the

Eunice Kennedy Shriver National Institute of Child Health and Human Development. The content is solely the responsibility of the authors and does not necessarily represent the official views of the CUPC or NIH. This material is also based upon work supported by the National Science Foundation Graduate Research Fellowship Program. Any opinions, findings, and conclusions or recommendations expressed in this material are those of the author and do not necessarily reflect the views of the National Science Foundation. The author would also like to thank the anonymous reviewer for helpful comments in preparing this chapter.

References

Adachi SA, Kimura F, Kusaka H, Inoue T, Ueda H (2012) Comparison of the impact of global climate changes and urbanization on summertime future climate in the Tokyo metropolitan area. *Journal of Applied Meteorology and Climatology* 51:2074–2075. doi:10.1175/jamc-d-12–0246.1

Adger WN (2003). Social capital, collective action, and adaptation to climate change. *Economic geography*, 79(4), pp. 387–404.

Aguayo-Téllez E, Martínez-Navarro J (2013). Internal and international migration in Mexico: 1995–2000. *Applied Economics*, 45(13), 1647–1661.

Alscher S (2010). Environmental factors in Mexican migration: The cases of Chiapas and Tlaxcala. In *Environment, forced migration and social vulnerability* (pp. 171–185). Springer Berlin Heidelberg.

Appendini K, Liverman D (1994). 'Agricultural policy, Climate Change and Food Security in Mexico', *Food Policy* 19, 149–164.

Auffhammer M, Vincent JR (2012). Unobserved time effects confound the identification of climate change impacts. *Proceedings of the National Academy of Sciences*, 109(30), pp. 11973–11974.

Bardsley DK, Hugo GJ (2010). Migration and climate change: examining thresholds of change to guide effective adaptation decision-making. *Population and Environment*, 32(2–3), 238–262. doi:10.1007/s11111-010-0126-9.

Barrios Puente, G, Perez F, and Gitter RJ, (2016). The Effect of Rainfall on Migration from Mexico to the United States. *International Migration Review*, 50(4), pp. 890–909.

Black R, Adger, WN, Arnell NW, Dercon S, Geddes A, Thomas DS (2011). The effect of environmental change on human migration. *Global Environmental Change-Human and Policy Dimensions*, 21, S3–S11. doi:10.1016/j.gloenvcha.2011.10.001.

Bodvarsson ÖB, Van den Berg, H (2009). *The economics of immigration*. Springer, Heidelberg, Germany.

Boyd R, Ibarraran ME (2009) Extreme climate events and adaptation: an exploratory analysis of drought in Mexico. *Environ Dev Econ* 14:371–395. doi:10.1017/s1355770x08004956

Calavita K (1992). Inside the state: The bracero program, immigration, and the I.N.S. New York: Routledge.

Carr DL, Lopez AC, Bilsborrow RE (2009) The population, agriculture, and environment nexus in Latin America: country-level evidence from the latter half of the twentieth century. *Population and Environment* 30:222–246. doi:10.1007/s11111-009-0090-4

Christensen JH, Hesselbjerg J, Kanikicharla K, Marshall G, Turner J (2013) Climate phenomena and their relevance for future regional climate change. In: Stocker TF, Qin D, Plattner GK, Tignor M, Allen SK, Boschung J, Nauels A, Xia Y, Bex V, Midgley PM (eds) Climate change 2013: The physical science basis. Contribution of Working Group I to the fifth assessment report of the Intergovernmental Panel on Climate Change. Cambridge University Press, New York, pp 1217–1308

Collins M, Knutti R, Arblaster J, Dufresne JL, Fichefet T, Friedlingstein P, Gao X, Gutowski WJ, Johns T, Krinner G, Shongwe M, Tebaldi C, Weaver AJ, Wehner M (2013) Long-term climate change: projections, commitments and irreversibility. In: Stocker TF, Qin D, Plattner GK, Tignor M, Allen SK, Boschung J, Nauels A, Xia Y, Bex V, Midgley PM (eds) Climate change 2013: the physical science basis. Contribution of working group I to the fifth assessment report of the Intergovernmental Panel on Climate Change. Cambridge University Press, New York, pp. 1029–1136

Connolly P (1999) Mexico City: our common future? *Environ Urban* 11:53–78. doi:10.1177/095624789901100116

Cornelius WA (1992). From sojourners to settlers: The changing profile of Mexican migration to the United States. In J. A. Bustamante, C. W. Reynolds, & R. A. Hinojosa Ojeda (Eds.), U.S.-Mexico relations: Labor market interdependence (pp. 155–195). Stanford, CA: Stanford University Press.

Curran SR, Rivero-Fuentes E (2003) Engendering migrant networks: The case of Mexican migration. *Demography* 40:289–307. doi:10.2307/3180802

de Janvry A, Sadoulet E (2001) Income strategies among rural households in Mexico: The role of off- farm activities. *World Dev* 29:467–480

de Sherbinin A, VanWey LK, McSweeney K, Aggarwal R, Barbieri A, Henry S, Walker R (2008). Rural household demographics, livelihoods and the environment. *Global environmental change*, *18*(1), 38–53.

Dow K, Berkhout F, Preston BL, Klein RJT, Midgley G, Shaw MR (2013). Commentary: Limits to adaptation. *Nature Climate Change*, 3(4), 305–307.

Durand J, Arias P (2000). La experiencia migrante: Iconografia de la migracion Mexico-Estados Unidos. Xalapa, Mexico: Altexto.

Durand, J, Massey DS, Zenteno RM (2001). Mexican immigration to the United States: Continuities and changes. *Latin American research review*, pp. 107–127.

Eakin, H (2000). Smallholder maize production and climatic risk: a case study from Mexico. *Climatic change*, *45*(1), pp. 19–36.

Eakin H (2005) Institutional change, climate risk, and rural vulnerability: Cases from central Mexico. *World Dev 33:1923–1938. doi:10.1016/j.worlddev.2005.06.005*

Endfield GH (2007) Archival explorations of climate variability and social vulnerability in colonial Mexico. *Climatic Change* 83:9–38. doi:10.1007/s10584-006-9125-3

Feng S, Krueger AB, Oppenheimer M (2010). Linkages among climate change, crop yields and Mexico–US cross-border migration. *Proceedings of the National Academy of Sciences*, *107*(32), pp. 14257–14262.

Feng S, Oppenheimer M (2012) Applying statistical models to the climate-migration relationship. *Proc Natl Acad Sci* 109:E2915

Findlay AM (2011). Migrant destinations in an era of environmental change. *Global Environmental Change*, *21*, S50-S58.

Fussell E (2004) Sources of Mexico's migration stream: Rural, urban, and border migrants to the United States. *Soc Forces* 82:937–967. doi:10.1353/sof.2004.0039

Fussell E, Massey DS (2004). The limits to cumulative causation: International migration from Mexican urban areas. *Demography*, 41(1), 151–171.

Gonzalez-Barrera A (2015). More Mexicans leaving than coming to the US. *Pew Research Center*, *19*.

Gray CL (2010). Gender, natural capital, and migration in the southern Ecuadorian Andes. *Environment and Planning A*, *42*(3), 678–696.

Gray CL, Mueller V (2012). Natural disasters and population mobility in Bangladesh. *Proceedings of the National Academy of Sciences*, 109(16), 6000–6005. doi:10.1073/pnas.1115944109.

Halliday T (2006). Migration, risk, and liquidity constraints in El Salvador. *Economic development and cultural change*, *54*(4), pp. 893–925.

Hamilton, ER (2015). Gendered disparities in Mexico-US migration by class, ethnicity, and geography. *Demographic Research*, *32*, 533.

Henry, S, Schoumaker B, Beauchemin C. (2004). The impact of rainfall on the first out-migration: A multi-level event-history analysis in Burkina Faso. *Population & Environment*, *25*(5), 423–460.

Hondagneu-Sotelo P (1994). *Gendered transitions: Mexican experiences of immigration*. Univ of California Press.

Howden SM, Soussana JF, Tubiello FN, Chhetri N, Dunlop M, Meinke H (2007). Adapting agriculture to climate change. *Proceedings of the National Academy of Sciences*, 104(50), 19691–19696. doi:10.1073/pnas.0701890104.

Hunter LM, Murray S, Riosmena F (2013) Rainfall patterns and U.S. migration from rural Mexico. *International Migration Review* 47:874–909

Hunter LM, David E (2011). Displacement, climate change and gender. *Migration and climate change*, 306–330.

IPCC (2013) Summary for Policymakers. In: Stocker TF, Qin D, Plattner GK, Tignor M, Allen SK, Boschung J, Nauels A, Xia Y, Bex V, Midgley PM (eds) Climate Change 2013: The Physical Science Basis. Contribution of Working Group I to the Fifth Assessment Report of the Intergovernmental Panel on Climate Change. Cambridge University Press, Cambridge, United Kingdom, pp 1–30

Kandel W, Parrado EA (2005). Restructuring of the US meat processing industry and new Hispanic migrant destinations. *Population and Development Review, 31*(3), pp. 447–471.

Keleman A, Hellin J, Bellon MR (2009). Maize diversity, rural development policy, and farmers' practices: lessons from Chiapas, Mexico. *Geographical Journal*, 175, 52–70. doi:10.1111/j.1475–4959. 2008.00314.x.

Koziell I, Saunders J (2001). *Living off biodiversity: Exploring livelihoods and biodiversity issues in natural resources management.*

Kunz Bolanos I, Valverde CV, Gonzalez JS (1996). "Cambios en la Estructura Ierarquica del Sistema Nacional de Asentamientos de Mexico." Estudios Demograficos y Urbanos 11:139–71.

Lerner, AM, Eakin H, Sweeney S. (2013). Understanding peri-urban maize production through an examination of household livelihoods in the Toluca Metropolitan Area, Mexico. *Journal of Rural Studies, 30*, 52–63.

Leyk S, Runfola D, Nawrotzki RJ, Hunter LM, Riosmena F (2017). Internal and International Mobility as Adaptation to Climatic Variability in Contemporary Mexico: Evidence from the Integration of Census and Satellite Data. *Population, Space and Place.*

Lindstrom DP, Lauster N (2001). Local economic opportunity and the competing risks of internal and US migration in Zacatecas, Mexico. *International Migration Review, 35*(4), pp. 1232–1256.

Lobell DB, Field CB (2007). Global scale climate — crop yield relationships and the impacts of recent warming. *Environmental Research Letters*, 2(1), 1–7. doi:10.1088/1748–9326/2/1/014002.

Lucas RE, Stark O (1985). Motivations to remit: Evidence from Botswana. *Journal of Political Economy, 93*(5), pp. 901–918.

MacLachlan I, Aguilar AG (1998) Maquiladora myths: Locational and structural change in Mexico's export manufacturing industry. *Professional Geographer* 50:315–331. doi:10.1111/0033–0124.00123

Martin P, Midgley E (2010). Immigration in America 2010. *Population Bulletin Update*, pp. 1–6.

Massey DS, Arango J, Hugo G, Kouaouci A, Pellegrino A, Taylor JE (1993) Theories of international migration — A review and appraisal. *Population and Development Review*, 19:431–466

Massey, DS, España FG (1987). The social process of international migration. *Science, 237*(4816), pp. 733–738.

Massey DS, Durand J, Malone NJ (2002). Beyond smoke and mirrors: Mexican immigration in an era of economic integration. New York: Russell Sage Foundation Publications.

Massey DS, Espinosa KE (1997). What's driving Mexico-US migration? A theoretical, empirical, and policy analysis. *American Journal of Sociology*, 102(4), 939–999. doi:10.1086/231037.

Massey DS, Riosmena F (2010). Undocumented migration from Latin America in an era of rising U.S. enforcement. *Annals of the American Academy of Political and Social Science*, 630, 294–321.

Massey DS, Sana M (2003). Patterns of US migration from Mexico, the Caribbean, and Central America. *Migraciones Internacionales, 2*(2).

McKenzie D, Rapoport H (2007). Network effects and the dynamics of migration and inequality: theory and evidence from Mexico. *Journal of Development Economics, 84*(1), pp. 1–24.

McLeman RA (2011). Settlement abandonment in the context of global environmental change. *Global Environmental Change*, 21, S108–S120.

McSweeney C, New M, Lizcano G (2008) UNDP climate change country profiles: Mexico. United Nations Development Programme, New York.

Meze-Hausken E (2000). Migration caused by climate change: how vulnerable are people inn dryland areas?. *Mitigation and Adaptation Strategies for Global Change*, 5(4), pp. 379–406.

Mueller, V., Gray, C. L., & Kosec, K. (2014). Heat stress increases long-term human migration in rural Pakistan. *Nature Climate Change*, 4(3), 182–185. doi:10.1038/nclimate2103.

Munshi, K. (2003). Networks in the modern economy: Mexican migrants in the US labor market. *The Quarterly Journal of Economics, 118*(2), 549–599.

Nawrotzki RJ, Riosmena F, Hunter LM (2013) Do rainfall deficits predict U.S.-bound migration from rural Mexico? Evidence from the Mexican census. *Population Research and Policy Review* 32:129–158. doi:10.1007/s11113-012-9251-8

Nawrotzki RJ, Riosmena F, Hunter LM, Runfola DM (2015a). Undocumented migration in response to climate change. *International Journal of Population Studies*, 1(1), p. 60.

Nawrotzki RJ, Hunter LM, Runfola DM, Riosmena F (2015b). Climate change as a migration driver from rural and urban Mexico. *Environmental Research Letters*, 10(11), 114023.

Nawrotzki RJ, Riosmena F, Hunter LM, Runfola DM (2015c). Amplification or suppression: Social networks and the climate change–migration association in rural Mexico. *Global Environmental Change*, 35, 463–474.

Nawrotzki RJ, DeWaard J (2016). Climate shocks and the timing of migration from Mexico. *Population and Environment*, 38(1), 72–100.

Nawrotzki RJ, Runfola DM, Hunter LM, Riosmena F (2016). Domestic and International Climate Migration from Rural Mexico. *Human Ecology*, 6(44), pp. 687–699.

Nawrotzki RJ, DeWaard J, Bakhtsiyarava M, Ha JT (2017). Climate shocks and rural-urban migration in Mexico: exploring nonlinearities and thresholds. *Climatic Change*, 140(2), 243–258.

Ngome, I, Foeken D (2012). "My garden is a great help": gender and urban gardening in Buea, Cameroon. *GeoJournal*, 77(1), 103–118.

Partida Bush V (1993) Niveles y tendencias de la migración interna en México a partir de las cifras censales, 1970–1990. *Revista Mexicana de Sociología*, 55:155–176

Passel JS, Cohn DV (2011). *Unauthorized immigrant population: National and state trends, 2010* (p. 31). Washington, DC: Pew Hispanic Center.

Revi A, Satterthwaite DE, Aragon-Durand F, Corfee-Morlot J, Kiunsi R, Pelling M, Roberts DC, Solecki W (2014). Urban Areas. Intergovernmental Panel on Climate Change. (2014). *Climate Change 2014 Impacts, Adaptation and Vulnerability: Regional Aspects*. Cambridge University Press.

Riosmena F, Massey DS (2012). Pathways to El Norte: origins, destinations, and characteristics of Mexican migrants to the United States. *International Migration Review*, 46(1), pp. 3–36.

Robertson R (2004) Relative prices and wage inequality: evidence from Mexico. *Journal of International Economics* 64:387–409. doi:10.1016/j.jinteco.2003.06.003

Romero-Lankao P (2010) Water in Mexico City: what will climate change bring to its history of water-related hazards and vulnerabilities? *Environment and Urbanization* 22:157–178. doi:10.1177/0956247809362636

Runfola DM, Romero-Lankao P, Jiang L, Hunter LM, Nawrotzki RJ, Sanchez L (2016). The influence of internal migration on exposure to extreme weather events in Mexico. *Society & Natural Resources*, 29(6), pp. 750–754.

Saldana-Zorrilla SO, Sandberg K (2009) Spatial econometric model of natural disaster impacts on human migration in vulnerable regions of Mexico. *Disasters* 33:591–607. doi:10.1111/j.0361–3666.2008.01089.x

Schmidt K (2016). Social Inequality and International Migration Related to Climate Stressors: The Case of Mexico. In *Environmental Migration and Social Inequality* (pp. 117–128). Springer International Publishing.

Schmidt-Verkerk K (2010). 'Buscando la vida'–How Do Perceptions of Increasingly Dry Weather Affect Migratory Behaviour in Zacatecas, Mexico?. In *Environment, forced migration and social vulnerability* (pp. 99–113). Springer Berlin Heidelberg.

Schoper JB, Lambert RJ, Vasilas BL (1987). Pollen viability, pollen shedding, and combining ability for tassel heat tolerance in maize. *Crop Science*, 27(1), pp. 27–31.

Stark O, Bloom DE (1985) The new economics of labor migration. *Am Econ Rev* 75:173–178

Villarreal A (2014). Explaining the decline in Mexico-US migration: The effect of the Great Recession. *Demography*, 51(6), pp. 2203–2228.

Villarreal A, Hamilton ER (2012). Rush to the border? Market liberalization and urban- and rural-origin internal migration in Mexico. *Social Science Research* 41:1275–1291. doi:10.1016/j.ssresearch.2012.02.007

Whetten NL, Burnight RG (1956) Internal migration in Mexico. *Rural Sociology* 21:140–151.

Wiggins S, Keilbach N, Preibisch K, Proctor S, Herrejon GR, Munoz GR (2002) Discussion - Agricultural policy reform and rural livelihoods in central Mexico. *Journal of Development Studies* 38:179–202. doi:1 0.1080/00220380412331322461

Winters P, Davis B, Corral L (2002) Assets, activities and income generation in rural Mexico: factoring in social and public capital. *Agricultural Economics* 27:139–156

World Bank. (2009). Mexico — Country Note on Climate Change Aspects in Agriculture. *Country Note on Climate Change Aspects in Agriculture*. Washington, DC. © World Bank. https://openknowledge.worldbank.org/handle/10986/9478 License: CC BY 3.0 IGO.

21

Transnational approaches to remittances, risk reduction, and disaster relief

Evidence from post-Typhoon Haiyan experiences of Filipino immigrants in Canada

Reiko Obokata and Luisa Veronis

Introduction

When Typhoon Haiyan (known locally as Typhoon Yolanda) struck the Philippines in November 2013, Filipino communities globally came together to contribute to disaster relief efforts through organizing fundraisers, or sending money and care packages (Chu and Jordan 2013; Esmaquel II 2014). In Canada, an estimated CAD $40 million was raised in the two weeks following the typhoon (Government of Canada 2013), and this amount only takes into account relief funds that flowed through official channels. The remittances provided by migrant communities are frequently discussed as a positive force for community development and for disaster recovery, seen by some as the answer to lifting migrants' home communities out of poverty, regardless of whether the evidence points to long-term developmental potential (see Castaneda 2013; de Haas 2005; Faist 2008). This chapter highlights how a transnational approach (see Levitt and Jaworsky 2007; Pessar and Mahler 2003; Yeoh and Ramdas 2014) to studying the environment-migration link is useful for better understanding the role that international migration plays in reducing environmental risk and vulnerability in migrants' home communities. In particular, it discusses the ways that remittances sent by international migrants help households and communities in the Philippines both reduce their environmental risk and recover after major disasters. Much like other socio-economic factors – e.g., social class, networks, land ownership and household size (Obokata et al. 2014) – being part of a transnational migrant household influences whether people migrate away from environmental risk. Specifically, having a member abroad who sends remittances can add to the resiliency of family members affected by environmental problems in the place of origin and provide more options to make mobility decisions, from the ability to stay home, to the ability to evacuate when needed. At the same time, it is important to note that a heavy burden is often placed on transnational migrants who feel an obligation to support their families and communities due to the neglect or corruption of their home governments, a situation that is amplified following major disasters such as Typhoon Haiyan. Moreover, emerging evidence suggests that remittances may serve to re-inscribe stratifications between migrant and non-migrant households, where those that had the capital to send a family member abroad in the first place are also those most able to cope in the face of environmental change and natural disasters.

The concept 'transnational social fields' has proved useful for untangling these transnational dynamics; it serves to highlight that the act of migration involves not only the individual who moves, but also non-migrant members of households (Carling 2008; Huang et al. 2008; Parrenas 2005), and the people and landscapes of wider communities in both origin and destination (Jackson et al. 2004; McKay 2005; Moran-Taylor and Taylor 2010). By taking into account the multiple social and spatial connections that migrants maintain and develop throughout the entire process of migration and settlement, scholars of environmental migration will be better equipped to understand the complexities of the mobility-immobility spectrum in the context of environmental challenges (see Black et al. 2013). To illustrate such ideas, we draw upon evidence from an exploratory study with newcomers (i.e., those arrived within the past 10 years) from the Philippines undertaken in Ottawa, Canada between December 2013 and March 2014. Data collection involved two key informant interviews with community leaders, and four focus groups and nine semi-structured personal interviews with Filipino immigrants, for a total of twenty-five participants. Participants' home communities in the Philippines ranged from all three major regions – Luzon, Visayas, and Mindanao. The findings of this study are presented for the first time in this chapter.

Remittances and risk reduction

Researchers have debated whether migrants' remittances should be considered a successful or sustainable form of development assistance as opposed to a form of conspicuous consumption (see Castaneda 2013; de Haas 2005; Faist 2008). Others have suggested that remittances can play a role in mitigating the environmental risk of family members who stay behind, thus aligning with those who see remittances as contributing to more than conspicuous consumption. In Vietnam, for example, it was found that because remittance income is generally not dependent on local environmental conditions, receiving remittances could assist in livelihood stability and risk reduction (Adger 1999). A study in Burkina Faso and Ghana found that households that receive international remittances have increased resiliency during natural disasters because of home improvements and greater access to communications (Mohapatra et al. 2012).

Our research similarly indicates that remittances sent from Canada to the Philippines during and after Typhoon Haiyan were used for risk reduction, and moreover, were used in some cases as a means to eliminate the need for the household to evacuate or re-locate. We were able to identify specifically how the relatives of Canadian Filipinos reacted to Typhoon Haiyan and how remittances from Canada were used by individual recipient households. In many cases, family members and friends evacuated temporarily to local public buildings, such as churches, while others traveled to Manila to shelter with relatives; but virtually all quickly returned home to rebuild. Few considered moving away permanently.[1] In these cases, for migrant households in the Philippines, remittances from family members play a role in reducing their vulnerability to environmental events and in increasing their ability to return home and rebuild afterward. For example, remittances from one of our participants allowed her relatives to build a second floor on their house so that they could go somewhere safe during almost monthly flooding incidents in their home. Whereas previously they had gone to a relative's home on higher ground when typhoons and flooding occurred, her remittances allowed the family to stay put. Now when it floods, she says, "they're OK . . . I tell them never mind the stuff, just go upstairs."

While remittances can play a role in making home improvements that reduce environmental risk, the literature is conflicting when it comes to the influence of land ownership; in some locations it increases the possibility of migrating, and in others it does not (Obokata et al. 2014). Land ownership should therefore not be considered a sole determinant of whether a household or individual migrates (whether temporarily or permanently); other factors such as geographical context, education levels, and social networks must also be taken into account. This is also the case when investigating the environmental risk of remittance-receiving households who own land or property. Existing research shows that overall, remittance-receiving households are better able to cope with environmental problems such as flooding and natural disasters (Adger 1999; Mohapatra et al. 2012; Predo 2010), but it is important to note that this ability is linked not only to the higher income provided by remittances, but also to factors such as education levels. That is, financial capital can contribute to increasing households' resilience when combined with human capital. One example is Predo's (2010) research in Ormoc, Philippines. He found that the higher a household's education level, annual income, and total landholding, the lower the household's vulnerability, which was in line with his predictions. However, contrary to expectation, he also found that vulnerability to flooding actually increased with house size, and that those with larger houses were those where one member of the family was working or living overseas (i.e., remittance-receiving households). Although existing research suggests that being part of a migrant household leads to risk reduction, this finding illuminates that this may only be the case insofar as having a family member overseas correlates to raising a household's level of education and annual income (or having higher levels of each to begin with). Indeed, migrant households who invest in bigger houses may potentially be increasing their exposure and vulnerability to extreme events.

The need to view home or land ownership as just one variable among others when assessing mobility outcomes and environmental risk was evident in our research. A participant who had previously worked as membership manager for a large humanitarian and disaster relief organization in the Philippines described two contrasting responses in the face of natural disasters depending on access to financial, social and human capital. On one hand, she explained that many Filipinos refuse to leave their homes in advance of typhoons because they are scared of leaving their possessions – an example where property ownership can impede mobility or migration, and decrease safety and security. Another participant, whose family lives in an area frequently affected by typhoons and whose family had helped evacuation efforts during Typhoon Haiyan, elaborated on the decision – and risk – of remaining at home this way: "they do not want to leave their house because that's the only place that they have. They go upstairs, they put their things upstairs, [but] then when the house is gone, everybody's gone." In contrast, the first participant described the following order she gave to her teenage sons who live without her in Cavite (a province adjacent to Manila):

> When I was talking to them during the typhoon wherein our floor almost got flooded, I told them, 'Don't even wait for the water to rise! You have to get out of that place, secure yourself, go to higher grounds! Just leave everything, just close the house, your safety is more important.'

These anecdotes suggest that property ownership may not be the determining factor in the decision to evacuate; rather, it is likely access to financial capital from remittances, along with human capital gained through formal education and experiential knowledge, that encourages some families to temporarily relocate. Furthermore, as international migrants residing in Canada, the participants' own perspectives of safety may have changed and had effects on the way they viewed their families' situations in the Philippines and encouraged them to respond.

A transnational perspective shows that environmental risk reduction is carried out both by household members who reside at home and those who reside abroad, and broadens our understanding of the factors that influence a household's actions in the face of flooding and disasters. Moreover, while remittances are a significant determining factor in the possible actions taken, it is necessary to look not just at the financial capital that is used by migrant households, but also the human capital.

Remittances and disaster relief: Typhoon Haiyan

Recent research has celebrated remittances as a "powerful mechanism to face disasters" (Le De et al. 2015: 668) because of their role in enabling households to quickly increase their security; to more specifically target community needs than does outside relief aid; and to increase empowerment because the money comes from within the (transnational) community. Disaster relief aid is perceived as important both by those who send and receive it, but emerging research also suggests that we must be wary of the burden that may be placed on migrants to solve all the problems of their households and communities, particularly in the face of state corruption (see Hammond 2010). Enthusiasm for the remarkable impact of remittances is warranted, but so is the need for caution in advocating remittances as a panacea.

This tension was evident in our research. Contributing to disaster relief was perceived as an important action for nearly all of the study participants, who each participated in relief efforts for Typhoon Haiyan and for other typhoons in the past. One of them put the reason for community action this way:

> Filipino communities in general, when big disasters happen, they really feel bad, whether they have family members that are affected or not, they feel almost obligated. Maybe they're thinking like, "Hey we're living here really well, I mean, not even wealthy, but we don't get floods and disasters here, I'm sure we can give some of our money, we can really help." And so, whether it's through church or other organizations, they just get together and at least give financially, directly to family members or to organizations or churches.

Acts of generosity by overseas Filipinos go beyond simple fundraising and should be seen as attempts to overcome institutional inadequacies at home. As one participant whose family was "back to zero" after Typhoon Haiyan put it: "all [the destruction] is still there, nobody's cleaned it because politicians, they're not helping others, they're just helping themselves." Another expanded: "even [to get] rice, just a little bit of Asian rice, [officials ask:] 'Did you vote? Did you vote for me?' If your name isn't there [on their list] you don't get anything."

This dynamic raises an important dialectic in the relationship between disasters and remittances. Without remittances, people affected by disasters may not receive the help they need from more official channels, but on the other hand, the assistance provided by remittances lets the government off the hook for providing for the needs of its citizens; responsibility for coping with disasters and managing risk is left up to the migrants and the international community. According to some of our study participants, this tactic is not even covert. One participant explained that her family did not receive relief aid following Typhoon Haiyan because government officials knew that they had family in Canada, and the assumption was that they would be receiving help from abroad. Being part of a migrant household thus does not always lead to risk reduction; in fact, it may increase the risk of those who stay behind, especially in the short-term after disasters when infrastructure is not in place to receive boxes and money from relatives, or for families whose relatives abroad are simply unable or unwilling to remit. Moreover, the stress placed on migrants to send money home leads to its own personal challenges. The pastor of a Filipino church in Ottawa described how a number of members of his congregation were crumbling under the weight of the enormous pressure they felt to send more and more money home, at a time when they themselves were struggling socially and economically to integrate into Canadian society. This burden, which is often hidden, reminds us that it may not be desirable to advocate remittances as the ideal solution for risk reduction and disaster relief, but to consider them as just one factor among others that can help communities in times of need.

Discussion

These results point to a number of significant issues and illuminate fruitful areas for future research. First, remittances from transnational Filipino migrants are playing a role in reducing the environmental risk of family members in the Philippines through home additions and/or by providing the financial security to evacuate homes without the overwhelming fear of losing property. This finding suggests that transnational migrant households may have more resilience in the face of environmental problems and that access to remittances may be one piece that influences potential migration decisions in the face of environmental challenges. At the same time, it is important to note that levels of human capital are also important in reducing environmental risk, and that families who are able to send one member abroad typically have more access to both financial and human capital even before migration occurs (Obokata et al. 2014; Stalker 2008). Nonetheless, future research on environmentally related migration should strive to consider the role of remittances in influencing mobility outcomes, whether on the potential to evacuate temporarily, re-locate more permanently, or to stay put.

It is also important to consider the plight of households that do not have a family member abroad. Given that migrant households are generally those that have some social, human, and/or economic capital in the first place, we must ask: are even deeper stratifications being created between migrant and non-migrant households when faced with environmental challenges? The complexity of transnational migration in both contributing to environmental risk reduction and relief through remittances – although not necessarily in the short term, as per one of the previous anecdotes – and to potentially creating deeper divisions between the haves and the have-nots merits further consideration. A promising area for future research would be to investigate differential mobility outcomes of environmental change on migrant households with access to remittances vs. non-migrant households with less access to capital.

While the impact of remittances is overwhelmingly positive for households that receive them, the conditions for their need are complicated. On one hand, the act of sending remittances allows migrants to be active agents in the process of securing, re-building and strengthening the homes and lives of their loved ones when re-building efforts would be much slower without them; yet on the other, the need for family and community members to receive remittances places responsibility squarely on migrants' shoulders to address the problems plaguing their home communities, letting governments eschew their responsibilities. This complicates the idea that remittances contribute to long-term development because it is necessary to weigh the benefits to transnational families and communities with the burdens that are simultaneously placed on them. Moreover, the idea of long-term development must take into account the non-migrant households who may not be receiving remittances and question whether imbalances are being created within the transnational community.

While exploratory, this research demonstrates that a transnational approach provides a useful framework for studying the environment-migration link. In the past, much literature has focused on environmental factors as "push or pull" variables, but transnationalism helps us view migration as a process in which multiple connections are maintained between the places of origin and destination, with insights into environmental risk reduction, disaster recovery, and migration outcomes for those that stay behind. This study also provides the groundwork for future research to investigate remittances as a complex variable in the environment-migration nexus.

Note

1 Readers are encouraged to compare this chapter with Chapter 22 by Elizabeth Fussell on post-Hurricane Katrina migration in this volume.

References

Adger W. N. (1999) "Social vulnerability to climate change and extremes in coastal Vietnam" World Development, 27(2) 249–269

Black R. Arnell N.W. Adger W. N. Thomas D. and Geddes A. (2013) "Migration, immobility and displacement outcomes following extreme events" Environmental Science and Policy 27S S32–S43

Carling J. (2008) "The human dynamics of migrant transnationalism" Ethnic and Racial Studies, 31(8) 1452–1477

Castaneda E. (2013) "Living in limbo: Transnational households, remittances and development" International Migration, 51(S1) e13–e35

Chu K. and Jordan M. (2013, Dec 1) "Philippine Typhoon Spurs Diaspora to Action — Overseas Filipinos Scramble to Aid Unreached Areas" The Wall Street Journal. (http://online.wsj.com/news/articles/SB10001424052702304355104579231290489111850) Accessed 1 September 2014

de Haas H. (2005) "International migration, remittances and development: Myths and facts" Third World Quarterly, 26(8) 1269–1284

Esmaquel II P. (2014, Apr 11) Canada on Haiyan: We helped because of Filipino-Canadians. Rappler. (www.rappler.com/nation/55258-canada-yolanda-haiyan-aid-filipino-canadians) Accessed 1 September 2014

Faist T. (2008) "Migrants as transnational development agents: An inquiry into the newest round of the migration-development nexus" Population, Space and Place, 14 21–42

Government of Canada (2013) Typhoon Haiyan – Questions and Answers. (www.international.gc.ca/development-developpement/humanitarian_response-situations_crises/haiyan/qa-qr.aspx#a14) Accessed 2 September 2014

Hammond L. (2010) "Obliged to give: Remittances and the maintenance of transnational networks between Somalis and home and abroad" Bildhaan: An International Journal of Somali Studies, 10 125–151

Huang S. Yeoh B. S. A. Lam T. (2008) "Asian transnational families in transition: The liminality of simultaneity" International Migration, 46(4) 3–13

Jackson P. Crang P. and Dwyer C. (2004) "Introduction: The spaces of transnationality" in Jackson P Crang P and Dwyer C eds. Transnational Spaces Routledge, New York 1–23

Le De L. Gaillard J. C. Friesen W. and Matautia Smith F. (2015) "Remittances in the face of disasters: A case study of rural Samoa" Environment, Development and Sustainability, 17(3) 653–672

Levitt P. and Jaworsky B.D. (2007) "Transnational migration studies: Past developments and future trends" Annual Review of Sociology, 33 129–156

McKay D. (2005) "Reading remittance landscapes: Female migration and agricultural transition in the Philippines" Geografisk Tidsskrift: Danish Journal of Geography, 105(1) 89–99

Mohapatra S. Joseph G. and Ratha D. (2012) "Remittances and natural disasters: ex-post response and contribution to ex-ante preparedness" Environment, Development and Sustainability, 14 365–387

Moran-Taylor M. J. and Taylor M. J. (2010) "Land and lena: Linking transnational migration, natural resources, and the environment in Guatemala" Population and Environment, 32 198–215

Obokata R.Veronis L. and McLeman R. (2014) "Empirical research on international environmental migration: a systematic review" Population and Environment, 36(1) 111–135

Parrenas R. (2005) "Long distance intimacy: Class, gender and intergenerational relations between mothers and children in Filipino transnational families" Global Networks, 5(4) 317–336

Pessar P. R. and Mahler S. J. (2003) "Transnational migration: Bringing gender in" International Migration Review, 37(3) 812–846

Predo C. (2010) "Adaptation of community and households to climate-related disaster: The case of storm surge and flooding experience in Ormoc and Cabalian Bay, Philippines" Economy and Environment Program for Southeast Asia: Climate Change Technical Reports

Stalker P. (2008) The no-nonsense guide to international migration, second edition Between the Lines, Toronto

Yeoh B. and Ramdas K. (2014) "Gender, migration, mobility and transnationalism" Gender, Place and Culture, 21(10) 1197–1213

22

Population displacements and migration patterns in response to Hurricane Katrina

Elizabeth Fussell

Introduction

Hurricane Katrina struck New Orleans and the Gulf Coast on August 29, 2005 and produced multiple migratory responses. First, it generated a large-scale evacuation of residents, some who left in anticipation of the storm's arrival, others in its wake. The widespread destruction of housing and infrastructure meant that many residents could not return to their homes for weeks or months, and some had no home left to which they could return. Consequently, return migration, a second type of migration, constituted a distinct migratory response that varied in its timing. Finally, new in-migration occurred as labor market sectors related to post-disaster recovery attracted workers. This churning of the population after a disaster is not unusual, but the scale of destruction wrought by Hurricane Katrina made it more visible, allowing researchers to collect and analyze data that shed light on the relationship between extreme environmental events and population mobility.

Although the slow recovery of New Orleans and other affected areas provide clear evidence that residents remained displaced for multiple years, many research activities ended after the first year. A few qualitative studies have investigated migration decision-making among householders affected by Hurricane Katrina (Fussell 2012; Litt 2012; Weber & Peek 2012). However, the goal of making generalizable conclusions about this environmental event and the people it set in motion is hampered by the lack of representative data following residents' migration trajectories over a longer period. Consequently, two questions remain unanswered. First, where are the New Orleanians who did not return after Hurricane Katrina? Second, who are the displaced New Orleanians? Answers to these descriptive questions can then be followed by investigations into why people returned or not, and the extent to which these environmentally related migrations were voluntary or compelled.

Several considerations should be noted before proceeding. First, most empirical research focuses on the City of New Orleans, the largest population center affected by Hurricane Katrina, and to a lesser extent the surrounding metropolitan area. This review reflects that geographic focus. Second, as already mentioned, very little research has been done on long-term population mobility since representative data on individuals and their residential mobility over multiple years are scarce due to logistical challenges in data collection. Therefore, long-term research mainly focuses on population recovery in New Orleans, including both returnees and newcomers, and neglecting those who did not return. Finally, migration in response to Hurricane Katrina, like any disaster, is produced by three factors: the hazard event, the susceptibility of the exposed place to that hazard, and the social vulnerability of the population living in that place (Wisner et al., 2004: 52). Therefore, what happened in New Orleans is not likely to be duplicated precisely in other places exposed to hurricanes or other hazardous events because each of these factors will differ. However, the social patterns observed after this extreme event point to important questions to be investigated and provide broader insights into environmental displacement and migration more generally.

The disaster and its effects on New Orleans' population

Hurricane Katrina set people in motion before it made landfall. About 70 percent of residents in the City of New Orleans[1] evacuated on their own in anticipation of Katrina's landfall (Elliott & Pais 2006). After Katrina's storm surge breached the levee system and flooded the below-sea-level city, most remaining residents were evacuated under the auspices of the Federal Emergency Management Agency (FEMA). The devastated city remained nearly vacant throughout September 2005. Residents' returns were impeded by storm debris on the roadways, lack of utility services, and the standing floodwater, which reached the rooftops of single story houses in some neighborhoods and needed to be physically pumped out once the levees were repaired. The "dewatering" of the city took six weeks and was prolonged when Hurricane Rita added rain to the standing floodwater on September 25. Housing damage was severe; approximately 71.5 percent of the 188,251 housing units in Orleans Parish were damaged, with 56 percent having major or severe damage (U.S. Department of Homeland Security 2006). Later, after the debris was cleared and utility services restored, many residents' returns were further impeded by the slow provision of rebuilding assistance to homeowners and owners of rental housing, especially affordable rental housing (U.S. Government Accountability Office 2010).

Kates et al. (2006) created an estimated timeline for New Orleans' reconstruction based on historical case studies of post-disaster reconstruction. They use the length of the emergency period – which lasted from the disaster event until the flood waters were removed six weeks later – to project the duration of the restoration and reconstruction periods, with each period expected to last about 10 times longer than the previous. They estimated that the restoration period – in which the built environment is made functional again – would last 60 weeks and the reconstruction period – in which the built environment is rebuilt, replaced or improved – would last 8–11 years. Three years after Hurricane Katrina, when the reconstruction period was well underway, Colten, Kates & Laska (2008) altered the recovery timeline by shortening the restoration period to reflect the strong commitment of federal resources, but lengthening the reconstruction period due to conflicts over the processes and goals of reconstruction. Whether New Orleans' recovery can ever be declared complete is stymied by the failure to define recovery goals by which to measure progress (Comfort et al. 2010; Olshansky et al. 2008). To date, neighborhood recovery of housing and population varies widely across the city, leading some to declare the housing recovery a secondary disaster (Adams 2013; Gill 2007; Kaiser Family Foundation 2010; Seidman 2013).

Early efforts to estimate the size of the New Orleans' population reveal the churning of population after such widespread destruction. Three population estimates dated December 3–4, 2005; January 1, 2006; and January 28–29, 2006 found that the increase in population over this two-month period corresponds with the return of utility services in most areas during December and the reopening of major universities and some primary and secondary schools in January

(Stone et al. 2007). The last of these population counts estimated the city-wide population to be 210,000 (±20,900), or about 37 percent of the 484,600 residents enumerated in the 2000 Census. This estimate included only residents who planned to spend 15 of the next 30 nights in a sampled home or in group quarters, such as hotels, cruise ships, or college dormitories, where many residents who lost homes were housed by their employers. When the daytime residential population was included – friends, family, and workers who planned to spend two hours or more in the dwelling – the population estimate was 262,200 (±33,500), or about 54 percent of the 2000 population. The difference between the resident and daytime population reflects daily population mobility at this time, as many residents rebuilding their homes were unable to live in them. By July 2006, the U.S. Census estimated New Orleans' population to be 223,000 (Frey, Singer & Park 2007), although demographers using different population estimation methods produced higher figures (Plyer, Bonaguro & Hodges 2010).

As recovery of the built environment proceeded, New Orleans became one of the fastest-growing U.S. cities with annual growth rates peaking at 17 percent between 2006 and 2007, and tapering to 1 percent between 2014 and 2015 (Figure 22.1). Despite this growth, New Orleans' population remains below its pre-Katrina size. Within the metropolitan area many residents have moved from the more devastated shoreline parishes to inland parishes. Consequently, the metropolitan area as a whole is closer to its pre-Katrina size (Plyer 2011). The incremental shifts of population inland might be viewed as an adaptive migration response that could reduce future vulnerability to rising sea levels and more frequent and intense cyclones and coastal storms.

In the year after Hurricane Katrina, 53 percent of pre-Katrina New Orleans metropolitan area residents had returned to (or were still in) the metropolitan area, but were not necessarily living in their pre-Katrina homes. Those who had not returned were located in Texas (18.3 percent), in other parts of Louisiana (12.3 percent), elsewhere in the South (11.7 percent) or outside the Southern U.S. (5.2 percent). African-Americans were less likely to have returned, as were young adults (ages 25–39), and those born outside of Louisiana (Sastry & Gregory 2014). These demographic differentials in return migration explain how New Orleans's population became "whiter, wealthier, and older" after Katrina (Frey, Singer & Park 2007; Fussell, Sastry & VanLandingham 2010). An analysis of New Orleans's "migration system" – the counties tied to New Orleans through in- and out-migration – shows that traditional out-migrant destinations became the source counties for in-migrants to New Orleans in the post-Katrina years, especially nearby urban counties (Curtis et al. 2015; Fussell et al. 2014. However, little more is known about the geography of the New Orleans "diaspora" (Fussell 2015).

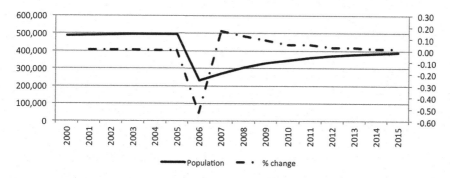

Figure 22.1 Population of New Orleans and annual percent change
Sources: U.S. Census Bureau (2011, 2015)

Disciplinary approaches to the study of mobility after Hurricane Katrina

Research on migration in response to Hurricane Katrina draws on two distinct research fields: demography and natural hazards research. Demographic research on post-Katrina migration primarily examines change in the size of the population of New Orleans, and the redistribution of the population throughout the U.S., using representative samples of the population to draw general conclusions. There is relatively little demographic research on disasters precisely because this type of data is difficult to obtain (Galea, Waxwell & Norris 2008). Natural hazards researchers tend to focus on the contexts and events that produce evacuation or migration behavior, typically relying on qualitative research methods in post-disaster settings that do not lend themselves to population-based sampling. They explore the lived experiences and decisions of disaster survivors, often focusing on social inequalities in disaster recovery. These two fields converge in research on environmental displacement and migration, particularly after rapid onset hazard events, and provide complementary insights.

Elements of each field are found in the frameworks and hypotheses that guide research on this topic. For example, the Foresight model of environmental migration conceptualizes an environmental event, like Hurricane Katrina, as a change that alters the macro-level demographic, economic, environmental, political, and social drivers of migration and thereby alters household level migration behavior (Black et al. 2011; Black et al. 2013). In this model, migration is but one of many adaptations to these structural changes; however, the model indicates that the social characteristics of individuals and households, as well as the contexts in which they live, make some people more likely to migrate than others. These sociodemographic differences in migration likelihoods are important for understanding which groups of people are most likely to become displaced or to migrate as a result of an environmental change.

The concept of social vulnerability informed much of the social science that occurred after Hurricane Katrina, particularly that which focused on evacuation responses and, to a lesser extent, residential mobility and new in-migration (Cutter et al. 2003; Cutter et al. 2006). While all three types of migration were produced when the disaster in New Orleans altered the structural drivers of migration, each type is distinct in the extent to which migrants were able to make decisions about the timing and destination of their moves (often described as migrant *agency*). In this way, the case of Hurricane Katrina's impact on the population of New Orleans illustrates the ways in which an environmental event operates both directly – in the case of evacuation – and indirectly – in the cases of return migration and new in-migration – on individuals' and households' decisions to migrate.

Evacuation outcomes after Hurricane Katrina

A rapid onset hazard event like Hurricane Katrina affects everyone in harm's way; however, the question of who evacuates in anticipation of the hazard is a product of the social and place-specific vulnerabilities of that population (Cutter et al. 2006; Laska & Morrow 2006/7). New Orleans residents were unequally vulnerable to disaster because of antecedent processes that were in place long before Hurricane Katrina ever formed. Historical land development patterns that left some areas of the city more highly exposed to flooding simultaneously created neighborhoods that were defined by race and class (Campanella 2006; Logan 2006). Cutter and colleagues found that the City of New Orleans was one of the most socially vulnerable parishes or counties affected by Katrina, with substantial variation in social vulnerability across the city

(Cutter et al. 2006; Finch, Emrich & Cutter 2010). Socially vulnerable census tracts had higher percentages of African American residents, low-income households, women residents, children under age 5, residents employed in the service sector or who were unemployed, women in the labor force, and residents living in high density housing units and renters (Finch, Emrich & Cutter 2010).

These socially vulnerable residents had the fewest resources to leave the city in anticipation of Hurricane Katrina and instead evacuated to local shelters, like the Superdome or the Ernest Morial Convention Center, or sheltered in place. Media images gave the impression that those who did not evacuate prior to the flood were disproportionately impoverished African Americans. Social scientists have found the picture to be more complicated, with evidence suggesting that a range of factors including race, class, age, gender, family statuses, employment, and social network composition influenced the evacuation timing of Gulf Coast residents (Elliott & Pais 2006; Groen & Polivka 2010; Haney, Elliott & Fussell 2010; Thiede & Brown 2013). Members of the most socially vulnerable groups were less likely to evacuate before the hurricane made landfall, and often had fewer options in terms of how to evacuate. For example, a Gallup survey conducted one month after Hurricane Katrina of adults registered with the Red Cross showed that African Americans were less likely than other racial groups to have evacuated with all family members, and were more likely to have left some family members behind (Haney, Elliott & Fussell 2010). By comparison, residents with higher incomes and family and friends living in places away from the storm's path were able to better protect themselves and their families.

Resource shortages combine with risk perception and unmet need for evacuation assistance to explain why so many people did not evacuate before the storm hit (Burnside, Miller & Rivera 2007; Trainor, Donner & Torres 2006). The Gallup survey cited previously showed that 49 percent of New Orleanians who did not evacuate said they did not think that the hurricane would be as bad as it was, and 21 percent reported they lacked finances or a car that would have allowed them to evacuate (Elliott & Pais 2006). A more disadvantaged group of Katrina evacuees surveyed in Houston area shelters found that half had not heard an evacuation order or had heard an order that lacked clear instructions, and the main reasons given for not evacuating before the storm were the lack of a car or other transportation (34 percent), underestimating how bad the storm would be (28 percent), and being physically unable to leave or having to care for someone who was physically unable to leave (12 percent) (Brodie et al. 2006).

Recall that it was not the weather event itself but the flood caused by the failure of the levees that made New Orleans uninhabitable, forcing evacuees into a sequence of stays in short-term, long-term, replacement, and reconstructed housing (Levine, Esnard & Sapat 2007). The Gallup survey of evacuees gives a sense of residents' different post-disaster housing trajectories one month after the storm. At this point, most emergency shelters had closed and shelter residents had transitioned to other housing. Among New Orleanians, 42 percent were in someone else's home; 53 percent were in an apartment, hotel, or shelter; and only 5 percent were in their pre-Katrina home (Elliott & Pais 2006). The implications of these post-disaster housing trajectories for long-term mobility have not been assessed, but several studies suggest that those who experienced prolonged instability and uncertainty in their housing arrangements often suffered in other life domains as well, such as mental and physical health, school attendance and attainment, and employment (Abramson et al. 2008; Fussell & Lowe 2014; Galea, Tracy, Norris & Coffey 2008; Mason 2012; Pardee 2012; Weber & Peek 2012). The effect of post-disaster housing on long-term recovery remains a gap in knowledge (Fussell 2015).

Return migration and displacement

The return migration to New Orleans is a second order mobility response to Hurricane Katrina, and the determinants of this movement are more complex. Residents' decisions to return or not were made at the evacuation destination and depended to a large extent on access to their pre-Katrina housing. For some, lack of access to housing in New Orleans and inadequate financial resources trapped them in the place to which they evacuated. For those who had access to housing in New Orleans, the return decision was complicated. Factors that influenced the calculus of return included housing and neighborhood damage, the delivery of insurance payments and rebuilding assistance to homeowners, inflated housing costs in the rental housing market, and the availability of employment, schools, and healthcare, as well as perceived hazard risk.

Neighborhood and housing damage was the first factor influencing return migration. In September 2006, after watching their city flood, displaced New Orleanians learned they would not be allowed to return home until the government declared their neighborhood open for occupancy. Neighborhood re-openings depended on the amount of flood and wind damage, the time needed to remove debris and restore utilities, and – perhaps most importantly – the resolution of highly political planning decisions about neighborhood investments (Olshansky et al. 2008). The first neighborhoods reopened were also the least damaged neighborhoods, which tended to be located in the sliver of high ground near the Mississippi River, where property values were high and more socially advantaged residents lived; the last to be reopened were the low-lying and less valuable neighborhoods, closer to Lake Ponchartrain, where more socially disadvantaged populations resided. Two notable exceptions to this spatial association between land elevation, property values, and socioeconomic status were the majority African American and low-income Lower Ninth Ward – which although located on higher ground near the Mississippi River, was inundated when the Industrial Canal levee broke – and the majority white, high-income Lakeview neighborhood built on landfill near Lake Ponchartrain and suffered deep flood waters. Despite these exceptions, residents' returns were stratified by flood depth and housing damage, and consequently, race and socioeconomic status (Finch, Emrich & Cutter 2010; Kamel 2012; Wang, Tang & Wang 2014).

The dispersal of private and public homeowners' insurance funds was a second factor in return migration. Homeowners with private insurance received payments relatively quickly and reliably so they could confidently make decisions about rebuilding or relocating. In contrast, the federal disaster assistance funds available to homeowners through Louisiana's Road Home Program (RHP) were only distributed several years after the disaster, with relatively meager grant amounts determined through convoluted and constantly changing rules (U.S. GAO 2010). Briefly, the RHP provided up to $150,000 per damaged home with funds to be used for rebuilding and flood mitigation or to compensate homeowners who chose to sell their properties to a state land trust and relocate (very few homeowners chose this option). The grant amounts for rebuilding depended on the lesser of two amounts: the cost of rebuilding the damaged home or the pre-storm value of the property. Consequently, homeowners in neighborhoods with lower property values received smaller grants even though their homes would cost as much to rebuild as a comparable home in a neighborhood with higher values (Green & Olshansky 2012). A lawsuit filed in November 2008 and settled in July 2011 found that the RHP discriminated against these African American homeowners and provided additional funds for home repairs (Greater New Orleans Fair Housing Coalition 2011). Bureaucratic delays in rebuilding assistance contributed to the prolonged return of these residents (Gotham 2015).

A third factor shaping return migration was rent inflation, a common occurrence after a disaster (Comerio 1998). Some factors contributing to this inflation are widely observed, but some were also unique to New Orleans. First, rental housing tends to be lower quality and therefore more susceptible to damage that prevents re-occupancy, and much of the rental property in New Orleans was permanently lost (Vigdor 2008). Second, re-occupancy is prohibited if a landlord cannot repair damage in a timely fashion, which may occur due to insufficient funds or a decision to upgrade the property. Third, competition for rental properties was stiff with pre-Katrina renters competing for a diminished number of rental units with homeowners who rented until their homes were rebuilt and with new in-migrants. Finally, residents of four large public housing projects – most of whom were female householders and their children – lost access to affordable housing when the Housing Authority of New Orleans decided to redevelop these as mixed income housing developments (Mitchell, Esnard & Sapat 2012). Since half of the occupied housing units in New Orleans before Hurricane Katrina were rental units, and since rental households were disproportionately headed by African Americans, women with children, or people with incomes below the poverty line (U.S. Census Bureau 2005), the delayed return of renters explains how the city became "whiter, older, and wealthier." It also suggests that renting is a particularly important component of post-disaster social vulnerability to displacement (Fothergill and Peek 2004).

Differentials in neighborhood population recovery remained large as reconstruction proceeded. In 2008, the more socially vulnerable pre-Katrina neighborhoods still had greater population losses, and the newly available homeowner rebuilding assistance grants did not appear to be speeding up repopulation in more damaged neighborhoods (Finch, Emrich & Cutter 2010). By 2010, those neighborhoods with the greatest population losses were mostly African American and low-income neighborhoods with more multi-unit residences, rental units, and subsidized housing that had experienced more housing damage and had received lower levels of FEMA assistance (Kamel 2012; Wang, Tang & Wang 2014). These studies indicate that in the first five years after Hurricane Katrina, disaster assistance was not able to overcome the differential in recovery between more and less socially vulnerable neighborhoods. However, between 2010 and 2013, the fastest growing neighborhoods were those that had been slowest to recover in earlier years (Mack & Plyer 2014). The opening of mixed-income housing developments in place of the shuttered public housing projects, the final dispersal of rebuilding assistance, and neighborhood gentrification by new residents will shape the new demographic profile of New Orleans.

In-migration of new residents

Disasters are rarely seen as a force attracting in-migration (Belcher & Bates 1983; Elliott 2015; Vale and Campanella 2005), but many new residents moved into New Orleans after Hurricane Katrina. Migrants were attracted to jobs and opportunities generated by the disaster recovery economy, most notably in construction. Construction employment recovered and exceeded its pre-Katrina numbers, even as total city-wide employment shrank, due to the massive influx of federal disaster assistance and insurance payments (Fussell & Diaz 2015). Many construction workers were unauthorized Latin American immigrants who arrived in New Orleans from other places throughout the U.S. (Vinck et al. 2009; Fussell 2009; Sisk & Bankston 2014). Whether or not they were unauthorized, many workers suffered from the chaos of the labor market and the city at that time, and were subject to wage theft, maltreatment, hazardous health exposures, and criminal victimization (Fussell 2009; Fussell 2015). Many workers stayed as long as the work lasted, and then moved on. However, enough stayed that the Latino population grew from 3.1 percent in 2005 to 5.6 percent in 2015 (Fussell & Diaz 2015).

Other in-migrant groups were less easily identifiable by a particular demographic trait, although young professionals, artists, and others were attracted by opportunities in the revitalized economy (Ehrenfeucht & Nelson 2012). A 2010 survey found that 9 percent of New Orleans residents had not been residents at the time of Hurricane Katrina (Kaiser Family Foundation 2010). Little is known about these post-disaster newcomers, but there is no doubt that they have contributed to the reconstruction and recovery of New Orleans even as they have changed its character. However, their arrival raises questions about whether post-disaster in-migrants contribute to the displacement of pre-Katrina residents by filling jobs and housing that residents would have accessed had they had the resources to return. This question was posed in racialized terms when many questioned whether Latino immigrants were "taking" jobs from displaced working class residents. An alternative explanation is that labor and immigration policies and practices facilitated the arrival of new and temporary in-migrants and discouraged the return of displaced residents (Delp, Podolsky & Aguilar 2009).

Conclusion: gains and gaps in knowledge about population mobility after disasters

Hurricane Katrina's impact on the population of New Orleans are consistent with two common hypotheses found in demographic and hazards research. The first is that natural hazards that threaten people and destroy housing and infrastructure generate displacement, return migration, and – a more novel finding – new in-migration. Second, disadvantaged populations were less able to evacuate in anticipation of the event, and returned to New Orleans later and in lower proportions. These outcomes are a direct function of the environmental event and an indirect function of the changes in the demographic, economic, environmental, political, and social drivers of migration. However, several empirical gaps remain unfilled.

First, although the vulnerability approach to understanding disaster impacts has informed much of the research agenda, it is difficult to draw robust conclusions given the methodological challenges associated with disaster research, especially research seeking to make generalizations about population change. For example, only a few of the surveys that seek to understand hazard impacts on populations use samples representative of the pre-disaster population, and those that do often lack pre- and post-event measures and the types of measures needed to evaluate sources of variation in disaster impacts and recovery (Galea, Waxwell & Norris, 2008). Consequently, although the research reviewed here has revealed that New Orleans residents were differentially mobile in the first year after Hurricane Katrina, there is much to be learned about why disasters do not uniformly affect populations and how they exacerbate pre-disaster inequalities.

Additionally, most research occurred within a year or two of Hurricane Katrina, so we know little about population groups displaced for longer periods and whether they returned or resettled elsewhere, and whether returning or remaining away resulted in better or worse social, economic, and health outcomes. Some studies using non-representative samples indicate that for some groups it was preferable to simply stay away from New Orleans (Bosick 2015; Graif 2016; Kirk 2009), but this is almost certainly not universally true, given that the expressed preference of at least half of pre-Katrina residents was to return to New Orleans in the first year. However, without representative population samples that observe residential mobility and social outcomes over a longer time frame, we cannot obtain a broader perspective on the unequal impacts of the disaster. Social scientists studying Hurricane Katrina's impact on New Orleans generated tremendous knowledge about disasters, displacement, and migration. However, it is also evident that representative population data and longitudinal studies are needed to fully understand the mobility consequences of disasters.

Acknowledgements

The author benefitted from National Institutes of Health Center Grant R24 HD041020 to the Population Studies and Training Center, Brown University.

Note

1 This chapter makes explicit differentiation between the City of New Orleans, which is delineated by the boundaries of Orleans Parish, and neighboring parishes that make up the wider metropolitan area of New Orleans. Louisiana parishes are equivalent to counties in other U.S. states.

References

Abramson, D., Stehling-Ariza, T., Garfield, R., & Redlener, I. (2008). Prevalence and predictors of mental health distress post-Katrina: Findings from the Gulf Coast Child and Family Health Study. *Disaster Medicine and Public Health Preparedness, 2*, 77–86.

Adams, V. (2013). *Markets of sorrow, labors of faith: New Orleans in the wake of Katrina.* Durham, NC: Duke University Press.

Belcher, J.C., & Bates, F.L. 1983. Aftermath of natural disasters: Coping through residential mobility. *Disasters, 7*(2), 118–128.

Black, R., Adger, W.N., Arnell, N.W., Dercon, S., Geddes, A., & Thomas, D. (2011). The effect of environmental change on human migration. *Global Environmental Change, 21*(Supplement 1), S3–S11.

Black, R., Arnell, N.W., Adger, W.N., Thomas, D., & Geddes, A. (2013). Migration, immobility and displacement outcomes following extreme events. *Environmental Science and Policy, 27*, 32–43.

Bosick, S.J. 2015. Pushed out on my own: The impact of Hurricane Katrina in the lives of low-income emerging adults." *Sociological Perspectives, 58*(2), 243–263.

Brodie, M., Weltzien, E., Altman, D., Blendon, R.J., & Benson, J.M. (2006). Experiences of Hurricane Katrina evacuees in Houston shelters: Implications for future planning. *American Journal of Public Health, 96*, 1402–1408.

Burnside, R., Miller, D.S., & Rivera, J.D. (2007). The impact of information and risk perception on the hurricane evacuation decision-making of greater New Orleans residents. *Sociological Spectrum, 27*, 727–740.

Campanella, R. (2006). *Geographies of New Orleans: Urban fabrics before the storm.* Lafayette, LA: University of Louisiana Press.

Colten, C., Kates, R.W., & Laska, S.B. (2008). Three years after Katrina: Lessons for community resilience. *Environment, 50*, 36–47.

Comerio, M.C. (1998). *Disaster hits home: New policy for urban housing recovery.* Berkeley, CA: University of California Press.

Comfort, L.K., Cigler, B.A., Birkland, T.A., & Nance, E. (2010). Retrospectives and prospectives on Hurricane Katrina: Five years and counting. *Public Administration Review, 70*, 669–678.

Curtis, K., Fussell, E., & DeWaard, J. (2015). Recovery Migration After Hurricanes Katrina and Rita: Spatial Concentration and Intensification in the Migration System. *Demography 52*: 1269–1293.

Cutter, S.L., Boruff, B.J., & Shirley, W.L. (2003). Social vulnerability to environmental hazards. *Social Science Quarterly, 84*, 242–261.

Cutter, S.L., Emrich, C.T., Mitchell, J.T., Boruff, B.J., Gall, M., Schmidtlein, M.C., Burton, C.G., & Melton, G. (2006). The long road home: Race, class, and recovery from Hurricane Katrina. *Environment, 48*, 8–20.

Delp, L., Podolsky, L., & Aguilar, T. (2009). Risk amid recovery: Occupational health and safety of Latino day laborers in the aftermath of the Gulf Coast hurricanes. *Organization & Environment, 22*(4), 479–490.

Ehrenfeucht, R., & Nelson, M. (2012). Young professionals as ambivalent change agents in New Orleans after the 2005 hurricanes. *Urban Studies, 50*, 825–841.

Elliott, J.R., & Pais, J. (2006). Race, class, and Hurricane Katrina: Social differences in human responses to disaster. *Social Science Research, 35*, 295–321.

Elliott, J.R. (2015). Natural hazards and residential mobility: General patterns and racially unequal outcomes in the United States. *Social Forces*, 93(4), 1723–1747.

Finch, C., Emrich, C.T., & Cutter, S.L. (2010). Disaster disparities and differential recovery in New Orleans. *Population & Environment*, 31, 179–202.

Fothergill, A., & Peek, L.A. (2004). Poverty and disasters in the United States: A review of recent sociological findings. *Natural Hazards*, 32, 89–110.

Frey, W.H., Singer, A., & Park, P. (2007). *Resettling New Orleans: The first full picture from the Census*. Washington, DC: The Brookings Institution.

Fussell, E. (2009). Hurricane chasers in New Orleans: Latino immigrants as a source of a rapid response labor force. *Hispanic Journal of Behavioral Sciences*, 31, 375–394.

Fussell, E., Sastry, N., & VanLandingham, M. (2010). Race, socio-economic status, and return migration to New Orleans after Hurricane Katrina. *Population & Environment*, 31, 20–42.

Fussell, E. (2011). The deportation threat dynamic and victimization of Latino migrants: Wage theft and robbery. *The Sociological Quarterly*, 52(4), 593–615.

Fussell, E. 2012. Help from family, friends, and strangers during Hurricane Katrina: Finding the limits of social networks. In L. Weber and L. Peek (Eds.) *Displaced: Life in the Katrina Diaspora* (pp.150–166). Austin, TX: Univeristy of Texas Press.

Fussell, E., Curtis, K., & DeWaard, J. (2014). Recovery migration to the city of New Orleans after Hurricane Katrina: A migration systems approach. *Population & Environment*, 35, 305–322.

Fussell, E., & Lowe, S. (2014). The impact of housing displacement on the mental health of low-income parents after Hurricane Katrina. *Social Science and Medicine*, 113, 137–144.

Fussell, E., & Diaz, L. (2015). Latinos in Metro New Orleans: Progress, problems, and potential. *The New Orleans Index at Ten*. Retrieved from www.datacenterresearch.org/

Fussell, E. (2015). The long-term recovery of New Orleans' population after Hurricane Katrina. *American Behavioral Scientist*, 59(10), 1231–1245.

Galea, S., Waxwell, A.R., & Norris, F. (2008). Sampling and design challenges in studying the mental health consequences of disasters. *International Journal of Methods in Psychiatric Research*, 17, 21–28.

Galea, S., Tracy, M., Norris, F., & Coffey, S.F. (2008). Financial and social circumstances and the incidence and course of PTSD in Mississippi during the first two years after Hurricane Katrina. *Journal of Traumatic Stress*, 21, 357–368.

Gill, D.A. (2007). Secondary trauma or secondary disaster? Insights from Hurricane Katrina. *Sociological Spectrum*, 27, 613–632.

Gotham, K.F. (2015). Limitations, legacies, and lessons: Post-Katrina rebuilding in retrospect and prospect. *American Behavioral Scientist*, 59(10), 1314–1326.

Graif, C. (2016). (Un)natural disaster: vulnerability, long-distance displacement, and the extended geography of neighborhood distress and attainment after Katrina. *Population & Environment*, 37(3), 288–318.

Green, T.F., & Olshansky, R.B. (2012). Rebuilding housing in New Orleans: The Road Home Program after the Hurricane Katrina disaster. *Housing Policy Debate*, 22, 75–99.

Greater New Orleans Fair Housing Coalition. (2011). *The Road Home: A Timeline*. Retrieved July 13, 2016 from www.gnofairhousing.org/2011/12/07/the-road-home-a-timeline/

Groen, J.A., & Polivka, A.E. (2010). Going home after Hurricane Katrina: Determinants of return migration and changes in affected areas. *Demography*, 47, 821–844.

Haney, T.J., Elliott, J.R., & Fussell, E. (2010). Families and hurricane response: Risk, roles, resources, race and religion. In D. Brunsma, D. Overfelt and J. S. Picou (Eds.), *The sociology of Katrina: Perspectives on a modern catastrophe, 2nd ed.* (pp. 77–102). Lanham, MD: Rowman & Littlefield.

Kates, R.W., Colten, C. E., Laska, S., & Leatherman, S. P. (2006). Reconstruction of New Orleans after Hurricane Katrina: A research perspective. *Proceedings of the National Academy of Science*, 103, 14653–14660.

Kaiser Family Foundation. (2010). *New Orleans five years after the storm: A New disaster amid recovery*. Retrieved from http://kff.org/other/poll-finding/new-orleans-five-years-after-the-storm-a-new-disaster-amid-recovery/.

Kamel, N. (2012). Marginalisation, federal assistance and repopulation patterns in the New Orleans metropolitan area following Hurricane Katrina. *Urban Studies*, 49, 3211–3231.

Kirk, D. (2009). A natural experiment on residential change and recidivism: Lessons from Hurricane Katrina. *American Sociological Review, 74*, 484–505.

Laska, S., & Morrow, B. H. (2006/7). Social vulnerabilities and Hurricane Katrina: An unnatural disaster in New Orleans. *Marine Technology Society Journal, 40*, 16–26.

Levine, J. N., Esnard, A. M., & Sapat, A. (2007). Population displacement and housing dilemmas due to catastrophic disasters. *Journal of Planning Literature, 22*, 3–15.

Litt, J. (2012). "We need to get together with each other": Women's narratives of help in Katrina's displacement. In L. Weber & L. Peek (Eds.), *Displaced: Life in the Katrina diaspora* (pp. 167–182). Austin, TX: University of Texas Press.

Logan, J. R. (2006). *The Impact of Katrina: Race and Class in Storm-Damaged Neighborhoods.* Retrieved from www.s4.brown.edu/katrina/report.pdf.

Mack, V., & Plyer, A. (2014). Neighborhood growth rates: Growth continues through 2014 in New Orleans neighborhoods. *The Data Center.* Retrieved from http://datacenterresearch.org.

Mason, B.J. (2012). The women of Renaissance Village: From homes in New Orleans to a trailer park in Baker, Louisiana. In L. Weber & L. Peek (Eds.), *Displaced: Life in the Katrina diaspora* (pp. 183–197). Austin, TX: University of Texas Press.

Mitchell, C.M., A.M. Esnard, & A. Sapat. (2012). Hurricane events and the displacement process in the United States. *Natural Hazards Review, 13,* 150–161.

Olshansky, R.B., Johnson, L.A., Horne, J., & Nee, B. (2008). Planning for the rebuilding of New Orleans. *Journal of the American Planning Association, 74, 273–287.*

Pardee, J.W. (2012). Living through displacement: Housing insecurity among low-income evacuees. In L. Weber & L. Peek (Eds.), *Displaced: Life in the Katrina diaspora* (pp. 63–78). Austin, TX: University of Texas Press.

Plyer, A., Bonaguro, J., & Hodges, K. (2010). Using administrative data to estimate population displacement and resettlement following a catastrophic U.S. disaster. *Population & Environment, 31*, 150–175.

Plyer, A. (2011). *What census 2010 reveals about population and housing in New Orleans and the metro area.* Greater New Orleans Community Data Center. Released March 17, 2011. Retrieved from www.datacenterresearch.org/

Sastry, N., & Gregory, J. (2014). The location of displaced New Orleans residents in the year after Hurricane Katrina. *Demography, 51*, 753–775.

Seidman, K.F. (2013). *Coming home to New Orleans: Neighborhood rebuilding after Katrina.* New York, NY: Oxford University Press.

Sisk, B., & Bankston, C.L. (2014). Hurricane Katrina, a construction boom, and a new labor force: Latino immigrants and the New Orleans construction industry, 2000 and 2006–2010. *Population Research and Policy Review, 33*, 309–334.

Stone, G., Lekht, A., Burris, N., & Williams, C. (2007). Data collection and communications in the public health response to a disaster: Rapid population estimate surveys and the daily dashboard in post-Katrina New Orleans. *Journal of Public Health Management Practice, 13*, 453–460.

Thiede, B.C., & Brown, D.L. (2013). Hurricane Katrina: Who stayed and why? *Population Research and Policy Review, 32*, 803–824.

Trainor, J.E., Donner, W., & Torres, M.R. (2006). There for the storm: Warning, response, and rescue among nonevacuees. In *Learning from Catastrophe: Quick Response Research in the Wake of Hurricane Katrina* (pp. 307–326). Boulder: Natural Hazards Center, University of Colorado.

U.S. Census Bureau. (2005). *American housing survey for the New Orleans metropolitan area: 2004.* Retrieved from www.census.gov/prod/2005pubs/h170-04-30.pdf.

U.S. Census Bureau. (2011). *Table 1. Intercensal Estimates of the Resident Population for Counties of Louisiana: April 1, 2000 to July 1, 2010.* Retrieved from www.census.gov.

U.S. Census Bureau. (2015). *Annual Estimates of the Resident Population: April 1, 2010 to July 1, 2014.* Retrieved from www.census.gov.

U.S. Department of Homeland Security. (2006). *Current Housing Unit Damage Estimates: Hurricanes Katrina, Rita, and Wilma.* Retrieved from www.huduser.org/publications/pdf/GulfCoast_Hsngdmgest.pdf.

U.S. Government Accountability Office. (2010). *Disaster assistance: Federal assistance for permanent housing primarily benefited homeowners; Opportunities exist to better target rental housing needs.* Report to Congressional Requesters GAO-10–17. Retrieved from www.gao.gov/products/GAO-10-17.

Vale, L.J., & Campanella, T.J. (2005). *The resilient city: How modern cities recover from disaster.* Oxford, UK: Oxford University Press.

Vigdor, J. (2008). The economic aftermath of Hurricane Katrina. *Journal of Economic Perspectives, 22,* 135–154.

Vinck, P., Pham, P.N., Fletcher, L.E., & Stover, E. (2009). Inequalities and prospects: Ethnicity and legal status in the construction labor force after Hurricane Katrina. *Organization & Environment, 22,* 470–480.

Wang, F., Tang, Q., & Wang, L. (2014). Post-Katrina population loss and uneven recovery in New Orleans, 2000–2010. *Geographical Review, 104,* 310–327.

Weber, L., & Peek, L. (2012). *Displaced: Life in the Katrina Diaspora.* Austin, TX: University of Texas Press.

Wisner, B., Blaikie, P., Cannon, T., & Davis, I. (2004). *At risk: Natural hazards, People's vulnerability, and disasters, 2nd ed.* Oxford, UK: Routledge Press.

23

A community-based model for resettlement

Lessons from coastal Louisiana

Julie K. Maldonado and Kristina Peterson

Three major reports released in 2014 – the Fifth Intergovernmental Panel on Climate Change Report; Third U.S. National Climate Assessment (NCA3); and the U.S. President's State, Local, and Tribal Leaders Task Force on Climate Preparedness and Resilience Report – affirmed how immediate and long-term anthropogenic climate change impacts, such as increased sea level rise, coastal erosion, and extreme weather events, are already causing, and will continue to cause, the displacement of entire communities. Yet, governments are either inconsistently implementing social protection policies or failing to create such policies at all, perpetuating a state of limbo for communities who have been trying to proactively relocate, some for over a generation.

In particular, with their lives, livelihoods, and knowledge systems intricately and intimately linked to the natural environment, Indigenous and other communities who have lived in a place for generations are particularly at risk of climate change impacts and ecological dispossession (Gautam et al. 2013; Whyte 2013). According to the NCA3:

> Climate change related impacts are forcing relocation of tribal and Indigenous communities, especially in coastal locations. These relocations, and the lack of governance mechanisms or funding to support them, are causing loss of community and culture, health impacts, and economic decline, further exacerbating tribal impoverishment.
>
> *(Bennett et al. 2014: 307; see also Bronen 2011; Bronen and Chapin 2013; Maldonado et al. 2013)*

Often, climate change is most impacting people who have already been made vulnerable and pushed to the fringes – geographically, politically, and socially – acting as a tipping point to the changes to which they have already been adapting. Communities in southeast coastal Louisiana are living this reality every day.

This chapter highlights the resettlement efforts of the Isle de Jean Charles Tribe, located in southeast coastal Louisiana, a region that is facing among the most rapid rate of land loss and relative sea level rise in the world. It is also a region that includes both tribal and non-tribal communities who have dwelled in place for generations, with their lifeway shaped by their subsistence and traditional practices, and spiritual connection to the land and water. The chapter aims to demonstrate that current vulnerability to climate change and other environmental hazards cannot be understood just as physical processes, but must be considered within a socio-historical context that has marginalized Indigenous communities since the colonial settler process began. It is not about one event or disaster, but the accumulation of multiple disasters and systemic violence – starting from colonization – over time.

The drastic environmental changes the Isle de Jean Charles Tribe has faced highlights the contradictions in our social, political, and economic systems, and the need for affected communities to make decisions under increasingly uncertain and complex conditions. Communities in the region are employing a vast range of adaptation strategies to stay in place, but in the case of Isle de Jean Charles, after many years of addressing the layers of systemic violence and land loss, the Tribal Council has recognized they are out of options for in-situ adaptation. The Council has prioritized the need to maintain the Tribe's community and culture, even if doing so means resettling together in a new location. This chapter will discuss the obstacles, challenges, and opportunities they have experienced in working towards proactive community-led resettlement to be an exemplar model of finding a new site of their choosing to sustain their community, bring people who have already been forced apart, back together, and maintain their family blood line connections as a Tribe, lifeway integrity, and sovereignty.

Layers of disasters

Environmental and technological disasters, extractive industries, river mismanagement, and climate change are drastically transforming coastal Louisiana's near-shore and landscape. While the river management system put in place in the 20th century by the U.S. Army Corps of Engineers (USACE) and local levee districts provided both flood control and economic benefits, such forms of management, control, and re-direction of the Mississippi River deprived the coastal system of much needed sediment and fresh water (Barry 1997; CPRA 2012; Freudenberg et al. 2009; Laska et al. 2005; Turner 1997). Instead of collecting along the coast, the sediment brought by the Mississippi River went into the Gulf of Mexico and dropped off the continental shelf to the bottom of the sea floor (Morris 2012).

The region's river management system began by draining the wetlands for agricultural production, then expanded with the construction of levees for flood control. Following, starting with the first coastal zone oil lease in 1921, oil and gas companies began dredging passageways through Louisiana's wetlands (Austin 2006; Turner 1997), resulting in approximately 25,000 miles of pipelines and 3,500 offshore production facilities in the central and western Gulf of Mexico's federal waters, three-quarters of which are off the coast of Louisiana (Freudenburg and Gramling 2011). The dredged passageways allow more water to rush in from the Gulf of Mexico during storms and high tide, leaving the once fertile lands barren from saltwater intrusion.

Southeast coastal Louisiana has experienced one of the world's highest rates of relative sea level rise – sediment subsidence combined with sea level rise – with an over 8-inch rise in the last 50 years, slightly faster than twice the global rate (Karl et al. 2009; Melillo et al. 2014; NOAA 2012). Recent data from the U.S. National Oceanic and Atmospheric Administration (NOAA) predict the region will experience an additional 4.3 feet of sea level rise by the end of this century (Marshall 2013; Osborn 2013). Hurricanes and storms have become more severe, resulting in accelerated rates of coastal land loss in recent years (Couvillion et al. 2011). Climate change-induced sea level rise and intensified hurricanes compound the effects of subsidence, in addition to oil and gas being extracted from the earth and the erosion from the salt water intrusion through the oil/gas canals (Burkett and Davidson 2012). The sea level rise and storms increase the salinity in estuaries and wetlands. Freshwater is now brackish and brackish water is now saltwater, impacting the fish that the tribes and other subsistence coastal communities have relied on for sustenance and food security for generations.

Since the onset of colonization, tribes in coastal Louisiana have accrued layers of chronic disasters and injustices (Laska et al. 2015; Maldonado forthcoming). Many of the tribes including Isle de Jean Charles moved to the high ground of bayou ridges, rich with forest, land appropriate for farms and livestock, and water rich with fish. The locale where the tribes settled after breaking from the 'trail of tears' were well inland from the Gulf and isolated enough for privacy and safe from discovery. The relationship with the land, water, and environment was crucial in their new home and led to the development of a wealth of knowledge bases. Now the once bio-diverse-rich home has been damaged. The Gulf continually moves inland with severe erosion and intense saltwater intrusion, the majority of the trees are dead and the tribes' traditional and medicinal plants, gardens, and trapping grounds, along with the animals, are gone. Retaining fishing livelihoods and community rituals is increasingly difficult: people no longer gather and share as they once did and the everyday traditions and lifeway practices that tied families and communities together with mutual aid and resiliency gradually diminish (Coastal Louisiana Tribal Communities 2012; Laska 2012; Laska et al. 2010; Maldonado et al. 2015; Peterson and Maldonado 2016) due to the continual scattering of the families by storms. Mutual aid was core to the communities' way of being. They used to build boats and houses together and trade crops and seafood; but with more people being forced to move and the soil and water contaminated with salt and heavy metals, they are losing essential lifeway practices, as well as diminished community capacity and resilience. What once was stable forest and grazing lands that grew abundant healthy foods and medicinal plants are now under water. Community health and economy suffer through these losses.

Whereas before they rarely experienced flooding from hurricanes, now with the land loss and disappearance of barrier islands to the south, flooding can occur just during high tide. The accruing disasters have forced more and more people to relocate. Many people left after hurricanes because of severe flood damage to their houses, lack of resources to elevate their houses, or they became tired of rebuilding or the skyrocketing flood insurance rates, which are sometimes greater than the value of a person's home and many cannot afford to pay. Some left to pursue other job opportunities because of the loss of fishing-based livelihoods, a result of a combination of severe environmental changes and a changing seafood industry flooded by lower-priced, subsidized, pond-raised imports. Wanting to stay together and maintain their community, many people coped with relocation by remaining as close as possible to a familiar landscape and to other people from their tribe, clustering together on slightly higher ground farther north.

In coastal Louisiana, residents' intimate Traditional Ecological Knowledge (TEK) of the surrounding waterways and landscape enables them to see the changes happening, document impacts, and identify intervention strategies (Peterson 2014). Once land becomes inundated in Louisiana, the title reverts back to the state, and is often then leased to oil companies. The same is true with oyster leases, as land is reclaimed by the state and neighboring oyster leases can be turned over to the state. Some residents therefore lease waters back from the state so their families can continue to access the water for fishing to maintain their livelihoods, food security, and an important cultural practice that connects them to their natural environment and resource base. They also reinvigorate their cultural traditions, adapt planting strategies, and form partnerships and coalitions (Maldonado 2014b; Maldonado et al. 2015). Local informal community leaders work together and advocate on each other's behalf, meeting with other communities and organizations to increase awareness and explore new options for restoration efforts (Peterson 2011; Peterson and Maldonado 2016).

Despite the layers of disasters and vulnerabilities, most communities are focused on staying in situ, and working to restore communities, cultures, and ancestral lands. However, with little land left and being at increasing risk of extreme weather events and being left out of government-led hurricane protection systems, the Isle de Jean Charles Tribal Council has decided that to maintain their culture, community, and lifeways, the best option for them is to move to another site, together as a tribe, so they can rebuild their community which has been forced to scatter back together and sustain their culture and autonomy in a new place.

Pursuing community-led resettlement

The Isle de Jean Charles Band of Biloxi-Chitimacha-Choctaw Indians is a state-recognized Native American tribe located on a narrow strip of land in Terrebonne Parish, Louisiana, approximately 80 miles southwest of New Orleans. Isle de Jean Charles (called the Island) is connected to the mainland by a narrow strip of asphalt that is quickly eroding away and floods during high tide or south winds. The Island settlement, established in the 1830s, is made up almost entirely of Isle de Jean Charles tribal members.

Following the 1830 Indian Removal Act (U.S. Congress 1830), tens of thousands of Indigenous people were forced out of their ancestral homelands along the Eastern seaboard. The tribes moved across the Mississippi River to lands in the west that were part of the Louisiana Purchase. During this time, Louisiana's densely forested bayous – a Choctaw word referring to a slow-moving stream that flows back and forth as the tide goes in and out – served as a "region of refuge" (Vélez-Ibáñez 2004: 7), or ecological shelter, for some Indigenous people from the Southeast. The ancestors established settlements at the southern ends of the bayous, with families living in small clusters and maintaining a subsistence culture based on fishing, trapping, hunting, and farming. The tribes had a wealth of resources, including barrier islands, extensive, life-giving estuaries, and an abundance of aquatic resources. Once people escaped down the bayous, they were physically and therefore socially isolated from communities and political relations farther north. This isolation reinforced and helped shape the tribes' relationship with the land, water, and place, as well as self-sufficiency.

From 2005–2015, Isle de Jean Charles severely flooded nearly a dozen times from eight hurricanes and storms, most recently from Hurricane Patricia in 2015, in addition to king tides and south winds that have also flooded the Island and the Island Road. The loss of landmass and barrier islands to the south of their community has decreased the natural protection against hurricanes and storms, and now Isle de Jean Charles has become the shock absorber for communities farther north. Only 320 of 22,400 acres (the estimated size of the territory in 2015) of land remain of the Island (State of Louisiana 2017). There were 78 houses and approximately 325 people living on Isle de Jean Charles in 2002 before Hurricane Lili; in 2012 there were about 25 houses and 70 people left, with more people being forced to relocate after each flooding event.

State reports have concluded that without restoration and flood mitigation actions, much of the tribes' lands would be gone before 2050, including all of Isle de Jean Charles (CPRA 2012). Isle de Jean Charles was originally included in the Morganza-to-the-Gulf of Mexico Hurricane Protection System, a flood control project to reduce hurricane and storm damage in coastal Louisiana, which was crafted by the USACE, the Louisiana Department of Transportation and Development, and the Terrebonne Levee and Conservation District. However, the community was cut out of the plan in 1998 because the USACE decided it was more economically feasible to relocate the people from Isle de Jean Charles than include them in the protection zone (USACE et al. 2013). The Morganza Environmental Impact Statement (EIS) acknowledged that leaving Isle de Jean Charles out of the proposed levee alignment and likely induced flooding during storm events when the protection system is closed is a potential environmental justice issue. However, the EIS went on to state: "Providing hurricane risk reduction for Isle de Jean Charles has been determined in previous Corps of Engineers analyses to be cost prohibitive" (USACE et al. 2013: 5.53). The EIS reported that impacts to the communities left out of the system "would be mitigated through 100% buyout and uniform relocation assistance" (USACE et al. 2013: 6.45). Without government support to mitigate the flooding and restore the land, the Isle de Jean Charles Tribal Council informed the USACE that they would like relocation assistance for their people, but as a community. The USACE worked with them to identify a site nearby where the community could rebuild. However, the USACE not being aware of who were members of the Tribe, counted non-tribal and members of another tribe in a negative "community" vote to determine if the Isle de Jean Charles Tribe would be offered relocation.[1]

Some residents perceived the government wanting residents to relocate so the oil industry could have free range over the area without interference. Individuals from local tribes grew up either with the personal experience or with the stories of family and friends having had their land confiscated. Oil and gas corporations, land speculators, and foresters came in with formal contracts written in English, often with private militia demanding families sign the documents which resulted in the taking their tribal and family lands. The USACE representatives and others involved failed to recognize the sensitive power dynamics of government representatives raising ideas about relocating a tribal community and what this sounded like to people whose ancestors fled for their lives a few generations prior during forced removals, and did not have the local knowledge of internal politics, which resulted in counting people from another tribe in the vote to relocate. The USACE informed the community that if they could find an appropriate ridge to build on, they would reconsider including the community in the hurricane protection system. However, the USACE's representatives did not listen to elders on the Island about where to take soil samples, maintaining instead that the cost-benefit ratio was not there to include the community in the levee system.[2]

The cost-benefit analysis used to make coastal restoration decisions does not account for the distribution of costs and benefits or important social and cultural factors, such as people's identity, beliefs, traditions, livelihoods, and sacred places (Cernea 2008; Oliver-Smith 2010). It does not include the social, psychological, and financial costs associated with moving fishing families inland, loss of local knowledge, and the mental stress of being removed from one's home and traditional life (Maldonado 2014a). These results stem, in part, from a lack of policies to fully include tribal or traditional knowledge or values in such analysis.

In 2009, making another attempt at relocation, Chief Naquin, the Traditional Chief of the Isle de Jean Charles Tribe, presented at a Terrebonne Parish Council meeting, but after less than five minutes, the Council silenced him. A Parish Council member stood up and raised the concern of property values decreasing if the Tribal community moved to Bourg, an area approximately 20 miles north of the Island, where the Tribal Council was considering raising funds to purchase an available property.[3] As the restoration process became an object of commodification and racial tension, the residents became further estranged and alienated from the physical environment. The greater community and the Tribe were denied the input of their local ecological knowledge, which could be an invaluable contribution to the restoration process (Bethel et al. 2011; Burley 2010; Thornton 2008).

Concerned that their lifeway and cultural community will be lost if tribal members are geographically separated, the Isle de Jean Charles Tribal Council has been proactively pursuing Tribal-led resettlement for nearly two decades. But there have been no funds for the lengthy and sensitive process of resettling an entire community, and there is no federal government agency delegated to support communities' proactive efforts (Bronen 2011; Maldonado et al. 2013). One distinct consequence is that if community leaders come to the decision that the community is too at-risk to continue to adapt in situ and decide to pursue resettlement, they could be cut off from funding to support their current existing infrastructure, and left in limbo between the time the decision is made to relocate and when such plans can be implemented, which is proving to take decades without the necessary institutional infrastructure (Laska and Peterson 2013; Marino 2012, 2015; Peterson and Maldonado 2016). Thus, when plans fall through, as happened with the USACE plan, communities are forced to start the process all over again, losing time that they can no longer afford.

Louisiana's 50-Year Master Plan for a Sustainable Coast had the option of voluntary relocation for individual households (CPRA 2012), but not communities. The U.S. Federal Emergency Management Agency's (FEMA) buyouts support individual, voluntary relocation. Organized on an individual basis – as opposed to a collective community re-settlement – the government disaster programs do not consider the disruptions to culture, sense of autonomy, and community values – including the place-based communal and environmental relations, that tribes value – that can occur when people must move in a piecemeal manner. Without one's community, the process to relocate individually is colonizing in and of itself and works to reinstate the forced assimilation policies. It is about more than just relocating people from one place to another, as if the same model could be used in any geographical or cultural context. Resettlement should be just that – re-establishing an intact community settlement that includes the key physical, economic, cultural, social, and spiritual infrastructure that enable the community to thrive in such a way as they determine, in a location that the community chooses and makes sense to them. It should envision a community that can thrive and resemble the positive attributes of the pre-dispersed community, so as to reunite those who have been displaced.

Conclusion

The Isle de Jean Charles Tribal Council, in partnership with the Lowlander Center,[4] has developed a culturally appropriate, sustainable, and community-based resettlement plan that includes ecosystem protection and rehabilitation to mitigate further degradation of their current and ancestral lands, and to once again be a self-sustaining community (Laska et al. 2014; Maldonado et al. 2015; Swan et al. 2015). The design is a vision of reinvigoration of culture, land, and biodiversity to contribute to the health of the entire web-of-life or 'seventh generation' community.

To move their efforts forward, with very limited resources, the tribal leaders have been vocal in high-level government discussions – and created their own governable spaces – engaging with policymakers, the media, non-profit and non-governmental organizations, practitioners, scholars, and students from the local to international levels. For example, leaders have spoken at forums on Capitol Hill in Washington, DC and at the United Nations in New York, and given interviews to media outlets around the world. In large part due to their advocacy efforts, the urgent issue of relocation was included as a key message in the NCA3 and in the President's State, Local, and Tribal Leaders Task Force on Climate Preparedness and Resilience, which recommended in its final report to the President the need to "[e]xplore Federal role in addressing climate change-related displacement, needs of affected communities, and institutional barriers to community relocation" (2014: 30).

The Tribe is out of time to wait for legislation and policies to be worked out. Faced with immediate threats of cultural genocide and health and safety concerns, and knowing that once the water overtakes their land it is too late, the Isle de Jean Charles Tribe is continuing to move forward to implement its plans, engage in partnership support, and be exemplar models of community-led actions. As an Indigenous leader working to address energy concerns on tribal lands recently noted at a Congressional briefing, "They are not going to be climate refugees, these folks are Indigenous scouts for a new way in the 21st century to be able to thrive with culture, values and dignity intact" (EESI 2015).

These efforts have now proven results – in January 2016, the Housing and Urban Development Agency of the U.S. government in partnership with the Rockefeller Foundation announced a $52 million grant award for the National Disaster Resilience Competition to support Isle de Jean Charles Tribe to resettle as a community, making them the first community to resettle together, as a community, in the continental U.S. in modern times. Renowned resettlement expert Anthony Oliver-Smith, member of the scientific committee on Integrated Research on Disaster Risk of the International Council for Science and former Munich Re Foundation Chair on Social Vulnerability at the United Nations University Institute on Environment and Human Security, commented that the Isle de Jean Charles Tribe's resettlement plan was one of the most inclusive of best principles for resettlement that he had ever seen.[5]

The Tribe, along with the Lowlander Center team, was able to achieve this with expertise of Tribal members and subject matter experts, all based on a volunteer basis and all of whom have contributed personal funds, resources, and time. The lack of funds becomes a hindrance for the team to access resources or to be present at essential meetings and conferences. In dialogue with other highly at-risk communities, this seems to be the norm; people are challenged with time commitments to family, work, and community while also having to dedicate an enormous amount of time to the development of resettlement plans. Furthermore, the Tribe is constantly dealing with ongoing chronic issues such as flooding. The population base is geographically disconnected, with many families being forced to disperse following impacts from hurricane after hurricane. They are mostly dispersed in a 50-mile span that follows the higher bayou ridges, as well as the extremely at-risk marsh region close to their original island home. Support networks are compromised due to distance, and often times by climate conditions. For the families still living on the Island, they have to travel further to reach their support system and resources that were once readily available right outside their door. Continuing colonial legacies and systemic violence set the foundation for the mounting layers of complexity, which are growing more intense with less resources to address them (Barrios 2016; Farmer 2003, 2004; Schuller 2016). The additional layers of resettlement planning and fundraising are in addition to the workload demanded by the chronic and daily disasters.

At the time of this writing, it is not known if the grant will actually be given to the Tribe due to conflict between the Fair Housing Act[6] and the necessity of the Tribe to resettle as a community entity. We honor the Fair Housing Act in terms of inclusion, but it also poses a distinct challenge because it is for individuals, not communities. This schism between two values (individual rights vs. community) is called a 'conflict with law'. For many tribes and culturally connected communities, the need to be recognized as a community, and not just individuals, calls for an exception from the Fair Housing Act to be considered.

Through their vision, indigeneity and generational roots of resilience (Whyte 2013, 2016), the Tribe is showing us a path away from cultural genocide. A powerful community of people, bound by tradition and blood ties, they are willing to take a courageous act of resettlement and provide a 'proof of concept' design so that others can learn from their work. They are showing us the path out of a culture-of-risk to a culture of sustainability that will counter the devastation caused by a heating planet.

Acknowledgments

Thank you to Robert McLeman for his editorial comments; to Melissa Watkinson, who helped bring out the complexities and power of the story; and most importantly, to the Isle de Jean Charles tribal members, who have spent days, hours, and years with us sharing stories, meals, laughter, and the importance of community.

Notes

1 Personal communication with Isle de Jean Charles tribal members.
2 Personal communication with Isle de Jean Charles tribal members.
3 Personal communication with the Traditional Chief and with local community members who attended the meeting.
4 A local non-governmental organization with a long-standing relationship with the tribe.
5 Comment made at meeting between members of the Isle de Jean Charles Resettlement Team and Council on Environmental Quality in Washington, DC, May 19, 2016.
6 For further information, www.justice.gov/crt/fair-housing-act-2

References

Austin, Diane. 2006. Cultural Exploitation, Land Loss and Hurricanes: A Recipe for Disaster. *American Anthropologist* 108(4):671–691.

Barrios, Roberto. 2016. Resilience: A commentary from the vantage point of anthropology. *Annals of Anthropological Practice* 40(1): 28–38.

Barry, John M. 1997. Rising Tide: the Great Mississippi Flood of 1927 and How It Changed America. New York: Simon and Schuster.

Bennett, T. M. Bull, Nancy G. Maynard, Patricia Cochran, Robert Gough, Kathy Lynn, Julie Maldonado, Garrit Voggesser, Susan Wotkyns, and Karen Cozzetto. 2014. Ch. 12: Indigenous Peoples, Lands, and Resources. *In* Climate Change Impacts in the United States: The Third National Climate Assessment. Jerry M. Melillo, Terese Richmond, and Gary W. Yohe, eds. Pp. 297–317. Washington, DC: U.S. Global Change Research Program. [Available online at http://nca2014.globalchange.gov/report/sectors/indigenous-peoples].

Bethel, Matthew B., Lynn F. Brien, Emily J. Danielson, Shirley B. Laska, John P. Troutman, William M. Boshart, Marco J. Giardino, and Maurice A. Phillips. 2011. Blending Geospatial Technology and Traditional Ecological Knowledge to Enhance Restoration Decision-Support Processes in Coastal Louisiana. CHART Publications. Paper 23:555–571. [Available online at http://scholarworks.uno.edu/chart_pubs/23].

Bronen, Robin. 2011. Climate-Induced Community Relocations: Creating an Adaptive Governance Framework Based in Human Rights Doctrine. *New York University Review of Law and Social Change* 35:356–406.

Bronen, Robin and F. Stuart Chapin III. 2013. Adaptive Governance and Institutional Strategies for Climate-induced Community Relocations in Alaska. *PNAS* 110(23):9320–9325.

Burkett, Virginia, and Margaret Davidson, eds. 2012. Coastal Impacts, Adaptation and Vulnerability: A Technical Input to the 2012 National Climate Assessment. Cooperative Report to the 2013 National Climate Assessment. [Available online at www.southernclimate.org/documents/resources/Coastal_Technical_Input_2012.pdf]

Burley, David. 2010. Losing Ground: Identity and Land Loss in Coastal Louisiana. Jackson: University Press of Mississippi.

Cernea, Michael M. 2008. The Impoverishment Risks and Reconstruction Model: Resettlement and Benefit-Sharing. Manila: Asian Development Bank.

Coastal Louisiana Tribal Communities. 2012. Stories of Change: Coastal Louisiana Tribal Communities' Experiences of a Transforming Environment (Grand Bayou, Grand Caillou/ Dulac, Isle de Jean Charles,

Pointe-au-Chien). Julie Koppel Maldonado, ed. Workshop Report Input Into the National Climate Assessment. Pointe-aux-Chenes, LA, January 22–27.

Couvillion, Brady A., John A. Barras, Gregory D. Steyer, William Sleavin, Michelle Fischer, Holly Beck, Nadine Trahan, Brad Griffin, and David Heckman. 2011. Land Area Change in Coastal Louisiana from 1932 to 2010: U.S. Geological Survey Scientific Investigations Map 3164. [Available online at http:// pubs.usgs.gov/sim/3164/downloads/SIM3164_Pamphlet.pdf].

CPRA [Coastal Protection and Restoration Authority of Louisiana]. 2012. Louisiana's Comprehensive Master Plan For a Sustainable Coast. Baton Rouge, LA: CPRA. [Available online at www. lacpra.org/assets/docs/2012%20Master%20Plan/Final%20Plan/2012%20Coastal%20Master%20 Plan.pdf].

EESI [Environmental and Energy Study Institute]. 2015. What If the Water Can't Be Stopped? Tribal Resilience Plans in an Age of Sea Level Rise. Congressional Briefing, Washington, DC. April 20. [Available online at www.eesi.org/briefings/view/042015tribal].

Farmer, Paul. 2003. Pathologies of Power: Health, Human Rights, and the New War on the Poor. Berkeley, CA: University of California Press.

——— 2004. An Anthropology of Structural Violence. *Current Anthropology* 45(3):305–325.

Freudenburg, William R., and Robert Gramling. 2011. Blowout in the Gulf: The BP Oil Spill Disaster and the Future of Energy in America. Cambridge, MA: The MIT Press.

Freudenberg, William R., Robert Gramling, Shirley Laska, and Kai T. Erikson. 2009. Catastrophe in the Making: The Engineering of Katrina and the Disasters of Tomorrow. Washington, DC: Island Press.

Gautam, Mahesh R., Karletta Chief, and William J. Smith Jr. 2013. Climate Change in Arid Lands and Native American Socioeconomic Vulnerability: The Case of the Pyramid Lake Paiute Tribe. *Climatic Change* 120(3):585–599.

Karl, Thomas R., Jerry M. Melillo, and Thomas C. Peterson, eds. 2009. Global Climate Change Impacts in the United States: A State of Knowledge Report from the US Global Change Research Program. Cambridge University Press.

Laska, Shirley. 2012. Dimensions of Resiliency: Essential, Exceptional, and Scale. *International Journal of Critical Infrastructure* 6(3): 246–276.

Laska, Shirley, George Wooddell, Ronald Hagelman, Robert Grambling, and Monica Teets Farris. 2005. At Risk: The Human, Community, and Infrastructure Resources of Coastal Louisiana. *Journal of Coastal Research* 44:90–111.

Laska, Shirley, Kristina Peterson, Michelle E. Alcina, Jonathan West, Ashey Volion, Brent Tranchina, and Richard Krajeski. 2010. Enhancing Gulf of Mexico Coastal Communities' Resiliency through Participatory Community Engagement. CHART Publications. Paper 21. [Available online at http://scholarworks.uno.edu/chart_pubs/21].

Laska, Shirley and Kristina Peterson. 2013. Between Now and Then: Tackling the Conundrum of Climate Change. CHART Publications. Paper 32: 5–8. [Available online at http://scholarworks.uno.edu/ chart_pubs/32].

Laska, Shirley Tony Laska, Bob Gough, Jack Martin, Albert Naquin, and Kristina Peterson. 2014. Proposal for Isle de Jean Charles Relocation Planning. Indigenous Roots for Sustainable Futures: Proactive Solutions for a Time of Change.

Laska, Shirley, Kristina Peterson, Crystlyn Rodrigue, Tia Cosse', Rosina Philippe, Olivia Burchett, and Richard Krajeski. 2015. "Layering" of Natural and Human Caused Disasters in the Context of Anticipated Climate Change Disasters: The Coastal Louisiana Experience. *In* Disasters' Impact on Livelihood and Cultural Survival: Losses, Opportunities, and Mitigation. Michèle Companion, ed. Boca Raton, FL: CRC Press.

Maldonado, Julie Koppel. Forthcoming. Corexit to Forget It: The Transformation of Coastal Louisiana into an Energy Sacrifice Zone. *In* ExtrACTION: Impacts, Engagements and Alternative Futures. Kirk Jalbert, Anna Willow, David Casagrande, Stephanie Paladino, and Jeanne Simonelli. New York: Left Coast Press.

——— 2014a A Multiple Knowledge Approach for Adaptation to Environmental Change: Lessons Learned from Coastal Louisiana's Tribal Communities. *Journal of Political Ecology* 21:61–82.

—— 2014b Everyday Practices and Symbolic Forms of Resistance: Adapting to Environmental Change in Coastal Louisiana. *In* Hazards, Risks, and Disasters in Society: A Cross-Disciplinary Overview. Andrew Collins, ed. Philadelphia, PA: Elsevier Inc.

Maldonado, Julie Koppel, Christine Shearer, Robin Bronen, Kristina Peterson, and Heather Lazrus. 2013. The Impact of Climate Change on Tribal Communities in the US: Displacement, Relocation, and Human Rights. *Climatic Change* 120(3):601–614.

Maldonado, Julie Koppel, Albert P. Naquin, Theresa Dardar, Shirell Parfait-Dardar, and Kelly Bagwell. 2015. Above the Rising Tide: Coastal Louisiana's Tribal Communities Apply Local Strategies and Knowledge to Adapt to Rapid Environmental Change. *In* Disasters' Impact on Livelihood and Cultural Survival: Losses, Opportunities, and Mitigation. Michèle Companion, ed. Boca Raton, FL: CRC Press.

Marino, Elizabeth. 2012. The Long History of Environmental Migration: Assessing Vulnerability Construction and Obstacles to Successful Relocation in Shishmaref, Alaska. *Global Environmental Change* 22(2):374–381.

—— 2015 Fierce Climate, Sacred Ground. An Ethnography of Climate Change in Shishmaref, Alaska. Fairbanks, AK: University of Alaska Press.

Marshall, Bob. 2013. New Research: Louisiana Coast Faces Highest Rate of Sea-Level Rise Worldwide. The Lens. February 21. [Available online at http://thelensnola.org/2013/02/21/new-research-louisiana-coast-faceshighest-rate-of-sea-level-rise-on-the-planet/].

Melillo, Jerry M., Terese (T.C.) Richmond, and Gary W. Yohe, eds. 2014 Climate Change Impacts in the United States: The Third National Climate Assessment. Washington, DC: U.S. Global Change Research Program.

Morris, Christopher. 2012. The Big Muddy: An Environmental History of the Mississippi and its Peoples from Hernando De Soto to Hurricane Katrina. New York: Oxford University Press.

NOAA [U.S. National Oceanic and Atmospheric Administration]. 2012. Global Sea Level Rise Scenarios for the United States National Climate Assessment. NOAA Technical Report OAR CPO-1. [Available online at http://scenarios.globalchange.gov/sites/default/files/NOAA_SLR_r3_0.pdf].

Oliver-Smith, Anthony. 2010. Defying Displacement: Grassroots Resistance and the Critique of Development. Austin, TX: University of Texas Press.

Osborn, Tim. 2013. Keynote Comments: Critical Needs for Community Resilience. Presentation at the Building Resilience Workshop IV: Adapting to Uncertainty Implementing Resilience in Times of Change. March 2–9, New Orleans, LA.

Peterson, Kristina J. 2011. Transforming Researchers and Practitioners: The Unanticipated Consequences (Significance) of Participatory Action Research (PAR). Ph.D. dissertation, Department of Urban Studies, University of New Orleans.

—— 2014. Community conversation with Point au Chien Tribe and the OGHS staff from Presbyterian Church (USA), Tribal Center. October 28.

Peterson, Kristina J. and Julie K. Maldonado. 2016. When Adaptation is Not Enough: Between Now and Then of Community-led Resettlement. *In* Anthropology and Climate Change, 2nd edition. Susan Crate and Mark Nuttall, eds. Pp. 336–353. New York: Routledge.

President's State, Local and Tribal Leaders Task Force on Climate Preparedness and Resilience. 2014. Recommendations to the President. Washington, DC. [Available online at www.whitehouse.gov/sites/default/files/docs/task_force_report_0.pdf].

Schuller, Mark. 2016. Humanitarian Aftershocks in Haiti. New Brunswick: Rutgers University Press.

State of Louisiana. 2017. Isle de Jean Charles Resettlement Project [website: http://isledejeancharles.la.gov/].

Swan, Colleen, Chief Albert P. Naquin, and Stanley Tom. 2015 Building Respectful Solutions. *Forced Migration Review: Disasters and Displacement in a Changing Climate*, Issue 49, pp. 100.

Thornton, Thomas F. 2008. Being and Place among the Tlingit. Seattle: University of Washington Press.

Turner, R.E. 1997. Wetland Loss in the Northern Gulf Of Mexico: Multiple Working Hypotheses. *Estuaries* 20(1):1–13.

USACE [United States Army Corps of Engineers], Louisiana Coastal Protection and Restoration Authority Board, and Terrebonne Levee and Conservation District. 2013. Final Revised Programmatic

Environmental Impact Statement. Morganza to the Gulf of Mexico, Louisiana. [Available online at www.mvn.usace.army.mil/Portals/56/docs/PD/Projects/MTG/FinalRevisedProgrammaticEISM-toG.pdf].

U.S. Congress. 1830. Twenty-First Congress. Session I. Chapter 148. Statute I. May 28. In A Century of Lawmaking for a New Nation: U.S. Congressional Documents and Debates, 1774–1875, Statutes at Large, 21st Congress, 1st Session. [Available online at http://memory.loc.gov/].

Vélez-Ibáñez, Carlos G. 2004. Regions of Refuge in the United States: Issues, Problems, and Concerns for the Future of Mexican-Origin Populations in the United States. *Human Organization* 63(1):1–20.

Whyte, Kyle Powys. 2013. Justice Forward: Tribes, Climate Adaptation and Responsibility in Indian Country. *Climatic Change* 120(3):517–530.

—— 2016. Indigeneity. *Keywords for Environmental Studies*. J. Adamson, W. Gleason, and D. Pellow, eds. New York: NYU Press. Chapter 43.

24

Social and cultural dimensions of environment-related mobility and planned relocations in the South Pacific

Dalila Gharbaoui

Intraregional differences in vulnerability to climate change in the Pacific

Pacific Island countries and territories (PICTs) share common features such as a high dependency on the Pacific Ocean and its resources, a relatively high exposure to natural disasters, high vulnerability to exogenous environmental and socio-economic changes, and a relatively low capacity to adapt to changes in climate (SPREP 2009). The Pacific region can be divided in three main zones (Figure 24.1) affected differently by climate change according to "resource endowments, size, and the state of economic development" (UNESCAP 2000).

The first zone, described as *Large High Islands* or *Melanesian Countries*[1] (includes Papua New Guinea, Solomon Islands, New Caledonia, Vanuatu, and Fiji), experiences a range of challenges that include rapid population growth, land degradation, deforestation, mining (often leading to water pollution), invasive species, and deterioration of fisheries due to coastal reef decomposition. The second zone, the *Mid-Sized High Islands of Polynesia and Micronesia and the Small High Island Territories of the United States* (includes Tonga, Samoa, French Polynesia, Palau, Federated States of Micronesia, Guam, American Samoa and the Northern Mariana Islands), is characterised by scarcity of land, extreme deforestation, loss of biodiversity, degradation of coral reefs and fisheries, and pollution of ground water and coasts by agriculture chemicals. Islands in this area are also prone to volcanic eruptions, earthquakes, droughts, and other disasters. Residents of the third zone, the *Small Islands* (includes Cook Islands, Kiribati, Tuvalu, Federated States of Micronesia, the Marshall Islands, Niue, and Nauru, as well as the Republic of Maldives in the Indian Ocean), are especially vulnerable to the effects of climate change. These promarily low-lying islands are highly exposed to storms, droughts, and limited fresh water access, but residents also have to cope with the consequences of ground water pollution from salt and agriculture,

Figure 24.1 Map of the Pacific Islands sub-regions

Used under Creative Commons license; map originally created by CartoGIS Services, College of Asia and the Pacific, The Australian National University

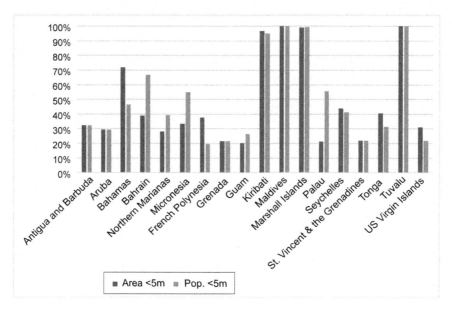

Figure 24.2 Percentage of land area and population below 5 m
Source: UN-Habitat (2015: 19)

and consequent food insecurity. High rates of population create additional challenges including rapid urbanisation in coastal areas and agricultural land unavailability.

Slow-onset environmental events: rising sea levels

Rising sea levels pose a range of challenges to low-lying and coastal regions around the world. Small island developing states (SIDS) are particulary threathened by inundation in low-lying areas with significant consequences such as substantial loss of territory (Figure 24.2). Many SIDS countries, due to their size, geography, and relative isolation and remoteness, have their very existence threatened. Key conclusions on the impacts of climate change on Small Island Developing States from the IPCC's Fifth Assessment Report (IPCC 2014) recognized as "virtually certain" that the rate of global average sea level rise has been accelerating since the 1950s, with the western Pacific experiencing a sea level rise up to four times the global average. The same report also observed that climate change is affecting the essential ecosystems on which the economic stability of the SIDS depend, posing risks to livelihoods, coastal settlements, infrastructure, ecosystems, and economic growth in the region. SIDS are especially exposed and vulnerable to sea level rise given that most socio-economic activity takes place in low-lying coastal areas (IPCC 2014: 1625).

Although rising sea levels in the SIDS are being generally driven by climate change, non-climate factors also play a role, including volcanic activity, subsidence, El Niño cycles, population growth, and sand mining (Balinuas and Soon 2002; Connell 2003).

Increased frequency and internsity of extreme rapid-onset events

There is a strong correlation between the frequency and intensity of extreme environmental events such as cyclones, hurricanes, typhoons, and climate change (UNEP 2007). The Pacific region is particularly exposed to these phenomena (Hay 2003). Forecasts estimate that climate variability, global average temperature rise, and sea warming will intensify and increase the frequency of natural disasters such as cyclones from 5–20% in the region (World Bank 2006). Evidence suggests the frequency of natural hazard events has increased in the region since the 1950s, and notably accelerated in the last decade. Increased intensity and frequency of tropical cyclones is a considerable concern in the Pacific. Cyclone Pam in 2015 and Cyclone Zoe in 2002 are examples of particularly destructive storms that have hit the region in recent decades (Shultz et al. 2016: 41), with Cyclone Winston, which hit Fiji in February 2016, ranking as one of the most powerful storms to ever strike the Pacific Islands region.

Since 1950, extreme environmental events have affected around 9.2 million people in the Pacific, with 9,811 reported deaths, and estimated damages of USD 3.2 billion (Framework for Resilient Development in the Pacific 2016: 17). The economic consequences of extreme natural disasters are expected to grow, but the scale of the impacts will vary by country. For example, a World Bank (2006) study estimated that annual damages from climate change and sea level rise could, for the state of Kiribati, could be equivalent to 17–34% of the country's Gross Domestic Product (GDP), but that for a high island as Viti Levu (Fiji), the average annual economic impact is expected to be much lower (about 2–4% of GDP by mid-century). During the last decade, some countries have experienced disasters and losses that have approached or exceeded their GDP. Estimates are that future economic loss and damage to key economic sectors, including agriculture, fisheries, and tourism could reach 34% of GDP in some countries (ADB 2013). In terms of economy, the Pacific countries will experience net negative impacts by 2050 in all climate change scenarios commonly used by climate scientists (ADB 2013). The costs of hard infrastructure needed to protect shorelines from future damage is not yet being fully accounted for in SIDS (SPREP 2009). In addition to economic risks, there also needs to be considered the non-economic implications of loss of family and community livelihoods, damage to housing and land, damage to cultural practices (such as burials), and the undermining of traditional governance system (Monnereau and Abraham 2013; Cantieri 2016). The livelihood and adaptation strategies of Pacific Islands residents often depend to a high degree on mobility, (UNFCCC 2012, UNHCR 2014), making it an important component of future socio-economic futures for the region.

Mobility in the Pacific: historical and cultural context, and current themes

Migration patterns in the Pacific, including those influenced by environmental factors, reflect complex decision-making processes involving multiple drivers (Shen and Gemenne 2011). Estimates of future climate-induced migration in the region often do not systematically consider evidence about how traditional and emergent forms of adaptation might minimize the impacts of climate change and therefore warrant consideration (Barnett and Webber 2010; Kniveton et al. 2008). Any assessments of human mobility in the context of climate change in the Pacific must also include the unpredicatable dimension of "perceptions" in order to reflect the complex and nuanced reality of the phenomenon. Mortreux and Barnett (2009) argue, for example, that decision-making process in response to climate change is highly shaped by "perceptions" of the affected population, which in turn are in turn reflective of their social circumstances. The decision to migrate is based on a multi-causal and complex process that is directly influenced by socioeconomic factors at the place of origin and perceptions of opportunities at place of destination (Connell and King 1990).

Further, perceptions and intention to migrate in the Pacific within the context of climate change should be contrasted with concerns about trapped populations:

> [S]ome people who do not intend to migrate may not have a choice in the future and may have to use migration as a survival strategy. Conversely, the intention to migrate may not translate into actual movements: people who intend to migrate may find themselves unable to do so, lacking the necessary means (for example, financial, social, and human capital).
>
> *(Zickgraf et al. 2016: 17)*

Barnett and Chamberlain (2010) argue that there will be large numbers of people unable to move away from the impacts of climate change in the Pacific, lacking the social and financial means to do so.

The Pacific region has a long tradition of environmentally induced migration and short-distance relocations of whole communities (Campbell, Goldsmith, and Koshy 2005: 3), and climate change is likely to exacerbate those long-term and immediate environmental risks that force people to move. Environmental variability and extreme events have always been a reality of life in Pacific Island communities Traditionally, Pacific Islanders have used a wide range of coping measures to sustain themselves in the face of the adverse effects of their environment, and Pacific cultures are embedded with a deep understanding of climate variability and patterns. Campbell (2010) has identified four main coping methods inherent in the long traditions of Pacific Island cultures: the maintenance of food security through surplus production, food storage, crop diversity, and food preservation; inter- and intra-community cooperation; environment-adapted settlement patterns and housing design; and the use of traditional environmental knowledge systems (Campbell 2006). These local adaptation strategies have been eroding over time, and disaster relief operations have contributed to this decline (Campbell 2010). Nonetheless, recent studies of adaptive capacity in the Cook Islands, Fiji, Samoa, and Vanuatu indicated that traditional coping methods are still used to deal with the environment hazards, with strategies that are still in use focusing on traditional methods, faith and religious beliefs, traditional governance and leadership systems, family and community involvement, and agriculture and food security (Fletcher et al. 2013).

Within this context, migration has been traditionally used as a coping method used to deal with environmental risks. As one study notes:

> Migration has always been an adaptation strategy to climate change in most [Pacific Island] countries and can become part of the solution in the face of climate change. [. . .] Seasonal and circular migration has always been used as adaptation strategy to cope with the natural annual change of seasons. This is particularly the case in rural areas at early stages of environmental degradation in reaction to slow-onset changes.
>
> *(Kniveton et al. 2008)*

For generations, Pacific Island communities' traditional adaptive strategies, culture, and practices have included retreating from coastal zones following extreme environmental events. For example, in Campbell, Goldsmith, and Koshy (2005), the Asia-Pacific Network for Global Change Research (APN) identified 86 historical cases involving population movements or relocation of communities (international and intra-national) between 1920 and 2004, includdng those that took place under colonial administration and under self-government. Such events were generated by a range of phenomena, including 37 caused by natural hazards, 13 by environmental degradation due to human actions such mining and nuclear testing, nine by conflicts, and nine by development projects.

Numerous studies have shown the importance of historical processes in order to better understand and address current and future climate-induced migration in the Pacific (e.g. Edwards 2013; McAdam and Ferris 2015; McAdam 2014; Campbell, Goldsmith, and Koshy 2005; Campbell 2010). Many traditional risk management and response strategies, such as customary land ownership structures, have been lost in the post-colonial era, leading in turn to the loss of shared social and cultural identities, spaces and meanings. At the same time, historical colonial ties help shape current patterns of migration, such as shown in mobility research in Tuvalu and the importance of trade agreements (Shen and Binns 2012). The adverse effects of climate change are likely to increasingly motivate islanders to migrate in order to cope with threats to their livelihoods. Therefore, human mobility in the Pacific in a changing climate needs to be understood in the context of both traditional and modern approaches to adaptation, and include consideration of traditional knowledge, cultural attitudes, values, and practices, and local expertise on community relocation as adaptive responses to extreme environmental events. Translating traditional knowledge into policy and finding ways to merge it with the best practices on planned relocation should be urgently addressed (Gharbaoui and Blocher 2016b).

Culture, place attachment, and customary land arrangements are other important factors often described in the literature on climate change and human mobility in the Pacific region (Barnett and Webber 2010). In a study of climate and migration in Tuvalu, Mortreux and Barnett (2009) found that migration decisions are shaped in a significant way by families' and communities' spiritual and social ties to their land. Land has been described by Pacific Islanders as "an extension of the self; and conversely the people are an extension of the land" (Ravuvu 1988).

The importance of customary land tenure is increasingly analyzed in studies on the human mobility and climate change nexus in the Pacific. However, its influence on mobility outcomes in the Pacific varies according to the context, as customary land systems are diverse in the region. A continuum of land rights arrangements that span from freehold to informal settlements may be found across Pacific Islands, and authors such as Mitchell et al. (2016) highlight the importance of accounting for such arrangements when assessing migration and relocation possibilities and outcomes under climate change. Looking ahead to the need for possible planned relocations due to climate change, Barry and Augustinus (2015) note that future tenure arrangements need to be found that best suit the cultural and economic needs of communities and of the larger state authority. Others highlight the importance of developing a "middle-ground approach" that includes negotiation at early stages of the relocation process including governments, local leaders, land owners, the communities being relocated and the hosting communities (Gharbaoui and Blocher 2016a). This recognizes the inherent tension in Pacific Islands of collective versus individual land rights.

Representations and portrayals of Pacific Islanders as "climate refugees" have been subject to heavy criticism from academics (McNamara and Gibson 2009). Farbotko (2010) provides a critical evaluation of debates on sea level rise, which she says have been dominated by western mythologies of islands being little more than laboratories and experimental spaces. Along these lines, Shen and Gemenne (2011) point out the critical need for population of the Pacific concerned by climate change to speak for themselves and, citing the case of Tuvaluan migration to New Zealand, point out that the reality of that migration is more complex than how it is portrayed in the media as a flight from rising sea levels. Rather than view themselves as refugees, Pacific Islanders increasingly call for the possibility of "migration with dignity" as the impacts of climate change take hold, which would allow for greater labour migration from SIDS to wealthier economies (McNamara 2015).

Current environmental migration and displacement in the region

There is varying evidence with respect to the role environmental factors, including climate change and sea level rise, currently play as drivers of migration in the Pacific Islands. Research done in 2015 by the Pacific Islands Forum Secretariat and United Nations University-Institute for Environment and Human Security (UNU-EHS) found that land degradation and deterioration of water conditions and infrastructure, combined with new economic and social challenges directly or indirectly linked to climate change, represent 17% of the reasons for which people migrate. A far more important driver is unemployment, cited by two-thirds of participants in that study (Corendea, Bello, and Bryar 2015: 12). In a different study, the Pacific Climate Change and Migration (PCCM) project[2] identified migration patterns and top international destinations for people living in Kiribati, Nauru, and Tuvalu between 2005 and 2015. It found that slow-onset environmental events have affected most households living in those countries (94% in Kiribati, 97% in Tuvalu, and 74% in Nauru), leading to migration either to ensure income or to find an alternative to land. However, only 23% of migrants in Kiribati and 8% in Tuvalu named climate change as being a reason for migrating. In a practical sense, international migration is at present not a widely available option for responding to climate risks. International migration opportunities for residents of Tuvalu, Kiribati, and Nauru are mostly limited to seasonal worker schemes in Australia and New Zealand, newly developed semi-skilled worker visa programs in Australia, educational or skilled labour migration to Australia, Fiji, and New Zealand. Although references are often made in the media to special migration programs that allow residents of Kiribati and Tuvalu to move to New Zealand, these actually add up to about 75 people per year. Although it is regularly cited as being highly exposed to the impacts of climate change and sea level rise, international migration from Kiribati is actually quite low: from 2005 to 2015, 1.3% of the population moved abroad. International migration rates are higher in Nauru and Tuvalu, where 10% and 15%, respectively, of people had migrated abroad (PCCM 2015).

Most documented examples of migration in the Pacific Region for climate-related reasons is internal, not international. Natural disasters and adverse impacts from strong El Niño Southern Oscillation (ENSO) events already lead to population displacements in many parts of the Pacific, and the scale of harm and number of people affected tend to be disproportionately high. In Papua New Guinea, for example, cyclones, flooding and earthquakes regularly cause internal displacements IOM (2015). Statistics from the Internal Displacement Monitoring Center (IDMC) suggest that 151,000 people were displaced in Papua New Guinea during the period 2008–2013, two-thirds of them by natural hazards (IDMC, NRC 2014: 5). As noted earlier, population growth and urbanisation rates in many Pacific Island nations are already high, and are expected to increase as a result of climate change. Modelling exercises carried out for PCCM (2015) that assume a medium climate change scenario (IPCC RCP 6) suggest that, in the 2050s, internal migration for Kiribati and Tuvalu will increase by 100% and 70%, respectively.

Recent ENSO-related weather events provide insights into the scale of vulnerability of Pacific small island states to climate-related disasters. An ENSO event in late 2015-early 2016 led to increased drought and food insecurity in parts of Fiji, Vanuatu, the Solomon Islands, and Papua New Guinea. In February 2016, a state of emergency was declared in the Marshall Islands as drought caused severe water shortages (Radio New Zealand 2016). The frequency of cyclones in the Pacific tends to go up during ENSO events; this was observed in 2015 with 21 storms of category 4 and 5 in the North Pacific, four more than the previous record of 17 in 1997 (NOAA

2015). It is thus not surprising that the latest, 2016 Global Report on Internal Displacements (GRID) that reports on internal displacement caused by sudden-onset disasters stated that:

> As in previous years, south and east Asia and the Pacific regions were worst-affected by displacement associated with disasters, and the vulnerable, coastal populations of small island developing states (SIDS) were disproportionately affected again.
>
> *(Bilak et al. 2016: p. 5)*

Tuvalu, Vanuatu, Micronesia, and Kiribati often figure in the top five most affected countries when it comes to disaster-induced displacement relative to population size. (Bilak et. al 2016) statistics for 2015 estimated displacement rates of 54,800 people displaced per 100,000 inhabitants in Tuvalu; 41,700 in Vanuatu; 6,500 in Micronesia; and 2,200 in Kiribati. Much of this was attributable to Cyclone Pam, a category 5 storm that struck in March 2015. Ten thousand people were displaced in Tuvalu, more than half its population. In Vanuatu, a quarter of the population was forced to move, and around 166,000 people required emergency assistance and shelter.

Internal migration and displacement due to climate change displacement will generate growing challenges to land and food security, state sovereignty, and culture preservation. There is no strong evidence linking climate change directly to conflict, but increasing human insecurity could conceivably act as a "threat multiplier" (Chapter 28, this volume) in countries such as Papua New Guinea, which has experienced past events of inter-community violence and consequent displacement (Corendea, Bello, and Bryar : 29). Competition over scarce socioeconomic and natural resources could lead to increased levels of violence and conflict between groups in the absence of adaptation measures.

Are planned relocations an answer?

Many countries in the Pacific region have actively considered planned relocation as an adaptation strategy to climate change and sea level rise (Gharbaoui and Blocher, 2016a). The relocation scenarios can take various forms. Local relocation that takes place within national boundaries is the most obvious option. In the context of the Pacific, the most likely scenarios would entail relocating coastal populations to more elevated land positions close to their existing locales (UNHCR 2008: 15). Doing so, however, would in many countries require moving people outside the boundaries of their traditionally held lands, which would raise a whole suite of social, economic, cultural and political challenges, and potentially generate conflicts over land use (Campbell, Goldsmith, and Koshy 2005,). The Pacific Regional Consultation organised by the Nansen Initiative thus suggested that relocation should be considered as a last resort option to be used only after other adaptation or mitigation measures have been considered (Nansen Initiative (2011).

Fiji has been a pioneer in developing guidelines for planned relocations. The Fijian government has identified 830 coastal and riverbank communities at risk of climate change (Turagaiviu 2015), including 45 communities that will need to be relocated within the next decade (Chandra 2015). The next section provides an overview of three examples of recent planned relocations, including two briefly described in recent studies by Charan, Kaur, and Singh (2017) and Cleaver and Hutt (2017), and a study of my own that is still ongoing, and now described to provide insights into the types of challenges faced in relocating communities in this region.

Vunidogoloa, Fiji

The village of Vunidogoloa, located in the province of Cakaudrove, was relocated in February 2014, the first village to be relocated under Fiji's Disaster Risk Reduction Programme. Several decades of gradual coastal erosion had made the site increasingly uninhabitable. In 2006, the Fijian government, after having been approached by the head of the Vunidogoloa community, confirmed that relocation would take place as an adaptive response to sea level rise. A new site for the village was found 1.5 km away, inland and uphill; the process of consultation and negotiation took several years, and was finally confirmed in 2012. Attachment to land was a major element that had to be considered in the relocation process. Sailosi Ramatu, head of the Vunidogoloa village observed: "It was not easy for the village community to relocate [. . .] especially true for older people that had lived in the village all their life, because the land is part of their culture and identity" (United Nations Office for the Coordination of Humanitarian Affairs 2014). The new site, named Kenani (the Promised Land) by the relocated community, was built to have approximately 30 houses, some fish ponds, farms, and a copra drier (Edwards 2013, RTCC 2014). It is notable that community members agreed to move to the new site only once the site was almost finalised and all the houses were completed, as it was crucial for the villagers to move all together as a community (Edwards 2013).

Tukuraki, Fiji

The village of Tukuraki in Ba, Viti Levu (Fiji main island) was hit by a landslide after heavy rains in January 2012, destroying 50% of the village homes and infrastructure. In December 2012, Cyclone Evan (category 4) destroyed those parts of the remaining village that were not destroyed by the previous disaster (SPC 2016). The Tukuraki village chief, Simione Deru, described the landslide as particularly destructive and mentioned that the disasters left villagers with very few resources, explaining that, "Since the accident some of us have moved to work in cane farms near the town. Others have found employment in the town just so they can survive" (Fox 2016).

Temporary shelters were found for residents after Cyclone Evan, and the Fiji government identified the village as being a potential candidate for future permanent relocation due to the risks associated with natural hazards and landslides (SPC 2016). In 2016, Tukuraki village was hit by Cyclone Winston (category 5), which forced residents to take emergency shelter in nearby caves. Following Cyclone Winston, Tukuraki was the first of 46 communities in Fiji to begin the process of relocation for disater-related reasons (Fox 2016). Fiji's National Disaster Management Office (NDMO) is in charge of the relocation, which is funded in part by the European Union through the Building Safety and Resilience in the Pacific Project (BSRP). A new site for Tukuraki village was selected in February 2014 after a geo-technical assessment was completed by the Fijian Mineral Resources Department (SPC 2016). The new site is approximately is 10 km from the original village, and the last 10 homes were being completed in mid-2017.

This relocation will allow the Tukuraki villagers to be re-unified as a community again. The new site provides villagers with full access to clean water, fish ponds, poultry farms, new homes and infrastructure, "retaining walls" surrounding the village, an evacuation centre, and a church (Cleaver and Hutt 2017). The Tukuraki chief, Simione Deru, explained that many villagers left the area after the repeated disasters, and hopes that they will return once the new village is finalised. He stated that the village relocation gives hope for the future generations:

At times we think about our old village where we were brought up, the place we used to play when we were kids. We miss it [. . .] Maybe the next generation they're going to grow up on this village, then they'll say this is our village.

(Fox 2016: n.p.)

Matawalu, Fiji

Matawalu Village in Ba province (Viti Levu) has a long history of river flooding. The village was severely hit by Cyclone Winston in 2016, which left some homes completely uninhabitable. Matawalu community members aim to relocate their village uphill by 2020 and, for that purpose, have developed a "Five Year Development plan" (2015–2020) funded by UNDP's Pacific Risk Resilience Program (PRRP).[3] The plan focuses on seven areas, including "improving flood prevention; sourcing water with a borehole and tanks and mineral water sources; community health; establishing an evacuation centre; developing roadside market stalls; youth workshops and awareness, and finally the planned village relocation" (UNDP 2014).

Qualitative data on the future planned relocation of Matawalu village and the potential land security challenges anticipated in coming years were collected personally in September 2017. The "middle-ground approach" to relocation (Gharbaoui and Blocher 2016a) was used as a framework in order to understand the role of customary chiefs, land owners, and community members in the relocation process. I conducted in-depth qualitative interviews with Matawalu's traditional customary chief and with 18 residents of Matawalu at very preliminary phase of the relocation process. At this point in time, negotiations had been initiated between Matawalu customary chief (and village headman) Josaia Rakoto (Figure 24.3) and the land owner of Kavula, the future hosting site.

Most Matawalu villagers are positive about moving their houses to the new site of Kavula, which is located uphill and less than one kilometer away from the original village site. The village headman explained that UN-Habitat has recently informed him that they will be funding the relocation of 25 houses, and has tasked him with negotiating the acquisition of the land that will be used for relocation.

The Matawalu village chief is also the customary chief of Kavula (Figure 24.4), which facilitates the negotiation process with the Kavula land owner. The negotiated *yaqona* (or price) was traditionally presented to the people of Kavula community, asking for their approval to allow the future relocation of 25 houses of some of the affected members of Matawalu village. The Matawalu village headman indicated that the negotiation over the new piece of land was facilitated by following the traditional protocol, and that discussions have consequently been smooth. The prior good relationship between the Matawalu customary chief and the Kavula landowner was another factor that simplified the process, as well as the fact that the Kavula landowner and community members also belong to the same *Mataqali* (or sub-clan) as the Matawalu villagers. Social relations are important aspects to consider when planning for village relocations in this part of the world. As the Matawalu customary chief underlined, "As I know that native Fijians honour traditional agreements, I believe that we will not face any problems with the Kavula landowner and community in the future". Even so, the negotiated agreement required some compromises; for example, the Kavula landowner and community have agreed to share their land, but only if residents of Kavula can occupy 12 of the 25 houses to be built, leaving Matawalu residents with only 13 houses to be rebuilt on the new site.

The Matawalu village headman is now facing the challenge of selecting which households will be moved from his community. As he perceives it, his choice will be based on his own

Figure 24.3 Matawalu customary chief, Josaia Rakoto, and his family
Credit: Author

judgement, in consultation with community members, to determine the households which are the most vulnerable but that also hardworking, reliable, and who have contributed well towards the village. At the same time, villagers of Matawalu are holding their own discussions about which households are the most vulnerable. The selection process is consequently raising tensions within the community and affecting community cohesion. Only one household of the 18 interviewed did not see any need to relocate, and would rather have their house rebuilt a few metres away from its current house. Most other villagers consider themselves vulnerable to flooding, and see relocation as the only way to provide their families with a sustainable future. Residents note that an alternative option of building seawalls would be too costly and thus not viable (Figures 24.5–24.7).

An important consideration for people of Matawalu who relocate to Kavula is to be able to continue to access the original village site and retain ownership of their current houses and farming lands. This would improve their current living status, as a house in Matawalu can some-times include two households, and so the relocation would allow each family to reside in one separate house in the short term and share the new house in Kavula only once the Matawalu home becomes uninhabitable in the future.

The example of Matawalu provides useful insights on the viability of so-called "staggered" relocation, such as that proposed by Zahir, Sarker, and Al-Mahud (2009), who proposed a sta-tistical approach that sees the relocation of part of an affected community whilst offering a local adaptation approach for those who do not move. The example of Matawalu suggests that relocating only a portion of a community can be highly problematic and can create tensions affecting community cohesion. Even though the final decision has not yet been made on which households in Matawalu are to be relocated, the cultural and social cohesion of the community is fraying, and splitting the community in this way threatens its collective structure. At this stage, the village chief and people of Matawalu have clearly expressed the need for UN-Habitat to be

Figure 24.4   Kavula, future hosting site of the Matawalu village
Credit: Author

Figure 24.5   Palm trees described by Matawalu villagers as "seawalls" protecting their homes from flooding by the nearby river. Piles of wood are also regularly added by the community to protect their homes.
Credit: Author

more actively involved in the vulnerability assessment, in the hope that the challenging decision of who will move and who will stay will be made in a more "scientific" manner (Figure 24.8). The chief and the villagers have also expressed concerns that UN-Habitat representatives have only ever contacted the village headman by phone, and have not once visited Matawalu in person. This lack of communication is creating more complexity in the relocation process, as the lack of clear and regular information leaves villagers with a lot of uncertainties and questions regarding their future relocation. For that reason, the customary chief and residents have stated that the timeframe and the next steps of the relocation process are not clear to them, and they are urging UN-Habitat to be involved in the selection of vulnerable houses in order to avoid internal tensions.

Figure 24.6 River bordering Matawalu village and causing flooding after heavy rains
Credit: Author

Figure 24.7 Matawalu village coastline impacted by flooding by the bordering river
Credit: Author

This case study shows how tensions about land can emerge within an affected community despite using a "middle-ground approach" to relocation that places traditional chiefs and the affected communities at the center of the relocation process and empowering them early in land negotiations. Tensions are arising within the community due to the lack of clear communication and information on the relocation process from the external stakeholder, UN-Habitat. For a "middle-ground approach" to relocation to work, it must have regular and clear communication, information, and support from external stakeholders, with regular and personal meetings in order to demystify the process for residents. Staggered relocations can evidently have negative impacts on community cohesion, reflecting Campbell's (2010) observation that community disarticulation could be considered as the most complex part of the displacement

Figures 24.8 Matawalu village member and his son in front of a village house damaged by flooding

Credit: Author

and reconstruction process. The importance of social aspects of relocation has previously been emphasized by Lieber (1977), and by Perry and Lindell (1997), who observed that specific attention should be given to social needs of populations forced to relocate and a particular emphasis should be placed on social networks that also need to be preserved. The preservation of community cohesion in relocation is particularly crucial in the context of the Pacific region (UNFCCC 2005), and it is critical that external stakeholders ensure that this element is central in any relocation planning. Once the relocation process is initiated, there is a strong need for all stakeholders involved in the process to regularly follow-up closely on the village's needs and to support the community by carrying out vulnerability assessments, if necessary.

Conclusion

Small Island Developing States in the Pacific are, by nature, extremely sensitive to environmental threats. The Pacific region as a whole is increasingly vulnerable to the impacts of climate change through accelerating rates of sea level rise and intensification in frequency and intensity of extreme environmental events. This poses challenges associated to both economic and non-economic loss and damages, including the loss of territories, customary lands, culture, identity, and resources.

Migration, displacement, and planned relocations in this region in response to environmental hazards, climate change and sea level rise are multi-causal and complex processes. The common representation in western literature of Pacific islanders as being "climate refugees" is not consistent with current international migration from the region. Although environmental factors do indeed stimulate migration and displacement, most of this takes place internally, within countries. As the impacts of climate change become manifest, internal migration rates are likely to rise, and the relocation of people from highly exposed coastal areas will become increasingly necessary. Key considerations going forward include necessity of taking into account the perceptions of individuals and communities, and the roles culture, place of attachment, and socio-cultural processes play in adaptation processes. Customary land tenure arrangements, which vary across countries, will raise additional challenges in state-led relocation initiatives. Examples from Fiji show that organized relocations can succeed, but are time-consuming and require considerable interaction between governments, external stakeholders, and affected communities to succeed. Situations where only part of an affected community is to be relocated are especially challenging, and even where communities are active participants from the early stages of the process, they require considerable support from external stakeholders if the process is to function without disrupting community cohesion. It is finally worth noting that most of the available literature on these issues has been generated by western academic institutions and researchers. Local and traditional knowledge and expertise is under-represented in published studies, suggesting an important opportunity to expand the presence and contribution of researchers from the Pacific.

Notes

1 Classifications based on United Nations Economic and Social Commission for Asia and the Pacific, "Ministerial Conference on Environment and Development in Asia and the Pacific 2000" Japan, Kitakyushu, 31 August–5 September 2000 www.unescap.org/MCED2000/pacific/SoE-pacific.htm#ove
2 Funded by the European Union and jointly implemented by the United Nations Economic and Social Commission for Asia and the Pacific (ESCAP), the International Labour Organization (ILO), and the United Nations Development Programme (UNDP). The United Nations University Institute for Environment and Human Security (UNU-EHS), UNESCAP, and the University of the South Pacific (USP)
3 PRRP, currently implemented in Solomon Islands, Vanuatu, Tonga and Fiji, is a US$16.1 million risk governance programme developed in partnership with the Australian Government Department for Foreign Affairs and Trade (DFAT) and the United Nations Development Programme (UNDP 2014)

Bibliography

Asia Development Bank (2013). *The economics of climate change in the Pacific.* Manila: ADB.

Asian Development Bank (n.d.) Regional cooperation on knowledge management, policy and institutional support of the Coral Triangle Initiative (www.coraltriangleinitiative.org/sites/default/files/resources/PNG%20SCTR_web%20copy.pdf)

AusAID (2008) Making land work – volume one: Reconciling customary land and development in the Pacific (www.ausaid.gov.au/publications/pdf/MLW_VolumeOne_Bookmarked.pdf) Canberra: AusAID.

Balinuas, S., & Soon, W. (2002). Is Tuvalu really sinking? *Pacific Magazine,* 28(2): 44–45, February.

Barnett J., & Chamberlain, N. (2010). Migration as climate change adaptation: Implications for the Pacific. In B. Burson (Ed.), Climate change and migration: South Pacific perspectives. Wellington, New Zealand: Institute of Policy Studies.

Barnett, J., & Webber, M. (2010). Accommodating migration to promote adaptation to climate change. *Policy Research Working Paper,* 5270, 62. Washington, DC: The World Bank.

Barry, M., & Augustinus, F. (2015). Framework for evaluating continuum of land rights scenarios, UN-Habitat, GLTN. www.ucalgary.ca/mikebarry/files/mikebarry/2-barryaugustinus-framework-for-evaluating-continuum-of-land-rights-scenarios-150915-review-copy.pdf

Bilak, A. Cardona-Fox, G. Ginnetti, J. Rushing, E. Scherer, I. Swain, M. Walicki, N. Yonetani, M. (2016). Global Report on Internal Displacement (GRID) Internal Displacement Monitoring Center (IDMC), Norwegian Refugee Council (NRC) (http://www.internal-displacement.org/assets/publications/2016/2016-global-report-internal-displacement-IDMC.pdf).

Black, R., Adger, W.N., Arnell, N.W., Dercon, S., Geddes, A. and Thomas, D. (2011) The effect of environmental change on human migration. *Global Environmental Change,* 21, S3–S11.

Bolatagici, L. (2016). After assessments, many more Fiji villages slated for relocation (www.pireport.org/articles/2016/04/21/after-assessments-many-more-fiji-villages-slated-relocation)

Bronen, R. and Chapin, F.S. (2013). Adaptive governance and institutional strategies for climate-induced community relocations in Alaska. *PNAS,* 110(23), 9320–9325.

Byamugisha, F. (2013) Sharing Africa's land for shared prosperity. A program to scale up reforms and investments (www.scribd.com/doc/144377306/Securing-Africa-s-Land-for-Shared-Prosperity) World Bank, Washington, DC.

Campbell, J.R., Goldsmith, M., & Koshy, K. (2005). Community relocation as an option for adaptation to the effects of climate change and climate variability in Pacific Island Countries (PICs). Kobe: Asia-Pacific Network for Global Change Research (APN).

Campbell, J. R. (2006). Traditional disaster reduction in Pacific Island communities. *GNS Science Report*, 38, 46.

Campbell, J. (2010). An overview of natural hazard planning in the Pacific Island region. *Australasian Journal of Disaster and Trauma Studies*, ISSN: 1174–4707, Volume 2010–1.

Cantieri, J. (2016, June). Rising sea threatens traditional leadership in Kiribati. *National Geographic* (http://voices.nationalgeographic.com/2016/06/02/rising-sea-threatens-traditional-leadership-in-kiribati/)

Chandra, T. (2015). 45 Fiji Villages likely to be relocated due to climate change. *Pacific Islands Report, Pacific Islands Development program (PIDP), Fiji Times* (http://pidp.eastwestcenter.org/pireport/2015/February/02-13-03.htm)

Charan, D., Kaur, M., & Singh, P. (2017). Customary land and climate change induced relocation—a case study of Vunidogoloa Village, Vanua Levu, Fiji. *Climate Change Adaptation in Pacific Countries, Climate Change Management Series (CCM)*, 19–33.

Cleaver, J., & Hutt, K. (2017). Village relocation provides new hope for Fiji's devastated Tukuraki. *Asia Pacific Report* (http://asiapacificreport.nz/2017/07/23/village-relocation-provides-new-hope-for-devastated-tukuraki/)

Connell, J., & King R. (1990). Island migration in a changing world. In *Small Worlds Global Lives : Islands and migration* (pp. 1–26). London: Pinter Publications.

Connell, J. (2003). Losing ground Tuvalu, the greenhouse effect and the garbage can. *Asia-Pacific View Point*, 44(2), 89–107.

Connell, J., & Lutkehaus, N. (2016). Another Manam? The forced migration of the population of Manam Island, Papua New Guinea, due to volcanic eruptions 2004/2005 Geneva, IOM.

Connell, J., & Lutkehaus, N. (2017). Environmental refugees? A tale of two resettlement projects in coastal Papua New Guinea. *Australian Geographer*, 48(1), 79–95.

Corendea, C., Bello, V., & Bryar, T. (2015). Pacific research project: Promoting human security and minimizing conflict associated with forced migration in the Pacific region (https://collections.unu.edu/view/UNU:3171)

Edwards, J. (2012). Location, location, relocation, the bula bulletin, April–May, p. 3. December 5, 2016 (newsletter-aprilmay2012.pdf)

Edwards, J. (2013a). The logistics of climate-induced resettlement: Lessons from the Carteret Islands, Papua New Guinea. *Refugee Survey Quarterly*, 32(3), 1 September 2013, 52–78 (https://doi.org/10.1093/rsq/hdt011)

Edwards, J. (2013). Financing the future wave of relocations (www.methodist.org.uk/media/757401/wcr-pcc-relocation-policy-fiji-jan13.pdf)

Edwards, J. (2014). Climate justice and the Pacific conference of churches: Moving the relocation agenda in the Pacific. In L. Andrianos, J. W. Sneep, G. Kerber, & R. Attfield (Eds.), *Sustainable alternatives for poverty reduction and eco-justice* (Vol. 1, p. 209). Newcastle, England: Cambridge Scholars Publishing.

FAO (2012). Voluntary guidelines on the responsible governance of tenure of land, fisheries and forests in the context of food security (www.fao.org/docrep/016/i2801e/i2801e.pdf)

Farbotko, C. (2010). Wishful sinking: Disappearing islands, climate refugees and cosmopolitan experimentation. *Asia Pacific Viewpoint*, 51(1), April, 47–60 (http://onlinelibrary.wiley.com/doi/10.1111/j.1467-8373.2010.001413.x/epdf?r3_referer=wol&tracking_action=preview_click&show_checkout=1&purchase_referrer=ro.uow.edu.au&purchase_site_license=LICENSE_DENIED)

Farbotko, C., & Lazrus, H. (2012). The first climate refugees? Contesting global narratives of climate change in Tuvalu. *Global Environmental Change*, 22, 382–390.

Fien, J., Sykes, H., & Yencken, D. (2000). *Environment, education and society in the Asia-Pacific: Local traditions and global discourses. Routledge Advances in Asia-Pacific Studies.* London and New York: Routledge.

FIG/GLTN (2010). The social tenure domain model. FIG Publication 52 (www.fig.net/pub/figpub/pub52/figpub52.htm) Copenhagen, Denmark.

Fletcher, S., Thiessen, J., Gero, A., Rumsey, M., Kuruppu, N., & Willets, J. (2013). Traditional coping strategies and disaster response: Examples from the South Pacific Region. *Journal of Environmental and Public Health*, 2013, Article ID 264503, 9 pages. http://dx.doi.org/10.1155/2013/264503

Foresight (2011). Migration and global environmental change: Future challenges and opportunities. Final Project Report (London, UK: UK Government Office for Science) 236.

Fox, L., (2016). Fiji relocates villages vulnerable to natural disasters as part of Cyclone Winston rebuild. *ABC News*, Press release, 9 September 2016 (www.abc.net.au/news/2016-09-09/fiji-relocates-villages-as-part-of-cyclone-winston-rebuild/7831630)

Fletcher, S., Thiessen, J., Gero, A., Rumsey, M., Kuruppu, N., & Willets, J. (2013). Traditional coping strategies and disaster response: Examples from the South Pacific Region. *Journal of Environmental and Public Health*, 2013, Article ID 264503, 9 pages. http://dx.doi.org/10.1155/2013/264503

Foresight (2011). Migration and global environmental change: Future challenges and opportunities. Final Project Report (London UK: UK Government Office for Science) 236.

Framework for Resilient Development in the Pacific (2016), An Integrated Approach to Address Climate Change and Disaster Risk Management (FRDP) 2017–2030, 11 September 2016 (http://www.forumsec.org/resources/uploads/embeds/file/Annex%201%20-%20Framework%20for%20Resilient%20Development%20in%20the%20Pacific.pdf)

Gemenne, F., & Blocher, J. (2016). How can migration support adaptation? Different options to test the migration-adaptation nexus migration, environment and climate change. Working Paper Series 1/2016 IOM, Geneva.

Gemenne, F., and Blocher, J. M. (2017). How can migration serve adaptation to climate change? Challenges to fleshing out a policy ideal. *The Geographic Journal*, 1–12.

Gharbaoui, D., & Blocher, J. (2016a). The reason land matters: Relocation as adaptation to climate change in Fiji Islands. In A. Milan, N. Cascone, B. Schraven, & K. Warner (Eds.), *Migration, risk management, and climate change – evidence and policy responses*. Berlin: Springer.

Gharbaoui, D., & Blocher, J. (2016b) The reason place matters; Climate change, planned relocation and land tenure in Fiji and Papua New Guinea. Macmillan Brown Centre for Pacific Studies, Pacific Policy Brief 2016/7, Policy Brief Series, University of Canterbury.

Government of Papua New Guinea (GoPNG) (2007). The National Land Development Taskforce report: Land administration, land dispute settlement, and customary land development. National Research Institute, Monograph 39, Port Moresby.

GoPNG (2012). Systems, process and institutions. PNG Decent Country Program. Monograph. Department of Labour and Industrial Relations, Port Moresby. Papua New Guinea Vision 2050, National Strategic Plan Taskforce. Papua New Guinea's Strategic Program for Climate Resilience. Recognised Seasonal Employer Policy: Inter-Agency Understanding Papua New Guinea.

Gravelle, G., & Mimura, N. (2008). Vulnerability assessment of sea-level rise in Viti Levu, Fiji Islands. *Sustainability Science*, 3(2), 171–180 (http://link.springer.com/article/10.1007/s11625-008-0052-2?no-access=true)

Hay, J.E. (2003). Climate variability and change and sea-level rise in the Pacific Islands region: A resource book for policy and decision makers, educators and other stakeholders, Apia, Samoa. (www.sprep.org/publication/pub_detail.asp?id=181)

Humanitarian Affairs (OCHA) (2014). Fiji: Building resilience in the face of climate change. Accessed 25 April 2016 (www.unocha.org/top-stories/all-stories/fijibuilding-resilience-face-climatechange)

Yonetani, M. Lavell, C. Bower E., Meneghetti, L. O'Connor K. (2015) Global Estimates 2015, People displaced by disasters, Internal Displacement Monitoring Center (IDMC) July.

International Disaster Database (2015). Brussels: Université catholique de Louvain (www.emdat.be)

IDMC, NRC (2014). Papua New Guinea: Invisible and neglected protracted displacement, 11 December (www.refworld.org/docid/548e9e564.html)

IOM (2015). Assessing the evidence: Migration, environment and climate change in Papua New Guinea (https://publications.iom.int/books/assessing-evidence-migration-environment-and-climate-change-papua-new-guinea)

IPCC (2014) Impacts, Adaptation, and Vulnerability. Part A: Global and Sectoral Aspects. Contribution of Working Group II to the Fifth Assessment Report of the Intergovernmental Panel on Climate Change (http://www.ipcc.ch/report/ar5/wg2/).

IRIN News (2013). Papua New Guinea government improves disaster preparedness funding (www.irin-news.org/report/98433/papua-new-guinea-government-improves-disaster-preparedness-funding)

Janif, S.Z., Nunn, P.D., Geraghty, P., Aalbersberg, W., Thomas, F.R. and Camailakeba, M. (2016). Value of traditional oral narratives in building climate-change resilience: Insights from rural communities in Fiji. *Ecology and Society*, 21(2), 7 (//www.ecologyandsociety.org/vol21/iss2/art7/#Relocation)

Johnson, R.W. (2013). *Fire mountains of the islands: A history of volcanic eruptions and disaster management in Papua New Guinea and the Solomon Islands.* Canberra: Australian National University Press.

Kirsch, S. (2001). Lost worlds – environmental disaster, culture loss, and the law. *Current Anthropology*, 42(2), 167.

Klein, R.J.T., Midgley, G.F., Preston, B.L., Alam, M., Berkhout, F.G.H., Dow, K., & Shaw, M.R. (2014). Adaptation opportunities, constraints and limits. In *Climate change 2014: Impacts, adaptation, and vulnerability. Part A: global and sectoral aspects.* Contribution of the Working Group II to the Fifth Assessment Report of the Intergovernmental Panel on Climate Change C. B. Field, V. R. Barros, D. J. Dokken et al. Cambridge, United Kingdom/New York, NY: Cambridge University Press, 899–943.

Kniveton, D., Schmidt-Verkerk, K., Smith, C., & Black, R. (2008). Climate change and migration: Improving methodologies to estimate flows. IOM Migration Research Series Paper No.33. Geneva, Switzerland: International Organisation for Migration (IOM).

Lieber, M. D. (1977). Exiles and migrants in oceania (Association for Social Anthropology in Oceania Monograph Series). Honolulu: The University Press of Hawaii.

López-Carr, D., & Marter-Kenyon, J. (2015). Human adaptation: Manage climate-induced resettlement. *Nature*, 517, 7534.

Lutkehaus, N.C. (2016). Finishing Kapui's name: Birth, death and the reproduction of Manam society, Papua New Guinea. In D. Lipset & E.K. Silverman (Eds.). *Mortuary dialogues: Death ritual and the reproduction of moral community in Pacific modernities.* New York and Oxford: Barghahn.

McAdam, J. (2014). Historical cross-border relocations in the Pacific: Lessons for planned relocations in the context of climate change. *Journal of Pacific History*, 301, 49.

McAdam, J., & Ferris, E. (2015). Planned relocations in the context of climate change: Unpacking the legal and conceptual issues. *Cambridge Journal of International and Comparative Law*, 137–66.

McNamara, K. E. (2015). Cross-border migration with dignity in Kiribati. *Forced Migration Review*, 49, 62.

McNamara, K., & Gibson, C. (2009). We do not want to leave our land': Pacific ambassadors at the United Nations resists the category of 'climate refugees'. *Geoforum*, 40(3), 475–83.

McNamara, K.E., & Combes, D. (2015). H.J. Int J Disaster Risk Sci, 6 315.

Mitchell, D.P., & Antonio, D., Storey, D., CheeHai, T., & Rosales-Kawasaki, L. (2016). Land tenure in Asia and the Pacific: Challenges, opportunities and way forward, February 23. Available at SSRN: https://ssrn.com/abstract=2737103

Mitchell, D., Orcherton, D., Numbasa, G., & McEvoy, D. (2016). The implications of land issues for climate resilient informal settlements in Fiji and Papua New Guinea (www.rics.org/Global/Land_Issues_Fiji_PNG_300316_dwl_aa.pdf)

Monnereau, I., & Abraham, S. (2013). Limits to autonomous adaptation in response to coastal erosion in Kosrae, Micronesia. *International Journal Of Global Warming*, 5(4), 416–32.

Mortreux, C, and J Barnett (2009) Climate change, migration and adaptation in Funafuti, Tuvalu. *Global Environmental Change*, 19: 105–112.

Mulina, K., Sukua, J., & Tibong, H. (2011, 6–29 September). Report on Madang volcanic hazards awareness program. *Rabaul Volcanological Observatory*.

Nalu, M. (2011a). The tragedy of Manam Islanders . . . Refugees in their own country (http://malumnalu.blogspot.com/)

Nansen Initiative. (2011). Conclusion: Nansen Initiative Pacific Regional Consultation. (http://www2. nanseninitiative.org/pacific-consultations-intergovernmental)

Nansen Initiative (2013). Human mobility, natural disasters and climate change in the Pacific: Report from the Nansen Initiative Pacific Regional Consultation 21–24 May 2013, Rarotonga, Cook Islands.

Nicholls, J. (2003). Case study on sea-level rise impacts, Working party on global and structural policies; OECD workshop on the benefits of climate policy: Improving information for policy makers (www. oecd.org/dataoecd/7/15/2483213.pdf)

NOAA (2015). November El Niño update: It's a small world, 12 November (https://goo.gl/Fgb0MB)

Pacific Climate Change and Migration project (PCCM) (2015). Key Findings: Climate Change and Migration in the Pacific: Links, attitudes, and future scenarios in Nauru, Tuvalu, and Kiribati, UNU-EHS, ESCAP. (https://i.unu.edu/media/ehs.unu.edu/news/11747/RZ_Pacific_EHS_ESCAP_151201.pdf)

Perry, M. (2005). Rising seas, disappearing islands to cause environmental refugees in a warming world, 24 November. (http://news.mongabay.com/2005/1124-reuters.html)

Perry, R.W., & Lindell, M.K. (1997). Principles for managing community relocation as a hazard mitigation measure. *Journal of Contingencies and Crisis Management*, 5(1), 53–56.

Radio New Zealand (2016). PNG government commended for establishing Manam resettlement authority (www.radionz.co.nz/international/pacific-news/163830/png-government-commended-for-establishing-manam-resettlement-authority)

Radio Australia (2012). Manam islanders displaced by volcano to re-settle (www.radioaustralia.net.au/international/radio/program/pacific-beat/manam-islanders-displaced-by-volcano-to-resettle/1020584)

Ravuvu, A.D. (1988). *Development or dependence: The pattern of change in a Fijian Village*. Suva: University of the South Pacific.

Report for Royal Institution of Chartered Surveyors (RICS) (2016). *The implications of land issues for climate resilient informal settlements in Fiji and Papua New Guinea*. London: RICS.

Responding to Climate Change (RTCC). (2014). Fiji village relocated under climate change programme (www.rtcc.org/2014/01/17/fiji-village-relocated-under-climate-changeprogramme/#sthash.dbj8Y9XN.dpuf)

Secretariat Pacific Community (2016) Tukuraki village relocation, News and Press release, 21 July 2016 (http://reliefweb.int/report/fiji/tukuraki-village-relocation)

Sendai Framework (2015). Sendai framework for disaster risk reduction 2015–2030 United Nations Office for Disaster Risk Reduction (UNISDR) (www.unisdr.org/files/43291_sendaiframeworkfordrren.pdf)

Serge, L., Nolan, A., Brown, A., & Clements, K. (2009). Conflict management processes for land-related conflict (www.forumsec.org/resources/uploads/attachments/documents/LMCM%204_1%20COMPLETE.pdf) Suva, Fiji: Pacific Islands Forum Secretariat.

Shen, S., & Binns, T. (2012). Pathways, motivations and challenges: Contemporary Tuvaluan migration to New Zealand. *GeoJournal*, 77, 63–82.

Shen, S., & Gemenne, F. (2011). Contrasted views on environmental change and migration: The case of Tuvaluan migration to New Zealand. *International Migration*, 49(S1), e224–e242.

Shisei, R. (2016). Manam Resettlement Bill passed (www.emtv.com.pg/article.aspx?slug=Manam-Resettlement-Bill-Passed---2&)

Shultz, J.M., Cohen, M.A., Hermosilla, S., Espinel, Z., & McLean, A. (2016). Disaster risk reduction and sustainable development for small island developing states. *Disaster Health*, 3(1), 32–44.

SPC (2016) Tukuraki Village Relocation, 21 July 2016 (http://www.spc.int/blog/tukuraki-village-relocation/)

SPREP (2009). Pacific adaptation to climate change; Cook Islands. Report of In-Country Consultations, p. 1 (www.sprep.org/att/irc/ecopies/countries/cook_islands/67.pdf)

Thaman K.H. (2000). Cultural rights: A personal perspective. In M. Wilson & P. Hunt (eds) *Culture, Rights, and Cultural Rights: Perspectives from the South Pacific*. Conference Proceedings for a colloquium by the UNESCO Office for Pacific Member States and the Centre for New Zealand Jurisprudence, (School of Law, University of Waikato, New Zealand), in October 1998, Huaia Publishers, Wellington, pp. 69–81.

Turagaiviu, E. (2015). 830 Fijian communities at risk from climate change. Fiji Broadcasting Corporation, 29 October. February 12, 2016 (www.fbc.com.fj/fiji/34377/-830-fijian-communities-at-risk-from-climate-change)

UNDP (2014). *Matawalu Village plans village relocation to reduce risks for residents.* United Nations Development Program Asia Pacific, 2 December 2014 (www.asia-pacific.undp.org/content/rbap/en/home/presscenter/pressreleases/2014/12/02/matawalu-village-plans-village-relocation-to-reduce-risks-for-residents-.html)

UNESCAP (2000). United Nations Economic and Social Commission for Asia and the Pacific, "Ministerial Conference on Environment and Development in Asia and the Pacific 2000" Japan, Kitakyushu, 31 August-5 September 2000, www.unescap.org/MCED2000/pacific/SoE-pacific.htm#ove

United Nations Framework Convention on Climate Change (UNFCCC). (2005). *Climate change small island developing states.* Bonn: UNFCC Secretariat. (http://unfccc.int/resource/docs/publications/cc_sids.pdf)

UN-Habitat (2008). Secure land rights for all (www.responsibleagroinvestment.org/sites/responsibleagroinvestment.org/files/Secure%20land%20rights%20for%20all-UN%20HABITAT.pdf)

UN-Habitat (2015). Urbanization and climate change in Small Island Developing States (https://sustainabledevelopment.un.org/content/documents/2169(UN-Habitat,%202015)%20SIDS_Urbanization.pdf).

United Nations Environment Programme (2007). IPCC Fourth Assessment Report (AR4) (www.ipcc.ch/pdf/assessment-report/ar4/syr/ar4_syr.pdf)

United Nations Framework Convention on Climate Change (2012) Slow-onset events, Technical Paper (http://unfccc.int/resource/docs/2012/tp/07.pdf)

United Nations High Commissioner for Refugees (UNHCR) (2008). *Climate change, human rights and forced human displacement: Meeting report,* Australia, 10 Dec 2008. Geneva: UNHCR.

United Nations Office of the High Commissioner for Refugees (UNHCR) (2014). *Planned relocations, disasters and climate change: Consolidating good practices and preparing for the future Background Document.* Geneva: UNHCR.

United Nations Office of the High Commissioner for Human Rights (UNOHCHR), Regional Office for the Pacific (2011, April). Protecting the human rights of internally displaced persons in natural disasters: Challenges in the Pacific. Discussion Paper, Suva.

United Nations Office for the Coordination of Humanitarian Affairs. (2014). Fiji: Building resilience face climate change. February 18, 2016 (www.unocha.org/topstories/ all-stories/fiji-building-resilience-face-climate-change)

Waide, S. (2014). 10 years after the eruption (www.PNGBlogs.com/2014)

WMO (2016, 18 February). 15 April 2017 (https://goo.gl/wiAUF)

World Bank (2006). Not if but when; adapting to natural hazards in the Pacific Islands region. The World Bank East Asia and Pacific Region Pacific Islands Country Management Unit (Policy Note)

Zahir, S., Sarker, R., & Al-Mahmud, Z. (2009). An interactive decision support system for implementing sustainable relocation strategies for adaptation to climate change: A multi-objective optimisation approach. *International Journal of Mathematics in Operational Research,* 1(3), 326–350.

Zickgraf, C., Vigil, S., De Longueville, F., Ozer, P., & Gemenne, F. (2016). The impact of vulnerability and resilience to environmental changes on mobility patterns in West Africa. KNOMAD Working Paper, 2016/04/01

Part III
Legal and policy considerations

25
Definitions and concepts

Benoît Mayer

Introduction

Many terms have been used to refer to individuals who are displaced in connection with environmental factors. Alternative qualificatives – "environmental," "ecological," "climate," etc. – have been combined with several substantives – "migrants," "refugees," "displaced persons," etc. – to form a myriad of ill-defined terms. Such terminological hesitancy is far from uncommon in a new field were many voices attempt to say similar things without necessarily using the same words. Yet, in relation to environmental migration, these terminological difficulties have continued for several decades and remain particularly intractable. Debates on the terminology to use when referring to individuals displaced in connection with environmental factors reflect deeper conceptual questions that this chapter seeks to explore, in particular the difficulty of attributing an individual decision to migration to one single cause in isolation from others.

There are important questions at stake in terminological choices. Although there is no unique understanding of these terminological choices, "refugee" (from the French past participle "réfugié," literally a "refuged" person) and "displaced persons" have a passive connotation suggesting that the person was *forced* to migrate, whereas "migrant" uses the active voice of the present participle so does not exclude that the person could have freely *decided* to migrate. While "migrant" can thus be used as a generic term, "refugee" is often taken to indicate a forced journey across an international border, and "displaced person" generally alludes to "internationally displaced persons," a term coined in the 1990s to refer essentially to people who could qualify as refugees if they were to cross an international border or to other individuals forcedly displaced within their own state. Adjoining "climate" as a qualificative to any such substantive, as in "climate migrants" or "climate refugees," suggests a narrower attribution of migration to environmental impacts of climate change, such as sea level rise or perhaps some hydro-meteorological natural disasters whose occurrence becomes more likely because of climate change. Attribution to climate change raises additional difficulties relating to evidence as well as to the probabilistic (rather than determinative) nature of climate change.

This chapter uses "environmental migrants" as a generic term to relate to populations displaced because of environmental factors. Defining environmental migrants is an essential preliminary step before assessing the scope of the phenomenon (e.g. put figures on "environmental migration") and proposing possible legal responses (e.g. a status of "environmental migrants"). However, any attempt at a specific definition of an environmental migrant faces many conceptual issues. It is rarely possible to attribute an individual migration to environmental factors in a convincing way.

The second section reviews the definitions proposed (or implied) in the literature. A third section discusses underlying conceptual issues that have impeded any attempt to define environmental migrants. A fourth section finally turns to alternative approaches to defining populations of concern on the basis of scenarios or protection needs.

The elusive definition of environmental migrants

At the most basic and almost tautological level, "environmental migrant" refers to people who migrate because of environmental factors. Many authors have sought to develop a more specific definition of environmental migrants – one which could actually help identify individuals as environmental migrants. An exhaustive list of such attempts is obviously beyond the scope of this chapter, but five representative illustrations can be mentioned.

1   In one of the first publications on the impact of environmental factors on migration, Hassam El-Hinnawi (1985: 4) suggested the term "environmental refugees" to refer to people "who have been forced to leave their traditional habitat, temporarily or permanently, because of a marked environmental disruption (natural and/or triggered by people) that jeopardised their existence and/or seriously affected the quality of their life."

2   Two decades later, a discussion note of the International Organization for Migration proposed a working definition that has largely been cited in subsequent publications. "Environmental migrants" were accordingly to refer to:

persons or groups of persons who, for compelling reasons of sudden or progressive changes in the environment that adversely affect their lives or living conditions, are obliged to leave their habitual homes, or choose to do so, either temporarily or permanently, and who move either within their country or abroad.

(IOM 2007: para. 6)

3   In 2008, Michel Prieur led a group of jurists to develop a proposal for a "Convention on the International Status of Environmentally-Displaced Persons." The latter were defined as "individuals, families and populations confronted with a sudden or gradual environment disaster that inexorably impacts their living conditions, resulting in their forced displacement, at the outset or throughout, from their habitual residence" (CRIDEAU 2008: article 2).

4   Two years thereafter, an influential article by Frank Biermann and Ingrid Boas called for working "towards a global governance system to protect climate refugees." "Climate refugees" were defined as:

people who have to leave their habitats, immediately or in the near future, because of sudden or gradual alterations in their natural environment related to at least one of three impacts of climate change: sea-level rise, extreme weather events, and drought and water scarcity.

(Biermann and Boas 2010: 67)

5   A more recent article by Eike Albrecht and Malte Paul Plewa defines a "climate-change refugee" as:

> an individual who is forced to flee his or her home and to relocate prospectively permanently in a different country, as the result of sudden or gradual environmental disruption which has made his or her homeland uninhabitable and which has, more likely than not, resulted from anthropogenic climate change, where that individual is either unable or unwilling to avail him- or herself of the protection of his or her home country.
>
> *(Albrecht and Plewa 2015: 80)*

These definitions address several questions often, although not always in similar fashion.

1   Environmental migrants are generally approached as individuals, but also, sometimes, as groups, or even as families or "populations" (CRIDEAU 2008), which could suggest some collective rights (e.g. possibly some rights to self-governance) or some individual rights to ensure belonging to a collective entity (e.g. a specific protection of cultural rights).
2   Environmental migrants have migrated, or possibly have to migrate "immediately or in the near future" (Biermann and Boas 2010: 67). It is slightly counter-intuitive to qualify a person who has not yet migrated as a migrant (or "refugee"), but this suggests that a status of environmental migrants could include the right to migrate. In practice, however, identifying individuals who will have to migrate in the near future is particularly problematic.
3   Their migration may be either temporary or permanent. Environmental migrants include, therefore, people in very different situations on a continuum between very short-term displacements (a few days) and people for whom permanent arrangements need to be made.
4   Their migration is forced as a matter of survival or in order to avoid serious loss of life quality, or could possibly follow from a choice (IOM 2007). These differences in the definitions cited above are of tremendous significance. Forced migration can be defined very narrowly if it is limited to matters of immediate and certain life or death. But all migrants, whether forced or not, have rights; many of them are exposed to human rights abuses as they enter unknown places.
5   Their migration is caused by a "marked environmental disruption" (El-Hinnawi 1985: 4), whether happening suddenly or gradually. Gradual environmental impacts such as sea level rise, happening at a very slow pace, may be particularly difficult to isolate from other factors. They may not cause migration as suddenly as a natural disaster, but rather through economic proxy factors.

Some definitions also require that environmental "refugees" cross the border of their state of origin (Albrecht and Plewa 2015), or that, to quality as "climate refugees," the environmental factor could be related to climate change (Biermann and Boas 2010, Albrecht and Plewa 2015). We leave these particularities aside in the following, focusing on environmental migrants in their generality.

Underlying conceptual issues

Such definitions are overly general and abstract, and they would be of little assistance in trying to identify an individual environmental migrant. Distinguishing individuals likely to migrate in the immediate future, for instance, would be quite problematic. Asserting whether an individual's migration is necessary for survival or to ensure minimal living quality, on the other hand, could also be particularly difficult. The distinction between voluntary and forced migration is not a dichotomy based on clear criteria, but rather a continuum (for instance, Hugo 1996). Whether migration is voluntary and forced cannot in practice be based on the individual's own feeling that there is no other option but to migration, as this would require an impossible guess in an individual's thoughts. Instead, an objective test would need to be used, based on an idea of what constitutes an acceptable threshold to prevail over other considerations. This would require the difficult definition of a threshold of harm (how much harm is likely to be suffered?) and a threshold of risk (how likely is this harm?).

However, by far the most problematic dimensions in implementing any definition of an environmental migrant would be to determine whether an individual's migration can be attributed to an environmental factor, and whether *that* particular factor "forces" this individual to migrate. We migrate, or do not migrate, at any given time in our life, by taking into account as many elements as we take into account in any important decision, including possibly expected economic opportunities or health care, options for education or leisure at different places, and the quality of the natural or socio-cultural environment and our readiness, or fears, to see different horizons. None of these factors operates in total isolation from the others.

Environmental factors may, however, lead to compelling considerations. Natural disasters most obviously force people to flee suddenly when their life is at risk. Slow-onset environmental changes effect individuals more gradually, most often through economic considerations. A gradual degradation of a grassland could make it more difficult to rear cattle, for instance, leading new generations to seek other sources of income elsewhere. By contrast, a sudden drought, or a flood, could force entire populations to leave at once.

Yet, even the strongest physical event only becomes a natural disaster in a given context. Exposure, vulnerability and resilience define whether and how individuals and societies are affected by any given environmental phenomenon. Thus, Olivia Dun and François Gemenne noted that "[t]he main reason for the lack of definition relating to migration caused by environmental degradation or change is linked to the difficulty of isolating environmental factors from other drivers of migration" (Dun and Gemenne 2007: 10). Likewise, a report on "Migration and Global Environmental Change" delivered to the British Foresight agency in 2011 concluded that, although environmental change will continue to affect migration, interactions between economic, social, political and environmental factors "means that it will rarely be possible to distinguish individuals for whom environmental factors are the sole driver ('environmental migrants')" (Foresight 2011: 9).

The latter quote, if taken seriously, suggests that the difficulty faced in adopting a meaningful definition of environmental migrants is actually a conceptual issue – the impossibility of recognizing environmental factors in individuals' experience of migration. Because migration scholars overwhelmingly suggest that environmental factors are only part of a cluster of causes, it is conceptually misleading to discuss something called "environmental migration" as if it is a distinct phenomenon. The difficulty is not in putting a name to it, but in trying to identify the "it" in the first place when environmental change does not create a distinct sort of migration. Definitions of environmental migrants will remain overly abstract, figures will remain inconsistent and policy proposals will remain irrelevant as long as we fail to understand that the influence of environmental factors on migration does not give rise to a distinct population of migrants.

Alternative approaches to defining populations of concern

Rather than seeking to define environmental migrants as a particular population of concern, recent developments have considered alternative perspectives. Some have relaxed the causal requirement and explored on multiple scenarios whereby a particular trigger (rather than an abstract cause) results in specific forms of migration (e.g. Kälin 2010). Other approaches have done completely away with causal attribution, focusing on the protection needs rather than on what induces them (e.g. Nansen Initiative 2015).

An influential list of scenarios was developed by Walter Kälin, the former Representative of the UN Secretary-General on the Human Rights of Internally Displaced Persons. In relation to "climate-induced displacement," Kälin distinguishes the five following scenarios:

1   "Sudden-onset disasters . . . trigger[ing] large-scale displacement";
2   "Slow-onset environmental degradation" which may first "prompt people to consider 'voluntary' displacement", then increasingly force permanent migration;
3   "So-called 'sinking' small island states", a "special case of slow-onset disasters";
4   The designation of certain areas as high-risk zones too dangerous for human habitation, forcing the evacuation or prohibiting the return of certain populations; and
5   "Unrest seriously disturbing public order, violence or even armed conflict" triggered by environmental changes. (Kälin 2010: 81)

These scenarios are archetypical but they do not constitute an exhaustive typology of the multiple migration scenarios that climate change effects. Like the concentric circles that an impact produces on a water surface, extending *ad infinitum* and *at absurdum* in time and space, environmental phenomena may translate in innumerable scenarios of migration. Measures adopted in response to environmental phenomena consist not only in designating zones as too dangerous for human habitation, but also in diverse infrastructural projects that involve the displacement and resettlement of populations, or in policies (e.g. towards climate change mitigation) translating in economic incentives that modify labour migration patterns.

Although it would be vain to try and identify each and every migration scenario, the main scenarios can be the object of specific research and, possibly, particular policy responses. Thus, nineteen scholars from climate change, migration and development studies co-authored an article calling for a renewed attention to protection challenges and opportunities related to "resettlement associated with climate change" (de Sherbinin et al. 2011). Likewise, the Nansen Initiative, first closely focused on the impact of climate change on transboundary migration, has gradually abandoned any causal attribution to climate change and explored protection issues related to cross-border displacement triggered by natural disasters (Nansen Initiative 2015).

This focus on migration scenarios diverted attention from causal attribution. Some authors argued that causal attribution should be set aside entirely (Nicholson 2014). The cause of migration is not a direct determinant of the protection needs at the place of destination, and giving priority to migrants related to a particular driver (whether persecution, climate change, or environmental factors) hinders the quest for an optimal distribution of concerns and protection resources towards all populations in need (Mayer 2016). Bertrand Russell's (1912: 1) stark critique of causation as "a relic of a bygone age, surviving . . . only because it is erroneously supposed to do no harm" resonate here.

Alexander Betts, in particular, argued that a debate focusing on particular drivers of migration "risks missing the point" (Betts 2013: 15). Beside the difficulty of attributing migration to a single driver such as environmental change, Betts notes that, "if the aim is to identify who should be entitled to asylum, then isolating a particular cause of movement is unimportant" (16). Doing away with causality entirely, Betts develops the concept of survival migration to relate to "persons who are outside their country of origin because of an existential threat for which they have no access to a domestic remedy or resolution" (23). Somewhat analogous arguments were made with regard to internal displacement through the concept of "crisis migration" developed by Susan Martin et al. (2014).

Conclusions

In the debate on environmental migrations, definitions are not just of a conventional nature. Elusive attempts to provide a specific definition of "environmental migrants" reveal conceptual issues – the difficulty of attributing migration to one factor in abstraction of others. One may certainly identify migration scenarios that are triggered or exacerbated by environmental drivers. Yet, there is a need to think carefully about what is gained and what is lost in putting emphasis on environmental rather than other factors (e.g. political, economic). The politics of causal attribution are politics of blame and exoneration. But while debating whether those millions risking their lives to cross international borders are "environmentally-displaced persons", "ecological migrants" or perhaps "economic refugees", one needs to keep in mind what really matters: that migrants, notwithstanding what drives them, are human beings.

References

Albrecht E. and Plewa M.P. (2015) "International Recognition of Environmental Refugees" Environmental Policy and Law 45 78–84.

Biermann F. and Boas I. (2010) "Preparing for a Warmer World: Towards a Global Governance System to Protect Climate Refugees" Global Environmental Politics 10 60–88.

Betts A. (2013) Survival Migration: Failed Governance and the Crisis of Displacement, Cornell University Press, Ithaca, NY.

CRIDEAU (2008) "Draft Convention on the International Status of Environmentally-Displaced Persons" Revue de Droit de l'Université de Sherbrooke 39 451–505.

De Sherbinin A. et al. (2011) "Preparing for Resettlement Associated with Climate Change" Science 334 456–457.

Dun O. and Gemenne F. (2007) "Defining 'environmental migration'" Forced Migration 31 10–11.

El-Hinnawi, E. (1985) Environmental Refugees. UNEP, Nairobi.

Foresight: Migration and Global Environmental Change (2011) Final Project Report, The Government Office for Science, London.

Hugo G. (1996) "Environmental Concerns and International Migration" International Migration Review 30 105.

IOM (International Organization for Migration) (2007) Discussion note: Migration and the environment. MC/INF/288.

Kälin W. (2010) "Conceptualizing Climate-Induced Migration" in McAdam J ed, Climate Change and Displacement: Multidisciplinary Perspectives, Oxford University Press 81–104.

Martin S, Weerasinghe S and Taylor A (2014) "What Is Crisis Migration?" Forced Migration Review 45 5–9.

Mayer B. (2016) The concept of climate migration: Advocacy and its prospects, Cheltenham, Edward Elgar.

Nansen Initiative (2015) Agenda for the protection of cross-border displaced persons in the context of disasters and climate change (https://www.nanseninitiative.org/).

Nicholson C. (2014) "Climate Change and the Politics of Causal Reasoning: The Case of Climate Change and Migration" The Geographical Journal 180 151.

Russel B. (1912) "On the notion of cause" Proceedings of the Aristotelian Society 13 1.

26

Human rights, environmental displacement and migration

Dug Cubie

Introduction

The need or desire to move from one place to the next as a result of changing environmental conditions has been a constant feature of life since the dawn of time; from swallows migrating each winter from cold northerly climes to warmer lands down south, to the majestic summer migration of wildebeest from the Serengeti in search of greener pastures in the Maasi Mara. Likewise, as noted by McLeman and Gemenne in Chapter 1, humans have undertaken vast journeys in search of new lands, opportunities and safety down through the centuries. Even in the comparatively recent past, the main limitations on large-scale human population movements were the distance and difficulty of terrain to traverse; but improved transportation, communications and infrastructure have significantly reduced, if not eliminated, these physical challenges. However, since the beginning of the 20th Century, human migration has increasingly become regulated, indeed dominated, by legal requirements and strictures. While migration opportunities abound for the resourceful and fortunate, for the majority of the world's population, the possibility of securing a dignified long-term migration pathway remains an almost insurmountable legal and physical challenge.

Concurrently, the interconnections between environmental degradation, global climate change, forced displacement and potential human rights violations have been increasingly recognised in recent years. By their nature, each of these topics entails a specific focus of research and enquiry across multiple disciplines, covering the sciences, social sciences and humanities. Just as George Bernard Shaw noted that 'England and America are two countries divided by a common language,' so too is the inter-disciplinary examination of the relationship between human rights, environmental displacement and migration. Lawyers and policy-makers may focus primarily on the obligations placed on States by the International Bill of Rights,[1] the 1951 Refugee Convention[2] or the UN Framework Convention on Climate Change;[3] while social scientists may focus more on the human impact of environmental degradation on communities and individuals. Additionally, specialists such as soil engineers, climatologists and physicists are essential not only to our understanding of the physical mechanisms at play, but the predicted scenarios to expect.

Yet we risk being separated by a common language. Terms such as 'resilience', 'adaptation', 'vulnerability' and 'human rights' all have different connotations and implications depending on the disciplinary lens adopted (Cannon 2008). This chapter therefore aims to provide a brief overview of the interconnected topics of human rights, environmental displacement and migration from the perspective of an international lawyer. The contribution commences by setting out the relevant bodies of international law, before examining current debates and scholarship surrounding the application of human rights norms to population movement arising from or influenced by environmental or climatic changes. The chapter concludes by highlighting recent scholarship on the need to ensure migration or adaptation with dignity (McAdam and Saul 2010).

Applicable bodies of international law

Conflict and humanitarian crises often provide the catalyst for people to uproot from their homes and communities in search of protection and an improved life elsewhere. It is therefore no surprise that the first High Commissioner for Refugees, the Norwegian explorer Fridtjof Nansen, was appointed in the aftermath of the First World War. Indeed, Nansen's initial task focused specifically on the millions of Russians who were not only displaced by the war and Soviet revolution, but by massive crop failures in the summer of 1921 (Cabanes 2014). The subsequent famine remains a stark reminder of the interplay between environmental conditions, human activities and population movements. Despite Nansen's untimely death in 1930, the work of his Office continued and following the horrors of the Second World War was re-established as the Office of the UN High Commissioner for Refugees. Throughout the second half of the 20th Century, in the face of Cold War rivalry, the popular perception of a 'refugee' solidified into that of an individual fleeing political persecution across an international border (Goodwin-Gill and McAdam 2007). It was not until the 1990s that the material assistance and protection needs of persons displaced within the borders of their own country were identified, in large part due to the ground-breaking work of Roberta Cohen and Francis Deng (Cohen and Deng 1998; Cohen 2004). Our legal and operational understanding of these two categories of persons, refugees and the internally displaced, therefore stems from the international framework developed in the 1950s and 1990s; with the protection of refugees clearly articulated in the 1951 Refugee Convention, and the rights of internally displaced persons set out in the (non-binding) 1998 UN Guiding Principles on Internal Displacement.[4]

In parallel to the development of international refugee and displaced persons law, the newly established United Nations drew up the 'International Bill of Rights', comprised of the 1948 Universal Declaration of Human Rights, and the 1966 International Covenants on Civil and Political Rights, and on Economic, Social and Cultural Rights (Kälin and Künzli 2009). These three key texts are supplemented by specific international human rights treaties, such as the 1979 Convention on the Elimination of All Forms of Discrimination Against Women (CEDAW)[5] and the 1989 Convention on the Rights of the Child (CRC).[6] While the concept of 'human rights' or the 'rights of man'[7] may be traced to the French and American revolutions in the late 18th Century, modern international human rights law is remarkable for two key reasons. First, the primary focus of the law is on the individual, not the sovereign state – in other words, the rights-holder rather than the duty-bearer. Secondly, the international framework is designed to promote domestic and international accountability mechanisms (Cubie and Hesselman 2015). While no global judicial body was created to adjudicate on human rights violations (Nowak 2007), the normative development of international human rights law led directly to the establishment of regional courts such as the European, Inter-American, and African Courts of Human Rights, as well as the internalisation of human rights norms into domestic legal regimes (Hathaway 2007).

In the context of population movements, Michel Prieur has stressed the fundamental point that: 'The flight of environmentally displaced persons is a manifestation of their fundamental right to life, expressed as the right to survive by fleeing' (Prieur 2010–2011, 247).

The final relevant body of international law and policy addresses our increasing awareness of the potential fragility of the global environment, and the impact which human activities can play. As the seminal Declaration of the UN Conference on the Human Environment, held in Stockholm in June 1972, stated:

> A point has been reached in history when we must shape our actions throughout the world with a more prudent care for their environmental consequences. Through ignorance or indifference we can do massive and irreversible harm to the earthly environment on which our life and well being depend.[8]

Over the past 40 years, the impact of acid rain, depletion of the ozone layer, radioactive materials and greenhouse gas emissions (to name just a few) have been felt keenly by local communities and by the international community as a whole. The development of distinct bodies of law covering the environment and climate change have attempted to ameliorate the worst excesses of human consumption (Alam et al. 2013). Of particular importance is the ultimate objective of the 1992 UN Framework Convention on Climate Change (UNFCCC), namely: 'the stabilization of greenhouse gas concentrations in the atmosphere at a level that would prevent dangerous anthropogenic interference with the climate system.'[9] Moreover, the process established by the UNFCCC has resulted in a broad range of international declarations and plans of action. In the context of migration, the most important is the 2011 Cancun Adaptation Framework, which invites States to undertake work on: 'Measures to enhance understanding, coordination and cooperation with regard to climate change induced displacement, migration and planned relocation, where appropriate, at the national, regional and international levels.'[10]

Nevertheless, with the exponential growth of expert actors and concomitant diversity of challenges arising in a globalised world, a key debate has arisen regarding the fragmentation of international law (ILC 2006). As noted by Martti Koskenniemi, the increasing specialisation of international law risks favouring a 'structural bias in the relevant functional expertise' (Koskenniemi 2007: 4). Yet the interconnections and need for dialogue between different disciplines addressing human rights, environmental displacement and migration are clear from both an operational perspective and from the standpoint of academic research. For example, Lisa Schipper and Mark Pelling have noted the dearth of coordination mechanisms and potential for conflict between actions taken to address disaster risk reduction, climate change and development (Schipper and Pelling 2006). Likewise, Thomalla et al. (2006) have argued that both the disaster risk reduction and climate change adaptation communities have ignored the underlying causes of vulnerability, while noting that these disciplines have largely developed and operated in isolation from each other. Therefore, the following section will briefly highlight some of the current debates and scholarship addressing the interconnections between human rights, environmental displacement and migration.

Current debates and scholarship

Causation and legal categorisation

Before one even considers which human rights are affected, a key challenge when examining the question of 'environmental displacement and migration' is the terminology itself. Dun and Gemenne (2008: 10) have highlighted the variety of terms currently in use, such as 'environmental migration, climate change-induced migration, ecological or environmental refugees, climate change migrants and environmentally-induced forced migrants.' Ferris, meanwhile, has noted the differential understandings of the terms 'displacement', 'relocation', 'resettlement' and 'evacuations' between humanitarian actors and those working in international development (Ferris 2011: 3–5). Moreover, there has been particular debate regarding whether or not the term 'refugee' is appropriate in the context of environmental or climate population movements. Biermann and Boas have argued: 'The term refugee has strong moral connotations of societal protection in most world cultures and religions. By using this term, the protection of climate refugees will receive the legitimacy and urgency it deserves' (Biermann and Boas 2010: 67). Conversely, Jane McAdam has forcefully argued that despite the harm caused by negative climate impacts such as sea level rise, this harm lacks a discriminatory element or an agent of persecution as envisaged in the 1951 Refugee Convention. While recognising the clear threat posed by climate change, McAdam argues that the refugee regime is the wrong paradigm to address such threats, not least since many putative 'climate refugees' such as the populations of the Pacific islands of Kiribati and Tuvalu have explicitly rejected the terminology of 'refugees' for their plight (McAdam 2009; 2011).

This terminological indeterminacy has generated a variety of approaches. In 2008, a group of researchers at the University of Limoges drafted a Convention on the International Status of Environmentally-Displaced Persons. While recognising that the international community was not particularly receptive to amending the existing 1951 Refugee Convention or adopting a new environmental agreement, the participants viewed their proposed text as an explicitly human rights-based treaty to fill 'legal gaps . . . that give rise to an imperative moral necessity to which states must respond' (Prieur 2010–2011: 248). In particular, the objective of the draft convention was to elaborate the rights of environmentally displaced persons, covering both their reception conditions as well as their eventual return to their place of habitual residence, in application of the principle of solidarity (Prieur et al. 2008). Alternatively, proposals have been advanced that 'climate migrants' should be provided with a specific legal status under the UNFCCC (Gibb and Ford 2012; Biermann and Boas 2010). Key benefits of identifying a specific legal category of persons in need of protection due to their environmental displacement are the concrete legal and policy actions which States and other actors would then be obliged to undertake, such as guaranteeing a defined legal status (either on an individual or group basis) and a framework of material assistance and protection activities in which obligations would be shared between the affected State and the international community (Hodgkinson and Young 2012: 8).

However, Jane McAdam (amongst others) has argued against the conclusion of a universal international convention on 'climate refugees' in favour of more flexible bilateral or regional approaches that reflect the differential migratory scenarios across the globe (McAdam 2011). McAdam subsequently identified three main legal or policy strategies that need to be enhanced: i) strengthening in-country adaptation to climate change; ii) implementing international standards on internal displacement; and iii) encouraging international labour mobility and lawful migration pathways (McAdam 2012). Similarly, Mayer has highlighted the impossibility of identifying a workable legal category for environmental displacement due to the complex and indirect causation of migration, decrying the 'conceptual and semantic chaos' that currently ensues (Mayer 2017).

It is generally recognised that the motivations for population movements range across a continuum of voluntary to forced migration, and that migratory decisions combine economic, social, environmental and security considerations (Hugo 1996; Renaud et al. 2007: 5–6; Biermann and Boas 2010). Indeed, the UN High Commissioner for Refugees has stressed that most people do not want to leave their communities and those that remain behind may in fact be the most vulnerable of all (UNHCR 2011: 573). Despite the difficulties in defining a specific legal category, Elizabeth Ferris has identified four broad displacement scenarios, namely: i) development-forced displacement and resettlement; ii) conflict-induced displacement; iii) climate change-induced displacement; and iv) disaster-induced displacement. Ferris focuses on the last two categories, and notes that: 'While people's experiences of being displaced might be similar, regardless of the causes which provoked their displacement, the international system responds in very different ways' (Ferris 2011: 6). This issue lies at the heart of the question of how best to protect persons affected by environmental or climatic hazards – if causation is hard to determine, how can one determine what legal status such displaced persons should receive?

Institutional mechanisms

Closely connected to the debate surrounding the legal status for environmentally or climate-displaced persons is the question of the domestic and international frameworks that need to be established to address such questions. Recognising the limitations of the current 1951 Refugee Convention to adequately address the protection needs of 'climate refugees', Biermann and Boas have called for a *sui generis* global governance regime for the recognition, protection and resettlement of climate refugees (Biermann and Boas 2010). They argue that such a regime should be based on five principles, namely: i) planned relocation and resettlement; ii) resettlement instead of temporary asylum; iii) collective rights for local populations; iv) international assistance for domestic measures; and v) international burden sharing. Biermann and Boas suggest that the appropriate institutional mechanism for establishing such a regime lies in the adoption of a Protocol to the UNFCCC on the Recognition, Protection and Resettlement of Climate Refugees which would reflect the agreed principles of common but differentiated responsibilities and the reimbursement of full incremental costs (Biermann and Boas 2010, 76).

Susannah Willcox likewise grounds her argument in collective transnational obligations, although those based in international human rights rather than the UNFCCC (Willcox 2012). Willcox highlights that States facing serious and imminent threats to their very existence as a result of climate change (for example rising sea levels and extreme weather events) have a right to self-determination derived from international human rights law. As a *jus cogens* right for the State concerned and an obligation *erga omnes* of the international community as a whole, Willcox argues that developed States have a particular responsibility to assist poorer developing States meet their human rights obligations in the context of climate change (Willcox 2012, 6–7). Moreover, Willcox concludes that international human rights law can achieve what the UNFCCC process cannot, namely: 'the implementation of transnational mechanisms for protecting and promoting fundamental rights, enforcing accountability, and compensating individuals and communities for climate change harms' (Willcox 2012, 13).

Such an approach reflects the fact that the majority of environmental or climate displacement is likely to occur within the borders of States, rather than across borders. In such circumstances, the institutional regime of the UN Guiding Principles on Internal Displacement provides a key normative framework for States (UN 1998). The UN Guiding Principles are premised on a State's primary obligation to respect, protect and fulfil the rights of all persons in its territory before, during or after a displacement event. As a non-binding international text, the UN Guiding Principles do not establish a new institutional regime for internal displacement, but focus primarily on the duties and responsibilities of States that should be addressed through their domestic law and policy. The UN General Assembly has likewise encouraged States to 'continue to develop and implement domestic legislation and policies dealing with all stages of displacement, including through the identification of a national focal point within the Government for issues of internal displacement, and through the allocation of budget resources' (UN 2008: para 11).

Separately, the governments of Norway and Switzerland established the 'Nansen Initiative' in 2011 in response to the call within Article 14(f) of the UNFCCC Cancun Adaptation Framework for States to consider climate change-induced displacement, migration and planned relocation.[11] The final report of the Nansen Initiative sets out an agenda for the protection of cross-border displaced persons in the context of disasters and climate change, which was endorsed by a global intergovernmental consultation held in Geneva during October 2015 (Nansen Initiative 2015). This 'Protection Agenda' highlights three priority areas for future action in the context of cross-border disaster-displacement:

i Collecting data and enhancing knowledge on cross-border disaster-displacement;
ii Enhancing the use of humanitarian protection measures for cross-border disaster-displaced persons; and
iii Strengthening the management of disaster displacement risk in the country of origin.
(Nansen Initiative 2015: 19)

Following the conclusion of the Nansen Initiative, which was driven by Walter Kälin as the Envoy of the Chairperson, it is noteworthy that the report prepared by the UN Secretary General in advance of the first ever World Humanitarian Summit (WHS) held in Istanbul during May 2016 called on States to prepare for cross-border displacement arising from disasters and climate change, and to:

Adopt an appropriate international framework, national legislation and regional cooperation frameworks by 2025 to ensure countries in disaster-prone regions are prepared to receive and protect those displaced across borders without refugee status.

(UN 2016, 7)

While the practical implementation of many of the commitments made at the WHS will take place over several years, a key institutional response was the establishment of the Platform on Disaster Displacement to follow-up the work of the Nansen Initiative and to advance the Protection Agenda for persons displaced by disasters and climate change. Led by the governments of Germany and Bangladesh, this multi-stakeholder initiative is intended to support States and other international actors in their implementation of the recommendations set out in the Protection Agenda.[12]

Climate change and human rights

Just as the debate surrounding the terminology and institutional mechanisms to assist and protect 'environmentally displaced' persons has received considerable academic and practitioner engagement over the past 10 years or so, so too have the linkages between environmental degradation, global climate change and human rights violations. This focus has built on insights gained from the Bhopal and Chernobyl disasters in the 1980s, which highlighted the human impact of industrial accidents that result in extensive environmental harm. As noted by Michel Prieur:

If the effects of disasters on the environment are issues of environmental law, the effects on humans belong to human rights law, with the particularity that they concern both classic human rights and the new human rights to the environment recognized both at the international level and in many national constitutions and laws.

(Prieur 2010–2011, 247)

The impact for future generations was specifically highlighted by Edith Brown Weiss in her pivotal 1987 paper on climate change, intergenerational equity and international law, in which she argued for a Declaration of the Planetary Rights and Obligations to Future Generations that would identify key principles of intergenerational equity to guide normative and policy developments in areas such as global climate change (Brown Weiss 1987). Despite the ongoing focus on environmental degradation and climate change at the international level, it took over 20 years before the potential human rights violations of climate change were authoritatively examined by the Office of the UN High Commissioner for Human Rights (OHCHR) in January 2009. The OHCHR report clearly identifies the relationship between the negative impacts of climate change, such as sea level rise and extreme weather events, on those countries, communities and individuals most vulnerable to its effects. In particular, the report notes:

> While the universal human rights treaties do not refer to a specific right to a safe and healthy environment, the United Nations human rights treaty bodies all recognize the intrinsic link between the environment and the realization of a range of human rights, such as the right to life, to health, to food, to water, and to housing.
>
> *(UN 2009: para. 18)*

Margaretha Wewerinke has argued that the lack of specific human rights clauses in international environmental and climate agreements, such as the UNFCCC, can potentially be rectified through general principles of international law, including the rules of treaty interpretation and the requirement to combat the fragmentation of international law (Wewerinke 2014). Although others have questioned how an approach predicated on human rights can improve our understanding of climate change or make measures to address it more effective (McInerney-Lankford 2009), the OHCHR report highlights the range of binding legal obligations which may be breached by climate change. Indeed, the serious threat posed to future generations by climate change is one of the key priorities of former UN High Commissioner for Human Rights, Mary Robinson (MRFCJ 2013). As argued by John Knox prior to his appointment as UN Special Rapporteur on Human Rights and the Environment:

> Applying human rights rhetoric to climate change may draw attention to its effects on particular communities, convince those not yet directly affected that it is a growing disaster on a scale similar to other great historical disasters, and make individuals and states more willing to take the hard choices needed to combat it.
>
> *(Knox 2009–2010: 166)*

Meanwhile, the UN Inter-Governmental Panel on Climate Change comprehensively examined the effects of extreme weather events in its 2012 Special Report on Managing the Risks of Extreme Events and Disasters to Advance Climate Change Adaptation (known as the SREX report). From the meteorological perspective, the SREX report highlighted that a changing climate leads to changes in the frequency, intensity, spatial extent, duration and timing of extreme weather and climate events, and can result in unprecedented extreme weather and climate events. Moreover, from the social and human perspective, the report noted that extreme and non-extreme weather or climate events affect vulnerability to future extreme events by modifying resilience, coping capacity, and adaptive capacity (IPCC 2012, 4–5). The increasing frequency and severity of hydro-meteorological events such as storms, flooding and heatwaves will therefore severely impact on human populations. It follows that potential human rights violations will occur, as identified by the OHCHR, and this may prompt or directly cause people to move to seek a more dignified life elsewhere. The following section, therefore, concludes by examining some of the current research specifically focusing on the human rights implications of environmental and/ or climate change displacement and migration.

Migration and adaptation with dignity

As noted by the International Law Commission, the principle of human dignity underpins all international human rights instruments and has been interpreted as providing the ultimate foundation of human rights law (ILC 2011: 258). Nasser has argued that a dominant theme of rights-based discourse is that a person's rights should not be violated as a result of forced displacement, since the international human rights regime ensures the principle of the inherent dignity of every human person (Nasser 2010). Indeed, one can argue that closer coordination and coherence between the human rights approaches of international legal and policy frameworks would help promote human dignity in the face of economic, social or environmental challenges (Cubie 2014; Scott and Picot 2014; Thorp 2014; Melamed, Scott and Mitchell 2012). Therefore, reflecting the acknowledged interconnections between human rights, environmental degradation, climate change and human migration, an increasing number of scholars and practitioners are focusing on the need to ensure that local populations can either migrate or adapt with dignity in the face of a changing environment.

Recognising the multi-causal factors influencing an individual's decision to migrate, Jane McAdam and Ben Saul coined the phrases 'displacement with dignity' and 'adaptation with dignity' in their 2010 research paper examining law and policy responses to climate change migration and security in Bangladesh. In their paper, they argue: 'adaptation with dignity requires not only a focus on defending sustainable livelihoods, but doing so in a way which enables people to live with their human rights respected' (McAdam and Saul 2010: 28). Moreover, when faced with the prospect of internal displacement, resettlement or relocation, those affected need to be actively involved in a participatory process, reflecting the provisions of the UN Guiding Principles on Internal Displacement. At a regional level, the African Union's Kampala Convention on Internally Displaced Persons in Africa provides a legally binding obligation on State Parties to: 'Take measures to protect and assist persons who have been internally displaced due to natural or human made disasters, including climate change.'[13] Moreover, State Parties must: 'Respect and ensure respect for the principles of humanity and human dignity of internally displaced persons.'[14] The recent focus on human dignity in the legal context of environmental and climate displacement provides an interesting and timely counterpart to social science research examining the importance of migration as a form of adaptation in the face of climate change (McLeman and Smit 2006; Renaud et al. 2007; Warner et al. 2012).

Meanwhile, if migration within a State is not a viable option, the Nansen Initiative's Protection Agenda on cross-border displacement has called for: 'Measures to help facilitate migration with dignity from countries or areas facing natural hazards or climate change impacts' (Nansen Initiative 2105: 18). Yet despite those displaced across borders retaining the protection of international human rights law, substantial gaps remain in the levels of existing protection for those displaced by disasters or climate change. Cohen and Bradley have identified four key challenges to human rights protection in the context of disaster displacement, namely: i) a lack of conceptual and definitional clarity; ii) limited legal protection; iii) gaps in institutional arrangements; and iv) inadequate consultation with potential victims (Cohen and Bradley 2010). Michelle Leighton has similarly highlighted a series of serious gaps in existing law and policy, including the need to differentiate between slow-onset and rapid-onset environmental disaster scenarios. Leighton identifies three key areas of concern: i) laws may only protect some but not all potential victims; ii) standards are often voluntary; and iii) the mechanisms for accountability lack clarity. She concludes that:

> governments should begin to clarify the rights of affected climate migrants and the responsibilities of host countries and countries of origin in their treatment of both persons who move as an immediate response to natural disaster and persons who migrate in response to a prolonged drought disaster, where either movement is motivated by a need for basic survival.
>
> *(Leighton 2010)*

Furthermore, while all persons affected by environmental degradation and climate change face particular challenges and potential human rights violations, it is also recognised that certain potentially 'vulnerable' groups may be especially at risk. Namrata Chindarkar has highlighted that climate change-induced migration, both voluntary and forced, is a gendered and socially embedded process. Chindarkar argues that the impacts of both climate change and adaptation processes can have a disproportionate effect on women; moreover this impact is likely to be worse in developing countries 'due to the greater economic and social gender divide' (Chindarkar 2012: 2). Chindarkar therefore proposes two frameworks: the first is an indicator framework to operationalise and examine vulnerability to climate change-induced migration and its gender dimensions; while the second is an analytical framework to examine gender and climate change-induced migration decisions. When the UN Special Rapporteur on the Human Rights of Migrants, François Crépeau, examined the issue of climate change-induced migration in 2012, he concluded that not only were specific regions of the world more vulnerable to the effects of climate change, but that particular groups living in these high-risk areas, such as women, children, minority groups and indigenous peoples, were more likely to be affected than others. The Special Rapporteur also noted that such vulnerabilities may be exacerbated by political and social factors within a country (UN 2012a).

To conclude, this overview has touched on some of the key areas of ongoing research and policy development, and the increasing scholarly and practitioner debate and engagement in the topic of human rights, environmental displacement and migration is to be welcomed. In particular, the identified gaps in protection of those most affected by climate change and environmental degradation provides a clear inter-disciplinary research agenda to ensure that vulnerable individuals and groups do not fall through the cracks of the emerging international, regional and domestic legal and policy frameworks. The Rio+20 World Summit outcome document, entitled *The Future We Want*, called on States to:

> promote and protect effectively the human rights and fundamental freedom of all migrants *regardless of migration status*, especially those of women and children, and to address international migration through international, regional or bilateral cooperation and dialogue and a comprehensive and balanced approach, recognizing the roles and responsibilities of

countries of origin, transit and destination in promoting and protecting the human rights of all migrants, and avoiding approaches that might aggravate their vulnerability.

(UN 2012b, emphasis added)

Recognising that this call applies equally to those displaced or who migrate due to environmental degradation and climate change is an important first step in moving towards more dignified and safer future for all.

Notes

1 The International Bill of Rights is comprised of three instruments: the *Universal Declaration of Human Rights* (adopted 10 December 1948) UNGA Res 217 A(III) (UHDR); the *International Covenant on Civil and Political Rights* (adopted 16 December 1966, entered into force 23 March 1976) 999 UNTS 171; and the *International Covenant on Economic, Social and Cultural Rights* (adopted 16 December 1966, entered into force 3 January 1976) 993 UNTS 3.
2 United Nations (1951), *Convention relating to the Status of Refugees* (adopted 28 July 1951, entered into force 22 April 1954) 189 UNTS 137.
3 United Nations (1992), *Framework Convention on Climate Change* (adopted 9 May 1992, entered into force 21 March 1994) 1771 UNTS 107 (UNFCCC).
4 United Nations, *Guiding Principles on Internal Displacement*, E/CN.4/1998/53/Add.2 (11 February 1998).
5 United Nations, *Convention on the Elimination of Discrimination Against Women* (adopted 18 December 1979, entered into force 3 September 1981) 1249 UNTS 13.
6 United Nations, *Convention on the Rights of the Child* (adopted 20 November 1989, entered into force 2 September 1990) 1577 UTS 3.
7 For a counterpoint to the gendered language of the time, see: Mary Wollstonecraft, *A Vindication of the Rights of Women* (1792) (Oxford University Press 2008).
8 United Nations (1973), *Declaration of the United Nations Conference on the Human Environment*, A/Conf.48/14/Rev. 1 (1973), para. 6.
9 United Nations (1992), *Framework Convention on Climate Change* (adopted 9 May 1992, entered into force 21 March 1994) 1771 UNTS 107 (UNFCCC), article 2.
10 United Nations (2011), *The Cancun Agreements: Outcome of the work of the Ad Hoc Working Group on Long-term Cooperative Action under the Convention*, Decision 1/CP.16, FCCC/CP/2010/7/Add.1 (15 March 2011), article 14(f).
11 *Ibid.*
12 See: http://disasterdisplacement.org Accessed 17 November 2017.
13 African Union (2009), *Convention for the Protection and Assistance of Internally Displaced Persons in Africa* ('Kampala Convention') (adopted 22 October 2009, entered into force 6 December 2012), article 5(4).
14 *Ibid.*, article 3(1)(c).

References

African Union (AU) (2009) *Convention for the Protection and Assistance of Internally Displaced Persons in Africa* ('Kampala Convention') (22 October 2009)

Alam S., Bhuiyan J. H., Chowdhury T. M. R., and Techera E. J. (eds) (2013) *Routledge Handbook of International Environmental Law* (Routledge)

Biermann F. and Boas I. (2010) 'Preparing for a Warmer World: Towards a Global Governance System to Protect Climate Refugees' 10(1) *Global Environmental Politics* 60–88

Brown Weiss E. (1987) 'Climate Change, Intergenerational Equity and International Law' reprinted with new introduction in: (2008) 9 *Vermont Journal of Environmental Law* 615–627

Cabanes B. (2014) 'The Tragedy of Being Stateless: Fridtjof Nansen and the Rights of Refugees' in Cabanes B. *The Great War and the Origins of Humanitarianism 1918–1924* (Cambridge University Press) 133–188

Cannon T. (2008) 'Reducing People's Vulnerability to Natural Hazards: Communities and Resilience' United Nations University, World Institute for Development Economic Research, Research Paper No. 2008/34

Chindarkar N. (2012) 'Gender and Climate Change-induced Migration: Proposing a Framework for Analysis' 7 *Environmental Research Letters* 025601

Cohen R. (2004) 'The Guiding Principles on Internal Displacement: An Innovation in International Standard Setting' 10 *Global Governance* 459–480

Cohen R. and Deng F. M. (1998) *Masses in Flight: The Global Crisis of Internal Displacement* (Washington, D.C.: The Brookings Institution)

Cohen R. and Bradley M. (2010) Disasters and Displacement: Gaps in Protection' 1 *Journal of International Humanitarian Legal Studies* 95–142

Cubie D. (2014) 'Promoting Dignity for All: Human Rights Approaches in the Post-2015 Climate Change, Disaster Risk Reduction and Sustainable Development Frameworks' 8(1) *Human Rights and International Legal Discourse* 36–51

Cubie D. and Hesselman M. (2015) 'Accountability for the Human Rights Implications of Natural Disasters: A Proposal for Systemic International Oversight' 33(1) *Netherlands Quarterly of Human Rights* 9–41

Dun O. and Gemenne F. (2008) 'Defining "Environmental Migration"' 31 *Forced Migration Review* 10–11

Ferris E. (2011) 'Climate Change and Internal Displacement: A Contribution to the Discussion', paper prepared for the UNHCR Roundtable in Bellagio, Italy, 22–26 February 2011 (www.brookings.edu/~/media/research/files/papers/2011/2/28-cc-displacement-ferris/0228_cc_displacement_ferris.pdf) Accessed 28 June 2016

Gibb C. and Ford J. (2012) 'Should the United Nations Framework Convention on Climate Change Recognize Climate Migrants?' 7 *Environmental Research Letters* 045601

Goodwin-Gill G. S. and McAdam J. (2007) *The Refugee in International Law* (3rd ed., Oxford University Press)

Hathaway O. A. (2007) 'Why Do Countries Commit to Human Rights Treaties?' 51(4) *Journal of Conflict Resolution* 588–621

Hodgkinson D. and Young, L. (2012) '"In the Face of Looming Catastrophe": A Convention for Climate Change Displaced Persons' (www.ccdpconvention.com) Accessed 28 June 2016

Hugo G. (1996) 'Environmental Concerns and International Migration' 30(1) *International Migration Review* 105–131

Inter-Governmental Panel on Climate Change (IPCC) (2012) *Summary for Policymakers. In: Managing the Risks of Extreme Events and Disasters to Advance Climate Change Adaptation* [Field, C. B. et al. (eds.)] A Special Report of Working Groups I and II of the Intergovernmental Panel on Climate Change

International Law Commission (ILC) (2006) *Fragmentation of International Law: Difficulties Arising from the Diversification and Expansion of International Law*, Report of the Study Group of the International Law Commission, Finalized by Martti Koskenniemi UN Doc. A/CN.4/L.682 (13 April 2006)

International Law Commission (ILC) (2011) Official Records of the General Assembly, Sixty-sixth Session, *Supplement No. 10* (A/66/10), Chapter IX: Protection of Persons in the Event of Disasters

Kälin W. and Künzli J. (2009) *The Law of International Human Rights Protection* (Oxford University Press)

Knox J. (2009–2010) 'Climate Change and Human Rights Law' 50 *Virginia Journal of International Law* 163–218

Koskenniemi M. (2007) 'The Fate of Public International Law: Between Technique and Politics' 70(1) *The Modern Law Review* 1–30

Leighton M. (2010) 'Climate Change and Migration: Key Issues for Legal Protection of Migrants and Displaced Persons' Study Team on Climate-Induced Migration, The German Marshall Fund of the United States (June 2010)

Mary Robinson Foundation: Climate Justice (MRFCJ) (2013) *Declaration on Climate Justice* (www.mrfcj.org/media/pdf/Declaration-on-Climate-Justice.pdf Accessed 28 June 2016

Mayer B. (2017 – forthcoming) 'Critical Perspective on the Identification of "Environmental Refugees" as a Category of Human Rights Concern' in Baldwin A. et al. (eds) *Climate Change, Migration and Human Rights: Law and Policy Perspectives* (Routledge)

McAdam J. and Saul B. (2010) 'Displacement with Dignity: International Law and Policy Responses to Climate Change Migration and Security in Bangladesh' Sydney Law School, Legal Studies Research Paper, No. 10/113

McAdam J. (2009) From Economic Refugees to Climate Refugees? 10 *Melbourne Journal of International Law* 579–595

McAdam J. (2011) 'Swimming Against the Tide: Why a Climate Change Displacement Treaty is Not *the* Answer' 23(1) *International Journal of Refugee Law* 2–27

McAdam J. (2012) 'Legal Solutions: If a Treaty is Not the Answer, Then What Is?' presentation at ClimMig Conference on Human Rights, Environmental Change, Migration and Displacement, Vienna, 20–21 September 2012 (www.humanrights.at/climmig/wp-content/uploads/McAdam-Jane_speech-20-Sept-2012.pdf) Accessed 28 June 2016

McInerney-Lankford S. (2009) 'Climate Change and Human Rights: an Introduction to Legal Issues' 33 *Harvard Environmental Law Review* 431–437

McLeman R. and Smit B. (2006) 'Migration as an Adaptation to Climate Change' 76 *Climatic Change* 31–53

Melamed C., Scott A. and Mitchell T. (2012) *Separated at Birth, Reunited in Rio? A Roadmap to Bring Environment and Development Back Together*, Overseas Development Institute (May 2012)

The Nansen Initiative (2015), *Global Consultation Conference Report*, Geneva, 12–13 October 2015

Naser M. M. (2010) 'Climate Change and Forced Displacement: Obligation of States under International Human Rights Law' 22 *Sri Lanka Journal of International Law* 117–163

Nowak M. (2007) 'The Need for a World Court of Human Rights' 7(1) *Human Rights Law Review* 251–259

Prieur M. (2010–2011) 'Draft Convention on the International Status of Environmentally-Displaced Persons' 42–43 *The Urban Lawyer* 247–257

Prieur M. et al. (2008) 'Draft Convention on the International Status of Environmentally-Displaced Persons' 12(4) *Revue Européenne de Droit de l'Environnement* 395–406

Renaud F. et al. (2007) *Control, Adapt or Flee: How to Face Environmental Migration?* UNU Institute for Environment and Human Security, InterSecTions No.5/2007

Schipper L. and Pelling M. (2006) 'Disaster Risk, Climate Change and International Development: Scope for, and Challenges to, Integration' 30(1) *Disasters* 19–38

Scott A. and Picot H. (2014) *Integrating Climate Change in the Post-2015 Development Agenda*, Climate & Development Knowledge Network (March 2014)

Thomalla F. et al. (2006) 'Reducing Hazard Vulnerability: Towards a Common Approach between Disaster Risk Reduction and Climate Adaptation' 30(1) *Disasters* 39–48

Thorp, T. (2014) 'In Search of Coherency in Negotiating Post-2015 International Climate, Development, and Disaster Risk Reduction Agreements' 25 *Fordham Environmental Law Review* 706–731

UNHCR (2011) 'Summary of Deliberations on Climate Change and Displacement' 23(3) *International Journal of Refugee Law* 561–574

United Nations (UN) (1951) *Convention relating to the Status of Refugees* (adopted 28 July 1951, entered into force 22 April 1954) 189 UNTS 137

United Nations (UN) (1973) *Declaration of the United Nations Conference on the Human Environment*, A/Conf.48/14/Rev. 1

United Nations (UN) (1992) *Framework Convention on Climate Change*, 1771 UNTS 107 / [1994] ATS 2 / 31 ILM 849

United Nations (UN) (1998) *Guiding Principles on Internal Displacement*, E/CN.4/1998/53/Add.2 (11 February 1998)

United Nations (UN) (2008) General Assembly Resolution A/RES/62/153, *Protection of and Assistance to Internally Displaced Persons* (6 March 2008)

United Nations (UN) (2009) *Report of the Office of the United Nations High Commissioner for Human Rights on the Relationship between Climate Change and Human Rights*, A/HRC/10/61 (15 January 2009)

United Nations (UN) (2011) *The Cancun Agreements: Outcome of the work of the Ad Hoc Working Group on Long-term Cooperative Action under the Convention*, Decision 1/CP.16, FCCC/CP/2010/7/Add.1 (15 March 2011)

United Nations (UN) (2012a) *Report of the Special Rapporteur on the Human Rights of Migrants*, A/67/299 (13 August 2012)

United Nations (UN) (2012b) General Assembly Resolution A/66/L.56, *The Future We Want* (24 July 2012)

United Nations (UN) (2016) *Agenda for Humanity: Annex to the Report of the Secretary-General for the World Humanitarian Summit* (advance, unedited version)

Warner K. et al. (2012) *Where the Rain Falls: Climate Change, Food and Livelihood Security, and Migration*, Global Policy Report

Wewerinke M. (2014) 'The Role of the UN Human Rights Council in Addressing Climate Change' 8(1) *Human Rights and International Legal Discourse* 10–35

Willcox S. (2012) 'A Rising Tide: The Implications of Climate Change Inundation for Human Rights and State Sovereignty' 9(1) *Essex Human Rights Review* 1–19

27

Climate, migration and displacement

Exploring the politics of preventative action

Craig A. Johnson

Climate change is just one of many issues where our security is linked to the rest of the world.

US President Barack Obama, 2016 State of the Union Address[1]

Introduction

There is now a growing consensus that anthropogenic emissions of greenhouse gases are leading to unprecedented transformations in the Earth's climate, and that climate change may soon displace large numbers of people living in the Global South.[2] In 2007, the British Aid charity Christian Aid (2007) called displacement due to climate change "the most urgent threat facing poor people in the developing world." Two years later, UN Secretary General Ban Ki-moon warned that

> migration is a likely consequence of climate change impacts. Populations will relocate due to more extreme weather including prolonged droughts, intensive storms and wildfire. In some cases, as with small island nations, whole countries are under threat. Protecting vulnerable communities must be a priority in both national and international adaptation efforts.[3]

Finally, in 2015, UN Secretary General (then the UN High Commissioner for Refugees) António Guterres observed that the "world today" is:

> at a crossroads. From a humanitarian perspective, this juncture is defined by two 'mega-problems': a seemingly uncontrollable multiplication of violent conflicts in an environment of global insecurity, and the pervasive and growing effects of natural hazards and climate change that are already shaping our present and will shape our future even more.[4]

Underlying these concerns is an assumption that climate change poses both a "human security threat" to populations facing the risk of environmental displacement and a broader "national security threat" to the sovereignty and stability of individual nation-states.[5] Within the national security field, particular attention has been paid to the idea that forced displacement and international migration will overwhelm the ability of sovereign nation-states to accommodate and absorb new flows of people displaced as a result of climate change. From a human security perspective, migration is seen as an adaptative strategy that builds assets, incomes and resilience to rapid-onset disasters and long-term environmental change. However, the ability of poor people to engage in migration is often constrained by national and international policies that effectively restrict the free movement of people, both within and across international borders (Zetter, 2007; Bakewell, 2008; de Haas, 2012).

By and large, the vast majority of writing about international policy on climate-induced displacement has been confined to a relatively narrow field of scholars, international aid workers, government officials and politicians, whose general aim has been to highlight the possibility that climate change may displace large numbers of people and to suggest possible strategies for preventing what could be a major humanitarian disaster. Among the most ambitious of these are calls for expanded immigration quotas and entitlements (e.g. Risse, 2009a; Johnson, 2012; Eckersley, 2015), reinterpretations of the refugee convention (e.g. Kolmannskog, 2008; Westra, 2009) and the targeted relocation of populations deemed most vulnerable to climate change (e.g. Biermann and Boas, 2008a, 2008b). Underlying all of these suggestions is an assumption that the international community has a moral responsibility to protect populations facing the risk of climate-induced displacement by facilitating out-migration from areas most vulnerable to climate change. However, facilitating out-migration (and immigration more generally) poses threats to national and international security, reflecting a more general tendency on the part of states and state bureaucracies to define and control their populations in relation to fixed social and spatial categories (Scott, 1998; Bakewell, 2008; de Haas, 2012).

This chapter explores the challenge of engaging in preventative action that expands the rights of national and international migrants to asylum, opportunity and freedom from the negative effects of climate change. It starts from the premise that *forced displacement* is a form of distress migration that obviates all but the most desperate of coping strategies (cf. de Haan, 1999; Deshingkar, 2005; McLeman and Smit, 2006; Perch-Nielson et al., 2008; de Sherbinin et al., 2008; Boano et al., 2008; Raleigh et al., 2008; IOM, 2009; Penz et al., 2011). *Economic migration*, on the other hand, implies the existence of forward and strategic planning on the part of households, communities, governments and policies. In reviewing the extant literature on climate, migration and displacement, the chapter makes the case that ambitious policy statements favouring preventative action through economic migration (e.g. expanding immigration quotas, relocating populations) have by and large undervalued or ignored the national – and increasingly nationalist – rhetoric that is now shaping the politics of immigration in Western liberal democracies. The chapter, therefore, highlights the need to situate the highly prescriptive policy literature on migration as preventative action more squarely in relation to the contemporary realpolitik of immigration and asylum.

The chapter proceeds as follows. The following section first outlines the national security literature on climate, migration and displacement, outlining the arguments and evidence that have been used in making the case that climate-induced displacement be treated as a national security issue. The chapter then compares and contrasts the national security framing of climate-induced displacement with (primarily) human security writing about livelihoods, household decision-making and economic migration. The following section then explores the policies that donors, international institutions and nation-states may use in supporting economic migration, highlighting the recognition that certain populations may be trapped as a result of climate change. The final section concludes the chapter by outlining major themes and tensions in the literature, including future trends for empirical research.

'The coming anarchy': climate, displacement and development[6]

When it is planned and supported through public policy, economic migration has been shown to provide an important means of diversifying and strengthening poor people's assets, livelihoods and income, thereby reducing household and systemic vulnerability to climate change (Biermann and Boas, 2008a; Johnson and Krishnamurthy, 2010; de Haan, 1999; Deshingkar, 2005; McLeman and Smit, 2006; Perch-Nielson et al., 2008; de Sherbinin et al., 2008, 2011b; Bogardi and Warner, 2009; Barnett and Webber, 2010; Foresight, 2011; de Haas, 2012; Adger et al., 2014; Suckall et al., 2016). However, governments frequently discourage migration, using labour codes, land use restrictions and other policy instruments as a means of controlling the movement and settlement of itinerant populations (cf. Bakewell, 2008; de Haas, 2012). Moreover, national and international debates about immigration and asylum policy have become increasingly hostile towards the rights of migrants, "asylum seekers" and refugees (Neumayer, 2006; Zetter, 2007; Johnson, 2013; Humble, 2014).

Arguably one of the most prominent themes that appears in the extant literature on climate, migration and displacement is the notion that climate-induced displacement is a threat to political stability and international security (e.g. Homer-Dixon, 1991; Kaplan, 1994; Reueney, 2007; WBGU, 2008). At the heart of this literature is a (largely speculative) assertion that population pressures and a changing climate pose the risk of triggering new and violent conflicts along ethnic, religious and nationalist lines (Homer-Dixon, 1991; Kaplan, 1994; Kahl, 2006; Christian Aid, 2007; Reuveny, 2007; WBGU, 2008). In the words of the German Advisory Council:

> climate change could exacerbate existing environmental crises such as drought, water scarcity and soil degradation, intensify land-use conflicts and trigger further environmentally induced migration. Rising global temperatures will jeopardize the bases of many people's livelihoods, especially in the developing regions, increase vulnerability to poverty and social deprivation, and thus put human security at risk. Particularly in weak and fragile states with poorly performing institutions and systems of government, climate change is also likely to overwhelm local capacities to adapt to changing environmental conditions and will thus reinforce the trend towards general instability that already exists in many societies and regions.
>
> *(WBGU, 2008: 1)*

Similarly, and more squarely directed towards the American security regime, Werz and Conley (2012: 7–8) warn that "Environmentally induced migration, resource conflicts, and unstable states will not only have an impact upon the nations where they occur, but also on the United States and the broader international community."

At the heart of this analysis are a number of causal assumptions about the factors affecting processes of state breakdown, "environmental conflict" and social unrest. One is an assumption that migration – and especially movements of people across national borders – will unleash new and otherwise dormant ethnic tensions rooted in race, religion, language and other social markers (Kaplan, 1994; Homer-Dixon, 1991; Reuveny, 2007; WBGU, 2008). A second is the "state breakdown thesis" that internal and international migration flows will overwhelm the ability of governments to undertake basic functions, including ones most important to development agendas (e.g. transportation, communication, water and sanitation) (Kaplan, 1994; Homer-Dixon, 1991; Kahl, 2006; Reuveny, 2007; WBGU, 2008). A third is that climate change will undermine the agricultural and natural resource base, forcing vulnerable rural populations into cities, whose capacity to provide even the most basic forms of public services is already highly constrained (Satterthwaite et al., 2010; Revi et al., 2014).

For many observers, the framing of climate-induced displacement as a national security threat has evoked considerable scepticism and alarm. A number of analysts, for instance, have questioned the ability of social science research to isolate the environmental determinants of migration in the absence of the historical and socio-economic factors that affect migration decisions and processes (e.g. Nordas and Gleditsch, 2007; Barnett and Adger, 2007; Hartmann, 2010; Gemenne, 2011; Adger et al., 2014; Bettini, 2015; Boas, 2015). In their crudest forms, environmental migration models appear to suggest that climate phenomena are the only or primary factors motivating migration when in fact a host of factors (including seasonality, wage rates, persecution, life cycles and *institutions*) may have equal or more bearing on the decision or not to migrate (Black, 2001; Castles, 2002; Boano et al., 2008; Hulme, 2008; Perch-Nielson et al., 2008; IOM, 2009; Black et al., 2011b; Gemenne, 2011; Adger et al., 2014; Bettini, 2015). At the very least, the lines of causality are more complex than they are sometimes construed in the literature, highlighting the need to scrutinize far more carefully the theories and assumptions being used to understand climate, migration and displacement (cf. Barnett and Adger, 2007; Nordas and Gleditsch, 2007; Hartmann, 2010; Gemenne, 2011; Bettini, 2015; Boas, 2015).

Others have argued that climate-displacement narratives (e.g. flooding and displacement due to sea level rise) are being used (somewhat disingenuously) as a means of "securitizing" wider policy objectives, such as immigration controls, asylum policy and foreign aid (Levy, 1995; Hartmann, 2010; Bettini, 2013, 2015; Oels, 2013; Boas, 2015; Boas and Rothe, 2016). The argument here is that migration is being subsumed by other objectives and being portrayed as a failure to adapt, particularly if it entails migration across international borders. For Bettini (2015: n.p.),

> The idea we should "solve" climate migration is rooted in a view of mobility as pathological, as the result of a failure to develop, to adapt to climate change, or to be more resilient.

Framed in this way, populations facing the threat of environmental displacement are seen as victims or threats, whose actions, movements and decisions need to be managed and controlled (cf. Levy, 1995; Hartmann, 2010; Bettini, 2013, 2015; Oels, 2013; Boas and Rothe, 2016). An alternative perspective that is rooted far more squarely in the human security paradigm is one that focuses less on questions of national security and stability and more on the factors affecting social agency and decisions regarding migration and adaptation to climate change.

Pathways out of poverty: migration, adaptation and climate change

Challenging the notion that migration is a threat to national and international security, considerable attention has been paid to the role of migration (and the remittances provided by migration) in building the incomes, assets and resilience of the poor (de Sherbinin, 2008; UNDP, 2009; Black et al., 2011b; de Haas, 2012; Adger et al., 2014; Suckall et al., 2016). For scholars investigating the role of climatic factors in migration processes and decisions, empirical work has shown that household assets, security of land title and the existence of social networks have strong bearing on whether vulnerable household members are able to engage in economic migration (McLeman and Smit, 2006; Perch-Nielson et al., 2008; Warner et al., 2009; de Sherbinin et al.,

2008; Foresight, 2011; Adger et al., 2014; Suckall et al., 2016). The Environmental Change and Forced Migration Scenarios Project (EACH-FOR, www.each-for.eu), for instance, found that wealthier households with secure land title and better quality housing were able to recover and rebuild in the wake of rapid-onset disasters, whereas poorer families were forced to seek shelter in urban areas (Warner et al., 2009). Similarly, McLeman and Smit (2006) found that agricultural labourers, tenant farmers and sharecroppers were more likely to engage in migration than landowners, suggesting that strong connections to land and livelihood may actually inhibit out-migration.

A related issue is the role of *in-situ* adaptation. Leaving aside the normative terms on which we might interpret migration (i.e. whether migration is interpreted as an opportunity or a failure to adapt – see ahead), empirical research has shown that household decisions about migration are strongly shaped by the viability (both real and perceived) of competing livelihood systems, particularly ones in food and agriculture (de Sherbinin et al., 2008; Warner et al., 2009; Johnson and Krishnamurthy, 2010; Black et al., 2011a, 2011b; Foresight, 2011; de Haas, 2012; Adger et al., 2014; Suckall et al., 2016). Here, important conceptual distinctions have been made between the temporary (or circular) patterns of migration that occur in a context of short-term climatic shocks (e.g. floods, windstorms) and the more permanent forms of resettlement that respond to long-term transformations in climatic conditions (McLeman and Smit, 2006; Warner et al., 2009; Johnson and Krishnamurthy, 2010; Foresight, 2011). Particular attention has been paid to the strategies households use in adapting to temporary shocks and stresses (e.g. a failed harvest) and the more permanent decisions involving migration to cities, regions and other countries (de Haan, 1999; McLeman and Smit, 2006; Warner et al., 2009; Foresight, 2011; Suckall et al., 2016).

Whether people are migrating in response to longer-term processes or shorter-term shocks has important implications for the kinds of development policies that might be used in facilitating adaptation to climate change (Heltberg et al., 2009; Johnson and Krishnamurthy, 2010; Coirolo et al., 2013; Johnson et al., 2013; Kuriakose et al., 2013; Panda, 2013). For shorter-term shocks, considerable attention has been paid to the role of insurance in pooling and reducing the risks of economic losses due to climate change (Heltberg et al., 2009; Kuriakose et al., 2013; Panda, 2013). Within agriculture, important distinctions have been made between crop insurance, which insures against actual crop losses, and index-based insurance, which insures against a pre-established index of rainfall, soil moisture, etc. below which compensation payments are made (Hetberg et al., 2009: 97–98). Although studies suggest that both forms of insurance can help pool the risks of losses due to climatic shocks, observations have also been made that the provision of insurance for climate-sensitive sectors and regions (e.g. rain-fed agriculture, sugar cane, paddy) may in fact exacerbate vulnerability to climate change (Heltberg et al., 2009; Coirolo et al., 2013; Panda, 2013; Weldegebriel and Prowse, 2013), raising difficult questions about whether and to what extent development policy can or should be encouraging diversification away from livelihoods that are dependent upon climate sensitive sectors and regions, such as forestry, fishing and sedentary agriculture.

A related question is whether development policy interventions are inadvertently exacerbating vulnerability to climate change. In recent years, development scholars have articulated the need to establish a continuum of "relief to development," in which humanitarian aid (e.g. medical treatment, food aid, cash provisioning and shelter) lays the foundations for investment in assets and income-generating activities that can reduce poverty and vulnerability to climate change (O'Brien et al., 2008; Johnson et al., 2013). However, trade-offs exist between the policies that donors, governments and other humanitarian agencies have used to rehabilitate lives and livelihoods and the factors affecting human vulnerability to climate change (Wisner et al., 2004; Moench, 2007 [2009]; O'Brien et al., 2008). First, efforts to promote "relief to development" (e.g. insurance, subsidies, compensation and reconstruction) create strong incentives to *relocate* and to *re-engage* in geographical areas whose exposure to natural disasters remains high (Wisner et al., 2004; Moench, 2007 [2009]; O'Brien et al., 2008). Second, efforts to mitigate and adapt to climate change can in and of themselves become drivers of displacement. De Sherbinin et al. (2011b), for instance, highlight the possibility that large-scale efforts to mitigate and adapt to climate change (e.g. building seawalls, coastal defences, biofuel projects) may inadvertently displace large numbers of people either as a result of planned resettlement or outright eviction.

A final theme that appears in more recent writing about climate change and migration is the prospect that certain populations will be "trapped" in areas adversely affected by climate change (Foresight, 2011; Adger et al., 2014; Humble, 2014; Suckall et al., 2016). At the heart of this literature is an observation that migration is structured and dependent upon complex networks of traders, intermediaries, moneylenders and states, whose transaction costs will be disproportionately high for the poor, particularly during times of crisis (de Haan, 1999; Foresight, 2011; de Haas, 2012; Humble, 2014; Suckall et al., 2016). As noted earlier, empirical studies have shown that wealthier households with secure land title and better quality housing appear better able to rebuild and recover from (relatively) short-term environmental shocks. For longer-term transformations, where existing livelihoods have become less viable, the opposite appears to be true, only the wealthiest individuals with extensive assets and social networks are able to cover the costs of permanent migration. Supporting this claim, the vast majority of migration that has been documented in the extant literature on human migration has occurred domestically – i.e. within nations – and the vast majority of international migration has been South-South (UNDP, 2009), suggesting that the ability of vulnerable populations to move to areas where living standards are considerably higher than the sending regions is limited. In the words of one analyst, "Growing numbers of people are becoming trapped in their own countries or in transit countries, or being forced to roam border areas, unable to access legal protection or basic social necessities" (Humble, 2014: 1).

Making the case for preventative action: economic migration, refugee protection and the politics of aid

The recognition that populations may be "trapped" within regions plagued by extreme poverty and environmental vulnerability has renewed calls for preventative action on the part of the international community (Risse, 2009a; Foresight, 2011; Johnson and Krishnamurthy, 2010; Johnson, 2012; Eckersley, 2015). At the international level, considerable attention has been paid to the challenge of rationalizing international refugee policy as a means of protecting populations displaced by climate change (Risse, 2009a, 2009b; Johnson and Krishnamurthy, 2010; McAdam and Saul, 2010; Barnett and Webber, 2010; de Sherbinin et al., 2011a, 2011b; Johnson, 2012; Eckersley, 2015).[7] Kolmannskog (2008) and Westra (2009), for instance, identify a number of conditions under which environmental factors may be used as grounds for protection under the Refugee Convention. One is the principle of non-refoulement, which holds that people cannot be returned to places where their lives or freedoms are under threat, conceivably as a result of climate change (Kolmannskog, 2008). A second is the notion that displacement due to climate change constitutes a form of persecution. Where it can be established that environmental degradation (e.g. draining of marshlands, etc.) is being intentionally used to harm populations on the basis of "race, religion, nationality, membership of a particular social group, or political opinion," such groups may conceivably claim protection on the grounds of political persecution (Kolmannskog, 2008; Westra, 2009).

The Convention therefore provides some scope for protecting populations whose homelands have been rendered permanently uninhabitable, but these provisions apply only to individuals seeking refugee status, which effectively precludes efforts to encourage voluntary resettlement in advance of displacement (cf. Biermann and Boas, 2008a). Moreover, the idea of revising the Convention to include new categories of refugee raises difficult ethical and political questions about the rights of populations currently recognized under the 1951 Convention (i.e. those facing persecution) and about the terms on which national governments may be expected to grant new rights of citizenship and asylum (Kolmannnskog, 2008; Biermann and Boas, 2008a; Johnson, 2012; Eckersley, 2015).

Recognizing the limitations of working through the existing refugee regime, a number of analysts have argued in favour of using long-term strategies aimed at supporting economic (as opposed to distress) migration (Risse, 2009a, 2009b; Johnson and Krishnamurthy, 2010; McAdam and Saul, 2010; Barnett and Webber, 2010; de Sherbinin et al, 2011a, 2011b; Foresight, 2011; Johnson, 2012; Eckersley, 2015). The UK government's "Foresight Report," for instance, argues that:

> The challenges of migration in the context of environmental change require a new strategic approach to policy. Policy makers will need to take action to reduce the impact of environmental change on communities yet must simultaneously plan for migration.
>
> *(Foresight, 2011: 7)*

Similarly, Barnett and Webber's background report to the 2010 World Development Report (World Bank, 2010) makes the following recommendation:

> Policy responses to minimize the risks associated with migration in response to climate change, and to maximize migration's contribution to adaptive capacity include: ensuring that migrants have the same rights and opportunities as host communities; reducing the costs of moving money and people between areas of origin and destination; facilitating mutual understanding among migrants and host communities; clarifying property rights where they are contested; ensuring that efforts to assist migrants include host communities; and strengthening regional and international emergency response systems
>
> *(Barnett and Webber, 2010: 2)*

Most ambitiously, Biermann and Boas (2008a) argue in favour of creating an entirely new protection regime that would be defined primarily on the rights and entitlements of populations facing the immediate and long-term threat of displacement dues to climate change. At the heart of their proposal is the notion that the international community would encourage "planned and voluntary resettlement and reintegration of affected populations over periods of many years and decades, as opposed to mere emergency response and disaster relief" (Biermann and Boas, 2008a: 3).

In principle, the idea of acting early to support economic migration provides an important means of diversifying and strengthening poor people's assets, livelihoods and income sources, thereby reducing vulnerability to rapid-onset disasters and long-term environmental change. In practice, it faces a number of logistical and ethical challenges. First, notwithstanding safeguards to ensure the wellbeing of affected populations, efforts to relocate communities run the risk of violating people's rights and freedoms, including the right to remain in areas adversely affected by climate change (Hulme, 2008; Raleigh et al., 2008; Johnson, 2012; Eckersley, 2015; cf. Cernea, 1997; Cernea and Schmidt-Soltau, 2006). Second, the idea of coordinating large-scale resettlements puts considerable faith in the ability of states and international "super-states" (Hulme, 2008), whose capacity cannot be taken for granted, particularly in areas plagued by chronic poverty, environmental degradation and civil strife (Brown et al., 2007; WBGU, 2008). Third, questions have been raised about the specific ways in which national governments and international institutions might support the needs of populations displaced as a result of climate change (e.g. Hulme, 2008; Risse, 2009a, 2009b; Johnson and Krishnamurthy, 2010; Johnson, 2012; Eckersley, 2015). Finally, questions have been raised about the logistical and methodological challenges of establishing whether displaced populations have in fact been displaced by climatic factors (cf. Black, 2001; Bell, 2004; Boano et al., 2008; Hulme, 2008; Hartmann, 2010; Gemenne, 2011; Bettini, 2015).

Given the speculative nature of climate-induced displacement, the vast majority of writing about relocation and refugee protection has focussed on the legal and normative-theoretical dimensions of policy, equity and human rights (e.g. Biermann and Boas, 2008a; Kolmannnskog, 2008; Risse, 2009a, 2009b; Westra, 2009; McAdam and Saul, 2010; Johnson, 2012; Eckersley, 2015). One important strand of scholarship has explored the language being used to describe "climate refugees," highlighting the political implications of labelling displaced populations as "refugees" (Bell, 2004; Boano et al., 2008; McAdam and Saul, 2010; Bettini, 2013, 2015; Eckersley, 2015; cf. Zetter, 2007). Another explores the rights and entitlements that may be used in protecting and accommodating populations displaced by climate change (Johnson and Krishnamurthy, 2010; McAdam and Saul, 2010; Eckersley, 2015). A third body of scholarship questions the assumption that economic migration is always or necessarily desirable, highlighting an obligation on the part of states and societies to ensure the non-separation of family, friends and other significant others during processes of displacement and resettlement (Risse, 2009a, 2009b; Johnson, 2012; Eckersley, 2015).

A final and critical point about the role of international policy is the apparent contradiction that exists between the ambitious policy statements favouring accommodation and protection on the part of Western industrialized states and the nationalist rhetoric that is now shaping the politics of immigration and asylum in the West. While political scientists and international development scholars have called upon industrialized countries to accommodate populations displaced as a result of climate change (c.f. Biermann and Boas, 2008a; Risse, 2009a, 2009b; Johnson, 2012; Eckersley, 2015), political discourses surrounding the rights of refugees and immigrants in western industrialized economies have narrowed considerably (cf. Neumayer, 2006; Zetter, 2007; Johnson, 2013; Humble, 2014). Notwithstanding the introduction of financial and legal instruments aimed at facilitating North-South transfers (e.g. the Green Climate Fund) and redressing the various costs of climate change (e.g. the UNFCCC's Loss and Damage mechanism), international efforts to expand immigration quotas on the basis of climate change are unlikely to thrive in this current geopolitical climate (cf. Neumayer, 2006; Zetter, 2007; Johnson, 2013; Humble, 2014).

Conclusions, implications and future research directions

This chapter has explored the implications of academic writing about climate, migration and displacement in the field of international development. It identifies a number of themes, tensions and empirical research questions that have important bearing on our understanding of human mobility and national security issues in the context of climate change. This section now concludes the chapter by outlining some of these core themes and tensions, outlining future questions for research and policy analysis.

One important theme that emerges from the analysis is a tension that clearly exists between national and human security writing about climate, migration and displacement. From a human security perspective, the framing of climate-induced displacement as a national security threat is something of a double-edged sword; on one hand, it has been used to justify international action on climate change and development issues; on the other, it frames these issues in a way that equates displaced populations with threats or (at best) victims of environmental factors, whose movements need to be managed and controlled (cf. Levy, 1995; Hartmann, 2010; Bettini, 2013, 2015; Oels, 2013; Boas and Rothe, 2016).

A second and related theme concerns the role of climatic factors in shaping migration processes and decisions. There is now a rich body of evidence that identifies the factors affecting processes of economic and distress migration. Here the focus on livelihoods, wage rates and assets provides an important lens for investigating and comparing the role of national and regional development policies in facilitating or undermining migration patterns and decisions. Similarly, the observation that certain populations will be "trapped" in areas plagued by chronic poverty and environmental vulnerability opens new lines of inquiry about the factors inhibiting and facilitating economic migration in the context of climate change. Methodologically, isolating climatic (as opposed to socio-economic and institutional) determinants of migration remains a challenge, highlighting the need for careful comparative and historical studies of migration.

A third theme concerns the policies that donors, national governments and international agencies might use in supporting and protecting populations being displaced or entrapped as a result of climate change. Underlying much of the normative and legal writing about climate, migration and displacement is the notion that states and societies have an obligation to assist vulnerable populations, possibly through the use of planned resettlement. On one hand, acting early to avert a climatic-humanitarian disaster seems perfectly reasonable. On the other, acting early without acknowledging or understanding the history of development-induced displacement runs the risk of exacerbating poverty and vulnerability. Here, a wealth of disastrous and successful histories of planned resettlement can provide useful analogues that may be used in informing future efforts to move vulnerable populations out of harm's way.

A fourth theme concerns the implications of what we might call the unintended consequences of development policy interventions. As noted earlier, there is now a sizeable body of evidence suggesting that humanitarian and development policies that are intended to help poor people rebuild and recover from natural disasters also often create perverse incentives to rebuild and relocate in areas and sectors that are highly vulnerable to future environmental change. In one sense, policies aimed at rebuilding the lives and livelihoods of displaced populations are an essential part of humanitarian and development policy. In another, they also run the risk of exacerbating future vulnerability to climate change. For scholars of humanitarian and development policy, critical questions can be asked about the conditions under which donors, NGOs, national governments and affected populations are able to balance these demands in ways that lead to disaster risk reduction.

A fifth and final theme concerns the coherence and possible policy convergence of aid and related development policy fields, such as trade, immigration and the environment. As noted earlier, policy integration now represents an important theme in international development policy and practice. On the question of humanitarian policy, an expansion of immigration quotas may be more effective – and more cost-effective – in assisting poor and vulnerable people than traditional aid transfers that are arguably more prone to misallocation and corruption (e.g. Clemens, 2010). However, ambitious efforts to expand immigration quotas need to take stock of the increasingly nationalist rhetoric that is now shaping the politics of immigration in Western liberal democracies. For scholars of political science and international development, identifying the conditions under which states are able to accommodate populations displaced by climate and environmental factors offers a promising line of inquiry. Focusing particularly on "Southern" States and South-South migration flows appears particularly fruitful in this regard.

Notes

1 www.whitehouse.gov/the-press-office/2016/01/12/remarks-president-barack-obama-%E2%80%93-prepared-delivery-state-union-address last accessed 21 May 2016.
2 Important recent contributions in the field include Byravan and Rajan (2006); Biermann and Boas (2008a, 2008b, 2010); Brown et al. (2007); Reuveny (2007); Burton (2008); Raleigh et al. (2008); the German Advisory Council (WBGU, 2008), the Norwegian Refugee Council (Kolmannskog 2008); Boano et al. (2008); Hulme (2008); Risse (2009a, 2009b); Barnett and Webber (2010); Hartmann (2010); McAdam and Saul (2010); Black et al. (2011a, 2011b); de Sherbinin et al. (2011a, 2011b); Gemenne (2011); Johnson (2012); Bettini (2013, 2015); Oels (2013); Adger et al., (2014); Eckersley (2015); Boas and Rothe (2016); and Suckall et al. (2016).
3 Downloaded 17 December 2012 from www.un.org/esa/population/migration/Opening_remarks_SG_Athens.pdf
4 Downloaded 20 September 2016 from www.unhcr.org/admin/hcspeeches/567139aa9/high-commissioner-dialogue-protection-challenges-understanding-addressing.html
5 For the purposes of this analysis, "human security" implies "the survival and dignity of human beings through freedom from fear and freedom from want" (Khagram et al. 2003, 292). "Structural security" or national security, on the other hand, implies the survival and territorial integrity of individual nation-states facing real and constructed threats to their sovereignty.
6 "The Coming Anarchy" is a reference to Robert Kaplan's controversial 1994 article of the same title that appeared in the magazine *Atlantic Monthly* (Kaplan, 1994), capturing what was arguably an emerging idea at the end of the Cold War that environmental factors can and should be treated as new threats to national and international security.
7 According to the UN High Commission for Refugees, a refugee is defined as a person who:

> owing to a well-founded fear of being persecuted for reasons of race, religion, nationality, membership of a particular social group, or political opinion, is outside the country of his nationality and is unable or, owing to such fear, is unwilling to avail himself of the protection of that country.

(CSR, Art. 1.A.2) (CSR, Art. 1.A.2) downloaded 5 July 2011 from www.unhcr.org.ua/main.php?article_id=5&view=full

Bibliography

Adger, W.N., Pulhin, J. M., Barnett, J., Dabelko, G. D., Hovelsrud, G. K., Levy, M., Oswald Spring, Ú. and Vogel, C. H. (2014) "Human security," in: C. B. Field, V. R. Barros, D. J. Dokken, K. J. Mach, M. D. Mastrandrea, T. E. Bilir, M. Chatterjee, K. L. Ebi, Y. O. Estrada, R. C. Genova, B. Girma, E. S. Kissel, A. N. Levy, S. MacCracken, P. R. Mastrandrea, and L. L. White (Ed) *Climate Change 2014: Impacts, Adaptation, and Vulnerability. Part A: Global and Sectoral Aspects. Contribution of Working Group II to the Fifth Assessment Report of the Intergovernmental Panel on Climate Change*. Cambridge, United Kingdom and New York, NY: Cambridge University Press, pp. 755–791.
Bakewell, O. (2008) "'Keeping them in their place': The ambivalent relationship between development and migration in Africa," *Third World Quarterly* (29):7, pp. 1341–58
Barnett, J. and Adger, W.N. (2007) 'Climate change, human security and violent conflict,' *Political Geography* (26): 639–655
Barnett, J. and Webber, M. (2010) "Accommodating Migration to Promote Adaptation to Climate Change," *Background Paper to the 2010 World Development Report. World Bank Policy Research Working Paper 5270*, Washington, DC: World Bank
Bell, D. (2004) "Environmental Refugees: What Rights? Which Duties?" *Res Publica* (10): pp. 135–52
Bettini, G. (2013) "Climate barbarians at the gate? A critique of apocalyptic narratives on 'climate refugees'" *Geoforum* (45), pp. 63–72

Bettini, G. (2015) "Climate migration' proved too political for the Paris agreement – and rightly so" https://theconversation.com/climate-migration-proved-too-political-for-the-paris-agreement-and-rightly-so-52133; last accessed 15 September 2016

Biermann, F. and I. Boas (2008a) 'Protecting climate refugees: The case for a global protocol,' *Environment* 50 (6), pp. 8–16.

Biermann, F. and I. Boas (2008b) "Response to Hulme," *Environment* 50 (6)

Biermann, F. and I. Boas (2010) "Preparing for a Warmer World: Towards a Global Governance System to Protect Climate Refugees," *Global Environmental Politics* 2010 10(1), pp. 60–88

Black, R. (2001) 'Environmental refugees: Myth or reality?' Available at http://www.unhcr.ch/refworld/pubs/pubon.htm

Black, R., S.R.G. Bennett, S.M. Thomas, and J.R. Beddington (2011a) "Climate change: migration as adaptation," *Nature* 478(7370), 447–449

Black, R., W.N. Adger, N.W. Arnell, S. Dercon, A. Geddes, and D. Thomas, (2011b) "The effect of environmental change on human migration," *Global Environmental Change*, 21(Suppl. 1), S3–S11

Boano, C., R. Zetter and T. Morris (2008) "Environmentally displaced people: Understanding the linkages between environmental change, livelihoods and forced migration" Forced Migration Policy Briefing 1 Refugees Studies Centre, Oxford University www.rsc.ox.ac.uk

Boas, I. (2015). *Climate Migration and Security: Securitisation as a Strategy in Climate Change Politics* New York and London: Routledge.

Boas, I., & Rothe, D. (2016) "From conflict to resilience? Explaining recent changes in climate security discourse and practice," *Environmental Politics* (25): 4, pp. 613–632

Bogardi, J. and K. Warner (2009) 'Here comes the flood,' *Nature Reports Climate Change* (3), pp. 9–11.

Brown, O., A. Hammill and R. McLeman (2007) 'Climate change as the 'new' security threat: implications for Africa,' *International Affairs* 83: 6, 1141–1154

Burton, I. (2008) "Beyond borders: The need for strategic global adaptation," *IIED Opinion* December 2008 www.iied.org/pubs

Byravan, S. and S.C. Rajan (2006) "Providing new homes for climate change exiles," *Climate Policy* (6), pp. 247–252

Castles, S. (2002) 'Environmental change and forced migration: making sense of the debate' Refugees Studies Centre Working Paper No. 70 University of Oxford

Cernea, M. M. (1997) "The risks and reconstruction model for resettling displaced populations," *World Development* (25): 10, pp. 1569–1589.

Cernea, M. and Schmidt-Soltau, K. (2006) "Poverty risks and national parks: Policy issues in conservation and resettlement," *World Development* (34): 100, pp. 1808–30.

Christian Aid (2007). Human Tide: The Real Migration Crisis London, May. Accessible at www.christian-aid.org.uk.

Clemens, M. (2010) "To help Haiti's earthquake victims, change US immigration laws," *Washington Post* 24 January 2010 www.washingtonpost.com/wp-dyn/content/article/2010/01/22/AR2010012202274.html

Coirolo, C., Commins, S., Haque, I., & Pierce, G. (2013) "Climate change and social protection in Bangladesh: Are existing programmes able to address the impacts of climate change?" *Development Policy Review*, (31): s2, pp. o74–o90

Corbridge, S. (1983) "Urban bias, rural bias, and industrialization: an appraisal of the work of Michael Lipton and Terry Byres," in J. Harriss (Ed) *Rural development: Theories of peasant economy and agrarian change.* London: Hutchinson, pp. 94–118

Couldrey, M. and Herson, M. (2008 Eds.) "Climate change and displacement," Special Issue of Forced Migration Review Issue 31, October 2008

de Haan, A. (1999) 'Livelihoods and poverty: The role of migration—a critical review of the migration literature,' *The Journal of Development Studies* (36): 2, pp. 1–47

de Haas, H. (2012) "The migration and development pendulum: A critical view on research and policy," *International Migration* (50):3, pp. 8–25.

de Sherbinin, A., Van Wey, L.K., McSweeney, K., Aggarwal, R., Barbieri, A., Henry, S., Hunter, L.M., Twine, W. and Walker, R. (2008) "Rural household demographics, livelihoods and the environment," *Global Environmental Change* (18): pp. 38–53

de Sherbinin, A., Warner, K., and Ehrhart, C. (2011a) "Casualties of Climate Change," *Scientific American* January: pp. 32–39

de Sherbinin, A., Castro, M., Gemenne, F., Cernea, M. M., Adamo, S., Fearnside, P. M., Krieger, G., Lahmani, S., Oliver-Smith, A., Pankhurst, A., Scudder, T., Singer, B., Tan, Y., Wannier, G., Boncour, P., Ehrhart, C., Hugo, G., Pandey, B. and Shi, G. (2011b) "Preparing for Resettlement Associated with Climate Change," *Science* (334) 28 October 2011, pp. 456–7

Deshingkar, P. (2005) "Maximizing the benefits of internal migration for development," www.preventtraffickingchina.org/english/Website_Files/Deshingkar.pdf; accessed 29 June 2009

Eckersley, R. (2015) "The Common but Differentiated Responsibility of States to Assist and Receive 'Climate Refugees,'" *European Journal of Political Theory* (14):4, pp. 481–500

Foresight: Migration and Global Environmental Change (2011) *Final Project Report: Executive Summary* The (UK) Government Office for Science, London

GEF (Global Environment Facility, 2007) *Linking Adaptation to Development* Downloaded 18 December 2012 at www.thegef.org/gef/sites/thegef.org/files/publication/Adaptation_brochure.pdf

Gemenne, F. (2011) "Why the numbers don't add up: A review of estimates and projections of people displaced by environmental changes," *Global Environmental Change* (21S): S41–S49

Hartmann, B. (2010) "Rethinking climate refugees and climate conflict: Rhetoric, reality and the politics of policy discourse," *Journal of International Development* (22): 233–246

Heltberg, R., Siegel, P.B. and Jorgensen, S.L. (2009) "Addressing human vulnerability to climate change: Toward a 'no-regrets' approach", *Global Environmental Change* 19(1): 89–99

Homer-Dixon T. (1991) "On the threshold: environmental changes as causes of acute conflict," *International Security* 16 (2): 76–116

Humble, A. (2014) "The rise of trapped populations," *Forced Migration Review* 45 February 2014 www.fmreview.org/crisis/humble.html; last accessed 6 June 2016

Hulme, M. (2008) "Commentary – Climate refugees: Cause for a new agreement?" *Environment* (50):6

IOM (International Organization for Migration) (2009) "Migration, climate change and the environment," *IOM Policy Brief* May 2009 www.iom.int/envmig Accessed 29 June 2009

Johnson, C. and Krishnamurthy, K. (2010) "Dealing with displacement: Can 'social protection' facilitate long-term adaptation to climate change? *Global Environmental Change* (20): 648–55

Johnson, C. (2012) "Governing climate displacement: The ethics and politics of human resettlement," *Environmental Politics* 21(2): 308–28

Johnson, C. (2013) "Accommodating 'climate refugees': Models of sovereignty and security in the international climate regime," in DK Vajpeyi (Ed.) *Climate change, sustainable development and human security: A comparative analysis* Toronto: Lexington Books, pp. 83–109

Johnson, C., Bansha Dulal, H., Prowse, M., Krishnamurthy, K., & Mitchell, T. (2013) "Social protection and climate change: emerging issues for research, policy and practice," *Development Policy Review* (31):s2, pp. o2–o18

Joppke, C. (1999) *Immigration and the Nation-State: The United States, Germany, and Great Britain* Oxford: Oxford University Press

Kahl, C. H. (2006) *States, Scarcity, and Civil Strife in the Developing World* Princeton, NJ: Princeton U.P

Kaplan, R. (1994) "The coming anarchy," *The Atlantic Monthly* www.theatlantic.com/magazine/archive/1994/02/the-coming-anarchy/304670/; last accesses 2 June 2016

Khagram, S., Clark, W. C., and Raad, D. F. (2003) "From the environment and human security to sustainable security and development," *Journal of Human Development* (4):2, pp. 289–313

Kolmannskog, V. O. (2008) *Future Floods of Refugees: A Comment on Climate Change, Conflict and Forced Migration* Oslo: Norwegian Refugee Council

Kuriakose, A. T., Heltberg, R., Wiseman, W., Costella, C., Cipryk, R., & Cornelius, S. (2013) "Climate-Responsive Social Protection" *Development Policy Review*, (31):s2, pp. o19–o34

Levy, M. A. (1995) "Is the environment a national security issue?" *International Security*, (20):2, 35–62

Lipton, M. (1983) "Why poor people stay poor," in J. Harriss (Ed) *Rural Development: Theories of Peasant Economy and Agrarian Change*. London: Hutchinson, pp. 66–81.

McAdam, J. and Saul, B. (2010) "Displacement with dignity: International law and policy responses to climate change migration and security in Bangladesh," *University of New South Wales Faculty of Law Research Series 2010*. Working Paper 63 (December 2010)

McGranahan, G., Balk, D. and Anderson, B. (2007) "The rising tide: assessing the risks of climate change and human settlements in low elevation coastal zones," *Environment and Urbanization* (19):1, pp. 17–37

McLeman, R. and Smit, B. (2006) "Migration as adaptation to climate change," *Climatic Change* (76): pp. 31–53

Moench, M. (2007 [2009]) Adapting to climate change and the risks associated with other natural hazards: Methods for moving from concepts to action," in E.L.F. Schipper and I. Burton (Eds.) *The Earthscan Reader on Adaptation to Climate Change* London: Earthscan, pp. 249–82

Myers N. (1993) "Environmental refugees in a globally warmed world," *BioScience* 43 752–61

Neumayer, E. (2006) "The environment: One more reason to keep immigrants out?" *Ecological Economics* (59): pp. 204–7

Nordas, R. and N. P. Gleditsch (2007) "Climate change and conflict," *Political Geography* (26), pp. 627–638

O'Brien, K. et al. (2008) "Disaster risk reduction, climate change adaptation and human security," A Commissioned Report for the Norwegian Ministry of Foreign Affairs available at www.preventionweb.net/files/7946_GECHSReport3081.pdf last accessed 6 June 2016

Oels, A., (2013) "Rendering climate change governable by risk: From probability to contingency," *Geoforum*, 45 (1), 17–29. doi:10.1016/j.geoforum.2011.09.007

Panda, A. (2013) "Climate Variability and the Role of Access to Crop Insurance as a Social-Protection Measure: Insights from India," *Development Policy Review*, 31(s2), o57–o73

Penz, P., J. Drydyk and P. Bose (2011) *Displacement by Development: Ethics, Rights and Responsibilities* Cambridge: Cambridge University Press

Perch-Nielson, S.L., Battig, M.B. and Imboden, D. (2008) "Exploring the link between climate change and migration," *Climatic Change* (91): 375–93.

Raleigh, Clionadh, Lisa Jordan and Idean Salehyan (2008) Assessing the Impact of Climate Change on Migration and Conflict Washington DC: World Bank

Reuveny, R. (2007) "Climate change-induced migration and violent conflict," *Political Geography* (26), pp. 656–673

Revi, A., D. Satterthwaite, F. Aragón-Durand, J. Corfee-Morlot, R.B.R. Kiunsi, M. Pelling, D.C. Roberts, and W. Solecki. (2014) "Urban areas," in Field, C.B., V.R. Barros, D.J. Dokken, K.J. Mach, M.D. Mastrandrea, T.E. Bilir, M. Chatterjee, K.L. Ebi, Y.O. Estrada, R.C. Genova, B. Girma, E.S. Kissel, A.N. Levy, S. MacCracken, P.R. Mastrandrea, and L.L. White (Eds) *Climate Change 2014: Impacts, Adaptation, and Vulnerability. Part A: Global and Sectoral Aspects. Contribution of Working Group II to the Fifth Assessment Report of the Intergovernmental Panel on Climate Change*. Cambridge, UK and New York: Cambridge University Press, pp. 535–612

Riddell, R. (2008) *Does Foreign Aid Really Work?* Oxford: Oxford University Press

Risse, M. (2009a) "The Right to Relocation: Disappearing Island Nations and Common Ownership of the Earth," *Ethics and International Affairs* (23): pp. 281–300

Risse, M. (2009b) Immigration, Ethics and the Capabilities Approach Published in: Human Development Research Paper (HDRP) Series, Vol. 34, No. 2009, downloaded 5 July 2011 at http://mpra.ub.uni-muenchen.de/19218/

Rothe, D. (2016) *Securitizing global warming: a climate of complexity* London and New York: Routledge

Satterthwaite, D., G. McGranahan and C. Tacoli (2010) "Urbanization and its implications for food and farming," *Philosophical Transactions of the Royal Society B*. 365: 2809–2820

Scott J. C. (1998) *Seeing Like a State: How Certain Schemes to Improve the Human Condition Have Failed* New Haven, CT: Yale University Press

Suckall, N., Fraser, E., & Forster, P. (2016) "Reduced migration under climate change: evidence from Malawi using an aspirations and capabilities framework," *Climate and Development*, 1–15 doi: http://dx.doi.org/10.1080/17565529.2016.1149441

UNDP (2008) Human Development Report 2007/08: Fighting Climate Change: Human Solidarity in a Divided World New York: Oxford University Press

UNDP (2009) "Summary: Overcoming barriers: Human mobility and development," *Human Development Report 2009* available at: http://hdr.undp.org/en/media/HDR_2009_EN_Summary.pdf

UNFCCC (2007) *Climate Change: Impacts, Vulnerabilities and Adaptation in Developing Countries* Downloaded from http://unfccc.int/adaptation/items/4159.php 10 June 2009

WBGU (German Advisory Council on Global Change) (2008) Climate Change as a Security Risk London: Earthscan

Warner, K., C. Ehrhart, A. de Sherbinin, S. Adamo and T. Chai-Onn (2009) In Search of Shelter: Mapping the Effects of Climate Change on Human Migration and Displacement CARE International and CIESEN, downloaded 17 March 2010 at http://ciesen.columbia.edu/publications.html

Weldegebriel, Z. B., & Prowse, M. (2013) "Climate-Change Adaptation in Ethiopia: To What Extent Does Social Protection Influence Livelihood Diversification?" *Development Policy Review, 31*(s2), o35–o56

Werz, M. and L. Conley (2012) *Climate change, migration and conflict: Addressing complex crisis scenarios in the 21st century* The Center for American Progress downloaded 16 November 2012 at www.americanprogress.org/wp-content/uploads/issues/2012/01/pdf/climate_migration.pdf

Westra, L. (2009) *Environmental Justice and the Rights of Ecological Refugees* London: Earthscan

Wisner, B., Blaikie, P., Cannon, T. and Davis, I. (2004) *At risk: Natural hazards, people's vulnerability and disasters* London and New York: Routledge

World Bank (2010) *World Development Report 2010: Development and Climate Change* Washington DC: The World Bank

Zetter, R. (2007) "More labels, fewer refugees: Remaking the refugee label in the era of globalization," *Journal of Refugee Studies* (20): 2, pp. 172–92

355

28

Environmental migration and international political security

Rhetoric, reality and questions

Stern Mwakalimi Kita and Clionadh Raleigh

Introduction

The perception that environmental migration poses a security threat is found across all levels of global governance, with migrants often being scapegoated as being sources of risk. Consider the following quotations:

> We must make no mistake. The facts are clear: climate change is real; it is accelerating in a dangerous manner; and it not only exacerbates threats to international peace and security, it is a threat to international peace and security.
>
> *Ban Ki-moon (2011: n.p.)*

> The (EU) Council recognizes climate change as a contributing factor to migration resulting from state fragility, insecurity and resource scarcity. By further analysing climate vulnerability links with fragility and security risk, the EU will be in a better position to identify areas where combined risks are particularly high and where there are critical opportunities for conflict prevention and resilience, including in the context of a wider migration challenge.
>
> *Council of the European Union (2016)*

> Leaving ancestral homelands, and in some cases the entire country, behind is unacceptable in the Pacific culture. External migration has a similar potential for conflict and unrest as internal migration, but adds a cultural and international dimension.
>
> *Pacific Small Island Developing States (2009)*

> When Mexico sends its people, they're not sending their best. They're not sending you. They're not sending you. They're sending people that have lots of problems, and they're bringing those problems with them. They're bringing drugs. They're bringing crime. They're rapists. And some, I assume, are good people.
>
> *Donald J. Trump (2015)*

Although there is little empirical evidence to link environmental migration to international security threats, as the preceding quotations suggest, there is a growing public narrative that presents environmental change as a source of political instability and conflict within developing nations, and which presents international migrants from developing nations as a potential source of international security risks. This chapter reviews the state of existing knowledge on the linkages between environment migration and security, and summarises emerging research directions. In doing so, we find that the purported connections between environmental change, migration and security are poorly substantiated in evidence, and that fears about climate-related migration becoming a driver of future conflict and instability should be tempered in the absence of further evidence.

Environmental change, migration and conflict

Conceptual connection

The environmental change, migration and conflict nexus can be interpreted in many different ways, including the following:

(i) Migration will lead to environmental degradation or stress that will result in conflict.
(ii) Environmental change or degradation will lead to migration, that will in turn lead to conflicts in the destination area; and
(iii) Environmental change or degradation will lead to conflict that generates migration that in turn contributes to diffusion or relocation of existing conflicts.

The final scenario has received the most attention within the climate security literature. Here, insecurity arising from competition due to resource scarcity or abundance may lead to migration (McLeman, 2011) through two distinct avenues. The first may referred to as the *scarcity-conflict* hypothesis, where competition may eventually lead to violent conflict as climate change creates resource scarcity in terms of quality, access or availability of key resources. Increased risks of disasters and environmental degradation would reduce state capacity to provide public services. This would impact directly on the livelihoods of communities and increase levels of poverty that may feed the likelihood of conflicts (Homer-Dixon, 1991; Barnett & Adger, 2007; Buhaug et al., 2008; Foresight, 2011). This is an especially large risk in developing countries such as East Timor, where 85% of the population depend on agriculture as a source of income; in such a situation, drought and other environment stresses might increase poverty levels and incentives for conflicts (Barnett & Adger, 2007). The conflict may further worsen resource scarcity, creating a feedback cycle.

The second avenue is *abundance-competition* hypothesis, where particular demographic groups extract economic rents for geographically concentrated resources; when such resources rise in demand and prices, competition may be created among the population leading to conflict, migration and further conflict.

In all scenarios, interpretations of the relationships between climate change, conflict and migration are built upon assumptions of correlated and coordinated negative impacts. Some interpretations directly privilege an outcome of conflict; others emphasize migration and environmental change. However, the available evidence from the literature remains inconclusive about the general and specific occurrence of any scenario (see Raleigh & Kniveton, 2012; Theisen et al., 2013; van Weezel, 2013; von Uexkull, 2014; Buhaug et al., 2015).

Links between climate change, scarcity and conflict

A number of studies show that environmental scarcity resulting from climate change may lead to or exacerbate conflict. Most of these studies compare historical data on rainfall, temperature and natural disasters with historical conflict data. Research in Africa provides several examples. There have been claims that in Nigeria, climate-induced food insecurity has led to an increase in cases of terrorist activities and general civil unrest (Aribigbola et. al., 2013). Focusing on small-scale conflict events in East Africa, Raleigh and Kniveton (2012) found that rainfall variability – manifested through extreme wet and extreme dry conditions – worsens conflicts. This study also finds that rebel conflicts are common in extreme dry conditions, while communal conflicts occur mostly in extreme wet situations. The interpretation is that rebel activity is highest in the dry season for strategic reasons, while communal conflicts and raiding are highest during seasons of 'plenty'. In a study of Sub-Saharan Africa, O'Loughlin et al. (2014) found that extremely high temperature significantly increase the risk of conflict, while precipitation variability fails to explain conflict occurrence, though there were variations in the influence of extreme temperature on conflict across regions and conflict type. Von Uexkull (2014) established a link between sustained drought and risk of violent civil conflict in Sub-Saharan Africa, largely in areas whose food production and income depend on rain-fed agriculture. However, data show that drought largely exacerbates existing conflicts in agricultural-dependent regions, as opposed to generating new conflicts. Werz and Hoffman (2016) argue that second-order effects of climate change such as agricultural production shortfalls and competition for food contribute to conflicts that result in increasing numbers of migrants. They therefore call for policy changes, including urgent broadening of the definition of national security for Europe so that threats emanating from global environmental change are considered. However, it is important to note that all of those studies strongly emphasize that political, socioeconomic and geographical factors influence the location and timing of conflicts more than either temperature or rainfall anomalies.

Other studies have focused on the impact that extreme climatic events such as floods have on a state's capacity to deal with conflict. Ghimire and Ferreira (2016) analysed flood and conflict data for 126 countries between 1985 and 2009 and observed that high magnitude floods do not cause new conflicts but can worsen existing conflicts. Further, the effect of floods is larger in countries that are chronically susceptible to conflicts. Why might this happen? One explanation provided is that disasters distract states' focus on conflict because efforts and resources – including military personnel – are channelled to responding to the disaster; this provides an opportunity for other conflict actors to expand their influence. Similar conclusions were reached by Eastin (2016), who analysed 224 armed conflicts occurring between 1946 and 2005 and found that occurrence of natural disasters prolong conflicts. He argues that disasters affect the state's capacity to deal with conflicts while at the same time strengthening rebel groups' ability to evade the state, thereby making peace efforts difficult. This point is reinforced by examples from the 2010 floods in Pakistan and 2009 floods in Somalia that allowed rebel groups to expand their influence (Ghimire & Ferreira, 2016).

Evidence to suggest climate change does not cause conflict

Using similar datasets from similar geographical locations, other scholars have found no link between environmental change and conflict. Using an event coincidence analysis, Schleussnera et al. (2016) found that 23% of outbreaks of conflicts in countries with highly fractionalised ethnic groups coincide robustly with climatic disasters such as heat waves and droughts. They also found a 9% global coincident rate of armed conflict outbreak and occurrence of natural disasters. However, it is important to note that their study does not show any evidence of armed conflicts being directly triggered by climate-related disasters, but simply an occasional and infrequent temporal coincidence. In a study on the link between environmental scarcity and conflict in 39 Sub-Saharan countries, Bell and Keys (2016) identified three socio-political conditions that explain the link between environmental scarcity and civil conflict: social vulnerability, unequal resource distribution and the capacity of the state. Noteworthy is that the study found no evidence that drought increases the risk of armed conflict in fragile states, even those where socio-political conditions favour conflict outbreak. A study by Hegre et al. (2016) found no significant effect of temperature anomalies on the risk of conflict, but the authors did suggest that climate change may lead to low socioeconomic growth that may lead to further conflict. This could also affect investment in climate change adaptation and mitigation, especially in low-income countries. In a study on Sub-Saharan Africa, Buhaug et al. (2015) analysed data on climate variability, food production and conflict over a 50-year period and found no effect of food production shocks on the likelihood of conflict, dispelling the position that harvest failure and bad weather conditions contribute to violence in Africa. They argue that political and socioeconomic factors such as corruption, market failures and government policies better explain occurrence of civil unrest in times of food crisis.

Investigating the possibility that climate affects conflict risk through economic challenges, van Weezel (2013) studied rainfall and conflict patterns between 1981 and 2010 in Sub-Saharan Africa and concluded that there is no robust link between rainfall failure, an important determinant of crop failure in Sub-Saharan Africa, and conflict onset, directly or indirectly. A study by Ayana et al. (2016) focused on pastoralists in East Africa, and found that livelihood stresses due to rainfall and forage yields fail to predict the occurrence and location of conflicts. Bergholt and Lujala (2012) have demonstrated that even the indirect link between climate change and conflict is suspect. The authors used historical data for the period 1980–2007 to show that severe and frequent climate-induced disasters create income shocks and affect Gross Domestic Product (GDP) growth of affected countries, but do not lead to conflict outbreaks directly or indirectly.

Many studies result in counterclaims by other scholars, with the ensuing debates often centering on data and methods. For example, when Burke et al. (2009) claimed that Sub-Saharan African temperature increases contributed to conflict outbreak in the region, Buhaug (2010) questioned the veracity of such claims given the restricted time period used in the study by Burke and colleagues (the years 1981–2002), and suggested that the study used a purposefully narrow definition of conflicts, and other methodological oddities. Buhaug therefore reached an opposite conclusion: climate change and variability are poor predictors of conflicts in Africa. After recalibrating their models, Burke and colleagues found that the purported relationship vanished, and accepted that their earlier results were wrong (Aldhous, 2010). In another study, Hsiang and Burke (2014: 42) examined 50 quantitative studies and found "strong support for a causal association between climatological changes and conflict across a range of geographies, a range of different time periods, a range of spatial scales and across climatic events of different duration." This led them to presume that the 'climate security' was firmly based in evidence. In response, Buhaug et al. (2014) identified three challenges with the study: across-study independence, causal homogeneity and sample representativeness. They employed the same method, but were not able to replicate the original results on climate change and conflicts using the same cases used by Hsiang and Burke (2014).

Is climate change a peacemaker?

Interestingly, other scholars have found climatic disasters reduce not only the occurrence of conflict, but may also lead to peace. Some hold that contrary to the resource scarcity hypothesis, conflicts are more common when critical resources such as water are abundant. Evidence from the drylands of Kenya indicates that during times of drought and water scarcity, there is less violence (Hartmann, 2010). Two other researchers studying pastoralist conflict in Kenya used historical and archival records to show that conflict intensity increases in times of abundance during the rainy season, and not during dry periods when resources are scarce (Witsenburg & Adano, 2009). Salehyan and Hendrix (2014) assessed the impact of climatic conditions on conflict prevalence across 165 countries and concluded that resource scarcity caused by extreme climatic events affects the capacity of rebel groups to organise and maintain their control over the population, hence leading to fewer conflict events.

In another study on climate-related natural disasters and civil conflicts that used global data from 1950 to around 2010, Sletteback (2012) found that disasters reduced the likelihood of conflict occurring. The study also found that conflict risk increases with population growth, but this increase is more rapid where no disaster occurs than where there is a disaster. Gartzke (2012) also found that global warming results in reduced interstate conflicts. The study further shows that one of the key factors contributing to global warming – economic development – also reduces the risk of conflicts among states.

Environmental scarcity, conflict and migration

Migration as a result of climate change might also create geopolitical problems and other conditions that increase the risk of conflicts in the destination area (Reuveny, 2007; Foresight, 2011; Theisen et al., 2013; Burrows & Kinney, 2016). Reuveny (2007: 659) argues that the likelihood of conflict increases where two or more of the following four potential conditions exist:

(i)   Where environmental migrants create *competition* over the available public goods and services leading to contest from the host,
(ii) Where *ethnic tension* exists between residents and migrants belonging to different ethnic groups,
(iii) Where there is *distrust* between the country the migrants are coming from and the destination country, and
(iv) Where there are pre-existing *fault lines* such as competition over land or jobs.

There may also be auxiliary conditions in receiving countries that make the likelihood of conflict high, such as low levels of development, existing conflicts and instability situation. Reuveny (2007) emphasises his point with evidence from past migration, some climate-induced and other not, which led to conflict in the destination area. These include the violence in India with the arrival of Bangladeshi environmental migrants in the 1980s and the war in Honduras in 1969 with the arrival of environmental migrants from El Salvador.

There is little question that environmental change can create, disturb or exacerbate migration patterns. According to a UN Environment Programme report (UNEP, 2011), recurrent drought in the Sahel, combined with social and economic factors, has caused northern pastoralists to migrate farther southwards into areas that are used by sedentary farmers, and the resulting increased food demand has led farmers to cultivate land that was traditionally used by pastoralists. Whether these cases have created increased competition and violent conflicts in the areas is a further leap, and often assertions of this nature ignore the local political context and previous conflicts. For example, a recent study in Nigeria of Fulani herdsmen who moved from the northern to the southern part of the country attributed their movement to drought, landslides, unusual weather, desertification and hunger caused by climatic factors, and suggested that the consequences included inter-communal conflicts between the Fulani and their hosts (Folami & Folami, 2013). However, Fulani occupy a significant part of the Middle Belt in Nigeria, and their contests with other groups over land occupation are a long-standing feature of the region. Further, the Fulani are in active contest within their large communities about political representation, local management and relative status, which is closely associated with violence across the area (Dimelu et al., 2016). Attributing violence or migration to climate without fully understanding the local contexts can lead to misrepresentations of reality.

Some scholars suggest that migration resulting from climate change will itself lead to conflicts. Examples that have been cited in the literature include the ethnic tensions and conflicts in India (attributed to Bangladeshi migrants), in Syria, in the Philippines during the period 1970–2000 and in Ethiopia from 1984–1985 (Burrows and Kinney, 2016; Ghimire et al., 2015). But there are significant political problems in all aforementioned cases that led to a number of destabilizing conditions, including migration. Often while concentrating on the climate-migration-conflict risk, these studies have overlooked crucial national and subnational factors such as the pre-existing war in Ethiopia, the ongoing insurgency in the Philippines, domestic political instability in Syria and conflicts in neighbouring countries, and demographic pressures by Bangladeshi migrants that pre-date environmental changes. The potential for migration and subsequent intergroup conflict was high in all of these cases, regardless of coincident environmental changes.

The conflict in Darfur is often cited as an illustration of how climate change will lead to conflicts and then migration (Christian Aid, 2007; De Juan, 2015). Drought in Sudan is argued to have led to competition between pastoralists and farmers that eventually led to the conflict (Brown, 2007; Christian Aid, 2007). De Juan (2015), while agreeing that the onset of the Darfur conflict was not directly linked to environmental scarcity but to the economic and political context, argues that long-term environmental change shaped the conflict by acting as a risk factor. Most scholars, however, agree that the Darfur conflict is a result of a combination of factors, including collapse of traditional social structures and normal mechanisms for dispute mediation and resolution, nationalisation of land, gross power and wealth inequalities, and policies that favoured large farm owners over rural farmers (Tacoli, 2009; Hartmann, 2010). While the claim that the Darfur conflict is linked to environmental degradation and change is highly contentious and has been shown to be flawed, the international NGO Christian Aid posit what Gemenne et al. (2014: 2) have called "dire apocalyptic visions" in one of its publications: "let Darfur stand as the starkest of warnings about what the future could bring" (Christian Aid, 2007: 2). Even in conflict situations, migration is not an automatic and uniform option for the population, nor is it in turn an automatic generator of further conflict. Poverty, extant threats, the presence of relief assistance, social networks, the likelihood of livelihood security and opportunity to return are just some of the factors that determine individuals' decisions whether to migrate or not and the duration and direction of such migration (Raleigh, 2011).

As was the case with Darfur, some scholars have attempted to make direct or indirect causal connections between climate change, migration and the civil unrest in Syria. Gleick (2014), Kelley et al. (2015) and Werrell et al. (2015) argue that, in addition to other political, economic, religious and social factors, environmental factors including water shortages, drought and the impacts of climate change and climate variability impact on hydrology contributed to the generation of conflict. They hold that the climate-induced 2007–2010 drought, which was the worst in instrumental record, led to food insecurity, loss of livelihoods and displacement of large populations. Most of those affected migrated to urban areas, and this 'environmental migration' increased urban pressure, including unemployment and resource scarcity resulting in political instability. Fröhlich (2016), however, through an empirical study with Syrian refugees finds that although environmental factors contributed to some migration, it was not the decisive factor but just one among several key factors. He also finds that poor governance in natural resource management worsened the water problem in Syria. As regards the initiation of conflict, his study finds that migrants were mostly marginalised and were not involved in the protests that led to the uprising. Fröhlich (2016) questioned whether the migrants in question originated in environmentally challenged regions of Syria in the first place; further, the question arises why drought would have triggered migration and violence in Syria but not in neighboring states that were also politically unstable.

While environmental change did not solely or principally contribute to the Syrian crisis, just like Darfur, the media and global leaders have capitalised on such studies, with some partly linking the migration crisis in Europe to conflicts resulting from environmental change in Syria (Fountain, 2015; Fröhlich, 2016). This has led to calls for policy options to address threats posed by environmental migration. In a 2015 senate report titled 'National security implications of climate-related risks and a changing climate,' the US Department of Defense (DoD) considers extreme climate events such as droughts and floods to be potential security risks and, citing the Gleick (2014) study on the Syrian conflict as an example, and argues that climate change "could result in increased intra- and inter-state migration, and generate other negative effects on human security" (DoD 2015: p. 4). During the opening of a Global Leadership in the Arctic conference on cooperation, innovation, engagement and resilience in Alaska in August 2015, US Secretary of State John Kerry expressed another 'apocalyptic vision' in the face of global environmental change:

> And we as leaders of countries will begin to witness what we call climate refugees moving – you think migration is a challenge to Europe today because of extremism, wait until you see what happens when there's an absence of water, an absence of food, or one tribe fighting against another for mere survival.[1]

Making sense of the debate

Despite the contradictory findings from the literature, we know that the environment – and possibly environmental change – has some impact on conflict and migration. Most scholars agree on an indirect causal link, but claims of a direct link remain contentious, with evidence existing to suggest that both more conflict and more peace may emerge in areas experiencing environmental stress. For both migration and conflict, direct links to environmental factors are questioned by most scholars. Both processes are ongoing and dynamic, so ascribing their occurrence to a single continuously changing environmental factor (such as weather or climate) is problematic, and most scholars see climate change to be just one of many factors that can cause migration (Foresight, 2011).

The literature on environmental security often pre-supposes a direct causal link between demographic movement and violence, for which there is limited evidence, and studies often ignore non-climatic factors in the causation of violence. We do know that environmental conditions can create opportunities and constraints for the emergence of violent actions, typically through strategic incentives (e.g. dry season and rebel activity) or livelihoods. Independent of subnational and national political, economic and social factors, there is little evidence that environmental change or scarcity leads to conflicts; rather, the evidence shows that some conflicts are over control of natural resource-rich areas (Black, 2001). Although disputes might arise over natural resources like water, there are few cases where such conflicts have turned violent in the absence of pre-existing political, economic or social tensions (Castles, 2002). Further, almost all research is concentrated on domestic movement and domestic conflict: there is very little evidence that environmental factors have any significant influence on international movement or in conflict.

The position taken in the IPCC's fifth assessment report (2014) is at present the most reliable one available. In it, the IPCC suggests that climate change can affect human security, thereby affecting migration patterns. Regarding conflicts, the IPCC suggests that climate change can indirectly lead to conflict by amplifying known drivers of conflicts such as poverty and economic shocks, an opinion that is presented with a medium level of confidence. The report concludes that current evidence does not conclusively show a link between climate change and armed conflict, but that most of the factors that increase the risk of conflict are sensitive to climate change (Adger et al., 2014).

Securitization of environmental migration

Migration has often been viewed to varying degrees as being a threat to national security and political stability (Homer-Dixon, 1991; Barnett, 2003; Brown, et al., 2007; Tacoli, 2009; McMichael et al., 2012). Recent decades have witnessed a growth in the *perception* that migration is a major security issue, and that certain categories of people pose threats to the sovereignty and success of countries. Such anti-migration sentiments can be a political strategy to promote social cohesion and muster support in 'native' populations, and claim legitimacy to represent such groups (White, 2011; Humphrey, 2013). The rhetoric of 'dangerous migrants' makes governments become increasingly concerned with border controls, stringent visa enforcement, and choosing what categories of migrants are the 'best' (Humphrey, 2013). The 2015–2016 European migration 'crisis' and the subsequent fear of uncontrolled waves of refugees that might include potential terrorists is a reason many believe that the United Kingdom's referendum on exiting the EU succeeded, that far-right parties in Europe have gained political ground, and that President Trump's calls for a wall between the US and Mexico helped him get elected.

Academic literature has sometimes been used to support these extreme views. In addition to previously mentioned invocation of research on the links between drought and the Syrian conflict, Homer-Dixon's (1999) 'degradation narrative' has also been historically influential. His work suggested that population growth, combined with scarcity of resources such as food and water, may lead to migration and violent conflicts. In turn, this leads to further environmental damage, persistent conflicts and high levels of poverty. States may become more fragmented or authoritarian as a result of the chronic conflicts, thereby affecting international security. These dystopian causal chains can be easily leveraged for popular media and political discourse.

Environmental migrants are specifically considered to be security threats as they are often believed to:

(i) 'Free-ride' on a state's collective goods and services,
(ii) Reflect weak border controls,
(iii) Bring new diseases and/or socially unacceptable ideologies from their countries of origin,
(iv) Negatively affect the economic wellbeing of the receiving country, and
(v) Generally act as a threat to the territorial integrity of states (Detraz & Windsor, 2014,: 130).

Countries are therefore expected to take measures to control environmental-induced migration (Detraz & Windsor, 2014). The placement of environmental migration within a security framework provides leeway for states to argue for stricter border controls and other national security responses, and creating political resistance to any possibility of adopting international obligations towards those migrating as a result of environmental factors (White, 2011; Nishimura, 2015). Anti-asylum lobbyists have tended to use climate refugee predictions as tools to advocate for restricting migration (Black, 2001; Morrissey, 2009), and securitization of environmental migration has been blamed for discriminatory practices against African and Bedouin migrants in Israel, as well for incentivizing nations to build border fences and exclusionary policies (Weinthal et al., 2015). As argued by Hartmann (2010), securitization of environmental migration may end up militarising not just climate policy but development aid as well. With emphasis on the security dimensions of environmental migration, it is difficult to find support for protection-based approaches to addressing environmental migration (Nishimura, 2015).

The securitization of climate change writ large is partly linked to the securitisation of migrants; this was done to create a sense of urgency in the international debate, and to prevent the likely developmental impacts of climate change and possible conflicts (Brown et al., 2007). Creating urgency around climate change and associated issues is a common strategy (see Lomborg, 2001) and designed to make the UN Security Council (UNSC) take a leading role in spurring states to take action on mitigation and adaptation (Scott, 2008). There has been growing interest in the UN General Assembly and Security Council to discuss climate change as a security concern and agreeing on non-security measures to address its impacts, especially on small island states (Brown et al., 2007; UN, 2009; Ki-moon, 2011; Gemenne et al., 2014). In a report to the 64th session of the UN General Assembly titled 'Climate Change and Its Possible Security Implications,' the UN Secretary General described climate change as a "threat multiplier" and called upon states to implement "threat minimisers" to address the security threats it poses (UN, 2009: 6). The UN Security Council (UNSC) held its first debate on climate change, energy and security on 17 April 2007 (Scott, 2008). Opening the second Security Council's major debate on climate change and security in 2011, the UN Secretary General argued that climate change "not only exacerbates threats to international peace and security; it is a threat to international peace and security" (Ki-moon, 2011: n.p.). The meeting resolved that the Secretary General should include contextual information on the possible security implication of climate change in his report to the UNSC.

Further evidence of the securitization of climate change is found in policy discussions in Europe over the past decade or so. In the United Kingdom, the government's chief scientist in 2004 argued that climate change poses a greater risk to national security than international terrorism (Brown et al., 2007). In a paper presented to the European Council in 2008, the EU High Representative for the Common Foreign and Security Policy argued that environmentally-induced migration may lead to increased cases of conflicts and called upon the EU to be prepared as "Europe must expect substantially increased migratory pressure" (CEC, 2008: 4). A 2016 EU Resolution considers climate change impacts to be a major threat to international security, and calls upon the UNSC to continue with its work on climate change, while also calling for member states to take measures to address the threat posed by climate change. While it does not recognize climate change as the sole factor leading to migration, the resolution encourages the seeking of opportunities for conflict prevention and resilience (Council of the European Union, 2016).

The environmental-migration-security narrative may bring both positive and negative developments. It may promote adaptation and adoption of practices that reduce environmental change, but there is also a wide scholarship that views the narrative as problematic, since by blaming conflicts on climate change, it thereby punishes victims of both, and shelters the perpetrators of conflicts from being held responsible. For example, the Sudanese state claimed that the conflict in Darfur was due to climate change, and therefore they could not be held responsible for it (Curtis, 2007). It also creates the potential that attention might be diverted away from what ought to be done in terms of adaptation, and lead to resources instead being given to military and security responses (Buckland, 2007). White (2011: 125–126) argues that viewing environmental migration as an international political security concern "saps energies away from scientific analyses of the phenomenon, from the development of integrative policy solutions devoted to adaptation to climate change already underway, and from efforts to mitigate greenhouse gas emissions." Nishimura (2015) suggests that it allows for blame to be shifted to the migrants and developing countries instead of focusing on the historic and current emissions that contribute to climate change; it also means that efforts to create a protection framework for climate change migrants become overridden by predictions of violent conflict, state failure, disease and mass displacements.

This may in part explain why national legislative activity in developed countries on climate-related migration has, to date, been limited. In one instance, the Australian Green Party tabled a 'Migration Amendment (Climate Refugees) Bill' as a way of legislating a climate refugee visa in 2007 (Federal Register of Registration, 2007), but this did not advance to law. In 2009, two American senators introduced a bill that explicitly described climate-induced migration as a security issue (White, 2011). The US National Security Strategy (White House, 2015) under the Obama administration included climate change as a security threat, arguing "climate change is an urgent and growing threat to our national security, contributing to increased natural disasters, refugee flows, and conflicts over basic resources like food and water" (p. 12). But while the EU, the US, Australia and other developed nations have worried about the security implications of environmental migration, potential source countries have used the climate change-migration-security argument to call upon wealthier nations to reduce their greenhouse gas emissions and provide greater financial support for adaptation. In 2009, for instance, a group of 12 Pacific Island states presented a resolution to the UN General Assembly which linked political instability to climate change so that the underlying causes could be addressed (Pacific Small Island Developing States, 2009). In short, the securitization argument can be potentially used in multiple ways.

Conclusions

The relationship between environmental change, migration and security continues to be actively debated, with the narrative that securitizes migration having significant political and public support. Despite little empirical evidence to support direct relationships between climate change, conflict and migration, the perception that environmental change leads to domestic and international insecurity is popular. Attempts to document connections between migration and insecurity, or climate change and insecurity, have been the focus of a considerable amount of recent research, but theories connecting migration to insecurity remain poorly formulated and lacking in empirical basis to substantiate them.

There are several possible ways in which connections between the environment, conflict and migration may develop. There is truth amidst the speculation: conflicts can and do cause migration; and contested access to environment goods and services – including water, land and resources – can exacerbate tense local political contexts. However, most empirical studies, including those reviewed in this chapter, find that environmental change makes a minor contribution to formation of conflicts, and is superceded by other factors. The prevailing conclusion from the current literature is that environmental change and environmental migration will not independently cause conflicts, but that either of the two may, in conjunction with other factors, catalyse conflict depending on local conditions.

This suggests that a direct, sequenced, causal relationship between environmental pressures, violence and migration may not actually exist; nor is there generalizable evidence that migration leads to violence in receiving areas. In comparison with receiving populations, distress migrants are typically weaker, fewer and usually preoccupied with integrating at their destination (Suhrke, 1993; Raleigh & Jordan, 2008). In simple terms, they are not looking to cause trouble.

Migration, with or without environmental change, will continue in the 21st century and beyond. Perceiving migration as a security risk that has to be controlled is not the best solution moving forward. Migration is an important part of people's livelihoods and is a common way of adapting to climate change, as authors elsewhere in this volume have shown. To 'silo' this complex issue away from the demographic, political, social and economic contexts in which it occurs is unhelpful. Scholars from developing regions suggest that a holistic approach is required where issues of environment, livelihoods, urban planning, conflict prevention and resolution, disaster management, climate smart development are considered as policy priorities (Myers, 1997; Reuveny, 2007; Morrissey, 2009; Tacoli, 2009; Foresight, 2011; White, 2011). The opposite approach – i.e. approaching the subject from a security perspective – contributes to a vicious cycle in policymaking: security issues attract the most attention from governments and policy makers, and aid money and other resources are typically allocated to what are considered pressing issues. In turn, advocates and those concerned with issues such as climate change, migration, land rights and livelihoods become incentivised to 'securitise' their rhetoric and link these factors to insecurity in some way in order to garner both attention and funds. This spiral has indirectly led to warnings about all manner of climate-migration 'security threats' that are largely without basis and distract us from the real human and societal cost of climate change, unplanned and unaided migration, and how environmental use and access feeds into persistent societal inequalities.

Note

1 Secretary Kerry's speech is no longer available at the US Department of State website; it was last accessed on 1 November 2016 at the following link: www.state.gov/secretary/remarks/2015/08/246489.htm

References

Adger, N., Pulhin, J.M., Barnett, J., Dabelko, G.D., Hovelsrud, G.K., Levy, M., Oswald Spring, Ú., and Vogel, C.H. 2014. Chapter 12: Human security. In *Climate change 2014: impacts, adaptation, and vulnerability, Working group II contribution to the IPCC fifth assessment report*. Cambridge: Cambridge University Press.

Aldhous, P., 2010. Civil war in Africa has no link to climate change. *New Scientist*, 207(2777), 11–11.

Aribigbola, A., Folami, O.M., and Folami, A.O., 2013. Climate change and insecurity are like a chain reaction. *Peace Review*, 25(4), 518–525.

Ayana, E.K., Ceccato, P., Fisher, J.R.B., and Defries, R., 2016. Examining the relationship between environmental factors and conflict in pastoralist areas of East Africa. *Science of the Total Environment*, 557–558, pp. 601–611.

Barnett, J., 2003. Security and climate change. *Global Environmental Change*, 13(1), 7–17.

Barnett, J., and Adger, N.W., 2007. Climate change, human security and violent conflict. *Political Geography*, 26(6), 639–655.

Bell, C., and Keys, P.W., 2016. Conditional relationships between drought and civil conflict in Sub-Saharan Africa. *Foreign Policy Analysis*, 00, 1–23.

Bergholt, D., and Lujala, P., 2012. Climate-related natural disasters, economic growth, and armed civil conflict. *Journal of Peace Research*, 49(1), 147–162.

Black, R., 2001. Environmental refugees: myth or reality? *New Issues in Refugee Research, Working Paper* No. 34. Geneva; UNHCR.

Brown, O., 2007. Climate change and forced migration: Observations, projections and implications. *Human Development Report 2007/08 background paper*. New York: UNDP. Available at: http://hdr.undp.org/en/reports/global/hdr2007-8/papers/brown_oli.pdf. [Accessed 22 February 2016].

Brown, O., Hammill, A., and McLeman, R., 2007. Climate change as the 'new' security threat: implications for Africa. *International Affairs*, 83(6), 1141–1154.

Buckland, B., 2007. A climate of war? Stopping the securitisation of global climate change. Geneva: International Peace Bureau. Available at http://ipb.org/i/pdf-files/A_Climate_of_War_Stopping_the_Securitisation_of_Climate_Change.pdf. [Accessed on 27 February 2016]

Buhaug, H. (2010). Climate not to blame for African civil wars. *Proceedings of the National Academy of Science*, 107(38), 16477–16482.

Buhaug, B., Gleditsch, N.P., and Theisen, O.M., 2008. Implications of climate change for armed conflict. Paper presented to the World Bank workshop on Social Dimensions of Climate Change, 25 February 2008, World Bank, Washington, DC. Available at: http://siteresources.worldbank.org/INTRANETSOCIALDEVELOPMENT/Resources/SDCCWorkingPaper_Conflict.pdf. [Accessed 29 February 2016].

Buhaug H. et al., 2014. One effect to rule them all? A Comment on climate and conflict. *Climatic Change*, 127(3), 391–397.

Buhaug, H., Benjaminsen, T.A., Sjaastad, E., and Theisen, O.M., 2015. Climate variability, food production shocks, and violent conflict in Sub-Saharan Africa. *Environmental Research Letters*, 10(12), 125015

Burke, M. B., Miguel, E., Satyanath, S., Dykema, J., and Lobell, D.B. 2009. Warming increases the risk of civil war in Africa. *Proceedings of the National Academy of Sciences*, 106(49), 20670–20274.

Burrows, K. and Kinney, P.L., 2016. Exploring the climate change, migration and conflict nexus. *International Journal of Environmental Research in Public Health*, 13(4), 1–17.

Castles, S., 2002. Environmental change and forced migration: making sense of the debate. *New Issues in Refugee Research Working Paper* No. 70. Geneva: UNHCR.

CEC, 2008. Climate change and international security. Paper from the High Representative and the European Commission to the European Council, S113/08, 14 March 2008. Available at: www.consilium.europa.eu/uedocs/cms_data/docs/pressdata/en/reports/99387.pdf [Accessed 2 March 2016]

Christian Aid, 2007. *Human tide: The real migration crisis – a Christian Aid report*. London: Christian Aid.

Council of the European Union, 2016. European climate diplomacy after COP21 — Council conclusions (15 February 2016). Available at: www.cop21.gouv.fr/wp-content/uploads/2016/02/Conclusions-Conseil-UE-sur-Diplo-climatique-15-02-2016.pdf [Accessed 4 March 2016]

Curtis, A., 2007. Don't blame climate change for Africa's conflicts. *New Scientist*, 196(2626), 24–24.

De Juan, A., 2015. Long-term environmental change and geographical patterns of violence in Darfur. *Political Geography*, 45, 22–33.

Detraz, N., and Windsor, L., 2014. Evaluating climate migration. *International Feminist Journal of Politics*, 16(1), 127–146.

Dimelu, M. B., Salifu, E. D., & Igbokwe, E. M. (2016). Resource use conflict in agrarian communities, management and challenges: A case of farmer-herdsmen conflict in Kogi State, Nigeria. *Journal of Rural Studies*, 46, 147–154.

DoD, 2015. National security implications of climate-related risks and a changing climate. Available at http://archive.defense.gov/pubs/150724-congressional-report-on-national-implications-of-climate-change.pdf?source=govdelivery [Accessed on 1 November 2016].

Eastin, J., 2016. Fuel to the fire: natural disasters and the duration of civil conflict. *International Interactions*, 42(2), 322–349.

Federal Register of Registration, 2007. Migration (Climate Refugees) Amendment Bill 2007. Available at www.legislation.gov.au/Details/C2007B00149/Explanatory%20Memorandum/Text [Accessed 24 August 2016]

Folami, O.M., and Folami, A.O., 2013. Climate change and inter-ethnic conflict in Nigeria. *Peace Review*, 25(1), 104–110.

Foresight, 2011. *Migration and global environmental change: future challenges and opportunities*. Final Project Report. London: The Government Office for Science.

Fountain, H., 2015. Researchers link Syrian conflict to a drought made worse by climate change. *The New York Times*, 2 March, 2015. Available at www.nytimes.com/2015/03/03/science/earth/study-links-syria-conflict-to-drought-caused-by-climate-change.html?_r=0 [Accessed on 3 November 2016]

Fröhlich, C.J., 2016. Climate migrants as protestors? Dispelling misconceptions about global environmental change in pre-revolutionary Syria. *Contemporary Levant*, 1(1), 38–50, DOI: 10.1080/20581831.2016.1149355

Gartzke, E., 2012. Could climate change precipitate peace? *Journal of Peace Research*, 49(1) 177–192.

Gemenne, F., Barnett, J., Adger, W. and Dabelko, G., 2014. Climate and security: evidence, emerging risks, and a new agenda. *Climatic Change*, 123(1), 1–9.

Ghimire, R., and Ferreira, S., 2016. Floods and armed conflict. *Environment and Development Economics*, 21(1), 23–52.

Ghimire, R., Ferreira, S., and Dorfman, J.H., 2015. Flood-induced displacement and civil conflict. *World Development*, 66, 614–628.

Gleick, P.H., 2014. Water, drought, climate change, and conflict in Syria. *Weather, Climate, and Society*, 6, pp. 331–340.

Hartmann, B., 2010. Rethinking climate refugees and climate conflict: rhetoric, reality and the politics of policy discourse. *Journal of International Development*, 22(2), 233–246.

Hegre, H., Buhaug, H., Calvin, K.V., Nordkvelle, J., Waldhoff, S.T., and Gilmore, E., 2016. Forecasting civil conflict along the shared socioeconomic pathways. *Environmental Research Letters*, 11(5), 054002.

Homer-Dixon, T.F., 1991. On the threshold: environmental changes as causes of acute conflict. *International Security*, 16(2), 76–116.

Homer-Dixon, T.F., 1999. *Environment scarcity and violence*. Princeton: Princeton University Press.

Hsiang, S., and Burke M., 2014. Climate, conflict, and social stability: what does the evidence say? *Climatic Change*, 123(1), 39–55.

Hsiang, S., Burke, M., and Miguel, E., 2014. Reconciling climate-conflict meta-analyses: reply to Buhaug et al. *Climatic Change*, 127(3), 399–405.

Humphrey, M., 2013. Migration, security and insecurity. *Journal of Intercultural Studies*, 34(2), 178–195.

IPCC. (2014). *Climate change 2014: impacts, adaptation and vulnerability: summary for policy makers*. Cambridge: Cambridge University Press.

Kelley, C.P., Mohtadi, S., Cane, M.A., Seager, R. and Kushnir, Y. 2015. Climate change in the Fertile Crescent and implications of the recent Syrian drought. *Proceedings of the National Academy of Science*, 112 (11), pp. 3241–3246

Ki-moon, B., 2011, United Nations Secretary General, 6587th UN Security Council Meeting Opening Remarks. Available at: www.un.org/apps/news/infocus/sgspeeches/search_full.asp?statID=1250 [Accessed on 10 February 2016]

Lomborg, B. 2001. *The skeptical environmentalist*. Cambridge: Cambridge University Press.

McLeman, R., 2011. Climate change, migration and critical international security considerations. *IOM Migration Research Series*, No. 42. Available at: http://publications.iom.int/system/files/pdf/mrs42.pdf [Accessed 12 February 2016]

McMichael, C. Barnett, J. and McMichael, A.J., 2012. An ill wind? Climate change, migration, and health. *Environmental Health Perspectives*, 120(5), 646–654.

Morrissey, J., 2009. *Environmental change and forced migration: a state of the art review*. Oxford: University of Oxford.

Myers, N., 1997. Environmental refugees. *Population and Environment*, 19(2), 167–182.

Nishimura, L., 2015. 'Climate change migrants': impediments to a protection framework and the need to incorporate migration into climate change adaptation strategies. *International Journal of Refugee Law*, 27(1), 107–134.

O'Loughlin, J., Linke, A.M., and Witmer, F.D.W., 2014. Effects of temperature and precipitation variability on the risk of violence in sub-Saharan Africa, 1980–2012. *Proceedings of the National Academy of Sciences of the United States of America*, 111(47), 16712–16717.

Pacific Small Island Developing States, 2009. Views on the possible security implications of climate change to be included in the report of the Secretary-General to the 64th Session of the United Nations

General Assembly. Available at www.un.org/esa/dsd/resources/res_pdfs/ga-64/cc-inputs/PSIDS_ CCIS.pdf [Accessed 25 August 2016]

Raleigh, C., and Jordan, L. 2008. *Assessing the impact of climate change on migration and conflict. Social dimensions of climate change.* Washington, DC: World Bank working paper.

Raleigh, C., & Kniveton, D., 2012. Come rain or shine: an analysis of conflict and climate variability in East Africa. *Journal of Peace Research*, 49(1), 51–64.

Raleigh, C., & Urdal, H., 2007. Climate change, environmental degradation and armed conflict. *Political Geography*, 26(6), 674–694.

Raleigh, C., 2011. The search for safety: the effects of conflict, poverty and ecological influences on migration in the developing world. *Global Environmental Change*, 21S, S82–S93.

Reuveny, R., 2007. Climate change-induced migration and violent conflict. *Political Geography*, 26, 656–673.

Salehyan, I., and Hendrix, C.S., 2014. Climate shocks and political violence. *Global Environmental Change*, 28, 239–250.

Schleussnera, C., Dongesa, J.F., Donnera, R.V., and Schellnhuber, H.J., 2016. Armed-conflict risks enhanced by climate-related disasters in ethnically fractionalized countries. *PNAS*, 113(33), 9216–9221.

Scott, S.V., 2008. Securitising climate change: international legal implications and obstacles. *Cambridge Review of International Affairs*, 21(4), 603–619.

Sletteback, R., 2012. Don't blame the weather! Climate-related natural disasters and civil conflict. *Journal of Peace Research*, 49(1), 163–176.

Stern, N., 2006, *The economics of climate change: The Stern review*. Cambridge: Cambridge University Press.

Suhrke, A., 1993. *Pressure points: Environmental degradation, migration and conflict.* Cambridge: American Academy of Arts and Science.

Tacoli, C., 2009. Crisis or adaptation? Migration and climate change in a context of high mobility. *Environment and Urbanisation*, 21(2), 513–525.

Theisen, O., Gleditsch, N., and Buhaug, H., 2013. Is climate change a driver of armed conflict? *Climatic Change*, 117(3), pp. 613–625.

Trump, D.J., 2015. US Republican Presidential Candidate presidential announcement speech, 16 June 2015. Available at: www.washingtonpost.com/news/post-politics/wp/2015/06/16/full-text-donald-trump-announces-a-presidential-bid/ [Accessed 24 August 2016].

UN, 2009. Climate change and its possible security implications: Report of the Secretary-General, sixty-fourth session, Available at www.securitycouncilreport.org/atf/cf/%7B65BFCF9B-6D27-4E9C-8CD3-CF6E4FF96FF9%7D/sg%20report%202009.pdf [Accessed on 2 November 2016].

UNEP, 2011. *Climate change, conflict and migration in the Sahel.* United Nations Environment Programme. Geneva: UNEP. Available at www.un.org/en/events/environmentconflictday/pdf/UNEP_Sahel_ EN.pdf [Accessed on 10 May 2016].

van Weezel, S., 2013. Economic shocks and civil conflict onset in Sub-Saharan Africa, 1981–2010. *Defence and Peace Economics*, 26(2), 153–177.

von Uexkull, N., 2014. Sustained drought, vulnerability and civil conflict in Sub-Saharan Africa. *Political Geography*, 43, 16–26.

Weinthal, E., Zawahri, N., and Sowers, J., 2015. Securitizing water, climate, and migration in Israel, Jordan, and Syria. *International Environmental Agreements: Politics, Law and Economics*, 15(3), 293–307.

Werrell, C.E., Femia, F., and Sternberg, T., 2015. Did we see it coming? State fragility, climate vulnerability, and the uprisings in Syria and Egypt. *SAIS Review of International Affairs*, 35(1), 29–46.

Werz, M., and Hoffman, M., 2016. Europe's twenty-first century challenge: climate change, migration and security. *European View*, 15(1), 145–154.

White, G., 2011. *Climate change and migration: Security and borders in a warming world.* New York: Oxford University Press.

White House, 2015. National Security Strategy. Available at www.whitehouse.gov/sites/default/files/ docs/2015_national_security_strategy.pdf [Accessed on 30 October 2016].

Witsenburg, K.M., and Adano, W.R., 2009. Of rain and raids: violent livestock raiding in Northern Kenya. *Civil Wars*, 11(4), 514–538.

29

Green grabbing-induced displacement

Sara Vigil[1]

Introduction

Land is a vital asset for the vast majority of populations in developing countries who still rely on agriculture for their livelihoods. However, pressures on farmland have increased dramatically in recent decades as a consequence of climate change, population pressure, and increased competition over scarce resources. Moreover, since the convergence of multiple global crises (financial, environmental, and food), there has been a deep revaluation of land and a rush to acquire it in what has been denominated as the 'global land grab', where land-intensive climate mitigation policies have played a considerable role. Whilst the study of the connections between the biophysical impacts of climate change and mobility have made substantial progress, very little attention has been given to the interactions between climate change policies, land grabs, and displacement. On one hand, environmental migration scholars have focused on natural disruptions such as sudden-onset and slow-onset environmental changes with very little attention to questions about access to natural resources as major determinants in these trends, and land has been disregarded in the tripartite classification of displacement by conflict, disasters, and development projects. On the other hand, despite some references to forced displacement associated with land grabs provided on a case-by-case manner by intergovernmental organizations, NGOs, and donors,[2] and the growing academic literature on land grabbing, the allusions to displacement and migration remain generally relegated to a secondary level calling for more empirical and theoretical work. Whilst those analysing the social consequences of land investments need to pay more attention to forced displacement outcomes, there is also a need for environmental migration scholars and practitioners to broaden the spectrum of their analyses.

The aim of this chapter is to give an overview of how these three major issues interrelate in order to show the urgency for research and policy to treat them concomitantly. The first part of the chapter introduces the phenomenon of land grabbing with a focus on its drivers, scale, and definitions. Second, it concentrates on the green components of this trend by focusing on critically examining the impacts of two major climate change policies: biofuels and forest carbon projects. Third, drawing upon agrarian studies and categories from political economy/ecology, the chapter reviews some of the main impacts of these policies on displacement. Finally, the chapter addresses some policy incoherences, protection mechanisms and gaps of what I refer to as 'green-grabbing induced displacement', concluding with some research implications for the field of environmental migration.

Land grabbing

The recent rush for land captured attention in the immediate aftermath of the global food price crisis of 2007–2008 with the release of a report by the NGO GRAIN entitled 'Seized' (GRAIN 2008). The main factors that have contributed to the recent wave of land grabbing stem from a combination between the spike in oil prices and the needs for renewable energy, food insecurity concerns of rich net-food importing countries, climate mitigation imperatives, and the need for private investors to diversify placements in an increasingly unpredictable market (Borras and Franco 2010b, Deininger and Byerlee 2011, De Schutter 2011). Although land acquisitions are far from being a new phenomenon, the trend has accelerated considerably to a magnitude unprecedented since colonial times. Whilst the proponents of land transactions refer to them as 'direct investment in agriculture' highlighting their potential for agricultural modernisation, employment creation, local food security, and green energy production (World Bank 2008), the retractors refer to them as 'land grabs', pointing to the various threats that these deals can pose to the environment, to local food security, to traditional livelihoods, and to local employment. Proponents, argue moreover, that the targeted land is under-utilised or even idle, yet these areas are often used for a variety of purposes (farming, pastoralism, grazing, or as a communal resource) and provide vital resources for the poor (Borras et al. 2010). Although there is still no agreed-upon definition, Borras and Franco (2012: 851)defined land grabs as:

> the capturing of control of relatively vast tracts of land and other natural resources through a variety of mechanisms and forms that involve large-scale capital that often shifts resource use orientation into extractive character, whether for international or domestic purposes, as capital's response to the convergence of food, energy and financial crises, climate change mitigation imperatives, and demands for resources from newer hubs of global capital.

The Tirana Declaration of 2011 gives specific criteria in order to determine which land deals can be considered as land grabs (Box 29.1). Even if not all land deals can be considered as land grabs, this chapter concentrates on those that fit these criteria.

Box 29.1   Definition of land grabbing by the Tirana Declaration*

Large-scale land grabs are acquisitions or concessions that that are one or more of the following:

1) In violation of human rights, particularly the equal rights of women;
2) Not based on free, prior and informed consent of the affected land-users;
3) Not based on a thorough assessment, or are in disregard of social, economic and environmental impacts, including the way they are gendered;
4) Not based on transparent contracts that specify clear and binding commitments about activities, employment and benefits sharing;

5) Not based on effective democratic planning, independent oversight and meaningful participation

Source: International Land Coalition (2011: 2)

* The International Land Coalition counts with more than 150 representatives from civil social organisations, social movements, grassroots organisations, international organisations, and governments from more than 45 countries in Africa, Latin America, North America, Asia and Europe.

Table 29.1 Target regions of large-scale land investments for agricultural ends

Region	Number of concluded deals	Total size of concluded deals (millions of hectares)
Africa	422	10.0
Asia	305	4.9
Latin America	146	4.5
Eastern Europe	96	5.1
Oceania	35	2.2
Total	1004	26.7

Source: Land Matrix (2017)

If we were to compare the phenomenon to colonial times, we see that new actors such as various transnational and national corporations, banks, hedge funds, and local political elites are now involved and that many of the transactions are undertaken through often legal but questionable means (Sassen 2013). Most of the targeted land is situated in Africa, but there is also an increasing expansion of the phenomenon in Asia and Latin America (see Table 29.1). Given the rapid extension of the phenomenon, and the lack of information and transparency surrounding these land transactions, it is extremely difficult to quantify the precise extent of this phenomenon. However, in 2009, the World Bank noted that in less than a year investors had expressed interest in approximately 56 million hectares of land globally (Deininger and Byerlee 2011). Moreover, data from the Land Matrix[3] conservatively estimates the amount of land acquired transnationally since the year 2000, in 63 low- and middle-income countries, at 40 million hectares (Land Matrix 2017). To these figures we must add the immense amount of land that changes hands within the same countries and the transactions that cover areas smaller than 200 hectares that are not counted in this data base.

Green grabbing

Green grabbing, defined as 'the appropriation of land and nature for environmental ends' (Fairhead et al. 2012: 238), arises as a particular concern within the broader issue of land grabs. Although this phenomenon builds on historical resource expropriations in the name of the environment, climate change has reinvigorated the trend considerably with novel discourses around climate mitigation being deployed as justifiers. The narrative underlying these policies posits that market instruments are the most cost-effective way to mitigate climate change and meet emission requirements (Liverman 2009) whilst also being compatible with socio-economic development. The logic of this 'economy of repair' is that unsustainable practices in one place can be repaired by sustainable ones in another (Fairhead et al. 2012, Leach et al. 2012). However, as we shall see, they come at a considerable cost for many of the most already socio-environmentally vulnerable populations (Marino and Ribot 2012). Today, on top of biodiversity conservation and eco-tourism, land-intensive climate mitigation policies such as biofuel production and forest carbon projects are becoming more and more prominent (Hunsberger et al. 2016).

Biofuels[4]

In recent years there has been a radical expansion for biomass-based energy from biofuels (Cotula et al. 2008). Following rising oil prices and commitments made to transition towards a green economy, many countries (with the European Union and the United States leading the trend), have endorsed biofuel targets and supported the production of ethanol and biodiesel through tax exemptions and other financial incentives. Although estimates vary, all sources agree that biofuels have been a main – if not the most important – driver of land grabbing. According to the International Land Coalition, biofuels were responsible for around 59% of all land grabs between 2000 and 2010 (Anseeuw et al. 2012). Data from the Land Matrix shows that 78% of all the recorded deals are for agricultural production, of which three quarters are for biofuels. 'Flex crops' – those that have multiple uses (food, feed, fuel, industrial material) – are now being used to cover both financial and climate risk (Borras et al. 2014: 7) allowing investors to sell in the food or biofuel market depending on market prices or opportunities for commercialisation (Diop et al. 2013: 65). However, first generation biofuels often compete with food production, lead to human rights violations, and do not guarantee greenhouse emissions savings due to their impacts on land use change and their use of fossil fuels for commercialisation and transportation (Cotula 2013). Moreover, since a large part of biofuel production takes place on forested land this creates a striking contradiction with efforts to protect forests.

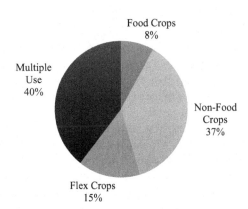

Figure 29.1 Agricultural drivers

Data source: Land Matrix (2017)

Forest carbon projects

Forests are crucial for climate stability, and also constitute a basic source of livelihoods for large part of the world's population.[5] Under the United Nations Framework Convention on Climate Change (UNFCCC), carbon offsets have become an increasingly popular measure to protect them. The afforestation and reforestation projects under the Clean Development Mechanism of the Kyoto Protocol aim to offset emissions. Moreover, the Reducing Emissions from Deforestation and Forest Degradation (REDD+)[6] project creates a framework by which companies and governments can be compensated economically for protecting forests. The logic behind these policies is that they would be able to contribute to mitigation, conservation, and poverty reduction concomitantly (Angelsen 2009). However, forest carbon projects have been criticized for 'leakage' as they can displace and/or postpone environmental damage from one site to another (McAfee 2012: 110, Dryzek 2013: 131) and 'activity leakage' can also occur when populations displaced for offsets move into other forested areas (Smith 2002). It is also worth noting that FAO's forest definition (also used by the UNFCCC) allows industrial tree monocultures to be considered a forest, which poses considerable problems.[7]

Impacts on displacement

Already in 2009, the United Nations High Commissioner for Human Rights warned that climate adaptation and mitigation may have negative implications on human rights such as the right to food or the rights of indigenous peoples and may even lead to expropriation and displacement (OHCHR 2009: 22–23). Up to date, however, we only possess case-by-case evidence on displacement resulting from such ventures and none concerning the processes and outcomes of these specific types of movements. Whilst the focus of land grabs has remained on the number of hectares involved, and its environmental impacts having receiving considerable attention, key social impacts on displacement are understudied in all regions and practically not included in global studies (Robledo-Abad et al. 2017: 9). In general terms, the influence of natural resource development on agricultural outcomes and migration decisions remains scarcely understood (Headey et al. 2008: 31).

How these policies impact the human mobility of local populations depends on a variety of factors ranging from the social and tenure arrangements already in place, the purpose of the project, the negotiation power of populations, the level of rule of law in the host country, and how the costs and benefits are distributed across populations (White et al. 2012). Depending on the project and on the context, local people may be included or excluded from land deals, and those who are included may be incorporated with either beneficial or adverse impacts (White et al. 2012: 663, McCarthy 2010). In order to better understand the root causes of land grabs on human mobility, it is important to first analyse these processes of inclusions and exclusion by drawing upon four basic questions of political economy: who owns what?, who does what?, who gets what?, and what do they do with it? (Bernstein 2010).[8] Property relations, entitlements over natural resources, and questions of benefit distribution are vital in understanding resulting mouvements in a context of overlapping land claims, unclear land rights, and uneven access to resources. How these root causes modulate who moves, who stays, and why depends on socio-economic status, demographic characteristics, off-farm labour opportunities, and social networks.

It is important to underline that many different types of movements happen alongside each other in a given space and time, and although some main scenarios can be traced, one is not necessarily exclusive from another. Additionally, in-migration dynamics often occur concomitantly to displacement in these areas, but it is the potential impact of the projects on the mobility of local people that will be the focus of analysis here.

Exclusion

The intellectual idea of displacement linked to land dispossession goes back to Marx's (1867–1894] 1976) notion of 'primitive accumulation' that is based primarily on the expropriation of the peasantry. The category of 'primitive accumulation' points both to a logic of extraction that can expropriate and impoverish and also to a mode of incorporating capitalist economies into non-capitalistic ones (Sassen 2010). Hidden behind what we often refer to as forced displacement, there is still often a process of separation between the workers and the ownership of the conditions for the realisation of their labour (Marx [1867–1894] 1976). The question of labour – both at the local level and in other sectors of the economy – is still today especially crucial in understanding how land deals impact displacement and migration.[9] The most iconic scenario of expulsion (Sassen 2014) tends to happen when *the land is needed but the labour is not* (Li 2011). The underlying assumption behind conservation initiatives is that human presence is negative and that the effects of displacement can be balanced by the gains of conservation (Agrawal and Redford 2009). As the number of protected areas has increased exponentially over the last three decades, environmental conservation has become an increasingly significant contributor to global forced migration (Geisler 2003, Chatty and Colchester 2002, Schmidt-Soltau 2009, Dowie 2009, Lunstrum et al. 2016). In REDD+ initiatives, the technical responses for forest protection focuses on the exclusion of people on the basis of 'rational' and 'scientific' forest management (Adams et al. 2016: 246). Following this assumption, the solution is presented to lie in displacing humans in order to save the climate and generate carbon credits.

Given that tropical forests are typically under the formal control of the government, it is relatively simple to expropriate inhabitants in the name of climate mitigation. When tenure is not formalised, populations can be labelled as illegal settlers and evicted without compensation. Moreover, populations with unclear or insecure tenure arrangements have scarce negotiation power. In the frame of REDD+ in Tanzania, Beymer-Farris and Basset (2012) found that who gets rights over forests is highly dependent on how 'the environmental problem' is portrayed. In the Rufji Delta, the state falsely portrayed inhabitants who had been occupying the land for millenia as recent migrants and poor stewards of the mangrove forest. This false portrayal has justified their expulsion, deprived them of their livelihoods, and created conflicts (Beymer-Farris and Basset 2012). Additionally, a study of REDD+ projects in Brazil, Indonesia, Vietnam, Cameroon, and Tanzania, has shown that although forest tenure has been receiving increased attention under REDD+, progress has often failed to materialise (Larson et al. 2013). Even in the rare cases where forests are formaly owned by customary land owners (as in Papua New Guinea), evidence shows that many landowners are not aware of their rights, leaving them vulnerable to exploitation and manipulation (Larson et al. 2013). In Kenya, the constitution recognises the rights of communities to own ancestral lands traditionally occupied by hunter-gatherers. Nonetheless, indigenous peoples from the Embobut forest, where an estimated 13,500 people live, have been suffering violent evictions (Survival International 2014, Lang 2014). Also, under the afforestation and reforestation schemes of a CDM project in Uganda, there have been allegedly evictions of around 20,000 residents who had been living there since 1975 (Carrere 2009).

Examples from biofuel evicting ventures come from Indonesia, Malaysia, Papua New Guinea, and India, where the exponential demand for palm oil has been displacing millions of indigenous communities from their lands in order to produce for export (Vigil 2015a, Rainforest Rescue 2017, Down to Earth 2014, Diop et al. 2013). The racialised dimensions of biofuel expulsions are visible in Colombia, where paramilitary forces have used fear and violence to force the displacement of Afro-Colombian communities for the production of sugarcane and cassava (War on Want 2008). Research on Indonesian palm oil has also underlined the gendered experiences of dispossession (White and White 2012). In Brazil, mega-farms for soy production are the extreme example of highly mechanized productions where the land is needed but the labour is not (Li 2011: 283). Estimates suggest that soybean cultivation displaces eleven agricultural workers for everyone who finds employment in the sector (Altieri and Pengue 2006: 14). In Honduras, thousands of small farmers were displaced from the north coast valley to make way for oil palm (Schwarze et al. 2002). Just as with other plantations and estates, one of the main reasons biofuel plantations have limited interaction with local economies is their embededdedness in the global market with their export orientation (Hall 2011).

Inclusion?

Although most early media reports and academic discussions assumed that most poor farmers would be automatically expelled from their land by land grabs (Hall et al. 2017: 468), there are also cases of inclusion of the populations in the land deals – when 'the land is needed and (some) labour is too' – with more gradual and less visible forms of displacement. Although some processes may not involve enclosure or 'accumulation by dispossession' (Harvey 2004: 73), the penetration of corporate capital may can have profound impacts on local livelihoods and mobility outcomes (Hall et al. 2017). The outcomes of inclusion for local populations are highly dependent on their terms of incorporation (McCarthy 2010).

Total dispossession from forests, in the name of forest carbon projects, could be mitigated through the participation of local communities in the implementation of the projects. However, in practice, many targeted countries still lack clear procedures for their participation (Corbera 2012: 615), with scarce involvement of local populations in REDD+ projects (GRAIN and WRM 2015). Moreover, result-based payments to local landholders have been slow to materialise (Sills et al. 2014). Since many of these projects are implemented in areas already affected by unequal land distribution and unclear land tenure, it is unlikely that the benefits from carbon storage will enhance equity (Chomba et al. 2016). As evidence from Nigeria shows, the 'carbonised exclusion' of local populations tends to actually allow elite capital accumulation and even further forest decline (Asiyanbi 2016). Given the scarce negociation power of the populations, their lack of de facto recognised rights, and the corruption of local elites, the distribution of benefits from these projects is often captured by local and international elites rather than distributed equally amongst local populations (Sills et al. 2014, Mwangi et al. 2015).

In the case of biofuels, if the land was really previously unused, then large-scale biofuel production might create employment and attract migration flows. However, whilst employment creation is often presented as the main benefit by of large-scale plantations by governments, investors, and local populations themselves, de facto employment creation tends to be scarce, seasonal, or unreliable (Cotula 2014, Al-Mahmood 2015). Even if different crops vary considerably in their labour requirements, they tend to be capital rather than labour intensive (De Schutter 2011). Crops such as sugar, palm oil, and soy, that could be produced at the small-farm level, tend to be produced in large-scale farms for export (Dauvergne and Neville 2010: 634). Maize, sugarcane, and sorghum are produced in highly mechanized ways and, in general, biofuels have a lower labour input than small-scale farming (Diop et al. 2013: 66).[10] For example, in Zambia a sugar cane producer can earn six times more income on a one hectare smallholding than on a wage for the same crop (Li 2011: 285). Moreover, promises in terms of employment are often neglected. In Mozambique, for example, a biofuels company that had estimated employment creation for 2,650 people had only created 35–40 full time jobs two years after its approval (Aabø and Kring 2012: 32–35). In Indonesia, those incapable of accessing the assets required for development of the oil palm business as smallholders tended to be adversely incorporated by being forced to sell their land and pushed into wage labour (McCarthy 2010). Importantly, in many targeted countries, labour rights are weak or not enforced, and the agricultural sector raises special issues of the seasonality and casual nature of labour (Cotula 2014). Another problematic issue is that those who lose land and those who get the jobs are often not the same people. This results from a combination of 'myths of the lazy native', the fact that some locals may still have access to some landholdings – hence other options (Li 2011: 286) – and that many locals are often involved in frontal conflicts with the companies. Although large-scale planations can provide permanent, salaried employment with higher wages than the standard incomes in the areas, such jobs are usually taken by highly qualified outsiders and hence do not improve local conditions (Hall et al. 2017: 12). Moreover, many employers prefer to recruit migrants because 'their social isolation and dependance makes them easier to discipline' (Li 2009: 631). Migrant labourers often work and live in extremely precarious conditions. For example, the working conditions of migrants have been of major concern in sugar plantations in Brazil (Wilkinson and Herrera 2010, Phillips 2007) and in Indonisian palm oil (Li 2011: 286).

Additionally, *adverse incorporation* can lead to *'in situ displacement'*, which occurs when people remain in place or suffer a prolonged multi-stage process of displacement (Hickey and du Toit 2013, Feldman and Geisler 2012). As Cernea has long argued, displacement also describes situations in which some people are deprived of their productive lands or income-generating assets without being physically evicted (Cernea 1999, 2005). A progressive loss of entitlements ultimately leading to migration is also a very recurrent outcome of how green grabs can affect human mobility (Feldman et al. 2003). In situ displacement occurs when REDD+ prevents communities from accessing forested areas and diminishes the area of cultivable land, with impacts on the livelihoods and food security of forest dependent communities unable to find alternative livelihoods. Biofuels can also 'displace in place' (Lubkemann 2008: 454) by shrinking the land availability for small holders' food production. Mobility is just one of the possible outcomes emanating from a multifaceted 'package of losses' including the loss of social networks and capital, economic and material goods and power, political and legal rights, and even of cultural moorings (Lubkemann 2008: 455). Lacking the necessary assets to make a move, many of those who lose land become 'involuntarily immobile' (Carling 2002). Moreover, the growing demand for biofuels rises the price of flex crops impacting food security and market and policy incentives to convert land into biofuel production will also tend to rise the value of land. Although this could bring opportunities to certain farmers, it can also translate into the displacement of people from their land (Cotula et al. 2008) and in the inability for the poorest to access needed farmland.

Winners and losers

In the name of climate change mitigation, we are experiencing an ongoing process of 'accumulation by dispossession'[11] (Harvey 2004: 73), 'accumulation by displacement' (Araghi 2009: 114) – inclusing in situ displacement – where the benefits of biofuels and forest carbon projects accrue to local elites and stakeholders that are able to manage their terms of incorporation (Dauvergne and Neville 2010, Boyd et al. 2007). Amongst those interested in forced displacement, there remains a tendency to analyse the drivers of displacement as a result of visible disruptions such as natural disasters, development projects, or civil wars and to understand movements following lack of tenure, market calamity, or debt as out-migration rather than as evictions. This means that the forces underlying and coercing people to move – such as land grabs – often remain invisible despite their very heavy impacts amongst the most vulnerable (Feldmand and Geisler 2012: 972). The consequences of these 'green' ventures in terms of exclusion, adverse incorporation or in situ displacement remain invisible root causes of what we still tend to analyse as labour migration (Sassen 2013).

Whilst many rural households have become increasingly mobile and no longer depend entirely on agriculture, farmers still account for approximately 60% of the population in most African and Asian countries where land grabs are taking place (Rigg 2006). Although migrant labour is necessary for industrial and service sectors, agricultural transitions have coincided with limited industrialization, high unemployment, and increasing poverty rates in urban areas. The often scarce available off-farm activities that have the highest potential for income generation are also those with the highest barriers to entry, and they are thus concentrated among middle-income and rich households. Concomitantly, distress livelihood diversification through the migration of the rural poor often generates little surplus that can lift households out of their pre-existent positions. As multiple studies have shown, access to land is closely linked to access to capital, with this access to capital ultimately determining the type of non-farm activities that households can undertake (Rigg 2006: 194). Even in scenarios of incorporation, households with more resources and landholdings may be better able to reap the benefits of contract farming and emerge as medium- or large-scale producers, while others may enter into debt, experiencing land loss and may or not be incorporated as wage labourers (Hall et al. 2017: 475).

The availability of off-farm opportunities – as well as the economic and social differentiation of the peasantry (Byres 2009; Borras 2009) – are thus greatly important in understanding why some groups, and not others, can take advantage of emerging green ventures (Dauvergne and Neville 2010: 633). Hence, who wins and who loses depends not only on state-civil society relationships, but also on social and economic differentiations within communities (Byres 2009, Dauvergne and Neville 2010, Hall 2013). Moreover, differentiations within households (especially in terms of age, education, and gender) also has a very influential role in terms of impacts. Labour opportunities may be more available for men or women, depending on the context, yet the elderly and the youngest member of the households are those most likely to remain in place.

Concerning destinations, and as occurs with other types of movements, migration tends to remain internal, inter-regional, and south-south. The main explanatory factor is that people need a higher amount of human, financial, social, and natural capital to be able to move longer distances. Additionally, policies (e.g. migration regimes) are much more likely to intervene in international movements than internal ones. However, countries with large initial agricultural populations, high rates of agricultural exits, and low growth rates may ignite international migration (Headey et al. 2008: 23). Yet, the routes of international migration are becoming increasingly difficult and the most vulnerable often end up in bonded labour and are even less protected when they cross national borders (Li 2009). Further expansion of biofuels or forest conservation projects will compete for scarce land resources in countries with economies incapable of absorbing the displaced labour they expel and where human rights protection is lacking. This will not only increase poverty in place and increase distress migration, but will also contribute to the 'planet of slums' (Davis 2007) where more than 32% of the urban populations around the world already live (UNHSP 2003).

Policy mechanisms, gaps, and incoherences

There have been attempts to control the negative impacts and processes of land grabbing through the development of codes of conduct and principles for responsible agricultural investment that respect rights, livelihoods and resources.[12] The most adequate instrument of protection to have emerged to date is the Voluntary Guidelines on the Responsible Governance of Tenure of Land, Fisheries and Forests (CFS and FAO 2012). Transparency in negotiations, respect for existing land rights, sharing of benefits, environmental sustainability, and adherence to national trade policies are the most frequently addressed challenges in order to attain 'win-win' outcomes. All of them seem to suggest that good governance norms would diminish the dispossession and forced displacement of rural communities. However, despite the well-intended rationale behind such principles, they still fail to question agro-industrial development *per se*, as if other possible development pathways, such as smallholder agriculture and family farming, would not be better suited to address our social and environmental challenges (Borras and Franco 2010). Large-scale biofuel plantations and monoculture tree plantations stimulate the industrialization of agriculture, which is at the very basis of many of our environmental problems today (McMichael 2009; De Schutter 2011). Moreover, these principles as well as those of Corporate Social Responsibility (CSR) are still too vague in a context where governments and elites of developing nations often take the side of investors for purposes of personal enrichment. Different discourses around climate change solutions, agricultural productivity, and migration, enhance certain descriptions of reality and legitimize certain tools while sidelining others. Market solutions to climate change mitigation tend to understand displacement as an inevitable consequence of sustainability that needs to be managed rather than as the evidence of development's uneven and unfair distribution of costs and benefits (Dwivedi 2002). The key question is not solely to regulate investment for equitable sharing, but rather how to best to use the land that is really idle or underutilized. A fine assessment of impacts should not only involve the number of jobs created or benefit sharing, but also an assessment of poverty reduction through alternative land uses (De Schutter 2009).

Although the UNFCCC and its Kyoto Protocol commit states to minimise adverse economic, social, and environmental impacts resulting from the implementation of measures taken to mitigate or adapt to climate change impacts ('response measures')' (OHCHR 2009: 22), human rights are still inadequately incorporated into the global climate change policy and legal framework, leaving communities affected by climate response measures vulnerable to the violations of their rights (Mayrhofer and Mersmann 2016: 71). The Paris Agreement includes human rights in its preamble,[13] but there is no clear roadmap of the specific measures needed in order to stay 'well below 2°C' (UNFCCC 2015: 2) Despite the evidence of the harmful effects of biofuels, many countries have specifically referred to their use as a part of their action to combat climate change in their INDCs (intended nationally-determined contributions). Moreover, the models of the Intergovernmental Panel on Climate Change (IPCC) tend to assume a significant global-scale deployment of negative emissions technologies in the second half of this century (IPCC 2014) if the target of 2°C is to be reached. These include bioenergy, combined with carbon capture and storage (BECCS). Given the impacts of biofuels and forest offsets to date, this uncertain roadmap for climate action is likely to drive green-grabbing induced displacement whilst adding supplementary stress on the environment. This creates policy incoherence between the goals of climate change policies, and those of international human rights law whilst also compromising the future of the Sustainable Development Goals.

Research directions

Climate mitigation interventions are necessary and inevitable, but without understanding their impacts, they can reproduce or deepen the very damages that they intend to repair (Barnett and O'Neill 2010). Although not generally recognised as a part of climate or environmental-induced displacement, the links with this category are twofold: i) when climate change policies drive such as acquisitions; and ii) when projects destroy the local land and the water resources, forcing people off their land in what could be seen as a form of tertiary displacement. The issue of land has been disregarded in the tripartite classification of displacement by conflict, disasters or development projects occluding the political economy of land at its centre stage (Thomson 2014). However, with both 'land grabs' and 'green grabs' on the rise, we can hypothesize that more and more people will be involuntarily displaced from their lands in the years to come in what I argue should be considered as a new category in the environmental migration debate (Vigil 2015a).

'Land grabbing'- and 'green grabbing'-induced migration and displacement force us to bring the politics of distribution and access to resources back in to our analysis by engaging with studies that examine uneven access to and control over resources (Carr 2005, Peet et al. 2010). While 'green grabbing' does not always result in the outright alienation of land, it does involve a restructuring of rules over access and management of resources, that can have deep alienating outcomes for the most vulnerable (Fairhead et al. 2012: 239). Moreover, for a fine understanding of migratory impacts, our analysis of migration from rural areas must be situated within a context of surplus labour in many countries of the Global South where climate impacts and green grabbing are taking place. Political ecology – with its focus on the relationship between people and their environment and its attention political economic forces – is a fundamental framing to answer questions as important as: How should scarce resources be allocated, to whom, and by what processes? How are choices made, by whom, and in whose interest? Who profits from changes in control over resources? (Vira 2015, Blaikie and Brookfield 1987, Robbins 2004), and how does all of this influence migration dynamics? In a warming planet, where fundamental resources will face increasing competition for multiple uses, it is not only how biophysical impacts of climate change will affect migration dynamics that we should question, but also *who* holds and is likely to hold these resources in the first place, and how this will affect human mobility. Collecting data on the displacement and migratory outcomes as well as on their processes and impacts is crucial for the formulation of sound policy recommendations that could mitigate their worst impacts.

Conclusions

Climate change will provoke adjustments in the value of natural resources in ways that are hard to predict (USAID 2014) and as its impacts worsen, struggles over use, management, and control of land can be expected to deepen, with consequential impacts for displacement. The green economy and the 'technology of repair' (Fairhead et al. 2012) proposes a managerial approach to solving the climate crisis which implies 'selling nature in order to save it' (McAfee 2012: 105). However, as we have seen, measures placing a priority on market-based solutions to address climate mitigation and environmental conservation are compounding conflicts over land (De Schutter 2009) and already forcing the displacement of many of the most socio-environmentally vulnerable populations. Moreover, green grabs imply a transfer of costs from global polluters in faraway places to local smallholders whose vulnerabilities are further expanded (cf. Araghi 2009) and shift the control of forests from the hands of local people to those of the global markets (Beymer-Farris and Basset 2012). These indirect impacts of climate policy should be urgently addressed in order to avoid 'green grabbing-induced displacement' (Vigil 2015a, 2015b), prevent further impoverishment through mobility in places lacking alternative employment, and protect the climate system at a broader scale. Notwithstanding very important context specificities, findings across all areas show that when land transactions fail to follow a human rights-based framework with full consideration of existing land rights, they result in added socio-environmental pressures that deeply can deeply affect forced displacement outcomes (Vigil 2016).

Continued large-scale land acquisitions that overlook customary rights and fail to develop environmentally sustainable practices, whilst providing viable livelihood diversification strategies, will increase competition for natural resources whilst decreasing the resilience of communities. When sustainability measures fail to acknowledge contentious land tenure claims, patterns of exclusion, and availability of alternative labour opportunities, they are unlikely to benefit the most vulnerable segments of society and to prevent further displacement and distress migration. The lack of research and evidence on the interlinkages between these three major challenges translates into these issues being addressed at best in pairs and by separate and often isolated governance structures. It is now time to assure policy coherence between disconnected governance structures taking into account the leakage effects of 'green' ventures, securing community and indigenous land rights and ensuring that human rights are fully taken into consideration. In order to achieve this, environmental migration studies need to take into account the interdependence of 'environmental migration' with other key areas of global relations including, of course, climate policies, but also agriculture and broader development issues.

Notes

1 The author would like to thank the editors of this book and the anonymous reviewer for their helpful comments and suggestions.
2 Cf. Land Deals Politics Initiative; World Bank; The United Nations Permanent Forum on Indigenous Issues (UNPFII); Food and Agriculture Organization of the United Nations, Oakland Institute, GRAIN.
3 The Land Matrix is a global and independent land monitoring initiative that promotes transparency and accountability in decisions over land and investment The Land Matrix monitors land deals that: i) Entail a transfer of rights to use, control, or ownership of land through sale, lease, or concession, ii) have been initiated since the year 2000; iii) cover an area of 200 hectares or more; and iv) imply the potential conversion of land from smallholder production, local community use or important ecosystem service provision to commercial use. (Land Matrix 2017).
4 Given its wide use, the term biofuels is maintained throughout the chapter. However, it is worth noting that critics use the term 'agrofuels', arguing that there is little of 'bio' in agricultural crops used for fuels.
5 Deforestation, occurring mostly in developing countries, accounts for 12–18% of annual global carbon dioxide emissions (Verbist et al. 2011).
6 The '+' stands for 'enhancing carbon stocks, sustainable forest management and conservation of forest carbon stcks' (REDD Desk 2016).
7 Forests are defined as: 'Land spanning more than 0.5 hectares of trees equipped with a minimum height of 5m at maturity in situ and a crown cover (or equivalent stocking level) of more than 10 percent' (FAO 2015: 3).
8 This framing is also useful for other land deals, independently from their motives.
9 Although employment creation is often presented as the main benefit by governments, investors, and local populations themselves, the information of employment generation, whether it be temporary or permanent, is surprisingly limited (Deininger and Byerlee 2011: 63).
10 The Mozambican biofuel assessment estimated that biodiesel production by smallholders has the capacity of creating 0.45–0.5 jobs per hectare, while the production of bioethanol by large-scale sugar plantations has only the potential of 0.2 jobs per hectare (Aabø and Kring 2012: 32–35).
11 Araghi uses the concept of 'accumulation by displacement' to point the double aspect of contemporary land grabs: i) the ongoing massive dispossession of the world's peasantries and the appropriation of the migratory surplus labour power, and ii) the accumulation of the spaces of 'surplus nature' (Araghi 2009: 114).

12 FAO, IFAD, UNCTAD and the World Bank developed a set of principles for responsible agricultural investment (PRAI). The United Nations Economic Commission for Africa, the African Union, the African Development Bank, and the EU, have also developed frameworks and guidelines.

13 Parties should, when taking action to address climate change, respect, promote and consider their respective obligations on human rights, the right to health, the rights of indigenous peoples, local communities, migrants, children, persons with disabilities and people in vulnerable situations and the right to development, as well as gender equality, empowerment of women and intergenerational equity.

(UNFCCC 2015)

References

Aabø, Ellen, and Thomas Kring. 2012. "The Political Economy of Large-Scale Agricultural Land Acquisitions: Implications for Food Security and Livelihoods/Employment Creation in Rural Mozambique." UNDP.

Adams, Cristina, Sidney T. Rodrigues, Miguel Calmon, and Chetan Kumar. 2016. "Impacts of Large-scale Forest Restoration on Socioeconomic Status and Local Livelihoods: What We Know and Do Not Know." *Biotropica* 48 (6):731–44.

Agrawal, Arun, and Kent Redford. 2009. "Conservation and Displacement: An Overview." *Conservation and Society* 7 (1): 1.

Al-Mahmood, Syed Zain. 2015. "Palm-Oil Migrant Workers Tell of Abuses on Malaysian Plantations." *Wall Street Journal*, July 26, sec. World. www.wsj.com/articles/palm-oil-migrant-workers-tell-of-abuses-on-malaysian-plantations-1437933321.

Altieri, Miguel, and Walter Pengue. 2006. "GM Soybean: Latin America's New Coloniser." *Seedling GRAIN*, 13–17.

Angelsen, Arild. 2009. "Realising REDD+. National Strategy and Policy Options." Indonesia: CIFOR. https://www.cifor.org/publications/pdf_files/Books/BAngelsen0902.pdf

Anseeuw, Ward, Alden Wily, Lorenzo Cotula, and Michael Taylor. 2012. "Land Rights and the Rush for Land. Findings of the Global Commercial Pressures on Land Reserach Project." International Land Coalition.

Araghi, Farshad. 2009. *The Invisible Hand and the Visible Foot : Peasants, Dispossession and Globalization.* Peasants and Globalization : Political Economy, Rural Transformation and the Agrarian Question. London: Routledge, Pp. 111–147.

Asiyanbi, Adeniyi P. 2016. "A Political Ecology of REDD+: Property Rights, Militarised Protectionism, and Carbonised Exclusion in Cross River." *Geoforum* 77 (December): 146–56.

Barnett, Jon, and Saffron O'Neill. 2010. "Maladaptation." *Global Environmental Change* 20 (2):211–13.

Blaikie, Piers, and Harold Brookfield. 1987. *Land Degradation and Society.* Development Studies. London [etc.]: Methuen.

Bernstein, Henry. 2010. *Class Dynamics of Agrarian Change.* Agrarian Change and Peasant Studies Series; Agrarian Change and Peasant Studies Series. Halifax, NS: Fernwood Pub.

Beymer-Farris, Betsy A., and Thomas J. Bassett. 2012. "The REDD Menace: Resurgent Protectionism in Tanzania's Mangrove Forests." *Adding Insult to Injury: Climate Change, Social Stratification, and the Inequities of Intervention* 22 (2): 332–41.

Blomley, Tom, Dilys Roe, Fred Nelson, and Fiona Flintan. 2013. "'Land Grabbing': Is Conservation Part of the Problem or the Solution?" IIED. http://pubs.iied.org/17166IIED/.

Borras, Saturnino M. 2009. "Agrarian Change and Peasant Studies: Changes, Continuities and Challenges – an Introduction." *Journal of Peasant Studies* 36 (1): 5–31.

Borras Jr, Saturnino, and Jennifer Franco. 2010a. "From Threat to Opportunity-Problems with the Idea of a Code of Conduct for Land-Grabbing." *Yale Hum. Rts. & Dev. LJ* 13: 507.

Borras Jr, Saturnino, and Jennifer Franco. 2010b. "Towards a Broader View of the Politics of Global Land Grab: Rethinking Land Issues, Reframing Resistance." *Initiatives in Critical Agrarian Studies Working Paper Series* 1.

Borras Jr, Saturnino, and Jennifer C. Franco. 2012. 'Global Land Grabbing and Trajectories of Agrarian Change: A Preliminary Analysis'. *Journal of Agrarian Change* 12 (1):34–59

Borras Jr., Saturnino M., Philip McMichael, and Ian Scoones. 2013. *The Politics of Biofuels, Land and Agrarian Change*. 1 online resource (408 pages). vols. Critical Agrarian Studies. London: Routledge.

Borras, Saturnino M., Jennifer C. Franco, Ryan Isakson, Les Levidow, and Pietje Vervest. 2014. "Towards Understanding the Politics of Flex Crops and Commodities: Implications for Research and Policy Advocacy." TNI. http://oro.open.ac.uk/40501/.

Boyd, Emily, Maria Gutierrez, and Manyu Chang. 2007. "Small-Scale Forest Carbon Projects: Adapting CDM to Low-Income Communities." *Global Environmental Change* 17 (2):250–59.

Byres, Terence J. 2009. "The Landlord Class, Peasant Differentiation, Class Struggle and the Transition to Capitalism: England, France and Prussia Compared." *The Journal of Peasant Studies* 36 (1): 33–54.

Carling, J-rgen. 2002. "Migration in the Age of Involuntary Immobility: Theoretical Reflections and Cape Verdean Experiences." *Journal of Ethnic and Migration Studies* 28 (1): 5–42.

Carr, Edward R. 2005. "Placing the Environment in Migration: Environment, Economy, and Power in Ghana's Central Region." *Environment and Planning A* 37 (5):925–46.

Carrere, Ricardo. 2009. "Carbon Sink Plantation in Uganda: Evicting People for Making Space for Trees." *Upsetting the Offset : The Political Economy of Carbon Markets*, 98–101.

Cernea, Michael. 2005. "'Restriction of Access' Is Displacement: A Broader Concept and Policy." *Forced Migration Review* 31: 48–49.

Cernea, Michael M. 1999 "Development's Painful Social Costs." In *The Development Dilemma Displacement in India*, edited by S. Parasuraman, 1–31. London: Palgrave Macmillan UK.

CFS and FAO. 2012. "Voluntary Guidelines on the Responsible Governance of Tenure of Land, Fisheries and Forests in the Context of National Food Security." Rome: FAO. www.fao.org/docrep/016/i2801e/i2801e.pdf.

Chatty, Dawn, and Marcus, Colchester. 2002. *Conservation and Mobile Indigenous Peoples: Displacement, Forced Settlement, and Sustainable Development*. Studies in Forced Migration; v. 10. New York: Berghahn Books.

Chomba, Susan, Juliet Kariuki, Jens Friis Lund, and Fergus Sinclair. 2016. "Roots of Inequity: How the Implementation of REDD+ Reinforces Past Injustices." *Land Use Policy* 50 (January): 202–13.

Corbera, Esteve. 2012. "Problematizing REDD+ as an Experiment in Payments for Ecosystem Services." *4/6 Climate Systems* 4 (6): 612–19.

Cotula, Lorenzo. 2013. "Food Versus Fuel: An Informed Introduction to Biofuels Agrofuels: Big Profits, Ruined Lives and Ecological Destruction." *Journal of Peasant Studies* 40 (1): 297–300.

Cotula, Lorenzo, Dyer, and Sonja Vermeulen. 2008. "Fuelling Exclusion? The Biofuels Boom and Poor People's Access to Land." IIED and FAO. http://pubs.iied.org/pdfs/12551IIED.pdf.

Cotula, Lorenzo, European Parliament, and Directorate-General for Internal Policies of the Union. 2014. *Addressing the Human Rights Impacts of "Land Grabbing"*. [Luxembourg]: [Publications Office].

Dauvergne, Peter, and Kate J. Neville. 2010. "Forests, Food, and Fuel in the Tropics: The Uneven Social and Ecological Consequences of the Emerging Political Economy of Biofuels." *The Journal of Peasant Studies* 37 (4): 631–60

Davis, Mike. 2007. *Planet of Slums*. London ; New York: Verso.

De Schutter, Olivier. 2009. "Large-Scale Land Acquisitions and Leases: A Set Core of Principles and Measures to Address Human Rights." United Nations Human Rights Council.

De Schutter, Olivier. 2011. "How Not to Think of Land-Grabbing: Three Critiques of Large-Scale Investments in Farmland." *The Journal of Peasant Studies* 38 (2): 249–79.

Deininger, Klaus W., and Derek Byerlee. 2011. *Rising Global Interest in Farmland: Can It Yield Sustainable and Equitable Benefits?* Agriculture and Rural Development. Washington, DC: World Bank.

Diop, Demba, Marina Blanco, Alessandro Flammini, Michel Schlaifer, Magdalena Anna ropiwnicka, and Martin Mautner Markhof. 2013. "Assessing the Impact of Biofuels Production on Developing Countries from the Point of View of Policy Coherence for Development." AETS. https://ec.europa.eu/europeaid/sites/devco/files/study-impact-assesment-biofuels-production-on-development-pcd-201302_en_2.pdf.

Down to Earth. 2014. "Indonesia on the Front Line: Impacts of Biofuel Expansion for People, Forests and Climate." www.downtoearth-indonesia.org/sites/downtoearth-indonesia.org/files/4-page%20 briefing-10-lowres-1234.pdf.

Dowie, Mark. 2009. "Conservation Refugees: The Hundred-Year Conflict Between Global Conservation and Native Peoples. Cambridge, MA: The MIT Press." *Global Environmental Politics* 10 (2): 122–24.

Dryzek, John S. 2013. *The Politics of the Earth.* Third Edition. Oxford: Oxford University Press.

Dwivedi, Ranjit. 2002. "Models and Methods in Development-Induced Displacement (Review Article)." *Development and Change* 33 (4): 709–32.

FAO. 2015. "Forest Resource Assessment." Working Paper. Food and Agriculture Organization of the United Nations. http://www.fao.org/docrep/017/ap862e/ap862e00.pdf.

Fairhead, James, Melissa Leach, and Ian Scoones. 2012. "Green Grabbing: A New Appropriation of Nature?" *Journal of Peasant Studies* 39 (2): 237–61.

Feldman, Shelley, and Charles Geisler. 2012. "Land Expropriation and Displacement in Bangladesh." *Journal of Peasant Studies* 39 (3–4): 971–93.

Feldman, Shelley, Charles Geisler, and Louise Silberling. 2003. "Moving Targets: Displacement, Impoverishment, and Development★." *International Social Science Journal* 55 (175): 7–13.

Geisler, Charles. 2003. "A New Kind of Trouble: Evictions in Eden★." *International Social Science Journal* 55 (175): 69–78.

GRAIN. 2008. "Seized! The 2008 Land Grab for Food and Financial Security." GRAIN. https://www. grain.org/article/entries/93-seized-the-2008-landgrab-for-food-and-financial-security.

GRAIN and WRM. 2015. "How REDD+ Projects Undermine Peasant Farming and Real Solutions to Climate Change." www.grain.org/article/entries/5322-how-redd-projects-undermine-peasant-farming-and-real-solutions-to-climate-change.

Hall, Derek. 2011. "Land Grabs, Land Control, and Southeast Asian Crop Booms." *Journal of Peasant Studies* 38 (4): 837–57.

Hall, Derek. 2013. "Primitive Accumulation, Accumulation by Dispossession and the Global Land Grab." *Third World Quarterly* 34 (9): 1582–1604.

Hall, Ruth, Ian Scoones, and Dzodzi Tsikata. 2017. "Plantations, Outgrowers and Commercial Farming in Africa: Agricultural Commercialisation and Implications for Agrarian Change." *The Journal of Peasant Studies*, March, 1–23.

Harvey, David. 2004. "The 'New' Imperialism: Accumulation by Dispossession." *Socialist Register*, no. 40:63–78.

Headey, Derek, Dirk Bezemer, and Peter B.Hazell. 2008. "Agricultural Exit Problems Causes and Consequences." 802. IFPRI Discussion Paper. IFPRI. http://ebrary.ifpri.org/utils/getfile/collection/p15738coll2/id/14204/filename/14153.pdf.

Hickey, Sam, and Andries du Toit. 2013. "Adverse Incorporation, Social Exclusion, and Chronic Poverty." In *Chronic Poverty: Concepts, Causes and Policy*, edited by Andrew Shepherd and Julia Brunt, 134–59. London: Palgrave Macmillan UK.

Hunsberger, Carol, Esteve Corbera, Saturnino M. Borras Jr, Jennifer C. Franco, Kevin Woods, Courtney Work, Romulo de la Rosa, Vuthy Eang, Roman Herre, Sai Sam Kham, Clara Park, Seng Sokheng, Max Spoor, Shwe Thein, Kyaw Thu Aung, Ratha Thuon and Chayan Vaddhanaphuti. 2016. "Climate Change Mitigation, Land Grabbing and Conflict: Towards a Landscape-Based and Collaborative Action Research Agenda." *Canadian Journal of Development Studies/Revue Canadienne d'études Du Développement*, 1–20.

International Land Coalition. 2011. "The Tirana Declaration." Tirana, Albania. www.landcoalition.org/sites/default/files/documents/resources/tiranadeclaration.pdf.

IPCC. 2014. "Climate Change 2014: Synthesis Report. Contribution of Working Groups I, II and III to the Fifth Assessment Report of the Intergovernmental Panel on Climate Change." Geneva, Switzerland. www.ipcc.ch/report/ar5/syr/.

'Land Deal Politics Initiative' (LDPI): Erasmus University Rotterdam. Accessed 30 November 2017. http://www.iss.nl/research/research_groups/political_economy_of_resources_environment_and_population_per/networks/land_deal_politics_ldpi/.

Land Matrix. 2017. Accessed February 1, 2017. www.landmatrix.org/en/

Lang, Chris. 2014. "Indigenous Peoples Evicted and Their Homes Set on Fire: Embobut Forest, Kenya | REDD-Monitor." Accessed February 1. www.redd-monitor.org/2014/01/24/indigenous-peoples-evicted-and-their-homes-set-on-fire-embobut-forest-kenya/.

Larson, Anne M., Maria Brockhaus, William D. Sunderlin, Amy Duchelle, Andrea Babon, Therese Dokken, Thu Thuy Pham, Thu Thuy Pham, I.A.P Resosudarmo, Galia Selaya, Abdon Awono, and Thu-Ba Huynh. 2013. "Land Tenure and REDD+: The Good, the Bad and the Ugly." *Global Environmental Change* 23 (3): 678–89.

Leach, Melissa, James Fairhead, and James Fraser. 2012. "Green Grabs and Biochar: Revaluing African Soils and Farming in the New Carbon Economy." *The Journal of Peasant Studies* 39 (2): 285–307.

Li, Tania Murray. 2009. "Exit from Agriculture: A Step Forward or a Step Backward for the Rural Poor?" *The Journal of Peasant Studies* 36 (3): 629–36.

———. 2010. "To Make Live or Let Die? Rural Dispossession and the Protection of Surplus Populations." *Antipode* 41 (January): 66–93.

———. 2011. "Centering Labor in the Land Grab Debate." *Journal of Peasant Studies* 38 (2): 281–98.

Liverman, Diana M. 2009. "Conventions of Climate Change: Constructions of Danger and the Dispossession of the Atmosphere." *Feature: Narratives of Climate Change* 35 (2): 279–96.

Lubkemann, Stephen C. 2008. "Involuntary Immobility: On a Theoretical Invisibility in Forced Migration Studies." *Journal of Refugee Studies* 21 (4): 454–75.

Lunstrum, Elizabeth, Pablo Bose, and Anna Zalik. 2016. "Environmental Displacement: The Common Ground of Climate Change, Extraction and Conservation." *Area* 48 (2): 130–33.

Marino, Elizabeth, and Jesse Ribot. 2012. "Special Issue Introduction: Adding Insult to Injury: Climate Change and the Inequities of Climate Intervention." *Adding Insult to Injury: Climate Change, Social Stratification, and the Inequities of Intervention* 22 (2): 323–28.

Marx, Karl. [1867–1894] 1976. *Capital: A Critique of Political Economy: A Critique of Political Economy / Karl Marx; Introduced by Ernest Mandeltranslated by Ben Fowkes [and David Fernbach].* 3 vols. Penguin Books. Harmondsworth: Penguin Books in association with New Left Review.

Mayrhofer, Monika, and Florian Mersmann. 2016. "Displaced, Evicted or Resettled by Climate Change Measures : Neglecting the Rights of Affected Communities in the Case of the Bujagali Hydropower Plant."

McAfee, Kathleen. 2012. "The Contradictory Logic of Global Ecosystem Services Markets." *Development and Change* 43 (1): 105–31.

McCarthy, John F. 2010. "Processes of Inclusion and Adverse Incorporation: Oil Palm and Agrarian Change in Sumatra, Indonesia." *The Journal of Peasant Studies* 37 (4): 821–50.

McMichael, Philip. 2009. "Contemporary Contradictions of the Global Development Project: Geopolitics, Global Ecology and the 'development Climate.'" *Third World Quarterly* 30 (1): 247–62.

Mwangi, Esther, Isla Duporge, and Andersson. 2015. "Can REDD+ Shift the Tide against Elite Capture of Forest Benefits? Probably Not." *CIFOR Forests News Blog.* August 25. http://blog.cifor.org/32241/can-redd-shift-the-tide-against-elite-capture-of-forest-benefits-probably-not?fnl=en.

OHCHR. 2009. "Report of the Office of the United Nations High Commissioner for Human Rights on the Relationship between Climate Change and Human Rights." A/HRC/10/61. OHCHR. https://documents-dds-ny.un.org/doc/UNDOC/GEN/G09/103/44/PDF/G0910344.pdf?OpenElement.

Peet, Richard, Paul Robbins, and Michael Watts. 2010. *Global Political Ecology.* 1st ed. London: Taylor & Francis.

Phillips, Tom. 2007. "Brazil's Ethanol Slaves: 200,000 Migrant Sugar Cutters Who Prop Up Renewable Energy Boom." *The Guardian*, March 9, sec. World news. www.theguardian.com/world/2007/mar/09/brazil.renewableenergy.

Rainforest Rescue. 2017. "Indonesia: Terror and Eviction for Palm Oil." Accessed February 4, 2017. www.rainforest-rescue.org/petitions/936.

REDD Desk. 2016. "What Is REDD+?" Accessed November 30, 2017. https://theredddesk.org/what-redd#toc-2.

Rigg, Jonathan. 2006. "Land, Farming, Livelihoods, and Poverty: Rethinking the Links in the Rural South." *World Development* 34 (1): 180–202.

Robbins, Paul. 2004. *Political Ecology: A Critical Introduction / Paul Robbins.* xxi, 242 p. vols. Critical Introductions to Geography. Malden, MA: Blackwell Pub.

Robledo-Abad, Carmenza, Hans-Jörg Althaus, Göran Berndes, Simon Bolwig, Esteve Corbera, Felix Creutzig, John Garcia-Ulloa, et al. 2017. "Bioenergy Production and Sustainable Development: Science Base for Policymaking Remains Limited." *GCB Bioenergy* 9 (3): 541–56.

Sassen, Saskia. 2010. "A Savage Sorting of Winners and Losers: Contemporary Versions of Primitive Accumulation." *Globalizations* 7 (1–2): 23–50.

———. 2013. "Land Grabs Today: Feeding the Disassembling of National Territory." *Globalizations* 10 (1): 25–46.

———. 2014. *Expulsions : Brutality and Complexity in the Global Economy : Brutality and Complexity in the Global Economy/Saskia Sassen.* 1 vol. (298 p.) vols. Cambridge, MA and London: The Belknap Press of Harvard University Press.

Schmidt-Soltau, Kai. 2009. "Is the Displacement of People from Parks Only 'Purported', or Is It Real?" *Conservation and Society* 7 (1): 46–55.

Schwarze, Reimund, John Niles, and Jacob Olander. 2002. "Understanding and Managing Leakage in Forest-Based Greenhouse-Gas-Mitigation Projects." *Philosophical Transactions: Mathematical, Physical & Engineering Sciences* 360 (1797): 1685–1703.

Sills, E. O., S. Atmadja, C. de Sassi, A. E. Duchelle, D. Kweka, I. a. P. Resosudarmo, W. D. Sunderlin, and (eds.). 2014. *REDD+ on the Ground: A Case Book of Subnational Initiatives across the Globe.* Center for International Forestry Research (CIFOR), Bogor, Indonesia.

Smith, John. 2002. "Afforestation and Reforestation in the Clean Development Mechanism of the Kyoto Protocol: Implications for Forests and Forest People." *Journal of Global Environment Issues* 2 (3/4): 322–43.

Survival International. 2014. "Kenyan Government Forcing Us into Extinction': Evictions of Sengwer Tribe Escalate." www.survivalinternational.org/news/9932, www.survivalinternational.org/news/9932.

The World Bank. 2008. "World Development Report 2008. Agriculture for Development." Washington, DC: The World Bank. https://siteresources.worldbank.org/INTWDR2008/Resources/WDR_00_book.pdf.

Thomson, Frances. 2014. "Why We Need the Concept of Land-Grab-Induced Displacement." *Journal of Internal Displacement* 4 (2): 42–65.

UNFCCC. 2015. "The Paris Agreement." https://unfccc.int/resource/docs/2015/cop21/eng/l09r01.pdf.

'UNPFII Recommendations Database'. n.d. Accessed 30 November 2017. https://esa.un.org/unpfiidata/UNPFII_Recommendations_Database_view.asp?editid=1827&editid2=&editid3=&TargetPageNumber=1&todo=readonly&masterkey=.

United Nations Human Settlements Programme (UNHSP), ed. 2003. *The Challenge of Slums: Global Report on Human Settlements, 2003.* London; Sterling, VA: Earthscan Publications.

USAID. 2014. "Climate Change, Property Rights, and Resource Governance: Emerging Implications for USG Policies and Programming." https://rmportal.net/news-events/news-usaid-rmp-featured-stories/climate-change-property-rights-resource-governance-emerging-implications-for-usg-policies-and-programming/view.

Verbist, Bruno, Marieke Vangoidsenhoven, Robert Dewulf, and Bart Muys. 2011. "Reducing Emissions from Deforestation and Degradation (REDD)." KLIMOS. https://ees.kuleuven.be/klimos/papers/wp3reddfinal.pdf.

Vira, Bhaskar. 2015. "Taking Natural Limits Seriously: Implications for Development Studies and the Environment: Debate: Taking Natural Limits Seriously." *Development and Change* 46 (4): 762–76.

Vigil, Sara. 2015a. "Displacement as a Consequence of Climate Change Mitigation Policies." *Disasters and Displacement in a Changing Climate*, no. 49: 43–45.

———. 2015b. "Une Cause Invisible de Migrations : La Tragédie de L'accaparement Des Terres." *Politiques Du Capital*, no. 64: 111–23.

———. 2016. *Without Rain or Land, Where Will Our People Go? Climate Change, Land Grabbing and Human Mobility. Insights from Senegal and Cambodia.* The Hague, The Netherlands: ISS. www.iss.nl/fileadmin/ASSETS/iss/Research_and_projects/Research_networks/ICAS/60-ICAS_CP_Vigil.pdf.

War on Want. 2008. "Fuelling Fear. The Human Costs of Biofuels in Colombia." http://media.waronwant. org/sites/default/files/Fuelling%20Fear.pdf.

White, Ben., Saturnino M. Borras Jr, Ruth. Hall, Ian. 2012. Scoones, and Wendy. Wolford. 2013. *The New Enclosures : Critical Perspectives on Corporate Land Deals*. Critical Agrarian Studies. London: Routledge.

White, Julia, and Ben White. 2012. "Gendered Experiences of Dispossession: Oil Palm Expansion in a Dayak Hibun Community in West Kalimantan." *The Journal of Peasant Studies* 39 (3–4): 995–1016.

Wilkinson, John, and Selena Herrera. 2010. "Biofuels in Brazil: Debates and Impacts." *The Journal of Peasant Studies* 37 (4): 749–68.

30

Climate-induced community relocations

Institutional challenges and human rights protections

Robin Bronen

Climate change

Climate change is most often associated with temperature changes in the Earth's atmosphere. The warmest six-year period in the 137-year temperature record occurred between 2011 and 2016. The hottest year ever recorded was 2016, followed by 2015 and 2014 (NOAA 2017). In the northern polar regions, temperatures are rising at twice the global average (Jeffries et al. 2015). The accelerated warming in the Arctic has tremendous implications, not only in the Arctic but throughout the world.

These temperature increases impact the hydrosphere, cryosphere, atmosphere and biosphere. As a consequence, numerous and diverse climate-induced environmental changes are occurring and affecting the totality of the environment where humans live, work and carry out their cultural traditions and ceremonies. Sea level rise and thawing permafrost are two climate-induced environmental changes, which combined with the loss of natural coastal barriers, such as sea ice, severely threaten coastal communities. Permafrost, permanently frozen soil that is the glue that makes land habitable in the Arctic, is thawing due to warming temperatures (Walsh et al. 2015).

Sea level rise is accelerating and expected to worsen over the next century due to increased rates of ice sheet mass loss from Antarctica and Greenland (Nicholls and Cazenave 2010). The Greenland Ice Sheet experienced extensive melting in 2012 and 2015. In 2012, melting occurred over more than 96% of the ice sheet, and in 2015, 50% of the ice sheet was melting. Melt season duration in 2015 was as much as 30–40 days longer than average in western, northwestern and northeastern Greenland (Jeffries et al. 2015). Increased ocean temperatures, causing ocean water to expand and glaciers to melt, also contribute to sea level rise (Nicholls and Cazenave 2010). Sea level rise contributes to flooding, sea surges, erosion and salinization of land and water (IPCC 2012).

Warming temperatures also affect ocean ecosystems and cause a loss of Arctic sea ice, the natural barrier that protects coastal communities from sea surges, erosion and floods. Arctic sea ice is decreasing in thickness and extent. Record minimum levels of Arctic sea ice have been recorded since 2007 (Jeffries et al. 2015). Minimum sea ice extent in September 2015 was 29% less than the average for 1981–2010 (NSIDC 2016).

The decrease in extent of Arctic sea ice coupled with warming temperatures has caused a delay in freezing of the Bering and Chukchi seas (Walsh et al. 2015, Shulski and Wendler 2007). Near shore pack ice has historically provided a protective barrier to coastal communities (Shulski and Wendler 2007). Since the 1980s, the Arctic seas are remaining ice-free approximately three weeks longer in the autumn (Hufford and Partain 2005). The delay in freezing of the Arctic seas has left many communities exposed to the autumnal storms that originate in the Pacific and occur primarily between August and early December (Walsh et al. 2015, Shulski and Wendler 2007). The loss of Arctic sea ice coupled with thawing permafrost is causing severe erosion and storm surges along the northern and western Alaska coasts.

Relocation

The combination of repeated extreme weather events, ongoing and accelerating rates of environmental change such as erosion, and the loss of protective coastal barriers is forcing coastal communities to choose to relocate as a long-term adaptation strategy. Community relocation is required to protect residents from climate-induced ecological changes, which cause extensive damage to infrastructure and repeatedly place people in danger (Bronen 2011). Relocation is a process whereby a community's residents, housing and public infrastructure are reconstructed in another location (Abhas 2010). In addition, relocation should also include rebuilding livelihoods and social networks. Relocation is always an adaptation strategy of last resort and a decision that must be made by the community faced with imminent threat from environmental hazard, when no other strategies can protect populations in the places where they currently live.

Alaska

Newtok, a Yup'ik Eskimo village, is located near the Bering Sea in western Alaska. Approximately 320 residents reside in about 60 houses (Cox 2007). The Ninglick River borders Newtok to the south; to the east is the Newtok River (USACE 2006). A combination of increased temperatures, thawing permafrost and decreased Arctic sea ice is causing accelerating erosion, moving the Ninglick River closer to the village (Cox 2007). The State of Alaska spent about $1.5 million to control the erosion between 1983 and 1989 (USACE 2008a). Despite these efforts, erosion associated with the movement of the Ninglick River was projected to reach the school, the largest structure in the community, by about 2017 (USACE 2008a).

Six extreme weather events between 1989 and 2006 exacerbated these gradual ecological changes. Five of these events precipitated U.S. Federal Emergency Management Agency (FEMA) disaster declarations (ASCG 2008). FEMA declared three disasters between October 2004 and May 2006 alone (ASCG 2008). These three storms accelerated the erosion and repeatedly "flooded the village water supply, caused raw sewage to be spread throughout the community, displaced residents from homes, destroyed subsistence food storage, and shut down essential utilities" (USACE 2008a, 5). Public infrastructure that was significantly damaged or destroyed included the village landfill, barge ramp, sewage treatment facility and fuel storage facilities (Bronen 2011). The only access to the community is by barge during the summer or by airplane. The barge landing, which allows for most delivery of supplies and heating fuel, no longer exists, creating a fuel crisis. Salt water is affecting the potable water (Cox 2007).

In 1994, the Newtok Traditional Council analyzed six potential relocation sites to start a relocation planning process. In September 1996, Newtok inhabitants voted – for the first of three times

– to relocate to Nelson Island, nine miles south of Newtok, remaining within their subsistence area (Cox 2007). Subsequent votes occurred in May 2001, and most recently in August 2003. Newtok obtained title to the preferred relocation site, which they named Mertarvik, through a land-exchange agreement negotiated with the U.S. Fish and Wildlife Service. Construction of pioneer infrastructure, including a multi-purpose evacuation center and barge landing, began at the relocation site in 2009. Federal grant funding through the Economic Development Corporation was the primary source of revenues. With no other infrastructure located at the relocation site, the barge landing was critical in order to provide the development of the relocation site (Bronen 2011).

State, federal and tribal government and nongovernmental agencies have issued numerous reports documenting the social-ecological crisis faced by Newtok residents and the habitability of the relocation site (Bronen 2011). Between 2006 and 2016, more than two dozen reports were completed by federal and state government agencies to document the environmental changes threatening the health and wellbeing of community residents, to identify the steps federal, state and tribal government entities need to take during the relocation process and to plan for the infrastructure development at the relocation site (Bronen 2011).

The Newtok Traditional Council (the Council) commissioned the Newtok Background for Relocation Report, which summarized the previous erosion studies, mapped the advancing Ninglick River to show the scope of erosion, documented the social-ecological impacts of erosion on the village and developed a tentative timeline for the short-term and long-term relocation of residences (Bronen 2011) The report also described the Council's evaluation of each potential village relocation site, including "collocation" to one of four existing communities or relocation to one of six potential new sites in the region close to Newtok. In addition, it contained the results of the 2003 resident survey, which asked Newtok residents to vote on relocation alternatives (Bronen 2011). This report was instrumental to the community's relocation effort because it provided background documentation to government agencies and officials to justify the village's relocation efforts and to support the Newtok Traditional Council's requests for government assistance in this process (Cox 2007).

In addition, the U.S. Army Corps of Engineers funded a report in 2008 that analyzed five alternative responses to the social, health and ecological crises facing Newtok village residents (USACE 2008b). These alternatives included: taking no action, staying in place with erosion and flood control, collocation, relocation funded and orchestrated solely by the Corps of Engineers and a collaborative relocation effort (USACE 2008b). The report found that a coordinated relocation effort was in the best interests of Newtok residents, explaining:

> With no Federal and state action, relocation efforts will be piecemeal and uncoordinated and will increase ultimate costs many times over a coordinated, efficient relocation plan. Local efforts will take many years and the existing significant risk to health, life, and property will continue in Newtok. The disintegration of these people as a distinct tribe may result from splitting the community in two or more locations for many years as they relocate under their own efforts.
>
> *(USACE 2008b)*

The Corps also specifically rejected the collocation alternative, finding that "[c]ollocation would destroy the Newtok community identity" (USACE 2008b).

The Corps also issued several reports that evaluated the habitability of Newtok's relocation site and confirmed the Council's conclusion that Mertarvik is a suitable relocation site (USACE 2008a, 2008b).

Newtok Planning Group

The Newtok Planning Group emerged in May 2006 from an ad hoc series of meetings. It is unique in Alaska in its multi-disciplinary and multi-jurisdictional structure and consists of about 25 state, federal and tribal governmental and nongovernmental agencies that all voluntarily collaborate to facilitate Newtok's relocation (Bronen 2011). From the Planning Group's inception, Newtok's tribal government has led the relocation effort. On June 9, 2011, the Newtok Traditional Council unanimously approved a set of guiding principles ("Maligtaquyarat") for the community's relocation to Mertarvik (AgnewBeck 2012).

These guiding principles are based on the Yup'ik way of life and are:

- Remain a distinct, unique community – our own community.
- Stay focused on our vision by taking small steps forward each day.
- Make decisions openly and as a community and look to elders for guidance.
- Build a healthy future for our youth.
- Our voice comes first – we have first and final say in making decisions and defining priorities.
- Share with and learn from our partners.
- No matter how long it takes, we will work together to provide support to our people in both Mertarvik and Newtok.
- Development should:
    - Reflect our cultural traditions.
    - Nurture our spiritual and physical wellbeing.
    - Respect and enhance the environment.
    - Be designed with local input from start to finish.
    - Be affordable for our people.
    - Hire community members first.
    - Use what we have first and use available funds wisely.
- Look for projects that build on our talents and strengthen our economy.

(AgnewBeck 2012, 4)

These guiding principles govern every aspect of the relocation process and have been integrated into the strategic relocation master plan, which guides federal and state government participation in the relocation effort (AgnewBeck 2012).

Governance

The institutional and statutory barriers to relocation are enormous. With no designated relocation funding, each government agency must follow its own budgetary and funding prioritization criteria to allocate funding for Newtok's relocation effort. The lack of a population base at the relocation site and the uncertainty of when and if people will be able to relocate because of the lack of any infrastructure has impacted Newtok's ability to receive state funding for capital expenditures at their relocation site. For example, Newtok's request for state funding for an airstrip, the only means of transportation to the relocation site, was initially placed at a lower prioritization than other communities seeking this funding where people are already living and need state funding to maintain and rebuild this infrastructure.

Despite these challenges, the Newtok Planning Group has been exceptionally creative in finding existing funding sources to support the relocation effort and in coordinating different funding streams to meet cost sharing eligibility requirements as well as increasing the revenue available for the relocation effort. For example, as a result of a presidential disaster declaration in November 2013 because of a storm that impacted Newtok, funding from the U.S. Federal Emergency Management Agency (FEMA) and the Alaska Division of Homeland Security and Emergency Management (DHS&EM), will focus on housing assistance. Newtok residents critically need homes to move to Mertarvik, their relocation site (DCRA 2016).

FEMA administers the Hazard Mitigation Grant Program (HMGP) to help communities implement hazard mitigation measures following a presidentially declared disaster. In order for a local government (city or tribe) to qualify for HMGP funds, it must have a FEMA-approved Local Hazard Mitigation Plan (LHMP). Because Newtok has an approved LHMP, the community was eligible to apply for an HMGP grant. Newtok's tribal government chose to pursue relocation of 12 structurally-sound homes to the relocation site (DCRA 2016).

However, due to the lack of a national and state institutional framework, the relocation process remains painfully slow, placing Newtok residents at great risk as erosion continues to accelerate and threaten them. This lack of a governance framework hampers the ability of local, regional and national government agencies to respond. If climate-induced environmental change renders the places where people live uninhabitable and causes land to disappear, new governance institutions need to be designed to determine whether people can be protected in place or require relocation. Funding mechanisms also need to be identified in order to facilitate a relocation process that ensures there is adequate funding for the relocation site as well as maintenance costs for infrstructure at the original community location (Bronen 2011, Bronen and Chapin 2013).

Recognizing this institutional gap and the complex challenges of climate-induced population displacement, the Bicameral Task Force on Climate Change recommended in their December 2013 report "Implementing the President's Action Plan: U.S. Department of the Interior":

> that the Administration devote special attention to the problems of communities that decide they have little choice but to relocate in the face of the impacts of climate change. Because the relocation of entire communities due to climate change is such an unprecedented need, there is no institutional framework within the U.S. to relocate communities, and agencies lack technical, organizational, and financial means to do so.
>
> *(United States Congress Bicameral Task Force on Climate Change 2013)*

Former President Obama's Task Force on Climate Preparedness and Resilience (Task Force) echoed this recommendation in November 2014 and affirmed that the federal government should take a lead role to establish a relocation institutional framework to respond to the complex challenges of climate-induced population displacement (White House 2014). How this will proceed under the Trump administration is not known at time of writing.

Creating an adaptive governance relocation framework based on human rights

A relocation institutional framework needs to determine the appropriate role of federal, state, local and tribal governments and outline the decision-making process for relocations – who decides relocation needs to occur and what steps do communities need to take to engage with government agencies to receive the technical assistance they will need to implement a relocation plan, including the building of critical infrastructure at their relocation site (Bronen 2011).

A relocation institutional framework also needs to outline the factors to determine when and if relocations should occur (Bronen 2015).

An adaptive governance relocation framework means that protection in the places where people live and work is always prioritized. Relocation of populations is always a last resort to respond to climate change threats and should not be implemented until other adaptation strategies to protect communities in place have been pursued. Consequently, a relocation institutional framework would incorporate all of the institutional mechanisms, such as sea walls and land use planning tools to protect people in place, and also create new mechanisms to implement a relocation process so that national, state, local and tribal governments can dynamically shift their efforts from protection in place to managed retreat, involving some threatened infrastructure and community relocation, involving the entire community (Bronen 2011, Bronen and Chapin 2013).

Implementing an adaptive governance relocation framework requires multi-level and diverse governmental and nongovernmental actors to engage in a collaborative process of knowledge production and problem solving (Bronen 2015). Adaptive capacity, an essential element of adaptive governance, is the ability to respond to social-ecological disturbances and maintain resilience when responding to rapid ecological change (Armitage and Plummer 2010). Adaptive capacity in social systems refers to the ability of institutions to balance power among interest groups and engage in an iterative learning process that can generate knowledge and be flexible in solving problems. Networks of multiple and diverse organizations are critical for building adaptive capacity (Bronen 2015).

Human rights protections must form the foundation of this adaptive governance framework. Four factors compel the creation of a specific human rights instrument to protect the rights of those living in communities that are no longer habitable due to climate-induced ecological change: 1) nation-state governments have a duty to protect populations that reside within their jurisdiction; 2) refugee law and the Guiding Principles on Internal Displacement do not provide human rights protections for planned community relocations; 3) relocation human rights guidelines must ensure the protection of collective rights because climate change impacts the habitability of entire communities whose residents will be forced to permanently relocate; and 4) the human rights of host communities must also be protected.

Nation-state governments have a duty to protect their citizens

Nation-state governments have an obligation to protect vulnerable populations from climate-induced ecological change, which threatens the civil, economic, social and cultural rights fundamental to the inherent dignity of individuals, as well as collective society. A nation-state government's protection of human rights is a critical threshold for that nation-state to claim sovereignty over its citizens and also is a minimum test for international legitimacy (Hathaway 1991; CISS 2001). International law defines sovereignty as the legal identity of a state and signifies a nation-state government's capacity to make authoritative decisions about the people and resources within its territory (Montevideo Convention on the Rights and Duties of States 1934). The duty to protect is inherent in the concept of sovereignty and implies that the nation-state government has the primary responsibility for the protection of populations within its jurisdiction (CISS 2001).

The duty to protect is also considered a seminal principle for United Nations membership and for the attainment of international peace and security (CISS 2001). Nation-state governments have a primary duty to protect the human rights, recognized in international human rights conventions, of their citizens if they are a party to these conventions (CISS 2001).

The duty to protect has three core principles (CISS 2001). Prevention is the most important and is defined as the responsibility to address the primary causes of crises that threaten human populations. The responsibility to react means that a nation-state government must respond appropriately to situations requiring humanitarian assistance. The third principle requires a nation-state government to provide resources to reconstruct after a humanitarian crisis occurs (CISS 2001).

International legal doctrine also specifically outlines the responsibilities of a nation-state government to protect internally displaced populations. The Inter-Agency Standing Committee (IASC) has defined the duties of a nation-state government to provide human rights protections to natural disaster victims (Brookings-Bern 2011). In this context, protection means securing the physical safety of natural disaster victims, and also securing all of the human rights guaranteed in international human rights law (UN Economic and Social Council, 2006). The obligation also includes the responsibility to minimize damage caused by natural hazards (UN Economic and Social Council, 2006, para. 4–8).

The Guiding Principles on Internal Displacement incorporate this sovereign responsibility to protect into a nation-state government's obligation to internally displaced populations. The responsibility includes the duty to provide safe access to housing "at the minimum, regardless of the circumstances, and without discrimination" (UNHCR 1998, 10). The Pinheiro Principles on Housing and Property Restitution echo the principle that nation-states have an obligation to guarantee human rights protections to persons affected by internal displacement and emphasize the obligation to protect human rights related to housing and property restitution (CHRE 2007).

The failure of the nation-state to protect its citizens is a human rights violation. The European Court of Human Rights found that government officials in Russia violated the right to life of community residents when they failed to implement land-planning and emergency relief policies even though they were aware of an increasing risk of a large-scale mudslide. The Court also noted that the population had not been adequately informed about the risk (Budayeva et al. 2008).

The duty to protect means that nation-state governments are responsible for implementing adaptation strategies. Communities will need a continuum of responses, from protection in place to community relocation, to adapt to climate-induced ecological change. Disaster and hazard mitigation are critical components of this continuum in order to assess vulnerabilities and develop disaster risk reduction and mitigation strategies (Bronen 2011, Bronen and Chapin 2013). Social ecological indicators can also assess vulnerability and guide the design of adaptation strategies. Traditional and local knowledge must be included. A human rights framework is critical to the design and implementation of these adaptation strategies to ensure that nation-state governments focus on the protection of freedoms that are fundamental to collective society, and that relocation only occurs when there are no other feasible solutions to protect vulnerable populations.

Lack of capacity and resources can limit a government's ability to protect the economic, social and cultural rights of populations within its jurisdiction (Zetter 2010). If human rights protections cannot be realized because of inadequate resources, then working for institutional capacity building through expansion or reform can be a part of the international obligations generated by the recognition of these rights. For example, if funding is required in order to ensure that populations have access to adequate housing, the international community needs to ensure that these funds are provided and that the community determines the location, layout and design of community housing:

> For developing countries, international cooperation is an essential component of the suc-
> cessful design and implementation of adaptation strategies. The United Nations Framework
> on Climate Change Convention clearly articulates the need for international cooperation

in the development and implementation of adaptation strategies, including planned relocations, and specifically states that developed country Parties shall: "[A]ssist the developing
country Parties that are particularly vulnerable to the adverse effects of climate change in
meeting costs of adaptation to those adverse effects."

(UNFCCC 1992, art. 4[1][b])

Communities displaced by climate impacts not protected by refugee law and the Guiding Principles on Internal Displacement

Existing human rights instruments fail to protect communities needing to relocate because of
climate-induced environmental change. The 1951 UN Convention Relating to the Status of
Refugees is the only treaty that creates an international structure to manage human migration.
The Convention provides for third country resettlement, human rights protections and humanitarian assistance for those fleeing persecution or torture in their country of origin and crossing a
nation-state border. The Convention initially applied to only those fleeing within Europe (UN
1951). The 1967 Protocol Relating to the Status of Refugees removed both the temporal and
geographic restrictions of the 1951 Convention, but kept the primary elements of the refugee
definition intact (UN 1967).

To be considered a refugee pursuant to the post-Protocol 1951 UN Convention, a person
must prove that they are unable or unwilling to return to their country of origin because they
have been singled out by a government actor or an actor the government cannot control and
persecuted on account of one of the five previously mentioned protected grounds. The definition
does not include environmental causes for flight from a person's country of origin (UN 1951).

Refugee law is based on the fundamental premise that the ordinary bonds between citi-
zen and state have been broken and a person is outside of their country of origin because the
nation-state government is unable or unwilling to protect them (Hathaway 1991). Refugees
need international intervention to ensure there is safe refuge because they can not turn to their
own governments for protection because nation-states are often the source of their persecution (Hathaway 1991). As a consequence, the 1951 Convention actually relieves a nation-state
government of its obligation to protect the human rights of its citizens and execute the necessary policies to enable populations who had fled its territory to return (Hathaway 1991). This
underlying premise of refugee law conflicts with the nation-state obligation to guarantee human
rights protections for all populations within its jurisdiction. In the situation of climate-induced
population displacement, which will primarily occur within countries, communities should still
be able to rely on national protection to respond to their humanitarian crisis.

Two international human rights documents that concern displacement are the Guiding
Principles of Internal Displacement and the Inter-Agency Standing Committee (IASC) Human
Rights Guidelines to Respond to Natural Disasters. Both documents outline the human rights
protections for populations that are internally displaced, but neither is adequate to address the
complex issues and human rights implications of climate-induced community relocations for
several reasons.

First, emergencies are clearly different from planned relocations. Neither the IASC guidelines nor the Guiding Principles on Internal Displacement provide for the prospective needs
of populations planning their permanent relocation and do not provide any guidance on how
communities can sustain themselves and create the necessary infrastructure to provide for basic
necessities without the assistance of humanitarian aid (Brookings-Bern 2011). Most importantly,
these documents do not clearly define a mechanism for communities to make the decisions

regarding the process of relocation. The IASC guidelines state the need for informed consent and participation in decisions regarding the relocation process, but as discussed later in this chapter, these principles are different from the ability to make decisions about the relocation (Brookings-Bern 2011).

The IASC Human Rights Guidelines to Respond to Natural Disasters were developed to respond to situations when pre-planning is not possible (Brookings-Bern 2011). The guidelines outline minimum core human rights obligations under the International Covenant on Economic, Social and Cultural Rights, such as the duty to provide food, shelter and health services, which a nation-state government must provide after the occurrence of a natural disaster (ICESCR 1966). However, the guidelines assume that humanitarian aid organizations will provide these basic necessities to populations displaced by natural disasters and do not describe how displaced populations can provide these basic necessities for themselves.

The Guiding Principles of Internal Displacement also do not provide sufficient human rights protections for those facing climate-induced community relocation. This document is not a binding international treaty or convention, but the UN General Assembly has recognized the Guiding Principles as "an important international framework for the protection of internally displaced persons" (UN General Assembly Resolution 2005). Although the Guiding Principles include persons displaced by natural disasters, the primary focus of these guidelines is displacement caused by the state's inability or unwillingness to protect populations from political, religious, ethnic or otherwise discriminatory persecution or violence. In comparison, as stated previously, those displaced by climate-induced ecological change should be able to continue to rely on State protection.

Second, both documents are based on the premise that populations may be able to return to their original home. Climate-induced ecological change will cause permanent population displacement. Enormous policy differences and human rights protections exist between temporary and permanent population displacement (Bronen 2011).

Relocation human rights guidelines must ensure the protection of collective rights

Climate-induced displacement will affect entire communities whose residents will collectively need protection from the threats caused by climate change. International human rights conventions, such as the UN Declaration on the Rights of Indigenous Peoples, recognize the rights of peoples collectively and that Indigenous peoples have the collective right to the fundamental freedoms articulated in the Universal Declaration of Human Rights and international law. Like these documents, a human rights instrument that addresses climate-induced population displacement must ensure the protection of collective rights because climate change impacts the habitability of entire communities whose residents will be forced to permanently relocate. These rights include the collective right to relocate as a community, as well as the collective right to make decisions regarding where and how a community will relocate.

The human rights of host communities must also be protected

The human rights of host communities must also be protected. A human rights instrument developed to respond to climate-induced displacement must also ensure that human rights protections are extended to those living in communities that provide sanctuary for those displaced by climate change. Host populations may experience shortages of water, food, sanitation, shelter and essential health services as a result of the increase in population. Schools may also be overburdened to provide educational services if there is an influx of displaced students. Human rights protections for host populations will ensure that host communities benefit from the relocation, preserve or improve their standard of living and also prevent conflicts and competition with the displaced populations (Abhas 2010).

Guiding human rights principles

The Peninsula Principles, a human rights document drafted in 2012 to address the human rights principles that need to adhere to the relocation of communities, create a common language to guide the international, national and local humanitarian response (Displacement Solutions 2013). The Peninsula Principles identify the appropriate human rights standards to guide national government actions when climate-induced ecological change threatens community habitability and the lives of community residents.

Collective self-determination

The right to self-determination is the cornerstone of the human rights principles that need to guide community relocations. Both the International Covenant on Economic, Social and Cultural Rights (ICESCR) and the International Covenant on Civil and Political Rights (ICCPR) establish that "all peoples have the right to self-determination" (ICCPR 1966, Article 1) by virtue of which "they freely determine their political status and freely pursue their economic, social and cultural development" (ICESCR 1966, Article 1). The inclusion of the right to self-determination in both treaties indicates that its importance spans all political, civil, economic, social and cultural rights.

The concept of self-determination has evolved since the creation of the United Nations in 1945 when the principle initially was interpreted to apply to the right of independence, non-interference and democracy of a nation-state in relation to other nation-state governments (Broderstad and Dahl 2004; UN Universal Declaration of Human Rights 1948). However, more recently the concept of self-determination has included the development of self-government institutions in Indigenous communities (Broderstad and Dahl 2004; UN Committee on Economic, Social and Cultural Rights 1991).

The UN Declaration on the Rights of Indigenous Peoples affirms that Indigenous peoples possess collective rights indispensable for their existence and wellbeing, including the right to collective self-determination and the collective right to the lands, territories and natural resources they have traditionally occupied and used (UN 2007, art.1). The collective right to self-determination ensures that Indigenous communities can determine their own identity, belong to "an indigenous community or nation, in accordance with the traditions and customs of the community or nation concerned" and make decisions about internal and local affairs (UN 2007, arts. 9, 33). The Declaration also provides that Indigenous peoples have the right to freely define and pursue their economic, social and cultural development. Similarly, the Convention for the Safeguarding of the Intangible Cultural Heritage also affirms the collective rights of communities to safeguard and respect their cultural heritage (UN 2006, art. 1).

In the context of climate-induced ecological change that threatens the habitability of entire communities, self-determination means that communities have the right to make decisions regarding adaptation strategies, which includes the right to make fundamental decisions about when, how and if relocation occurs.

Several existing international human rights documents include the right to participate in decision-making processes and the right to adequate and meaningful consultation as a means to ensure human rights protections. Informed consent and participation alone do not constitute effective self-determination, and are insufficient to protect the human rights of those threatened by climate-induced ecological change. These principles are part of the World Bank (2004) guidelines on involuntary resettlement and have been unable to prevent the social fragmentation and impoverishment that has plagued involuntary resettlements caused by World Bank-funded projects (Oliver-Smith 2009).

The failure to fully consider the welfare of the population and empower people of a community to make decisions regarding critical elements of a relocation, including site selection and community layout, are the principal reasons why relocations have been unsuccessful(Abhas 2010). Community relocations are more likely to be successful when affected communities participate in critical relocation and implementation decisions, such as identification of basic needs and settlement planning (Abhas 2010). For these reasons, communities faced with climate-induced ecological threats must have the authority to decide to relocate or not. Collective self-determination ensures that communities are empowered to make the critical decisions affecting their relocation.

Right to relocation

The right to relocate is a fundamental component of the right to self-determination when climate-induced ecological changes threaten the lives of people and cause degraded community habitability. The right to relocate, as with other human rights, is an entitlement when relocation is the only feasible solution to protect the human right to life, as well as the right to basic necessities inherent in living a life of dignity (Moyn 2010).

Several international legal instruments support the right to relocate, including the Universal Declaration of Human Rights and the Pinheiro Principles, which both state that everyone has the right to freedom of movement and residence (UN 2007, CHRE 2007). Although this right has been interpreted to mean that no one shall be arbitrarily or unlawfully forced to remain within a certain territory, area or region and that no one shall be arbitrarily or unlawfully forced to leave a certain territory, area or region, this right also includes the right to movement when threatened by environmental events (CHRE 2007). The human rights guidelines to respond to natural disasters interpret the right to life to mean that people affected by natural disasters should be allowed to relocate to other parts of the country (Brookings-Bern 2011).

Right to subsistence and food

Human rights doctrine explicitly states that the right to food and the right to be free from hunger are indispensible to human dignity and critically connected to other fundamental rights.[1] The right to food is concerned with an individual's lack of food, and also with the economic or physical reasons that people do not have access to food.[2]

States have the primary responsibility to promote and protect the right to food.[3] States have the duty to provide food "[w]henever an individual or group is unable, for reasons beyond their control, to enjoy the right to adequate food by the means at their disposal". This obligation also applies for persons who are victims of natural or other disasters.[4]

The right to subsistence, an element of the right to self-determination defined in both the International Covenant on Economic, Social and Cultural Rights and the International Covenant on Civil and Political Rights, is one of the essential human rights connected to the right to food.[5] For Indigenous peoples, the right to food is a collective right, and fundamentally connected to sovereignty, rights to land and territories, health, subsistence, treaties, economic development and culture.[6] For these reasons, the community of Newtok has chosen its relocation sites in order to maintain connection to traditional locations used for subsistence activities. Mertarvik, the relocation site for the residents of Newtok, is only 9 miles from the current location of the community, and is located across the Ninglick River from Newtok so that the community has easy access to navigable waters leading to their traditional fishing grounds of the river and the Bering Sea.

Right to work/economic development/improved standard of living

Human development goals which improve the economic and social conditions of community residents – including in the areas of education, employment, vocational training and retraining, housing, sanitation, health and social security – required to relocate must be incorporated into community relocation planning.[7]

The Newtok tribal government is incorporating workforce development opportunities and improved living standards in their relocation efforts. Newtok residents are using recently acquired construction skills to build the housing and public infrastructure at their relocation site. In addition, the relocation site will have access to economic development opportunities for fishing and construction.

Right to housing/property

Three human rights principles apply to community relocations and the right to housing: 1) right to replacement housing; 2) right to habitable housing; and 3) the right to choose the place of one's residence. The right to habitable housing means the housing provides adequate protection from weather hazards and is located away from hazardous zones. The human right to property, defined in the Universal Declaration of Human Rights, includes the right to land ownership as well as housing. (Brookings-Bern 2011) The Pinheiro Principles specifically outline the human rights principles that must guide land, housing and property restitution, which is viewed as an essential remedy for displacement (CHRE 2007). Although the principles are premised on the unlawful or arbitrary taking of housing, land or property, they outline a method for restitution which is highly relevant to those who lose their housing land or property due to climate change.

States' governments need to enact policies and laws to ensure that housing, land and property restitution procedures, institutions and mechanisms are within a legally sound, coherent and practical framework which should bring displacement to a permanent, sustainable and just end and fully compatible with international human rights, refugee and humanitarian law and related standards (CHRE 2007). Principles that must be included within these laws include non-discrimination in housing restitution (CHRE 2007). All displaced persons must also have the right to full and effective compensation as an integral component of the relocation process (Leckie 2009).

Land is the critical issue for all peoples needing to relocate. The right to land ownership restitution requires that specific arrangements be made to recognize claims to land title and ownership, especially for Indigenous peoples who may not have formal land titles and who may own land collectively.

Conclusion

Newtok's tribal government and the work of the Newtok Planning Group provide a model for other communities facing relocation as a consequence of climate change. The tribal government's role as a leader in the relocation process ensures that the community's culture and the collective and individual human rights of community residents are central to the relocation process. As climate change causes increasing frequency of extreme weather events and ongoing ecological change which renders entire communities uninhabitable and requires community relocation, human rights protections need to infuse the relocation process. In this way, communities will be able to collectively protect their cultural cohesion even though they have experienced the enormous loss of the land to which they are connected.

Notes

1 United Nations Committee on Economic, Social and Cultural Rights, General Comment 12: The Right to Adequate Food, para. 1, U.N. Doc. E/C.12/1995/5 (May 12, 1999).
2 United Nations Committee on Economic, Social and Cultural Rights, General Comment 12: The Right to Adequate Food, para. 4–5, U.N. Doc. E/C.12/1995/5 (May 12, 1999).
3 United Nations Human Rights Committee, The Right to Food, A/HRC/RES/16/27 para. 11 (2011).
4 United Nations Committee on Economic, Social and Cultural Rights, General Comment 12: The Right to Adequate Food, para. 12, U.N. Doc. E/C.12/1995/5 (May 12, 1999).
5 United Nations International Covenant on Economic, Social and Cultural Rights, opened for signature Dec. 16, 1966, G.A. Res. 2200A (XXI), U.N. GAOR, 21st Sess., Supp. No. 16, U.N. Doc. A/6316 (1966), 993 U.N.T.S. 3 (entered into force Jan. 3, 1976).
6 United Nations General Assembly, Report of the Office of the United Nations High Commissioner for Human Rights on the relationship between climate change and human rights (October 22, 2008) https://documents-dds-ny.un.org/doc/UNDOC/GEN/G09/103/44/PDF/G0910344.pdf?Open Element.
7 United Nations Declaration on the Rights of Indigenous Peoples, art. 21, G.A. Res. 61/295, U.N. Doc. A/RES/61/295 (Sept. 13, 2007).

References

Abhas, K.J. (2010) *Safer Homes, Stronger Communities A Handbook for Reconstructing after Natural Disasters Global Facility for Disaster Reduction and Recovery*. Washington, DC: World Bank.

AgnewBeck (2012) *Strategic Management Plan Newtok to Mertarvik*. Anchorage, AL: AgnewBeck. https://www.commerce.alaska.gov/web/Portals/4/pub/Mertarvik_Strategic_Management_Plan.pdf [Last accessed 29 November 2017].

Armitage, D., and Plummer, R. (2010) Adapting and transforming: governance for navigating change. Pages 287–302 *in* D. Armitage and R. Plummer, editors. *Adaptive capacity and environmental governance*. Springer, Berlin, Germany. http://dx.doi.org/10.1007/978-3-642-12194-4_14

ASCG (Arctic Slope Consulting Group) (2008) *Village of Newtok, Local Hazards Mitigation Plan* (ASCG Inc. of Alaska Bechtol Planning and Development, Newtok), www.commerce.state.ak.us/dca/planning/pub/Newtok_HMP.pdf.

Broderstad, E.G. and Dahl, J. (2004) Political systems. In Einarsson, N., Larsen, J. N., Nilsson, A., Young, O. (eds) *Arctic Human Development Report* Akureyri: Stefansson Arctic Institute.

Bronen, R. (2011) Climate-Induced Community Relocations: Creating an Adaptive Governance Framework Based in Human Rights Doctrine. *N.Y.U Review of Law and Social Change* 35(2) 101–148.

Bronen, R. and Chapin, F.S. (2013) "Adaptive Governance and Institutional Strategies for Climate-induced Community Relocations in Alaska," *Proceedings of the National Academy of Sciences*, Washington, DC.

Bronen, R. (2015) Climate-Induced Community Relocations: Using Integrated Social-Ecological Assessments to Foster Adaptation and Resilience. *Ecology and Society* 20(3) 36.

Brookings-Bern (Brookings-Bern Project on Internal Displacement) (2011) *IASC Operational Guidelines on the Protection of Persons In Situations of Natural Disasters*. Washington, DC: Brookings-Bern Project on Internal Displacement.

Budayeva and others v. Russia, 2008. Applications nos. 15339/02, 21166/02, 20058/02, 11673/02 and 1534/02, European Court of Human Rights.

CISS (Canadian International Commission on Intervention and State Sovereignty) 2001. *Responsibility to Protect*. Canada: International Development Research Centre.

CHRE (Center on Housing, Rights & Evictions) 2007. *The Pinheiro Principles Switzerland: Center on Housing, Rights & Evictions.* Available From: www.unhcr.org.ua/img/uploads/docs/PinheiroPrinciples.pdf

Cox, S., 2007. *An Overview of Erosion, Flooding, and Relocation Efforts in the Native Village of Newtok.* Anchorage, AL: Alaska Department of Commerce, Community and Economic Development.

DCRA (Alaska Division of Community and Regional Affairs) (2016) Newtok Planning Group Mertarvik Housing, accessed August 9, 2016 www.commerce.alaska.gov/web/dcra/PlanningLandManagement//NewtokPlanningGroup/MertarvikHousing.aspx

Displacement Solutions (2013). *The Peninsula Principles on Climate Displacement Within States.* Mornington Peninsula, Australia.

Docherty, B., and Giannini T., 2009. Confronting a Rising Tide: A Proposal for a Convention on Climate Change Refugees *Harvard Environmental Law Review* 33 359–360.

Hathaway, J.C. (1991).Reconceiving Refugee Law as Human Rights Protection, *Journal of Refugee Studies* 23 113–131.

Hufford, G., and Partain, J. (2005) *Climate Change and Short-Term Forecasting for Alaskan Northern Coasts.* Anchorage: National Weather Service.

ICCPR (International Covenant on Civil and Political Rights) (1966), *opened for signature* Dec. 16, 1966, G.A. Res. 2200A (XXI), U.N. GAOR, 21st Sess., Supp. No. 16, U.N. Doc. A/6316 (1966), 993 U.N.T.S. 3 (entered into force March 23, 1976).

ICESCR (International Covenant on Economic, Social and Cultural Rights) (1966), art. 2, *opened for signature* Dec. 16, 1966, G.A. Res. 2200A (XXI), U.N. GAOR, 21st Sess., Supp. No. 16, U.N. Doc. A/6316 (1966), 993 U.N.T.S. 3 (entered into force Jan. 3, 1976).

IPCC (Intergovernmental Panel on Climate Change) (2012) Summary for Policymakers. Pages 3–21 *in* C.B. Field, V. Barros, T.F. Stocker, D. Qin, D.J. Dokken, K.L. Ebi, M.D. Mastrandrea, K.J. Mach, G.-K. Plattner, S.K. Allen, M. Tignor, and P.M. Midgley, editors. *Managing the Risks of Extreme Events and Disasters to Advance Climate Change Adaptation: A Special Report of Working Groups I and II of the Intergovernmental Panel on Climate Change.* Cambridge, UK, and New York, NY: Cambridge University Press.

Jeffries, M.O., Richter-Menge, J., and Overland, J.E. (2015) Arctic Report Card 2015 NOAA, Washington DC.

Leckie, S. (2009) Climate-Related Disasters and Displacement: Homes for Lost Homes, Lands for Lost Lands. Pages 119–132 *in*: J.M.Guzmán, G. Martine, G. McGranahan, D. Schensul, and C.Tacoli, editors. *Population Dynamics and Climate Change.* New York and London, United Nations Population Fund and International Institute for Environment and Development.

Montevideo Convention on the Rights and Duties of States (1934) *opened for signature* July 13, 1934 (entered into force December 26, 1934).

Moyn, S. 2010. *The Last Utopia: Human Rights in History.* Cambridge, MA: Harvard University Press.

Nicholls, R.J., and Cazenave, A. (2010) Sea-level rise and its impact on coastal zones. *Science* 328 (1517).

NOAA National Centers for Environmental Information, State of the Climate: National Overview for Annual 2016 (2017) retrieved as of January 25, 2017, www.ncdc.noaa.gov/soc/national/201613.

NSIDC (National Snow and Ice Data Center) (2016) Arctic Sea Ice News & Analysis, published online March 2016, retrieved May 14, 2016 fromhttps://nsidc.org/arcticseaicenews/2016/03/

Oliver-Smith, A. (2009) Introduction. In: A.Oliver-Smith, editor *Development & Dispossession* Santa Fe, NM: School for Advanced Research Press.

Shulski, M., and Wendler, G. (2007) *The Climate of Alaska.* Anchorage, AK: University of Alaska Press.

UN (1951). *UN Convention Relating to the Status of Refugees.* New York: United Nations General Assembly.

UN (1948) *Universal Declaration of Human Rights.* New York: United Nations General Assembly.

UN (1967) *Protocol Relating to the Status of Refugees.* New York: United Nations General Assembly.

UNFCCC (UN Framework Convention on Climate Change) (1992) *Framework Convention on Climate Change*. New York: United Nations General Assembly.

UN (2006). *Convention for the Safeguarding of the Intangible Cultural Heritage*. New York: United Nations General Assembly.

UN (2007). Universal Declaration on the Rights of Indigenous Peoples. New York: United Nations General Assembly.

UN Committee on Economic, Social and Cultural Rights (1991) Fact Sheet No. 16 (Rev. 1) 4.

UN Economic and Social Council (2006) Specific Groups and Individuals: Mass Exoduses and Displaced Persons, Report of the Representative of the Secretary-General on the human rights of internally displaced persons, Walter Kalin, COMMISSION ON HUMAN RIGHTS, sixty-second session, E/CN.4/2006/71

UN General Assembly Resolution (2005) 60/1, UN Doc A/Res/60/1, October 24.

UNHCR (United Nations High Commissioner on Refugees) (1998) *Guiding Principles on Internal Displacement*, E/CN.4/1998/53/Add.2

USACE (United States Army Corps of Engineers) (2006). Relocation Planning Project Master Plan: Kivalina, Alaska. http://www.poa.usace.army.mil/Portals/34/docs/civilworks/reports/KivalinaMasterPlanMainReportJune2006.pdf

USACE (2008a) Revised environmental assessment: Finding of no significant impact: Newtok Evacuation Center: Mertarvik, Nelson Island, Alaska. (U.S. Army Corps of Engineers, Alaska, Anchorage), www.commerce.state.ak.us/dca/planning/pub/Newtok_Evacuation_Center_EA_&_FONSI_July_08.pdf.

USACE (2008b) Section 117 Project fact sheet. (U.S. Army Corps of Engineers, Alaska, Anchorage), www.commerce.state.ak.us/dca/planning/pub/Newtok_Sec_117.pdf.

United States Congress Bicameral Task Force on Climate Change (2013) *Implementing the President's Action Plan: U.S. Department of the Interior*. Washington, DC: United States Congress.

Walsh, J.E., Anisimov, O., Hagen, J.O.M., Jakobsson, T., Oerlemans, J. Prowse, T.D., Romanovsky, V., Savelieva, N., Serreze, M., Shiklomanov, A., Shiklomanov, I., Solomon S., Arendt, A., Atkinson, D., Demuth, M.N., Dowdeswell, J., Dyurgerov, M., Glazovsky, A., Koerner, R.M., Meier, M., Reeh, N., Sigurosson, O., Steffen, K., and Truffer, M. (2015) Cryosphere and Hydrology In *Arctic Climate Impact Assessment*. New York: Cambridge University Press.

White House (2014) *President's State, Local and Tribal Leader's Task Force on Climate Preparedness and Resilience, Recommendations to the President*. Washington, DC: White House.

World Bank (2004) *Involuntary Resettlement Sourcebook: Planning and Implementation in Development Projects*. Washington, DC: World Bank.

Zetter, R. (2010) Protecting People Displaced by Climate Change: Some Conceptual Challenges. In: McAdam, J. (ed.) *Climate Change and Displacement: Multi-Disciplinary Perspectives*, Oxford: Hart Publishing.

31

UNHCR's perspectives and activities on displacement in the context of climate change

Marine Franck

Climate change and displacement are intrinsically and increasingly linked, and have long been of concern to the Office of the United Nations High Commissioner for Refugees (UNHCR), consistent with its protection responsibilities for refugees, stateless persons and internally displaced persons.

A 2009 United Nations Environment Programme (UNEP) study suggested that between 1990 and 2009, there had been at least 18 violent conflicts fuelled by natural resources exploitation and that natural resources-related conflicts experienced an earlier and higher probability of relapse than others.[1]

More broadly, disasters linked to natural hazards, including the adverse impacts of climate change, are also drivers of contemporary displacement. Disaster displacement often occurs in the context of natural hazards such as earthquakes, tropical storms, drought, tsunamis, flooding, glacial lake outburst floods and landslides. The fifth report of the United Nations Intergovernmental Panel on Climate Change[2] projects that the effects of climate change will increase the displacement of people. In addition, populations lacking the resources for voluntary migration are often more exposed to extreme weather events, particularly in low-income developing countries.

The Nansen Initiative's Protection Agenda, the Sendai Framework for Disaster Risk Reduction Framework 2015–2030 and the UNFCCC COP 21 meeting in Paris in December 2015 represent important milestones in clarifying the displacement-related implications of natural hazards, disasters and climate change, and the manner in which States can marshal international support for responses going beyond "humanitarian approaches". One of the most important lessons derived from the Nansen Initiative is that States *can* prevent and prepare for increased disaster displacement in the future when the right policies are in place.

Between 2008 and 2015, more than 203.4 million people were displaced by disasterse (IDMC GRID 2016). The likelihood of being displaced by disasters has doubled since the 1970s. Looking to the future, there is high agreement among scientists that disasters are expected to become more frequent and more severe. Climate change, in combination with other factors, is projected to contribute to increased displacement.

The vast majority of displacement associated with disasters in 2015 took place in low and lower-middle income economies (IDMC GRID 2016). These countries have relatively little capacity to meet the protection and assistance needs of internally displaced persons (IDPs), or to invest in climate adaptation and disaster risk reduction measures that would either prevent displacement or mitigate the impacts of disasters.

Climate change can also exacerbate competition over scarce resources such as water, food and energy, and act as an accelerator of armed conflict. Environmental degradation is among factors behind many of today's conflicts, from Darfur to Somalia to Iraq and Syria. Climate change sows seeds for conflict which may result in displacement, but it also makes displacement much worse when it happens.

The vast majority of people displaced in this context are internally displaced. If they cross a border, they are not normally considered refugees under the 1951 Convention on the Status of Refugees. The 1951 Convention describes a "well-founded fear of persecution" based on five grounds: race, religion, nationality, membership of a particular social group and political opinion.[3] There is a legal gap to assist and protect people who cross borders in the context of disasters and climate change.

UNHCR believes the response to address the whole spectrum of human mobility (from voluntary migration to forced displacement) in the context of disasters and climate change requires consultation and coordination with different inter-agency or state-led initiatives that address climate change and disaster displacement. UNHCR's particular role and expertise lies in protection of people displaced internally and across borders.

From 2013 to 2016, UNHCR has coordinated the informal Advisory Group on Climate Change and Human Mobility composed of the International Organization for Migration (IOM), the United Nations University Institute for Environment and Human Security (UNU-EHS), the United Nations Development Programme (UNDP), the Norwegian Refugee Council and its Internal Displacement Monitoring Centre (NRC/IDMC), Refugees International (RI), the University of Liège (ULg) and the Arab Network for Environment and Development (RAED), which shares most recent available knowledge with UNFCCC parties. UNHCR, through the Advisory Group, has been instrumental in securing human mobility language in the COP 21 Paris Agreement including the creation of a task force on displacement within the Warsaw International Mechanism, which has the objective to develop recommendations to avert, minimize and address displacement.

UNHCR has been actively involved in the work of the High-Level Committee on Programmes (HLCP) working group on climate change (WGCC). The One UN strategy of the WGCC has proved efficiency in bringing together various stakeholders to collaborate on climate change and human mobility under the leadership of UNHCR and IOM. In the UNFCCC Lima COP 20 (2014) and Paris COP 21 (2015), UNHCR and IOM have run joint exhibit booth to disseminate relevant publications and have organized high-level side events together with other UN and non-UN partners to alert and provide guidance on ways to avert, minimize and address climate-related displacement.

People who are *internally displaced* in the context of climate change and disasters are in need of timely assistance and protection alongside durable solutions. People who are displaced within their countries are legally protected by national laws and international humanitarian and human rights law, as reflected in the Guiding Principles on Internal Displacement and, in the case of Africa, by the African Union Convention for the Protection and Assistance of Internally Displaced Persons in Africa (the Kampala Convention) that specifically addresses internal displacement caused by natural disasters. Internally displaced persons – whether they return to their homes, settle elsewhere in the country or try to integrate locally where they are displaced – usually face continuing problems and risks, and require support beyond the acute crisis period of a disaster. Achieving a solution is therefore a gradual and complex process requiring timely and coordinated efforts to address humanitarian, development and human rights concerns, including measures to prepare for or prevent further displacement.

Under the arrangements for IDPs, UNHCR is the Global Protection Cluster lead. However, at the country level in disaster situations or complex emergencies without significant displacement, the three protection-mandated agencies (UNHCR, UNICEF and OHCHR) will consult closely (including with the RC or HC) and agree which agency among the three intervene depending on specific contexts. UNHCR provided protection and shelter coordination during the response to the earthquake in Haiti in 2010, the droughts in Somalia from 2011–2012, floods in Pakistan in 2010 and 2012, storms and flooding in Myanmar in 2013, typhoons in the Philippines in 2011 and 2013, the floods and landslides in Afghanistan in 2014 and floods in Malawi and Mozambique in 2015, among others.

Enhancing the resilience of people of concern and the communities hosting them is also a concern to UNHCR as a means to avoid secondary displacement. Beginning in the 1990s, UNHCR became increasingly aware of the environmental challenges associated with hosting a large population in a small area. Competition over scarce natural resource, such as firewood, water and grazing land, has the potential to generate animosity and occasionally to spark friction or conflict between refugees and host communities.

In some cases, the impacts of climate change may make life unsustainable or render certain areas uninhabitable owing to high exposure to extreme or frequent hazards or by severely limiting livelihoods options. In all cases, States must prioritize appropriate mitigation, adaptation and other preventative measures to allow populations at risk of displacement to remain in their homes. However, in some cases, States will need to take measures to protect people who are at risk of displacement due to climate change-related hazards and permanently relocate them to safer areas.

Planned relocation, if implemented in consultation with, and with respect for the rights of, the people and communities involved can protect vulnerable populations from climate risks and impacts through settling them in safer, more secure locations. However, where not properly planned and implemented, relocation can result in protracted or secondary displacement and related human rights violations. Where planned relocation related to climate change cannot be avoided, its scale should be minimized and the process should always involve affected communities, fully protect their rights, and support them to fully restore their standard of living. UNHCR, the Brookings Institution and Georgetown University's Institute for the Study of International Migration (ISIM) and IOM have drafted with relevant stakeholders guidance to the effect that planned relocation is a participatory rights-based process, involving both relocating and host communities, and taking into consideration their specific needs, rights and conditions of vulnerability.

In the case of *cross-border displacement in the context of climate change and disasters*, rather than calling for a new binding international convention on cross-border disaster displacement, UNHCR supports an approach that focuses on the integration of effective practices by States and (sub-) regional organizations into their own normative frameworks and practices in accordance with their specific situations and challenges.

UNHCR was closely engaged in the Nansen Initiative (2012–2015), a State-led, bottom-up consultative process intended to build consensus on key principles and elements to address the protection and assistance needs of persons displaced across borders in the context of disasters, including the adverse effects of climate change. A key outcome of this process is the Agenda for the Protection of Cross-Border Displaced Persons in the Context of Disasters and Climate

Change (Protection Agenda), which presents a comprehensive approach on how to both prevent and address disaster displacement (both internal and cross-border). It highlights the need for policy integration and enhanced coordination across humanitarian response, disaster risk reduction, climate change adaptation and development action areas. The Protection Agenda consolidates a broad set of effective practices and policy options that can be used by States and others to reduce and manage disaster displacement, and to better protect and assist disaster displaced persons.

The Platform on Disaster Displacement was launched at Wold Humanitarian Summit on 23 May 2016 and started work on 1 July 2016 with the objective to follow up on the Nansen Initiative and to implement the recommendations of the Protection Agenda, with the aim to better prevent an prepare for displacement and to respond to situations when people are forced to flee across a border. The Platform builds partnerships between policymakers, practitioners and researchers and constitutes a multi-stakeholder forum for dialogue and information sharing, as well as policy and normative development.

It also works with UNHCR and continues to consolidate, enhance use and further the application of Humanitarian Protection Measures, including UNHCR's Guidelines on Temporary Protection or Stay Arrangements (TPSAs) as responses to humanitarian crises and complex or mixed population movements. UNHCR formally involved in this Platform's institutional arrangements.

Overall, UNHCR is committed to working closely with States and relevant stakeholders in addressing this issue, hand in hand, in particular to avert and minimize displacement and to better protect and assist disaster-displaced children, women and men.

For more information:

- UNHCR's Environment, Disasters and Climate Change web portal: www.unhcr.org/environment-disasters-and-climate-change.html
- UNHCR, the environment and climate change Overview report, 2015: www.unhcr.org/unhcr-climate-change-overview.html
- UNHCR's Guidelines on Temporary Protection or Stay Arrangements www.unhcr.org/protection/environment/542e99fd9/unhcr-temporary-protection-stay-arrangements-2014.html
- Guidance on Planned Relocation www.unhcr.org/protection/environment/562f798d9/planned-relocation-guidance-october-2015.html
- Latest submission to the UNFCCC www.unhcr.org/protection/environment/57459e3d7/warsaw-international-mechanism-executive-committee-wim-excom-work-plan.html
- IDMC Global Report on Internal Displacement (GRID) 2016: www.internal-displacement.org/globalreport2016/
- Platform on Disaster Displacement website www.disasterdisplacement.org
- Nansen Initiative website https://nanseninitiative.org/
- Global Protection Cluster web portal: www.globalprotectioncluster.org/en/tools-and-guidance/essential-protection-guidance-and-tools/protection-in-natural-disasters-essential-guidance-and-tools.html

Notes

1 United Nations Environment Programme (UNEP), *From Conflict to Peacebuilding: The Role of Natural Resources and the Environment*, 2009, p. 5, cited in United Nations, *The Challenge of Sustaining Peace*, Report of the Advisory Group of Experts for the 2015 review of the United Nations

peacebuilding architecture, 29 June 2015, p. 15, available at www.un.org/pga/wp-content/uploads/ sites/3/2015/07/300615_The-Challenge-of-Sustaining-Peace.pdf.

2 Intergovernmental Panel on Climate Change (IPCC), *Climate Change 2014 Synthesis Report: Summary for Policymakers*, 2014, available at www.ipcc.ch/pdf/assessment-report/ar5/syr/AR5_SYR_FINAL_ SPM.pdf.

3 United Nations High Commissioners for Refugees (UNHCR), *Handbook and guidelines on procedures and criteria for determining refugee status*, 2011, p. 11- p. 19, available at http://www.unhcr.org/3d58e13b4. pdf.

32

Environmental change and human mobility

Perspectives from the World Bank

Susan F. Martin, Jonas Bergmann, Hanspeter Wyss and Kanta Kumari Rigaud

Introduction

Human mobility in the context of environmental change is a critical issue from a development perspective. This holds true both against the background of the Sustainable Development Goals (SDGs) as well as of the World Bank's twin goals of eradicating extreme poverty and boosting shared prosperity. As a result, the World Bank's Global Knowledge Partnership on Migration and Development (KNOMAD) established a thematic working group on environmental change and migration, displacement and relocation that aims to improve the evidence base for policy making and practice in this critical area. Deriving sustainable solutions for individuals, households and communities affected by environmental change requires improved understanding of the ways in which environmental change, in conjunction with other stressors, intersects with development to make people more or less vulnerable or resilient to both acute environmental events and ongoing environmental processes. The converse is also true; there is need for greater understanding of the ways that migration, displacement and planned relocation affect the resilience and vulnerability of those who move in the context of environmental change. This chapter first expands on this understanding of the nexus between environmental change, human mobility and development. It then outlines the general approach of the World Bank to this nexus and some selected specific activities in which the World Bank is engaged related to environmental migration, displacement and planned relocation.

The nexus between environmental change, mobility and development

The linkages between environmental change, human mobility and development are significant.

First, human mobility is already an important global phenomenon with substantial development implications. In the case of displacement, for instance, development concerns complement humanitarian short-term responses, but transcend them in scope and time horizon. The World Bank has published two reports on the linkages of development and mobility (World Bank 2016a, 2016b) as well as guidance on preventive resettlement and population retreat from at-risk areas (Correa et al. 2011, Koskinen-Lewis et al. 2016). They highlight that migrants as well as displaced and relocated persons have their own specific vulnerabilities, yet also present specific potentials that require tailored approaches in order to maximize their sustainable development prospects as well as those of their host communities.

Second, while a share of the global movements of people has traditionally occurred in the context of environmental influences, climate change will significantly alter the magnitude of environmental degradation and hazards that human beings and systems face (IPCC 2014; World Bank 2014). Climate change will increase risks from both slow-onset and sudden-onset hazards that work together with other stressors such as pollution, often in areas with growing populations. The scientific community has therefore emphasized the potential role of climate change on current and future patterns of human movements (IPCC 2014).

Third, this amplification of risks through climate change is particularly concerning for development actors, since vulnerability to climate impacts is highest in poorer countries (ND-GAIN 2017; WRI 2016). Most migration and displacement in the context of changing environments and climate variability over the past two decades has happened in less wealthy countries outside of the Organisation for Economic Co-operation and Development (OECD) (McLeman et al. 2016). Lower adaptive capacities, already stretched resources and weak governance systems, often combined with population growth, higher exposure and sensitivity, make distress migration and displacement as well as planned relocation more probable and challenging in many low and middle-income countries. They need better mechanisms to identify vulnerabilities as early as possible, as well as resources to enhance benefits and reduce costs associated with movements.

Fourth, both mobility and non-mobility related to environmental change have important implications for the vulnerability and resilience of concerned populations that need to be managed carefully (Martin & Bergmann, 2017). Some of the development potentials and challenges associated with movements in the context of environmental change are known (Martin 2010); they often resemble those of labor migration, irregular migration, forced displacement or development-induced resettlement. On the one hand, the occurrences of slow-onset and sudden-onset disasters are intrinsically tied to poverty; on the other, disasters perpetuate or create poverty (Hallegatte et al. 2017). A natural hazard can turn into a disaster depending on the characteristics of the event and the exposure, but also on the underlying vulnerability of affected populations. Poor people will frequently be affected more detrimentally by environmental change: Their livelihoods often depend directly on increasingly threatened ecosystem goods and services. They are nearly twice as likely to live in fragile housing in vulnerable areas, often work in sectors highly susceptible to climate impacts, and tend to receive less recovery support after disasters (idem).

The development implications of the environmental change-mobility nexus are complex and require a nuanced approach. On the one hand, pre-existing levels of vulnerability and resilience mediate the extent to which environmental changes cause movement as well as the types of mobility that occur. On the other hand, mobility itself affects the vulnerability and resilience of those who move, their families and host communities (Martin & Bergmann, 2017). For some of the people facing increasing climate pressures and limited options to adapt in place, migration can be an adaptation strategy (Adger et al. 2014, McLeman 2016), as recognized by the Intergovernmental Panel on Climate Change (IPCC) and in the Cancún Adaptation Framework of the UN Framework Convention on Climate Change (UNFCCC). Under positive circumstances, migration helps affected individuals to move out of harm's way and secure livelihoods despite adverse environmental conditions (Foresight 2011). It is often also seen as a household and community risk management strategy that builds resilience by providing diversified sources of income (Mohapatra et al. 2012).

In more negative circumstances, however, environmental change can lead to movements that increase vulnerabilities. Past experience shows that planned relocation of at-risk populations, similarly to resettlement, brings about substantial risks for human security (Cernea & McDowell, 2000). Risks also tend to be high when movements occur unexpectedly and in distress, as is often the case with displacement (Melde, Laczko, and Gemenne 2017). However, less desperate examples of movements can also entail increasing risks of human rights violations and human insecurity, poverty, loss of social and cultural ties, and other adverse consequences. This is particularly true under a changing climate: On the one hand, people are expected to continue moving into locations that are themselves at high risk from climate impacts such as coastal cities with already stretched resources (Foresight 2011). On the other hand, with the lack of political will to bridge current gaps in protection frameworks for displacement related to environmental change likely to persist, risks will be particularly acute for those compelled to move outside regular pathways.

Finally, the most vulnerable groups tend to have least opportunities to adapt locally or move away from risk, and when moving they tend to do so under adverse circumstances (Adger et al. 2014: 767). Maladaptation, as well as lacking means or failure to adapt, can lead to situations where people are unable or unwilling to move away from risks. These groups will experience drastic pressures on their resilience and wellbeing (Foresight 2011).

Engagement by the World Bank

From a development perspective, these implications for the vulnerability and resilience of large populations must be taken seriously in view of achieving the SDGs and the World Bank's twin goals on poverty reduction and shared prosperity. While the issue has recently come to feature prominently in national, regional and international debate (Gemenne et al. 2016), it is still insufficiently incorporated in long-term development planning for climate resilience. There is need for more evidence-based knowledge and norm setting in this area if the international community is to be prepared to address human mobility in the context of climate change adequately.

The World Bank engages with environmental mobility through research and financing. Through the Climate Change Action Plan, it (2016c: 1) commits to "scaling up climate action, integrating climate change across its operations, and working more closely with others." In Africa, for instance, some of the key activities include the Africa Climate Business Plan (World Bank 2016d), community based adaptation schemes, as well as planning the investment phase of the West Africa Coastal Erosion Response. Separately, the World Bank has also supported $748 million of lending operations on migration over the past 15 years. A range of migration projects address, among other things, skill development, job search, recruitment and placement, access to social and public services in the destination and origin countries, and protection of workers' rights (Word Bank 2016b). In its 2016 replenishment, the World Bank's fund for the poorest (the International Development Association's IDA18) established a regional sub-window for refugees, pledging $2 billion additional financing for refugees and their host communities. It also announced a $2.5 billion effort to enhance job creation and quality especially for high-risk contexts such as migration (World Bank 2016e).

In terms of research, several World Bank reports provide insights into the environmental change-mobility nexus. The "Turn Down the Heat" Series (World Bank 2012, 2014; PIK 2013) showed that the Middle East and North Africa will likely face accelerated migration flows to urban areas and social conflict because of climate change. Latin America and the Caribbean will experience climate impacts that can trigger displacement and migration from agricultural communities, while Southeast Asia will see significant coastal impacts on natural resources that put pressures on coastal cities. The Shock Waves report (Hallegatte et al. 2015) showed that migration and remittances can play a key role in managing shocks. Yet migration requires resources and assets that the poorest lack, and remittances tend to benefit non-poor people more than poor people. The "High and Dry" study (World Bank 2016f: 19) explored the "thirsty origins of migration and conflict" due to increases in water variability and expanding water deficits with climate change. It showed that a 1 percent reduction in precipitation is associated with a 0.59 percent increase in the urbanization rate. The "Confronting Drought in Africa's Drylands" report (Cervigni & Morris 2016) found that investments in drylands can only secure resilient livelihoods for about half of the people in their place of habitual residence in the region. Another recent report investigated the impact of natural disasters on the poor and showed that increasing resilience of affected populations "is good economics" over the long-term (Hallegatte et al. 2017: 11). Work is underway at the World Bank to characterize how much, where, and when internal migration patterns could be influenced by slow-onset climate change impacts, in an effort to inform upstream dialogue and the longer-term planning for climate resilient development.

KNOMAD's activities are embedded in the broader World Bank actions on climate change and development. KNOMAD's thematic working group on environmental change and migration has focused its work on several dimensions of the nexus, including the determinants of movements and the impacts of mobility on those who move, those who are left behind and those in host communities. It has been investing in its three objectives, namely a) increasing understanding of the impact of environmental change on migration through a combination of stock taking of the literature, expert consultation, research and stakeholder dialogue; b) increasing policy-relevant knowledge and information on environmental change and migration; and c) ensuring that knowledge on the relationship between environmental change and migration is available to policy-makers within the World Bank, other international organizations, governments and nongovernmental organizations.

In particular, KNOMAD has aimed to strengthen the evidence base by improving data and methodologies for understanding the linkages between environmental change and mobility (e.g. KNOMAD 2014, 2015a; Banerjee et al. 2017; Bylander 2016; Zickgraf et al. 2016; Martin & Bergmann 2017). KNOMAD's activities have emphasized the need for longitudinal and quantitatively sound research on the long-term impacts of climate change on human mobility (KNOMAD 2015b, 2016). Longitudinal research is particularly important in understanding the effects of slow-onset environmental processes, such as rising sea levels, and recurrent acute environmental events, such as floods and cyclones, by identifying tipping points influencing the decision to migrate. Such research designs would also improve understanding of the long-term effects of different migration-related adaptation strategies. These strategies may aim at reducing emigration pressures to permit people to remain in place where sensible, while also facilitate migration as part of a mix of strategies to promote adaptive capacity where needed. Understanding the long-term impacts of these adaptation and resilience building initiatives will help policymakers and practitioners undertake better planning and implementation.

KNOMAD has also focused on the ways in which resilience and vulnerability affect and are affected by mobility, with a particular interest in how to ensure that the most vulnerable are protected. In this context, KNOMAD has sought to improve understanding of South-South movements, both internal and cross-border, recognizing that the vast majority of affected persons will move internally or into other developing countries. Drawing from the experience of the World Bank with resettlement in context of development projects, KNOMAD has collaborated with several partners to develop guidelines and a toolbox on planned in the context of environmental change as well as helping governments improve their related planning processes and institutional frameworks (Brookings Institution, Georgetown University, and UNHCR 2015; UNHCR, Georgetown University, and IOM 2017).

In conclusion, approaching migration, displacement and relocation related to environmental change from an explicit development perspective provides an indispensable lens. Human mobility in general is already an important global phenomenon with significant development implications and increasingly approached from a development perspective. While a share of the global movements of people has traditionally occurred in the context of environmental influences, climate change will significantly alter the magnitude of environmental degradation and hazards that human beings and systems face. This amplification of risks through climate change is particularly concerning from a development perspective, since on the one hand, vulnerability to climate impacts is highest in poorer countries. On the other hand, both mobility and non-mobility related to environmental change have important implications for the vulnerability and resilience of large numbers of concerned people that need to be managed thoughtfully. The development challenge implied here is complex and requires a nuanced approach; it must not be ignored if the international community is to meet the Sustainable Development Goals and the World Bank's twin goals on poverty reduction and shared prosperity.

Acknowledgements

Paivi Koskinen, Senior Social Development Specialist, and Andrew Roberts, Senior Operations Officer, both with Social Urban, Rural and Resilience Global Practice at the World Bank, are thanked for their constructive comments on this chapter.

References

Adger, W.N.; J.M. Pulhin; J. Barnett; G.D. Dabelko; G.K. Hovelsrud; M. Levy; Ú. Oswald Spring & C.H. Vogel. 2014. "Human security." in *Climate Change 2014: Impacts, Adaptation, and Vulnerability. Part A: Global and Sectoral Aspects. Contribution of Working Group II to the Fifth Assessment Report of the Intergovernmental Panel on Climate Change* Cambridge University Press, Cambridge, United Kingdom and New York, NY, USA, pp. 755–791.

Banerjee, S.; D. Kniveton; R. Black; S. Bisht; P. Jyoti Das; B. Mahapatra; S. Tuladhar. 2017. Do Financial Remittances Build Household-Level Adaptive Capacity? A Case Study of Flood-Affected Households in India. KNOMAD Working Paper 16, January 2017.

Brookings Institution, Georgetown University, and UNHCR. 2015. *Guidance on Protecting People from Disasters and Environmental Change through Planned Relocation.* Available at: http://www.unhcr.org/protection/environment/562f798d9/planned-relocation-guidance-october-2015.html.

Bylander, M. 2016. Cambodian Migration to Thailand: The Role of Environmental Shocks and Stress, KNOMAD Working Paper 7, January 2016. Available at www.knomad.org/publications.

Cernea, M. M. & McDowell, C., 2000. *Risks and Reconstruction. Experiences of Resettlers and Refugees.* Washington, DC: World Bank.

Cervigni, R. & Morris, M., 2016. *Confronting Drought in Africa's Drylands: Opportunities for Enhancing Resilience.* Washington, DC: World Bank; and Agence Française de Développement. Available at: https://openknowledge.worldbank.org/handle/10986/23576.

Correa, E.; F. Ramírez & H. Sanahuja, 2011. *Populations at Risk of Disaster: A Resettlement Guide.* Washington, DC: World Bank & GFDRR.

Foresight, 2011. *Migration and Global Environmental Change: Future Challenges and Opportunities.* Government Office for Science. Available at: www.gov.uk/government/uploads/system/uploads/attachment_data/file/287717/11-1116-migration-and-global-environmental-change.pdf.

Gemenne, F., Zickgraf, C. & Ionesco, D., 2016. *The State of Environmental Migration 2016 — a Review of 2015.* ESSAIS. Presses Universitaires de Liège.

Hallegatte, S.; M. Bangalore; L. Bonzanigo; M. Fay; T. Kane; U. Narloch; J. Rozenberg; D. Treguer & A. Vogt-Schilb, 2015. *Shock Waves: Managing the Impacts of Climate Change on Poverty*. Washington, DC: World Bank Publications.

Hallegatte, S.; A. Vogt-Schilb; M. Bangalore; J. Rozenberg, 2017. *Unbreakable: Building the Resilience of the Poor in the Face of Natural Disasters*. Washington, DC. Available at: https://openknowledge.worldbank.org/handle/10986/25335.

IPCC, 2014. Climate Change 2014: Impacts, Adaptation, and Vulnerability. Part A: Global and Sectoral Aspects. Contribution of Working Group II to the Fifth Assessment Report of the Intergovernmental Panel on Climate Change [Field, C.B., V.R. Barros, D.J. Dokken, K.J. Mach, M.D. Mastrandrea, T.E. Bilir, M. Chatterjee, K.L. Ebi, Y.O. Estrada, R.C. Genova, B. Girma, E.S. Kissel, A.N. Levy, S. MacCracken, P.R. Mastrandrea, and L.L. White (eds.)]. Cambridge University Press, Cambridge, United Kingdom and New York, NY, USA, 1132 pp.

KNOMAD, 2014. International Symposium on Environmental Change and Migration, May 28–29 2014, Symposium Report. Available at: www.knomad.org/thematic-working-groups/environmental-change-and-migration.

KNOMAD, 2015a. Environmental Change and Migration: State of the Evidence. Bibliography available at www.knomad.org/docs/environmental_change/Environmental%20Change%20and%20Migration%20Literature%20Review.pdf.

KNOMAD, 2015b. Longitudinal Research on Environmental Change and Migration, Report of the Seminar, March 19–20, 2015. Available at: www.knomad.org/thematic working groups/environmental-change-and-migration. KNOMAD, 2016. Quantitative Assessments of Environmentally-Induced Migration, Report of Seminar, May 9–10, 2016. Available at www.knomad.org/thematic-working-groups/environmental-change-and-migration.

KNOMAD. 2016. *Summary Report on Workshop 'Quantitative Assessment of Environmentally-Induced Migration' May 9/10, 2016*. Washington, D.C. Available at http://www.knomad.org/sites/default/files/2017-03/KNOMAD%20Workshop_QuantitativeAssessments_Report%20May%202016%28final%20version%29.pdf.

Koskinen-Lewis, P., A. de Carvalho; C. M. Dias; C. Fernandes; O. Diogo; L. Taulealo; F. Evalu & N. Simi, 2016. Managing Population Retreat from At-Risk Areas. SISRI Knowledge note no. 3. Small Island States Resilience Initiative. The World Bank and Global Facility for Disaster Reduction and Recovery (GFDRR). Washington, DC.

Martin, S. F., 2010. Climate Change, Migration, and Governance. *Global Governance*, 16(3), pp. 397–414. www.jstor.org/stable/29764954.

Martin, S. F. & Bergmann, J., 2017. *Environmental Change and Human Mobility: Reducing Vulnerability and Increasing Resilience*. KNOMAD Policy Brief, 6 April.

McLeman, Robert A. 2016. "Migration as Adaptation: Conceptual Origins, Recent Developments, and Future Directions." In *Migration, Risk Management and Climate Change: Evidence and Policy Responses*, edited by A. Milan, B. Schraven, K. Warner, and N. Cascone. Dordrecht.

McLeman, R.; M. Opatowski; B. Borova & M. Walton-Roberts, 2016. Environmental migration and displacement. What we know and don't know. Available at: www.laurierenvironmentalmigration.com/wp-content/uploads/2015/11/WLU-Environmental-Migration-Background-Report.pdf.

Melde, S., Laczko, F. & Gemenne, F. (eds.). 2017. *Making Mobility Work For Adaptation to Environmental Changes*. IOM 2017, Geneva.

Mohapatra, S., Joseph, G. and Ratha, D., 2012. Remittances and natural disasters: ex-post response and contribution to ex-ante preparedness." *Environment, Development and Sustainability* 14(3), pp. 365–387.

ND-GAIN, 2017. Notre Dame Global Adaptation Index, section vulnerability, data from 2015. Available at: http://index.gain.org/ranking/vulnerability.

PIK, 2013. *Potsdam Institute for Climate Impact Research and Climate Analytics. Turn Down the Heat: Climate Extremes, Regional Impacts, and the Case for Resilience*. Washington, DC: World Bank. Available at: https://openknowledge.worldbank.org/handle/10986/14000.

UNHCR, Georgetown University, and IOM. 2017. *A toolbox: Planning Relocations to Protect People from Disasters and Environmental Change*. Available at: http://www.unhcr.org/596f1bb47.pdf.

World Bank. 2012. *Turn Down the Heat: Why a 4°C Warmer World Must Be Avoided.* Washington, DC. Available at: https://openknowledge.worldbank.org/handle/10986/11860.

World Bank, 2014. *Turn Down the Heat: Confronting the New Climate Normal.* Washington, DC: World Bank. Available at: https://openknowledge.worldbank.org/handle/10986/20595.

World Bank, 2016a. *Forcibly Displaced: Toward a Development Approach Supporting Refugees, the Internally Displaced, and Their Hosts.* Washington, DC: World Bank. Available at: https://openknowledge.worldbank.org/handle/10986/25016.

World Bank, 2016b. *Migration and Development: A Role for the World Bank.* Washington, DC: World Bank. Available at: http://pubdocs.worldbank.org/en/468881473870347506/Migration-and-Development-Report-Sept2016.pdf.

World Bank, 2016c. *World Bank Group Climate Action Plan 2016-2020.* April 7, 2016. Available at: https://openknowledge.worldbank.org/bitstream/handle/10986/24451/K8860.pdf?sequence=2.

World Bank, 2016d. *Accelerating Climate-Resilient and Low-Carbon Development — The Africa Climate Business Plan.* Available at http://documents.worldbank.org/curated/en/401711468185370301/pdf/101130-REPLACEMENT-FILE-SAME-BOX-PUBLIC-K8545.pdf.

World Bank, 2016e. *Global Community Makes Record $75 Billion Commitment to End Extreme Poverty.* Press Release, December 15, 2016.

World Bank, 2016f. *High and Dry: Climate Change, Water, and the Economy.* Washington, DC: World Bank. Available at: https://openknowledge.worldbank.org/handle/10986/23665.

WRI, 2016. *World Risk Report 2016. Alliance Development Works & UNU-EHS.* Available at: http://weltrisikobericht.de/wp-content/uploads/2016/08/WorldRiskReport2016.pdf.

Zickgraf, C.; S. Vigil; F. de Longueville; P. Ozer & F. Gemenne, 2016. The Impact of Vulnerability and Resilience to Environmental Changes on Mobility Patterns in West Africa, KNOMAD Working Paper 14; Available at www.knomad.org/publications.

33

Human mobility in the Anthropocene

Perspectives from UN Environment

Oli Brown and Brian Wittbold

Introduction

We live in an era of unprecedented human mobility: movement of ideas, values, money and, increasingly, of people. Increased human mobility and migration in the twenty-first century is spurred by, and also drives, economic growth and interdependency at the national, regional and global levels. 250 million people live and work outside the country of their birth, while 750 million people migrate within their own countries (World Bank, 2015).

When properly managed, migration has immense potential as a driver of human development and progress, spreading ideas and connecting the world. However, when migration is unmanaged and people are forced from their homes as result of negligence, crisis or compulsion, the issue can become politically divisive and societies forego the tremendous benefits that migration can otherwise offer. Indeed, protracted violent conflicts, climatic pressures and meteorological disasters have contributed to an upsurge in displacement and forced migration in recent years, adding urgency and complexity to the current global discussion on migration and displacement.

By mid-2017, an unprecedented 65.6 million people around the world had been forced from their homes, including nearly 21.3 million refugees (UNHCR, 2017). Fleeing from war, persecution and unmitigated destitution in Yemen, Syria, Iraq, Afghanistan, the Democratic Republic of Congo and elsewhere, affected populations have continued to surge as conflict and violence endure and new crises emerge. Nearly 7 million new cases of internal displacement due to conflict were recorded 2016. Analysis of civil wars over the past 70 years indicate that at least 40 per cent are linked to the contested control or use of natural resources such as land, water, minerals or oil (UNEP, 2009). The effects are not limited to countries directly involved in conflicts, but reverberate across regions with destabilizing consequences. Globally, the burden of hosting refugees is disproportionately shared, with a mere six countries hosting over one-third of the world's total refugee population.[1]

As the magnitude of conflict-induced displacement continued togrow at an unprecedented rate between 2011 and 2015, annual displacement attributable to natural disasters now accounts for a far greater proportion of the global caseload of people forced to leave their homes. Research shows that since 2008, disasters have displaced an average of 26.4 million people each year – the equivalent to one person per second (IFRC, 2016). In 2016 alone, some 24.2 million people were displaced by disasters brought on by sudden-onset natural hazards in 118 countries and territories (IDMC, 2017: 31). While it is increasingly difficult to determine the immediate causes of displacement and disentangle the various social, political, environmental and economic drivers of conflicts and disasters, these staggering statistics attest to the truly global scale of a challenge faced by developing and developed countries alike.

Indeed, recent demographic trends across the globe put humanity on a crash course with disasters that will undoubtedly be accompanied by increased displacement. Rapid population growth and our activities have upset ecological balances and pushed planetary boundaries so profoundly that scientists now suggest that we have entered "the Anthropocene", a new geological epoch that recognizes humans as the dominant influence on the climate and environment. With the human population predicted to peak at more than 9 billion by the middle of this century, this new epoch is characterized by a state of ecological disequilibrium that is likely to bear witness to the largest mass extinction of biodiversity since the dinosaurs (WWF, 2016).

Human-caused environmental change and environmental degradation – desertification, deforestation, land degradation, ocean acidification, climate change and water scarcity – are fundamentally redrawing the map of our world. The health of terrestrial and marine ecosystems and the continued availability of the critical services they provide affect where people are able to find sustenance and pursue livelihoods to sustain themselves, and ultimately where they are able to live (UNEP 2017). Their degradation may result in the collapse of fragile and complex life support systems, undermining self-sufficiency and resilience. Indeed, it is increasingly recognized by policy makers that environmental degradation and mismanagement can be root causes of populations' deprivation, destitution and vulnerability, ultimately contributing to the desperation that fuels forced migration.

The interlacing trends of climate change, population growth, rising consumption and environmental degradation may lead to greater numbers of people displaced in the future. The most commonly cited figure is that there could be as many as 200 million people displaced for environmental reasons by 2050.[2] That would mean that, in a world of 9 billion people, 1 in 45 would have been forced from home for environmental reasons.

Clearly, addressing such displacement could prove to be a defining environmental management challenge of the twenty-first century. Having created the Anthropocene, humanity must now acknowledge the imperative of responsible environmental stewardship, ensuring that we strive towards a safe planet on which we can all live.

Relevance of migration and displacement to the UN Environment

The links between the environment and displacement are multi-directional and complex, but make a compelling case for engagement from the United Nations Environment Programme (henceforth UN Environment). Not only do environmental factors have the potential to contribute to migration and displacement, but they also emerge as consequences of population movement. As such, the environmental dimensions of migration and displacement may manifest themselves differently across ecosystems and countries of origin, transit and destination.

UN Environment is the leading global environmental authority that sets the global environmental agenda, promotes the coherent implementation of the environmental dimension of sustainable development within the United Nations system and serves as an authoritative advocate for the global environment. UN Environment's mission is "to provide leadership and encourage partnership in caring for the Environment by inspiring, informing, and enabling nations and peoples to improve their quality of life without compromising that of future generations."[3]

The environmental community of which UN Environment is a part has an important role to play in building understanding and supporting mitigation of the ecological drivers of displacement, strengthening the capacity of communities and countries to develop appropriate policies and strategies to pre-empt and withstand shocks from environmental change, and helping to plan the resettlement of communities that stand to be displaced by unavoidable environmental change. Five broad areas of concern underlay UN Environment's past and future activities with respect to environment and migration:

i   **Environmental degradation:** Environmental degradation can drive displacement – desertification, deforestation, land degradation, climate change, water scarcity and extreme weather events (droughts, floods, etc.) – presenting a form of "forced displacement" by making lives or livelihoods untenable in marginal areas.

ii   **Development-induced displacement:** Population displacements and migration can result not only from development activity's alteration of the use of the physical landscape, but also from planned population redistribution and resulting interaction between humans and the environment. The issue is particularly visible in developing countries where large-scale infrastructure projects are fueled by capital-intensive investment supported by states and global corporations. Mega projects conceived to meet society's growing demand for water, food, energy and transportation have contributed to uprooting populations and undermining the self-sufficiency and resilience of local communities.

iii   **Natural resource management and conflicts:** Environmental degradation and conflicts over the access to, and use of, natural resources can indirectly lead to further internal displacement and refugee flows. The most vulnerable groups are frequently "trapped in place" or move within their own country, where governments may be unwilling to adequately safeguard their rights. Displacement itself can have environmental impacts, causing environmental degradation (e.g. rapid urbanization or poorly managed refugee camps, pressure on scarce water, energy and food resources, uncontrolled waste disposal). This can bring incoming refugees/migrants into direct competition – and occasion violent conflict – with local communities.

iv   **Urbanization:** The world's urban population is on a trajectory to triple in the next few years, with the result that one third of the world's population is expected to live in urban areas by 2050 (UNDESA, 2014). As urban areas grow and expand, Earth's natural systems and the interactions between populations and their environments will continue to evolve, presenting a wide range of challenges.

v   **Climate change:** Climate change and growing pressure on natural resources could dramatically increase the flows of displaced people. The Paris Agreement, Article 8 on loss and damage, and the related UN Framework Convention on Climate Change (UNFCCC) Conference of Parties (COP) decision give a new mandate to address displacement related to the adverse impacts of climate change. The COP decision, para. 50, requests the Executive Committee of Warsaw International Mechanism to establish a task force to develop recommendations for integrated approaches to avert, minimize and address displacement related to the adverse impacts of climate change. This COP decision can feed into national adaptation plans, bringing human mobility into the national planning.

Engagement by UN Environment

UN Environment has worked on issues around the environmental causes and consequences of environmental migration and displacement for many years. In fact the very term "environmental refugee" was coined in a 1985 UN Environment publication. UN Environment's core mission of ensuring coherent implementation of the environmental dimensions of sustainable development represents a critical contribution to ensuring the stability, resilience and overall welfare of communities and populations, mitigating drivers of forced migration and enabling more self-reliant permanence. From this perspective, more than 30 years of work helping countries to improve their environmental management, particularly in marginal areas, are not easily condensed into a short list. However, this work has formed three main strands.

First, UN Environment has sought to raise the profile of environmental issues in the debates around forced migration and displacement. In 2008, UN Environment collaborated with Oxford University to publish a special issue of the Forced Migration review dedicated to environmentally induced migration, featuring a foreword by the executive director, a joint lead article with the International Organization for Migration as well as 37 contributions by UN, academic, international and local actors exploring the extent of the potential migration crisis, community adaptation and coping strategies, and the search for solutions.

In 2009, UN Environment, the IOM, United Nations University and the Munich Re Foundation developed the Climate Change, Migration and Environment Alliance (CCEMA), a multi-stakeholder partnership with objective of mainstreaming environmental and climate change considerations into migration management policies and practices, and to bring migration issues into global environmental and climate change discourse. The Alliance was launched at COP15 in Copenhagen, but activities halted soon after launch as a result of funding and coordination challenges.

This work continues with the active involvement of UN Environment in the follow-up to the New York Declaration for Refugees and Migrants which was adopted by Heads of State and Government on 19 September 2016 at the UN Summit on Addressing Large Movements of Refugees and Migrants. This set in motion a process to develop a Global Compact for Safe, Orderly and Regular Migration (GCM) to be considered for adoption at an intergovernmental conference on international migration in 2018. The New York Declaration for Refugees and Migrants (Resolution 71/1) expresses the political will of world leaders to save lives, protect rights and share responsibility on a global scale. In December 2016, UN Environment joined the Global Migration Group, an interagency group of two dozen UN agencies, funds and programs working together to coordinate the UN's approach to all aspects of migration.

The second strand has been to advance the collective knowledge base on how better environmental management can address the root causes of forced migration and displacement. The example of the draining and partial recovery of the Iraqi marshlands (Box 33.1) underlines just how critical sustainable environmental management is to people's livelihoods and way of life. In 2012, for example, UN Environment partnered with the Office for the Coordination of Humanitarian Affairs, the United Nations University, the International Organization for Migration and CILSS (the Permanent Interstate Committee for Drought Control in the Sahel) to analyse climate trends and identify at risk populations in the Sahel which helped to inform the UN integrated strategy on the Sahel.

Our collective action on the global environment is largely organized through dozens, if not hundreds, of Multilateral Environmental Agreements. Some of these, such as the UN Convention on Combating Desertification, have already developed programs to combat displacement. Meanwhile, migration issues have been formally integrated into the Paris Agreement on Climate Change with the creation of a task force to develop approaches to prevent, minimize and address climate change displacement. No doubt there is much more that can be done to integrate displacement issues into present and future agreements. Ultimately, creating the conditions in which people can live lives of dignity and safety in their own homes and homelands should become a driving objective of global environmental policy.

Box 33.1   Reviving the Iraqi marshlands

In the 1950s, the Marshlands of Mesopotamia (Al-Ahwar) in southern Iraq were a vast landscape home to half a million people known as the Ma'dan, or "Marsh Arabs". They lived in secluded villages of reed houses, supporting their livelihoods by fishing, growing rice and raising water buffalo.

However, starting in the 1970s, the Marshlands were devastated as a result of upstream dam construction and agriculture, oil exploration, military operations and most directly by the deliberate drainage of the wetlands by Saddam Hussein as an act of reprisal for the 1991 uprisings against his regime. By 2003, 90 per cent of the Marshlands had been lost and just 20,000 Ma'dan remained. It is estimated that up to 100,000 Marsh Arabs had fled to refugee camps in Iran, and another 100,000 were internally displaced in Iraq. The extensive ecological damage to the area, with the accompanying displacement of much of the indigenous population, remains one of Iraq's major humanitarian and environmental challenges.[4]

In 2001, UN Environment sounded the alarm bell on the demise of the marshlands which brought its plight to the international spotlight. Following the Iraq War in 2003, UN Environment launched a project to help restore the marshlands by supporting the development of a rehabilitation strategy, building the capacity of decision makers, demonstrating environmentally sound technologies and monitoring the condition of the marshlands. This was followed with a joint project with the UNESCO in 2009 to support the designation of the marshlands as World Heritage Site. It included the development of a management plan that reflected the unique historical, cultural, environmental, hydrological and socio-economic characteristics of the region.

Since 2003, the wetlands have started to recover, though drought, upstream dam building and continuing conflict have hindered the process. Tens of thousands of the Ma'dan people are now returning to their ancestral homes. In July 2016, with the support of UN Environment, the marshlands were inscribed as the first mixed cultural and natural World Heritage Site in the Middle East.

The third area of work has been to work with the humanitarian community to help reduce the environmental footprint of humanitarian action. Since the early 1990s, UN Environment has supported a Joint Environment Unit with the Office for the Coordination of Humanitarian Affairs. This has given it a compelling voice within the humanitarian community to disseminate low carbon, low impact technologies, as well as to share best practice approaches to assessment, planning and camp management to ensure that humanitarian responses to the refugee and displacement crises are not exacerbating the situation or inadvertently undermining progress of resilience building and stabilization programming.

Dealing with environmental displacement

Ultimately, displacement is not just a political challenge. As the case of the Iraqi Marshland shows, we need to think of it also as a development challenge and, critically, an environmental management challenge. The scale of possible future displacement under even moderate climate change scenarios means that political, environment, humanitarian and development actors must work together.

Fundamentally, we have to find a way of moving away from recurring crises. It is not acceptable in this day and age to have more than 125 million people needing humanitarian assistance (OCHA, 2016). Environmental degradation and mismanagement are at the root of many of the political, economic and social drivers of displacement. We need to better understand, prepare for and seek appropriate and just solutions to mitigate and adapt to those complex and interdependent factors. Ultimately, unless we can deal with long-term environmental vulnerability, huge numbers of people displaced every year could become our "new normal". Fundamentally, we have to find a way of doing more than just responding to recurring crises.

The next few years will be critical for the development of a more effective, compassionate and rights-based approach to human displacement. We need to work more proactively to reduce risks and avoid merely reactive responses. We need, in other words, to do more fire prevention and less firefighting.

Notes

1 By mid-2017, Ethiopia, Uganda, Iran, Lebanon, Pakistan, and Turkey were hosting over 8 million refugees combined. See http://www.unhcr.org/figures-at-a-glance.html
2 While estimates of the numbers of displaced people by 2050 vary from 25 million to 1 billion environmental migrants, 200 million is the most frequently cited number (Brown, 2008). A more detailed discussion on the various numbers that have been proposed can be found in: (Ionesco, Mokhnacheva. & Gemenne, 2017).
3 UNEP Organization Profile, p. 1 (http://staging.unep.org/PDF/UNEPOrganizationProfile.pdf).
4 UNEP in Iraq Post-Conflict Assessment, Clean-up and Reconstruction (https://wedocs.unep.org/bitstream/handle/20.500.11822/17462/UNEP_Iraq.pdf?sequence=1&isAllowed=y).

References

Brown, O. (2008) 'The Numbers Game', in *Forced Migration Review: Climate Change and Displacement*: Oxford, Refugee Studies CentreIFRC (2016) *World Disasters Report, 2016* (http://www.ifrc.org/Global/Documents/Secretariat/201610/WDR%202016-FINAL_web.pdf), Geneva: International Federation of Red Cross and Red Crescent Societies

IDMC (2017), *Global Report on Internal Displacement, 2017* (accessed 10 June 2017: http://idp-key-resources.org/documents/0000/d04384/000.pdf) Oslo: Internal Displacement Monitoring Centre

Ionesco, D., Mokhnacheva, D. & Gemenne, F. (2017) *The Atlas of Environmental Migration*, London: Earthscan p: 12–15

OCHA (2016) *Global Humanitarian Overview – 2016*, New York: Office for the Coordination of Humanitarian Affairs

UNDESA (2014) *World Urbanization Prospects*, 2014 Revision, New York: UN Division for Economic and Social Affairs

UNEP (2007) *UNEP in Iraq: Post-Conflict Assessment, Clean-up and Reconstruction*, Nairobi: UNEP

UNEP (2009) *From Conflict to Peacebuilding: The Role of Natural Resources and the Environment*, Geneva: UNEP. Years have been updated by the author

UNEP (2017) *Frontiers Report*, Nairobi: UNEP

UNHCR (2017) *Figures at a Glance* (accessed 26 November 2017: www.unhcr.org); United Nations High Commissioner for Refugees

World Bank (2015) *Migration, Remittances, Diaspora and Development*, web.worldbank.org

WWF (2016) *Living Planet Report, 2016: Risk and Resilience in New Era* (accessed 12 June 2017: www.wwf.org.uk), Switzerland: Worldwide Fund for Nature

34

Platform on Disaster Displacement, follow-up to the Nansen Initiative

Addressing the protection needs of persons displaced across borders in the context of disasters and climate change

*The Platform on Disaster Displacement**

Disaster displacement

Disaster displacement is a reality and among the biggest humanitarian challenges facing States and the international community in the 21st century. On average, 25.4 million people are displaced each year in the context of sudden-onset disasters, according to estimates by the Internal Displacement Monitoring Centre[1], and there is evidence that climate change is already increasing the frequency and intensity of natural hazards. Disaster displacement risks have doubled since 1970 and are likely to continue to grow. Those who cross borders to avoid the impacts of disasters caused by natural hazards and the adverse effects of climate change are in need of protection and assistance, but in many cases their needs may not be met due to legal and other gaps. There are limited legal options in international law for persons displaced in the context of disasters to be admitted and allowed to stay in a foreign country.

The Nansen Initiative

In view of this important challenge and given the lack of an obvious organization or forum with a specific mandate to address it, Norway and Switzerland, together with other States, launched the Nansen Initiative in 2012. They pledged to build consensus on key principles and elements on how to better protect people displaced across borders in the context of disasters and climate change. The Nansen Initiative embarked on a process of regional consultations with a wide variety of stakeholders, such as government officials, affected populations, international organizations, academia and civil society groups in seven sub-regions of the world.[2] This consultative process highlighted a general lack of preparedness, leading to *ad hoc* responses in most cases of cross-border disaster-displacement. At the same time, the Nansen Initiative strengthened the knowledge base through research and better data, and gathered a large number of existing domestic and regionally specific effective practices and approaches.

The outcome of the Nansen Initiative consultative process is a toolbox of effective practices, the *Agenda for the protection of cross-border displaced persons in the context of disasters and climate change*.[3] The Protection Agenda was endorsed by more than 100 governmental delegations during a Global Consultation in October 2015 and is the first attempt by States to build consensus on how to address cross-border disaster-displacement at the international level.

The Platform on Disaster Displacement

To follow up on the work started by the Nansen Initiative and to support States in implementing the recommendations of the Protection Agenda, the Platform on Disaster Displacement (PDD or the Platform) was launched at the World Humanitarian Summit in May 2016. The objective of the PDD is to strengthen the protection of people displaced across borders in the context of disasters, including those linked to the effects of climate change, and to prevent or reduce disaster displacement risks. While being a state-led process, with Germany and Bangladesh as Chair and Vice-Chair for 2016–2017, a key working principle of the Platform is multi-stakeholder involvement and strong partnerships between policymakers, practitioners and researchers. This approach promotes collective outcomes and stronger links between policy, normative, technical and operational work. In this sense, the Platform constitutes a forum for dialogue, information sharing, and policy and normative development on disaster displacement.

PDD perspective

The Platform on Disaster Displacement adopted the conceptual framework on disaster displacement developed by the Nansen Initiative through the Protection Agenda. By definition, disaster displacement is multi-causal. The risk of displacement is a function of the mix of exposure to a natural hazard, the characteristics of the hazard itself and the vulnerability of an individual or a community. Moreover, disaster displacement often occurs in a complex context of rapid population growth in hazard-prone areas, poor land and urban planning, armed conflict and violence, weak governance, poverty and inequality, which weakens resilience, increases vulnerabilities and exacerbates the impacts of natural hazards and climate change.

Disaster displacement has devastating impacts on individuals, their families and livelihoods. It exacerbates pre-existing vulnerabilities and raises multiple protection concerns. Forced displacement related to disasters also undermines the development of many States, in particular Least Developed Countries (LDCs), Small Island Developing States (SIDS), Landlocked Developing Countries (LLDCs) and middle-income countries, all facing specific challenges.

Although international law is almost silent on whether States have an obligation to admit disaster displaced persons, and under what conditions, the Nansen Initiative consultative process identified at least 50 States[4] that have already developed and used a wide set of tools and practices to admit or refrain from returning foreigners in the aftermath of disasters. Defined as 'humanitarian protection measures'[5] in the Protection Agenda, these tools and practices are based on, for example, regular migration categories, free movement of persons agreements, pastoralist transhumance arrangements and human rights or even refugee law for the admission and stay of cross-border disaster-displaced persons.

Besides protection and assistance measures, the Protection Agenda, with its comprehensive approach to disaster displacement, also proposes measures to manage disaster displacement risks in the country of origin. These include effective practices from all over the world that aim to reduce vulnerability and build resilience to disaster displacement risk, facilitate migration with dignity, conduct planned relocation out of hazardous areas and address the needs of internally displaced persons.

Rather than calling for a new binding international convention on cross-border disaster-displacement, the Nansen Initiative Protection Agenda and the Platform promote an approach that focuses on the integration of such *effective practices* to prevent, reduce and address disaster displacement by States and (sub-)regional organizations into their own policy and normative frameworks, in accordance with their specific situations.

PDD strategic priorities and workplan

Working from Geneva, the Platform is built on three pillars: a Steering Group comprised of States, a Coordination Unit and an Advisory Committee comprised of individuals and representatives of international and regional organizations with expertise in relevant disciplines such as humanitarian assistance, human rights, migration management, protection, disaster risk reduction, climate change action and development. The United Nations High Commissioner for Refugees (UNHCR) and the International Organization for Migration (IOM) are standing inviters to the Steering Group and are key operational partners in implementing the PDD 2016–2019 Strategic Framework and Workplan.[6] Under the leadership of Member States, the Platform works towards four Strategic Priorities based on the recommendations of the Protection Agenda and endorsed by the PDD Steering Group:

I   Address knowledge and data gaps.
II   Enhance the use of identified effective practices at the national, regional and international levels.
III Promote policy coherence and mainstreaming of human mobility challenges in, and across, relevant policy and action areas.
IV   Promote policy and normative development in gap areas.

Knowledge and data gaps on disaster displacement persist, especially regarding the numbers and dynamics of cross-border movements, human mobility in slow-onset hazard contexts, solutions provided to displaced persons, and current and projected displacement risks. By linking up with existing data collection mechanisms and mapping and consolidating existing information management systems, the Platform seeks to propose measures to address such gaps. The aim is to strengthen data collection and information systems at the global, regional and national levels. Such systems need to collect and consolidate time-series disaggregated data regarding the overall number of people displaced, both internally and across international borders, in the context of disasters and climate change, based on clear criteria and effective methods, in order to provide a sound evidence base for policy development and decisions.

The Nansen Initiative Protection Agenda proposes a number of humanitarian protection measures for admission and stay, providing examples of how States can address the protection needs of cross-border disaster-displaced persons. These tools and practices can also be enhanced and integrated within and across regional and national policies on disaster risk reduction, climate change adaptation, human rights or development. In this context, PDD supports, among others, workshops, capacity building and training measures. The Platform also promotes *effective practices* for the protection of internally displaced persons as well as efforts to disseminate and operationalize the *'Guidance on Planned Relocation'*[7] and to develop options for regular and legal migration as an adaptation strategy to climate change under the *Cancun Adaptation Framework*.[8]

Given the enormous challenges that disaster displacement generates, bilateral, regional and international cooperation is crucial. The Platform promotes coherence and enhanced cooperation across relevant *global policy dialogues*, such as the United Nations Framework Convention on Climate Change (UNFCCC); the Sustainable Development Goals (SDGs); the Agenda for Humanity; the Global Forum for Migration and Development (GFMD); the Sendai Framework for Disaster Risk Reduction 2015-2030; the New York Declaration for Refugees and Migrants, including the Global Compact for safe, orderly and regular migration; and the Global Compact on Refugees. The Platform also seeks to engage in regional processes like the Regional Consultative Processes (RCPs) on Migration and supports implementation of regional policies and frameworks, such as the *Framework for Resilient Development in the Pacific 2017–2030*, the *2012 IGAD Regional Migration Policy Framework (RMPF)*, and the *2014 Brazil Declaration and Plan of Action*. The Platform engages in these processes through its Steering Group, Advisory Committee and Coordination Unit, as well as the Envoy of the Chair.

Following the Protection Agenda's recommendation that *policy and normative development* to address the protection gap for disaster displaced persons is likely to see more progress at the domestic and regional levels, the Platform seeks to identify and promote safe and legal pathways and protection measures in this context. In the Americas, for example, Member Countries of the Regional Conference on Migration (RCM) adopted *A Guide to Effective Practices for RCM Member Countries: protection for persons moving across borders in the context of disasters* in November 2016, which was developed under the Nansen Initiative.[9] This RCM Guide is a unique and unprecedented document. It is the first time that such a guide on admission and stay has been developed at the regional level to cover the protection needs of cross-border disaster-displaced persons. The PDD aims to support similar processes in other regions, such as South America, the Greater Horn of Africa and the Pacific.

Notes

* This chapter has been drafted by the Coordination Unit of the Platform on Disaster Displacement and the views and opinions expressed do not necessarily reflect the official policy or position of the Chair or the Steering Group members of the Platform on Disaster Displacement.

1 See the *2016 Global Report on Internal Displacement* (GRID), page 14, available at: http://www.internal-displacement.org/assets/publications/2016/2016-global-report-internal-displacement-IDMC.pdf.

2 To learn more about the Nansen Initiative Consultations, visit the Nansen Initiative at: www.nansen-initiative.org/#consultations.

3 The Nansen Initiative (2015), *Agenda for the protection of cross-border displaced persons in the context of disasters and climate change Volume I*, available at: http://disasterdisplacement.org/wp-content/uploads/2014/08/EN_Protection_Agenda_Volume_I_-low_res.pdf

4 The Nansen Initiative identified 53 such countries and since the purpose of the Nansen Initiative consultative process was to identify effective practices and policy options for disaster displaced persons and not to develop an exhaustive list of such cases, the number is likely higher. For a mapping of these 53 countries, please see: The Nansen Initiative (2015), *Agenda for the protection of cross-border displaced persons in the context of disasters and climate change Volume I*, page 50, available at: http://disasterdisplacement.org/wp-content/uploads/2014/08/EN_Protection_Agenda_Volume_I_-low_res.pdf

5 'Humanitarian protection measures' (HPM) refer to laws, policies and practices used by States to permit the admission and stay of cross-border disaster-displaced persons on their territory. HPM should not be equated with subsidiary and complementary protection as generally used in refugee and similar contexts, although in some circumstances the latter forms of protection might also be relevant in disaster contexts. : The Nansen Initiative (2015), *Agenda for the protection of cross-border displaced persons in the context of disasters and climate change Volume I*, page 26, available at: http://disasterdisplacement.org/wp-content/uploads/2014/08/EN_Protection_Agenda_Volume_I_-low_res.pdf

6 To consult the Platform on Disaster Displacement Workplan 2016–2019, please visit the PDD website at: http://disasterdisplacement.org/wp-content/uploads/2015/02/15012017-PDD-Workplan.pdf

7 UNHCR-Georgetown University-Brookings (2015), *Guidance on protecting people from disasters and environmental change through planned relocation*, available at: www.unhcr.org/protection/environment/562f798d9/planned-relocation-guidance-october-2015.html.

8 The Cancun Climate Change Adaptation Framework as part of the Cancun Agreements (paragraphs 11–35) was adopted at the 2010 Climate Change Conference of the Parties in Cancun, Mexico (COP 16/ CMP 6), available at: http://unfccc.int/resource/docs/2010/cop16/eng/07a01.pdf#page=4.

9 To read the RCM Guide to Effective Practice, please visit the PDD website at: http://disasterdisplacement.org/wp-content/uploads/2016/11/PROTECTION-FOR-PERSONS-MOVING-IN-THE-CONTEXT-OF-DISASTERS.pdf

35

A moment of opportunity to define the global governance of environmental migration

Perspectives from the International Organization for Migration

Mariam Traore Chazalnoel and Dina Ionesco

Introduction

In the past ten years, issues related to climate change and environmental degradation and their consequences on the migration of people have gained increasing visibility on the global policy agenda, as a question of concern to both global North and global South countries. This rising interest has led to the inclusion of environmental migration considerations within key global policy developments, most notably the global climate negotiations under the United Nations Framework Convention on Climate Change (UNFCCC)[1] – including the landmark Paris Climate Agreement.[2] In addition, global migration policy is starting to take into account climate and environmental issues, with the topic being discussed as part of the development of a global compact for safe, orderly and regular migration[3] – the first intergovernmental negotiated process on migration developed within the United Nations. These developments are occurring within the wider context of efforts to achieve the targets set out in the Sustainable Development Goals (SDGs) – an overarching framework that offers opportunities to take account of environmental migration issues in goals on reducing inequalities, energy, water, climate change, lands, and oceans.[4] It seems that after a decade of advocacy efforts from stakeholders such as Small Island Developing States (SIDS), intergovernmental organizations, non-governmental organizations (NGOs), civil society and academia, meaningful efforts to define how a coherent global governance of environmental migration would look are underway.

The following overview describes activities and institutional developments related to environmental migration issues within the International Organization for Migration (IOM), reflecting heightened interest from member states; highlights IOM's key messaging around potential opportunities associated with environmental migration; and reflects on how IOM's institutional approach can inform the environmental migration governance at the global level.

Institutional developments within the International Organization for Migration: a barometer of states' interest in environmental migration

Looking into how environmental migration has gained prominence within the IOM – the largest intergovernmental organization with a mandate solely dedicated to migration questions – allows us to analyze how states that are members of the organization have progressively assigned importance to a topic that they saw as increasingly relevant, highlighting the need to develop new thinking to respond to identified challenges.

The IOM, established in 1951, is a United Nations organization mandated to deal with all migration dimensions, from humanitarian responses to forced displacement of people in cases of conflict and natural disasters to border management and economic migration. It is in the context of this broad mandate that the IOM has developed since the early 1990s a comprehensive programme of work on questions related to migration and displacement in connection with environmental changes, implemented by a large network of field offices and with activities focusing on: research and advocacy, legal protection, policy and legislation development, capacity building of policy-makers and practitioners, communication and partnership development, and provision of direct assistance to migrants affected by adverse environmental impacts.[5]

Despite the development of a number of activities pertaining to environmental migration over the past 25 years, it is in the last decade that IOM's portfolio on that topic has particularly expanded. This is largely due to the growing interest of IOM's member states[6] in better understanding the nature of environmental migration and its impacts in both origin and destination countries, in order to develop policy responses and programmes to directly support those migrants. This heightened states' interest confirms that issues of environmental migration are a challenge of great importance to both developing countries – which are asking the organization to provide technical support and capacity building – and developed countries that finance IOM.

IOM has as a result reshaped its structure to formally establish a Migration, Environment and Climate Change Division that is tasked with thematic oversight. IOM has developed institutional views and analyses on terminology, definitions and legal frameworks[7] in order to respond to member states' expressed needs and to fulfil three institutional objectives: (1) to prevent forced migration linked to environmental and climate change; (2) to assist, protect and reduce vulnerabilities of migrants; and (3) to facilitate migration as an adaptation strategy to the adverse impacts of climate change.[8] In addition, IOM provides technical support to global policy processes on both environmental and migration tracks. On the environmental side, IOM is one of the expert members of the Taskforce on Displacement under the auspices of the Warsaw International Mechanism of the UNFCCC, and is a standing invitee and direct implementer of the Platform on Disaster Displacement. On the migration side, IOM jointly serves the negotiations of the Global Compact for Migration by providing required technical and policy expertise alongside the United Nations Secretariat, represented by a Special Representative of the Secretary General (SRSG).[9]

The necessity to promote a balanced message on climate migration: encouraging positive action

IOM's flexible mandate allows the organization to develop activities pertaining to both forced and voluntary forms of environmental migration. This is an important consideration as it allows the organization to encourage strategic thinking and implementation of activities linked to leveraging the positive aspects of environmental migration – a vital complement to more alarmist views that envision environmental migration as being a purely negative and forced phenomenon undertaken out of despair, that needs to be curtailed. This means, among other things, encouraging planned and well-managed migration policies and programmes to provide alternative opportunities to environmental migrants, thereby reducing pressure on stretched ecosystems, or encouraging migrant communities' investments in environmental sustainability and climate adaptation.[10] Thus, without minimizing the grave impacts of environmental degradation on migration, and vice versa, one of IOM's key objectives is to support a broader reflection of how well-designed policies can benefit migrants and states in the context of environmental degradation, and to allow for the active involvement of migrants, diasporas and migrant-hosting communities as actors which can positively contribute to climate change adaptation and sustainable development efforts.

Shaping the global governance of environmental migration: Seizing historical opportunities

The global policy landscape is at a crossroads, with the implementation of the Paris Climate Agreement on climate change, the development of the first intergovernmental agreement on migration within the United Nations (i.e. the Global Compact for safe, orderly and regular migration) and the Global Sustainable Development Goals agenda, which together encompass many different dimensions of environmental migration. There is thus an urgent need to encourage the consideration of environmental migration issues in a "mirror" process (i.e. to include migration in climate and environmental policy tracks and to include climate and environmental questions in migration policy tracks) within each of these in order to achieve meaningful global governance of environmental migration to be achieved. However, it is important to remember that both environmental issues and migration questions are highly politically sensitive topics, as they touch upon national sovereignty of states. A the same time, such challenges cannot be solved by states in isolation, and so these political sensitivities should not be allowed to become an obstacle to constructive interstate dialogue.

In a context where states' interest and opinions do not necessarily align, both the Global Compact for Migration and the work undertaken within the UNFCCC negotiations process offer an important window of opportunity for states to analyze, compare and understand existing knowledge, practices and possible ways forward in non-binding spaces; and to do so not only at the global level, but also through regional, national and local consultations. Doing so offers states the opportunity to propose actionable commitments as well as means of implementation and follow-up frameworks, while simultaneously acknowledging formally the necessity to address environmental drivers of migration and offering guidance on how to do so, including on ways to maximize potential benefits. Achievements made at the global policy level would, in turn, increase legitimacy and generate additional financial means to address environmental migration on the long term at the national level.

Conclusion

The current global policy context offers a momentous opportunity to develop and define a global governance strategy for environmental migration that would address emerging challenges and strive to reap potential benefits. For such an outcome to materialize, there is a necessity to encourage highest levels of convergence between two often distinct and separate worlds: migration policy, and environmental and climate policy. We should therefore aim at developing enhanced coherence between the UNFCCC climate negotiations process and the Global Compact for Migration process, in order to maximize resources and develop comprehensive responses that transcend narrow policy boundaries.

Notes

1 Dina Ionesco, Daria Mokhnacheva, François Gemenne, *The Atlas of Environmental Migration* (London: Routledge 2017), 112–113.
2 The Preamble of the Climate Agreement refers to the necessity to protect the rights of migrants when taking action on climate change and the Paris Agreement also mandates the creation of a Taskforce on climate-related displacement. <http://unfccc.int/paris_agreement/items/9485.php>. Accessed 28 June 2017.
3 Environmental Migration Portal, 'UN Summit for Refugees and Migrants' (International Organization of Migration, No date assigned). <https://environmentalmigration.iom.int/un-summit-refugees-and-migrants> Accessed 25 June 2017.
4 The following SDGs are of particular relevance to address climate and migration questions: 7 (Affordable and clean energy), 10 (Reduced inequalities), 11 (Sustainable cities and communities), 13 (Climate action), 14 (Life below water) and 15 (Life on land) of the "17 Goals to Transform Our World": The United Nations, Sustainable Development Goals (United Nations, No date assigned). <www.un.org/sustainabledevelopment/sustainable-development-goals/> Accessed 28 June 2017.
5 For a detailed historical outline of the development of climate migration work within IOM, see D. Ionesco and M. Traore Chazalnoël 'The Role of the International Organization for Migration in the International Governance of Environmental Migration' in Kerstin Rosenow-Williams, François Gemenne (eds.), *Organizational Perspectives on Environmental Migration* (Routledge 2015); D. Ionesco 'L'OIM et la gouvernance des migrations environnementales', in Christel Cournil Chloé Vlassopoulos Coordinateur (eds), Mobilité humaine et environnement, (Editions Quæ 2015); and International Organization for Migration (IOM) *Outlook on Migration, Environment and Climate Change* (International Organization for Migration, 2014).
6 IOM's member States have requested yearly updates on IOM's work on environmental migration since 2014, requesting the organization to step up activities on that specific topic, through the IOM Standing Committee for Programmes and Finance. <www.environmentalmigration.iom.int/iom-and-migration-environment-and-climate-change-mecc> Accessed 28 June 2017.
7 For a full analysis of the IOM's legal work on climate migration see Gervais Appave, Alice Sironi, Mariam Traore Chazalnoël, Dina Ionesco, Daria Mokhnacheva 'Organizational Perspectives: IOM's role and perspectives on Climate Change, Migration and the Law' in Benoit Mayer and François Crépeau, eds., *Research Handbook on Climate Change, Migration and the Law* (Edward Elgar, forthcoming in September 2017).
8 International Organization for Migration (IOM) *Outlook on Migration, Environment and Climate Change* (International Organization for Migration, 2014).
9 The United Nations, 'Modalities for the intergovernmental negotiations of the global compact for safe, orderly and regular migration' (United Nations General Assembly A/71/L.58, New York, 2017).
10 The International Organization for Migration 'Migration as an Adaptation Strategy to Climate Change' (The United Nations Migration Agency, No date assigned). <https://weblog.iom.int/migration-adaptation-strategy-climate-change> Accessed 03 May 2017.

36

Where do we go from here?

Reflections on the future of environmental migration and displacement research

Lori M. Hunter

What an exciting time to be examining migration-environment connections – and a desperately important one. McLeman and Gemenne note the timeliness of this collection in their introductory chapter, and their comments are certainly on the mark. As we witness the rapid pace of contemporary social and environmental change, anxiety can mount and nerves can fray. Yet as a research community, we *do* have pathways for response – and respond we have. At this juncture, it's useful to reflect on where we've come, where we need to go, and what requires our future attention.

This incredible collection of writing demonstrates how far we've come as a research community. For example, important progress in theory development is outlined by Piguet (Chapter 2), and the continuing expansion into new dimensions of migration-environment links is represented by the focus on immobility by Zickgraf (Chapter 5). Methodological advancements are covered including geospatial methodologies (de Sherbinin and Bai, Chapter 6) as well as description of the important insights offered by qualitative investigation (Gemenne, Chapter 9). Additional case studies from across the globe – from China to Mexico – further boost understanding of the migration-climate linkages, and important policy issues, such as human rights, prevention, and green grabs, are also represented.

All of this work is critical, and bringing these various dimensions together within one volume is to be applauded. As we well know, our planet is supporting 7.5 billion people, and in developing regions, about 1 in 5 persons lives on less than $1.25 per day. High poverty and high fertility often intersect in particularly fragile places; conflict often adds a further layer of challenge. And of course, as our climate changes, decreasing rainfall and increasing temperature will have particularly dire consequences for global citizens with an already precarious existence. These challenges must motivate us to continue adding to scientific understanding of the migration-environment linkages, and that this understanding reaches beyond the academic community to inform efforts to improve wellbeing. This collection takes us in those directions.

What we know (about environmental migration and displacement)

Migration is a longstanding adaptive strategy in the face of environmental pressures

Our research community has done excellent work positioning contemporary environmental migration as the most recent example of a long-standing livelihood strategy. From pastoralists in East Africa (Blocher, Chapter 15) to North American Dust Bowl migration, movement has historically been one of a variety of responses to environmental scarcity. While climate change is intensifying environmental pressures in many regions, migration should also be usefully considered within its historical context.

An environmental 'signal' is often identifiable when predicting migration, particularly in rural regions

Beyond historical references, substantial research has now identified significant precipitation and/or temperature predictors of contemporary migration, although the magnitude and directionality varies. For example, recent research finds that rising temperatures reduce migration in Bolivia, but increase migration in Brazil and Uruguay (Thiede, Gray and Mueller 2016). In South Africa, some work finds that local temperature increases and precipitation declines are related to greater out-migration (Mastrorillo et al. 2016), although other research finds that out-migration is more likely from households with access to greater natural resources which suggests less climate strain (Hunter et al. 2014). The variety of empirical evidence provided by this volume's chapters adds to this important body of research.

Context matters

These varied findings clearly demonstrate that context matters, and that environmental factors interact with social, economic, political, and cultural ones to influence migration decision-making and potential. A useful framework put forward by the Foresight project and summarized by Black et al. (2011) has offered excellent conceptual guidance for researchers exploring these complex socio-ecological interactions. This framework is presented in streamlined form within this collection's introductory chapter.

The migration-environment connection is characterized by a continuum

Although migration is a longstanding livelihood strategy, much contemporary environmental migration is far from voluntary. While acute events such as natural disasters can yield displacement, chronic environmental strain such as drought can ultimately result in migration also of an involuntary nature.

Environmental/climate 'refugees' is an alarmist term

I believe further energy spent debating "climate refugees" vs. "environmental migrants" is energy ill-spent. For several years following the introduction of the "environmental/climate refugee" narrative into popular discourse, debate raged within scholarly outlets regarding definitional issues. At this point, among researchers, we understand that "refugee" inaccurately represents most migration-environment linkages. We need not continue to debate this among ourselves, although room still remains for scholars to step into the public dialogue (more ahead).

What we might let go, and pursue next

Give up on far-reaching generalizations

While researchers involved in earlier case studies occasionally called for efforts to generalize, it's time for us to let go of ambitions for a broadly applicable theory. Local context is so critical in shaping the migration-environment connection that we may be best served expanding and refining conceptual frameworks such as that provided by Black et al. (2011). Such frameworks can continue to usefully guide future research.

Move beyond temperature and precipitation signals

The vast expansion in available data offers exciting opportunities. But perhaps we continue to rush too quickly into using available data without carefully considering how to push understanding beyond temperature or precipitation "effects". It's now time to take the increasingly accessible environmental data and examine their interactions with important socio-demographic and other factors to add important layers of depth to understanding.

Explore axes of differentiation

As an example of interactions with socio-demographic factors, migration as a social process is highly gendered. We also know that livelihood activities tend to be highly gendered. And, as such, it's surprising we know so little about the *gender* dimensions of migration-environment connections, particularly as related to livelihood migration. Chapter 10 (Pearce) and Chapter 11 (Gioli and Milan) in this collection offer important contributions in this regard. *Race* and *class* represent other important factors that distinguish intentions and/or capacity to migrate or otherwise adapt to environmental strain. In particular, *indigenous voices* have long been overlooked and should be brought more centrally into the broader scientific and public dialogue. Again, this collection offers progress here through Chapter 30 by Bronen.

Put social networks back in

Household-level axes of differentiation also exist. For example, it's well-documented that social networks influence migration decision-making, and it's likely that migration in response to environmental conditions is shaped by existing social connections. But, again, only a handful of studies have centrally integrated consideration of these networks. To move forward in this regard, Simon's review of research on migration-climate connections in Mexico (Chapter 20) provides insights on integrating consideration of networks' effects.

Consider the system

For the most part, we have typically built quantitative models that predict the likelihood of migration or the volume of migration flows. After the prediction, however, we stop. Migration is clearly part of a system, one that influences sending and receiving areas beyond the immediate term, but in shaping trajectories of people and places. Yet few studies have explored migration through a systems framework. This approach has substantial utility as well as possible extensions such as inclusion of feedback loops, remittances, and such.

What about wealthier settings?

For logical reasons, most migration-environment work has focused on less developed settings. In these regions, households may be particularly vulnerable to climate impacts. Some research focuses on immigration to Europe, particularly from climate-stressed African settings, but virtually no scholarship has explored internal movement. In the U.S., Hurricane Katrina has both received substantial research attention, nicely summarized by Fussell (Chapter 22). The potential displacement due to sea level rise has also been explored (Curtis and Bergmans, Chapter 8). Yet there's a wide variety of additional topics such as the implications for internal migration of urban heat islands, climate-related infrastructure impacts, regional water scarcity, and agricultural decline. These are all of relevance in wealthier settings, as well.

Keep developing and engaging innovative methods

It's so inspirational to see methodological innovations such as the use of mobile phone data to determine patterns of human mobility before and after extreme events (Lu et al. 2016). Never shy away from new, exciting approaches to our work!

Future challenges even bigger than filling research gaps

As a scholarly community, we have work to do beyond filling gaps in knowledge. We must set our sights high and work toward making inroads into demography writ-large as well as into climate science. We must also do better at engaging the public and policymakers.

The environment must be better integrated into demographic science

The absence of environmental factors within demography was brought to the general attention of population scholars two decades ago. In her presidential address to the Population Association of America, Anne Pebley argued that within demographic research, environmental considerations had been typically comingled with broader issues of economic development and population growth (Pebley 1998). Substantial progress has been made since then, but gone are the days when population-environment researchers can speak only to each other; environmental change is far too significant within global demographic dynamics. Jane Menken and I recently made this argument using Thomas Kuhn's (1962) famously postulated contention in *The Structure of Scientific Revolutions* that researchers follow *normal science* until a crisis level of unexplainable anomalies is reached – i.e., anomalies that push the limits of current paradigms. Perhaps climate change is causing population science's paradigms to become increasingly outdated in their exclusion of environmental factors (Hunter and Menken 2015). Our community is key to expanding demography's *normal science*.

Reach out to other scholarly communities

Migration-environment researchers have long integrated multiple perspectives into our work. For example, we've long considered vulnerability and adaptation central concepts for the hazards research community. But now that we've tapped into these perspectives, we must do a better job at reaching out to cognate communities to ensure *our* insights influence *their* intellectual trajectories. We should publish in journals and attend conferences of the hazards community, public health researchers, refugee scholars, climate scientists, experts on global environmental change, and so on. We should also work within our own institutions to ensure that activities outside of our disciplinary silo are valued.

Policy considerations and frameworks deserve more focus

Frameworks such as the United Nation's Sustainable Development Goals offer an opportunity to structure and apply our research and findings. The IPCC is increasingly seeking input from social scientists and we have much to offer. Part III of this collection offers important background on a variety of legal and policy perspectives. Let's be inspired by, and contribute to, these global efforts in order to maximize the contribution of population-environment research.

Speak out

Finally, our findings are important; we must share what we've learned and not hide within the ivory tower's sheltered walls. This is challenging since most of us are not taught how to engage the public, the media, or policymakers. Graduate training gives short shrift to such important activities. Yet organizations such as the Population Reference Bureau, among others, offer opportunities to learn about these processes of engagement. Opportunities such as "Academic Minute" and "Why Social Science?" facilitate dissemination. The need for such engagement is demonstrated by the dominance of alarmist perspectives in public dialogue on migration-environment linkages over the past many years. But conversation and rational policy should be based on insights from sound research. As a community, we have indeed generated broad understandings of migration-environment connections as well as highly detailed case studies. Let's now ask: How can these best inform policy to improve human and environmental wellbeing?

It's been exciting to watch our community's research progress over the past two decades, and it'll be exciting to watch the upcoming progress as we expand our inquiry and apply our knowledge. I'm proud to be part of the migration-environment research community. This is indeed an exciting time to be examining these connections – as well as a desperately important one. Keep up the incredible work – our future needs you.

References

Black, R., Adger, W. N., Arnell, N. W., Dercon, S., Geddes, A., & Thomas, D. (2011). The effect of environmental change on human migration. *Global Environmental Change, 21*, S3–S11.

Hunter, L. M., & Menken, J. (2015). Will climate change shift demography's' normal science'? *Vienna Yearbook of Population Research, 13*, 23–28.

Hunter, L. M., Nawrotzki, R., Leyk, S., Maclaurin, G. J., Twine, W., Collinson, M., & Erasmus, B. (2014). Rural outmigration, natural capital, and livelihoods in South Africa. *Population, space and place, 20*(5), 402–420.

Kuhn, T. (1962). *The Structure of Scientific Revolutions*. Chicago: The University of Chicago Press.

Lu, X., Wrathall, D. J., Sundsøy, P. R., Nadiruzzaman, M., Wetter, E., Iqbal, A., . . . Bengtsson, L. (2016). Unveiling hidden migration and mobility patterns in climate stressed regions: A longitudinal study of six million anonymous mobile phone users in Bangladesh. *Global Environmental Change, 38*, 1–7.

Mastrorillo, M., Licker, R., Bohra-Mishra, P., Fagiolo, G., Estes, L. D., & Oppenheimer, M. (2016). The influence of climate variability on internal migration flows in South Africa. *Global Environmental Change, 39*, 155–169.

Pebley, A. R. (1998). Demography and the environment. *Demography, 35*(4), 377–389.

Thiede, B., Gray, C., & Mueller, V. (2016). Climate variability and inter-provincial migration in South America, 1970–2011. *Global Environmental Change, 41*, 228–240.

Index

Printed in the United States
by Baker & Taylor Publisher Services